W9-DAN-195

Henry James
1917-1959

a reference guide

A
Reference
Publication
in
Literature

Jack Salzman
Editor

Henry James
1917-1959

a reference guide

KRISTIN PRUITT McCOLGAN

G.K.HALL&CO.

70 LINCOLN STREET, BOSTON, MASS.

Copyright © 1979 by Kristin Pruitt McColgan

Library of Congress Cataloging in Publication Data

McColgan, Kristin Pruitt.
  Henry James, 1917-1959.

  (A Reference publication in literature)
  Includes index.
  1. James, Henry, 1843-1916—Bibliography. I. Title.
II. Series.
Z8447.M32   [PS2123]   016.813'4   78-27118
ISBN 0-8161-7851-8

This publication is printed on permanent/durable acid-free paper
MANUFACTURED IN THE UNITED STATES OF AMERICA

To my family,
with love and appreciation

Contents

INTRODUCTION ix

LIST OF MAJOR BIBLIOGRAPHIC SOURCES xv

PRINCIPAL WORKS BY HENRY JAMES (1843-1916). . . . xvii

WRITINGS ABOUT HENRY JAMES, 1917-1959 1

APPENDIX A
   Critical Anthologies (Post 1959) Referenced in
   the Text 339

APPENDIX B
   Dissertations Not Listed in <u>Dissertation Abstracts</u> . 341

INDEX 345

Introduction

I. BIOGRAPHY

On April 15, 1843, Henry James, Jr. was born in New York City, the second child and son of a scholar/theologian and the grandson of an Irish immigrant who made in his adopted country a considerable fortune in tobacco and salt processing and real estate. Henry, like his siblings William, Garth Wilkinson, Robertson, and Alice, was reared in an atmosphere of intellectual speculation and financial ease. The family adopted no specific creed and gave allegiance to no organized religion, although Henry James, Sr. was a disciple of Swedenborg. The children's formal education was inconsistent, involving a series of tutors and a number of schools at home and abroad; and it was "liberal," directly introducing the youngsters to masterpieces of art, music and literature as the family shuffled between the New World and the Old, as well as between Manhattan and Albany, New York, and Newport, Rhode Island, where for a time James studied art with William Morris Hunt before enrolling in 1862 in Harvard Law School. In Newport, James received what he was to call an "obscure hurt" while operating a fire pump, an injury which provided the physical basis for his non-participation in the Civil War, a decision apparently supported by his emotional antipathy to the conflict.

In 1864, James turned his attention to a literary career and began writing reviews, essays and fiction for such periodicals as The North American Review, The Nation, and The Atlantic Monthly. After several years in Boston and Cambridge, where Henry was a companion of Charles Eliot Norton and William Dean Howells, he made his first journey as an adult to Europe in 1869. In 1870, while in England, he learned of the death of his beloved cousin, Minny Temple, who was to provide the inspiration for the creation of such heroines as Isabel Archer and Milly Theale. James returned to Cambridge in April, 1870, and his first novel, Watch and Ward, was serialized in The Atlantic Monthly, August–December, 1871.

During the next few years, James alternated between Europe and America, finally leaving the country of his birth in 1875 to spend a year in Paris learning more about his chosen craft from a French circle of writers which included Flaubert, Zola, and Turgenev, before settling permanently in England in 1876. In that same year, James' first novel in book form, <u>Roderick Hudson</u>, was published.

During the years in London, 1876-1897, James established himself as a literary mandarin in polite English society, endured the death of his parents, and experimented for five of those years writing for the stage. This flirtation with the drama culminated in a major personal and professional crisis at the performance of <u>Guy Domville</u> on January 5, 1895, when James the playwright was jeered by the audience.

In 1897 James retired to Lamb House, Rye, thereafter using dictation as his preferred mode of composition and creating the works that solidified his popular reputation as obscure, indirect and stylistically unintelligible. During 1904-1905, James returned to America to give a lecture tour, subsequently recording impressions of this trip in <u>The American Scene</u>. Back at Lamb House, he began revising his works and writing prefaces for the collected New York edition, which began appearing in 1907.

During the final years of his life, James wrote his memoirs and witnessed the onset of World War I. In 1915, disillusioned over America's failure to support the Allied cause, James made a moral declaration by becoming a naturalized British citizen. He was awarded the Order of Merit by King George V early the following year, prior to his death, caused by a stroke and pneumonia, on February 28, 1916.

II. CRITICAL TRENDS, 1917-1959

Several excellent surveys of Jamesian scholarship exist.[1] Therefore, I will attempt only a general discussion of critical trends during the period from 1917 to 1959--years that are the most lively in Jamesian scholarship and among the more animated in the history of American criticism. Unlike Melville, James was never ignored by scholars, although at times the treatment he received at their hands might have recommended the virtues of anonymity.

For many years after his death, the majority of published statements were either anecdotes involving James, descriptions of his personality and/or manner, or reminiscences about his behavior, not evaluations of his literary productions. James the notorious "diner-out" overshadowed James the artist and craftsman. Critical investigations of his works were the exception. Two critics who did pursue such an approach, Joseph Warren Beach and Percy Lubbock, pioneered the study of James' method. <u>The Little Review</u> and <u>Egoist</u> numbers devoted to James provided a forum for authors like Pound and Eliot to explain the importance and influence of James.

Introduction

In the mid-1920's, Van Wyck Brooks fired the salvo in what was to
become the major controversy in Jamesian criticism over the next two
decades. He aggressively expounded the theory that James' expatriation was ruinous to his art. A few years later, critics like Vernon
Parrington and Granville Hicks denounced James' failure to depict the
economic and social upheavals in the larger society and his preoccupation with what they viewed as the vacuous, corrupt upper class.
The 1934 issue of Hound and Horn dedicated to James briefly distract-
ed attention from his choice of England as a residence and from his
choice of the leisure class as a characteristic subject to more compelling issues. This collection offered dissenting views to the
common claim that the complexity of James' style camouflaged weaknesses in his selection of themes and in his artistry. However, if
the Marxist thesis was by now passé, the thesis of Edmund Wilson's
"The Ambiguity of Henry James" conveyed a no less emotionally-charged
position in its suggestion that the governess in The Turn of the
Screw exhibited a neurosis which was James' own; immediately other
critics began speculating about such Freudian implications of James'
"obscure hurt," and his failure to marry and to deal explicitly with
sexual matters became suspect.

Not until 1943, the centenary of James' birth, did the maverick
articles focusing on James' writings become the standard production;
new editions, often with illuminating introductions, began to crop
up; and what came to be termed the "James revival" was underway. By
1950, individual works (along with The Turn of the Screw and James'
later novels, which, prior to that time, had received the bulk of
critical attention) were being scrutinized. James' themes, techniques
and style were now receiving their just due.

It is a tribute to Henry James that his work has survived the
vagaries of nationalistic, political and literary movements and that
he has, in the past quarter century, been recognized as a superior
craftsman whose art justifies the flood of criticism which it has
elicited. Many eminent critics have offered sensitive, provocative
analyses of James and his art, and one must respect both the quantity
and, in many cases, the quality of the comment he has inspired.

Some authors, for one or more of a variety of reasons, must wait
for recognition from the reading public. Certainly James' critical
preeminence over the past twenty-five years would have cheered the
author who had sought public approval during his lifetime without any
great measure of success. Nevertheless, it now appears certain that
James will never have the public appeal of a Hemingway or even a
Faulkner. His gift for character analysis is expressed in too subtle
a form; his style is too complicated and prolix to be easily readable. Indeed, James did not court wide acceptance: He was, in a
sense, an elitist, seeking with singleminded fervor to create in his
art a perfection which precludes broad popularity. For many, James
is and will remain the author of "that ghost story I didn't understand." Even now, he is capable of provoking antagonism as well as

adoration, just as he was in 1920: "Across a vast gulf those who like Henry James view with contempt those who do not, and in return those who do not like him view with incredulity those who do." (See "The Gulf of Henry James," 1920.B3.) Still, Henry James can rest assured that he has secured his position as a major figure in American literature, and that he has provided his detractors as well as his supporters with a good deal of amusement along the way.

III. FORMAT, ANNOTATIONS AND EXCLUSIONS

This Reference Guide provides an annotated listing of books and articles about Henry James which appeared between 1917 and 1959. Entries are chronologically arranged according to year of publication. For each year, works wholly or substantially about James (i.e., books, dissertations) are entered under the heading "A. Books," and articles, reviews and portions of books are contained in section "B. Shorter Writings." Within each category, items are arranged alphabetically according to author. When there is more than one anonymous work or work by a particular author, material from periodicals, chronologically presented, precedes that from books.

A few comments about my purposes and practices in the annotations: First, they are intended to be descriptive rather than evaluative, and I have frequently used direct quotations in characterizing the content of the source. Second, I have, whenever possible, noted subsequent reprintings of the items referenced. Finally, I have personally examined all of the material annotated, with the exception of dissertations, for which I relied on the abstracts in Dissertation Abstracts (unless otherwise noted), and of entries marked with an asterisk (*), for which I have, in most instances, supplied information from a secondary source. Material which, according to an interlibrary loan search, was unlocatable or unobtainable is so labeled.

The index lists authors, titles of periodicals, titles of book chapters where relevant to James, titles of books and annotated dissertations on James, titles of James' novels and collections of his works for which I have annotated the introductions. I have also indexed selected general topics (e.g., bibliography, biography, expatriation, criticism and literary theory), and significant treatments of James' individual works. The numbers in the index refer to the year and entry number of a specific item; for example, 1956.B5 directs the reader to the year 1956, to the fifth entry in category B, for shorter writings.

When I began this project, I had grandiose hopes of tracking down even the most obscure and inaccessible references to James and his works. Now, my fantasy tempered by the massive numbers of books and articles surveyed, and made wiser by the repeated experience of uncovering new sources just when I had expectations of at last concluding my research, I am aware that to claim my compilation is exhaustive would smack of arrogance. Nonetheless, I have sought in this volume to annotate all the significant and substantial commentary on James within the scope of coverage. I have deliberately excluded certain items: As a rule, I omitted those dissertations not abstracted in Dissertation Abstracts (which are, however, listed chronologically in Appendix B), and excerpts from teachers' manuals. Other than reviews included in the bibliographies enumerated on pp. xv-xvi, and with the exceptions noted, reviews of works on James were not annotated. However, a list of selected reviews (compiled from Book Review Index, Comprehensive Index to Little Magazines and American Literature) is appended to citations of major works on James. I summarized theatrical reviews of adaptations of James' works, such as The Heiress and The Innocents, when they made a useful statement about the original source or about James. Rather than eliminate an entry because it contained only passing reference to James, I have tried, whenever possible, to indicate the nature of that reference. In general, then, my touchstone has been the potential utility of the entry to the reader.

I am indebted to the following libraries for use of their facilities and the assistance of their interlibrary loan staffs: Rochester Public Library, Rochester, Minn.; Kansas City Public Library, Kansas City, Mo.; University of Missouri at Kansas City General Library, Kansas City, Mo.; and, above all, University of Texas General Libraries, including the Humanities Research Center, Austin, Tex. I also owe thanks to my friend and colleague, Dr. Dorothy Scura, to my sister and colleague, Dr. Virginia Pruitt, and to my husband, Dr. Ed McColgan, for suggestions and assistance in proofreading.

NOTE

1. See Joseph Warren Beach's introduction to the revised edition of The Method of Henry James (1954.A1); Philip Rahv's "Attitudes to Henry James" (1943.B39); Heidi Specker's "The Change of Emphasis in the Criticism of Henry James" (1948.B43); Robert Spiller's "Henry James" in Eight American Authors: A Review of Research and Criticism (1956.B70), and Robert Gale's essay by the same title in the revised edition of that volume (Edited by James Woodress. The Norton Library. New York: W. W. Norton and Co., 1971); Edward Stone's The Battle and the Books: Some Aspects of Henry James (Athens, Ohio: Ohio University Press, 1964). More detailed examinations can be found in dissertations by William T. Stafford, "The American Critics of Henry James: 1864-1943" (University of Kentucky, 1956); and by J. Scholes, "American and British Criticism of Henry James: 1916-1953" (University of North Carolina, 1961).

Major Bibliographic Sources

Modern Humanities Research Association Annual Bibliography of English Language and Literature, excluding reviews of books on James, unless listed elsewhere.

Modern Language Association Annual Bibliography, International Bibliography.

CORNELIA P. KELLEY, The Early Development of Henry James (1930.A1).

LYON RICHARDSON, Henry James: Representative Selections, with Introduction, Bibliography, and Notes (1941.B15).

SIMON NOWELL-SMITH, The Legend of the Master (1947.A2).

THOMAS JOHNSON, "Henry James," in Literary History of the United States (1948.B23), and the supplemental listing by Richard Ludwig (1959.B59).

EUNICE HAMILTON, "Biographical and Critical Studies of Henry James, 1941-1948" (1949.B19), and Viola Dunbar's addenda (1950.B30).

LEWIS LEARY, comp., Articles on American Literature, 1900-1950 (1954.B30), and the sequel, Articles on American Literature, 1950-1967 (Durham, N.C.: Duke University Press, 1970).

ROBERT SPILLER, "Henry James," in Eight American Authors: A Review of Research and Criticism (1956.B70), and the subsequent essay by Robert Gale in the revised edition of that work, edited by James Woodress (The Norton Library. New York: W. W. Norton and Co., 1971).

MAURICE BEEBE and WILLIAM STAFFORD, "Criticism of Henry James: A Selected Checklist with an Index to Studies of Separate Works" (1957.B2), and the revised and updated version in Modern Fiction Studies, 12 (1966).

JARVIS A. THURSTON et al., Short Fiction Criticism: A Checklist of Interpretation Since 1925 of Stories and Novelettes (American, British, Continental) 1800-1958 (The Swallow Checklists of Criticism and Explication. Denver: Alan Swallow, 1960).

JAMES BERT SCHOLES, "American and British Criticism of Henry James: 1916–1953" (Ph.D. dissertation, University of North Carolina at Chapel Hill, 1961).

C. HUGH HOLMAN, comp., The American Novel Through Henry James (Goldentree Bibliographies. Edited by O. B. Hardison, Jr. New York: Appleton-Century-Crofts, 1966).

DONNA GERSTENBERGER and GEORGE HENDRICK, The American Novel: 1789–1959. A Checklist of Twentieth-Century Criticism (Denver: Alan Swallow, 1967).

JAMES WOODRESS, Dissertations in American Literature, 1891–1966 (Durham, N.C.: Duke University Press, 1968).

BEATRICE RICKS, comp., Henry James: A Bibliography of Secondary Works (Scarecrow Author Bibliographies, Number 24. Metuchen, N.J.: The Scarecrow Press, 1975).

MARION SADER, ed., A Comprehensive Index to Little Magazines: 1890–1970 (Vol. 4. Millwood, New York: Kraus-Thomson Organization, 1976), excluding reviews of books on James, unless listed elsewhere.

Principal Works by Henry James *

A Passionate Pilgrim, 1875 ("A Passionate Pilgrim," "The Last of the
   Valerii," "Eugene Pickering," "The Madonna of the Future," "The
   Romance of Certain Old Clothes," "Madame de Mauves")

Transatlantic Sketches, 1875

Roderick Hudson, 1875

The American, 1877

French Poets and Novelists, 1878

Watch and Ward, 1878

The Europeans, 1878

Daisy Miller, 1878

An International Episode, 1879

The Madonna of the Future, 1879 ("The Madonna of the Future," "Longstaff's Marriage," "Madame de Mauves," "Eugene Pickering," "The
   Diary of A Man of Fifty," "Benvolio")

Confidence, 1879

Hawthorne, 1879

The Diary of A Man of Fifty, 1880 ("The Diary of A Man of Fifty,"
   "A Bundle of Letters")

Washington Square, 1880

The Portrait of A Lady, 1881

Daisy Miller: A Comedy, 1883

The Siege of London, 1883

Portraits of Places, 1883

---

*For this list of James' major published works (excluding those
published between 1917 and 1959 which are reviewed in the text) and
the date of first authorized edition, I am indebted to Edel and Laurence, 1957.A3.

<u>A Little Tour in France</u>, 1884

<u>Tales of Three Cities</u>, 1884 ("The Impressions of a Cousin," "Lady Barbarina," "A New England Winter")

<u>The Author of Beltraffio</u>, 1885 ("The Author of Beltraffio," "Pandora," "Georgina's Reasons," "The Path of Duty," "Four Meetings")

<u>Stories Revived</u>, 1885 ("The Author of 'Beltraffio,'" "Pandora," "The Path of Duty," "A Light Man," "A Day of Days," "Georgina's Reasons," "A Passionate Pilgrim," "A Landscape-Painter," "Rose-Agathe," "Poor Richard," "The Last of the Valerii," "Master Eustace," "The Romance of Certain Old Clothes," "A Most Extraordinary Case")

<u>The Bostonians</u>, 1886

<u>The Princess Casamassima</u>, 1886

<u>Partial Portraits</u>, 1888

<u>The Reverberator</u>, 1888

<u>The Aspern Papers</u>, 1888 ("The Aspern Papers," "Louisa Pallant," "The Modern Warning")

<u>A London Life</u>, 1889 ("A London Life," "The Patagonia," "The Liar," "Mrs. Temperly")

<u>The Tragic Muse</u>, 1890

<u>The Lesson of the Master</u>, 1892 ("The Lesson of the Master," "The Marriages," "The Pupil," "Brooksmith," "The Solution," "Sir Edmund Orme")

<u>The Real Thing</u>, 1893 ("The Real Thing," "Sir Dominick Ferrand," "Nona Vincent," "The Chaperone," "Greville Fane")

<u>Picture and Text</u>, 1893

<u>The Private Life</u>, 1893 ("The Private Life," "The Wheel of Time," "Lord Beaupre," "The Visits," "Collaboration," "Owen Wingrave")

<u>Essays in London and Elsewhere</u>, 1893

<u>The Wheel of Time</u>, 1893 ("The Wheel of Time," "Collaboration," "Owen Wingrave")

<u>Theatricals</u>, 1894

<u>Theatricals, Second Series</u>, 1894

<u>Terminations</u>, 1895 ("The Death of the Lion," "The Coxon Fund," "The Middle Years," "The Altar of the Dead")

<u>Embarrassments</u>, 1896 ("The Figure in the Carpet," "Glasses," "The Next Time," "The Way It Came")

<u>The Other House</u>, 1896

<u>The Spoils of Poynton</u>, 1897

<u>What Maisie Knew</u>, 1897

Principal Works by Henry James

In the Cage, 1898

The Two Magics, 1898 ("The Turn of the Screw," "Covering End")

The Awkward Age, 1899

The Soft Side, 1900 ("The Great Good Place," "'Europe,'" "Paste,"
     "The Real Right Thing," "The Great Condition," "The Tree of
     Knowledge," "The Abasement of the Northmores," "The Given Case,"
     "John Delavoy," "The Third Person," "Maud-Evelyn," "Miss Gunton
     of Poughkeepsie")

The Sacred Fount, 1901

The Wings of the Dove, 1902

The Better Sort, 1903 ("Broken Wings," "The Beldonald Holbein," "The
     Two Faces," "The Tone of Time," "The Special Type," "Mrs. Medwin,"
     "Flickerbridge," "The Story in It," "The Beast in the Jungle,"
     "The Birthplace," "The Papers")

The Ambassadors, 1903

William Wetmore Story and His Friends, 1903

The Golden Bowl, 1904

The Question of Our Speech, The Lesson of Balzac, 1905

English Hours, 1905

The American Scene, 1907

The Novels and Tales of Henry James, "New York Edition," 1907-09

Views and Reviews, 1908

Julia Bride, 1909

Italian Hours, 1909

The Finer Grain, 1910 ("The Velvet Glove," "Mora Montravers," "A
     Round of Visits," "Crapy Cornelia," "The Bench of Desolation")

The Outcry, 1911

A Small Boy and Others, 1913

Notes of a Son and Brother, 1914

Notes on Novelists, 1914

The Question of the Mind, 1915

The Ivory Tower, 1917

The Sense of the Past, 1917

The Middle Years, 1917

Gabrielle de Bergerac, 1918

Within the Rim, 1919

Master Eustace, 1920 ("Master Eustace," "Longstaff's Marriage,"
     "Théodolinde," "A Light Man," "Benvolio")

Writings about Henry James, 1917-1959

1917 A BOOKS - NONE

1917 B SHORTER WRITINGS

1   ANON. "The Secret of Henry James's Style as Revealed by His
     Typist." Current Opinion, 63 (August), 118.
         Bosanquet's revelations (see 1917.B4) concerning James'
     later method of dictating rather than writing out his nov-
     els in longhand may solve the mystery of his style. For
     James, dictation was the simpler, more inspiring procedure.

2   ANON. "Henry James' Failure as a Dramatist Exposed by a Lon-
     don Critic." Current Opinion, 63 (October), 247.
         With reference to a derogatory review of James' The Out-
     cry in which the author is criticized for his choice of
     subjects and complex style, concludes that James' strengths
     as a novelist caused his failure as a dramatist.

3   BENNETT, ARNOLD. "Henry James," in Books and Persons: Being
     Comments on a Past Epoch: 1908-1911. London: Chatto and
     Windus, pp. 263-66.
         Reprints articles from a series which appeared in New
     Age, 1908-1911. Although James is a first-rate craftsman
     and an admirable critic, his themes are not particularly
     significant, he lacks emotional vigor, and he has a conven-
     tional and ambivalent attitude towards life. When he does
     choose an important subject, he "never fairly bites it and
     makes it bleed."

4   BOSANQUET, THEODORA. "Henry James." Fortnightly Review, NS
     101 (June), 995-1009.
         Reminiscence of Bosanquet's stint as James' amanuensis,
     including description of his dictation methods, the writing
     of the prefaces, his reticence to discuss his work, his rec-
     reational activities. Understanding of an artist's tempera-
     ment is vital to an understanding of his works. Reprinted:
     1917.B5-6.

1917

5   BOSANQUET, THEODORA. "Henry James as a Literary Artist."
    Bookman (New York), 45 (August), 571-81.
        Reprint of 1917.B4.

6   BOSANQUET, THEODORA. "Henry James." Living Age, 294 (11 Au-
    gust), 346-57.
        Reprint of 1917.B4.

7   BROOKE, STOPFORD. Life and Letters of Stopford Brooke.
    Edited by L. P. Jacks. New York: Charles Scribner's Sons,
    pp. 528-29.
        Referring to a preface by James in a letter dated August,
    1897, Brooke describes James' style as "involved and tor-
    mented," difficult to understand.

8   BURRELL, JOHN ANGUS. "Henry James: A Rhapsody of Youth."
    Dial, 63 (27 September), 260-62.
        For a youth "fresh in the experience of knowing Henry
    James," that author depicts life, displays a strong moral
    element and portrays "spiritually alive" characters.

9   DALY, JOSEPH FRANCIS. The Life of Augustin Daly. New York:
    The Macmillan Co., pp. 551-54, 566.
        Reprints letters and excerpts from letters from James to
    Daly in which production of "Mrs. Jasper," written by James
    at Daly's recommendation, is discussed. The comedy was not
    staged because "Augustin lost faith" in the piece.

10 FOLLETT, WILSON. "Henry James and the Untold Story." Dial,
    63 (6 December), 579-81.
        In The Ivory Tower and The Sense of the Past, the effect
    of incompleteness makes James the hero, the center of in-
    terest, and demonstrates the fusion of an "appreciation of
    life" with "a particular kind of fictional method." The
    Ivory Tower is a study of money, and The Sense of the Past
    an affirmation of the superiority of the present as well
    as "the rounding out...of the international novel as Henry
    James created it."

11 FREEMAN, JOHN. "Henry James," in The Moderns: Essays in Lit-
    erary Criticism. New York: Thomas Y. Crowell Co.; London:
    Robert Scott, 1916, pp. 219-41.
        Tribute to James, concentrating on the later work.
    James has had an immense influence on art and criticism of
    our time and demonstrates in his writings the "curiosity of
    a girl, the imagination of a poet, the reasoning mind of a
    man."

1917

12   HUNEKER, JAMES GIBBONS. "A Note on Henry James," in <u>Unicorns</u>.
New York: Charles Scribner's Sons, pp. 53-66.
James deviated from English traditions in the novel and
is a "distinctly American novelist, a psychologist of extraordinary power and divination." Responds to Ford Madox
Ford's study, "stuffed with startling things," and rejects
the notion that James is a moralist. Reprinted: 1922.B9.

13   K., Q. "Henry James's Workshop." <u>New Republic</u>, 13 (1 December), 119-21.
James' sketches for unfinished novels throw interesting
light on the literary process. His notes demonstrate the
importance of logic in the creative process, his tendency
to withhold some of the material for later use, his passion
for the scenic.

14   LITTELL, PHILIP. "Books and Things." <u>New Republic</u>, 13
(29 December), 254.
James' autobiography has some invaluable parts but demonstrates sensibilities too finely attuned and a mood of
"anxious receptivity." Discusses occasional reactions
against James' way of viewing life and way of writing
English. James lived with his adopted England in "a sacred
twitter." Reprinted: 1919.B9.

15   MacCARTHY, DESMOND. "Money, Birth, and Henry James." <u>New
Statesman</u>, 9 (21 July), 375-76.
<u>The Outcry</u> explores "different attitudes of those ap-
parently enjoying such immense immunities towards money"
and, despite its charm, fails as a result of poor acting
and bad dialogue.

16   SCARBOROUGH, DOROTHY. "Modern Ghosts," in <u>The Supernatural
in Modern English Fiction</u>. New York: G. P. Putnam's Sons,
The Knickerbocker Press, pp. 86, 91, 109.
<u>The Turn of the Screw</u> is a "remarkable example of the ob-
jective ghost story." Describes Quint and Jessell as
"characters of unmitigated evil."

17   SCARBOROUGH, DOROTHY. "Supernatural Life," in <u>The Supernatural in Modern English Fiction</u>. New York: G. P. Putnam's
Sons, The Knickerbocker Press, p. 204.
James based <u>The Turn of the Screw</u> on an occurrence "reported to the Psychical Society, of a spectral old woman
corrupting the mind of a child."

1917

18   SCOTT, DIXON. "Henry James," in <u>Men of Letters</u>. Second edi-
     tion. London and New York: Hodder and Stoughton, pp. 78-
     110. Reprinted: 1923.
          Reprints three essays on James. The essential design in
     James is his "simplicity," his "innocence, eagerness, hon-
     esty...," but "technical mutiny" perverted his chosen aims.
     Originally appeared in <u>Bookman</u>, March, 1913. <u>A Small Boy
     and Others</u> shows James' "amazed adoration of the ordinary."
     Originally appeared in <u>Manchester Guardian</u>, May, 1913. In
     the confessional <u>Notes of a Son and Brother</u>, there is a
     distinction between the interest of the subject and the
     arts of the narrator, and thus the work is fallible as
     autobiography. Originally appeared in <u>Manchester Guardian</u>,
     1914.

19   SHERMAN, STUART PRATT. "The Aesthetic Idealism of Henry
     James." <u>Nation</u>, 104 (5 April), 393-99.
          The dominant element of James' art is his absolute and
     exclusive adoration of beauty, and his importance derives
     from the fact that "he is the first novelist writing in
     English to offer us on a grand scale a purely aesthetic
     criticism of modern society and modern fiction." James'
     passion for beauty determines his style and form. Re-
     printed: 1917.B20; 1945.A1.

20   SHERMAN, STUART PRATT. "The Aesthetic Idealism of Henry
     James," in <u>On Contemporary Literature</u>. New York: Henry
     Holt and Co., pp. 226-55.
          Reprint of 1917.B19.

21   WYATT, EDITH FRANKLIN. "Henry James: An Impression," in
     <u>Great Companions</u>. New York: D. Appleton and Co., pp. 83-
     99. Reprinted: Essay Index Reprint Series. Freeport,
     N.Y.: Books for Libraries Press, 1966.
          Reminiscences of James and appreciative commentary on
     his art. The fascination of James' characters is in the
     "essential stuff" of their natures; their inner motives
     are clearly displayed. For them, acquiescence is an act
     of high vision, courage. Originally appeared in <u>North
     American Review</u>, 203 (April 1916), 592-99.

<u>1918 A BOOKS</u>

1   BEACH, JOSEPH WARREN. <u>The Method of Henry James</u>. New Haven,
     Conn.: Yale University Press, 289 pp. Revised: 1954.A1.
          Study of James' story-telling techniques, his novel-
     istic methods. "Part I: The Method" is a theoretical

examination of James' method in its final form, with chapters on "Idea," "Picture," "Revelation," "Suspense," "Point of View," "Dialogue," "Drama," "Eliminations," "Tone," "Romance," and "Ethics." "Part II: The Method of Henry James" demonstrates the evolution of James' method in longer narratives, the process by which he assumed his technique, concentrating on the early excursions and investigations. Chapters include "Obscure Beginnings," "Early Prime," "Non-Canonical," "Achievement: The Spoils of Poynton," "Technical Exercises," "Full Prime," and "The Figure in the Carpet." Ultimately, James dispensed with anything that obscured the rigorous simplicity of design. Partially reprinted: "The Figure in the Carpet," 1945.A1; "Full Prime," in Albert E. Stone, ed. Twentieth Century Interpretations of "The Ambassadors," pp. 37-42; "From The Method of Henry James," in William Stafford, ed. Perspectives on James's "The Portrait of a Lady," pp. 45-50. Reviewed: Thomas Pearce Baily, Sewanee Review, 26 (October 1918), 510-12; Nation, 108 (11 January 1919), 59; Springfield Republican (5 May 1918), p. 15.

1918 B SHORTER WRITINGS

1 BOSANQUET, THEODORA. "The Revised Version." Little Review, 5 (August), 56-62.
   The difference in revised versions of novels for the New York edition is due largely to James' use of dictation, and although the revisions lack the simplicity and smoothness of their predecessors, they are "always richer and more alive." Includes two versions of an excerpt from Four Meetings to indicate general direction of revisions.

2 BOWEN, EDWIN W. "Henry James, the Realist: An Appreciation." Methodist Review, 101 [Fifth series, 34] (May), 410-19.
   Surveys James' accomplishments as one of the early exponents of realism. James is the master of the "story of serious situation" and the first American author to "introduce realism into the impressionistic short story."

3 CAIRNS, WILLIAM B. "Character-Portrayal in the Work of Henry James." University of Wisconsin Studies in Language and Literature, no. 2, pp. 314-22.
   James' characters are more important than his plots, and in his novels persons with different training and standards are allowed to see each other's peculiarities. Points out James' use of the "register" or "reflector" of others and of the action, discusses his use of members of higher

levels of society. James' characters are both intensely real and emotionally appealing, and he presents life "very much as we have known it to be."

4   ELIOT, T. S. "In Memory of Henry James." Egoist, 5 (January), 1-2.
     Only an American can properly appreciate James, who, as a critic, "preyed not upon ideas, but upon living beings.... He had a mind so fine that no idea could violate it." James maintains a consistent point of view and his native wit profited from his being a foreigner. Views James as "a continuator of the New England genius" and suggests relationship with Hawthorne: Both preferred the "deeper psychology" and perceived characters through the relation of two or more people to each other. James shows the most evident influence of Hawthorne at the beginning and end of his career. Reprinted: 1918.B5-6; 1943.B19; 1945.A1.

5   ELIOT, T. S. "The Hawthorne Aspect." Little Review, 5 (August), 47-53.
     Partial reprint of 1918.B4.

6   ELIOT, T. S. "In Memory." Little Review, 5 (August), 44-47.
     Partial reprint of 1918.B4.

7   FOLLETT, HELEN T. and WILSON FOLLETT. "Henry James," in Some Modern Novelists: Appreciations and Estimates. New York: Henry Holt and Co., pp. 75-98. Reprinted: Freeport, N.Y.: Books for Libraries Press, 1967.
     Appreciation of James, which bemoans the "rough gauntlet of criticisms, reviews, notices, parodies" in his later years. Praise James' style, originality. James' philosophy of the social conscience can be summed up in the term "Renunciation, which the soul does that it might live up to itself." Originally appeared in Atlantic Monthly, 117 (June 1916), 801-11.

8   FOLLETT, WILSON. "The Realistic Spirit: II," in The Modern Novel. New York: Alfred A. Knopf, pp. 161-66 and passim. Reprinted: 1923.
     In discussing the mood of impartiality in contemporary fiction, describes James as a writer "animated from the earliest years by this very impulse of curiosity," which became his "philosophy of art and life."

9   GILMAN, LAWRENCE. "Henry James in Reverie." North American Review, 207 (January), 130-35.

The weaknesses in James' reminiscences in <u>The Middle</u>
<u>Years</u> are caused by his lack of a "sense of relative sig-
nificance," a "profound defect in Henry James' art."

10   GOMEZ, ENRIQUE. "The Two Unfinished Novels." <u>Egoist</u>, 5
(January), 3-4.
     <u>The Sense of the Past</u> and <u>The Ivory Tower</u> are generally
dull, although the "scenarios, the word of mouth by which
James revealed his plans...are intensely interesting."

11   HACKETT, FRANCIS. "Henry James," in <u>Horizons: A Book of</u>
<u>Criticism</u>. New York: B. W. Huebsch, pp. 74-82.
     In an essay which originally appeared in the literary
review of <u>The Chicago Evening Post</u> (2 December 1910), asserts that despite James' relative lack of popularity and
his reputation as a "detached bachelor," he was true to his
nature, though one may not appreciate that nature.

12   HACKETT, FRANCIS. "A Stylist on Tour," in <u>Horizons: A Book</u>
<u>of Criticism</u>. New York: B. W. Huebsch, pp. 268-73.
     James' style submits civilized conversation to intense
scrutiny, although simplicity would have been preferable.
<u>The American</u> Scene demonstrates the value of his meticulous-
ness, preserves the beauty of America. Originally appeared
in <u>New Republic</u>, 2 (1 May 1915), 320-21.

13   HOLLIDAY, ROBERT CORTES. "Henry James, Himself," in <u>Walking-</u>
<u>Stick Papers</u>. New York: George H. Doran Co., pp. 121-29.
     Describes James as "a rather amusing though not undis-
tinguished figure." Reports observations of and conversations with James in an American bookstore.

14   HOWELLS, WILLIAM DEAN. "Introduction," in <u>Daisy Miller; An</u>
<u>International Episode</u>. By Henry James. New York: Boni
and Liveright, pp. i-ix.
     Daisy Miller is James' most memorable heroine and repre-
sents the "effect of the American attitude toward woman-
hood." Cites James as the inventor of the international
American girl.

15   K., Q. "Before the Play." <u>New Republic</u>, 16 (7 September),
172.
     <u>The Other House</u> illustrates the differences between the
novelist's and dramatist's crafts.

16   MAYNE, ETHEL COBURN. "Henry James (As seen from the 'Yellow
Book')." <u>Little Review</u>, 5 (August), 1-4.

1918

What the "Yellow Book" group found especially stimulat-
ing about James was "the new world he took us to." James'
strongest work, remarkable for its subtlety and the quality
of fable, was written in his middle period. Points out
that James was highly specialized, writing about relations
in a drawing-room world, not "a working-model of the universe." See 1918.B21.

17 MICHAUD, RÉGIS. "L'art de Henry James," in Mystiques et
    réalistes anglo-saxon d'Emerson à Bernard Shaw. Paris:
    Librairie Armand Colin, pp. 105-32. (French)
       James' notes represent the evolution of the conscience
    of an artist, the history of his method of creating. Dis-
    cusses James' manner, subject matter, and characters.
    James found a psychological theme and a romantic motif.

18 ORAGE, A. R. "Henry James and the Ghostly." Little Review,
    5 (August), 41-43.
       The difference in William James' and Henry James'
    methods and life styles is due to the fact that Henry dealt
    with the subconscious in the province of art, William with
    the conscious in the province of science. Henry aimed at
    representation, not theorizing, and his "method of dealing
    with real persons shades into his dealing with ghosts," in
    which he "rose to the perfection of his observation." Re-
    printed: 1953.B45.

19 POUND, EZRA. "'The Middle Years.'" Egoist, 5 (January), 2-3.
       Only an American who has lived abroad can appreciate
    James' writings to their fullest. Concludes that "the
    essence of James is that he is always 'settling-in.'" Re-
    printed: 1918.B22; 1920.B27; 1934.B24.

20 POUND, EZRA. "Brief Note." Little Review, 5 (August), 6-9.
       James' death signals the end of an era. He attempted
    "to make three nations intelligible to each other" and
    portrayed major conflicts and national qualities in his
    works. Discusses James as a "hater of tyranny." Re-
    printed: 1920.B27; 1934.B24; in Leon Edel, ed. Henry
    James: A Collection of Critical Essays, pp. 27-30.

21 POUND, EZRA. "In Explanation." Little Review, 5 (August), 5-6.
       Introduction to essays, 1918.B20, B22-24. Answers
    Mayne's objections (in 1918.B16) to Notes on Novelists.
    Reprinted: 1920.B27; 1934.B24.

22 POUND, EZRA. "'The Middle Years.'" Little Review, 5 (August),
     39-41.
          Reprint of 1918.B19.

23 POUND, EZRA. "The Notes to 'The Ivory Tower.'" Little Review,
     5 (August), 62-64; (September), 50-53.
          Presents the generalities found in James' notes for The
     Ivory Tower, reviews in outline form James' plan for con-
     structing the novel. The notes are a "landmark" in the
     "history of the novel as written in English." Reprinted:
     1920.B27.

24 POUND, EZRA. "A Shake Down." Little Review, 5 (August), 9-39.
          Discussion of James' various styles, his faults, his
     preoccupation with major forces in the analyses of national
     qualities. Calls James "the great true recorder." Sug-
     gests what of James to read and includes notes on novels
     and stories in the order of their publication, with some
     lengthier explications. Proposes a five or six volume
     edition of James "so selected as to hold its own inter-
     nationally." Reprinted: 1920.B27; 1934.B24.

25 RODKER, JOHN. "The Notes on Novelists." Little Review, 5
     (August), 53-56.
          James' criticisms of contemporary writers are both fair
     and astute. Reviews James' judgments, suggests that his
     article on "The New Novel" is not on "such sure ground" in
     that it fails to recognize D. H. Lawrence's preeminence.

26 WALEY, ARTHUR. "'The Turn of the Screw.'" Egoist, 5 (Janu-
     ary), 4.
          In The Turn of the Screw, the ghosts are the embodiment
     of the contamination of Miles and Flora in a story that
     deals with the interior life of the children.

27 WARD, GENEVIEVE and RICHARD WHITEING. Both Sides of the Cur-
     tain. London: Cassell and Co., pp. 274-75.
          James' dramas were too "literary," and therefore unac-
     ceptable to British audiences.

28 WARD, MRS. HUMPHRY. "London in the Eighties," and "The Villa
     Barberini. Henry James," in A Writer's Recollections
     (1856-1900). Glasgow: W. Collins Sons and Co., pp. 193-
     96, 323-36.
          Recounts association with James, whom Mrs. Ward met in
     London in 1882 and whose visit with the Wards at Villa
     Barberini is described. Summarizes "the general mark left
     on me by his fruitful and stainless life." Notes James'

1918

wide knowledge, his relationship with Italian country people, quotes from his letter on Ward's 'Elenor,' discusses
his novelistic method. "Technique--presentation--were then
immensely important to him...." Concludes that at the core
of James' work is the man, "with whose delicate, ironic
mind and most human heart we are in contact."

1919 A BOOKS - NONE

1919 B SHORTER WRITINGS

1   BOYNTON, PERCY H. "The Rise of Fiction; William Dean How-
     ells," in A History of American Literature. Boston and New
     York: Ginn and Co., pp. 422-24 and passim.
        James is an international novelist, and a master in his
     field, however limited. But "normal, healthy human beings
     ...are seldom to be encountered in the pages of Henry
     James." Describes The Awkward Age as "a piece of Swiss
     carving on ivory."

2   CLARK, A. F. BRUCE. "Henry James." University Magazine
     (Montreal), 18 (February), 45-68.
        James showed unusual artistic independence from the
     novel-reading public and from contemporary influences.
     Chronological examination of the growth of James' concep-
     tion of the novel in typical novels and critical essays.
     Concludes that James' "originality, conscientiousness, and
     moral refinement still await due recognition."

3   CORNELIUS, R. D. "The Clearness of Henry James." Sewanee
     Review, 27 (January), 1-8.
        Makes a case for James' simplification of complicated
     material, pointing out characteristics that contribute to
     clarity. James' works reveal an "artistic clearness that
     is satisfying to a careful and interested reader."

4   EAGLE, SOLOMON [pseud.]. "Henry James' Obscurity," in Books
     in General. New York: Alfred A. Knopf, pp. 195-200.
        See 1919.B14.

5   EDGAR, PELHAM. "Henry James and His Method." Proceedings
     and Transactions of the Royal Society of Canada, series 3,
     12 (December 1918; March 1919), section II, 225-40.
        Uses James to exemplify effective methods of composi-
     tion, discusses the realization of theme in The Ivory
     Tower, studies The Ambassadors as an example of the disci-
     pline James applied to his novels, mentions weaknesses in

10

that work but calls it "his greatest achievement in fiction...." Considers James' indebtedness to writers like
Balzac and Flaubert.

6   GUEDALLA, PHILIP. "The Crowner's Quest." New Statesman, 12
(15 February), 421-22.
    With the Little Review James number, "the coroner spir-
it...invaded the quiet chambers of literary criticism."
The reviewers ignore the humor and the "rich purity" of
James' middle period and venerate the "rococo" of his later
period. Divides James' work into that of "James I,
James II, and the Old Pretender." Reprinted: 1921.B11.

7   JOHNSON, ARTHUR. "A Comparison of Manners." New Republic,
20 (27 August), 113-15.
    As concerns "manners," Melville's writing is "almost
uniquely comparable" to that of James. Both grope for
thoroughness. Questions whether James as a child might
have read Melville.

8   LITTELL, PHILIP. "Henry James's Quality," in Books and Things.
New York: Harcourt, Brace and Howe, pp. 215-23.
    James improved in his ability to depict human relation-
ships and create characters. Discusses James' four "supreme novels," The Awkward Age, The Wings of the Dove, The
Ambassadors, and The Golden Bowl, in which the presence of
vigilant observers leaves the protagonists without adequate
friendships. Originally appeared in New Republic, 6
(11 March 1916), 152-54.

9   LITTELL, PHILIP. "The Middle Years," in Books and Things.
New York: Harcourt, Brace and Howe, pp. 224-29.
Reprint of 1917.B14.

10 LYND, ROBERT. "Henry James," in Old and New Masters. New
York: Charles Scribner's Sons, pp. 70-85.
    James lived for his tastes rather than his passions and
is "The Novelist of Grains and Scruples." Praises James'
skill, his critical judgment. Discusses "The Artist at
Work" in The Sense of the Past and The Ivory Tower. In
"How He Was Born Again," compares James' British naturalization to Christian conversion, and suggests that the autobiography is remarkably egocentric.

11 MENCKEN, H. L. The American Language: An Inquiry into the
Development of English in the United States. New York:
Alfred A. Knopf, passim. Reprinted: 1921; 1923; fourth
edition corrected, enlarged, and rewritten, 1936;

1919

reprinted: 1937. Abridged, with annotations and new material, by Raven I. McDavid, Jr., with the assistance of David W. Maurer, 1963.
  Refers to James' view of "'vulgarisms'" in "The Question of Our Speech" and his dislike of the "persistent r-sound" in American speech.

12 MORDELL, ALBERT. "Foreword," in Travelling Companions. By Henry James. New York: Boni and Liveright, pp. vii-ix.
  The seven stories included in the volume, written between 1868 and 1874, show the influence of Hawthorne and romanticism and reveal a simplicity which neither baffles nor tires the reader.

13 MORDELL, ALBERT. "Preface," in A Landscape Painter. By Henry James. New York: Scott and Seltzer, pp. 1-4.
  The four tales included in the volume, "A Landscape Painter," "Poor Richard," "A Day of Days," and "A Most Extraordinary Case," display exceptionally mature thought and clear style.

14 SQUIRE, SIR JOHN COLLINGS. "Henry James's Obscurity," in Books in General. New York: Alfred A. Knopf, pp. 195-200.
  Discusses James' lack of public popularity. James' obscurity was a result of his desire for clarity. "In an age of sloppy writing he stood for accuracy of craftmanship...." See 1919.B4.

15 WAUGH, ARTHUR. "The Art of Henry James," in Tradition and Change: Studies in Contemporary Literature. New York: E. P. Dutton and Co., pp. 246-52.
  James developed from a national novelist into a proponent of "the novel of analytic impressionism" and bridged the gap between the Victorian giants and the eager, experimental Georgians.

16 WILLIAMS, HAROLD. "A Note on American Novelists," in Modern English Writers: Being a Study of Imaginative Literature, 1890-1914. New York: Alfred A. Knopf, pp. 455-56, 458-67.
  For James, life had too much the air of a museum art exhibit, his characters were too polished and sterile, his psychology superficial. His influence results from the emphasis on point of view.

17 [WOOLF, VIRGINIA.] "Henry James: A Last Glimpse." Living Age, 301 (31 May), 541-43.

James' "Within the Rim" was written in support of the
beauties of civilization threatened by war, and is "the
best statement yet made of the largest point of view."
Reprinted: 1942.B8.

1920 A BOOKS

1 LILJEGREN, S. B. American and European in the Works of Henry
     James. Lund: Lund Universitets Arsskrift, 66 pp.
        James' interest in America and Europe and their inter-
     relations is a predominant theme in his works. Discusses
     influences on theme and looks at The American, Daisy Miller,
     The Portrait of a Lady to demonstrate the contrast between
     cultures and the personality differences which the two
     worlds create. "The perfect accordance of his work with
     his theory of the 'point of view' is most easily understood
     in the light of his 'double consciousness'" of America and
     Europe.

1920 B SHORTER WRITINGS

1 ANON. "Henry James's Failure as a Dramatist." Literary Di-
     gest, 65 (8 May), 48.
        Briefly surveys James' dramatic ventures, with emphasis
     on Guy Domville. "How to fail gloriously as a dramatist is
     one way of treating a period of five years in the life of
     Henry James...."

2 ANON. "The Illuminating Letters of Henry James." Current
     Opinion, 68 (May), 676-78.
        Using excerpts from James' correspondence, asserts that
     the value of the letters is in showing "the everyday lov-
     able, witty, humorous, human Henry James, as well as James
     the novelist, James the critic, James the dramatist, James
     the artist in life as in literature.

3 ANON. "The Gulf of Henry James." Nation, 111 (20 October),
     441.
        The gulf between James' critics and supporters can be
     attributed to his attempt to write courtly romances in a
     democratic age. "Decorum...damns Henry James with the
     larger public."

4 BENNETT, ARNOLD. "Henry James," in Things That Have Inter-
     ested Me. First series. New York: George H. Doran Co.,
     pp. 323-32.

13

1920

James' letters exhibit his "lovable personality," but
his novels lack interest because they are rarely "about
anything," and "lack ecstasy, guts." Recalls his meetings
with James and appends critical review he wrote of the
first performance of Guy Domville.

5   BOSANQUET, THEODORA. "The Record of Henry James." Yale Re-
    view, NS 10 (October), 143-56.
        Reviews the critical reception of the letters of James,
    which are a magnificent achievement in an age which has
    lost the capacity for such effort. James' view of the art
    of correspondence was as broad as that of conversation.
    The foundation of the letters is his faith in his literary
    calling.

6   BOYD, ERNEST AUGUSTUS. "Henry James Self-Revealed." Freeman,
    1 (25 August), 563-64.
        In reference to Lubbock's edition of James' letters
    (1920.B20), "only a mouse emerges from the mountain of
    words of which the letters are composed." James' corre-
    spondence confirms the low regard in which he is held with
    the general public, demonstrating him to be an "intellec-
    tual hypochondriac," and is the "reductio ad absurdum of
    the 'literary gent.'" See 1920.B7, B9. Reprinted:
    1927.B2.

7   BRAGDON, CLAUDE. "The Letters of Henry James." Freeman, 1
    (8 September), 619.
        In order to appreciate a talent like James', one must
    possess with him a "community of consciousness." Boyd
    (see 1920.B6) revealed himself.

8   BROOKS, VAN WYCK. "Our Illustrious Expatriate." Freeman, 1
    (28 April), 164-65.
        The style of James' letters is deliberately concealing,
    obscure, and protective. They reveal his obsession with
    America, his "evasion of all the major experiences of
    life...." However, "as compositions, as exercises in
    prose...they are of supreme significance."

9   COWARD, T. R. "The Letters of Henry James." Freeman, 1
    (8 September), 618-19.
        Boyd (see 1920.B6) denounces James as a man without
    judging the letters as they reveal and elucidate the works
    of James the artist. Nevertheless, the correspondence
    fails to display the "glorious, intuitive genius" of James.

10   EGAN, MAURICE FRANCIS. "The Revelation of an Artist in Lit-
     erature." Catholic World, 111 (June), 289-300.
          James' letters are of little interest to Catholics be-
     cause they fail to treat "the union of the human soul with
     God." Suggests that the letters show little of the spir-
     itual element in James, and discusses some of the topics
     and attitudes expressed therein.

11   FORD, FORD MADOX [pseud.]. "Thus to Revisit...." Dial, 69
     (July), 52-60; (August), 132-41; (September), 239-46.
          See 1920.B16.

12   GILMAN, LAWRENCE. "The Letters of Henry James." North Ameri-
     can Review, 211 (May), 682-90.
          James' letters are "matchless for their prodigal and
     eager flow of sympathy, their inexhaustible kindliness,
     their ample and exquisite tenderness...." Sees James'
     expatriation as natural and necessary in view of his
     "loathing of America."

13   GOSSE, EDMUND. "Henry James." London Mercury, 1 (April),
     673-84; 2 (May), 29-41.
          Essentially a biographical account of James, based in
     part on personal reminiscences, with brief chronological
     discussions of his novels. Gosse met James in 1880, and
     their friendship, the details of which are related, con-
     tinued until James' fatal illness. "Henry James, at the
     age of seventy, had not begun to reveal himself behind the
     mask which spoke in the tones of a world of imaginary char-
     acters." Reprinted: 1920.B14; 1922.B5.

14   _____. "Henry James." Scribner's Magazine, 67 (April), 422-
     30; (May), 548-57.
          Reprint of 1920.B13.

15   HIND, CHARLES LEWIS. "Henry James," in Authors and I. New
     York: John Lane Co., pp. 161-65.
          Criticizes the overinvolved style and characters who
     have analyzed their feelings out of existence in James'
     novels. Recalls his initial meeting with James at Henry
     Harland's flat, his visits at Lamb House. James is more
     impressive as a man than as an author.

16   HUEFFER, FORD MADOX. "Thus to Revisit...." Dial, 69 (July),
     52-60; (August), 132-41; (September), 239-46.
          In the English literary world, Conrad and James are the
     outstanding figures of the past quarter century "for the
     history of definite, conscious...contagious aesthetic

1920

effect." James found a new form for the English novel, viewing the artist as a receptive instrument recording his sense of the Truth. Reminisces about conversations with James. <u>See</u> 1920.B11.

17 HUNEKER, J. G. "The Lesson of the Master." <u>Bookman</u> (New York), 51 (May), 364-68.
    The letters of James reveal the social side of the cosmopolitan author and illuminate his writings and his characters, thus serving as an introduction to his life and work. "He was well-nigh the typical 'Uncle' of fiction and footlights...."

18 JAMES, WILLIAM. <u>The Letters of William James</u>. Edited by Henry James II. 2 vols. Boston: Atlantic Monthly Press, passim.
    Includes letters to Henry James, 1867 to 1908. Introduction presents biographical information about the James family.

19 LITTELL, PHILIP. "Books and Things." <u>New Republic</u>, 23 (9 June), 63-64.
    The primary interest in James' letters is that of "contact with an extraordinary human being...." The overall impression yielded by the correspondence is one of "great loneliness in the midst of so much affection received and given."

20 LUBBOCK, PERCY. "Introduction," in <u>The Letters of Henry James</u>. Edited by Percy Lubbock. Vol. 1. New York: Charles Scribner's Sons, pp. xiii-xxxi.
    Although the letters of James offer as comprehensive a picture of him as we can hope to possess, they only suggest the revealing aspects of his chosen profession. "...The central fact of all, the fact that gave everything else its meaning to himself, is that of which least is told." Discusses the different strains in James' artistic experience and interpersonal relations, notes the change in tone of letters over the years, considers his expatriation. The later letters give the flavor of James' conversation, with its "grandiose courtesy, his luxuriant phraseology, his relish for some extravagantly colloquial turn embedded in a Ciceronian period, his humor at once so majestic and so burly." Reprinted: as "The Mind of the Artist," 1945.A1.

21 MacCARTHY, DESMOND. "Henry James." <u>New Statesman</u>, 15 (15 May), 162-64.

1920

Reminiscence of James, "above all a novelist of dis-
tinctions," whom MacCarthy knew for fifteen years. Describes the essence of James as "his apprehensively tender
clutch upon others, his immense preoccupation with the
surface of things and his exclusive devotion to his art."
See 1931.B17.

22 MATTHEWS, BRANDER. "Henry James and The Theatre." Bookman
(New York), 51 (June), 389-95.
With reference to James' letters and prefaces, discusses
James' experiment with the dramatic form. The secret to
his failure at playwrighting is his detestation of the
audience he was aiming to amuse, the absence of solidarity
between author and spectators. Reprinted: 1923.B15.

23 MENCKEN, H. L. "Notes in the Margin." Smart Set, 63 (November), 140-41.
"Henry James would have been vastly improved by a few
whiffs" from the Chicago stockyards. He went the wrong
direction in his escape from New England and "was confronted by a culture more solid and assured than his own.
It kept him shaky all his life long." Reprinted: 1949.B39.

24 MOSES, MONTROSE J. "Henry James as a Letter Writer." Outlook, 125 (26 May), 167-68.
The letters of James portray him as a fascinating
friend, an individual pursuing artistic perfection. They
reveal his passion for life and his humanity and offer a
guide to methods of plot and character evolution.

25 MOULT, THOMAS. "Dedicated to Art." English Review, 31
(August), 183-86.
James' singleminded dedication to art resulted in his
separation from life itself, which provides the natural
material for art, and caused him to be rejected by the
reading public.

26 NADAL, ELIRMAN SYME. "Personal Recollections of Henry James."
Scribner's Magazine, 68 (July), 89-97.
Reminiscence of his friendship with James, which began
shortly after both had arrived in England to live, including description of James' personal qualities and ideas, and
with occasional reference to his works as they reveal his
opinions. Deals with James primarily as a social creature
rather than as a novelist.

1920

27   POUND, EZRA. "Henry James," in <u>Instigations</u>. New York: Boni
      and Liveright, pp. 106-67. Reprinted: Chicago: Henry
      Regnery Co., 1960; Essay Index Reprint Series. Freeport,
      N.Y.: Books for Libraries Press, 1967.
           Reprints of 1918.B19-21, B23-24.

28   SAMPSON, GEORGE. "Letters in Criticism." <u>Bookman</u> (London),
      58 (May), 76-77.
           James was a critic rather than a novelist, a spectator
      rather than a participant, and a fanatic on the subject of
      form.

29   WALKLEY, ARTHUR BINGHAM. "Henry James and His Letters."
      <u>Fortnightly Review</u>, NS 107 (June), 864-73.
           Discusses, with the aid of the letters, selected as-
      pects of James the literary artist. Correspondence re-
      veals a man who lived absolutely, dedicatedly for
      literature and demonstrates that the attention James could
      not gain from others in the reading public he was unable
      to give himself.

30   WHARTON, EDITH. "Henry James in His Letters." <u>Quarterly Re-
      view</u> (London), 234 (July), 188-202.
           Notes personal characteristics evident in James' let-
      ters: his concern for the recipient, his affection. Con-
      siders the difficulties of editing the correspondence,
      describes James in conversation, points out the "quality of
      fun" in his talk. James as a man of letters had unshake-
      able faith in the novelist's art, and he excelled in allu-
      sion, comment and reminiscence rather than in correspond-
      ence. Partially reprinted: in Leon Edel, ed. <u>Henry James:
      A Collection of Critical Essays</u>, pp. 31-36.

31   WHITFORD, ROBERT CALVIN. "The Letters of Henry James." <u>South
      Atlantic Quarterly</u>, 19 (October), 371-72.
           James' individuality is represented in Lubbock's excel-
      lent edition of the letters (1920.B20), which reveal the
      author's character development from 1869-1915 and show his
      growing concern for style and aesthetic questions. James
      occasionally "rubs the American eagle's neck-feathers the
      wrong way."

32   [WOOLF, VIRGINIA.] "The Letters of Henry James." <u>Times Lit-
      erary Supplement</u> (8 April), pp. 217-18.
           James' letters give a clear and controlled picture of
      his experiences in Europe and suggest his love of life.
      The reader may derive from the later letters an idea of
      "the complex figure of the artist in his completeness."
      Reprinted: 1942.B8.

1921 A BOOKS - NONE

1921 B SHORTER WRITINGS

1   ANON. "Novels of Henry James." Living Age, 310 (30 July),
    267-71.
        Events are calculated in James' work to reveal some
    concealed state of mind. His world is an ideal one, set-
    ting up unrealizable standards, and his characters exist
    in "a vibrating air of sympathy," in which the highest
    moments come from "shared perception."

2   ANON. "A Reviewer's Notebook." Freeman, 3 (24 August), 574-
    75.
        James is one of the "young old men" of the literary
    scene "who seem to have been born with ink in their veins."
    Suggests that there is something depressing in "the decay
    of Henry James" which makes more remarkable "the cheerful,
    if rather inky, vigour of his prime." See 1922.B1.

3   BEACH, JOSEPH WARREN. "Henry James," in The Cambridge History
    of American Literature. Edited by William Peterfield Trent
    et al. Cambridge, England: At the University Press; New
    York: The Macmillan Co., vol. 3, pp. 96-108; vol. 4,
    pp. 671-75. Reprint, 1936.
        "Henry James was born an American and died an English-
    man." Discusses James' passion for Europe associated with
    his love for the art of representation, but suggests that
    his theme ultimately possessed as much American character
    as European setting. Considers three periods of James'
    writing in terms of his treatment of the American theme.
    Includes a biographical sketch of the James family, dis-
    cusses Henry's literary career with reference to form and
    treatment, and assesses the influence of other novelists,
    concluding that the style and tone of Walter Pater's writ-
    ing "more nearly anticipate the style of James than do those
    of any other writer, English or French."

4   BENSON, EDWARD FREDERIC. "An Archaeological Excursion," in
    Our Family Affairs, 1867-1896. New York: George H. Doran
    Co., pp. 272-75.
        Records James' reaction to Benson's manuscript Dodo:
    "He wrote me the most careful and kindly of letters...."

5   BRADFORD, GAMALIEL. "Portrait of Henry James." North American
    Review, 213 (February), 211-24.
        James provides an example of passion for art injuring
    itself, distracting the author from the variety and richness

1921

of life in general. Considers James in regard to "common concerns of men," like sports, business, religion, politics. Only in the area of human relations does James seem alive as a man. Reprinted: 1922.B3.

6   CONRAD, JOSEPH. "Henry James: An Appreciation," in <u>Notes on Life and Letters</u>. London: J. M. Dent and Sons, pp. 13-23; Garden City, N.Y.: Doubleday, Page and Co., pp. 11-19.
     James chronicles "personal contests desperate in their silence," examines human conduct. Describes the novelist as "a historian, the preserver, the keeper, the expounder, of human experience," and James as "the historian of fine consciences." His characters' final triumphs occur in "an energetic act of renunciation," and his novels "remain with the sense of the life still going on...." Originally appeared in <u>North American Review</u>, 180 (January 1905), 102-108; 203 (April 1916), 585-91. Reprinted: 1945.A1; in Leon Edel, ed. <u>Henry James: A Collection of Critical Essays</u>, pp. 11-17.

7   DAVRAY, HENRY D. "Un déraciné angloaméricain: Henry James, d'après sa correspondance." <u>Mercure de France</u>, 146 (15 February), 68-84. (French)
     Discusses James' interval in Paris and his attitudes towards French authors and movements, particularly naturalism, as evidenced in his correspondence. Despite differences in their theories of art, James shows understanding and impartiality in assessing the naturalists.

8   de CHAIGNON la ROSE, PIERRE. "Preface," in <u>Notes and Reviews by Henry James</u>. Edited by Pierre de Chaignon la Rose. Cambridge, Mass.: Dunster House, pp. v-xvi. Reprinted: Essay Index Reprint Series. Freeport, N.Y.: Books for Libraries Press, 1968.
     In introducing this collection of twenty-five unsigned book reviews by James which appeared in <u>Nation</u> and <u>North American Review</u>, considers the general literary task of book reviewing, and suggests that James' emphasis on technical problems made it impossible for him to be a great critic. Nevertheless, time has confirmed most of James' judgments, and the reviews reveal "charm," "discriminating intelligence," and "supremely endearing 'fineness.'"

9   EDGAR, PELHAM. "The Letters of Henry James." <u>Queen's Quarterly</u>, 28 (January), 283-87.
     Reviews the scope and variety of James' correspondence, which demonstrates his "thrilling response to life" and

preoccupation with art and its principles. Notes "the
sympathetic qualities, the grave Olympian urbanities, that
constitute the human basis of these admirable letters."

10   FORD, FORD MADOX [pseud.]. "Two Americans--Henry James and
     Stephen Crane." The Literary Review, 1 (19 March), 1-2;
     (26 March), 1-2.
         See 1921.B12.

11   GUEDALLA, PHILIP. "Some Critics," in Supers and Supermen:
     Studies in Politics, History and Letters. New York:
     Alfred A. Knopf, pp. 42-46.
         Reprint of 1919.B6.

12   HUEFFER, FORD MADOX. "Two Americans--Henry James and Stephen
     Crane." The Literary Review, 1 (19 March), 1-2; (26 March),
     1-2.
         Despite the angry critical response to previous judgment
     of James as an American, Hueffer reiterates his position
     and gives evidence for it. James' attitude towards Stephen
     Crane was uncomfortable, although he recognized his coun-
     tryman's genius. James' characteristic attitude towards
     other literary personalities had three levels: "superfi-
     cial benevolences," underneath which was a layer of "nervous
     cruelty," and finally a depth of "religious, mystical bene-
     volence." See 1921.B10.

13   LUBBOCK, PERCY. The Craft of Fiction. New York: Charles
     Scribner's Sons, pp. 156-202. Reprint, Compass Books.
     New York: The Viking Press, 1957.
         Defines point of view as the "method by which the pic-
     ture of the mind is fully dramatized." James represents
     his subject by letting his reader watch the thought itself
     rather than telling the reader what is there. Shows how
     this technique is put into effect in The Ambassadors. "It
     is a purely pictorial subject, covering Strether's field of
     vision and bounded by its limits...." Although the novel
     is a story told from one man's point of view, the point of
     view itself is something for the reader to confront and
     watch actively. Everything in the novel is dramatically
     rendered. Describes James' use of dramatic technique in
     The Wings of the Dove, the subject of which is Milly's ef-
     fect on the relationship between Kate and Densher: "Not to
     walk straight up to the fact and put it into phrases, but
     to surround the fact, and so to detach it inviolate--such
     is Henry James's manner of dramatizing it." Examines The
     Awkward Age, a story treated "as pure drama" in which
     "everything is immediate and particular..." and in which

1921

> "method becomes as consistent and homogeneous as it ever
> may in fiction." Labels James "the only real scholar in
> the art" of fiction. Partially reprinted: 1952.B33; as
> "The Point of View: The Ambassadors," in Leon Edel, ed.
> Henry James: A Collection of Critical Essays, pp. 37-46.

14   LUCAS, E. V., ed. Edwin Austin Abbey, The Record of His Life
     and Work. 2 vols. London: Methuen and Co., passim.
       Recounts details of the association between Edwin Austin
     Abbey and James, including James' views of the artist whose
     work he saw as "'characteristically American.'" Quotes ex-
     cerpts from James' remarks on Abbey's genius.

15   MATTHEWS, BRANDER. "Henry James, Book Reviewer." New York
     Times Book Review (12 June), p. 2.
       The specimens of James' early manner in de Chaignon la
     Rose's edition of Notes and Reviews (see 1921.B8) show the
     author to be "resolutely clear and conscientiously clever"
     and demonstrate his critical penetration. The reviews are
     generally within the established traditions, with evidence
     of independence and frankness. Notes subjects of reviews.

*16 MILLS, J. SAXON. Sir Edward Cook. London: Constable and
     Co. Excerpted in 1947.A2.
       Reprints James' response to assistant editor Edward
     Cook's invitation to submit his list of "'the hundred best
     books'" to Pall Mall Magazine.

17   PHELPS, WILLIAM LYON. "Henry James, Reviewer." The Literary
     Review, 1 (4 June), 4.
       James' literary judgments have stood the test of time
     well, and his criticisms serve as models. He does not show
     off, yet he is constantly attempting in imagination to re-
     write the works he reviews. Discusses James' attitude
     towards Trollope, whose success defied analysis in James'
     opinion.

18   RANDELL, WILFRID L. "Henry James as Humanist." Fortnightly
     Review, NS 110 (September), 458-69.
       James was a humanist whose attention "is focussed upon
     democracy rather than upon aristocracy." Analyzes The
     Princess Casamassima, an example of James' wider range.
     Also refers to In the Cage, several other short stories,
     and three characters in The Golden Bowl to demonstrate
     "the strong interest of a great novelist in humanity under
     varied aspects."

1921

19 VAN DOREN, CARL. "Henry James," in The American Novel. New
    York: The Macmillan Co., pp. 188-220. Revised and en-
    larged, 1940; reprinted: 1970.
        Biographical sketch with brief discussions of individual
    works, emphasizing the "international situation," for James
    roughly equivalent to the frontier. James' sensitivity to
    national differences caused him to neglect the universal
    human similarities which transcend nationality. He tried,
    "in a democratic way, to write courtly romances."

20 WALKLEY, ARTHUR BINGHAM. "Henry James and the Theatre," in
    Pastiche and Prejudice. London: William Heinemann,
    pp. 155-59. Reprinted: Essay Index Reprint Series. Free-
    port, N.Y.: Books for Libraries Press, 1970.
        James was not coarse enough or tough enough for success
    in the theatre and was unable to turn himself into "a
    simple-minded writer." However, he used what he learned
    while afflicted with the "theatrical malady."

21 WALKLEY, ARTHUR BINGHAM. "Talk at the Martello Tower," in
    Pastiche and Prejudice. London: William Heinemann,
    pp. 206-10. Reprinted: Essay Index Reprint Series. Free-
    port, N.Y.: Books for Libraries Press, 1970.
        Dialogue between Selina and Patty, with reference to
    James' letters and especially his concept of point of view.
    "The method of Henry James was good for Henry James."

22 [WOOLF, VIRGINIA.] "Henry James' Ghost Stories." Times Lit-
    erary Supplement (22 December), pp. 849-50.
        Critiques "Owen Wingrave," "The Friends of the Friends,"
    and The Turn of the Screw, and suggests that "the stories
    in which Henry James uses the supernatural effectively
    are...those where some quality in a character or in a situ-
    ation can only be given its fullest meaning by being cut
    free from facts." Concludes that "that courtly, worldly,
    sentimental old gentleman can still make us afraid of the
    dark." Reprinted: 1921.B23; in Leon Edel, ed. Henry James:
    A Collection of Critical Essays, pp. 47-54.

23 WOOLF, VIRGINIA. "The Ghost Stories," in Granite and Rainbow.
    New York: Harcourt, Brace and World, pp. 65-72. Re-
    printed: 1958.
        Reprint of unsigned article in Times Literary Supplement,
    1921.B22.

1922

1922 A BOOKS

1 PERRY, BLISS. <u>Commemorative Tribute to Henry James.</u> Academy
   Notes and Monographs. New York: The DeVinne Press, 5 pp.
       In an essay prepared for the American Academy of Arts
   and Letters, suggests that James, despite his penetration
   in New England character, was everywhere, except possibly
   London, a "'visiting mind,'" "subject of complete theory
   of deracination." Remarks on James' absolute devotion to
   his craft, his individual dialect which became increasingly
   apparent in his later works. "In his three score books
   there are delicious, poignant moments where the spirit of
   life itself flutters like a wild creature, half-caught,
   half-escaping."

1922 B SHORTER WRITINGS

1 ANON. "A Reviewer's Notebook." <u>Freeman</u>, 4 (8 February),
   526-27.
       Continuation of 1921.B2. Queries what James' American
   destiny might have been and if he would have survived more
   effectually there. Illustrates James' ambivalent views on
   emigration of the artist from America in biography of W. W.
   Story and <u>The Sense of the Past</u>.

2 AYSCOUGH, JOHN. "Of Some Americans." <u>Catholic World</u>, 116
   (October), 41-55.
       In discussing Irving, Hawthorne, Poe, Howells, Bret
   Harte and James as stylists, describes James' work as "the
   undesirable climax of containing hardly anything but craftsmanship." Like Jane Austen, James chose to be a miniaturist,
   but he failed to achieve her mastery in his chosen form.
   "...One questions if he were so much a great author as a
   first-rate man of letters."

3 BRADFORD, GAMALIEL. "Henry James," in <u>American Portraits:
   1875-1900</u>. New York: Houghton Mifflin Co., pp. 171-96.
       Reprint of 1921.B5.

4 CANBY, HENRY SEIDEL. "Henry James," in <u>Definitions: Essays
   in Contemporary Criticism</u>. First series. New York: Harcourt, Brace and Co., pp. 278-81. Reprinted: Port Washington, N.Y.: Kennikat Press, 1967.
       James as a literary phenomenon "represented a sensitive
   mind's reaction against the obviousness of the life that one
   finds in most American 'best sellers.'" Considers James
   the greatest craftsman among American novelists and the
   greatest critic since Poe. His novels offer analysis of

life. "...As a writer of fine, imaginative criticism of the intellect as it moves through the complexities of modern civilization, he yields to no one of our time."

5   GOSSE, EDMUND. "Henry James," in Aspects and Impressions. New York: Cassell and Co., pp. 17-53.
Reprint of 1920.B13.

6   HERRICK, ROBERT. "Tolstoi and Henry James." Yale Review, NS 12 (October), 181-86.
Review of Lubbock's The Craft of Fiction (see 1921.B13) reveals some critical limitations in Lubbock's method and performance, including his critical observations of Tolstoi. He is strongest in his treatment of James. "...If ever artist was made not born, if ever an imaginative writer created with a laborious, even irritable self-consciousness of his process, it was Henry James."

7   HOWE, M. A. DeWOLFE. Memories of a Hostess: A Chronicle of Eminent Friendships Drawn Chiefly from the Diaries of Mrs. Jas. T. Fields. Boston: The Atlantic Monthly Press, pp. 297-301 and passim.
An excerpt from Mrs. Field's diary, Monday, September 13, 1898, describes a day with Henry James at Rye, accompanied by Sarah Orne Jewett, for whose writings James expressed appreciation.

8   HUNEKER, JAMES GIBBONS. Letters of James Gibbons Huneker. Edited by Josephine Huneker. New York: Charles Scribner's Sons, passim.
Passing references to James. Calls Rebecca West's study of the author "'sassy.'"

9   HUNEKER, JAMES GIBBONS. "A Note on Henry James," in Modern English Essays: 1870-1920. Edited by Ernest Rhys. Vol. 5. New York: E. P. Dutton and Co., pp. 64-76.
Reprint of 1917.B12.

10 HUNEKER, JAMES GIBBONS. Steeplejack. Vol. 2. New York: Charles Scribner's Sons, passim.
Passing references to James, whom Huneker met only once in New York and whom James mistook for Scribner.

11 MANLY, JOHN MATTHEWS and EDITH RICKERT. "The Old Masters: Howells and James," in Contemporary American Literature: Bibliographies and Study Outlines. New York: Harcourt, Brace and Co., pp. 81-87. Reprinted: 1929.

1922

Biographical sketch of James, suggestions for reading, bibliography of writings by James, bibliography of "studies and reviews."

12 MICHAUD, RÉGIS. "William et Henry James d'après leur correspondance." Revue de France, 5 (September), 141-59. (French)
Describes James as "the most original novelist in the United States" and as "a professional globe-trotter." Discusses his reasons for expatriation, his eagerness for culture, his interim in France and relations with the realists there, his individual, subjective technique. "The case of the two Jameses is well made to discourage deterministic monism of literary inheritance." Similar factors resulted in different products and contradictory attitudes in William and Henry James.

13 ORAGE, ALFRED RICHARD. "Henry James," in Readers and Writers (1917-1921). London: George Allen and Unwin, pp. 22-27.
Coincidence and momentary sympathy were responsible for James' affiliation with the Yellow Book writers, but he was unwilling to be identified with the tendencies of the school. James "mentalised phenomenon" and was "in love with the next world, or the next state of consciousness...." Concludes that "nobody is likely to be happier 'dead' than Henry James."

14 PENNELL, JOSEPH. "Adventures of an Illustrator. II: In London with Henry James." Century, 103 (February), 543-48.
The illustrator of "A Little Tour of France" and other non-fictional pieces by James attempts to reveal "some traits and facts about James which have been ignored or omitted by others who never worked with him half as much as I have worked with him." Reprinted: 1925.B13.

15 SCHELLING, FELIX E. "Some Forgotten Tales of Henry James," in Appraisements and Asperities as to Some Contemporary Writers. Philadelphia: J. B. Lippincott Co., 169-74.
James possesses sympathetic powers which enable him to "sink himself in the point of view, if not in the personality" of his characters. Reviews Master Eustace and A Landscape Painter, which contain stories of unequal merit, although all demonstrate distinctive style.

16 TICKNOR, CAROLINE. "Henry James's 'Bostonians,'" in Glimpses of Authors. Boston: Houghton Mifflin Co., pp. 243-56.
Reprints and discusses a letter on The Bostonians which shows James' method of outlining a prospective work. The

novel failed because of lack of interest by those outside
Boston and the fact that Bostonians didn't relish the picture of social life it depicted. Quotes from James' later
letters which detail his decision to be "of England as well
as in England."

1923 A BOOKS - NONE

1923 B SHORTER WRITINGS

1   ANON. "Letters and Comment." Yale Review, NS 13 (October),
     206-208.
          Reprints letter from Robert Herrick apologizing for sug-
     gesting (in 1923.B11) that Lubbock "either suppressed or
     shifted his material" in edition of the letters (1920.B20).
     James is responsible for choosing for posterity the decor-
     ous "and quite colorless...record of his life," either by
     destroying some material or refraining from self-revela-
     tion." Reprints unpublished letter from James to Mrs. F.
     C. Prindle.

2   BEER, THOMAS. "London to Cuba," in Stephen Crane: A Study in
     American Letters. New York: Alfred A. Knopf, pp. 169-72.
          Character sketch of James, with reference to relation-
     ship with Crane. James "was a colored and complicated
     ritual that demanded of spectators a reverence unfailingly
     accorded." Despite his ridiculous qualities, he had many
     admirers. "This plain and limited old bachelor commanded
     the world to respect him and the world obeyed. He was so
     kind." Reprinted: 1945.A1.

3   BETHURUM, DOROTHY. "Morality and Henry James." Sewanee Re-
     view, 31 (July), 324-30.
          Disagreement with Sherman's comment that for James there
     are only aesthetic questions (see 1917.B19). Moral judg-
     ments are implicit in James' works. Illustrates from The
     Portrait of a Lady and The Ambassadors James' setting the
     moral question forth in the lives of his characters. The
     moral sense is bound up in a sense of the beautiful.

4   BLANCHE, JACQUES-ÉMILE. "Henry James." La Revue Européenne
     (August), pp. 23-48; (September), pp. 39-63. (French)
          A discussion of James as an individual and as an artist,
     based on personal association. Describes James as a "rare
     artist...a man of the world; like Marcel Proust, a 'diner
     out,' a brilliant 'conversationalist.'" Considers James
     as an observer of the wealthy, and discusses several works,

1923

including <u>The American</u>, <u>The Awkward Age</u>, <u>Daisy Miller</u>, <u>The Ambassadors</u>, <u>The Wings of the Dove</u>. Recounts anecdotes involving James, describes a visit at Lamb House, comments on Lubbock's edition of James' letters (see 1920.B20) and translates three of James' letters into French. Revised: 1928.B3. <u>See also</u> 1937.B1.

5 BROOKS, VAN WYCK. "Henry James: The First Phase." <u>Dial</u>, 74 (May), 433-50.
James was essentially a product of a "sensuous education in the Old World" provided by his father. Briefly describes the character and philosophy of Henry James, Sr., the novelist's early desire for European culture, his isolation from the commonplace and vulgar in America. After his boyhood trip to Europe, James' "affections had been fixed irretrievably upon the Old World."

6 BROOKS, VAN WYCK. "Henry James: The American Scene." <u>Dial</u>, 75 (July), 29-42.
To the end of James' life, America signified failure and destruction. James, emerging from the '60's, was "inspired by the sacred terror of his own individuality," and in his first period as novelist he defends personal freedom, liberty, and represents America as the eclipse of one's finest possibilities.

7 BROOKS, VAN WYCK. "Henry James: An International Episode." <u>Dial</u>, 75 (September), 225-38.
One cannot advance as a novelist without being saturated in the atmosphere of one's own country: "The great writer is the voice of his own people...." Although James understood this, he had to escape from America.

8 ELIOT, T. S. "Lettre d'Angleterre." <u>Nouvelle Revue Française</u>, 21 (1 November), 621. (French)
Tribute to James, whose works "constitute a whole.... Their lesson is a single lesson."

9 FOLLETT, WILSON. "The Simplicity of Henry James: Some Notes on a Discovery." <u>American Review Magazine</u>, 1 (May-June), 315-25.
Deplores cultish attitudes of James' admirers, and attempts to make him intelligible to a broader group. Hypothesizes that James "spent his whole life in a ruthless pursuit of the simplicity which was no part of him inherently...until he had won it and made it his own...." The key to the ultimate simplicity of his art is <u>The Sacred Fount</u>, which is interpreted as a parable of the relation

between reality and art, with the narrator being "the artistic conscience of Henry James objectified in a person."
For James, "every story exists for the occupancy of a certain in-dwelling idea or principle.... This is the way of
simplicity, the way of sense."

10   GOMME, LAURENCE, comp. "American First Editions: A Series of
Bibliographic Check-Lists Edited by Merle Johnson and
Frederick M. Hopkins. Henry James, 1843-1916." Publish-
er's Weekly, 104 (11 August), 498-99.
Listing of publications of American first editions of
James.

11   HERRICK, ROBERT. "A Visit to Henry James." Yale Review, NS
12 (July), 724-41; NS 13 (October), 206-208.
Description of a visit at Lamb House in 1907. Recalls
conversations with James concerning revisions of works for
the New York edition, and compares the "fresh, young man's
rendering of life in The American with the retouched style"
of the later version. For the artist, "there should be
some sort of conscience which forbids him to lay hands on
the offspring of his youth." Reprinted: 1923.B12.

12   HERRICK, ROBERT. "A Visit to Henry James," in The Manly Anni-
versary Studies in Language and Literature. Chicago:
University of Chicago Press, pp. 229-42.
Reprint of 1923.B11.

13   KRANS, HORATIO S. "Henry James," in The New International
Encyclopaedia. Vol. 12. New York: Dodd, Mead and Co.,
p. 552.
Biographical sketch and discussion of James' development
of character and his "practice of the realistic method."
Labels James "the inventor of the artistic society novel,"
and lists selected works by James and a few critical studies.

14   LEE, VERNON [pseud.]. "Henry James," in The Handling of Words
and Other Studies in Literary Psychology. New York:
Dodd, Mead and Co., pp. 241-51.
See 1921.B18.

15   MATTHEWS, BRANDER. "Henry James and the Theatre," in Play-
wrights on Playmaking, and Other Studies of the Stage.
New York: Charles Scribner's Sons, pp. 187-204.
Reprint of 1920.B22.

1923

*16   MOORE, GEORGE. <u>Avowals</u>. London: William Heinemann. Ex-
       cerpted in 1947.A2.
          Includes physical description of James, who appeared
       to be a man who viewed women "with literary rather than
       personal interest," and notes his views on a point in Wal-
       ter Pater's <u>Marius the Epicurean</u> (quotation from 1947.A2).

17   O'BRIEN, E. J. "Henry James," in <u>The Advance of the American
       Short Story</u>. New York: Dodd, Mead and Co., pp. 117-38.
          Sketches James' early environment and education, notes
       influence of other authors, discusses literary method and
       conception of the relations between art and life. De-
       scribes James as "the one detached impersonal social his-
       torian on a large scale of our time," and the key to his
       literary approach as "silent seeing without unnecessary
       action."

18   PAGET, VIOLET. "Henry James," in <u>The Handling of Words and
       Other Studies in Literary Psychology</u>. New York: Dodd,
       Mead and Co., pp. 241-51. Reprinted: A Bison Book. Lin-
       coln: University of Nebraska Press, 1969.
          Analysis of the use of single words and simple combina-
       tions of words in a 500 word excerpt from <u>The Ambassadors</u>.
       Enumerates parts of speech, noting the preponderance of
       "personal" words, of pronouns which shift in case, demand-
       ing the reader's attention. Originally appeared in <u>English
       Review</u>, 5 (June 1910), 427-41. <u>See</u> 1923.B14.

19   PATTEE, FRED L. "Following the Civil War," in <u>The Development
       of the American Short Story</u>. New York: Biblo and Tannen,
       pp. 191-208.
          Views James as "the dominant figure in a literary move-
       ment which was little short of a revolution," the one who
       brought a cosmopolitan air to American fiction. In the
       short story, he was naturally critical and scientific, but
       his early environment and training made him romantic. He
       conceived of short-length fiction as a picture, with a
       fundamentally historical purpose, and his shorter pieces,
       among which is his most valuable work, initiated an empha-
       sis on subtle character analysis.

20   PHELPS, WILLIAM LYON. "Henry James--America's Analytical Nov-
       elist." <u>Ladies' Home Journal</u>, 40 (November), 23, 174-75.
          Discusses James' dedication to the life of the novelist,
       describes him as an affectionate, lovable man. Makes
       suggestions to novice readers concerning order in which
       they might approach James. Touches on James' style, his
       influence on other writers, his mastery of literary criti-
       cism. Reprinted: 1924.B13.

21 SHAW, GEORGE BERNARD. "Mr. Shaw on Printed Plays." <u>Times</u>
   <u>Literary Supplement</u> (17 May), p. 339.
   In arguing that the writer must make his play intelligible to the reader, cites James' dramatic works as an example of "literary language which is perfectly intelligible
   to the eye, yet utterly unintelligible to the ear even when
   it is easily speakable by the mouth."

22 TREVELYAN, JANET PENROSE. <u>The Life of Mrs. Humphry Ward</u>. New
   York: Dodd, Mead and Co., passim.
   James' visit with Mrs. Ward in London, 1884, "laid the
   foundation of a friendship that was to ripen into one of
   the most precious of all Mrs. Ward's possessions." Numerous references to the association between James and
   Mrs. Ward, who corresponded for years, are included, along
   with a photograph of James and Mrs. Ward in the garden at
   Stocks.

1924 A BOOKS

1 BOSANQUET, THEODORA. <u>Henry James at Work</u>. The Hogarth Essays.
   London: The Hogarth Press, 33 pp.
   Reminiscences about her relationship with James as his
   amanuensis. Describes James' work habits, the surroundings
   at Lamb House, the "free, involved, unanswered talk," her
   involvement in preparation of the New York edition, "re-
   trieval of neglected opportunities for adequate 'render-
   ings.'" James' primary recreation was the "cultivation of
   friendships," which often provided ideas for his writing.
   "Wherever he might have lived and whatever human interactions he might have observed, he would in all probability
   have reached much the same conclusion that he arrived at by
   way of America, France and England." Restatement of material in 1917.B4; 1954.B6-7.

1924 B SHORTER WRITINGS

1 BENSON, ARTHUR CHRISTOPHER. "Henry James," in <u>Memories and</u>
   <u>Friends</u>. New York: G. P. Putnam's Sons, pp. 214-28.
   Recollections of James, whom Benson met in 1884. Con-
   versing with the author "was like being present at the
   actual construction of a little palace of thought, of im-
   provised yet perfect design." James was absorbed in art
   and life alike.

1924

2   BREWSTER, DOROTHY and JOHN ANGUS BURRELL. "Paris and the Pu-
     ritan," in Dead Reckonings in Fiction. New York: Long-
     mans, Green and Co., pp. 19-41.
        Both The Ambassadors and Anatole France's The Red Lily
     are concerned with relations of the accepted, convention-
     alized order, but from different points of view. The
     Ambassadors is "a comedy of irony wherein the gods are
     pitted against an unsuspecting Puritan from Massachusetts."

3   COLVIN, SIR SIDNEY. "Robert Louis Stevenson and Henry James,
     with Some Letters of Mrs. R. L. Stevenson." Scribner's
     Magazine, 75 (March), 315-26.
        Colvin reprints letters, including the one James wrote
     to Mrs. Stevenson when he first learned of Robert Louis
     Stevenson's death, and seeks to "make the circumstances
     both of the friendship and the contrast" apparent through
     reminiscence and quotation. Although the differences be-
     tween Stevenson and James were those of temperament, ex-
     perience, and birth, they were both emotional, lovable
     men.

4   CROTHERS, SAMUEL McCHORD. "Henry James," in Later Years of
     the Saturday Club, 1870-1920. Edited by Mark Anthony
     DeWolfe Howe. Boston: Houghton Mifflin Co., pp. 385-90.
        In the memoirs of various club members by fellow mem-
     bers, Crothers recalls James breaking news of the San
     Francisco earthquake to his nephew while on board ship.
     Describes James' "extemporaneous" style of speech, calls
     him an "inspired improvisator." Argues with the view of
     James as thwarted by his expatriation.

5   EDGAR, PELHAM. "The Art of Henry James." National and En-
     glish Review, 83 (July), 730-39.
        Discusses James' choice of subject and search for the
     ideal method to display his chosen theme. James' major
     concern was "the revelation of human relations in a given
     situation," and his plea "is merely that the writer should
     give more concern to the ordering of his material."

6   ELIOT, T. S. "A Prediction in Regard to Three English Authors."
     Vanity Fair, 21 (February), 29, 98.
        It is necessary to read all of James in order to grasp
     the unity and progression in his works. Suggests that
     James was often criticized for failing to do things he was
     not trying to do and concludes that he "did not provide us
     with 'ideas,' but with another world of thought and feel-
     ing." Reprinted: as "A Prediction," in Leon Edel, ed.
     Henry James: A Collection of Critical Essays, pp. 55-56.

7   FIRKINS, OSCAR W. W. D. Howells, A Study. Cambridge, Mass.:
     Harvard University Press, passim.
        Using James and Tolstoi as examples, suggests that "the
     differences between realists are minimized," and, in dis-
     cussing Howell's style, compares him with James, in whom
     "the impression of literature is transcendent."

8   HARVITT, HÉLÈNE. "How Henry James Revised Roderick Hudson:
     A Study in Style." Publications of the Modern Language
     Association, 39 (March), 203-27.
        A study of the nature of the revisions of Roderick Hud-
     son for the New York edition reveals that James made few
     radical changes but minutely revised style, resulting in
     a greater tendency to analyze which almost became affecta-
     tion. The effect is a "feeling of effort" which spoils
     the youthful production. See 1925.B10.

*9 HASTINGS, KATHERINE. "William James of Albany, New York, and
     His Descendants." New York Genealogical and Biographical
     Record. Cited in 1956.B70, p. 373.
        This title, which gives full genealogy of the James
     family, is noncirculating at all known locations.

10 KENTON, EDNA. "Henry James to the Ruminant Reader: The Turn
     of the Screw." The Arts, 6 (November), 245-55.
        Interprets The Turn of the Screw through the character
     of the narrator-governess, who is "pathetically trying to
     harmonize her own disharmonies by creating discords outside
     herself." Cites James' characterization of the tale as
     "'an amusette to catch those not easily caught'" as evi-
     dence that he was attempting to trap the reader into be-
     lieving the governess' story. In this nouvelle, "the
     protection of character...reached its apotheosis." Re-
     printed: in Gerald Willen, ed. A Casebook on Henry James's
     "The Turn of the Screw," pp. 102-14.

11 McLANE, JAMES. "A Henry James Letter." Yale Review, NS 14
     (October), 205-208.
        Lubbock's edition of James' letters (1920.B20) lacks the
     "rare humor and rich allusion" prevalent in the novels and
     tales. Questions whether more spontaneous letters were
     rejected or withheld from publication. Reprints a previ-
     ously unpublished letter from James to Mrs. Thomas Sergeant
     Perry in which he states his attitude towards British nat-
     uralization.

12 PALACHE, JOHN G. "The Critical Faculty of Henry James." Uni-
     versity of California Chronicle, 26 (October), 399-410.

1924

Considers James' view of the art of the novel and certain of its practitioners. James' ideas had their origin
in a "personal internationalism" free from the dominant
influence of either French or English schools of thought.
"It all comes down to a general belief...in the excellence
of French critical theory and devotion to the fine technique of art, with...his response to the special social
features of English personality and character."

13 PHELPS, WILLIAM LYON. "James," in Howells, James, Bryant,
and Other Essays. New York: The Macmillan Co., pp. 123-
55.
Reprint of 1923.B20.

14 SICHEL, WALTER. "The Three 'L's,'" in The Sands of Time:
Recollections and Reflections. New York: George H. Doran
Co., p. 181; Hutchinson and Co., 1923.
Recounts two anecdotes concerning James, whose "psychol
ogy, his subtle simplicity, his meticulous analyses over-
powered not only us but himself."

15 TOOKER, L. FRANK. "As I Saw It from an Editor's Desk. X:
The Fiction of the Magazine." Century, NS 86 (June), 260-
71.
A member of the editorial staff of Century when The Bos
tonians was serialized discusses James' reputation with
serial readers, his habit of ignoring the reader, his concern for artistic background, his passion to depict life
truly. Cites evidence that James was unemotional by nature, "unperterbed by any concern in humanity."

16 WARD, ALFRED C. "Henry James: 'The Turn of the Screw,'" in
Aspects of the Modern Short Story. London: University of
London Press, pp. 89-101.
James viewed fiction as a cooperative venture between
author and reader, and in The Turn of the Screw he refused
to depict stereotyped ghosts. Discusses how James solved
the problem of conveying a sense of evil rather than merel:
stating it.

1925 A BOOKS

1 BROOKS, VAN WYCK. The Pilgrimage of Henry James. New York:
E. P. Dutton and Co., 177 pp. Reprinted: New York: Octa-
gon Books, 1972.
An early expression of the theory that expatriation
ruined James' art. Describes James' dissatisfaction with

America, which signified "calamity, destruction, oblivion"
for the artist, his European visits and eventual decision
to settle in London, where he felt an alien and lost touch
with life itself. Views James as an "immortal symbol" of
yearning for the Old World, who, through his exile, lost
"the basis of a novelist's life as he had once conceived
it: a firm knowledge of the phenomenal world, a living
sense of objective reality." James was unable to hold on
to the "power of instinctive perception" and the "artist's
faculty of disinterested judgment." Partially reprinted:
in "Two Phases of Henry James," 1945.A1. Reviewed: Joseph
Collins, Bookman (New York), 61 (June 1925), 477; Ernest
Boyd, Independent, 114 (18 April 1925), 448; Gilbert Seldes,
Nation, 121 (12 August 1925), 191; H. B. Fuller, New York
Times Book Review (19 April 1925), p. 4.

1925 B SHORTER WRITINGS

1   AIKEN, CONRAD. Review of Theodora Bosanquet, Henry James at
    Work; Walt Whitman, Criticism: An Unpublished Essay. Cri-
    terion, 3 (April), 465-68.
       Notes contrast between James and Whitman, isolates "de-
    votion to refinement" as a major principle of James' life
    and work. His view of art was exclusively aesthetic. Re-
    printed: 1958.B1.

2   BEER, THOMAS. "The Princess Far Away." Saturday Review of
    Literature, 1 (25 April), 701-702, 707.
       Disagrees with Brooks (see 1925.A1) that James was inex-
    perienced in life. Rather, he was "driven to replace his
    own limited imagination by a subconscious cross reference
    to something he once read." His limitation shows in his
    revulsion over "the ruthlessness of science--which is art."
    James continued to pursue an impossible civility, and for
    him Europe remained a fairy tale, "The Princess," to the
    end.

3   CHEVALLEZ, ABEL. "Henry James and the Psychological Novel,"
    in The Modern English Novel. Translated by Ben Ray Redman.
    New York: Alfred A. Knopf, pp. 109-16.
       James is a master psychological novelist, a specialist
    in "the elegant, cultivated, cosmopolitan life," whose best
    works were written between 1880 and 1890. In attempting to
    show the result of James' doctrine and practice, contrasts
    the earlier and later styles. James' influence has been
    "as much moral as intellectual," as much that of "a man as
    that of a man of letters." Originally published as Le
    roman anglais de notre temps, 1921.

1925

4   EDGAR, PELHAM. "Three Novels of Henry James." <u>Dalhousie Re-</u>
     <u>view</u>, 4 (January), 467-75.
        After an introductory statement of the various compo-
     nents available to the writer of fiction, illustrates "the
     manner in which organization may serve to enrich theme" in
     <u>The Ambassadors, The Wings of the Dove</u> and <u>The Golden Bowl</u>.
     Notes cooperation of dramatic and pictorial methods in the
     three novels, and shows how James manipulated the elements
     at his disposal to achieve the effect of unity.

*5   ELLIOT, W. G. <u>In My Anecdotage</u>. London: Philip Allan and
     Co. Excerpted in 1947.A2.
        One of the cast members of <u>Guy Domville</u> recalls James'
     effort to suggest the proper portrayal of character.

6   ELLIS, STEWART MARSH. "February Reverie: Henry James--Thomas
     Moore," in <u>Mainly Victorian</u>. London: Hutchinson and Co.,
     pp. 205-208.
        James' best writing can be found in the short stories,
     often "perfect examples of literary skill and craftsman-
     ship."

7   FITZROY, ALMERIC. Entry for January 5, 1906, in <u>Memoirs of</u>
     <u>Sir Almeric FitzRoy</u>. London: Hutchinson and Co., p. 278.
        Mentions having tea with James, "anchorite and novelist,"
     whose "spiritual enchantments" are the "fruit of sheer
     loneliness of soul."

8   FORBES-ROBERTSON, SIR JOHNSTON. <u>A Player Under Three Reigns</u>.
     London: T. F. Unwin, pp. 246-50.
        Reminisces about his acquaintance with James, and de-
     scribes the circumstances surrounding his production of
     James' <u>The High Bid</u> (<u>Covering End</u>), "an enchanting tale...
     admirably suited for the stage" which "proved of far too
     delicate a fibre and literary elegance to appeal to a gen-
     eral public."

9   FRIERSON, WILLIAM C. "Henry James," in <u>L'Influence du natural-</u>
     <u>isme francais sur les romanciers anglais de 1885 à 1900</u>.
     Paris: Marcel Giard, pp. 190-205. (French)
        Considers the influence of the Flaubert group on James'
     literary technique, and discusses the distinction between
     the naturalistic and experimental novel. James was averse
     to characteristic practices of naturalists but possessed
     certain similarities with them.

10   HAVENS, RAYMOND D. "The Revision of <u>Roderick Hudson</u>." <u>Pub-</u>
     <u>lications of the Modern Language Association</u>, 40 (June),
     433-34.

Harvitt (see 1924.B8) quotes from a later revised version rather than the first edition of Roderick Hudson, which demonstrates that "minute and fastidious correction was an early habit with Henry James." Changes in the 1882 edition of the novel correct the impression that James' revisions were towards more involved and less effective style and reveal the artist at work just before the zenith of his powers.

11   KENTON, EDNA. "Henry James and Mr. Van Wyck Brooks." Bookman (New York), 62 (October), 153-57.
      Brooks' The Pilgrimage of Henry James (1925.A1) is built on a syllogism lacking a middle term: "All expatriates are failures. _____ was an expatriate. Therefore,___ ___ _____ was a failure." Brooks has "rewritten" James, and attempted to fit the author to a theory.

12   KNIGHT, GRANT C. "The Most Memorable Children," in Superlatives. New York: Alfred A. Knopf, pp. 139-52.
      Discusses difficulty of creating three-dimensional young characters, and describes James' portrayal of children in What Maisie Knew, Daisy Miller, and The Turn of the Screw. Miles and Flora are "the most memorable children in fiction."

13   PENNELL, JOSEPH. "Chapter XXIX: Henry James; I Meet Him; The Faust Article in The Century; Illustrate A Little Tour in France and Two Other Books By Him; James Plays in London and Wagners Operas at Bayreuth," in The Adventures of an Illustrator: Mostly in Following His Authors in America and Europe. Boston: Little, Brown, and Co., pp. 258-67.
      Reprint of 1922.B14.

14   ROSCOE, E. S. "Henry James at the Reform Club." Bookman (New York), 60 (January), 584-85.
      Describes James' daily routine as a member of the Reform Club, London, where he was a tenant in November 1900, and where he spent varying intervals while in London until 1912. Conversation revealed James to be a man of extraordinary insight and kindliness, with a sense of humor about social life.

15   WAGENKNECHT, EDWARD. "Of Henry James and Howells, 1925." Virginia Quarterly Review, 1 (October), 453-60.
      Brooks' thesis (see 1925.A1) "has just enough truth to make it misleading." The style, "richly tapestried," of the later works is the "fulfillment, not the erasure, of his earlier promise."

1925

16   WHARTON, EDITH. <u>The Writing of Fiction</u>. New York: Charles
      Scribner's Sons, pp. 37, 45, 91, 107.
         James was the first to formulate the principle of unity
of vision and the "last great master of the eerie in English." James and Conrad experimented with the problem of
"tumbling in and out of their characters' minds," and Wharton discusses how James sought verisimilitude in this
regard by confining details of picture to the range and
capacity of the viewer.

17   WILSON, EDMUND. "A Novel of Henry Adams." <u>New Republic</u>, 44
      (14 October), 203.
         Adams' novel Democracy suggests the earlier novels of
James and possesses an interesting similarity to <u>The Bos-
tonians</u> in the nature of heroes. Both figures display the
authors' criticisms of democracy, their moral indignation.

1926 A BOOKS

1   HUGHES, HERBERT LELAND. <u>Theory and Practice in Henry James</u>.
      Ann Arbor, Mich.: Edwards Brothers, 120 pp.
         Presentation of James' theory of prose fiction and dem-
onstration of its application. Part I deals with theory,
as seen in James' reviews, magazine articles, letters, essays and prefaces, and Part II explicates James' practice
of the principles. Each part includes sections on "Art and
the Artist," "Themes and Subject-matter," "Definition,
Purpose and Scope," "Morality and Meaning," "Form and
Plot," "Character and Setting," "Style and Method," "Romance and Realism." Concludes that James generally practices his own announced theories, which were rather well-
developed from the start and showed "scarcely any special
growth and development...." James is "a significant, a
powerful, a great novelist."

1926 B SHORTER WRITINGS

1   AUBREY, G. JEAN, ed. <u>Twenty Letters to Joseph Conrad</u>. London:
      The First Editions Club, n.p.
         Prefatory statement describes the relationship between
Conrad and James as one "not only of artistic sympathy, but
of true affection." Reprints three letters from James to
Conrad.

2   BENSON, ARTHUR CHRISTOPHER. <u>The Diary of A. C. Benson</u>.
      Edited by Percy Lubbock. New York: Longmans, Green and
Co., passim.

Describes visit with James at Lamb House in diary entry
of January 17, 1900, gives account of conversation with
James and Thomas Hardy in 1904, and recalls a 1915 lunch
with James, who "leaves a deep impression of majesty,
beauty and greatness."

3 BENSON, ARTHUR CHRISTOPHER. "Lamb House, Rye," in <u>Rambles
and Reflections</u>. New York: G. P. Putnam's Sons, pp. 29-37.
Detailed description of Rye and Lamb House and recollections of visits there with James. "...Somehow the house is
pervaded by his personality, his benign kindness, his noble
presence, his rich sympathy, his generous outlook."

*4 CARR, MRS. J. COMYNS. <u>Reminiscences</u>. Edited by Eve Adam.
London: Hutchinson and Co. Excerpted in 1947.A2.
Recollections of James, with reference to his relation-
ship with the Millar boys, one of whom was his godson.

5 CONRAD, JESSIE. "The Early Years," in <u>Joseph Conrad As I Knew
Him</u>. London: William Heinemann, p. 48.
Recalls meeting Henry James and her son's calling him
"'an elegant fowl.'"

6 GODLEY, A. D. <u>Reliquiae</u>. Edited by C. R. L. Fletcher. Vol.
2. New York and London: Oxford University Press, pp. 250-
51. (Latin)
Commendatory speech for James, recipient of an honorary
degree, Doctor of Letters, from Oxford University, June 26,
1912.

7 GREGORY, ALYSE. "A Superb Brief," in <u>American Criticism: 1926</u>.
Edited by William A. Drake. New York: Harcourt, Brace and
Co., pp. 95-100.
Points out the persuasiveness of Brooks' argument (<u>see</u>
1925.A1), which has the weakness of viewing James' works
from a social scientific point of view. Praises James'
sophisticated intercourse, his subtle interpretations of
the human predicament. Brooks, like William James, displays a patronizing attitude of the social reformer to the
artist. Originally appeared in <u>Dial</u>, 79 (September 1925),
477.

8 HELLMAN, GEORGE S. "Stevenson and Henry James: The Rare
Friendship Between Two Famous Stylists." <u>Century</u>, NS 89
(January), 336-45.
Robert Louis Stevenson and James were in philosophical
and professional sympathy, and their letters reveal their

1926

    appreciation and admiration for each other's art. Discusses similarities between Stevenson and Mark Ambient of "The Author of Beltraffio" and James' way of handling a theme based on an actual occurence.

*9   HIND, C. LEWIS. Naphtali. London: John Lane, The Bodley Head. Excerpted in 1947.A2.
    An acquaintance's recollections of James, including reports on his response to Hind's praising his canary.

*10   HUNT, VIOLET. The Flurried Years. London: Hurst and Blackett. Excerpted in 1947.A2.
    Includes an account of James uninviting Violet Hunt for a weekend in Rye when he heard rumors of an illicit association with F. M. Hueffer, and a description of his conversation about the war when he "talked Army, thought Army, and died Army—quite suddenly" (quotation from 1947.A2).

*11   MICHAUD, RÉGIS. Le roman américain d'aujourd'hui. Cited in 1930.A1, p. 303.
    See 1928.B18.

12   MICHAUD, RÉGIS. "Un splendide exile: Henry James," in Panorama de la litterature américaine contemporaine. Paris: Kra, pp. 115-20. (French)
    James' expatriation was destined. Biographical summary with commentary on how and why James chose Europe, England over France. James' focus was the study of consciences. "Nothing interested him more than the forms of thought and the expression capable of seizing them."

13   MORGAN, LOUISE. "The Weakness of Henry James." Outlook (London), 57 (6 February), 89.
    James' undeservedly high reputation during his lifetime was due to "his obsessing weakness," especially to the snobbery which caused him to emphasize the wrong things, thereby obscuring his point. "In arriving at an absolute and unimpeachable exquisiteness he becomes simply vulgar."

14   ORCUTT, WILLIAM DANA. "Friends Through Type," in In Quest of the Perfect Book: Reminiscences and Reflections of a Bookman. Boston: Little, Brown and Co., pp. 86-90.
    Describes James as a "genial and enjoyable dinner companion," and Lamb House as "a perfect expression of the host...." James' conversation was more intelligible than his books.

15 PERRY, F. M. "Henry James: Master of Indirection," in <u>Story-</u>
    <u>Writing: Lessons from the Masters</u>. New York: Henry Holt
    and Co., pp. 140-79.
      Discusses elements of James' style, his descriptive
    method, his attitude towards and use of dialogue. For
    James, truth is a matter of values, and he opts for the
    spirit rather than formal rectitude. The difficulties of
    style sharpen the reader's imagination and create a part-
    nership with the author.

16 POUND, EZRA. "Moeurs Contemporaines, VII," in <u>Personae</u>. A
    New Directions Book. New York: James Laughlin, p. 181.
    Reprinted: 1950.
      Alludes to James. "They will come no more,/The old men
    with beautiful manners."

*17 WALBROOK, H. M. <u>A Playgoer's Wanderings</u>. London: L. Parsons.
    Excerpted in 1947.A2.
      Includes remarks on James' assessment of <u>Guy Domville</u>
    several years after the failure of the play.

18 WATERLOW, STANLEY P. "Memories of Henry James." <u>New States-</u>
    <u>man</u>, 26 (6 February), 514-15.
      Although James' individual vision is admirable, his art
    has something "neuter and sterile" about it. James shrank
    from the common and unclean in favor of the safe, well-to-
    do environment. His art is rooted in puritanism.

19 WILLIAMS, STANLEY THOMAS. "Henry James," in <u>The Pageant of</u>
    <u>America: The American Spirit in Letters</u>. London: Oxford
    University Press; New Haven, Conn.: Yale University Press,
    pp. 261-64.
      Illustrated account of James' life and work, which con-
    siders his "detachment from rough experience," his in-
    dividual style, the influence of Flaubert and Eliot.
    "...here was a human soul that trusted utterly in art as
    the secret of life...."

1927 A BOOKS

1 EDGAR, PELHAM. <u>Henry James: Man and Author</u>. Boston:
    Houghton Mifflin Co., 351 pp. Reprinted: 1964.
      Biographical summary of James' career and critical
    analysis of his works, both fiction and non-fiction. Con-
    siders the American short stories, "Short Stories: General
    Group," "The Literary and Artistic Group," "The Supernatu-
    ral Group," and "Converted Dramas," with lengthier

1927

treatments of The Spoils of Poynton, "The Figure in the Carpet," and What Maisie Knew. In the chapter on "The Letters, The Prefaces and Literary Criticism," discusses James' early style, his concern for his craft, and techniques such as progressive revelation, use of dialogue. Critiques the major novels. Suggests that by the time James was thirty, he "had absorbed all the American impressions that his nature was capable of receiving," and that he always considered the best interests of his art. Reviewed: Conrad Aiken, New York Herald Tribune Book Review (27 February 1927), p. 5; P. A. Hutchison, New York Times Book Review (13 February 1927), p. 2; E. S. Bates, Saturday Review of Literature, 4 (3 September 1927), 89; Times Literary Supplement (6 January 1927), p. 1; Yale Review, NS 17 (October 1927), 185.

2 GARNIER, M. R. Henry James et la France. Paris: Librairie Ancienne Honoré Champion, 216 pp. (French)
Study of James' lifelong relationship to France, the country and its writers. Considers influence on James of French authors, with emphasis on the realism of Flaubert and the master of the analytical novel, Paul Bourget. Reviews contemporary French literature, discusses James as a "rousing witness" and friend during the war, and his reputation in France following his death. As a result of his reading, voyages and social activity, "Henry James was without doubt with France at the heart of his existence, in many respects."

1927 B SHORTER WRITINGS

1 AUBRY, G. JEAN. "Tales of Unrest 1895-1904," in Joseph Conrad, Life and Letters. Vol. 1. Garden City, N.Y.: Doubleday, Page and Co., pp. 201-202.
Conrad describes his reaction to The Spoils of Poynton: "It's Henry James and nothing but Henry James."

2 BOYD, ERNEST AUGUSTUS. "Henry James," in Literary Blasphemies. New York: Harper and Brothers, pp. 213-26.
Reprint of 1920.B6.

3 CHARTERIS, EVAN. John Sargent. New York: Charles Scribner's Sons, passim.
References to James' relationship to Sargent, who was his friend and painter of his portrait, and a member of the same social group of intellectual, artistic individuals in England, 1885. Remarks on their attitudes towards the war and Sargent's reaction to James' death.

4 DEMUTH, CHARLES. Charles Demuth. Edited by A. E. Gallatin.
   New York: W. E. Rudge, n.p.
       Reproductions of watercolor illustrations for James'
   "The Beast in the Jungle" and The Turn of the Screw. Those
   for the latter also appeared in 1924.B10.

5 FORSTER, E. M. "Pattern and Rhythm," in Aspects of the Novel,
   New York: Harcourt, Brace and World, pp. 153-64.
       A study of The Ambassadors reveals its pattern is that
   of an hourglass, with Strether and Chad changing places.
   At the center of the hourglass shape is Paris, the scale by
   which human sensibility is measured. James made sacrifices
   in order to preserve this pattern in limiting both the numbers of human beings and their attributes, thereby losing
   many readers. Reprinted: 1952.B22; as "The Ambassadors,"
   in Leon Edel, ed. Henry James: A Collection of Critical
   Essays, pp. 72-78.

6 GEROULD, KATHERINE FULLERTON. "Stream of Consciousness."
   Saturday Review of Literature, 4 (22 October), 233-35.
       James initiated the stream of consciousness method in
   English fiction, recording the thoughts of his characters
   "exactly as they go on in the mind." James used mental
   rather than rhetorical rhythms increasingly to determine
   his characters' feelings about the world and finally employed the syntax of solitary reflection in his later
   manner.

7 LIVESAY, J. F. B. "Henry James and His Critics." Dalhousie
   Review, 7 (April), 80-88.
       Considers James' method, his concern with character
   rather than plot which precludes wide popularity. Despite
   the intricate style of the later period, "no one more
   valued clear-thinking and essential clarity of statement
   than Henry James, much indebted as he was to the French
   school." Reviews Pelham Edgar's book (1927.A1).

8 [READ, HERBERT.] "The Significance of Henry James." Times
   Literary Supplement (6 January), pp. 1-2.
       The phrase "'moral dignity'" summarizes the significance
   of James, who adhered to the personal rather than the public aspects of Puritanism. James is the "master of indirect method" who posed numerous problems "in the philosophy of criticism," which concern "the novel itself, its
   form and features; the moral responsibility of the novelist, and...the attitude which the artist ought to adopt
   towards the particular crisis which civilization has now
   reached." James' evolution is similar to the historical

1927

development of the art of fiction. His greatest technical
advance was the realization that "in order to create personalities and set them in action...it is necessary to
repeat, on another plane, an analogous rhythm or pattern."
Reprinted: 1929.B5; 1938.B13; 1956.B58.

9   SAMPSON, MARTIN W. "Introduction," in Daisy Miller and An
     International Episode. New York: The Macmillan Co.,
     pp. v-xv.
        Description of James' method in Daisy Miller, and in-
     terpretation of Daisy's repudiation of convention. James
     is best known for one of his least subtle achievements and
     one of his simplest characters.

10   WILSON, EDMUND. "The Exploration of James." New Republic,
     50 (16 March), 112-13.
        Reviews Henry James: Man and Author (1927.A1). De-
     spite thematic and technical boldness, James wrote fiction
     under many personal and public inhibitions. He is con-
     cerned with the "perhaps essentially American-type of man
     who is foredoomed to remain a spectator of life and never
     to experience either its suffering or its joy." His pro-
     tagonists are the feminine equivalent of this type, intel-
     ligent and sensitive, "but with some Puritan blindness of
     the senses or atrophy of the emotions."

1928 A BOOKS - NONE

1928 B SHORTER WRITINGS

*1   ANON. "Two Frontiersmen." Nation, 90 (April), 422-23.
        Cited in Beatrice Ricks, comp. Henry James: A Bibliography
     of Secondary Works, #3527.
        Appears in Nation, 90 (28 April 1910).

2   BENNETT, ARNOLD. "Two Reputations," in Savour of Life: Es-
     says in Gusto. New York: Doubleday, Doran and Co.,
     pp. 117-21.
        Edgar's book (see 1927.A1) characterized as "painstak-
     ing, thorough, ingenious, infrequently illuminating, and
     not succulent." Suggests that James "knew everything about
     writing novels--except how to keep my attention," but ex-
     tols him as a literary critic. "...In the fastidiousness
     of his taste he rather repudiated life." Reprinted: in
     Albert E. Stone, ed. Twentieth Century Interpretations of
     "The Ambassadors," pp. 28-29.

3   BLANCHE, JACQUES-ÉMILE. "Henry James," in Mes Modèles.
      Paris: Stock, pp. 143-83. (French)
         Revised and abridged version of 1923.B4. Emphasizes
      James' attachment to Europe and its relationship to his
      writing. "James remained an American in spite of all."
      Recounts conversation with Walter Berry about whether James
      was "un grand esprit" (as in 1923.B4), and concludes that
      he is an "esthetic curiosity," "a great artist of the
      twentieth century, as narrator."

4   BROWN, IVOR. "The Theatre: Through the Mill." Saturday
      Review (London), 146 (7 July), 14.
         Review of Arts Theatre Club production of The Tragic
      Muse reveals a scenario that "was painted on a broad can-
      vas."

5   CHISLETT, WILLIAM, JR. "Henry James: His Range and Accom-
      plishments," in Moderns and Near-Moderns: Essays on Henry
      James, Stockton, Shaw, and Others. New York: The Grafton
      Press, pp. 11-66.
         Overview of the scope and variety of works by James, who
      is viewed as a storyteller as well as a character-drawer
      and psychologist. Discusses views of America in The Ameri-
      can Scene, other travel books, critical works, biography,
      letters. Briefly annotates dramas, short stories and nov-
      els, and notes differences of critical opinion on James.

6   DRAPER, MURIEL. "I Meet Henry James." Harper's Magazine,
      156 (March), 416-21.
         Recalls her childhood ambition to meet James, a "genius,"
      and describes their eventual encounter in London, 1912, and
      his subsequent visits to her home. Reprinted: 1929.B1.

7   GRABO, CARL H. "Excellence of the Point of View in James'
      'The Ambassadors,'" in The Technique of the Novel. New
      York: Charles Scribner's Sons, pp. 81-94. Reprinted: New
      York: Gordian Press, 1964.
         Discusses James' use of point of view in The Ambassadors,
      the reasons behind his choice of technique. Distinguishes
      James' approach from a "psychoanalytic" method.

8   GRABO, CARL H. "Fusion of Exposition in Narrative," in The
      Technique of the Novel. New York: Charles Scribner's
      Sons, pp. 106-108. Reprinted: New York: Gordian Press,
      1964.
         The Wings of the Dove demonstrates the "obligation which
      rests upon the author to transmute the composite elements
      of his story to pure narrative."

1928

9   GRABO, CARL H. "Principles Governing the Selection of Detail,
     and the Relation of Detail to Realistic Effects," in The
     Technique of the Novel. New York: Charles Scribner's
     Sons, p. 238. Reprinted: New York: Gordian Press, 1964.
       Contrasts Willa Cather's The Lost Lady and James' The
     Wings of the Dove in illustrating the "due subordination
     of visual detail...."

10   GRABO, CARL H. "The Technique of James's 'The Turn of the
     Screw,'" in The Technique of the Novel. New York: Charles
     Scribner's Sons, pp. 204-14. Reprinted: New York: Gor-
     dian Press, 1964.
       Examines James' method in The Turn of the Screw, the
     "most powerful and moving ghost story in English," enumer-
     ates examples of "technical dexterity," and discusses the
     effective tempo of the tale.

11   HARDY, FLORENCE EMILY. The Early Life of Thomas Hardy, 1840-
     1891. New York: The Macmillan Co., passim.
       Mentions Hardy's meetings with James, and reprints a
     letter in which Hardy comments on the "minutiae of manners"
     in The Reverberator.

*12 HEYNEMAN, J. H. "Henry James." World Today, 52 (September),
     348-50. Cited in International Index to Periodicals.
     Edited by Alice F. Muench et al. Vol. 5 (January 1928-
     June 1931), p. 1056.

13   HOWELLS, WILLIAM DEAN. Life in Letters of William Dean How-
     ells. Edited by Mildred Howells. 2 vols. New York:
     Doubleday, Doran and Co., passim.
       Reprints 22 letters from Howells to James, whom Howells
     considers "extremely gifted--gifted enough to do better
     than any one yet has done toward making us a real American
     novel." Includes segment from "Editor's Easy Chair," an
     effort to substantiate James' essential Americanness, in
     which he calls James an "inalienably American soul" and
     "The American James"; Howells' reminiscence of his friend-
     ship with James as Cambridge neighbors; and their discus-
     sion of principles of fiction.

14   KENTON, EDNA. "The 'Plays' of Henry James." Theatre Arts,
     12 (May), 347-52.
       James wrote dramas "for the sake of getting into the
     exact centre of dramatic form," not to get into the thea-
     tre. Briefly reviews James' dramatic output. "Henry James
     the Dramatist, concerned with the 'great Action,' Henry

James the Scenic Painter, intent on background and objects, and Henry James the Recorder of the 'subject...'" came to be fused into "James the Novelist."

15 LEWIS, J. H. "The Difficulties of Henry James." Poet Lore, 39 (Spring), 117-19.
James, "the greyhound of literature" and "the master of the indirect," inspires intense reactions in readers. With him, there is no middle ground.

*16 LUBBOCK, PERCY. Mary Cholmondeley. London: Jonathan Cape. Excerpted in 1947.A2.
Recounts relationship between James and Rhoda Broughton. "It was beautiful to see them together, complicated cosmopolitanized America and barbarous old Britain...." (quotation from 1947.A2).

17 LUCAS, E. V. The Colvins and Their Friends. New York: Charles Scribner's Sons, p. 161.
Mrs. Robert Louis Stevenson characterizes The Princess Casamassima as "'different, with the thrill of life, the beating of the pulse that you miss in the others.'"

18 MICHAUD, RÉGIS. "Henry James, Edith Wharton, William Dean Howells and 'American Society on Parade,'" in The American Novel Today: A Social and Psychological Study. Boston: Little, Brown and Co., pp. 47-54.
James, Wharton and Howells carried on the tradition of the novels of intrigue, character and manners. James' "indictment of his native country marked the parting of the ways between the ancient and the modern, between tradition and evolution, culture and spontaneity." Discusses James' method, and suggests that he possessed an "American taste for prodigality" and combined the attitudes of transcendentalist and detective. Translation of 1926.B11.

19 OXFORD and ASQUITH, EARL OF. "Anglo-American Relations before the War: Henry James," in Memories and Reflections, 1852-1927. Vol. 1. London: Cassell and Co., pp. 279-83.
One of James' oldest friends notes his sympathy with the Allies and reprints a 1915 letter from James requesting naturalization.

20 THOMPSON, E. R. "Henry James and Max Beerbohm," in Portraits of the New Century (The First Ten Years). Garden City, N.Y.: Doubleday, Doran and Co., pp. 282-99.
James' defense of civilization was "his little axe" to grind. His mental attitudes were Edwardian rather than Victorian: He was "creedless, and so a pessimist."

1928

21   WILLIAMS, ORLO. "The Ambassadors." Criterion, 8 (September),
      47-64.
          Attempts to show that there was a weakness in James'
      attitude to moral values. In The Ambassadors, James turned
      away from the obvious struggle for Chad's body to Streth-
      er's soul. "...He sheered off any direct treatment of
      those human conflicts and passions which must be the essen-
      tial groundwork of the novelist's art."

1929 A BOOKS

1   BORCHERS, LOTTE. Frauengestalten und Frauenprobleme bei Henry
     James. Berlin: Franz Schaetzell, 159 pp.
         A published dissertation (Greifswald, 1929) in German
     which analyzes the types of women in James' fiction. Part
     I, "Types of Women in James," has sections on "National
     Types," covering the European and the American; "Social
     Types," like "the worldly woman," "the society woman,"
     "the woman of the people," "the bourgeois woman;" "Spirit-
     ual Types," such as "the stupid woman" and "the intelligent
     woman"; and "Moral Types," including the "morally upstand-
     ing woman" and the "fallen woman." Also considers James'
     ideal of women. Part II, dealing with the problems of
     women in James, includes chapters on "Marriage," "The Woman
     and the Child," "The Unmarried Woman," and "Critics of
     Women." In conclusion, discusses James' personal relations
     with women.

2   ROBERTS, MORRIS. Henry James's Criticism. Cambridge, Mass.:
     Harvard University Press, 131 pp. Reprinted: New York:
     Haskell House, 1965.
         A chronological study of James' development as a critic
     and examination of his criticism, generally on 19th century
     English and French fiction, unmatched in English "for cer-
     tain qualities of style or for the just and vivid communi-
     cation of literary quality." Section I deals with the
     early reviews (1864-1872); Section II deals with "French
     Poets and Novelists" (1872-1883), a period which served as
     James' apprenticeship both in writing and in absorption of
     fictional material; Section III covers "Partial Portraits
     and Essays in London" (1883-1894), when the artist has
     "supplanted the legislator and judge" and criticism has
     evolved into a fine art; and Section IV, on "Prefaces and
     Notes on Novelists," discusses James' view of art and
     imagination. Concludes that the most conspicuous thing
     about James' theory of art is "Faith in the logic of imagi-
     nation, in the validity and sufficiency of an inner process

which is at once intellectual and imaginative...." Reviewed: Austin Warren, American Literature, 2 (March
1930), 187-89; Matthew Josephson, Hound and Horn, 3 (January-March 1930), 281-84; William Troy, New York Times
Book Review (10 August 1930), p. 2; Times Literary Supplement (5 December 1929), p. 1037.

1929 B SHORTER WRITINGS

1   DRAPER, MURIEL. "I Meet Henry James," in Music at Midnight.
     New York: Harper and Brothers, pp. 87-96.
        Reprint of 1928.B6.

2   HOARE, D. M. "A Note on Henry James." New Adelphi, 2
     (March-May), 247-48.
        The Ambassadors, The Wings of the Dove, and The Golden
     Bowl strongly suggest that James' primary concern was not
     in the interested study of society but in the fundamental
     problem of "morals," of the value of sincerity and integ-
     rity contrasted with conventional views of them.

3   KRUTCH, JOSEPH WOOD. "Life, Art and Peace," in The Modern
     Temper: A Study and a Confession. New York: Harcourt,
     Brace and Co., pp. 155-60.
        To James, "life was...an art, and in art all styles are
     good provided that they are consistent and harmonious with-
     in themselves." He adopted an aesthetic attitude which
     judges individuals according to their success or failure
     in developing in their chosen style.

4   LEISY, ERNEST ERWIN. American Literature: An Interpretive
     Survey. New York: Thomas Y. Crowell Co., pp. 193-200 and
     passim.
        Surveys James' work in three periods, and examines char-
     acteristics of his work as displayed in The American.
     Judges James' most significant contribution to be his the-
     oretical principles on the art of fiction. "The work of
     James presents, on a grand scale, aesthetic criticism of
     the leisure class in modern society."

5   READ, HERBERT. "Henry James," in The Sense of Glory: Essays
     in Criticism. Cambridge, England: Cambridge University
     Press, pp. 206-28.
        Reprint of unsigned article in Times Literary Supple-
     ment, 1927.B8.

1929

6   READ, FORREST. <u>Walter de la Mare: A Critical Study</u>. New
    York: Henry Holt and Co., pp. 69-73, 126-29, 221-24.
        James' approach in <u>What Maisie Knew</u> is similar to de la
    Mare's in <u>The Almond Tree</u>, and the circumstances in "The
    Next Time" resemble those in de la Mare's <u>The Return</u>.

7   SHERMAN, STUART PRATT. "Henry James," in <u>The Columbia Univer-
    sity Course in Literature: Writers of Modern America</u>.
    Vol. 18. New York: Columbia University Press, pp. 218-33.
        Mentions the vacillations of James' critical reputation,
    and describes him as the first novelist writing in English
    to offer, on a large scale, "a purely esthetic criticism
    of modern society and modern fiction." In James, the con-
    trolling principle is his sense of style and the aesthetic
    ideal, the consecration to beauty, in conduct.

8   WALBROOK, H. M. "Henry James and the Theatre." <u>London Mer-
    cury</u>, 20 (October), 612-16.
        James was a failure as a playwright because he worked
    on plays not with a sense of enthusiasm but with the spirit
    of a repugnant task, and because he adhered too strictly to
    the ideal that the essential ingredient of good drama is
    not "action" but "character."

<u>1930 A BOOKS</u>

1   KELLEY, CORNELIA PULSIFER. <u>The Early Development of Henry
    James</u>. University of Illinois Studies in Language and
    Literature. Vol. 15, nos. 1 and 2. Urbana: University
    of Illinois Press, 309 pp. Revised, 1965.
        Asserts that it is necessary to study James' develop-
    ment, to examine the "long, laborious apprenticeship to the
    masters of his craft...," his reviews, travel sketches, and
    early tales. Uses a chronological approach with emphasis
    on the early work, beginning in 1864. "Inter-chapters"
    supply chronological facts and dates as background, fol-
    lowed by chapters investigating James' inner development.
    Divides work into three distinct phases: 1864-1869, which
    receives the greatest emphasis, and during which period
    "James as a critic outweighed James as a writer of origi-
    nal fiction in bulk and often in idea and expression";
    1869-1875; and 1875-1881. Shows James emerging as the
    novelist he had <u>made</u> himself, and concludes that with <u>The
    Portrait of a Lady</u> James had reconciled both art and life
    in a novel. Includes a "Bibliography of the Early Devel-
    opment of Henry James." Partially reprinted: "From <u>The
    Early Development of Henry James</u>," in William Stafford, ed.

Perspectives on James's "The Portrait of a Lady," pp. 51-
62. Reviewed: E. E. Leisy, American Literature, 3 (January 1932), 487-88; James McLane, New England Quarterly,
4 (July 1931), 577-78.

2 PHILLIPS, LEROY. A Bibliography of the Writings of Henry
James. New York: Coward-McCann, 196 pp. Reprinted:
New York: Burt Franklin, 1968. Enlarged edition of 1906
publication, Boston: Houghton Mifflin.
   Describes title pages, gives collations and other bibliographical data on both English and American first
editions of James' works, and notes subsequent editions
printed from new types or plates. Describes books to which
James contributed or for which he wrote prefaces or introductions, printed but "unpublished" dramas, and short-
title entries of collected editions of his works and of
periodical contributions. Appends an alphabetical list of
titles.

1930 B SHORTER WRITINGS

1 BEERBOHM, MAX. "Jacobean and Shavian," in Around Theatres.
New York: Alfred A. Knopf, pp. 260-65, 323-26.
   The central figure of Shaw's The Doctor's Dilemma is
like Roderick Hudson, an artistic genius unendowed with
any "moral sense." James' primary subject is "Civilization, and a high state of it," and the common denominator
of his characters is "The passion of conscience." Reprinted: in Leon Edel, ed. Henry James: A Collection of
Critical Essays, pp. 18-26.

2 BENEDICT, CLARE. The Benedicts Abroad. London: Ellis,
passim.
   Benedict reprints the journals of her mother, Clara
Woolson Benedict, which include numerous references to the
family's association with James. Also includes extracts
of letters from James "as a kind of brilliant commentary,
and in some instances, amplification, of my mother's narrative."

3 BENSON, EDWARD FREDERIC. "Introduction," in Henry James:
Letters to A. C. Benson and Auguste Monod. New York:
Charles Scribner's Sons, pp. v-ix. Reprinted: New York:
Haskell House, 1969.
   James' letters to A. C. Benson display his affection for
his friends and his devotion to art. Stylistically, the
correspondence represents "the intermediate stage between
his talk and the printed page." Reviewed: Garreta Busey,

1930

New York Herald Tribune Books (21 December 1930), p. 2;
Osburt Burdett, Saturday Review (London), 150 (13 Septem-
ber 1930), 319; Hansell Baugh, Sewanee Review, 39 (October-
December 1931), 504-507; Times Literary Supplement (25
September 1930), p. 749.

4   BENSON, EDWARD FREDERIC. "The Movement of the Nineties," in
    As We Were: A Victorian Peep Show. London: Longmans,
    Green and Co., pp. 277-84.
        Although James attributed the source of The Turn of the
    Screw to Benson's father, "neither my mother nor my brother
    nor I had the faintest recollection of any tale of my
    father's which resembled it." Recalls association with
    James, relates anecdotes involving James, and discusses his
    style.

*5 BROOKFIELD, ARTHUR MONTAGU. Annals of a Chequered Life. Lon-
    don: John Murray. Excerpted in 1947.A2.
        Notes James' description of Anne Thackeray Ritchie as
    possessing "'every possible good quality except common
    sense'" (quotation from 1947.A2).

6   BROUN, HEYWOOD. "Introduction," in The Turn of the Screw and
    The Lesson of the Master. Modern Library. New York:
    Random House, pp. v-ix.
        Describes how he came to read The Turn of the Screw and
    his initial reaction to it.

*7 DIXON, ELLA HEPWORTH. As I Knew Them. London: Hutchinson
    and Co. Excerpted in 1947.A2.
        Describes James as "the most profoundly sad-looking man
    I have ever seen," with "age-old and world-weary" visionary
    eyes (quotations from 1947.A2).

8   EDEL, LEON. "A Note on the Translations of H. James in
    France." Revue Anglo-Américaine, 7 (August), 539-40.
        With the publication of four volumes of James in 1929,
    French readers showed renewed interest in a writer who had
    "intimate" relations with France and whose novels show
    French influences. "Among those who follow English litera-
    ture in France Henry James has always been highly respect-
    ed."

9   GARLAND, HAMLIN. "Roadside Meetings of a Literary Nomad: IX.
    Bret Harte with A Monacle--Henry James, Lover of America."
    Sections 77-80. Bookman (New York), 71 (July), 427-32.
        Although Howells and James are associated in the public
    mind, they are alike only "in the broad sense of being

students of manners rather than writers of romance." Recounts correspondence with James, a visit to Rye, and conversations with James on topics such as the conditions of
authorship in America, his assessment of other writers,
and his wish to have remained an American. Reprinted:
1930.B10.

10   GARLAND, HAMLIN. "Henry James at Rye," in Roadside Meetings.
     New York: The Macmillan Co., pp. 454-65.
          Reprint of 1930.B9.

11   GERBER, JOHN C. "Foreword," in The Ambassadors. Edited by
     Martin W. Sampson and John C. Gerber. Harper's Modern
     Classics. New York: Harper and Row, pp. xv-xviii. Re-
     printed: 1948.
          Reviews background of novel's composition and points out
     ten compositional problems of The Ambassadors. Notes
     James' high regard for the novel and concludes that "In
     several very real senses Strether was James and the novel
     is an autobiography."

12   GIDE, ANDRÉ. "Henry James." Yale Review, NS 19 (March), 641-
     43.
          James appeals to the intelligence of his readers, and
     his characters exist on the level of functioning intellect,
     lacking "all the shaggy, tangled undergrowth, all the wild
     darkness...." Concludes that James' novels are "marvels
     of composition, but that is all." Reprinted: 1945.A1.

13   HARDY, FLORENCE EMILY. The Later Years of Thomas Hardy, 1892-
     1928. New York: The Macmillan Co., pp. 7-8, 46, 137, 168-
     69. Reprinted: New York: St. Martin's Press, 1962.
          Notes James' and Robert Louis Stevenson's description of
     Hardy's Tess of the D'Urbervilles as "'vile.'" On James,
     Hardy remarked in a letter that "'It is remarkable that a
     writer who has no grain of poetry, or humour, or spontane-
     ity in his productions, can yet be a good novelist.'"

14   JOSEPHSON, MATTHEW. "The Education of Henry James," in Por-
     trait of the Artist as an American. New York: Harcourt,
     Brace and World, pp. 70-97. Reprinted: New York: Octagon
     Books, 1964.
          James' career was "a quarrel with--if not barbarism,
     then--provincialism." Concentrates on James' awareness of
     the American environment and his response to it, and con-
     cludes that the dominant theme of James' early writings
     was the American as artist or as the pilgrim of culture.

1930

15   JOSEPHSON, MATTHEW. "A 'Passionate Pilgrim,'" in <u>Portrait of</u>
     <u>the Artist as an American</u>. New York: Harcourt, Brace and
     World, pp. 98-138. Reprinted: New York: Octagon Books,
     1964.
          James is primarily a "man...of sensibility" who yearned
     for "sanctuaries of the beautiful." He was a supporter of
     civilization, but for him America represented civilization
     at a low ebb.

16   JOSEPHSON, MATTHEW. "The Return of Henry James," in <u>Portrait</u>
     <u>of the Artist as an American</u>. New York: Harcourt, Brace
     and World, pp. 265-88. Reprinted: New York: Octagon
     Books, 1964.
          Account of James' activities and impressions on his re-
     turn to America, which resulted in <u>The American Scene</u>, a
     criticism of "the gregarious, moral customs which the
     mechanized society tended to, and the unconscionable tempo
     at which life was lived."

17   MacCARTHY, DESMOND. "The World of Henry James." <u>Life and</u>
     <u>Letters</u>, 5 (November), 352-65.
          Reconstructs his fifteen year friendship with James,
     analyzes James as an author and describes him as a conver-
     sationalist. James' choice of theme was cases of con-
     science, and he was above all the "novelist of distinc-
     tions." Reprinted: 1931.B15-16.

18   McGILL, V. J. "Henry James: Master Detective." <u>Bookman</u>
     (New York), 72 (November), 251-56.
          In a novel like <u>The Golden Bowl</u>, each primary character
     becomes an accomplished detective in an attempt to solve
     the mysteries of personalities, and readers must actively
     participate in the solution. Points out James' adherence
     to necessary elements of the detective story. James,
     "though quite above the mechanical level of the customary
     detective story, still carries on as a first-rate sleuth
     in the more difficult province of the 'stream of conscious-
     ness.'"

19   NEVINS, ALLAN. <u>Henry White, Thirty Years of American Diplo-</u>
     <u>macy</u>. New York and London: Harper and Brothers, 91-93 and
     passim.
          Remarks on James' affection for Henry and (especially)
     Mrs. White, whom he met in the '80's and with whom he cor-
     responded, in letters which include "some self-revelatory
     passages, fuller and more intimate." Mrs. White possessed
     some of the qualities of Maria Gostrey and Maggie Verver.
     Reprints excerpts from some of James' letters.

20 PARRINGTON, VERNON LOUIS. "Henry James and the Nostalgia of
    Culture," in <u>Main Currents in American Thought</u>. Vol. 3.
    New York: Harcourt, Brace and World, 239-41. Reprinted:
    1959.
        James, a "forerunner of modern expressionism," fled to
    Europe from the vulgarities of the Gilded Age on the basis
    that the American atmosphere was uncongenial to the artist.
    Explains James' career in light of his expatriation, and
    describes him not as a realist but as a "self-deceived
    romantic," who, "wandering between worlds...found a home
    nowhere." Reprinted: 1945.A1.

21 PATTEE, FRED LEWIS. <u>The New American Literature: 1890-1930</u>.
    New York: The Century Co., passim.
        Describes James as "the classic example of émigré Ameri-
    can..." who "had been taken over by the English as one of
    their own."

22 SAMPSON, MARTIN W. "Introduction," in <u>The Ambassadors</u>.
    Edited by Martin W. Sampson and John C. Gerber. Harper's
    Modern Classics. New York: Harper and Row, pp. iii-xiii.
    Reprinted: 1948.
        Provides suggestions on the "process of reading" <u>The
    Ambassadors</u>, which displays "intellectual and moral refine-
    ment...." Discusses significant aspects of James' aims and
    methods, his use of point of view, summarizes the novel,
    and comments on the underlying theme, the recognition of a
    great meaning in life by Strether.

23 WALBROOK, H. M. "The Novels of Henry James." <u>Fortnightly
    Review</u>, NS 127 (May), 680-91.
        In the "contrast between the young civilisation of his
    native land and the older ones of Europe," James' sympa-
    thies were with the Old World. James, the most interna-
    tional American novelist, "cultivated difficulty" because
    he was intrigued by the problems of art.

<u>1931 A BOOKS</u>

1   EDEL, LEON. <u>Les années dramatiques</u>. Paris: Jouve and Cie,
    264 pp. (French)
        Examination of James' "evolution" during the period in
    which he wrote for the theatre. The crucial difference in
    James' early and late fiction is largely due to his drama-
    tic experiment during years "of great moral conflict."
    Includes chapters on "The Dramatic Muse," "Justification of
    the Theatre," "Guy Domville," "The Old Pretender," "The
    Last Years," and a bibliography.

1931

2   EDEL, LEON. Prefaces of Henry James. Paris: Jouve and Cie,
     136 pp.
          Exposition of James' theories and methods in fiction as
     articulated in the prefaces for the New York edition, which
     reveal James' attitude toward life as that of "observer and
     notetaker, of imaginative creative artist." Chapter I
     calls the prefaces "leisurely, quiet utterances of a man
     who, in his old age, holds his craft in his hand and sur-
     veys it with detachment." Describes James at the time he
     composed the prefaces in Chapter II, "Writing the Pref-
     aces." Chapter III, "The Art of Fiction," considers James'
     essay by that title and the way in which his views were
     enlarged despite the maintenance of a core of concepts, as
     illustrated in the prefaces. Other chapters include "The
     Origin of the Story," on James' analysis of his method;
     "The Telling of the Story," on James' point of view; "Ob-
     servations," on James' attitude toward the novel; and "The
     Figure in the Carpet," on remarks in the prefaces which
     illuminate James' pattern. Includes a bibliography of un-
     published material on James and reprints a letter from
     James to Mrs. Linton.

1931 B SHORTER WRITINGS

1   BEACH, JOSEPH WARREN. "The Novel from James to Joyce." Na-
     tion, 132 (10 June), 634-36.
          James, representative of the extreme in "dramatic" ten-
     dencies, is similar to Joyce in his "infinite expansion of
     the moment," although Joyce carried techniques such as
     self-effacement and subjective close-ups further.

*2   BOAS, RALPH PHILIP. The Study and Appreciation of Literature.
     New York: Harcourt, Brace and World, passim. Cited in
     Beatrice Ricks, comp. Henry James: A Bibliography of
     Secondary Works, #1954.

3   DeMILLE, GEORGE E. "Henry James," in Literary Criticism in
     America: A Preliminary Survey. New York: The Dial Press,
     pp. 158-81.
          James' criticism, basically technical, reveals a moral-
     istic bias, "masked by intelligent rationalization." De-
     scribes James as "master of the critical sneer," and com-
     pares James and Poe as critics.

4   FORD, FORD MADOX [pseud.]. "Three Americans and a Pole."
     Scribner's Magazine, 90 (October), 379-86.
          See 1931.B11.

1931

5   FORD, FORD MADOX [pseud.]. "Rye Road," in Return to Yesterday. London: V. Gollancz, pp. 202-18; New York: Horace
Liveright, 1932.
      See 1931.B12.

6   GARLAND, HAMLIN. "Henry James in America," in Companions on
the Trail. New York: The Macmillan Co., pp. 256-64.
      Recalls meetings with James during his 1904 visit to
America. Describes James' physical appearance and mannner,
and notes his impressions of Chicago.

7   GOSSE, EDMUND. The Life and Letters of Sir Edmund Gosse.
Edited by Evan Charteris. London: William Heinemann,
passim.
      Reprints eleven letters from Gosse to James. Passing
references to James made in other letters and in the biographical remarks.

8   HALE, E. E. "The Impressionism of Henry James." Faculty Papers of Union College, 2 (January), 3-17.
      Discussion of Impressionism in the life of James. Notes
his frequent use of the term "impression," and asserts that
James constantly received, stored and expressed impressions.
Examines the influence of the Newport group, 1859, especially William Hunt, the painter, and John La Farge, his
pupil, on James' artistic form. James' attitude is that
one "should be alive to the crowded impressions of life,
instead of arranging one's ideas in any definite or sche-
matic way..." and "that a work of art should be the definite portrait of such a keenly perceived impression."

9   HARRIS, JOEL CHANDLER. "Provinciality in Literature--a De-
fence of Boston," in Joel Chandler Harris: Editor and
Essayist: Miscellaneous Literary, Political, and Social
Writings. Edited by Julia Collier Harris. Chapel Hill:
University of North Carolina Press, pp. 186-91.
      Reacts against James' charge in the Hawthorne essay that
American literature is provincial, and describes James as
the "most delightful literary snob of the period." His
essay, although well-written and clever, is a study of New
England social life rather than a study of Hawthorne.

10   HERRICK, ROBERT. "Henry James," in American Writers on American Fiction. Edited by J. A. Macy. New York: Horace
Liveright, pp. 298-316.
      James demonstrated the nostalgic spirit for the "ances-
tral home of Western culture," and the majority of his
works illustrate some aspect of his obsession with the

1931

meaning of England for the American consciousness. Describes several types of American characters in James'
novels.

11   HUEFFER, FORD MADOX. "Three Americans and a Pole." Scribner's Magazine, 90 (October), 379-86.
         Recalls his association with four foreigners in England,
Crane, W. H. Hudson, Conrad and James. Describes James'
manner with acquaintances and friends, his relations with
Conrad and Crane. See 1931.B4.

12   HUEFFER, FORD MADOX. "Rye Road," in Return to Yesterday.
London: V. Gollancz, pp. 202-218; New York: Horace Liveright, 1932.
         Reminiscences of personal experiences with and impres-
sions of James, who portrayed "an immense--and an increasingly tragic--picture of leisured society that is fairly
unavailing, materialistic, emasculated--and doomed." In
discussing experiments with technique of the novel that he
and Conrad were engaged in, suggests "James was performing
the miracles after whose secrets we were merely groping,"
although he rarely revealed his aims and methods. James
"knew consummately one form of life; to that he restricted
himself." See 1931.B5. Reprinted: as "The Old Man," in
1945.A1.

13   KNIGHT, GRANT COCHRON. "The Triumph of Realism: Henry James,"
in The Novel in English. New York: Richard R. Smith,
pp. 276-87.
         Characterizes James as a "born dramatist rather than a
born novelist," who viewed "the spectacle of ideas, the
collision of situations, the tableau of motives." Discusses James' three periods and selected representative
works from each.

14   LEWISOHN, LUDWIG. "Where Henry James Never Entered." This
Quarter, 4 (December), 318-33.
         An attempt "to define the character of Henry James and
of his art and to establish...the psychical identity of
the man and the artist." The impetus of James' art and
life was "flight," and his theme was "frustration." James
"as stylist, master of form, creator of a body of memorable
work" is to date the "most eminent" American man of letters. Reprinted: 1932.B21.

15   MacCARTHY, DESMOND. "The World of Henry James." Living Age,
339 (January), 491-98.
         Reprint of 1930.B17.

16   MacCARTHY, DESMOND. "The World of Henry James." Saturday
     Review of Literature, 8 (29 August), 81-83.
         Reprint of 1930.B17.

17   MacCARTHY, DESMOND. "Henry James," in Portraits. New York:
     Oxford University Press, pp. 149-69. Reprinted: 1954.
         Expanded version of 1920.B21. Classes James with
     Proust, Balzac, and Dostoevsky in his "passion for final-
     ity in research and statement," in James' case directed
     towards man's social nature. James is "the most metaphor-
     ical of writers and 'metaphysical.'"

*18 ROBERTSON, W. GRAHAM. Time Was. London: Hamish Hamilton.
     In United States, entitled Life Was Worth Living. Ex-
     cerpted in 1947.A2.
         "In the 'nineties he was in appearance almost remark-
     ably unremarkable..."; James' authentic "face was not
     'delivered' until he was a comparatively old man, so that
     for the greater part of his life he went about in dis-
     guise" (quotations from 1947.A2). Gives account of open-
     ing night of Guy Domville.

19   ROURKE, CONSTANCE. "The American," in American Humor: A
     Study of the National Character. New York: Harcourt,
     Brace and Co., pp. 235-65.
         An examination of Christopher Newman in The American as
     a national type, who, though defeated, achieved a recogni-
     tion, "that laden balance of mind and feeling from which
     an enduring philosophical comedy may spring." Concludes
     that James expanded the realm of national comedy, devel-
     oped new subject matter for the novel in his emphasis on
     the internal view, and "discovered the international
     scene...'for literature.'" Reprinted: 1945.A1.

20   SMITH, LOGAN PEARSALL. "Robert Bridges: Recollections," in
     Society for Pure English Tract No. 35. Oxford: Clarendon
     Press, pp. 491-92.
         Mentions refusal of James on being invited to join the
     Society for Pure English, and reprints a portion of his
     reply.

21   SMITH, S. STEPHENSON. "The Psychological Novel," in The Craft
     of the Critic. New York: Thomas Y. Crowell Co., pp. 185-
     90.
         James' world, although "mentally normal," is "curiously
     stagnant." Views The Golden Bowl and The Wings of the Dove
     as "masterpieces in the field of the psychological novel,"
     and concludes that James moved "toward a full, almost

1931

lyrical expression of his own incredibly rich observations
of the highly civilized social world...."

22 TROY, WILLIAM. "Henry James and Young Writers." Bookman (New
York), 73 (June), 351-58.
James illuminates the novelist's proper relation to values. What writers can learn from James is not anything
distinctly represented in his achievement, nothing implicit
in his style or technique, not his 'philosophy' or beliefs.
"What they can learn from him is the deepest meaning of the
phrase 'the integrity of the artist.'" Reprinted: as "The
New Generation," in Leon Edel, ed. Henry James: A Collection of Critical Essays, pp. 79-91.

1932 A BOOKS

1 ROBINS, ELIZABETH. Theatre and Friendship: Some Henry James
Letters, with a Commentary. New York: G. P. Putnam's
Sons, 303 pp. Reprinted: Freeport, N.Y.: Books for Libraries Press, 1969.
Includes over 150 letters and notes written by James,
dated through 1911, to Elizabeth Robins, an actress, with
comments and explanation. The correspondence provides
evidence of James' interest in the theatre aside from his
dramatic writings; confirms his broad knowledge of plays,
playwrights and acting; and has additional human interest.
Reviewed: Richard P. Blackmur, Hound and Horn, 6 (January-
March 1933), 330-34; C. H. Grattan, Nation, 135 (12 October
1932), 335; Constance Rourke, New Republic, 72 (19 October
1932), 265; Leon Edel, Saturday Review of Literature, 9
(12 November 1932), 236; Times Literary Supplement (21 July
1932), p. 529.

1932 B SHORTER WRITINGS

1 ATHERTON, GERTRUDE. Adventures of a Novelist. New York:
Horace Liveright; London: Jonathan Cape, 279-80, 363-65
and passim.
Recounts her first reading of James and being "in love"
with him, and describes meetings where he "talked coher-
ently, brilliantly, illuminatingly."

2 BAKER, ERNEST A. and JAMES PACKMAN. "Henry James," in A
Guide to the Best Fiction. New York: The Macmillan Co.,
pp. 263-66.
List of 37 entries under James in a compilation of the
most "notable prose fiction in English," with brief

notations of the "contents, nature, and style of each book,"
and general bibliographic information with date of publication in book form.

3   BEACH, JOSEPH WARREN. "Point of View: James," in The Twen-
    tieth-Century Novel: Studies in Technique. New York: The
    Century Co., pp. 193-204.
        The restricted point of view contributes to realization
    of the dramatic ideal, the method of direct presentation
    rather than explanation by the author. Compares point of
    view in Crime and Punishment and The American, which dem-
    onstrate technical similarities.

4   BEACH, JOSEPH WARREN. "Point of View: James and Others," in
    The Twentieth-Century Novel: Studies in Technique. New
    York: The Century Co., pp. 204-17.
        The single point of view in the later novels of James
    is a natural outgrowth of his search for singleness of
    impression. Analyzes The Ambassadors as single point of
    view fiction.

5   BEACH, JOSEPH WARREN. "Point of View: James, Stendhal," in
    The Twentieth-Century Novel: Studies in Technique. New
    York: The Century Co., pp. 218-28.
        The technique of single point of view serves an aesthet-
    ic purpose, and James' system "implies that men are crea-
    tures living mainly in reflection...." Briefly compares
    James and Stendhal.

6   BEACH, JOSEPH WARREN. "Subjective Drama: James," in The
    Twentieth-Century Novel: Studies in Technique. New York:
    The Century Co., pp. 177-92.
        James uses the consciousness of his characters as a me-
    dium for explanation and comment. Discusses James' method
    of characterization and exposition using examples from The
    Wings of the Dove and The Ambassadors.

7   BENNETT, ARNOLD. The Journal of Arnold Bennett, 1896-1910.
    Vol. 1. New York: The Viking Press, p. 206.
        The plot of The Ambassadors is "clumsily managed" and
    the book is "not quite worth the great trouble of reading
    it."

*8 BLOMFIELD, SIR REGINALD. Memoirs of an Architect. New York
    and London: The Macmillan Co. Excerpted in 1947.A2.
        Recollections of James in Rye, where he first stayed in
    Blomfield's cottage. Describes James as "kind-hearted and
    sympathetic...modest and even diffident...yet conscious of
    what was due to him" (quotation from 1947.A2).

1932

9   BROOKS, VAN WYCK. "Henry James as a Reviewer," in <u>Sketches in Criticism</u>. New York: E. P. Dutton and Co., pp. 190-96.

Although the reviews demonstrate the "vigour" of James' "prime," he paid the "penalty" of expatriation. "There is something oppressive in the spectacle of what we can only consider the decay of Henry James." Reviews show James' devotion to his career and his preoccupation with problems of method.

10   CESTRE, CHARLES. "La France dans l'oeuvre de Henry James." <u>Revue Anglo-Américaine</u>, 10 (October), 1-13, 112-22. (French)

A study of the influence of France and its artists, especially Balzac, on James' works, with emphasis on <u>The American</u>, <u>Madame de Mauves</u>, <u>The Portrait of a Lady</u> and <u>Roderick Hudson</u>. James deviated from the French realists on moral grounds, although he was not puritanical.

11   COLLINS, NORMAN. "Henry James," in <u>The Facts of Fiction</u>. London: Victor Gollancz, pp. 228-36.

James exemplifies what the psychological novelists were trying to do: "...He gave the novel new nerves of sensitiveness, he taught it to explore the mind for the little half resolutions and misgivings as well as for the decisions and rejections that ultimately make for action."

12   DICKINSON, THOMAS H. "Henry James," in <u>The Making of American Literature</u>. New York: The Century Co., pp. 580-89.

Discusses James' interest in the international scene and in subtleties of character, and briefly surveys his fiction according to two periods. Concludes that James was a "product only of culture and civilization" who was unable to "survive the collapse of the order that had made him."

13   EDGAR, PELHAM. "Henry James, the Essential Novelist." <u>Queen's Quarterly</u>, 39 (May), 181-92.

Examination of James' strengths and weaknesses as a writer, with attention to critical objections such as those of Van Wyck Brooks and H. G. Wells. Considers James a "pioneer," with each successive work being an "experiment in design." Analyzes <u>The Wings of the Dove</u>, and annotates other novels of the same period to demonstrate the "variety of attack" which differentiates them. Reprinted: 1933.B6; as "The Essential Novelist?" in Leon Edel, ed. <u>Henry James: A Collection of Critical Essays</u>, pp. 92-101.

14   FULLERTON, BRADFORD M. Selective Bibliography of American
      Literature, 1775-1900: A Brief Estimate of the More Im-
      portant American Authors. New York: W. F. Payson,
      pp. 159-61.
          James' poor reputation with the average reader was
      caused by his slow plot development and involved style.
      Lists "representative" works of James with date of publi-
      cation of each.

15   GRATTAN, CLINTON HARTLEY. "The Calm within the Cyclone."
      Nation, 134 (17 February), 201-203.
          The major flaw in James is his emphasis on representa-
      tives of a highly specialized group, his preoccupation with
      characters from the leisure class. His focus is the calm
      spot at the center of the storm, inhabited by cultivated
      individuals. He is only dimly aware of the cyclone which
      surrounds his characters.

16   GRATTAN, CLINTON HARTLEY. "Henry James," in The Three
      Jameses: A Family of Minds. Henry James, Sr., William
      James, Henry James. New York: New York University Press,
      pp. 208-357. Reprinted: 1962.
          Biographical account of James, with an effort to assess
      the meaning and influence of elements in his background.
      Attempts to see relationships in the intellectual his-
      tories of Henry, Sr., William and Henry James. Includes
      lengthier discussions of the "great novels," including The
      Portrait of a Lady, The Awkward Age, The Sacred Fount, The
      Wings of the Dove, The Ambassadors, and The Golden Bowl,
      followed by a summary of James' artistic theory and char-
      acteristic themes. James is a "proponent of the intellect
      in its most self-conscious, discriminating and analytical
      development." Reviewed: Richard P. Blackmur, Hound and
      Horn, 6 (January-March 1933), 335; Constance Rourke, New
      Republic, 72 (19 October 1932), 265; B. R. Redman, New York
      Herald Tribune Books (23 October 1932), p. 1; Herschel
      Brickell, North American Review, 234 (December 1932), 574;
      Leon Edel, Saturday Review of Literature, 9 (12 November
      1932), 236.

17   HENDERSON, ARCHIBALD. "Shaw as a Man of 'Letters,'" in
      Bernard Shaw, Playboy and Prophet. New York and London:
      D. Appleton and Co., pp. 766-67.
          Recounts James' response to Henderson's query about one
      of Shaw's anti-American tirades.

1932

18   HUGHES, HELEN SARD and ROBERT MORSS LOVETT. "Henry James,"
       in The History of the Novel in England. Boston: Houghton
       Mifflin Co., pp. 337-46.
          James' influence on the fiction of his period resulted
       from his emphasis on aesthetic concerns. James' novels
       culminate in an "aesthetic apotheosis of the novel of man-
       ners."

19   JOHNSON, MERLE. "Henry James," in American First Editions:
       Bibliographic Checklists of the Works of 146 American
       Authors. Revised and enlarged. New York: R. R. Bowker
       Co., pp. 197-201.
          Identification of American books in first editions or
       "first state." Chronological listing, including place and
       date of publication. See 1936.B10.

20   LARRABEE, HAROLD A. "The Jameses: Financier, Heretic,
       Philosopher." The American Scholar, 1 (October), 401-13.
          Historical account of James' grandfather and father,
       which concludes that Henry James, Sr.'s inheritance made
       him a rebel against social and theological standards of
       his time.

21   LEWISOHN, LUDWIG. "The Rise of the Novel," in Expression in
       America. New York: Harper and Brothers, pp. 233-72.
          Reprint of 1931.B14.

22   LOWELL, JAMES RUSSELL. "To Henry James," in New Letters of
       James Russell Lowell. Edited by M. A. DeWolfe Howe. New
       York: Harper and Brothers, pp. 234-37.
          Reprints two 1878 letters from Lowell to James in which
       he praises The Europeans and The American and makes de-
       tailed suggestions, particularly about wording.

23   LUCAS, E. V. Reading, Writing and Remembering: A Literary
       Record. New York: Harper and Brothers, pp. 183-85 and
       passim.
          Recalls meeting with James at Lady Colvin's, where he
       "was very malicious about other guests," describes his
       "approaches" as "crablike," and praises his précis of The
       Ambassadors.

24   QUINN, ARTHUR HOBSON. "Liberality," in The Soul of America:
       Yesterday and Today. Philadelphia: University of Pennsyl-
       vania Press, passim.
          James' English Hours is an example of "observations of
       national characteristics" and "distinction of style."

25   ROBERTS, MORLEY. "Meetings with Some Men of Letters."
     Queen's Quarterly, 39 (February), 65-70.
          Rather uncomplimentary description of interactions with
     James at Rye, for whom Roberts "never found" the key. "It
     became humourously clear that he regarded me as a savage...."

26   ROTHENSTEIN, WILLIAM. "Henry James in Paris," in Men and Mem-
     ories. New York: Coward-McCann, pp. 81-82.
          Recollections of James around 1880, when "He was not...
     so massive as he became later, either in person or man-
     ner...." Describes James in Paris as "an arresting talker"
     whose speech was "slow and exact...."

27   SHERMAN, STUART PRATT. "The Special Case of Henry James," in
     The Emotional Discovery of America and Other Essays. New
     York: Farrar and Rinehart, pp. 35-47. Reprinted: Free-
     port, N.Y.: Books for Libraries Press, 1970.
          In an essay that originally appeared in The Weekly Re-
     view (7 July 1920), suggests that while James' letters
     show his relationships with his fellow artists, Lubbock
     (see 1920.B20) unduly emphasized the "sexagenarian out-
     look." Discusses differences in style between the two vol-
     umes of letters, the movement towards the "vraie vérité"
     of the "impressionist," and the "grand climax of disillu-
     sion and of moral commitment and passion."

28   WALPOLE, HUGH. "Henry James's High Hat," in The Apple Trees:
     Four Reminiscences. Waltham Saint Lawrence, Berkshire:
     The Golden Cockerel Press, pp. 38-63.
          Recalls details of the 70th birthday gathering for
     James, discusses the writing about James by his acquaint-
     ances. "I loved him, was frightened by him, was bored by
     him, was staggered by his intricacies, altogether enslaved
     by his kindness, generosity, child-like purity of his af-
     fections, his unswerving loyalties, his sly and Puck-like
     sense of humour." Remarks on James' "Puritan American
     conscience," his relations with his friends, his conversa-
     tional style, his "absorption in life perpetual...his
     passion for his art overwhelming." Concludes that James
     was "the best and greatest [man] I have ever known."

1933 A BOOKS - NONE

1933 B SHORTER WRITINGS

  1   CANTWELL, ROBERT. "No Landmarks." Symposium, 4 (January),
      70-84.

1933

James' statement in his Hawthorne essay on the inadequacies of American life has prejudiced many critics
against him. Supports the literal truth of James' assessment of social institutions in America, which were in flux,
as opposed to the more permanent landmarks of Europe.
James' perception of social change caused him to avoid re-
lying on any particular system of morality and create an
involved technique for relating characters to each other.
James became "the analyst and dramatist of the general."
Reprinted: 1937.B3.

2 CUNLIFFE, J. W. "Georgian Novelists," in English Literature
in the Twentieth Century. New York: The Macmillan Co.,
pp. 204-207. Reprinted: Essay Index Reprint Series.
Freeport, N.Y.: Books for Libraries Press, 1967.
James criticized the lack of "treatment, composition,
structure, fusion, a center of interest," in the Georgian
novelists, which he attributed to the influence of Tolstoi, but congratulated them for their courageous treatment
of the sexual question and the "genial force of their sat-
uration in and possession of their material."

3 DANIELS, EARL. "Bibliography of Henry James." Times Literary
Supplement (20 April), p. 276.
Note on the printing history of Terminations and The
Spoils of Poynton, regarding their spurious claim to being
first editions. Reprinted: 1933.B4.

4 DANIELS, EARL. "James Editions." Saturday Review of Literature, 10 (23 September), 128.
Reprint of 1933.B3.

5 EDEL, LEON. "The Exile of Henry James." University of Toronto Quarterly, 2 (July), 520-32.
James "went to Europe because he could create in Europe," not because he was unable to create in America.
Draws parallel to contemporary Canadian artist, and mentions other American artists who chose to reside in Europe.
James remains "the most important prototype of the cosmo-
politan who is...bound to shake off America for Europe."

6 EDGAR, PELHAM. "The Essential Novelist? Henry James," in
The Art of the Novel: From 1700 to the Present Time. New
York: The Macmillan Co., pp. 172-83.
Reprint of 1932.B13.

*7   FIELD, MICHAEL. Works and Days. Edited by T. and D. C.
        Sturge Moore. London: John Murray. Excerpted in 1947.A2.
        James described George Meredith and Thomas Hardy as
        "Meredith the Obscure and the Amazing Hardy" (quotation
        from 1947.A2).

8   GREENE, GRAHAM. "Henry James--An Aspect," in Contemporary
        Essays: 1933. Edited by Sylva Norman. London: E. Math-
        ews and Marrot, pp. 65-75. Reprinted: Essay Index Reprint
        Series. Freeport, N.Y.: Books for Libraries Press, 1968.
        James, who loved tradition and age, thought Catholicism
        appealing as an aesthetic form and found certain dogmas
        attractive. Perhaps his ignorance of the rules of the
        Catholic church, as in "The Altar of the Dead," indicate a
        fear of conversion. His novels are saved from deep cyni-
        cism by "the religious sense," although his beliefs were
        never codified into a system or stated in a philosophy.
        Reprinted: 1951.B28. See also 1951.B26.

9   HICKS, GRANVILLE. "Fugitives," in The Great Tradition: An
        Interpretation of American Literature Since the Civil War.
        New York: The Macmillan Co., pp. 100, 105-24.
        A partial explanation for James' expatriation is that
        he needed the sanctions of an "established, leisure class
        on his individual tastes and activities." Although his
        technique is outstanding, for him the writing process was
        a game and his created world almost wholly abstract.

10   PERRY, RALPH BARTON. "Henry James in Italy." Harvard Gradu-
        ate Magazine, 41 (June), 189-200.
        Reprints four letters exchanged between William and
        Henry during winter of 1869-1870, while both were in the
        experimental stages of their respective vocations.

*11 SUTRO, ALFRED. Celebrities and Simple Souls. London: Gerald
        Duckworth and Co. Excerpted in 1947.A2.
        Despite the characteristic hesitations and mannerisms
        of his speech, James "never came even near to being a
        bore" (quotation from 1947.A2). Includes anecdote in which
        James professed to desire public popularity.

12   WALPOLE, HUGH. "Mr. Oddy," in All Souls' Night: A Book of
        Stories. New York: Doubleday, Doran and Co., pp. 109-30.
        A fictional reminiscence of James in his later years.

1934

1934 A BOOKS - NONE

1934 B SHORTER WRITINGS

1   ARVIN, NEWTON. "Henry James and the Almighty Dollar." Hound
     and Horn, 7 (April-May), 434-43.
          James, who was almost altogether lacking in historic
     understanding, became "the chronicler of a festering soci-
     ety." He exposed both Americans and Europeans at their
     weakest point, a "gross preoccupation with money," drama-
     tized chiefly in the marriage market. Illustrates James'
     use of this theme in his novels.

2   BLACKMUR, RICHARD P. "The Critical Prefaces." Hound and
     Horn, 7 (April-May), 444-77.
          For James, the prefaces were a "kind of epitaph or
     series of inscriptions for the major monument of his life,"
     and they are the most "sustained and eloquent and original
     piece of literary criticism in existence." Defines the
     scope and nature of the preface, which is "the story of a
     story," and discusses its concern with expressing the re-
     lation between life and art. Summarizes the primary
     themes that provide the unifying context of the prefaces,
     such as "Finding of Subjects," "The Indirect Approach,"
     and "The Relation of Art and the Artist," and lists some
     of the more important subjects discussed in the prefaces,
     indicating where they can be located and the general di-
     rection of the discussion. Analyzes the Preface to The
     Ambassadors. Reprinted: 1934.B3; 1935.B4; 1955.B10.

3   BLACKMUR, RICHARD P. "Introduction," in The Art of the Novel:
     Critical Prefaces, by Henry James. New York: Charles
     Scribner's Sons, pp. vii-xxxix. Reprinted: 1960.
          Reprint of 1934.B2.

4   BOUGHTON, ALICE. "A Note by His Photographer." Hound and
     Horn, 7 (April-May), 478-79.
          Reminiscences of James' photographer on his sitting for
     his photograph. Describes James as "dignified and impres-
     sive, with manners almost courtly, and wearing a top hat
     several sizes too big."

5   BURR, A. R. "Her Brothers (Introduction)," in Alice James:
     Her Brothers--Her Journal. New York: Dodd, Mead and Co.,
     pp. 3-82.
          Biographical account of the James family, including
     discussion of the literary heritage Henry James, Sr. be-
     queathed to his children, of Henry's English life, and his

relationship with the American members of his family.
After a brief description of Alice, reprints her journal.
Reviewed: William Troy, Nation, 138 (13 June 1934), 682;
C. H. Gratton, New York Times Book Review (20 May 1934),
p. 3; R. B. Perry, Saturday Review of Literature, 10
(16 June 1934), 749; Graham Greene, Spectator, 153 (28 September 1934), 446.

6   CANTWELL, ROBERT. "A Little Reality." Hound and Horn, 7
     (April-May), 494-505.
         James' early years offer clues to the later works, with
     concern for the relationship between members of upper and
     lower classes. He didn't yet know that he could only write
     of the bourgeoise "if he shut his eyes and closed his ears
     to most of its activities...." James "wanted reality, yes,
     but just a little of it, just enough to prompt his imagina-
     tion and yet not too much, not too many of the dull par-
     ticulars that would drag his story down."

7   CANTWELL, ROBERT. "The Return of Henry James." New Republic,
     81 (12 December), 119-21.
         James evolved a theory about the author's relation to
     the social order and lived it through. He viewed without
     indignation the corrupt and doomed leisure class. His work
     ran "counter to the main stream of English fiction of his
     time, emphasizing form in a period when the novel had be-
     come hasty and sprawling."

8   DUNLAP, GEORGE A. "The Political Life of the City," in The
     City in the American Novel, 1789-1900. Philadelphia:
     University of Pennsylvania Press; pp. 160-62.
         In The Bostonians, James makes interesting use of the
     political material of the women's movement, although he
     emphasizes the social side of woman's life. His work is
     instructive on the progress of an important movement in
     Boston's history.

9   DUNLAP, GEORGE A. "The Social Life of the City," in The City
     in the American Novel, 1789-1900. Philadelphia: Univer-
     sity of Pennsylvania Press, pp. 102-103.
         In Washington Square, a "tiresome story," with, however,
     memorable character portrayal of the heroine, social rank
     is an important factor in the novel's development.

10   ELLIOTT, MAUD HOWE. My Cousin, F. Marion Crawford. New York:
     The Macmillan Co., passim.
         James recorded the "Anglo-American colony of Rome at the
     time when Louisa Ward and Thomas Crawford settled there..."

1934

in the biography of W. W. Story. Refers to James' association with the Crawford family.

11 FERGUSSON, FRANCIS. "The Drama in The Golden Bowl." Hound
    and Horn, 7 (April–May), 407-13.
        James' understanding of the term "romantic" suggested
    "Art, in the sense of craftsmanship; the work of art, and
    perhaps also the 'other actual': which the work of art
    imitates." Analyzes The Golden Bowl as a "drama without
    a stage and an ethical debate without abstract concepts."
    See 1955.B32.

12 GOODSPEED, E. J. "A Footnote to Daisy Miller." Atlantic
    Monthly, 153 (February), 252-53.
        The story James heard in 1877 of an American girl, Julia
    Newberry, who died in Rome in 1876, suggested Daisy Miller
    to him and explains the "strange and sad end of the story."

13 HARTWICK, HARRY. "Caviar to the General," in The Foreground
    of American Fiction. New York: American Book Co., pp. 341-
    68.
        Concerns James' attitude towards dilemmas of conscience,
    duty, and moral integrity, his "humanistic standard of
    judicious restraint," and concludes that the key to James
    is obedience to an internal law of necessity, sacrificing
    the valuable in favor of the priceless.

14 HAYS, H. R. "Henry James, the Satirist." Hound and Horn, 7
    (April–May), 514-22.
        James satirized behaviors foreign to him but also his
    own. Considers characteristics of the satiric attitude
    and character types in James, who, in the later novels,
    "instead of attaining individual life, self-consciously
    work James' theories of national characteristics," result-
    ing in "satiric comedy," not tragic pathos.

15 HOGARTH, BASIL. The Technique of Novel Writing. London:
    John Lane, The Bodley Head, passim.
        Passing references to James. In The Outcry, "dialogue
    overshadows everything else...."

16 KENTON, EDNA, ed. "The Ambassadors: Project of Novel." By
    Henry James. Hound and Horn, 7 (April–May), 541-62.
        The manuscript of this "huge, confidential preface"
    sheds light on James' method of writing and the sequence
    of the process, and proves that James' prefaces were not
    written post factum.

1934

17   KENTON, EDNA. "Henry James in the World." <u>Hound and Horn</u>, 7
      (April-May), 506-13.
          Interpretations of James' decision to settle in England
      are colored by resentment against criticism of America.
      James speaks of dispatriation, "a kind of detachment in
      viewpoint of, not severance of interest in, the birthland,"
      which was necessary in order to eliminate provincialism in
      favor of a more general subject. Reprinted: 1945.A1.

18   KENTON, EDNA. "Some Bibliographical Notes on Henry James."
      <u>Hound and Horn</u>, 7 (April-May), 535-40.
          Listing of Russian translations of James, bibliographi-
      cal comments on "Pandora" and "Georgina's Reasons," bib-
      liographical information on "Browning in Westminster Abbey,"
      "Paste," "The Pall Mall Gazette as a New Field for Re-
      search," and "The Pennell Contribution to James's Bibliog-
      raphy."

19   LEIGHTON, LAWRENCE. "Armor against Time," <u>Hound and Horn</u>, 7
      (April-May), 373-84.
          Differences between <u>Portraits of Places</u> and <u>The American
      Scene</u> verify James' "growth of sensibility." In the
      greater detachment and honesty of the later work are clues
      to James' expatriation, his search for an international
      style, his commitment to his art. America became the sym-
      bol of what James had missed, the romance of the unexplored.
      He was basically a man "out of sympathy with this modern
      time.... His answer was his self-devotion as an artist."

20   LEWIS, WYNDHAM. "Henry James: The Arch-Enemy of 'Low Com-
      pany,'" in <u>Men Without Art</u>. New York: Russell and Rus-
      sell, 138-57. Reprinted: 1964.
          James, "the great genteel classic" and idealist, was a
      supporter of private values, of "aestheticism" as opposed
      to outside public values.

21   MOORE, MARIANNE. "Henry James as a Characteristic American."
      <u>Hound and Horn</u>, 7 (April-May), 363-72.
          An examination of personality characteristics shared by
      James which are typically American. Mentions his idealism,
      warmth, affection for family and country. "If good-nature
      and reciprocity are American traits, Henry James was a
      characteristic American...." Reprinted: 1937.B11;
      1955.B53.

22   ORCUTT, WILLIAM DANA. "Celebrities Off Parade: Henry James."
      <u>Christian Science Monitor</u>, 26 (23 August), 12.

1934

James' work displayed a "literary innovation," painstaking analysis and observation. Describes Lamb House and his association with James, who interested him more as a person, less and less as a writer. Reprinted: 1935.B18.

23 POUND, EZRA. ABC of Reading. New Haven, Conn.: Yale University Press, pp. 63, 77.
A "text-book" consideration of "How to Read." "You can learn something of a great writer's attitude toward the art of the novel in the prefaces of Henry James' collected edition." Describes them as "the one extant great treatise of novel writing in English."

24 POUND, EZRA. "Henry James," in Make It New: Essays by Ezra Pound. London: Faber and Faber, pp. 251-307.
Reprint of 1918.B19-21, B24.

25 SARAWAK, RANEE MARGARET of. Good Morning and Good Night. London: Constable and Co., pp. 246-47, 273-75, 291.
Recalls initial meeting with James in London, his kindness to her son, and a visit to his flat.

26 SPENDER, STEPHEN. "The School of Experience in the Early Novels." Hound and Horn, 7 (April-May), 417-33.
Hypothesizes that the artist must eventually come to terms with the objective, factual life around him and use symbols to represent that reality. James' early works "form a full museum of objects which were at first observed and which were later in his work used as symbols for describing states of mind in his characters." Discusses Roderick Hudson, Madame de Mauves, The American, The Princess Casamassima as observations of European society, after which James portrayed inner experience by means of objective imagery. Reprinted: 1935.B25.

27 SPENDER, STEPHEN. "A Modern Writer in Search of a Moral Subject." London Mercury, 31 (December), 128-33.
James' writing shows the course of a great deal of contemporary literature, and he revolutionized "the manner of presenting the scene in the novel and the relation of the described scene to the emotional development of the characters." James' greatest contribution to the novel is his perception that "passionate activity is intellectual activity." The contradiction in James which afflicts many modern writers is that although he was a rebel against the corruption of his day, he was also an individualist with a private system of conduct, and thus ultimately became a supporter of the system which made this existence possible.

He was a political-moral artist "without a realistic subject drawn from contemporary life to correspond with his
ultimate ethical subject...." Reprinted: 1935.B21; as
"The Contemporary Subject, in Leon Edel, ed. Henry James:
A Collection of Critical Essays, pp. 102-10.

28   SWINNERTON, FRANK. "Artful Virtuosity: Henry James," in The
     Georgian Literary Scene: A Panorama. London: William
     Heinemann, pp. 19-40.
         James, through longevity, taste, and technical skill,
     became a "Panjandrum." Discusses James' three periods
     and his artistic theory, sketches his major literary out-
     put, and briefly comments on individual novels. Despite
     the virtuosity of his art, James' work was inferior in
     "character and experience," and he made a fetish of re-
     finement. "If only the people in these books had been
     interesting...."

29   VAN PATTEN, NATHAN. "Henry James," in An Index to Bibliog-
     raphies and Bibliographical Contributions Relating to the
     Work of American and British Authors, 1923-1932. London:
     Humphrey Milford, p. 133.
         Alphabetical listing of seven enumerative and descrip-
     tive bibliographies of James, including Merle Johnson
     (1932.B19) and LeRoy Phillips (1930.A2).

30   WALPOLE, HUGH. "England," in Tendencies of the Modern Novel.
     London: George Allen and Unwin, pp. 16-18.
         In discussion of the contemporary English novel, de-
     scribes Quint in The Turn of the Screw as one of those
     characters "born of their creators' personalities," yet
     "definitely alive beyond the experience and characteris-
     tics" of the novelist.

31   WARREN, AUSTIN. "William and Henry," in The Elder Henry
     James. New York: The Macmillan Co., pp. 127-53. Re-
     printed: New York: Octagon Books, 1970.
         "Detached from trade and from party, from the bigotries
     of patriotism and religion," William and Henry "were to
     cultivate nothing less ample than the universally human."
     Discusses characteristics which isolated the family, chron-
     icles the children's schooling, comments on the boy's
     selection of career. Henry had the necessary freedom for
     development and learned that "experience is not enough:
     it must be interpreted."

1934

32 WELLS, H. G. "Digression about Novels," in Experiment in
    Autobiography: Discoveries and Conclusions of a Very
    Ordinary Brain (Since 1886). New York: The Macmillan
    Co., 410-15.
        Recounts substance of discussions with James concerning
    the art of the novel, whose attitude towards the craft was
    "by nature and education unsympathetic" with that of Wells.
    Illustrates by describing James' objections to Marriage
    and quoting from a letter on the same topic.

33 WESTCOTT, GLENWAY. "A Sentimental Contribution." Hound and
    Horn, 7 (April-May), 523-34.
        Reflections on the influence James' writing had on him
    personally, particularly in terms of its moral effect.
    The work of James is "a truer abstract autobiography of
    his age, a more thorough account of the mentality of its
    governing classes," and moves from lower to higher levels,
    keeping the moral issues clear.

34 WHARTON, EDITH. "A Backward Glance." Ladies' Home Journal,
    51 (February), 19, 73, 78, 80.
        Retrospective account of her friendship with James and
    its "stimulating and enlightening" influence. Describes
    the author both as a personality and as a conversational-
    ist, and suggests that his talk and his writing supple-
    mented each other. Includes anecdotes, character observa-
    tions. See 1920.B30 for a similar discussion of James'
    conversational habits. Reprinted: 1934.B35.

35 WHARTON, EDITH. A Backward Glance. New York: D. Appleton-
    Century Co., pp. 169-96.
        Reprint of 1934.B34.

36 WHEELWRIGHT, JOHN. "Henry James and Stanford White." Hound
    and Horn, 7 (April-May), 480-93.
        Presentation of James' views on archeological architec-
    ture and one of its practitioners, Stanford White, whom
    James identified as "the best man of the lot," and who
    "showed up the whole New Yorker attempt at architecture as
    a mistake." He believed that "it is impossible to build a
    decent city upon an unworkable plan, by the mere accumula-
    tion of decent objects." References primarily to The Amer-
    ican Scene.

37 WILSON, EDMUND. "The Ambiguity of Henry James." Hound and
    Horn, 7 (April-May), 385-406.
        With reference to Kenton's hypothesis (1924.B10), of-
    fers a Freudian interpretation of The Turn of the Screw,

suggesting that "the governess...is a neurotic case of sex
repression, and that the ghosts are not real ghosts but
hallucinations of the governess." Quint is viewed as a
debased image of the master, and the conclusion develops
as a result of the governess falling in love with Miles
and frightening him to death. The story is thus a characterization of a "thwarted Anglo-Saxon spinster," of which
there are other examples in James' works. Examines The
Sacred Fount as a companion piece to The Turn of the Screw,
in which James was dramatizing the "frustration of his own
life without quite being willing to confess it...." James'
experiment as a dramatist provoked the principal crisis in
his life, an unsuccessful "effort to make himself felt,"
after which his central observer undergoes "diminution,"
is rarely a complete, full-grown person, and sex becomes
an "obsession." Concludes that "His work is incomplete as
his experience was; but it is in no respect second-rate,
and he can be judged only in the company of the greatest."
Reprinted: 1938.B16; 1945.A1; 1948.B56. Revised:
1948.B57.

1935 A BOOKS

1   SNELL, EDWIN MARION. The Modern Fables of Henry James. Cam-
    bridge, Mass.: Harvard University Press, 75 pp. Reprinted:
    New York: Russell and Russell, 1967.
        "The peculiar quality of Henry James, throughout life,
    was his detachment." As a novelist, James belongs with the
    fabulists, who present impartially their unavoidable real-
    ities in terms of a half-invented world, which we accept
    because it consistently possesses symbols drawn from the
    chaotic life from which it seems so far removed. Part I
    considers the influence of James' early environment; Part
    II investigates his early experiments, which showed him
    his inadequacy within limits of conventional forms; and
    Part III discusses his approach which finally dictated the
    peculiar method of his later fiction. Describes the domi-
    nant motif in James as the "individual's coming to compre-
    hend, through some situation, his real position in indus-
    trialized society." Briefly analyzes a number of James'
    novels to substantiate his thesis. Reviewed: Stanley T.
    Williams, New England Quarterly, 8 (December 1935), 623-24.

1935

1935 B SHORTER WRITINGS

1   AIKEN, CONRAD. Review of <u>Alice James: Her Brothers: Her</u>
       <u>Journal</u>. <u>Criterion</u>, 14 (January), 313-15.
          Alice was Henry James' "New England conscience and con-
       sciousness," a "democrat and a skeptic." Reprinted:
       1958.B2.

2   AIKEN, CONRAD. Review of <u>The Art of the Novel: Critical</u>
       <u>Prefaces</u>. <u>Criterion</u>, 14 (July), 667-69.
          Blackmur's edition of the prefaces is "the most impor-
       tant single book of English criticism--practical criticism
       --since the time of Arnold...." Describes James as a
       "great <u>specialist</u> in criticism," and the prefaces as "the
       most fascinating critical adventure of our time, and the
       profoundest." Reprinted: 1958.B3.

*3   BAILEY, JOHN. <u>Letters and Diaries</u>. Edited by his wife.
       London: John Murray. Excerpted in 1947.A2.
          Includes James' remarks on George Sand, comments on the
       war, criticism of Tennyson, and judgment of his effective-
       ness as a hospital visitor.

4   BLACKMUR, RICHARD P. "The Critical Prefaces of Henry James,"
       in <u>The Double Agent: Essays in Craft and Elucidation</u>.
       New York: Arrow Eds., pp. 234-68. Reprinted, enlarged
       edition: Gloucester, Mass.: Peter Smith, 1962.
       Reprint of 1934.B2.

*5   BLATHWAYT, RAYMOND. <u>Looking Down the Years</u>. London: George
       Allen and Unwin. Excerpted in 1947.A2.
          Remarks on James' attitude towards the "intolerance" of
       the Church.

6   FORD, FORD MADOX [pseud.]. "Techniques." <u>Southern Review</u>, 1
       (July), 20-35.
          See 1935.B9.

7   FORD, FORD MADOX [pseud.]. "Henry James." <u>American Mercury</u>,
       36 (November), 315-27.
          See 1935.B10.

8   HATCHER, HARLAN HENTHORNE. "America Catches Step," in <u>Creat-</u>
       <u>ing the American Novel</u>. New York: Farrar and Rinehart,
       pp. 13-14.
          James was an "isolated and specialized genius separated
       from and with little influence in the development of the
       American novel" except in matters of technique.

9   HUEFFER, FORD MADOX. "Techniques." <u>Southern Review</u>, 1 (July),
     20-35.
         Examines the techniques of the Impressionists, whose
     ideal was rendering rather than reporting, from Flaubert
     on; James' contact with the French novelists; and his
     transmission of many of their concepts to England. Crane,
     Conrad and James are the "protagonists of literary Impres-
     sionism in Anglo-Saxondom." <u>See</u> 1935.B6.

10   HUEFFER, FORD MADOX. "Henry James." <u>American Mercury</u>, 36
     (November), 315-27.
         Relates a vignette concerning James which provides the
     basis for proposing that he studied every aspect of a mat-
     ter, that he knew the "privileged" but also many details
     of the lower class, that he had knowledge of certain sub-
     jects (e.g. esoteric sin and sexual indulgence) even if he
     didn't write of them. Also suggests that he (Hueffer) was
     the model for Morton [sic] Densher. <u>See</u> 1935.B7.

11   LINN, JAMES W. and H. W. TAYLOR. <u>A Foreword to Fiction</u>. New
     York: D. Appleton-Century Co., pp. 39-43, 113-15 and
     passim.
         In considering the stream of consciousness, discusses
     James' use of representation of the mind using "a formal
     if somewhat colloquial rhetoric." Contrasts the styles of
     James and Conrad with the "classic" styles of Fielding and
     Hemingway.

12   MacCARTHY, DESMOND. <u>Experience</u>. New York: Oxford University
     Press, pp. 151-52. Reprinted: Freeport, N.Y.: Books for
     Libraries Press, 1968.
         Discussion of Percy Lubbock, who was influenced by
     James, characterized as "horrified at the offhand wasteful
     callousness of the world and whose imagination often liked
     to rest beside considerate, scrupulous people in the quiet
     garden of tradition."

13   MALLET, CHARLES. <u>Anthony Hope and His Books: Being the Au-
     thorised Life of Sir Anthony Hope Hawkins</u>. London:
     Hutchinson and Co., p. 230 and passim. Reprinted: Port
     Washington, N.Y.: Kennikat Press, 1968.
         In diary entry for February 29, 1916, Hope records death
     of James, whom he had met in the 1890's and whom he de-
     scribes as "kindly, modest, always seemingly a little up-
     set by the noise of this world."

1935

14   MASON, A. E. W. "<u>Guy Domville</u>," in <u>Sir George Alexander and</u>
     <u>the St. James's Theatre</u>. New York and London: Benjamin
     Blom, pp. 67-71.
         Account of the <u>Guy Domville</u> episode. Describes James
     as writing "with infinite care uneventful novels which
     reflected faithfully the milder scenes of those well-
     mannered Victorian days."

15   MATTHIESSEN, F. O. <u>The Achievement of T. S. Eliot: An Essay</u>
     <u>on the Nature of Poetry</u>. London and New York: Oxford
     University Press, pp. 8-9, 14-15, 54-55, 69-70 and passim.
     Reprinted: 1947; 1958.
         Eliot was indebted to James in his reflections on the
     art of the novel, his demand for reader participation and
     his point of view. He saw the similarity between James
     and the metaphysical poets.

16   MOWAT, ROBERT BALMAIN. "On Both Sides of the Atlantic," in
     <u>Americans in England</u>. New York: Houghton Mifflin Co.,
     pp. 213-26.
         James "was an American through and through," the "con-
     tinuator of the great New England school...." Biographi-
     cal study of James' relationship to England, towards which
     he held an attitude both observant and critical.

17   ORAGE, ALFRED RICHARD. "James' Play of Minds," in <u>Selected</u>
     <u>Essays and Critical Writings</u>. Edited by H. Read and D.
     Saurat. London: Stanley Nott, pp. 85-88.
         James was interested in the borderline between physical
     and psychic worlds, and his stories are "the psychological
     accompaniments played by a subtle mind to tunes too fami-
     liar to need to be sung," in which the reader must "imag-
     ine" the implied story as James translates it.

18   ORCUTT, WILLIAM DANA. "From a Publisher's Easy Chair," in
     <u>Celebrities Off Parade</u>. Chicago and New York: Willett,
     Clark and Co., pp. 192-233.
         Reprint of 1934.B22.

19   PERRY, BLISS. <u>And Gladly Teach: Reminiscences</u>. Boston:
     Houghton Mifflin Co., pp. 224-25 and passim.
         Recalls after dinner reading by Howells of passage from
     <u>The American Scene</u>, just after its publication. Other
     passing references to James.

20   PERRY, RALPH BARTON. <u>Thought and Character of William James</u>.
     2 vols. Boston: Little, Brown and Co., passim.

1935

Includes several letters to and from Henry and William. Mentions the brothers' boyhood and education, Henry's early European experiences, the move to Europe, his impressions of America and comments on William, using quotations from Henry James' letters and autobiographical works.

21 SPENDER, STEPHEN. "Henry James and the Contemporary Subject," in The Destructive Element. London: Jonathan Cape, pp. 189-200. Reprinted: Boston: Houghton Mifflin Co., 1936; 1938; 1953.
Reprint of 1934.B27.

22 SPENDER, STEPHEN. "Introduction," in The Destructive Element. London: Jonathan Cape, pp. 11-21. Reprinted: Boston: Houghton Mifflin Co., 1936; 1938; 1953.
James is an outstanding artist "who developed an inner world of his own through his art" both because of the decadence of European society and the power of his own individuality. Sees James as one of a line (with Yeats, Joyce, Pound, Eliot) who derived much from the Celtic and Continental traditions as well as the Anglo-Saxon heritage, who all create legends or return to a tradition that seemed to be dying, who confront the destructive element, "the experience of an all-pervading Present which is a world without belief." As a group, these writers deal with moral subjects, and their difficulty is primarily a technical one.

23 SPENDER, STEPHEN. "The Ivory Tower and The Sense of the Past," in The Destructive Element. London: Jonathan Cape, pp. 99-110. Reprinted: Boston: Houghton Mifflin Co., 1936; 1938; 1953.
The Ivory Tower, different from the works immediately preceding it in its American setting and completely contemporary subject, demonstrates the completion of "the circle of his life's artistic achievement, and returns to...the 'School of Experience'...." The Sense of the Past, with its obsession about time, is "typical of a whole school of modern literature."

24 SPENDER, STEPHEN. "Life as Art and Art as Life," in The Destructive Element. London: Jonathan Cape, pp. 47-66. Reprinted: Boston: Houghton Mifflin Co., 1936; 1938; 1953.
Examination of the relationship between those novels which provided the "school of his experience" and those which followed his dramatic period. In his later works, James used the method of indirect presentation and realized

1935

that "Art, which is merely a reflexion of life, is either
not Art but <u>rapportage</u>, or else Death Art."

25   SPENDER, STEPHEN. "The School of Experience in the Early
Novels of Henry James," in <u>The Destructive Element</u>. Lon-
don: Jonathan Cape, pp. 23-46. Reprinted: Boston:
Houghton Mifflin Co., 1936; 1938; 1953.
Reprint of 1934.B26.

26   SPENDER, STEPHEN. "The Unconscious," in <u>The Destructive Ele-
ment</u>. London: Jonathan Cape, pp. 67-98. Reprinted:
Boston: Houghton Mifflin Co., 1936; 1938; 1953.
Examination of the characters, plots, structure and
method of <u>The Ambassadors</u>, <u>The Wings of the Dove</u> and <u>The
Golden Bowl</u>, in which "fatal intelligence" is the "enemy
to action." Remarks on <u>The Golden Bowl</u> are reprinted in
1945.A1.

*27 STURGIS, HOWARD OVERING. <u>Belchamber</u>. Introduction by Gerard
Hopkins. New York and London: Oxford University Press.
Cited in 1947.A2, p. 175.

28   WHITALL, JAMES. <u>English Years</u>. New York: Harcourt, Brace
and Co., 22-23, 60-63, 94-95, 142-49.
Describes effort to meet James, "the most important
literary light in Chelsea," culminating in their eventual
encounter at Mrs. Van Rensselaer's, which Whitall describes.

29   ZABEL, MORTON D. "The Poetics of Henry James." <u>Poetry: A
Magazine of Verse</u>, 45 (February), 270-76.
Examination of James' influence on contemporary English
and American poets and his indirect perception of their
problem, based on his comments in the prefaces. Discusses
James' "efforts toward limitation and concretion," his
subtle and refined use of language, and his characters who
embody the "modern sensibility" and ultimately retreat "to
the final authority of selfhood." This parallels the
dilemma of modern poets: "the rescue of personality from
an excess of sophistication, erudition, self-indulgence,
and privilege." Reprinted: 1945.A1.

1936 A BOOKS - NONE

1936 B SHORTER WRITINGS

1   ADAMS, MRS. H. <u>The Letters of Mrs. Henry Adams, 1865-1883</u>.
Edited by Ward Thoron. Boston: Little, Brown and Co.,
passim.

Numerous references to social interactions with James, a personal friend of the Adams. Cites Countess Lewenhaupt as calling James "'the nicest Englishman I ever knew.'"

*2   ANSTEY, F. (THOMAS ANSTEY GUTHRIE). A Long Retrospect. New York and London: Oxford University Press. Excerpted in 1947.A2.
      Retrospective account of James, his meticulously precise conversations, with numerous references to his dramatic period.

3   BEERBOHM, MAX. "The Mote in the Middle Distance," in A Christmas Garland. New York: Oxford University Press, pp. 3-10. Reprinted: London: William Heinemann, 1950.
      An essay modelled on Jamesian style, first published in a 1912 edition of Saturday Review (London). Reprinted: 1945.A1.

4   BRADLEY, A. C. "Henry James as I Knew Him." John O'London's Weekly (18 December), pp. 505-506.
      Recollections of association with James by a neighbor in Rye. Describes the author's social activities, his tea table talk, his view of America; gives examples of his "abounding kindness of heart." Includes several vignettes which reveal the "human side" of the novelist.

5   BRUSSELL, I. R. "Henry James," in Anglo-American First Editions, Part Two, West to East, 1786-1930. London: Constable and Co.; New York: R. R. Bowker Co., pp. 58-90.
      Bibliographic descriptions of first editions of James' works which were initially published in England. Comparative dates of publication noted where relevant. Includes list of books by James published in America prior to the English publication, and notes sources of information concerning dates of publication.

6   CHESTERTON, G. K. "Friendship and Foolery," in The Autobiography of G. K. Chesterton. New York: Sheed and Ward, pp. 222-28.
      Reflections on a summer in Rye, living next to Lamb House. Describes James' speech as "gracefully groping," and James himself as "stately and courteous." Discusses H. G. Wells' reaction to James.

7   FOLLETT, WILSON. "Henry James's Portrait of Henry James." New York Times Book Review (23 August), pp. 2, 16.
      The Sacred Fount, a "stupendous parody," has as its subject James as a writer, who has reduced his philosophy

of fiction to "the graphic simplicity of a diagram." Proposes to extract "the wild, weird fun" of the work, which is discussed in terms of groupings of characters. The detective who works out the pattern "is being Henry James's perfect novelist." This "definitive parable of life and the artist" was omitted from the New York edition because it was not so much a novel as fiction with a purpose.

8 GREENE, GRAHAM. "Henry James: The Private Universe," in The English Novelists. Edited by Derek Verschoyle. London: Chatto and Windus, pp. 215-28.
   An attempt "to track the instinctive, the poetic writer back to the source of his fantasies," to reveal his dominant theme. James shared with his father and siblings a sense that evil was overwhelmingly part of his universe. Suggests a relation between this "private fantasy" and James' family background. Concludes that the justice of his pity ranks him with the greatest creative writers. "He is as solitary in the history of the novel as Shakespeare in the history of poetry." Reprinted: 1951.B27; in Leon Edel, ed. Henry James: A Collection of Critical Essays, pp. 111-22. See also 1950.B41.

9 HARTWICK, HARRY. "Henry James," in A History of American Letters. By Walter Fuller Taylor. New York: American Book Co., pp. 556-59.
   Bibliography includes works by James, texts, biography, and criticism.

10 JOHNSON, MERLE. "Henry James," in Merle Johnson's American First Editions. Bibliographic Checklist of the Works of 199 American Authors. Third edition. Revised by Jacob Blanck. New York: R. R. Bowker Co., pp. 260-64.
   Chronological listing (name of work; date and place of publication) of first editions of James' works with occasional further bibliographic description of the volumes. Checklist present in standardized form. A representative selection of minor productions follows the main body. Magazine appearances omitted. See 1932.B19

11 QUINN, ARTHUR HOBSON. "Henry James and the Fiction of International Relations," in American Fiction: An Historical and Critical Survey. New York: D. Appleton Century Co., pp. 279-304.
   Biographical sketch and survey of James' literary career, beginning with the short stories and including discussion of the major novels. James was more important in

the development of realism than in the impact of his international novels, which lack completeness in their represen-
tations of Americans.

12   SMITH, JANET ADAM. "Henry James and R. L. Stevenson." <u>London</u>
     <u>Mercury</u>, 34 (September), 412-20.
          James and Robert Louis Stevenson are linked not only by
     bonds of personal affection but also by a common interest
     in the craft of fiction and the art of literature, as well
     as by a need for each other as the two most conscious nov-
     elists of their time in England. Offers biographical de-
     tails and points out "themes" of their friendship;
     describes the similarities in mood and outlook, the dif-
     ferences in aim, method, and attitude towards life between
     the two men. <u>See</u> 1948.A3.

13   TAYLOR, WALTER FULLER. "Fiction as Fine Art: Henry James
     (1843-1916)," in <u>A History of American Letters</u>. New York:
     American Book Co., pp. 289-94. Revised edition: <u>The Story</u>
     <u>of American Letters</u>. Chicago: Henry Regnery Co., 1956.
          James' full-length novels follow a development similar
     to that of the novelettes, from fiction of manner to minute
     analysis of complex states of mind with painstaking tech-
     nique. James' belief that life is primarily an art influ-
     enced his choice of subject matter and method, and he had a
     great, though indirect, influence on American fiction.

1937 A BOOKS - NONE

1937 B SHORTER WRITINGS

1   BLANCHE, JACQUES-ÉMILE. "Henry James," in <u>Portraits of a</u>
     <u>Lifetime</u>. Translated and edited by Walter Clement. Lon-
     don: J. M. Dent and Sons, pp. 160-66 and passim.
          Recollections of relationship with his friend James,
     whose portrait Blanche painted. Criticizes Sargent's por-
     trait of James as lacking "psychological insight." De-
     scribes James in conversation, comparing his sentence to
     Proust's, and suggests that "'The Pattern in the Carpet'...
     matches his marvelous conversation and his correspondence."
     Restatement of 1923.B4; 1928.B3.

2   CANTWELL, ROBERT. "A Warning to Pre-war Novelists." <u>New</u>
     <u>Republic</u>, 91 (23 June), 177-80.
          "Owen Wingrave" is "a kind of laboratory specimen for a
     study of the relationship between a writer's observation
     of the normal and everyday life of his environment...and

the looming social conflicts that exert their pressure upon him." An anti-war story that investigates the means of social control, it is written as a ghost story.

3   CANTWELL, ROBERT. "No Landmarks," in Literary Opinion in America. Edited by Morton D. Zabel. New York: Harper and Brothers, pp. 530-41.
        Reprint of 1933.B1.

4   CLEMENS, CYRIL. "Bret Hart and Henry James as seen by Marie Belloc Lowndes." Mark Twain Quarterly, 2 (Fall), 21-23.
        Marie Belloc Lowndes recalls her acquaintance with James, refutes Brooks' theory of expatriation (see 1925.A1), and describes James' conversational manner.

5   COLUM, MRS. MARY MAGUIRE. "The Outside Literatures in English," in From These Roots: The Ideas That Have Made Modern Literature. New York: Charles Scribner's Sons, pp. 301-11.
        Although James theoretically supported the doctrines of realism, his technique was actually a move away from realsim. What James contributed was "his method, his material-- a small, detached, over-privileged, cultivated international group," characters in whom "instincts have been refined away in motive forces of immense psychological complexity."

6   FORD, FORD MADOX [pseud.]. "Henry James: The Master." American Mercury, 36 (November), 315-27.
        See 1937.B7.

7   HUEFFER, FORD MADOX. "Henry James: The Master." American Mercury, 36 (November), 315-27.
        Points out innumerability of James' stories which sprang from "germs." See 1937.B6. Reprinted: 1937.B8.

8   HUEFFER, FORD MADOX. "Henry James: The Master," in Portraits from Life. Boston: Houghton Mifflin Co., pp. 1-20. Reprinted: A Gateway Edition. Chicago: Henry Regnery Co., 1960.
        Reprint of 1937.B7. See 1937.B6.

9   LEAVIS, F. R. "Henry James." Scrutiny, 5 (March), 398-417.
        Blackmur's edition of James' prefaces (see 1934.B3) is "disappointing." James' later indirectness accounts for the unsatisfactoriness of the prefaces. Something went wrong with James' development: he penetrated English manners too thoroughly and lost the full sense of life and his moral taste in expressing his specialized interest. Describes The Portrait of a Lady as his "finest achievement."

1937

*10   MILLAR, C. C. HOYER. George du Maurier and Others. London:
       Cassell and Co. Excerpted in 1947.A2.
            James appeared to have "just come from an ultra-smart
       wedding ceremony" (quotation from 1947.A2). Recounts sev-
       eral anecdotes involving James.

11   MOORE, MARIANNE. "Henry James as a Characteristic American,"
       in Literary Opinion in America. Edited by Morton D. Zabel.
       New York: Harper and Brothers, pp. 225-33. Reprinted:
       1951; Harper Torchbook. Vol. 2. New York: Harper and
       Row, 1962, pp. 395-401.
            Reprint of 1934.B21.

12   MULLER, HERBERT. Modern Fiction: A Study in Values. New
       York: Funk and Wagnalls Co., passim.
            James was a writer who "brewed genteel little tempests
       in exquisite teapots" and wrote "ultra-refined and dis-
       tilled novels."

13   RAHV, PHILIP. "The Cult of Experience in American Writing,"
       in Literary Opinion in America. Edited by Morton D. Zabel.
       New York: Harper and Brothers. Reprinted: 1951; Harper
       Torchbooks. Vol. 2. New York: Harper and Row, 1962,
       pp. 550-60.
            With reference to Strether's injunction to "'Live'" in
       The Ambassadors, examines "the long-standing American habit
       of playing hide and seek with experience...." James es-
       poused "the rights of the private man, ...the rights of per-
       sonality, whose openness to experience provides the sole
       effective guaranty of its development." Views Strether's
       appeal "as the compositional key to the whole modern move-
       ment in American writing," the search for experience being
       the unifying motif of literary productions. Reprinted:
       1940.B9. See also 1959.B74.

14   ROUTH, HAROLD VICTOR. "George Romanes," in Towards the Twen-
       tieth Century: Essays in the Spiritual History of the
       Nineteenth. New York: The Macmillan Co., pp. 335-36,
       339.
            In discussion of the "Edwardian spirit," asserts that
       James' "complex and labyrinthine novels attract those
       interested in the manners of the vanished, if not imaginary
       class, or in the arts of transforming experience into moral
       speculation." In James, "the interest generally ends with
       technics of the intellect."

1937

15   WALDOCK, A. J. A.   "Henry James," in James Joyce, and Others.
     London: Williams and Norgate, pp. 1-29. Reprinted:
     Freeport, N.Y.: Books for Libraries Press, 1967.
          James technically reached his goal in the last three
     completed novels. Briefly reviews his career as a novel-
     ist, concentrating on the middle period as containing
     James' most popular works and suggesting reasons for their
     popularity. The main principle of the later method was
     the use of consciousness as a medium for exposition.

16   WINTERS, YVOR.   "Henry James and the Relation of Morals to
     Manners." American Review, 9 (October), 482-503.
          James believed there is a moral sense, conceived of as
     "essentially American," which can be cultivated by associa-
     tion with Europe but weakened or destroyed by excess of
     such association, and he portrayed the contact of the Amer-
     ican moral character, divorced from any body of American
     manners, with European manners. For James, plot was viewed
     almost entirely in terms of ethical choice and consequen-
     ces. Reprinted: 1938.B17; 1947.B50.

1938 A BOOKS - NONE

1938 B SHORTER WRITINGS

1   ADAMS, HENRY. Letters of Henry Adams (1892-1918). Edited by
     Worthington Chauncy Ford. 2 vols. Boston: Houghton
     Mifflin Co., passim.
          James pretended "to belong to a world which is extinct
     as Queen Elizabeth." Includes several letters to James
     and brief judgments of a few of his works.

2   ANTHONY, KATHERINE. "An American Author," in Louisa May Al-
     cott. New York: Alfred A. Knopf, pp. 174-79.
          "Except for the difference made by more extensive travel
     and schooling, young Henry James was a family product on
     the order of Louisa." Discusses James' review of Alcott's
     Moods, and concludes that "the mutual influence was per-
     haps stronger than anyone realized."

3   BAKER, ERNEST A. "Henry James," in The History of the English
     Novel. Vol. 9. London: H. F. and G. Witherby, pp. 243-87.
          James' influence has been primarily in the realm of
     method. Comments on the early novels and tales and on
     James' later development, technical innovations, and view
     of art. Illustrates James' techniques in The Spoils of
     Poynton, and examines What Maisie Knew, The Awkward Age,
     The Wings of the Dove, The Ambassadors and The Golden Bowl.

1938

4   BARRIE, JAMES M. The Greenwood Hat: Being a Memoir of James
    Anon (1885-1887). Privately printed, 1930. New York:
    Charles Scribner's Sons, pp. 240-42.
        Reminiscence of James at the Reform Club, where the two
    conversed during haircuts, although each would have pre-
    ferred privacy.

5   BOGAN, LOUISE. "James on a Revolutionary Theme." Nation,
    146 (23 April), 471-74.
        The criticism of The Princess Casamassima is colored by
    the critics' biases and fails to perceive James' design.
    Examines the character of the princess and Hyacinth, and
    concludes that Hyacinth, detached to the end, chooses the
    only solution for the artist, death. Reprinted: 1955.B14.

6   FORBES, ELIZABETH LIVERMORE. "Dramatic Lustrum: A Study on
    the Effect of Henry James's Theatrical Experience on His
    Later Novels." New England Quarterly, 11 (March), 108-20.
        The period from 1889-1896 was one "of great value" for
    James. Traces his dramatic career, and suggests that "The
    development of his work after the dramatic years shows how
    he exploited the possibilities of each [drama and novel] to
    the enhancement of the other.

7   HAYCRAFT, HOWARD. "Henry James, Jr.," in American Authors.
    Edited by Stanley J. Kunitz. New York: H. W. Wilson Co.,
    pp. 410-13.
        A biographical survey, in which James' mental and phy-
    sical health problems in 1905 are seen as a result of his
    regrets over expatriation, career choice, bachelorhood,
    and in which his goal is described as "achieving an accu-
    mulation of psychological forces, a progression d'effet."
    Includes chronological list of principal works and brief
    bibliography of critical studies.

8   HOARE, DOROTHY MACKENZIE. "Henry James," in Some Studies in
    the Modern Novel. London: Chatto and Windus, pp. 3-25.
        James' primary interest became "the triumph of individ-
    ual integrity through intelligent renunciation." Compares
    passages in Roderick Hudson and The Wings of the Dove to
    demonstrate the looser writing and "strong romantic sen-
    sibility" of the early works and his later striving for
    more precise definition.

9   JORDAN, ELIZABETH. "Mr. James and the London Season," in
    Three Rousing Cheers. New York: D. Appleton-Century Co.,
    pp. 195-221.
        Recalls first meeting with James at a dinner party in
    London and subsequent encounters "at the height of the

1938

London season" and later in America. Describes James'
demeanor, character, and conversation.

10   JORDAN, ELIZABETH. "'The Whole Family,'" in Three Rousing
      Cheers. New York: D. Appleton-Century Co., pp. 250-80.
         Account of the composition of the composite novel, The
      Whole Family, including the text of several letters from
      James, one of the contributors, to Jordan, the editor.
      The project turned into an "epoch-making row" and "was a
      mess."

11   LEAVIS, QUEENIE D. "Henry James's Heiress: The Importance
      of Edith Wharton." Scrutiny, 7 (December), 261-76.
         Edith Wharton's association with James and admiration
      for his work "provided her with a spring-board from which
      to take off as an artist."

12   NEFF, JOHN C. "Henry James the Reporter." New Mexico Quar-
      terly, 8 (February), 9-14.
         James, besides being a creative genius, "was a reporter"
      in the vein of a contemporary novelist who draws from
      actual experiences. Enumerates ways in which James used
      real life, actual persons in his works.

13   READ, HERBERT. "Particular Studies: Henry James," in Col-
      lected Essays in Literary Criticism. London: Faber and
      Faber, pp. 354-68.
         Reprint of 1927.B8 which omits the final paragraph of
      original version. See 1956.B58.

14   TWEEDY, KATHERINE. "Jane Austen's Novel and the Novel of
      Henry James." Vassar Journal of Undergraduate Studies, 11
      (May), 74-82.
         Compares James, "the most literary of writers," to Jane
      Austen, "the most unliterary." Points out differences in
      structure, style, and characters, and similarities in their
      intense concentration on what they knew, their delineation
      of relationships, their portrayal of the behaviors of peo-
      ple in contemporary society.

15   WILSON, EDMUND. "The Last Phase of Henry James." Partisan
      Review, 4 (February), 3-8.
         Despite critical theory to the contrary, "it is the
      American who finally dominates in Henry James," although
      his picture of Americans is mixed. James' return to his
      native land in 1904 revealed a crude, corrupt, phony
      "nightmare of the American rich," represented in "The
      Jolly Corner" and The Ivory Tower.

16   WILSON, EDMUND. "The Ambiguity of Henry James," in <u>The Triple</u>
      <u>Thinkers: Ten Essays on Literature</u>. New York: Harcourt,
      Brace and Co., pp. 122-64.
          Reprint of 1934.B37.

17   WINTERS, YVOR. "Maule's Well; or Henry James and the Relation
      of Morals to Manners," in <u>Maule's Curse: Seven Studies in</u>
      <u>the History of American Obscurantism</u>. Norfolk, Conn.:
      Swallow Press, pp. 169-216. Reprinted: 1947.
          Reprint of 1937.B16.

1939 A BOOKS

*1   DIFFENÉ, PATRICIA. <u>Henry James: Versuch einer Würdigung</u>
      <u>seiner Eigenart</u>. Bochum-Langendreer: Pöppinghaus.
      (German)
          Originally a dissertation (University of Marburg, 1939).
      According to Rev. W. Fischer, <u>Anglia Beiblatt</u>, 52 (1939-
      40), 121, a stylistic analysis of James' work, in particu-
      lar his theoretical writings, in an attempt to demonstrate
      that James is neither limited in subject matter nor diffi-
      cult to read.

1939 B SHORTER WRITINGS

1   B., H. S. "Henry James: American Criticism." <u>Notes and</u>
      <u>Queries</u>, 176 (7 January), 8.
          Requests information on the present opinion of James
      "among American men of letters." <u>See</u> 1939.B2.

2   CATALANI, G. "Henry James: American Criticism." <u>Notes and</u>
      <u>Queries</u>, 176 (18 March), 194-95.
          Americans have never forgiven James his "so-called 'ex-
      patriation,'" and "he never can become a popular author in
      the United States," despite wide admiration for his artis-
      tic devotion and ideals. <u>See</u> 1939.B1.

3   EDEL, LEON. "Henry James Discoveries." <u>Times Literary Sup-</u>
      <u>plement</u> (29 July), p. 460.
          Gives background concerning and reprints a letter from
      James dealing with a discussion of one of his novels at
      the summer school of Deerfield, which reiterates views ex-
      pounded in "The Art of Fiction." Also identifies an un-
      signed article on the London theatres in <u>Scribner's Maga-</u>
      <u>zine</u>, 1881, as James', which indicates "there was no break
      in the novelist's prolific periodical output over almost
      half a century."

1939

4   KNIGHTS, L. C. "Henry James and the Trapped Spectator."
    Southern Review, 4 (Winter), 600-15.
        Examination of the ways in which James apprehended the
    isolation of the individual, and, in his later novels,
    presented the character who is "merely a watcher, unable
    to participate freely and fully in human experience."
    Analyzes In the Cage and "The Beast in the Jungle" as ex-
    amples of his thesis. Reprinted: in Explorations: Essays
    in Criticism. New York: G. W. Stewart, 1946, pp. 155-69.

5   MARSH, EDWARD. "Henry James," in A Number of People: A Book
    of Reminiscences. New York and London: Harper and Broth-
    ers, pp. 114-21.
        Account of occasional meetings with James, who "though
    the kindliest of men...never hid the workings of his crit-
    ical sense." Reprints letter from James written the day
    after Rupert Brooke's death.

6   MAUGHAM, SOMERSET. "Introduction," in Teller of Tales: 100
    Short Stories from the United States, England, France,
    Russia and Germany. New York: Doubleday, Doran and Co.,
    pp. xxxiv-xxxvii.
        Personal recollections of James, the "most distinguished
    literary figure that America has produced." He was not
    successful at being a very great writer because "his expe-
    rience was inadequate and his sympathies were imperfect."
    See 1952.B46.

7   MAXSE, MARY. "Henry James: A Master of His Art." National
    Review (London), 113 (December), 773-78.
        James' tales arose from his subconscious, and his major
    preoccupation appeared to be "the reaction of human charac-
    ter to the storm and stress of life," although James him-
    self was "almost a hermit." The Portrait of a Lady and
    What Maisie Knew illustrate his ability to construct char-
    acters.

8   PHELPS, WILLIAM LYON. "Henry James," in Autobiography with
    Letters. London and New York: Oxford University Press,
    pp. 550-57.
        Impressions of and anecdotes about James, whose con-
    versational and written style he describes as "verbose
    reticence."

9   SMITH, BERNARD. "The Quest of Beauty," in Forces in American
    Criticism: A Study in the History of American Literary
    Thought. New York: Harcourt, Brace and Co., pp. 185-228.

James and Poe represented the aesthetic tradition in criticism, with their interest in craft rather than ideology, their preoccupation with form. James' was "a theory of art for the sake of consciousness, and consciousness for its own sake...."

10 SMITH, LOGAN PEARSALL. "The Expatriates," in Unforgotten Years. Boston: Little, Brown and Co., pp. 263-96.
Expatriates like Whistler, Mary Cassatt, Edith Wharton, and James are "more likely to be remembered than those who stayed at home." Other passing references to James and his portrayal of American women in Europe.

11 SMITH, LOGAN PEARSALL. "Paris," in Unforgotten Years. Boston: Little, Brown and Co., pp. 218-20.
Account of conversation with James concerning Smith's volume of short stories about Oxford, and James' comment on the "'Loneliness'" of the artist.

1940 A BOOKS - NONE

1940 B SHORTER WRITINGS

*1 ASTELDI, MARIA L. Studi di letteratura inglese. Cited in 1956.B70, p. 406.

2 BAIN, JAMES S. A Bookseller Looks Back: The Story of the Bains. London: Macmillan and Co., passim.
James Bain in his notebook mentions James' return from Boston "'to London, from which, thank Heaven, my absence is only temporary.'" Remarks on James as a collector of French literature, notes his intricate "analytical" style, recounts an anecdote about James receiving the Order of Merit.

3 BENSON, EDWARD FREDERIC. Final Edition. London and New York: D. Appleton-Century Co., pp. 6-13 and passim.
Recalls visit at Rye with James, an old family friend, and describes the author's method of composition and the "incomparable richness" of his speech. "Friends and literature were his passions...."

4 BROOKS, VAN WYCK. "Henry James of Boston." Saturday Review of Literature, 22 (13 July), 3-4, 16-17.
Examination of James' theme dealing with New World characters looking for the romance of Europe, thirsting for culture, who generally came to grief. "And this

1940

innocence was American innocence at the mercy of the dark
old world that so charmed it, deceived it, destroyed it,
and cast it away." James' picture of Americans was ex-
tremely limited.

5   BROOKS, VAN WYCK. "Henry James in England." Story, 17
     (September-October), 2-8, 96-97.
         A consideration of the effect of expatriation on James'
     art. His failure to "root himself in England" explains
     events of the middle years, his vague anxieties, the nature
     of the later work, and his abandonment of the novel to
     write drama. His concern with form and technique rather
     than content and characters caused him to become "a huge
     arachnid, pouncing on the tiny air blown particle and
     wrapping it round and round." Reprinted: 1940.B6.

6   BROOKS, VAN WYCK. "Henry James in England," in New England:
     Indian Summer, 1865-1915. New York: E. P. Dutton and Co.,
     pp. 395-408.
         Reprint of 1940.B5.

7   BROOKS, VAN WYCK. "Howells and James," in New England: In-
     dian Summer, 1865-1915. New York: E. P. Dutton and Co.,
     pp. 224-49.
         James and Howells "had almost everything in common"
     and formed a triumverate with Thomas Sergeant Perry.
     Traces growth of realistic method in American precursors
     of Howells and James, and discusses their qualified ad-
     herence to realism in later writings.

8   CHAPMAN, R. W. "False Scent." Times Literary Supplement
     (19 October), p. 531.
         Gives an example of a "form of ambiguity" in a sentence
     of James which he labels "false scent." See 1940.B11, B16.

9   RAHV, PHILIP. "The Cult of Experience in American Writing."
     Partisan Review, 7 (November-December), 412-24.
         Reprint of 1937.B13.

10   REID, FORREST. Private Road. London: Faber and Faber,
     pp. 65-73.
         Records James' reaction, that of "repressed exaspera-
     tion," to Reid's The Garden God, dedicated to James, and
     Reid's "sympathy with the moral and spiritual qualities
     that were the standards by which all his [James'] charac-
     ters were judged."

1941

11   RITCHIE, G. S. "False Scent." <u>Times Literary Supplement</u>
      (26 October), p. 543.
            Identifies term "false scent" as coming from <u>The King's</u>
      <u>English</u> (1906). <u>See</u> 1940.B8.

12   SMYTH, ETHEL. <u>Impressions that Remained</u>. 2 vols. London:
      Longmans, Green and Co. Reprinted: New York: Alfred A.
      Knopf, 1946, pp. 67, 506.
            Mentions the works of James in reference to the exas-
      peration of cracking "your brain about something you know
      is really quite simple." Also reprints an 1891 letter
      noting "Henry James's lamentations over the British
      brain...in the Dresden Gallery...."

13   SMYTH, ETHEL. <u>What Happened Next</u>. London: Longmans, Green
      and Co., pp. 205, 301.
            Mentions attendance of James, a "cherished" friend, at
      performance of chamber music, and recalls a remark he made
      "about the profound curtsey I launched, when 'called,' at
      the Royal Box!"

14   WALPOLE, HUGH. "Henry James, A Reminiscence." <u>Horizon</u>, 1
      (February), 74-80.
            A friend contradicts the modern critical portrait of
      James as "the stuttering word-spinning priest of Nothing-
      ness."

15   WOOLF, VIRGINIA. <u>Roger Fry: A Biography</u>. New York: Har-
      court, Brace and Co., pp. 273-74.
            Records Fry's impressions of <u>Confidence</u> and description
      of James as "a man who has a standard. He never wanders
      from the idea...."

16   YOUNG, G. M. "False Scent." <u>Times Literary Supplement</u>
      (26 October), p. 543.
            Gives classic example of "false scent" from <u>I Samuel</u>.
      <u>See</u> 1940.B8.

1941 A BOOKS - NONE

1941 B SHORTER WRITINGS

  1   AUDEN, WYSTAN HUGH. "At the Grave of Henry James." <u>Horizon</u>,
      3 (June), 379-83.
            A poetic tribute praising James as a disciplined artist,
      "poet of the difficult," "master of nuance and scruple,"
      and "a great and talkative man." Reprinted: 1941.B2;
      1945.A1.

1941

2   AUDEN, WYSTAN HUGH. "At the Grave of Henry James." <u>Partisan</u>
    <u>Review</u>, 7 (July-August), 266-70.
        Reprint of 1941.B1.

3   BURKE, KENNETH. <u>The Philosophy of Literary Form: Studies in</u>
    <u>Symbolic Action</u>. Baton Rouge: Louisiana State University
    Press, passim.
        Refers to James in illustrating his critical principles.

4   EDEL, LEON. "Henry James: The War Chapter, 1914-1916."
    <u>University of Toronto Quarterly</u>, 10 (January), 125-38.
        Description of James' activities and emotional reactions
    during the war years. Suggests that James' decision to
    become a British citizen has been disproportionately mag-
    nified, and calls "Within the Rim" and "The Question of the
    Mind" "the most autobiographical of the war essays."

5   FAGIN, N. B. "Another Reading of <u>The Turn of the Screw</u>."
    <u>Modern Language Notes</u>, 56 (March), 196-202.
        Points out the influence of Hawthorne on James' develop-
    ment as an artist, and hypothesizes that <u>The Turn of the</u>
    <u>Screw</u> is a simple allegory of the type that intrigued
    Hawthorne, one which dramatizes "the conflict between Good
    and Evil. The apparitions are personifications of evil....
    The governess...is a sort of Guardian Angel...." Reprint-
    ed: in Gerald Willen, ed. <u>A Casebook on "The Turn of the</u>
    Screw</u>," pp. 154-59.

6   HART, JAMES D. <u>The Oxford Companion to American Literature,</u>
    <u>1941-1965</u>. London: Oxford University Press, pp. 363-65.
        Biographical sketch with reference to James' works,
    concluding that "his influence in the history of the novel,
    in which he was a pioneer of psychological realism and
    formal architectonics, and the master of a rich, highly
    complex prose style and an extremely sensitive apprecia-
    tion of values of character," is unquestionable.

7   KEES, WELDON. "Henry James at Newport." <u>Poetry</u>, 59 (Octo-
    ber), 16-17.
        A poem which characterizes "The mild cosmopolites" who
    "nursed nostalgia on the sun-warmed rocks,/ Exquisite,
    sterile, easily distressed,/ Thought much of Paris, died/
    While he lived out their deaths."

8   LERNER, DANIEL. "The Influence of Turgenev on Henry James."
    <u>Slavonic and East European Review</u>, 20 (American series, I),
    28-54.

1941

The relationship between Turgenev and James is traced
from the latter's earliest contact with Turgenev's work
during his year in Paris (1875-1876); their "basic agree-
ment in aesthetic and theory of the novel" is discussed;
and several works (selected short stories and Roderick
Hudson, The American, The Portrait of a Lady, and The
Princess Casamassima) are examined to show the influence
of Turgenev on James' developing art.

9   MATTHIESSEN, F. O. "From Hawthorne to James to Eliot," in
     American Renaissance: Art and Expression in the Age of
     Emerson and Whitman. New York: Oxford University Press,
     pp. 351-68.
        James' moral sense "drew little direct nourishment from
     any widely accepted ethical system," and his characters
     are generally isolated from the "social violence and
     chaos" of the real world and from "dependence upon a world
     overhead."

10   MATTHIESSEN, F. O. "Hawthorne and James," in American Ren-
     aissance: Art and Expression in the Age of Emerson and
     Whitman. New York: Oxford University Press, pp. 292-305.
        Examination of fundamental connections between Hawthorne
     and James in order to clarify Hawthorne's contribution to
     James' writing, including their mutual moral interest,
     common character types, "links in the hidden chain that
     bound them together." Considers "how very closely some of
     James' first experiments follow Hawthorne's model," e.g.
     "The Romance of Certain Old Clothes," "The Last of the
     Valerii," Roderick Hudson and The Europeans.

11   MONROE, ELIZABETH N. The Novel and Society: A Critical
     Study of the Modern Novel. Chapel Hill: University of
     North Carolina Press, pp. 120-30 and passim.
        In Edith Wharton's work, in contrast to that of James,
     "the moral sense does not depend on contact with an old
     civilization for its highest development, and unlimited
     freedom is not presupposed for the characters in whom it
     is being observed."

12   NARKEVICH, A. IU. "Genri Dzhems (25 let so dnia smerti).
     [Henry James (25th anniversary of his death).] Litera-
     turnoe obozrenie, no. 4, p. 79. (Russian)
        Provides bibliographical information, listing studies
     of James translated into Russian and studies of James in
     Russian periodicals.

1941

13 PACEY, W. C. D. "Henry James and His French Contemporaries."
    <u>American Literature</u>, 13 (November), 240-56.
    From James' reviews and articles on French writers, it
    is apparent that "it was their renderings of sense-impres-
    sions and their technical dexterity which attracted him,
    and their lack of moral and intellectual insight...which
    repelled him." His greatest divergence from the French
    school is characterized as the "relative emphasis upon
    external and the internal in human behavior." Includes
    discussion of French influence on James' work.

14 RANDALL, D. A. and J. T. WINTERICH. "James, Henry: 'The
    Portrait of a Lady.'" <u>Publisher's Weekly</u>, 140 (19 July),
    186-87.
    Bibliographical data (compiled by Randall) concerning
    various editions of <u>The Portrait of a Lady</u>, and informa-
    tion (by Winterich) about the writing of the novel, in-
    cluding responses of Robert Louis Stevenson and A. C.
    Benson.

15 RICHARDSON, LYON. "Introduction," in <u>Henry James: Represen-
    tative Selections, with Introduction, Bibliography, and
    Notes</u>. American Writers Series. New York: American Book
    Co., pp. ix-xc. Reprinted: Urbana: University of Illi-
    nois Press, 1966.
    Reviews and responds to past criticisms of James, and
    provides a biocritical summary. In "The Matrix," assesses
    the influence of James' family and educational background,
    and describes his reviews and essays of the early years as
    "original, carefully studied contributions to the field of
    literary comment." "The Craftsman" includes discussion of
    major novels, many short stories, and their critical re-
    ception; and illustration of the "germ" or conception
    which James developed into a finished work. "Choice of
    Narrator" suggests that James sought increasingly to hide
    himself from the reader. James' "Style" is described as
    personal and subjective. In "Presiding Patterns of
    Thought," major themes in James' works are considered,
    such as his internationalism, the portrayal of women in
    his fiction, and certain social and political concepts.
    Concludes that James was "responsive to the conviction
    that good taste, goodness, beauty and truth are one, that
    all life has relationship in a common unity, that the fate
    of worldly affairs as well as of art rests in the hands of
    the exceptionally gifted, and that responsible institu-
    tions of age and dignity serve noble purposes." A "Bib-
    liography" (xci-cxi) and "Chronological Table and Selected
    Bibliography of Works of Henry James" (cxii-cxxii) are

included. Reviewed: Joseph Warren Beach, American Literature, 14 (March 1942), 91-94; Conrad Wright, Jr., New England Quarterly, 15 (September 1942), 572; New York Times
Book Review (11 January 1942), p. 18.

16 WOLFF, R. L. "The Genesis of The Turn of the Screw." American Literature, 13 (March), 1-8.
Identifies the "distinguished host" about whom James
speaks in his Preface to The Turn of the Screw as Edward
White Benson, Archbishop of Canterbury, and suggests that
a possible source for the tale is a picture by T. Grif-
fith, "The Haunted House," which appeared in a special
Christmas issue of Black and White in 1891, in which
James' "Sir Edmund Orme" was also published.

1942 A BOOKS

1 NOEL, FRANCE. Henry James, peintre de la femme. Alençon:
Poulet-Malassis, 259 pp. (French)
Originally a dissertation (University of Paris, 1942).
James is a painter of women in that he knows how to repro-
duce the complexities of the feminine soul and the plural-
ity of their personalities. During his apprenticeship,
James' presentation of women was exaggerated; however, he
moved toward a conception of the woman's role in the novel,
and his female characters undergo moral evolution. Examines James' changing portraits of heroines, with examples
from his works. Concludes that "the evolution of his
feminine personalities has been a progress in the truth,
towards beauty and life, but also towards complexity."
Appends a list of female characters in James' works.

1942 B SHORTER WRITINGS

1 BLACKMUR, RICHARD P. "The Sacred Fount." Kenyon Review, 4
(Autumn), 328-52.
Analysis of The Sacred Fount, James' most difficult
work in terms of obscure style and subtlety, in an attempt
to demonstrate that the difficulty "is due not to the conception and execution of the artist but to the readers'
powers of attenion [sic]." James' version of the ghost
story in this novel is a development of "the fable and
mystery into a new and rational imaginative form capable
of general use," and the work stands as "the last lucid
nightmare of James's hallucinated struggle with his conscience as a novelist."

1942

2   DURHAM, F. H. "Henry James' Dramatizations of His Novels."
      Bulletin of the Citadel, 6 (November), 51-64.
        James was unsuccessful as a playwright, but his experi-
      ence with drama increased his sense of form and his ability
      to characterize in subsequent novels. Compares novelette
      and play of Daisy Miller to illustrate why the latter
      failed, and concludes that James "was revolted by the in-
      formality...of practical play production," and "was more
      interested in form and technique, in the objective and
      minute analysis of the nuances of personality."

3   FRIERSON, WILLIAM COLEMAN. "Henry James's Version of the
      Experimental Novel," in The English Novel in Transition,
      1885-1940. Norman: University of Oklahoma Press,
      pp. 107-15.
        Defines the "experimental novel" as referring to the
      principle of logical deduction and "follow through" that
      Zola and the naturalists required, and suggests that the
      major portion of James' fiction meets the criteria. James
      introduced into English "the beauties of psychological
      reason,...the beauties of not overdogmatic logic," and
      showed the potential of a logical art-form in the novel.

4   GEROULD, GORDON HALL. "Explorers of the Inner Life," in
      Patterns of English and American Fiction: A History.
      Boston: Little, Brown and Co., pp. 438-61. Reprinted:
      New York: Russell and Russell, 1966.
        James was an "innovator as an explorer of the inner
      consciousness of his characters," and his expatriation was
      advantageous to his art. He discovered fresh themes and
      techniques for fiction, which he viewed as an aesthetic
      entity.

5   NEWBOLT, HENRY. The Later Life and Letters of Sir Henry New-
      bolt. Edited by Margaret Newbolt. London: Faber and
      Faber, passim.
        Professes intrigue of the "attractiveness of Henry in
      life and to some extent on paper, combined so incredibly
      with a lack of all possible artistic gifts," and describes
      a dinner party at which he met James and James at the
      Browning Centenary Lectures.

6   NUHN, FERNER. "The Enchanted Kingdom of Henry James," in The
      Wind Blew from the East: A Study in the Orientation of
      American Culture. New York: Harper and Brothers, pp. 87-
      163.
        Seeks the cause of James' "lifelong passion for other-
      ness," and suggests that the element in his life which

ruled the rest like an enchantment was the element of place. "James had connected culture with place--another place--and it was for that reason that he disconnected spirit with form," America with Europe. Traces this divorce in the international novels, emphasizing The Princess Casamassima and The Golden Bowl.

7 PERRY, RALPH BARTON. "The James Collection." Harvard University Library Notes, 4 (March), 74-79.
Account of the relations between the James family and Harvard University, and a description of the collection, which covers a century, donated to the Harvard Library by Henry James II.

8 WOOLF, VIRGINIA. "Henry James," in The Death of the Moth and Other Essays. New York: Harcourt, Brace and Co., pp. 129-55.
Reprints 1919.B17, 1920.B32. "The Old Order" is an appreciative review of The Middle Years.

1943 A BOOKS - NONE

1943 B SHORTER WRITINGS

1 ADAMS, J. R. "'At Isella': Some Horrible Printing Corrected." Mark Twain Quarterly, 5 (Spring), 10, 23.
The text of "At Isella," published in The Galaxy in August 1871, was disfigured by errors. Provides corrections, thereby giving the first accurate text of the story.

2 ADAMS, J. R. "Henry James: Citizen of Two Countries: An Anglo-American Vision." Times Literary Supplement (17 April), pp. 188, 190.
James' autobiographical works offer an intense personal analysis and description of artistic evolution, a "portrait of an imagination in development." Illustrates difference between early and late James by comparing essay on George Sand in French Poets and Novelists and one written to Mrs. Wharton in 1912. Concludes that James possessed a "hard core" of Americanism, despite many accretions, which never faded, and that it, like his style, was unique.

3 ADENEY, MARCUS. "For H. J." Horizon, 8 (November), [296].
A sonnet in memory of James: "We boiled our water, dressed our fears in white,/ Then waited for your words to sound the hours." "...in the otherness of your intent/ The lost years say what they have always meant."

1943

4   ANON. "The Death of Henry James." <u>Times Literary Supplement</u>
     (17 April), p. 187.
         Lurking behind James' "faith that civilization was
     built on rock," his beloved ideal, was an ancient evil,
     a beast which, when it attacked, left nothing for James
     but to die.

5   ANON. "A Henry James Centenary Exhibition." <u>Colby Library</u>
     <u>Quarterly</u>, 1 (June), 34-44.
         Describes the Colby library exhibition of James' books
     in honor of the centenary of his birth, with brief accounts
     of the circumstances surrounding composition of several
     previously unpublished letters, reprinted here.

6   ANON. "Memorabilia." <u>Notes and Queries</u>, 184 (5 June), 327-28.
         Includes James' comments on Rosetti, and suggests that
     "what went in at one end as Rossetti might come out at the
     other as 'Roderick Hudson.'"

7   ANON. "Memorabilia." <u>Notes and Queries</u>, 185 (3 July), 1-2.
         Quotes from James' essay on Arnold in <u>English Illus-</u>
     <u>trated Magazine</u>, January 1884, previously unprinted, which
     "is easily among the best things written on Arnold." <u>See</u>
     1943.B34.

8   BARZUN, JACQUES. "James the Melodramatist." <u>Kenyon Review</u>,
     5 (Autumn), 508-21.
         Despite his elaborate and refined presentation, James
     displays characteristics of a melodramatist in his moral
     view of individuals turning out either good or evil and in
     his addiction to violent plots. He was obsessed with the
     "wickedness of being cold, of deliberately sacrificing
     others to one's lust, of taking advantage of another
     through legal or social or emotional privilege." Labels
     his an "aesthetic melodrama." Notes his allegiance to
     Balzac, who used melodrama for the purposes "of nerving
     men to face life and of keeping the reader going." Re-
     printed: 1945.A1; 1956.B8.

9   BEMENT, DOUGLAS and ROSS M. TAYLOR. "Henry James: Miss
     Wenham," in <u>The Fabric of Fiction</u>. New York: Harcourt,
     Brace and World, p. 264.
         Excerpt from "Flickerbridge" in <u>The Better Sort</u>, fol-
     lowed by "three points of analysis" concerning James' de-
     lineation of Miss Wenham and effects of the figures of
     speech.

100

1943

10   BLACKMUR, RICHARD P. "In the Country of the Blue." <u>Kenyon</u>
      <u>Review</u>, 5 (Autumn), 595-617.
          An examination of James' presentation of the theme of
      the artist, who is "incompletely a man, though in his art
      he may envisage man completely." Suggests that the tales
      of the artist occupy an intermediate position in James'
      career, looking "back to the conditions of life in general
      and forward to the prophecy of life beyond and under, or
      at any rate in spite of, the mutilating conditions."
      James chose to represent the artist because he embodies
      the central struggle of man as an individual in conflict
      with society. Analyzes "The Figure in the Carpet," "The
      Private Life," "The Death of the Lion," "The Next Time,"
      and "The Lesson of the Master," the best and clearest
      fable of literary life. Reprinted: 1945.A1.

11   BYNNER, WITTER. "On Henry James' Centennial: Lasting Impres-
      sions of a Great American Writer." <u>Saturday Review of</u>
      <u>Literature</u>, 26 (22 May), 23, 26, 28.
          Records the first paragraph which James spoke to him on
      their meeting in New York, 1904, reminisces about James'
      manner of speaking, and reprints "an interview," which
      appeared in <u>The Critic</u> as "A Word or Two with Henry James"
      (February 1905).

12   CANBY, HENRY SEIDEL. <u>Walt Whitman, An American: A Study in</u>
      <u>Biography</u>. Boston: Houghton Mifflin Co., p. 281.
          Calls James' review of "Drum-Taps" in 1865 a "searching,
      caustic, somewhat condescending" piece, "in which every-
      thing is reasonably true except James' account of Walt
      Whitman's emotions...."

13   CLEMENS, CYRIL. "Henry James, 1843-1916." <u>Mark Twain Quar-</u>
      <u>terly</u>, 5 (Spring), 1.
          Brief biographical sketch of James, with mention of his
      mastery of the technique of fiction and his emphasis on
      the contrast between leisure class English and American
      individuals.

14   CLEMENS, CYRIL. "A Visit to Henry James' Old Home." <u>Mark</u>
      <u>Twain Quarterly</u>, 5 (Spring), 9.
          Recalls a visit to James' home to call on E. F. Benson
      and his conversation with Benson about James.

15   COOPER, HAROLD. "Trollope and Henry James in 1868." <u>Modern</u>
      <u>Language Notes</u>, 58 (November), 558.
          Trollope published two anonymous novels in 1867 and
      1868, which James identified in a review in <u>Nation</u> as being

1943

by the "'author of "Barchester Towers"'" and demonstrating
that Trollope had "'exhausted his vein.'"

16   DAICHES, DAVID. "Sensibility and Technique: Preface to a
      Critique." Kenyon Review, 5 (Autumn), 569-79.
      The distinction between the moderns and earlier novel-
      ists is that the former portray a type of experience fil-
      tered through an individual sensibility, while the latter
      attempt to provide a refined "literary exemplum of a public
      truth." James "is in the tradition of the modern novel of
      sensibility and...his technique is dependent on his sen-
      sibility." His stories would change in meaning if told in
      any other way. Defines term "sensibility" from a study of
      James' practice of the art of fiction, and compares Rod-
      erick Hudson and The Portrait of a Lady to show the devel-
      opment of James' method as a novelist of moral sensibility,
      based on a sense of "aesthetic significance."

17   de la ROCHE, MAZO. "Reading Henry James Aloud." Mark Twain
      Quarterly, 5 (Spring), 8.
      James "always seems to know where he stands in every
      question of life." He was too balanced for hopelessness,
      even in contemporary society.

18   EDEL, LEON. "Henry James and the Poets." Poetry, 62 (Sep-
      tember), 328-34.
      On the occasion of three recent poems in which James is
      a subject, suggests that "It is in his passionate and de-
      voted search for the artistic forms capable of containing
      and expressing the complexities of life and thought, in
      the intensity of his embrace of the artist life, that Henry
      James fascinates and will continue to fascinate poets...."

19   ELIOT, T. S. "Henry James," in The Shock of Recognition: The
      Development of Literature in the United States. Edited by
      Edmund Wilson. New York: Doubleday, Doran and Co.,
      pp. 854-65.
      Reprint of "In Memory" and "The Hawthorne Aspect,"
      1918.B4.

20   FERGUSSON, FRANCIS. "James's Idea of Dramatic Form." Kenyon
      Review, 5 (Autumn), 495-507.
      James sought to learn the laws of the theatre derived
      from the audience's habits and tastes, but his attempts
      approximated cold, hard Jonsonian farce. In the late nov-
      els, James made great discoveries in dramatic form and
      technique. Examines how some of the ideas from the criti-
      cal prefaces might be applied to drama and what basic con-
      ceptions of dramatic form they constitute.

21   H. J. "Henry James and Dumas, <u>fils</u>." <u>Notes and Queries</u>, 185
      (28 August), 132-33.
         "...In some measure both 'Roderick Hudson' and 'The
      Princess Casamassima' were influenced by 'L'Affaire Clem-
      enceau.'" Quotes extensively from James' review of that
      work by Dumas <u>fils</u>.

22   HALIFAX, VISCOUNT. "The British Ambassador Pays Tribute."
      <u>Mark Twain Quarterly</u>, 5 (Spring), cover.
         Though James wrote in English, his closest affinities
      in fiction were with Balzac and Turgenev. He suffered
      "the fate of the pioneer in technique that people should
      judge him not for what he has done but for what they think
      he is trying to do."

23   JENNINGS, RICHARD. "Fair Comment." <u>Nineteenth Century</u>, 133
      (May), 230.
         James "ruined" the "simplicity" of the earlier works
      "by imposing upon them the parenthetic clauses, the tor-
      tured syntax, of his last period."

24   JORDAN, ELIZABETH. "Henry James at Dinner." <u>Mark Twain Quar-</u>
      <u>terly</u>, 5 (Spring), 7.
         James' "habit of speech," particularly the repetition
      of groups of three or four words, never changing a word,
      is his most memorable characteristic.

25   KAZIN, ALFRED. "Our Passion Is Our Task." <u>New Republic</u>, 108
      (15 February), 215-18.
         Despite the devotion of William and Henry James to
      each other, "their essential antipathy of spirit," or at
      least "non-recognition," went "deeper still." Examination
      of the temperaments and positions of William and Henry in
      the family. "For the elder James the center of existence
      was the self that seeks to know God and to be sublimated
      in Him; William's theory of knowledge began with the know-
      ing mind that initiates the ideas to which the test of
      experience is to be applied; Henry found his technical--
      and moral--triumph in the central Jamesian intelligence
      which sifts the experiences of all the other characters
      and organizes them." Reprinted: 1955.B44.

26   KELLEY, CORNELIA PULSIFER. "Henry James on Zola." <u>Colby</u>
      <u>Library Quarterly</u>, 1 (June), 44-51.
         Provides background on and reprints a review by James,
      previously unavailable in America, of Zola's <u>Nana</u>, in
      which James presents his opinion of Zola's realism and
      which distinguishes between James' understanding of the
      French and of the Anglo-Saxon temperament.

1943

27   LESLIE, SHANE.   "A Note on Henry James." Horizon, 7 (June),
         405-13.
              Reminiscence of first meeting with James at a luncheon
         in 1914, where he condemned the Kaiser to some of his sup-
         porters. Reprints eleven selections from letters written
         by James to an intimate friend between 1903 and 1914.

28   LOWNDES, MARIE BELLOC.   "Henry James in War Time." Mark
         Twain Quarterly, 5 (Spring), 8.
              Although James had earlier protested that he would never
         become a British citizen, his pro-Ally sympathies reversed
         this resolve.

29   MACHEN, ARTHUR.   "Arthur Machen Pays Tribute." Mark Twain
         Quarterly, 5 (Spring), 8.
              Despite criticisms of James' excessive attempts to get
         the shade of meaning exactly right, views The Turn of the
         Screw as "one of the finest...tales of supernatural horror
         in the language."

30   MacKENZIE, COMPTON.   "Henry James." Life and Letters, 39
         (December), 147-55.
              Retrospective account of his acquaintance with James,
         whom he met in 1890, when he was seven years old. De-
         scribes the experience of hearing him speak as "incommu-
         nicable," and suggests that Gosse came closest to express-
         ing James' "abundant personality within the confines of
         the printed page." Reprinted: 1944.B7; 1950.B55.

31   MARSHALL, MARGARET.   "Notes by the Way." Nation, 156
         (24 April), 599, 602.
              Reflections on James' position as a reviewer for Nation,
         his role as an American, and the "persistent refusal of
         Americans to recognize James' achievement.

32   MATTHIESSEN, F. O.   "James and the Plastic Arts." Kenyon
         Review, 5 (Autumn), 533-50.
              Hypothesizes that "by seeing life in pictures, he
         [James] found his organic form." He reached the apex of
         his use of "plastic resources" in the last three completed
         novels. "Art puts a frame around experience in the sense
         of selecting a significant design, and, by thus concentrat-
         ing upon it, enabling us to share in the essence without
         being distracted by irrelevant details." Analyzes The Am-
         bassadors, The Wings of the Dove, The Golden Bowl, and The
         Ivory Tower in terms of their use of art and objet d'art.

33   MEMORABILIST. "Arnold on Ruskin; and Henry James." Notes
      and Queries, 185 (3 July), 17.
         Quotes comparative passages from Ruskin and James, and
      quotes Herbert Read's remark in The Sense of Glory
      (1929.B5) that "among the influences on the young Henry
      James's style is that of 'a temperate Ruskin.'"

34   MEMORABILIST. "Henry James on the Poetry of Arnold." Notes
      and Queries, 185 (14 August), 106.
         Quotes in entirety James' remarks on Arnold from English
      Illustrated Magazine, January 1884. See 1943.B7.

35   MORGAN, CHARLES. The House of Macmillan, 1843-1943. New
      York: The Macmillan Co., passim.
         References to James' association with the Macmillan
      publishing concern, including editorial assessment of
      James' French Poets and Novelists as "'prosaic to the last
      degree, and as criticism not at all interesting...,'"
      though it was nevertheless accepted for publication. Notes
      publication of the collected edition of James' works,
      which "failed."

36   MORTIMER, RAYMOND. "Henry James." Horizon, 7 (May), 314-29.
         James, contrary to most of his fellow writers who were
      interested in naturalism or sociological analysis, concen-
      trated on composition at the expense of representation.
      Comments on The Ambassadors, The Wings of the Dove, and
      The Golden Bowl, and concludes that James is loved or
      hated on the basis of his style.

37   ORCUTT, WILLIAM DANA. "From My Library Walls." Christian
      Science Monitor, 35 (17 August), 10.
         James "profoundly affected the literature of his epoch."
      Describes his reaction to Roderick Hudson, his first meet-
      ing with James, and a visit at Lamb House which gave him a
      new appreciation for the real man. Reprinted: 1945.B36.

38   PORTER, KATHERINE ANNE. "The Days Before." Kenyon Review, 5
      (Autumn), 481-94.
         Rejects the tendency to ally James with the New England
      or Puritan tradition, and, through an analysis of his
      youth, concludes that James acquired a worldly knowledge,
      "the end product of that education which began with the
      inward life, the early inculcated love of virtue for its
      own sake, a deep belief in human affections and natural
      goodness, a childhood of extraordinary freedom and privi-
      lege, lived in a small world of fostering care." See
      1952.B56.

1943

39   RAHV, PHILIP. "Attitudes to Henry James." New Republic,
     108 (15 February), 220-24.
        Comments on prevalent critical views, such as those of
     Parrington and Brooks, as depreciations whose assumptions
     are basic to our culture. James is an example of a writer
     who "mastered that 'principle of growth,'" and lifted the
     international theme "to a level of conscious experience
     and aesthetic possession not previously attained." His
     work displays the contradiction of search for and with-
     drawal from experience, or at least a dread of it in its
     natural state. Reprinted: 1945.A1; 1949.B46; also in
     Lewis Leary, ed. American Literary Essays. New York:
     Thomas Y. Crowell Co., 1960, pp. 153-58; and in Rahv's
     Literature and the Sixth Sense. Boston: Houghton Mifflin
     Co., 1969, pp. 95-103.

40   RAHV, PHILIP. "The Heiress of All the Ages," Partisan Re-
     view, 10 (May-June), 227-47.
        Analysis of the "principal heroine" who dominates
     James' international novels, the "pilgrim" who "learns to
     adjust European attitudes to the needs of her personality,"
     and who moves "between innocence and experience...."
     Sketches the development of this character type in the
     conflict between two cultures in James' works. The evolu-
     tion of this heroine suggests James' belief in the American
     fate. Reprinted: 1949.B47; in Rahv's Literature and the
     Sixth Sense. Boston: Houghton Mifflin Co., 1969, pp. 104-
     25; partially reprinted in Lyall H. Powers, ed. Studies in
     "The Portrait of a Lady," pp. 19-27; and in William Staf-
     ford, ed. Perspectives on James's "The Portrait of a
     Lady," pp. 139-47.

41   ROSENZWEIG, SAUL. "The Ghost of Henry James." Character and
     Personality, 12 (December), 79-100.
        A psychoanalytic study of James with emphasis on the
     supernatural stories James wrote during the final third of
     his life. The ghosts "point...to the irrepressible unlived
     life." Sees evidence of James' sense of powerlessness re-
     sulting from his adolescent injury in "The Story of a
     Year," and views James' visit to America in 1904 as actu-
     ated by "an impulse to repair, if possible, the injury and
     to complete the unfinished experience of his youth." Con-
     cludes that "Suffering from childhood with a keen sense of
     inadequacy, he experienced...an injury that sharply crys-
     tallized this attitude into a passional death. The ghost
     which as an apotheosis of his unlived life appears re-
     peatedly in his later tales was liberated from this
     'death.'" Reconstructs this view in Oedipal terms as well.
     Reprinted: 1944.B15.

42 RUSSELL, JOHN. "Henry James and his Architect." <u>Architectur-</u>
    <u>al Review</u>, 93 (March), 69-72.
        James lived in a house "congruous with himself, a
    connoisseur." Describes the search for and acquisition of
    Lamb House, aided by architect Edward Warren, and its sub-
    sequent remodelling.

43 RUSSELL, JOHN. "Henry James and the Leaning Tower." <u>New</u>
    <u>Statesman and Nation</u>, 25 (17 April), 254-55.
        Sketches James' life during wartime and his progress
    toward naturalization as seen in letters to Edward Warren,
    James' friend and architect. James was passionately proud
    of England, yet remained a "moral barometer."

44 SMITH, LOGAN PEARSALL. "Saved from the Salvage." <u>Horizon</u>, 7
    (March), 150, 154-55.
        <u>The Aspern Papers</u>, <u>The Spoils of Poynton</u> and James'
    later stories are composed "of memories, surmises, of
    appearances, of relations; ---and of abysses; of misgivings
    also...."

45 SMITH, LOGAN PEARSALL. "Slices of Cake." <u>New Statesman and</u>
    <u>Nation</u>, 25 (15 June), 367-68.
        Describes his conversations with James about the war
    and about becoming a naturalized British citizen, James'
    introduction to George Santayana, and his attitude towards
    the English.

46 SMITH, LOGAN PEARSALL. "Notes on Henry James." <u>Atlantic</u>
    <u>Monthly</u>, 172 (August), 75-77.
        Informal, retrospective essay in which Smith recounts
    two meetings with James, one a luncheon with him and Edith
    Wharton in 1914 and the other a gathering at Smith's at
    which George Santayana was present. Basically the same
    material as 1943.B45.

47 STEWART, RANDALL. "The Moral Aspects of Henry James's 'In-
    ternational Situation.'" <u>University of Kansas City Review</u>,
    9 (Winter), 109-13.
        Hypothesizes that "if in James's works America is 'cul-
    turally' inferior to Europe, Europe is morally inferior to
    America," and moral values assume preeminence in James.
    Analyzes Americans exposed to the influences of Europe in
    the major novels.

1943

48   STOVALL, FLOYD. "From Realism to Naturalism," in American
      Idealism. Norman: University of Oklahoma Press, pp. 121-
      23.
           In discussing realism in fiction, describes James as a
      novelist who "placed the small section of American life
      that he knew under the microscope and described it with
      the minuteness and cold detachment of a bacteriologist."
      Views James' expatriation as a manifestation of the Ameri-
      can characteristic "of turning one's back upon what is in
      order to seek for what might be, or ought to be...."

49   SWEENEY, J. L. "The Demuth Pictures." Kenyon Review, 5
      (Autumn), 522-32.
           The water colors by Charles Demuth, completed in 1918
      and 1919 under the "literary spell" of The Turn of the
      Screw and "The Beast in the Jungle," are important for the
      "light they throw on James's literary method by illustrat-
      ing it through an analogous approach in the materials of
      another art."

50   SWINNERTON, FRANK A. "Henry James." Spectator, 170
      (9 April), 336.
           James' dramatic technique, his method of viewing his
      material in scenes and pictures, was formed when, as a
      child, he used four sheets, three lined for writing the
      story, the fourth blank for a drawing. James' attitude
      was to remain separate from the picture and communicate
      his story indirectly. The Spoils of Poynton and The Am-
      bassadors come closest to James' ideal of detached tech-
      nical perfection. See 1943.B51.

51   SWINNERTON, FRANK. "A Superb Performance." Mark Twain Quar-
      terly, 5 (Spring), 2.
           An abridged version of 1943.B50.

52   TROY, WILLIAM. "The Altar of Henry James." New Republic,
      108 (15 February), 228-30.
           Questions what James' altar was, "the particular object
      of piety to which he was able to devote himself at the
      end," and suggests that a symbolic approach to James' work
      is more meaningful than dividing works into periods. Dis-
      cusses symbol of the garden in several works as an example,
      and analyzes "The Altar of the Dead." Concludes that "...
      his altar--what would it be but the sometimes splendid and
      exultant, sometimes mangled and ignoble, body of humanity
      stretched out in imagination in time and space?" Re-
      printed: 1945.A1.

1943

53 VIVAS, ELISEO. "Henry and William (Two Notes)." Kenyon Re-
    view, 5 (Autumn), 580-94.
        Although William and Henry James were back to back in
    moral conceptions, there is a similarity between them in
    "the way they conceive the mind's mode of apprehension,
    in which they conceive the process...through which the
    mind enters into relations with its world." Investigates
    Henry's illustration in his work of William's doctrine of
    the stream of consciousness. Reprinted: 1955.B70.

54 WADE, ALLEN. "Henry James as Dramatic Critic." Theatre Arts,
    27 (December), 735-40.
        Survey of James' lifelong relationship with the theatre,
    both as playgoer and playwright. Considers his attitude to
    British productions, his comments on theatrical perform-
    ances, his opinion of Ibsen. James urged the importance of
    a standard in dramatic criticism. Reprinted: 1948.B52.

55 WARREN, AUSTIN. "Myth and Dialectic in the Later Novels."
    Kenyon Review, 5 (Autumn), 551-68.
        Considers influences on James' later method, including
    his use of dictation, the experience with the drama, the
    influence of "symbolisme," by way of Maeterlinck and Ibsen.
    James' late novels intermix "reality and symbolism," and
    the closest counterparts can be found in poetic drama, in
    which are "adumbrated close conversation and the metaphor."
    James' use of narrative followed by dialogue is a technical
    analogue to epistemological and metaphysical modes of
    knowing, dialectic and myth, the former a cerebral process
    attacked from without, the latter an intuitive, imaginative
    process reached through images and symbols. Analyzes these
    two modes in James' later novels, with emphasis on his use
    of the "extended conceit" and "emblematic perception."
    Concludes that James' achievement "in his maturity is a
    series of 'metaphysical' novels in which, working as a
    poet, he incarnates the interrelations between the con-
    scious and the unconscious, between the social and the
    subjective." Reprinted: 1948.B54; in Leon Edel, ed.
    Henry James: A Collection of Critical Essays, pp. 123-38.

56 WEBER, C. J. "Henry James and Thomas Hardy." Mark Twain
    Quarterly, 5 (Spring), 3-4.
        James and Hardy, who both appeared in print in March
    1865 for the first time, had "strikingly different goals,
    Hardy writing of simple, uncultured man and James of
    gracious culture." Notes some of their comments regarding
    each other which emphasize their dissimilarity.

1943

57 WELLS, H. G. "Wells and Henry James." New Statesman and
    Nation, 25 (12 June), 385.
        Response to Logan Pearsall Smith's suggestion that Wells
    "pilloried my old friend" in Boon. Calls his parody "good-
    tempered guying of the Master's style."

58 WILLIAMS, BLANCHE. "The Depth of Henry James." Mark Twain
    Quarterly, 5 (Spring) 5-6.
        Depth is a permanent characteristic of James' work, and
    the quality which explains why he preferred an older civ-
    ilization. He required a setting of depth, which he found
    in Europe.

59 ZABEL, MORTON D. "Henry James' Place." Nation, 156
    (24 April), 596-99.
        Suggests that Washington Place, Henry's birthplace, be
    renamed Henry James Place and that Number Two be marked,
    and predicts the eventual publication of a complete, cheap
    edition of James' fiction and a complete reprinting of his
    non-fiction.

1944 A BOOKS

1 FOLEY, RICHARD NICHOLAS. Criticism in American Periodicals
   of the Works of Henry James from 1866-1916. Washington,
   D.C.: Catholic University of America Press, 175 pp.
   Reprinted: Folcroft, Pa.: Folcroft Press, 1970.
       Originally a dissertation (Catholic University, 1943).
   Traces James' reputation among reviewers during his lifetime, and relates important critical ideas in periodicals
   which were responsible for the status of, and changes in,
   attitudes towards James. Includes "all the significant
   and typical comment in American periodical criticism,"
   chronologically arranged from the first discoverable comment on James in February 1866 to his death. The survey
   is divided into 47 sections, each devoted to the reviews
   of a single book or to the books published in one year,
   with summaries of opinions on James and his work. In the
   conclusion, gives overview of critical reputation, discusses common ideas about James' works which emerge from
   the reviews, and makes observations concerning the quality
   of criticism by different magazines and critics. Study
   reveals "that criticism written when his books were published anticipated accepted critical opinion today." Reviewed: L. N. Richardson, American Literature, 17
   (March 1945), 95-96.

1944

2   MATTHIESSEN, F. O. Henry James: The Major Phase. New York:
    Oxford University Press, 190 pp. Reprinted: A Galaxy
    Book. New York: Oxford University Press, 1963.
        A study of James' later works, concentrating on The
    Ambassadors, The Wings of the Dove, The Golden Bowl and
    The Ivory Tower, in conjunction with information supplied
    by the notebooks. Subject is "the pursuit" of ideas James
    had several years earlier to "their created embodiment" in
    the late novels. The key to James' work is in "the intri-
    cate and fascinating designs of his final and major phase."
    Includes chapters on "The Art of Reflection," James' de-
    velopment as revealed in his notebooks, each of the last
    three completed novels, "'The American Scene' and 'The
    Ivory Tower,'" and other late shorter works. Concludes
    that James "was, to the end, the absorbed spectator" who
    expressed a "humane consciousness" and showed an intense
    spiritual awareness. Appendix reprints "The Painter's
    Sponge and Varnish Bottle" (see 1944.B9). Partially re-
    printed: as "The Ambassadors," 1945.A1; also in Albert E.
    Stone, ed. Twentieth Century Interpretations of "The
    Ambassadors," pp. 43-48. Reviewed: Joseph Warren Beach,
    American Literature, 17 (March 1945), 93-95; Philip Rahv,
    Kenyon Review, 7 (Spring 1945), 311-15; R. B. Heilman, New
    England Quarterly, 18 (June 1945), 268; Lionel Trilling,
    New York Times Book Review (26 November 1944), p. 3; John
    Berryman, Sewanee Review, 53 (Spring 1945), 291-97.

1944 B SHORTER WRITINGS

1   ANON. "With Two Countries." Time, 44 (4 December), 100-104.
        A survey of James' reputation reveals that "Fifty years
    ago young ladies...knew that Henry James was the greatest
    American writer of fiction. Thirty years ago, he could
    scarcely get his work published. Twenty years ago he was
    damned as an expatriate.... Ten years ago Marxist critics
    condemned him as the arch apologist of the ruling class.
    Now some critics are again saying that James is the great-
    est of modern novelists."

2   BOGAN, LOUISE. "The Silver Clue." Nation, 159 (23 December),
    775-76.
        The revival of interest in James may be due to present
    interest in the international scene rather than the "cen-
    tral values in James." Suggests that Matthiessen (see
    1944.A2) might label his phase "past-master," since James
    had been "major" for at least twenty years when he entered
    his "last and greatest powers of thought and expression."
    Reprinted: 1955.B16.

1944

*3   CASTIGLIONI, GIULIO. <u>Maestri del Pensiera e dell' educazione</u>.
     <u>Profili</u>. Cited in 1956.B70, p. 406.

4   CLEMENS, KATHERINE. "Alice James, Neglected Sister." <u>Mark
     Twain Quarterly</u>, 6 (Summer-Fall), 6-7.
          Prints selected comments from Alice's "witty" notebooks,
     full of caustic reminiscences and anecdotes, and discusses
     some of her views, including those concerning her brothers.

5   GOHDES, CLARENCE. <u>American Literature in Nineteenth Century
     England</u>. New York: Columbia University Press, passim.
          In discussion of booktrade and periodicals, refers to
     James as an author frequently represented in English peri-
     odicals, and mentions him as contributor to <u>Literature</u>, an
     "Anglo-American journal."

6   GREGORY, HORACE and MARYA ZATURENSKA. "The Vein of Comedy in
     E. A. Robinson's Poetry." <u>American Bookman</u>, 1 (Fall),
     53-55.
          Compares E. A. Robinson's Captain Craig and James' Lam-
     bert Strether, and suggests that James and Robinson "in-
     habited the same moral climate...."

7   MacKENZIE, COMPTON. "My Meetings with Henry James." <u>Mark
     Twain Quarterly</u>, 6 (Summer-Fall), 1-5.
          Reprint of 1943.B30.

8   MATTHIESSEN, F. O. "Henry James's Portrait of the Artist."
     <u>Partisan Review</u>, 11 (Winter), 71-87.
          Points out James' concern with the nature of art and
     life of the artist, and discusses the stories which deal
     with "problems of the writer and his audience, of the lack
     of intelligent appreciation and the demands of his craft.
     They also dramatize the...relation of the artist to soci-
     ety." Provides synopses of stories of the artist and sug-
     gests their genesis in James' life and thought and the
     relation of characters to real life models. Reprinted:
     1944.B10.

9   MATTHIESSEN, F. O. "The Painter's Sponge and Varnish Bottle:
     Henry James' Revision of <u>The Portrait of a Lady</u>." <u>Ameri-
     can Bookman</u>, 1 (Winter), 49-68.
          James' revisions, which "constituted a <u>re-seeing</u> of the
     problems of his craft," have been ignored. Examines
     changes made in <u>The Portrait of a Lady</u> for the New York
     edition, including "pervasive colloquialization," greater
     concreteness, and analogues with art rather than with the

stage. "The best way...to judge the final value of James'
rewriting is to relate it in each case to the character
involved...." Isabel emerges as one of his fullest expres-
sions of inner reliance in the presence of adversity. Reprinted in "Appendix," 1944.A2; also in William Stafford,
ed. Perspectives on James's "The Portrait of a Lady,"
pp. 63-88.

10 MATTHIESSEN, F. O. "Introduction," in Henry James: Stories
    of Writers and Artists by Henry James. Edited by F. O.
    Matthiessen. Norfolk, Conn.: New Directions Press,
    pp. 1-17.
        Reprint of 1944.B8. Reviewed: John Berryman, Sewanee
    Review, 53 (Spring 1945), 291-97.

11 MAUROIS, ANDRÉ. "The Gilded Age: Conclusion," in The Miracle
    of America. Translated by Denver Lindley and Jane Hastings
    Hickok Lindley. New York: Harper and Brothers, p. 346.
        James was "seduced by European culture" but continued to
    be "more American than he himself suspected. The exotic
    tree, dug up and replanted beneath other skies, if it
    flourishes at all, continues to put forth flowers of its
    own kind."

12 PORTER, KATHERINE ANNE, ALLEN TATE and MARK VAN DOREN. "Dis-
    cussion," in The New Invitation to Learning. Edited by
    Mark Van Doren. New York: New Home Library, pp. 221-35.
        Panel discussion of whether events in The Turn of the
    Screw are in the mind of the governess or have objective
    reality. Agree that only she sees Jessel and Quint as
    physical presences, and question her motivation. In the
    tale, the theme is knowledge of good and evil, and the
    apparitions represent a great force of undefined malig-
    nancy. Reprinted: as "James: 'The Turn of the Screw':
    A Radio Symposium," in Gerald Willen, ed. A Casebook on
    "The Turn of the Screw," pp. 160-70.

13 QVAMME, B. "Henry James." Edda (Oslo), 44 (January-June),
    73-85. (Norwegian)
        James remained a New Englander with his emphasis on
    ideals. Earlier works possess greater vitality. Criti-
    cizes unreal picture of super-sensitive upper-class, "a
    world of cathedrals and castles" where no one even eats,
    and describes James as an aesthete with an old-maidenlike
    avoidance of sex. Concludes that the "long journey through
    the desert of his books is worth it, because of the high
    points."

1944

14   RAHV, PHILIP. "A Biographical Introduction," in <u>The Great</u>
     <u>Short Novels of Henry James</u>. Edited by Philip Rahv. New
     York: Dial Press, pp. vii-xiii. Reprinted: Apollo Edi-
     tions. New York: Dial Press, 1965.
         James presents a group of American characters "who stand
     in a vital and crucial relation to the national life."
     Gives biographical summary, emphasizing James' relationship
     to Europe, with discussion of the international theme and
     heroine.

15   ROSENZWEIG, SAUL. "The Ghost of Henry James." <u>Partisan Re-</u>
     <u>view</u>, 11 (Fall), 436-55.
         Reprint of 1943.B41.

16   SPENDER, STEPHEN. "A World Where the Victor Belonged to the
     Spoils." <u>New York Times Book Review</u> (12 March), p. 3.
         Discusses James' attitude towards the "doom-ridden tra-
     dition" of Europe, delineates the paradox which obstructs
     understanding of James and the fact that his characters are
     often too clever to understand one another. Analyzes <u>The</u>
     <u>Spoils of Poynton</u> as an excellent example of James, who is
     a moralist.

17   WILSON, EDMUND. "A Treatise on Tales of Horror." <u>New Yorker</u>,
     20 (27 May), 67-74.
         In considering the revival of interest in horror tales,
     suggests that "James...was unconscious of having raised
     something more frightening than the ghosts he had contem-
     plated" in <u>The Turn of the Screw</u>, and describes "The Jolly
     Corner" as "James's other best ghost story."

18   WILSON, EDMUND. "The Vogue of Henry James." <u>New Yorker</u>, 20
     (25 November), 92-97.
         With the upsurge of interest in James, there is need
     for a complete, cheap edition of James' work like that
     brought out by Macmillan in the 1920's.

1945 A BOOKS

1   DUPEE, F. W., ed. <u>The Question of Henry James: A Collection</u>
    <u>of Critical Essays</u>. London: Allen Wingate; New York:
    Henry Holt and Co., 324 pp.
        In the "Introduction" (pp. ix-xvi), asserts that James
    had a classical conception of imagination as the "organizer
    and intensifier of life" and recognized the importance of
    concrete experience and the value of method. Summarizes
    critical controversy surrounding James' work. "In his

novels the innocent people, who are usually Americans, are
confronted with the possibilities for good and evil in a
life of superior cultivation and superior enjoyment; while
the worldly people, who are usually Europeans or European-
ized Americans, are acted upon, changed, sometimes even
destroyed, by the singular power of innocence." Reprints
"The Aesthetic Idealism of Henry James," 1917.B19 (pp. 70-
91); "The Figure in the Carpet," 1918.A1 (pp. 92-104); "In
Memory," 1918.B4 (pp. 108-19); "The Mind of an Artist,"
1920.B20 (pp. 54-69); "The Historian of Fine Consciences,"
1921.B6 (pp. 44-46); "Henry James and Stephen Crane,"
1923.B2 (pp. 105-107); "Two Phases of Henry James,"
1925.A1 (pp. 120-27); "Henry James," 1930.B12 (pp. 251-53);
"Henry James and the Nostalgia of Culture," 1930.B20
(pp. 128-30); "The Old Man," 1931.B12 (pp. 47-53); "The
American," 1931.B19 (pp. 138-59); "Henry James in the
World," 1934.B17 (pp. 131-37); "The Ambiguity of Henry
James," 1934.B37 (pp. 160-90); "The Golden Bowl," 1935.B26
(pp. 236-45); "The Poetics of Henry James," 1935.B29
(pp. 212-17); "The Mote in the Middle Distance," 1936.B3
(pp. 40-43); "At the Grave of Henry James," 1941.B1
(pp. 246-50); "Henry James, Melodramatist," 1943.B8
(pp. 254-66); "In the Country of the Blue," 1943.B10
(pp. 191-211); "Attitudes Toward Henry James," 1943.B39
(pp. 273-80); "The Altar of Henry James," 1943.B52
(pp. 267-72); "The Ambassadors," 1944.A2 (pp. 218-35).
Also reprints Thomas Wentworth Higginson's "Henry James,
Jr." (pp. 1-5), which originally appeared in The Literary
World, 10 (22 November, 1879), 383-84; also in Short
Studies of American Authors. Boston: Ticknor and Fields,
1880, pp. 51-60. Also reprints William Dean Howells' "Mr.
Henry James's Later Work" (pp. 6-19), which originally appeared in North American Review, 176 (January 1903), 125-
37; also in North American Review, 203 (April 1916), 572-
84. Also reprints Frank Moore Colby's "In Darkest James"
(pp. 20-27), which originally appeared in Bookman, 16
(November 1902), 259-60; also in Imaginary Obligations.
New York; 1904, pp. 321-35. Also reprints Herbert Croly's
"Henry James and His Countrymen" (pp. 28-39), which originally appeared in Lamp, 28 (February 1904), 47-53. Dupee
includes "Bibliography" (pp. 281-97), reprinted from
1941.B15. Reviewed: Lorna Reynolds, Dublin Magazine, NS
23 (July-September 1948), 53-55; James Grossman, Nation,
161 (17 November 1945), 525; Alfred Kazin, New York Times
Book Review (2 December 1945), p. 4; G. F. Whicher, New
York Herald Tribune Weekly Book Review (6 January 1946),
p. 5.

1945

1945 B SHORTER WRITINGS

1   ANON. "The Modern Henry James." <u>Newsweek</u>, 26 (22 October),
     106, 109-10.
         Essay-review of Fadiman's <u>The Short Stories of Henry</u>
     <u>James</u> (<u>see</u> 1945.B10) and Rahv's edition of <u>The Bostonians</u>
     (<u>see</u> 1945.B37), described as "long" and "tedious." "Nei-
     ther its satire nor its Sapphic implications will shock
     any one, even in Boston, today."

2   BARRELL, CHARLES WISNER. "Genesis of a Henry James Story."
     <u>Shakespeare Fellowship Quarterly</u>, 6: 63-64.
         Describes the incident which provided the Source for
     "The Birthplace" and James' development of the germinal
     idea. James "was a complete disbeliever in the orthodox
     story of William of Stratford as the actual Shakespeare."

3   BLACKMUR, RICHARD P. "The Sphinx and the Housecat." <u>Accent</u>,
     6 (Autumn), 60-63.
         The most distinguished American authors assumed a pos-
     ture of abjectness faced with the society of their time.
     Compares James and Melville in this respect, and suggests
     that, for the most part, James' defense was to provide
     psychic distance by writing ghost stories, fables and
     fantasies. In <u>The Wings of the Dove</u>, <u>The Sacred Fount</u>,
     and "The Bench of Desolation," he attempted a direct rep-
     resentation of evil. Concludes that "It is only the lesser
     writers who can be taken as they come and go. It is the
     sphinx gives meaning to the housecat."

4   BROWN, E. K. "The Fiction of Henry James." <u>Yale Review</u>, NS
     34 (Spring), 536-39.
         Questions whether "refinement or enlargment of conscious-
     ness is the main power of great fiction," as Matthiessen
     suggests (<u>see</u> 1944.A2). Notes shortcomings of the "major
     phase."

5   BROWN, E. K. "James and Conrad." <u>Yale Review</u>, NS 35 (Decem-
     ber), 265-85.
         James' weakness in presenting the "objective theatre"
     in <u>The Ambassadors</u> is in contrast to Conrad's capacity to
     make the reader <u>see</u> in <u>Lord Jim</u> or <u>Nostromo</u>. Analyzes
     James' method in <u>The Wings of the Dove</u>, in which Milly is
     approached from a distance rather than being in the fore-
     ground, thereby excluding us from full participation in
     her tragic experience, which is the core of the subject.
     Considers how the effect of intense grief is more fully

achieved in The Golden Bowl. The later James novels lack
the vitality which Conrad's great works possess.

6   CANBY, HENRY SEIDEL. "The Timelessness of Henry James."
     Saturday Review of Literature, 28 (20 October), 9-10.
         James recorded the backward reaching of an America which
     was still becoming, is equal to Hawthorne and Twain in
     power and insight, and should be judged a timeless author.

7 . CLEMENS, CYRIL. "A Chat with William Lyon Phelps." Mark
     Twain Quarterly, 6 (Winter-Spring), 5-7.
         In a discussion of authors, suggests that although James
     wished for a wider audience, he refused to change his
     methods in order to secure one. Recalls two incidents in-
     volving James.

8   COWLEY, MALCOLM. "The Two Henry Jameses." New Republic, 112
     (5 February), 177-80.
         Discussion of the dispute about the quality of James'
     later novels, which Cowley considers his best. Matthies-
     sen (see 1944.A2) has not answered all the objections to
     these works but instead has introduced totally different
     arguments. The worst stylistic aspect of the later novels
     is the inversions, especially noticeable in very short
     phrases.

9   FADIMAN, CLIFTON. "The Revival of Interest in Henry James."
     New York Herald Tribune Weekly Book Review, 21 (14 Janu-
     ary), 1-2.
         Restatement of material in 1945.B10. Despite his limit-
     ations, James is "wonderfully near to us," a truly modern
     writer.

10   FADIMAN, CLIFTON. "Introduction," in The Short Stories of
     Henry James. Edited by Clifton Fadiman. Modern Library.
     New York: Random House, pp. ix-xx.
         Gives biographical details in "Vita Brevis." "Nothing
     has happened to him [James] except everything...that he
     could observe, relate, weigh, judge." Sketches the pro-
     gression of James' career, from which he "ended as a great
     creative novelist and critic." "Ars Longa" lists five
     points in the case against James, followed by a defense of
     his prose, form and subtlety, his portrayal of interna-
     tional viewpoint, and his style. James lacks the range of
     Tolstoi or Balzac but compensates in depth. Volume in-
     cludes interpretive notes on each of the short stories
     (see 1945.B11-27). See also 1945.B9. Reprinted:
     1955.B30.

1945

11 FADIMAN, CLIFTON. "A Note on 'A Bundle of Letters,'" in The
    Short Stories of Henry James. Edited by Clifton Fadiman.
    Modern Library. New York: Random House, pp. 78-81.
       "A Bundle of Letters" is a dramatization of "the plight
    of a silk purse that was unable to make itself into a
    sow's ear." The desire for "ultraprovincial experience,
    for the past, for the wider horizon" is handled with "ami-
    able satire."

12 FADIMAN, CLIFTON. "A Note on 'Brooksmith,'" in The Short
    Stories of Henry James. Edited by Clifton Fadiman. Mod-
    ern Library. New York: Random House, pp. 291-92.
       "Brooksmith" is "virtually all tone, bearing a frail
    minimum of content." The theme concerns "the unwilling-
    ness or inability of society to sustain the artist," an
    individual "born into a world in which he never can be
    thoroughly at home."

13 FADIMAN, CLIFTON. "A Note on 'Europe,'" in The Short Stories
    of Henry James. Edited by Clifton Fadiman. Modern Li-
    brary. New York: Random House, pp. 382-84.
       "Europe" modifies the theme of the international rela-
    tionship, and examines "the life-denying power of American
    Puritanism," symbolized in Mrs. Rimmle. See 1948.B16.

14 FADIMAN, CLIFTON. "A Note on 'Four Meetings,'" in The Short
    Stories of Henry James. Edited by Clifton Fadiman. Mod-
    ern Library. New York: Random House, pp. 37-38.
       Caroline Spenser represents the minority enjoined "to
    experience for the community as a whole the thirst and the
    slaking of the thirst for the traditional...." It is a
    counterfeit Europe which she pursues, and for which she
    sacrifices her chance to experience reality.

15 FADIMAN, CLIFTON. "A Note on 'Louisa Pallant,'" in The Short
    Stories of Henry James. Edited by Clifton Fadiman. Mod-
    ern Library. New York: Random House, pp. 123-25.
       In "Louisa Pallant," "the true action takes the form of
    a moral crisis, the story being a bitter tragi-comedy of
    conscience." The themes of the tale are those of money-
    marriage and the nature of evil.

16 FADIMAN, CLIFTON. "A Note on 'Mrs. Medwin,'" in The Short
    Stories of Henry James. Edited by Clifton Fadiman. Mod-
    ern Library. New York: Random House, pp. 484-85.
       The "frail and...quite cynical story...throws some
    light on the question of James's snobbery and Anglomania."

Suggests that "The basic James...was an understander," for
whom "an attitude and analysis" constantly conflicted.

17 FADIMAN, CLIFTON. "A Note on 'The Altar of the Dead,'" in
    The Short Stories of Henry James. Edited by Clifton Fadi-
    man. Modern Library. New York: Random House, pp. 358-60.
        In "The Altar of the Dead," the allegiance of the two
    characters "to their dead comes out of a sense of the full-
    ness of life, rather than out of any perverse interest in
    the smell of mortality. The story is crowded, not with
    terror, but with love," and "administers the quietest and
    gravest rebuke to whatever is spurious" in existence.

18 FADIMAN, CLIFTON. "A Note on 'The Beast in the Jungle,'" in
    The Short Stories of Henry James. Edited by Clifton Fadi-
    man. Modern Library. New York: Random House, pp. 598-
    602.
        Sees "The Beast in the Jungle" as "the best of James'
    shorter fictions, combining concentration of effect with
    inclusiveness of meaning." The subject of the tale is
    "the life we have missed," and Marcher represents an "un
    Faust...man the coward, not the hero, of experience." His
    failure is "mankind's general failure. It is the failure
    to communicate." Reprinted: 1955.B30.

19 FADIMAN, CLIFTON. "A Note on 'The Birthplace,'" in The Short
    Stories of Henry James. Edited by Clifton Fadiman. Modern
    Library. New York: Random House, pp. 546-47.
        "The Birthplace" deals with recognition of "the nature
    of greatness, and also the manner in which greatness is
    honored by human beings who retain the old fashioned vir-
    tue of intellectual scrupulousness, or dishonored by the
    more numerous ones who merely pay lip-service to that vir-
    tue." Tale has deeply moral implications despite comedic
    tone.

20 FADIMAN, CLIFTON. "A Note on 'The Great Good Place,'" in The
    Short Stories of Henry James. Edited by Clifton Fadiman.
    Modern Library. New York: Random House, pp. 413-15.
        "The Great Good Place" is a departure from realism,
    creating a world, a "theoretically achievable Utopia," and
    stands as "criticism of a whole culture" developed on a
    miniature scale. Reprinted: 1948.B17.

21 FADIMAN, CLIFTON. "A Note on 'The Jolly Corner,'" in The
    Short Stories of Henry James. Edited by Clifton Fadiman.
    Modern Library. New York: Random House, pp. 641-44.

1945

Suggests connection between "The Jolly Corner" and
James' own experience, relating the tale to James' adol-
escent injury, his "sense of impotence." The story is a
"working-out of the impulses of James' own unlived life."
The American self which Brydon-James rejected, "the active,
dominating, Faustian self, comes to light at the end of a
long life in the form of the specter in the house on the
Jolly Corner." Or, the ghost may represent the America
from which James retreated.

22 FADIMAN, CLIFTON. "A Note on 'The Liar,'" in The Short
    Stories of Henry James. Edited by Clifton Fadiman. Mod-
    ern Library. New York: Random House, pp. 183-86.
       "The Liar" is "a story about lying as a passion," but
    also a love story. Notes wittiness of tale and describes
    James' kind of wit.

23 FADIMAN, CLIFTON. "A Note on 'The Middle Years,'" in The
    Short Stories of Henry James. Edited by Clifton Fadiman.
    Modern Library. New York: Random House, pp. 316-18.
       The tale "embodies one of the recurrent visions of
    James's dream life," dramatizing "the relation between
    master and disciple." In "The Middle Years," the artist
    "comes to perceive, in the very hour of his death, the
    meaninglessness of the cry for a second chance."

24 FADIMAN, CLIFTON. "A Note on 'The Pupil,'" in The Short S
    Stories of Henry James. Edited by Clifton Fadiman. Modern
    Library. New York: Random House, pp. 268-72.
       Describes James' "control" in "The Pupil," a narrative
    of "troubling beauty," and his aim to "make" rather than
    "sell characters." Views Morgan's as "the tragedy of ex-
    cessive sensibility...." Contrasts the "almost febrile
    awareness of the boy and the basic stupidity...of his
    family," and discusses the relationship between Morgan and
    Pemberton.

25 FADIMAN, CLIFTON. "A Note on 'The Real Thing,'" in The Short
    Stories of Henry James. Edited by Clifton Fadiman. Mod-
    ern Library. New York: Random House, pp. 216-17.
       "The Real Thing" is concerned with the problem of the
    artist class, and specifically with "the nature of real-
    ity." The tale "expresses amusingly...the old truth that
    art is a transformation of reality, not a mere reflection
    of the thing itself. Mrs. Monarch is a true lady, but for
    that very reason she cannot be a fine model of a true
    lady."

26   FADIMAN, CLIFTON. "A Note on 'The Tone of Time,'" in The
     Short Stories of Henry James. Edited by Clifton Fadiman.
     Modern Library. New York: Random House, pp. 457-59.
         "The Tone of Time" develops the situation of two women
     fighting for a man, or the painted image of a man, with
     "delicate irony." Praises James' rendering of Mary Tredick
     and Mrs. Bridgenorth, a dramatization of "his insights into
     the psychology of women."

27   FADIMAN, CLIFTON. "A Note on 'The Tree of Knowledge,'" in The
     Short Stories of Henry James. Edited by Clifton Fadiman.
     Modern Library. New York: Random House, pp. 432-34.
         Criticizes "The Tree of Knowledge" as "'snobbish,'"
     sympathetically portraying individuals "who feel themselves
     superior to most other people," "'unreal,'" and "'over-
     refined.'" Nevertheless, "it wrings the last possible
     droplet of effect out of a theme that to the quick view
     would seem to have nothing in it."

28   GETTMANN, ROYAL A. "Henry James's Revision of The American."
     American Literature, 16 (January), 279-95.
         Comparison of first and final editions of The American
     with attention to prose style, characters, and plot, in an
     attempt to suggest thereby, and from the prefaces, the
     general nature of James' revisions. James moved towards
     the more concrete and specific. "The greatest stylistic
     difference between the two versions of The American is the
     marked increase in the figures of speech." No essential
     changes were made in the characters. Concludes that "It
     is wrong...to assume that James the Reviser mercilessly
     manhandled the works of James the First."

29   GROSSMAN, JAMES. "The Face in the Mountain." Nation, 161
     (September), 230-32.
         Suggests a similarity between James and George Kaufman,
     who also wrote about arts and the life of the artist.
     Compares "The Death of the Lion" and Kaufman's plays, in-
     cluding "Once in a Lifetime," which depict the excellent
     artist acted upon by his environment but unsuccessfully
     acting upon it. James and Kaufman viewed the public taste
     with cynicism, but from different points of view.

30   HAVENS, R. D. "A Misprint in 'The Awkward Age.'" Modern
     Language Notes, 60 (November), 497.
         Points out a misprint in the crucial thirtieth chapter
     of The Awkward Age, in which the context calls for the
     word "bad" rather than "big," for the badness of the vol-
     ume "is what seals Nanda's fate with Vanderbank."

1945

31 LANIER, SIDNEY. "Lecture X [of the Johns Hopkins Lectures]," in The English Novel and Essays on Literature. Edited by Clarence Gohdes and Kemp Malone. Baltimore: Johns Hopkins Press, pp. 198-200.
    Excerpt from Daisy Miller, which offers in Daisy's brother a "portrait of the modern American boy."

32 LeCLAIR, ROBERT C. Three American Travellers in England: James Russell Lowell, Henry Adams, Henry James. Philadelphia: Lancaster Press, pp. 123-215.
    Originally a dissertation (University of Pennsylvania, 1944). In "Influence of the Early Years, 1843-1860," studies influences in James' early life on his attitude towards England and America. Discusses family background, childhood experiences, foreign travel, and eclectic education, and concludes that James was "strongly under the influence of European culture, taste and tradition...." "A Formative Decade, 1860-70" deals with events between the family's return from Europe and the next trip abroad, an interim "of education, motivation and experiment...." Discusses James' impression of England as found in the first four essays of Transatlantic Sketches and a few letters in "The Traveller and his English Sketches." "Londonization" deals with the period in Paris and the return to England. Other topics include consideration of James' transition from traveller to permanent resident as revealed in the sketches, and the maturation of James' views about Europe. James studies the English mind as represented in social order, customs, traditions, and codes of human behavior. Reviewed: H. Blodgett, American Literature, 18 (January 1947), 340-41; Robert E. Spiller, New England Quarterly, 22 (March 1949), 129-30.

33 MacCOLL, D. S. Life, Work and Setting of Philip Wilson Steer. London: Faber and Faber, pp. 4, 7, 57, 71.
    Philip Wilson Steer, like James and other English associates, "remained a bachelor of art," and is briefly compared to a Jamesian character.

34 MATTHIESSEN, F. O. "Not Quite the Real Thing." New Republic, 113 (3 December), 766-68.
    Despite the "discriminating remarks" in Fadiman's introduction to his volume of short stories (see 1945.B10), he makes some major errors and is shaky on James' development, which was not the result of mere imitation of Hawthorne. "James was not a thinker; his realm is consciousness and sensibility, not ideas." Reprinted: 1952.B45.

35 MAUROIS, ANDRÉ. "Henry James," in Études américaines. New
York: Editions de la Maison Francaise, pp. 119-28.
(French)
Discusses reaction of young college professor to his
suggestion that James was an American writer who would
survive. James was not an aesthete; rather, he introduced
moral values into his art. James, like Proust, has not
been accepted as an artist by his fellow countrymen. Reprinted: 1947.B33.

36 ORCUTT, WILLIAM DANA. "The Redundancy of Henry James," in
From My Library Walls: A Kaleidoscope of Memories. New
York: Longmans, Green and Co., pp. 134-38.
Reprint of 1943.B37.

37 RAHV, PHILIP. "Introduction," in The Bostonians. New York:
Dial Press, pp. v-ix.
The Bostonians is James' "only full-length narrative...
uniformly American." Discusses lack of public interest in
the work, explainable in terms of the "dictatorship of
gentility" which rejected the "astringent tone, and ironic
play of ideas...." Considers James' attitude towards the
novel, his reticence to revise it. In Basil Ransom, James
anticipated a major twentieth-century tendency: "Criticism
of modern civilization is rooted in traditionalist principles."

38 RUSSELL, JOHN. "Books in General." New Statesman and Nation,
29 (26 May), 339.
"Only perfection contented Henry James." Gives examples
of James' impatience with improvisation. Reviews Matthiessen's Henry James: The Major Phase (see 1944.A2).

39 SCHNEIDER, ISIDOR. "The Rediscovery of Henry James." New
Masses, 55 (29 May), 23-24.
Discussion of factors which confused James' recognition
as a major writer: his dealing with restricted group
from the inside, his sentence structures, his expatriation.

40 STEVENS, GEORGE. "The Return of Henry James." Saturday Review of Literature, 28 (3 March), 7-8, 30, 32-33.
Questions whether there is really a James revival, a
"resurgence of public interest" in his work. James en-
couraged the idea that literature was for the elite, and
his relationship with his audience was an anomalous one.
Concludes that his appeal is a matter of temperament, and
his characters frequently live in his books but not beyond
them, a result of "his bringing everything to consciousness."

1945

41   TRILLING, LIONEL. "A Note on Art and Neurosis." <u>Partisan</u>
     <u>Review</u>, 12 (Winter), 41-48.
         Takes issue with Rosenzweig's point that "genius is
     inextricably linked with disability" (<u>see</u> 1943.B41). His
     thesis that James had a castration complex "is not the
     same thing as disclosing the roots of James's power or
     providing an insight into the sources of his genius."

42   WILSON, JAMES SOUTHALL. "Henry James and Herman Melville."
     <u>Virginia Quarterly Review</u>, 21 (Spring), 281-86.
         In James' novels, "the frank, natural, simple American
     view triumphs...." Suggests possible connection between
     Melville and James in "the origins of the 'transcendental
     morality' that is so richly a part of the work of each."

43   YOUNG, VERNON. "The Question of James." <u>Arizona Quarterly</u>,
     1 (Winter), 57-62.
         James' popularity is due in part to greater social
     and psychological insight in society. Dupee's compila-
     tion of critical articles (<u>see</u> 1945.A1) "consummates...
     the reclamation of James from the Philistine dissenters...,"
     at least for the intellectual minority.

<u>1946 A BOOKS - NONE</u>

<u>1946 B SHORTER WRITINGS</u>

1   ANDERSON, QUENTIN. "Henry James and the New Jerusalem: Of
     Morality and Style." <u>Kenyon Review</u>, 8 (August), 515-66.
         A reading of James in terms of his father's works,
     based on the hypothesis that Henry James, Sr.'s beliefs
     about man and nature defined the realm in which his son
     excelled. Describes the theology of the elder James and
     applies it to selected works of the novelist. By use of
     parallel passages, suggests their agreement about the
     function of the artist and his spiritual individuality.
     James "was an inveterate allegorist who dramatized again
     and again the two great alternatives offered man: renun-
     ciation of the Eve or other self, and appropriation of
     'God-in-us' (conscience) in the hope of making the self
     absolute. In the theologian these alternatives represent
     two ways of viewing the basic human situation." Analyzes
     the final three completed novels in view of their spirit-
     ual meaning in order to instigate a reappraisal of James'
     "moral temper."

1946

2 ANON. "Henry James and the English Association." Scrutiny,
   14 (December), 131-33.
       Reprints a 1912 letter from James to John Bailey declin-
   ing the offered chairmanship of the English Association.
   James' refusal, his "unnecessary scruple, or moroseness,
   or timidity" is termed "regrettable."

3 AUDEN, WYSTAN HUGH. "Henry James's 'The American Scene.'"
   Horizon, 15 (February), 77-90.
       The American Scene reflects James' self-understanding
   and critical literary acumen and "is only the latest, most
   ambitious, and best of a series of topographical writings,
   beginning in 1870 with sketches of Saratoga and Newport."
   Suggests that the reader approach this book, which offers
   observations of a tourist, as "a prose poem of the first
   order," and praises James' handling of social objects and
   mental ideas. "It is harder for an American than it is
   for a European to become a good writer, but if he succeeds,
   he contributes something unique; he sees something and
   says it in a way that no one before him has said it."
   Reprinted: 1946.B4.

4 AUDEN, WYSTAN HUGH. "Introduction," in The American Scene.
   Edited by Wystan Hugh Auden. New York: Charles Scribner's Sons, pp. v-xxiii.
       Reprint of 1946.B3.

5 BEERBOHM, MAX. "An Incident," in Mainly on the Air. Enlarged
   edition. London: William Heinemann, pp. 119-20. Reprinted: 1957.
       Recalls meeting with James on the way to his club and
   declining to accompany James because of his impatience to
   read one of his short stories, his "preferring the Master's
   work to the Master." See 1956.B35.

6 BERTI, LUIGO. "Saggio su Henry James." Inventario, 1 (Au-
   tumn-Winter), 30-69. (Italian)
       Provides a biographical sketch of James, suggests his
   relationship to Balzac in their common desire to establish
   a national history of tradition and culture, and sees Balzac in the character of Rowland Mallet in Roderick Hudson.
   Discusses James' handling of romantic situations, and
   describes his characters as living in a sad, proper tranquillity of contemporary high society. Concludes that
   James revolutionized the novel with his poetry and construction of scenes in psychological narratives.

1946

7   BOIT, LOUISE. "Henry James as Landlord." <u>Atlantic Monthly</u>,
178 (August), 118-21.
Reprint of letters from James to the tenant of Lamb
House during James' 1904 visit to America, which show him
to be a "very kind and considerate and charming" landlord.

8   BOWEN, ELIZABETH. <u>English Novelists</u>. London: William Collins, pp. 41-43.
Characterizes James as "the analyst of civilisation,"
and notes fascination with the "phenomenon of the English
conscience." Under the surface of his works is the "simple pattern of the morality play." James provided the
transition from the nineteenth century to the twentieth
century.

9   BROWN, E. K. "Two Formulas for Fiction: Henry James and
H. G. Wells." <u>College English</u>, 8 (October), 7-17.
Consideration of the divergent views of the novel of
James and Wells; supplies details of the association of
the two artists and their controversy. Wells' experimental fiction lacked unity and verged on propaganda, and
he deplored James' many omissions on the side of substance,
his desire for unity and homogeneity of form. Sets forth
James' formula for fiction as displayed in <u>The Portrait of
a Lady</u>, and suggests how Wells would have treated the material differently.

10   BURLINGAME, ROGER. "Best-Sellers," in <u>Of Making Many Books:
A Hundred Years of Reading, Writing and Publishing</u>. New
York: Charles Scribner's Sons, pp. 134-35.
Records Bliss Perry's irritation upon reading <u>The Sa-
cred Fount</u>, whose author he calls "'a juggler with the
English language'" and "'exasperating.'"

11   BURNHAM, PHILIP. "View of America." <u>Commonweal</u>, 45 (25 October), 36-40, 42.
Analysis of <u>The American Scene</u>, in which "James proclaims his basic critical judgment of America's cultural
vacuity with a warm and unambiguous and surprising hearti-
ness...." Considers James' "norms of culture," discusses
the errors as well as the "inescapable truth" of his
charge of America's lack of culture, and applies James'
principles to contemporary society.

12   DERLETH, AUGUST. "The Imaginative Story," in <u>Writing Fiction</u>.
Boston: The Writer, pp. 101, 114.
In presenting how to write imaginative fiction, terms
<u>The Turn of the Screw</u>, a "moral ghost story."

1946

13 GARNETT, DAVID. "Introduction," in <u>Fourteen Stories by Henry</u>
    <u>James</u>. Edited by David Garnett. London: Rupert Hart-
    Davis, pp. vii-xi.
        Reviews James' development as a short story writer,
    which he describes as "slow," and characterizes the early
    work as "...contrived stories with little imagination or
    knowledge of human beings." James "had no unusual under-
    standing of psychology, no abnormal faculty of analysing
    the human soul. His characters are just as much alive as
    the people we meet in hotels or at houses of our friends,
    but no more."

14 HOSKINS, KATHERINE. "Henry James and the Future of the Novel."
    <u>Sewanee Review</u>, 54 (Winter), 87-101.
        For the post-war novelists, "there is no chap-book on
    novel writing comparable in illustrative material, theory
    and particularity to James's prefaces...his essay on Bal-
    zac and...'The Art of Fiction.'" Discusses aspects of
    James' method, including his use of a center of conscious-
    ness, his treatment of social class, his search for pre-
    cision of meaning.

15 HOXIE, ELIZABETH F. "Mrs. Grundy Adopts Daisy Miller." <u>New</u>
    <u>England Quarterly</u>, 19 (December), 474-84.
        Views Daisy Miller's behavior from a social-historical
    perspective. Daisy helped to set standards of decorum in
    America and became an authoritative example to writers of
    etiquette in the later nineteenth century of an American
    girl in Europe, condemned for her naturalness and lack of
    inhibition. Mentions fictional counterparts whose charac-
    teristics Daisy came to absorb.

16 JONES-EVANS, MERVYN. "Henry James's Year in France." <u>Hori-</u>
    <u>zon</u>, 14 (July), 52-60.
        Description of James' 1875 year in Paris, where he met
    and conversed with his literary idols, whom he found to be
    a closed circle, "not open to outside opinions and influ-
    ences." Nevertheless, James profited from his association,
    gleaning from it a "sense of analysis" and knowledge of
    certain fundamentals of his art. Reprinted: 1953.B33.

17 KEOWN, ERIC. "At the Play." <u>Punch</u>, 211 (6 November), 408.
        Review of two-act play adapted from James' <u>The Turn of</u>
    <u>the Screw</u> by Allan Turpin, which "no amateur of high-level
    horrifics should miss...."

1946

18   LEAVIS, F. R. "George Eliot (IV): 'Daniel Deronda' and 'The
      Portrait of a Lady.'" Scrutiny, 14 (December), 102-31.
          James' Isabel Archer is a variation, perhaps unconscious,
      of George Eliot's Gwendolen Harleth in Daniel Deronda.
      Eliot's portrayal of her heroine is more complete and spe-
      cific than James', whose approach is more subtle and ironic.
      Considers the differences between Gwendolen and Isabel,
      points out Osmond's relationship to Eliot's Grandcourt, and
      concludes that James "fails to produce the fable that gives
      inevitability and moral significance."

19   LOWNDES, MARIE BELLOC. "XVI," in The Merry Wives of Westmin-
      ster. London: Macmillan and Co., pp. 183-95.
          An account of her "affectionate friendship with Henry
      James." Remarks on James' opinion of contemporary English
      writers, his association with Turgenev, his desire for
      "commonplace" affection. Discusses relationships with
      Elizabeth Robins, Fanny Prothero, and Rhoda Broughton, and
      describes James' reaction to the war and the memorial serv-
      ice in his honor.

20   McCULLOUGH, BRUCE WALKER. "The Novelist in Search of Perfec-
      tion," in Representative English Novelists: Defoe to Con-
      rad. New York: Harper and Brothers, pp. 274-302.
          James provided a transition between the Victorian and
      modern eras, representing the broadminded attitude towards
      foreign literature as a "student of contrasting cultures."
      Distinguishes between science and art to elucidate James'
      approach to the novel, which he conceived of as "neither
      an impersonal rendering of life nor a personal autobiogra-
      phy."

21   MELLQUIST, JEROME. "From Henry James to Paul Rosenfeld."
      Sewanee Review, 54 (October), 691-98.
          A review of James' art criticism with reference to
      Transatlantic Sketches, Picture and Text, the biography of
      William Wetmore Story, reminiscences, and selected novels
      reveals that James "remains the elegant tourist...the keen
      and appreciative black and white connoisseur" when he
      writes about art.

22   NOWELL-SMITH, SIMON. "Mr. H____." Times Literary Supplement
      (28 December), p. 643.
          Asks readers for clues or confirmation of suspicion that
      the "Mr. H____" referred to by Flaubert in a letter to
      George Sand is James.

1946

23 PEACOCK, RONALD. "Henry James and the Drama," in The Poet in the Theatre. New York: George Routledge and Sons, pp. 21-38.

Questions why James was attracted to writing for the theatre, surveys his dramatic career, and concludes that the novel corresponded better to what James wished to convey, that in fiction he produced "drama" apart from the conditions of the stage. "Henry James has exploited in a form that is subtly compounded of two techniques one of the varieties of drama that life holds, and the stage cannot."

24 PUTT, S. GORLEY. "A Henry James Jubilee: I." Cornhill Magazine, 162 (Winter), 187-99.

The source of The Princess Casamassima is not Dickens but James' "own endless capacity for warm-hearted observation." The book should not be read as a political tract but as an illustration of Hyacinth's private dreams and public sympathies. See 1947.B37.

25 PUTT, S. GORLEY. "The Wings of the Dove: A Note on Henry James," in Orion: A Miscellany. Edited by C. Day Lewis et al. Vol. 3. London: Nicholson and Watson, pp. 120-43.

Synopsis of The Wings of the Dove, in which James attempted to display "the individual consciousness in its most secret development...." The primary interest in the novels can be found in the relationship between antithetical types, "mutually inimical and even destructive."

26 ROBERTS, MORRIS. "Henry James and the Art of Foreshortening." Review of English Studies, 22 (July), 207-14.

With great economy, James dramatized small incidents without their "being expanded into a scene and dialogue," thereby creating movement and a sense of drama. "... There are no decorative or moralizing digressions in James, and there is always a necessity of 'foreshortening'; of giving the sense of present action without an elaborated scene." In the later novels, the demands of drama resulted in a peculiar handling of time, in which dramatic time and real time interact, as seen in the interval between Books II and III of The Golden Bowl.

27 ROSENFELD, PAUL. "The Henry James Revival: The Expatriate Comes Home." Commonweal, 43 (11 January), 329-32.

Traces James' reputation during his lifetime, from the sympathetic response of readers until The Tragic Muse, when his public fell off. Attributes present revival in part to decline of naturalism and suggests several other possible influences.

1946

28   SHORT, R. W. "The Sentence Structure of Henry James." <u>Ameri-</u>
      <u>can Literature</u>, 18 (May), 71-88.
            Observations about sentence structure in novels written
      between 1901 and 1904, attempting to elucidate "the artis-
      tic intentions of James...." Suggests that James' is "a
      complexity that is not of <u>idea</u>, but of relationship between
      ideas." Techniques discussed include sentence order,
      parentheses, emphasis on relationships between expressions,
      grammatical ambiguity, and stylization. Sees a similarity
      between James' writing and euphuistic prose; however, "Un-
      like the Euphuists, he controlled the tides of association
      with a moonlike vigor."

29   TINTNER, ADELINE R. "The Spoils of Henry James." <u>Publications</u>
      <u>of the Modern Language Association</u>, 61 (March), <u>239-51.</u>
            With reference to Matthiessen's (<u>see</u> 1943.B32) and War-
      ren's (1943.B55) studies on art in James' novels, suggests
      that the "over-all meaning is that the work of art embodies
      and incorporates civilization as it was available to James,"
      and serves as "an attempt to balance the material aspect of
      civilization, art--with its spiritual aspect, life." Sur-
      veys the meaning of art in James' fiction, from the early
      period when the museum world determines "certain fixed
      modes of experience permitted in the presence of art and
      under its aegis," to the change in James' attitude signaled
      in <u>The Portrait of a Lady</u>, in which "society itself is val-
      ued only in so far as it is potential stuff for the tradi-
      tional art of the future," and finally to fiction from 1884-
      1901, when the work of art becomes secularized and contem-
      poraneous, and serves as a touchstone for judging human
      values in its molding of formal life. Relates James' dev-
      elopment to changes in the artistic climate and James'
      presentation of artists in his fiction, discusses later
      works in terms of the clues art gives to individual motives
      and drives. "As art dictated to behavior in the early fic-
      tion, and life dictated to art in the middle fiction, the
      final adjustment is a reconciliation between them." Re-
      printed: in Leon Edel, ed. <u>Henry James: A Collection of</u>
      <u>Critical Essays</u>, pp. 139-55.

30   TRILLING, LIONEL. "Dreiser and the Liberal Mind." <u>Nation</u>,
      162 (20 April), 466-72.
            Juxtaposition of James and Dreiser, with conclusion
      that James has been unfairly judged because he was "a
      traitor to the reality of the odors of the shop" and con-
      sidered what ought to be rather than what is.

31   WILDE, OSCAR. <u>Selected Works</u>. Edited by Richard Aldington.
        London: William Heinemann, p. 39.
            In dialogue, <u>The Decay of Lying</u>: "Mr. Henry James
        writes fiction as if it were a painful duty, and wastes
        upon mean motives and imperceptible 'points of view' his
        neat literary style, his felicitous phrases, his swift
        and caustic satire."

32   WILSON, EDMUND. "Henry James and Auden in America." <u>New
        Yorker</u>, 22 (28 September), 85-87.
            Reviews Auden's edition of <u>The American Scene</u> (1946.B4),
        a "magnificently brilliant and solid" book with acute
        judgment of American life and awareness of economic and
        political influences, and gives background surrounding its
        writing. The work exudes "old-fashioned American patriot-
        ism" and "is one of the best books about modern America."

1947

1947 A BOOKS

1   MATTHIESSEN, F. O. <u>The James Family: Including Selections
        from the Writings of Henry James, Senior, William, Henry,
        and Alice James</u>. New York: Alfred A. Knopf, 730 pp.
            A biography of the James family, who, as a striking,
        varied group, represented significant cultural elements of
        their time and facets of American intellectual history.
        Through a comprehensive "anthology" of letters, journals
        and essays by family members, connected by editorial com-
        mentary from the "director" of the narrative, Matthiessen
        attempts to "uncover the sources of their [William's and
        Henry's] seminal ideas in the matrix that formed them,"
        and suggests implications of ideas through juxtaposition,
        comparison and contrast. Includes a survey of James'
        career and discussions of his "inwardness" as an artist,
        his reactions to Europe, his ideas about art. William and
        Henry shared a "belief in nothing less than the sacredness
        of the individual." Reviewed: Richard P. Blackmur, <u>Ken-
        yon Review</u>, 10 (Spring 1948), 313-17; F. W. Dupee, <u>Nation</u>,
        165 (1 November 1947), 477; H. A. Larrabee, <u>New England
        Quarterly</u>, 22 (March 1949), 108-110; H. S. Canby, <u>Saturday
        Review of Literature</u>, 31 (24 January 1948), 9; Henry Bam-
        ford Parkes, <u>Sewanee Review</u>, 56 (Spring 1948), 323-28;
        E. K. Brown, <u>Yale Review</u>, NS 37 (Spring 1948), 532.

1947

2   NOWELL-SMITH, SIMON. The Legend of the Master. London:
    Constable and Co.; New York: Charles Scribner's Sons,
    1948, 222 pp.
        A collection of anecdotes and written portraits of
    James. In "The Legend," Nowell-Smith discusses what por-
    tion of the picture of James is distorted, embellished,
    or otherwise inaccurate. "Henry James's chroniclers can-
    not always be trusted to represent him faithfully." In-
    cludes excerpts from hostile witnesses as well as friendly
    and neutral ones. In "The Master," explains that the work
    deals not with James' literary achievement but rather with
    his literary endeavors only insofar as they contributed to
    the legend, the point being to show James as others saw
    him. Arrangement of chapters is by subject, including
    topics on "Talk," "Social Occasions," "Of Persons," "Of
    Peoples," "Public and Private," and "The Novelist." Re-
    viewed: Stanley Edgar Hyman, Hudson Review, 2 (Winter
    1950), 600; Lionel Trilling, Kenyon Review, 10 (Summer
    1948), 507-10; Leon Edel, New England Quarterly, 21 (De-
    cember 1948), 544-47; Times Literary Supplement (17 Janu-
    ary 1948), p. 34.

1947 B SHORTER WRITINGS

1   ANDERSON, QUENTIN. "The Two Henry Jameses." Scrutiny, 14
    (September), 242-51.
        Further investigation of the idea that James "based an
    extensive system of symbolism" on the theology and psy-
    chology, the "secular mysticism," of his father. (See
    1946.B1.) Discusses some of the tenets of the elder James'
    system, supplies instances of the novelist's use of his
    father's work, and examines the transmutation of the fa-
    ther's ideas into dramatic and symbolic form in the son's
    works. The Ambassadors, The Wings of the Dove and The
    Golden Bowl were "planned as a single poem embracing the
    history of mankind" and represent three stages in the ex-
    perience of the race which are paralleled by three stages
    in the moral career of the individual.

2   ANDERSON, QUENTIN. "Henry James, His Symbolism and his
    Critics." Scrutiny, 15 (December), 12-19.
        Few readers conceive of James "as a moralist who em-
    ployed symbols in a schematic way," and critics frequently
    "stress the artist's alienation from his society...as a
    stylist, a personality, a moral agent." James tried to
    break down the barrier between the artist and society.
    Suggests how James symbolized the universality of con-
    sciousness and the unity of humanity.

3   ANON. "Catalogue of Henry James Exhibition, October 24–
     December 8, 1946." Grolier Club Gazette, 2 (February),
     251-67.
         Listing of first editions, manuscripts, typescripts and
     portraits in the exhibition.

4   ANON. "The Heiress: Play Based on James's Novel Joins Broad-
     way's String of Sober Hits." Life, 23 (3 November), 149-
     50, 153.
         The production "is not first-class James, but it is
     first-class theatre."

5   ANON. "The Intellectual Jameses." Newsweek, 30 (3 November),
     93-94.
         Description of Henry James, Sr. and his "magnificent
     family of minds." Notes James' obsession for form, and
     calls the notebooks "a record of a great artist's mind at
     work."

6   AUDEN, WYSTAN HUGH. "Address on Henry James by W. H. Auden,
     October 24, 1947." Grolier Club Gazette, 2 (February),
     208-25.
         The effect of James' expatriation is exaggerated, and
     he has had a greater influence on English than American
     writers. Considers James an example of personal integrity,
     who did not give in to the temptation to popularize his
     work. He offered proper answers to the obligation of the
     artist in pursuing his vocation: "He must become inter-
     national, and he must stand alone."

7   BRODIN, PIERRE. "Presence de Henry James," in Écrivains
     américains du xxe siècle. Paris: Horizons de France,
     pp. 173-84. (French)
         Discusses James' reputation in America, the recent re-
     vival, and why he occupied a relatively unimportant place
     as a writer among his own people. Considers the two prob-
     lems, "a double paradox," that of his expatriation, and
     the fact that, after 1900, he wrote novels of analysis in
     which direct narration was renounced, and the public could
     not understand his works. Suggests that James was ahead
     of his time technically, points out differences between
     his psychological approach and that of the American natu-
     ralists, and mentions the progress of the international
     spirit in literature in America. "Like Proust, James is
     the painter of worlds and of women. Like him, he studies
     the most subtle nuances, the subtleties, the scruples, the
     secret thoughts, the unexpressed or only partially con-
     scious passions." Contemporary critics see James as a

1947

"painter of manners and admirable moralist, an intelligent
and powerful critic of his country and his time."

8   BROOKS, VAN WYCK. "Exodus to Europe: New York," in The
    Times of Melville and Whitman. New York: E. P. Dutton and
    Co., pp. 310-12.
       Reference to James in discussion of expatriation of
    artists.

9   CRANKSHAW, EDWARD. "James the Obscured." National Review,
    129 (July), 73-77.
       Critical appraisal of James has been "completely non-
    sensical," and the most recent examinations propagate the
    "legend of obscurity which surrounds the stories and the
    man," thereby deterring readers. The only way to counter-
    act the obscurity is to turn to James himself, beginning
    first with the letters which give an idea of the man be-
    hind the artist, and then to the novels.

10 EDEL, LEON. "Introduction," in The Other House. Edited by
    Leon Edel. London: Shenval Press, pp. vii-xxi.
       Supplies bibliographical and background information on
    the play-turned-novel-turned-play, the neglect of which is
    surprising since "it is unique in the great body of James's
    work." Considers influence of Ibsen on the portrayal of
    Rose Armiger and other elements of the drama. Reviewed:
    Rosemary Paris, Furioso, 4 (Winter 1949), 82-84; Ernest
    Jones, Nation, 167 (4 December 1948), 643; Ben R. Redman,
    Saturday Review of Literature, 31 (18 September 1948), 32.

11 FADIMAN, CLIFTON. "Address on Henry James by Clifton Fadiman,
    November 21, 1946." Grolier Club Gazette, 2 (February),
    227-51.
       Questions what is permanent about James to provoke new
    interest and study, and describes him as "one expression
    of everything which is opposed to our time," with his in-
    terest in the individual, in relationships, in creation
    rather than destruction and technology. Concludes that
    James' novels will survive because his are truly created
    characters, projected rather than sold, as are those of
    modern writers.

12 FARRELL, JAMES T. "Literature and Morality: A Crucial Ques-
    tion of Our Times," in Literature and Morality, New York:
    World Publishing Co., Vanguard Press, pp. 6-7.
       Notes James' role in bringing "the problems of litera-
    ture and morality" to public attention, and contrasts
    James and Tolstoi as moralists.

1947

13 GEISMAR, MAXWELL. The Last of the Provincials: The American Novel, 1915-1925. London: Secker and Warburg, passim.
Notes influence of James and his school on Fitzgerald's and Cather's use of the "sensitive observer."

14 GREENE, GRAHAM. "Introduction," in The Portrait of a Lady. Edited by Graham Greene. World Classics Double Volume. London: Oxford University Press, pp. v-xi.
Compares plots and heroines of The Portrait of a Lady and The Wings of the Dove. James' primary interest in both is with "the idea of treachery, the 'Judas complex.'" Reprinted: 1951.B31.

15 THE GROLIER CLUB. One Hundred Influential American Books Printed Before 1900: Exhibition at the Grolier Club. April 18-June 16, 1947, pp. 10, 115-16. Reprinted: New York: Kraus Reprint Corporation, 1967.
In an exhibition of works "chosen on the basis of their influence on the life and culture of the people," includes James' The Portrait of a Lady in first English and American editions. The book "supplies laymen with a representative sample of the work of this novelists' novelist."

16 GURKO, LEO. "Chicago, Yoknapatawpha County, and Points South," in The Angry Decade. New York: Dodd, Mead and Co., pp. 129-32.
In both The Golden Bowl and Absalom, Absalom, "the style is complex, and used as a mesh to strain not so much events as certain rarefied states of consciousness down to their molecular components."

17 HACKETT, FRANCIS. "Henry James Revisited," in On Judging Books: In General and in Particular. New York: The John Day Co., pp. 247-49.
Reviews Matthiessen's Henry James: The Major Phase (1944.A2) and Rahv's The Great Short Novels of Henry James (1944.B14). Characterizes James' work as "the drama of human dignity...restricted...to a society that he could ideally control." Originally a New York Times essay, 1944.

18 HEILMAN, R. B. "The Freudian Reading of The Turn of the Screw." Modern Language Notes, 62 (November), 433-35.
The Freudian reading of The Turn of the Screw, propounded by Edmund Wilson (1934.B37) and Edna Kenton (1924.B10), contradicts both the story and the Preface, both internal and external evidence. Cites evidence against assertion that the ghosts are seen only by the

1947

governess and that Miles' dismissal from school is insignificant, and points out other inadequacies of the Freudian point of view, especially the irreconcilable unqualified
initial picture of the governess. "...A great deal of unnecessary mystery has been made of the apparent ambiguity
of the story.... Most of it is a by-product of James's
method: his indirection; his refusal, in his fear of
anticlimax, to define the evil; his rigid adherence to
point of view."

19 LEAVIS, F. R. "The Appreciation of Henry James." Scrutiny,
    14 (Spring), 229-37.
        Refutes Matthiessens' view of the later phase as "major"
    (see 1944.A2), and suggests that the last three completed
    novels display "general feebleness...as to suggest senil-
    ity" due to "an over-developed technical preoccupation...."

20 LEAVIS, F. R. "Henry James's First Novel." Scrutiny, 14
    (Spring), 295-301.
        Analyzes the strengths and weaknesses of Roderick Hud-
    son, "an extremely interesting and extremely distinguished
    novel," remarkable for its maturity and presenting complex
    attitudes towards the international theme. Notes James'
    debt to Dickens. Although minor, the novel is "a most
    interesting success."

21 LEAVIS, QUEENIE D. "Henry James: The Stories." Scrutiny,
    14 (Spring), 223-29.
        In a review of Garnett's edition of short stories (see
    1946.B13), questions whether the reader unfamiliar with
    James will be motivated by Garnett's selection to explore
    James further. Only three stories are among the best of
    James' work, and Garnett misinterprets and misrepresents
    James and his development, giving false views of the na-
    ture of his art.

22 LEAVIS, QUEENIE D. "The Institution of Henry James."
    Scrutiny, 15 (December), 68-74.
        Comments on Dupee's The Question of Henry James
    (1945.A1), in which the interest is "less intrinsic than
    historical."

23 LEVY, B. M. "'The High Bid' and the Forbes-Robertsons."
    College English, 8 (March), 284-92.
        An examination of the play in different stages of
    development from a one-act play, Summersoft, to a sub-
    stantial short story, Covering End, and ultimately to a

three-act comedy of manners, The High Bid, "is...curiously
revealing of its author's mind."

24   LIDDELL, ROBERT. "The Expansion of Situation: 'The Spoils
      of Poynton,'" in A Treatise on the Novel. London: Jona-
      than Cape, pp. 72-76. Reprinted: 1963.
          "Henry James made his great novels out of little scraps
      of other people's talk." Discusses James' development of
      The Spoils of Poynton from a dinner table conversation.

25   LIDDELL, ROBERT. "The 'Hallucination' Theory of The Turn of
      the Screw," in A Treatise on the Novel. London: Jonathan
      Cape, pp. 138-45. Reprinted: 1963.
          Refutes Wilson's theory (see 1934.B37) as "perverted
      ingenuity" on the basis of external and internal evidence,
      and suggests that the governess displays "balance and
      courage in the most frightful circumstances. It is from
      literary antecedents, possibly Jane Eyre, and not from
      James' or the governess' abnormal psychology that the re-
      lationship between her and the ghosts arises." Reprinted:
      in Robert Liddell on the Novel. Chicago: University of
      Chicago Press, 1969, pp. 128-35.

26   LIDDELL, ROBERT. "The Novelist as Mystic: 'The Song of Henry
      James,'" in A Treatise on the Novel. London: Jonathan
      Cape, pp. 87-89. Reprinted: 1963.
          After giving William James' definition of mystical ex-
      perience, examines a Henry James letter, a "colloquy with
      his genius," which "throws some light on the mystical na-
      ture of the creative act." Reprinted: in Robert Liddell
      on the Novel. Chicago: University of Chicago Press,
      1969, pp. 77-79.

27   LIDDELL, ROBERT. "A Plot Successfully Deduced from One Epi-
      sode: 'The Ambassadors,'" in A Treatise on the Novel.
      London: Jonathan Cape, pp. 82-84. Reprinted: 1963.
          The Ambassadors springs from a single incident, from
      which James inquired, "'What would be the story to which
      it would most inevitably form the centre?'"

28   LIDDELL, ROBERT. "The Upholstery of Galsworthy, Contrasted
      with Henry James," in A Treatise on the Novel. London:
      Jonathan Cape, pp. 125-27. Reprinted: 1963.
          Illustrates Galsworthy's method of distinguishing char-
      acter in The Forsyte Saga, "not looking...at the external
      world through the eyes of the soul," in contrast to
      James' method in The Spoils of Poynton, in which he gives
      little detailed description of the furnishings of Poynton.

1947

29   LUBBOCK, PERCY. <u>Portrait of Edith Wharton</u>. New York: D.
     Appleton Century Co., passim. Reprinted: New York:
     Kraus Reprint Corporation, 1969.
        Recalls James' relationship with Edith, as "the master
     of her art," host during her visits at Lamb House, and a
     visitor with Howard Sturgis at Queen's Acre. "She was his
     equal friend, and the only woman of whom this could be
     said."

30   McLUHAN, H. M. "The Southern Quality," in <u>Southern Vanguard</u>.
     Edited by Allen Tate. New York: Prentice-Hall, pp. 100-
     21.
        James "belonged to a society suffering from the last
     stages of elephantiasis of the will," and dealt only with
     the fringes of this society, "dominant women and effete
     men." Discusses qualities present in contemporary southern
     writing absent in a writer like James, and refers to James'
     view of the South.

31   MATTHIESSEN, F. O. "Introduction," in <u>The American Novels and
     Stories of Henry James</u>. Edited by F. O. Matthiessen. New
     York: Alfred A. Knopf, pp. vii-xxvii.
        The stories of James which have America as their locale
     form a clear, compact "cross-section" of his canon. They
     provide examples of the evolution of James' style, reveal
     his attitude on the prospects for American fiction, and
     present opinions on the manners of the time. Surveys the
     works included in the volume and discusses characteristic
     themes. Reviewed: Philip Rahv, <u>New York Times Book Re-
     view</u> (2 March 1947), p. 32; Ben R. Redman, <u>Saturday Review
     of Literature</u>, 30 (12 April 1947), 66.

32   MATTHIESSEN, F. O. and KENNETH MURDOCK. "Introduction," in
     <u>The Notebooks of Henry James</u>. Edited by F. O. Matthiessen
     and Kenneth Murdock. New York: Oxford University Press,
     pp. ix-xx. Reprinted: New York: George Braziller, 1955,
     1961.
        After 1878, James either discusses or mentions all the
     completed novels and the majority of the short stories in
     his notebooks. Surveys the scope and contents of these
     journals, discusses James' activities and literary output
     at the time he began them, and considers the uses of the
     notebooks throughout the rest of his career. Notes his
     concern with technical problems, such as progression into
     central consciousness and dramatic dialogue. The note-
     books stand as an "informal companion volume to the pre-
     faces." Also reprints three related documents, including
     a sketch for <u>The Sense of the Past</u>, a project for <u>The</u>

Ambassadors, and a "Chronological List of James's Chief Publications." Reviewed: Clarence Gohdes, American Literature, 20 (March 1948), 64-65; Richard P. Blackmur, Kenyon Review, 10 (Spring 1948), 313-17; F. W. Dupee, Nation, 165 (20 December 1947), 685; Newton Arvin, New England Quarterly, 21 (March 1948), 110-11; William Troy, Partisan Review, 15 (March 1948), 377-79; Morris Roberts, Sewanee Review, 56 (Summer 1948), 510-14.

33 MAUROIS, ANDRÉ. "Écrivains américains." Revue de Paris, 54 (April), 9-24.
    Reprint of 1945.B35.

34 MORRIS, LLOYD R. "Melancholy of the Masters," in Postscript to Yesterday. New York: Random House, pp. 89-96.
    James visited America in 1904 "in quest of exotic experience...." Describes his observations of and reactions to his homeland and its repudiation of past, obsession for money, lack of a sustaining social order, and vast public indifference.

35 NORMAN, SYLVA (Mrs. Edmund C. Blunden). "Before the Dissolution." Fortnightly Review, NS 161 (May), 380-82.
    James' short stories are reminiscent of his longer fictional works and display a parallel development.

36 OLIVER, CLINTON FORREST. "Henry James as a Social Critic." Antioch Review, 7 (June), 243-58.
    Both The Bostonians and The Princess Casamassima show complete and open treatment of social themes, the former displaying the theme of reform, the latter dealing with the theme of revolution. Having rejected these two alternative solutions of the social and cultural problems, James reached a creative impasse. Hence, these were the last of his novels in the 19th century realistic tradition. He ultimately concluded "that the moral renovation of the private individual through the civilizing agency of art must lie at the center of any hope for a better world."

37 PUTT, S. GORLEY. "A Henry James Jubilee: II." Cornhill Magazine, 162 (Spring), 284-97.
    The Bostonians resembles The Princess Casamassima in the struggle between political concepts and private inclinations. Describes Olive Chancellor as "one of the great tragic heroines of fiction...," a victim of complex self-delusion. The point of both novels is that one cannot contribute to the solution of political or societal problems until one has come to terms with the immediate social environment. See 1946.B24.

1947

38   RAHV, PHILIP. "Henry James: The Banquet of Initiation," in
     <u>Discovery of Europe: The Story of American Experience in</u>
     <u>the Old World</u>. Boston: Houghton Mifflin Co., Riverside
     Press, pp. 269-71.
         James depicted the collision of New World innocence and
     Old World experience. "...Chief of our paleface novelists,
     he converted the trans-Atlantic relation into a subject of
     major fiction."

39   ROBERTS, MORRIS. "Henry James's Final Period." <u>Yale Review</u>,
     NS 37 (Autumn), 60-67.
         James' is "an art of compression" and abbreviated ideas,
     and his late fiction pictures a corrupted world from a
     moralist's rather than a psychologist's point of view.
     Considers some misleading ideas about the difficulty of
     James' works, which are elaborate but wholly intelligible,
     discusses <u>The Sacred Fount</u> as an "example of sheer sus-
     pense," and describes James' characters as "lovers of
     life."

40   ROBINSON, EDWIN ARLINGTON. <u>Untriangulated Stars. Letters of</u>
     <u>E. A. Robinson to Harry de Forest Smith, 1890-1905</u>. Edited
     by Denham Sutcliffe. Cambridge, Mass.: Harvard University
     Press, p. 239.
         In a letter of 1896, states that after reading "The
     Lesson of the Master" he concluded that "H. J. is a geni-
     us."

41   RODITI, EDOUARD. "Fiction as Allegory," in <u>Oscar Wilde</u>.
     Norfolk, Conn.: New Directions Press, pp. 99-124.
         Comparison and contrast of James' and Wilde's handling
     of the theme of art and the artist in "The Model Million-
     aire" and "The Real Thing," and "The Portrait of Mr. W. H."
     and "The Figure in the Carpet."

42   SMITH, F. E. "'The Beast in the Jungle': The Limits of
     Method." <u>Perspective</u>, 1 (Autumn), 33-40.
         James' concern with method was hazardous, and in "The
     Beast in the Jungle" technique hampers rather than en-
     riches theme of the changing relationship between Marcher
     and May Bartram. Nevertheless, the story is a "fascinat-
     ing study in irony."

43   SNELL, GEORGE. "Henry James: Life Refracted by Tempera-
     ment," in <u>The Shapers of American Fiction, 1798-1947</u>. New
     York: E. P. Dutton and Co., pp. 129-40. Reprinted: New
     York: Cooper Square Publishers, 1961.

1947

James' tragic theme, traceable to Hawthorne, is that
"the good life is the inner life; but those who live it
cannot compete with the 'animal' people, before whom they
eventually go down in defeat." The significance of his
later works is a result of their moral level, in spite of
near-unreadability. "...James has in him a strong element
of the feminine principle. Life without action interests
him inordinately."

44 STEIN, GERTRUDE. "Henry James," in Four in America. New
    Haven: Yale University Press, pp. 119-59. Reprinted:
    Freeport, N.Y.: Books for Libraries Press, 1969.
        A "Steinish" discussion, divided into "Duet," Vols. II-
    XXIV, which considers an artist's attachment to what he is
    saying, the sense of being connected to it. You may write
    what you are writing, or what you are going to be writing.
    James "saw he could write both ways at once which he
    did...," being a "general." Impressionistic ramblings
    about James' name and artistic identity.

45 SWAN, MICHAEL. "Note to the Present Edition," in What Maisie
    Knew. Chiltern Library, No. 9. London: John Lehmann,
    n.p.
        Mentions James' "air-tight structures" and "mastery of
    fundamental statement" gained from his theatrical experi-
    ence. In What Maisie Knew, James attempted "thorough
    examination of a small thing."

46 UZZELL, THOMAS H. "Appendix: The Theories of James, Wharton,
    and Glasgow," in The Technique of the Novel. New York:
    J. B. Lippincott Co., pp. 276-88.
        James' pronouncements on fictional method are more val-
    uable to him than to other writers. Singles out theories
    of viewpoint and indirect approach as "devices which...
    have been accepted without examination by writers and
    critics."

47 WALDOCK, A. J. A. "Mr. Edmund Wilson and The Turn of the
    Screw." Modern Language Notes, 62 (May), 331-34.
        Rebuttal of Wilson's theory (1934.B37) as untenable
    both on general grounds and in view of details of The Turn
    of the Screw. "How did the governess succeed in project-
    ing on vacancy, out of her subconscious mind, a perfectly
    precise, point-by-point image of a man, then dead, whom
    she had never seen in her life and never heard of?" Re-
    printed: in Gerald Willen, ed. A Casebook on "The Turn
    of the Screw," pp. 171-73.

141

1947

48   WERTHAM, FREDERIC. "Henry James' 'The Beast in the Jungle,'"
      in The World Within: Fiction Illuminating Neuroses of Our
      Time. Edited by Mary L. Aswell. New York: McGraw-Hill,
      pp. 105, 160-61.
           "The Beast in the Jungle" is an almost archetypal study
      of the neurotic, and "the best story ever written about
      neurosis." Analyzes the tale, and interprets the Beast as
      "an abstraction derived from the reality which is the
      Jungle of his [Marcher's] unconscious."

49   WILSON, EDMUND. "New Documents on the Jameses." New Yorker,
      23 (13 December), 119-25.
           The importance of James' notebooks (1947.B32) is in
      the "revelation...of Henry James's attitude toward his
      work and his method of producing his novels," although they
      show few emotions related to personal associations.

50   WINTERS, YVOR. "Maule's Well: or Henry James and the Rela-
      tion of Morals to Manners," in In Defense of Reason.
      University of Denver Press, pp. 300-43.
           Reprint of 1937.B16.

1948 A BOOKS

1   ANDREAS, OSBORN. Henry James and the Expanding Horizon: A
      Study of the Meaning and Basic Themes of James's Fiction.
      Seattle: University of Washington Press, 194 pp. Re-
      printed: 1953.
           An examination of James' themes informed by the princi-
      ple that he was a "great humanist" and the "novelist of
      consciousness," whose fiction attempts to define the most
      conscious person, to portray the "sense of being alive."
      Considers in detail nine themes prevalent in James' works,
      including the effect of emotional cannibalism, skepticism
      about the value of personal love, the sense of the past,
      conflict between values, the international theme and the
      mystery of personal identity. Concludes that James recog-
      nized "that sensitivity to other persons expands the con-
      sciousness," and suggests that "James makes a luminous
      addition to our powers of awareness." Reviewed: Leon
      Edel, American Literature, 21 (March 1949-January 1950),
      362-63; John Lucas, Furioso, 4 (Spring 1949), 63-67;
      Stanley Edgar Hyman, Hudson Review, 2 (Winter 1950), 606-
      607; Leon Edel, New England Quarterly, 23 (June 1950),
      245-49; Morris Roberts, Sewanee Review, 57 (Summer 1949),
      521-25.

2 MILANO, PAOLO. <u>Henry James, o il proscritto voluntario</u>.
Preface by Giorgio Monicelli. Milan: Arnoldo Mondador
Editore, 170 pp. (Italian)
Preface provides a biographical sketch and recreation of
James' writing routine towards the end of his life. Milano
views James as "a voluntary exile," who found repugnant any
direct contact with the outside world, a characteristic
which influenced his portrayal of characters, who lack the
third dimension of "reality," and which caused his desper-
ate attempts to become a part of Europe he adored but did
not fully understand. Labels James the originator of modern psychological realism, who influenced Joyce, Stein,
Hemingway and Faulkner.

3 SMITH, JANET ADAM, ed. <u>Henry James and Robert Louis Steven-
son: A Record of Friendship and Criticism</u>. London:
Rupert Hart-Davis, 284 pp.
In introduction, restates ideas in 1936.B12. The vol-
ume includes James' "The Art of Fiction," Stevenson's
"A Humble Remonstrance," and over forty letters exchanged
between the two men. Reviewed: John Lucas, <u>Furioso</u>, 4
(Fall 1949), 93-100; Leon Edel, <u>New England Quarterly</u>, 23
(June 1950), 245-49; David Daiches, <u>New York Times Book
Review</u> (19 June 1949), p. 8.

1948 B SHORTER WRITINGS

1 ANON. "What Henry James Went Through." <u>Time</u>, 51 (3 May),
100, 102-103.
Terms James "the Winston Spencer Churchill of fiction,"
the "battered but undefeated champion" of novelists.
Nowell-Smith's compilation (<u>see</u> 1947.A2) is "as absorbing
as a good mystery story."

2 ANON. "Cher Maître and Mon Bon." <u>Times Literary Supplement</u>
(25 September), p. 540.
James reflected on the art of fiction rather than on
the raw material of fiction. Bemoans James' inability to
feel, to let himself go. He was "the scholar and the poet
of passive states of consciousness" who was unable to
penetrate the limits of "'mon bon,'" the self.

3 AUDEN, WYSTAN HUGH. "Henry James and the Artist in America."
<u>Harper's Magazine</u>, 197 (July), 36-40.
James provided an antidote to the contemporary denial
of free will and moral responsibility and consistently
displayed integrity both as an artist and as an individual.
Restatement of ideas in 1947.B6.

1948

4   BEACH, JOSEPH WARREN. "The Sacred and Solitary Refuge."
     <u>Furioso</u>, 3 (Winter), 23-37.
         With James' notebooks (1947.B32), we have the greatest
     source "for study of the imaginative process," a record of
     his struggle to be a successful stage writer and his com-
     pensations for failing, and bits of autobiography. Al-
     though James does not emphasize the truth about individuals
     in typical situations, he is a realist in his attempt to
     give "convincing particularity to all the circumstances of
     the story...." Concludes that it is a privilege "to be
     able to follow the stages of that mysterious process by
     which, out of the...stuff of life, is fashioned, by in-
     finite patient strokes of art, the ordered cosmos, the
     brave new world of the imagination." Reprinted: 1948.B5.

5   BEACH, JOSEPH WARREN. "The Witness of the Notebooks," in
     <u>Forms of Modern Fiction</u>. Edited by William Van O'Connor.
     Minneapolis: University of Minnesota Press, 46-60.
         Reprint of 1948.B4.

6   BLACKMUR, RICHARD P. "Henry James," in <u>Literary History of
     the United States</u>. Edited by Robert Spiller et al. Vol.
     2. New York: The Macmillan Co., pp. 1039-64. Reprinted:
     1953; third edition, revised, 1963.
         James deviated from the "literal record of a Howells
     and the philosophical naturalism of a Zola," and provided
     the "interregnum between the effective dominance of the old
     Christian-classical ideal through old European institutions
     and the rise to role of the succeeding ideal...." Details
     the struggle to realize "life as emotion and to create it
     as art," and the eventual recognition that "life had to be
     sacrificed to art." Isolates four periods of James' ca-
     reer; discusses the international theme, in which James
     "set the two kinds of society he knew against each other
     for balance and contrast and mutual criticism," and the
     theme of the artist and society; and analyzes the relation
     of form to substance in James' work. Generalizes that
     "James's work constitutes a great single anarchic rebellion
     against society...in the combined names of decency, inno-
     cence, candor, good will, and the passionate heroism of
     true vocation."

7   BOGAN, LOUISE. "The Portrait of New England." <u>Nation</u>, 161
     (1 December), 582-83.
         <u>The Bostonians</u>, because it was never rewritten, is "per-
     fect 'early James.'" Briefly analyzes characters, de-
     scribes background of the novel, terms the tone as one of
     "high comedy," and suggests that the work fills a gap in
     our native literature. Reprinted: 1955.B15.

1948

8   BRODIN, PIERRE. "Henry James," in <u>Les maitres de la littéra-</u>
    <u>ture américaine</u>. Paris: Horizons de France, pp. 353-444.
    (French)
        Includes a biocritical survey of James and his writing,
    with synopses of shorter works as well as major novels,
    discussion of James as a man, examination of James as a
    psychologist and artist, and presentation of critical
    views of his work. Adopts a perspective towards James
    based on his position as "the painter and the social moral-
    ist, who wished to be the Balzac of his time; the psychol-
    ogist, who broods over the tragedy of sensibility, of the
    domination of sensitive souls by strong souls; the artist,
    who has widened the scope of the novel, and, in his por-
    traits of writers and painters, has developed in delicate-
    ly shaded terms his conception of Art and the problems of
    the artist." Appends bibliography of critical works on
    James, pp. 489-491.

9   BURNHAM, DAVID. "Fiction is Art--Plus." <u>Commonweal</u>, 48
    (14 May), 106-109.
        Demonstrates James' study of writers is from the point
    of view of a fellow practitioner. "Nothing was simple to
    Henry James, no surface opaque," as exemplified in his
    criticism of authors like Balzac and Emerson. He called
    for the fusion of idea and form but also demanded moral
    content.

10 CANBY, HENRY SEIDEL. "The Return of Henry James." <u>Saturday</u>
    <u>Review of Literature</u>, 31 (24 January), 9-10, 34-35.
        Revival of interest in James can be accounted for by
    the following facts: (1) his style is no longer too dif-
    ficult for his readers; (2) he portrayed a timeless human
    situation; (3) his craft has caused renewed interest in
    his work; (4) his formula for fiction includes moral val-
    ues, omitted by other authors.

11 CHEW, SAMUEL C. "The Modern Novel," in <u>A Literary History of</u>
    <u>England</u>. Edited by Albert C. Baugh. New York: Appleton-
    Century-Crofts, pp. 1547-51.
        James is included in the survey of English literature
    because "he was, by temperament and taste, long residence,
    and passionate devotion to the country of his adoption, an
    Englishman," and because he "turned the course of the
    novel into new directions...." Biographical account with
    brief critical discussion of important works in the three
    phases of James' career.

1948

12   COWIE, ALEXANDER. "Henry James," in <u>The Rise of the American</u>
        <u>Novel</u>. New York: American Book Co., pp. 702-42. Re
        printed: 1951.
            James, who disputed the view of form and substance as
        separate in art, was one of the late nineteenth-century
        writers who attempted to correct the haphazard structure
        of the novel. Examines similarities between Hawthorne and
        James, for whom "the implications and inferences were the
        main thing...," and considers the critical controversy
        surrounding James' work, the argument against James as a
        man. Sketches literary career, with some discussion of
        individual works, and analyzes James' method. Concludes
        that "the 'day' of James bids fair to extend far into the
        future." Includes bibliography, pp. 861-62.

13   DUNBAR, VIOLA. "A Note on the Genesis of <u>Daisy Miller</u>."
        <u>Philological Quarterly</u>, 27 (April), 184-86.
            Two of James' travel sketches, "Swiss Notes" (<u>Nation</u>,
        1872), which mentions the novel <u>Paule Méré</u> where "spon-
        taneity passes for impropriety" resulting in the heroine's
        death, and "The After-Season at Rome" (<u>Nation</u>, 1873), de-
        scribing an afternoon James spent in a Protestant cemetery
        in Rome (where Daisy is also buried), help to explain the
        development of <u>Daisy Miller</u>. See 1950.B65.

14   DUNBAR, VIOLA. "A Source for <u>Roderick Hudson</u>." <u>Modern Lan-</u>
        <u>guage Notes</u>, 63 (May), 303-10.
            Suggests direct influence of Alexander Dumas <u>fils</u>'
        L'Affaire Clemenceau; mémoire de l'accusé, which James
        enthusiastically reviewed for <u>Nation</u>, October 11, 1866, on
        the plot, characters and ideas of <u>Roderick Hudson</u>.

15   EDEL, LEON. "The James Revival." <u>Atlantic Monthly</u>, 182
        (September), 96-98.
            Gives background of James' lack of public popularity,
        and remarks on the "semi-anonymity" resulting from his
        having destroyed many of his letters and papers. "...
        While our vision of the man has constantly been enlarged,
        it remains still out of focus since we lack those primary
        materials which would answer certain questions and clarify
        certain judgments" which are at present tentative.

16   FADIMAN, CLIFTON. "En kommentar till 'Europa.'" <u>Bonniers</u>
        <u>Litterära Magasin</u> (Stockholm), 17 (February), 99-100.
        (Swedish)
            Translation of 1945.B13.

17   FADIMAN, CLIFTON. "On James's 'The Great Good Place,'" in
      Readings for Liberal Education. Edited by L. G. Locke,
      W. Gibson and G. Arms. Vol. 2. New York: Holt, Rinehart
      and Winston, pp. 298-99.
          Reprint of 1945.B20.

18   FIEDLER, LESLIE A. "Adolescence and Maturity in the American
      Novel," in An End to Innocence: Essays on Culture and
      Politics. Boston: Beacon Press, pp. 196-97, 199-200.
          James taught that "a novel is not what its author says
      happened in it, but what is really rendered." Describes
      James, Faulkner and Melville as creating a tradition which
      "combines an overall moral maturity with a failure to
      achieve mature attitudes toward sex...."

19   FINCH, GEORGE A. "James as a Traveler," in Portraits of
      Places. New York: Lear Publishers, pp. 15-31.
          James' love of travel is associated with his desire to
      gather impressions, and he realized he could make more
      fiction out of his experiences in Europe, unless he ex-
      amined the underneath surface of American life, which he
      was unprepared to do. Travel sketches occupy a middle
      ground between the letters and fiction, demonstrating at-
      titudes similar to those of the letters but lacking their
      spontaneity and sharpness.

20   GREENE, GRAHAM. "Kensington to Samoa." New Statesman and
      Nation, 36 (27 November), 468.
          Review of Smith's work, 1948.A3. Examination of both
      sides of the correspondence between James and Robert Louis
      Stevenson illuminates their relationship. "James was
      capable of oriental courtesy to his inferiors, but the
      praise he gives to Stevenson has the directness and warmth
      of equality."

21   HEILMAN, R. B. "'The Turn of the Screw' as Poem." University
      of Kansas City Review, 14 (Summer), 277-89.
          An analysis of verbal and imagistic patterns in The
      Turn of the Screw suggests the theme of the tale is the
      "struggle of evil to possess the human soul," the subject
      being the dual nature of man expressed in broadly reli-
      gious, even Christian terms. The story shows the trans-
      formation from one extreme to the other, culminating in a
      kind of Black Easter, and is a "poem about evil." Re-
      printed: in William Van O'Connor, ed. The Forms of Mod-
      ern Fiction, pp. 211-28 (see 1948.B5); also in Gerald
      Willen, ed. A Casebook on "The Turn of the Screw,"
      pp. 174-88.

1948

22   HODGE, ALAN. "Note," in The Awkward Age. Edited by Alan
     Hodge. Novel Library. London: Hamish Hamilton, pp. vii-
     x.
          By the end of the nineteenth century, James was con-
     cerned with the "decay of European society" which he had
     previously admired. Discusses details of composition and
     publication of The Awkward Age, developed "with a welcome
     simplicity of expression."

23   JOHNSON, THOMAS H. "Henry James," in Literary History of the
     United States. Edited by Robert Spiller et al. Vol. 3.
     New York: The Macmillan Co., pp. 584-90. Reprinted:
     1953; third edition, revised, 1963.
          A bibliography which includes listings of "Separate
     Works," "Collected Works," "Edited Texts and Reprints,"
     "Biography and Criticism," "Primary Sources," and "Bibli-
     ography." Supplement, 1959.B59.

24   JONES, HOWARD MUMFORD. The Theory of American Literature.
     Ithaca, N.Y.: Cornell University Press, passim.
          Passing references to James' view of America as lacking
     material for fiction.

25   LEAVIS, F. R. "Henry James and the Function of Criticism."
     Scrutiny, 15 (Spring), 98-104.
          Doubts that James identified himself so completely with
     his father's system as Quentin Anderson suggests (see
     1947.B1). Anderson's work "doesn't...deal satisfactorily
     with the critical bearings of the fact he establishes" and
     accepts value judgments and conventional consensus that
     rate the later novels so highly. James' greatest works
     are tragic, and at odds with the essential optimism of his
     father. Reprinted: 1952.B31.

26   LEAVIS, F. R. "The Novel as Dramatic Poem (III): The Euro-
     peans." Scrutiny, 15 (Summer), 209-21.
          The Europeans is a moral fable which investigates the
     standards of civilization on a comparative basis. Felix
     represents the less critical, more appreciative view of
     America, "a person of radical responsibility" and with
     "the virtues of artistic temperament." Eugenia suggests
     the more positively and characteristically European hier-
     archical order and status. Analyzes the characters in the
     novel as they embody different cultural ideals.

27   LEAVIS, F. R. "'The Portrait of a Lady' Reprinted." Scru-
     tiny, 15 (Summer), 235-41.

The Portrait of a Lady and Daniel Deronda provide an
"illuminating instance of 'influence'" and reveal the
central line of the English novelistic tradition. The
weakness in James' novel is that he admires Isabel too
much to treat her with a clear, consistent irony. See
1946.B18.

28   LEAVIS, F. R. "The Great Tradition" and "Henry James," in
     The Great Tradition: George Eliot, Henry James, Joseph
     Conrad. London: Chatto and Windus, pp. 1-27, 126-72.
     Reprinted: Garden City, N.Y.: Doubleday and Co., 1954;
     Harmondsworth: Penguin Books, 1962.
        In introductory chapter, explains that James, along with
     Jane Austen, George Eliot and Joseph Conrad, was a novel-
     ist who "not only changed the possibilities of the art"
     but promoted "human awareness." All were concerned with
     technical form and a moral tradition. Labels James a
     "poet-novelist" and The Portrait of a Lady one of the great
     novels of the language. Points out Dickens' influence on
     Roderick Hudson, examines the relationship of feminism to
     the conscience in The Bostonians, analyzes the characters
     as revealing discrimination in values in The Europeans,
     and discusses the success of James' characters in The Por-
     trait of a Lady. Addresses the problem of what went wrong
     in James' later period. Restatement of ideas in 1946.B18;
     1947.B19-20; 1948.B26.

29   LIND, S. E. "Henry James." Times Literary Supplement
     (27 November), p. 667.
        Suggests a reexamination of James' aims in the notebooks
     (with reference to 1947.B32), since James distinguished
     between "journal" and "notebook," as revealed in his review
     of Hawthorne's French and Italian Notebooks. Three of
     James' notebooks are, in fact, journals, containing trivial
     notations.

30   MARCHAND, LESLIE. "The Symington Collection." Journal of
     Rutgers University Library, 12 (December), 1-15.
        Description of the Symington collection of manuscripts
     and books of late nineteenth-century English writers, in-
     cluding a few manuscript letters by James, housed at Rut-
     gers University Library.

31   MATTHIESSEN, F. O. "Salzburg: July and August," in From the
     Heart of Europe. New York: Oxford University Press,
     pp. 44-46.
        James and Dreiser represent "pivotal contrast of our
     modern literature." Describes The Portrait of a Lady as

1948

one of the most original examinations of "the American's
discovery of Europe," and analyzes James' appeal for the
modern reader.

32 MILLER, BETTY. "Miss Savage and Miss Bartram." Nineteenth
Century, 144 (November), 285-92.
Relationship between John Marcher and Miss Bartram in
"The Beast in the Jungle" in many ways parallels that of
Samuel Butler and his friend, Miss Savage, as revealed in
correspondence. Although James was not necessarily familiar with Butler's private life, "it is characteristic of
the writer of genius that he will describe...the lives and
circumstances of people wholly unknown to him."

33 NEIDER, CHARLES. "Introduction," in Short Novels of the Masters. New York: Rinehart and Co., pp. 11-17.
James is termed a "feminine" artist in the line of
Sterne, Thackeray and Hawthorne, whose chief attributes
are "subtlety of insight and nuance, a high intellectual
quality, and remoteness from the cruder if more basic concerns of life." Discusses the motivation for James' flight
from fact: "One senses the latent homosexuality in almost
all of James's work."

34 O'FAOLAIN, SEAN. The Short Story. London: William Collins'
Sons and Co., pp. 162-64, 186-89.
James' stories demonstrate "how much less important
character is than incident...." Illustrates with "The
Real Thing" and "The Pupil" the idea that "construction
plus situation" offers all that is needed for plot, and
describes "The Beast in the Jungle" as a squandering of
words.

35 PARKES, HENRY BAMFORD. "The James Brothers." Sewanee Review,
56 (Spring), 323-28.
Considers uniqueness of James family in displaying creative genius in several family members, and suggests that
William and Henry were "alike in that the fundamental pre-
mise of all their activity was an acceptance of the moral
freedom of the individual human being," which William ex-
plored in philosophical terms and Henry in aesthetic.
Analyzes brothers as proponents of individualism, and
concludes that "the Jamesian view of life is of central
importance to the culture of our time."

36 PRITCHETT, V. S. "Books in General." New Statesman and Nation, 36 (2 October), 285.

James' notebooks (1947.B32) "belong to the working
kind" and demonstrate the author's observant nature. "They
confirm that the word was totally his form of life, as if
sentences rather than blood ran in his veins." Reprinted:
1953.B49.

37   PUTT, S. GORLEY. "The Passionate Pilgrim: An Aspect of
     Henry James." The Wind and the Rain (London), pp. 227-37.
        Examines motives behind James' passionate pilgrimage,
     discusses the presentation of England in "The [sic] Pas-
     sionate Pilgrim" and compares it with that in "Flicker-
     bridge," and notes the increasing detachment in character-
     ization. James' "unfortunate preoccupation" with the in-
     ternational theme was an attempt to "'externalize'" his
     own personal reaction to defection. "A mixed attitude is
     more apparent in later work, as that self-suspicion seems
     to grow and to shadow Henry James' descriptive style with
     doubt."

38   READ, HERBERT. "Introduction," in The Wings of the Dove.
     Edited by Herbert Read. Century Library, No. 7. London:
     Eyre and Spottiswoode, pp. v-vii.
        James' evolution, a reaching after perfection, is rep-
     resented in The Ambassadors and The Golden Bowl. In The
     Wings of the Dove, a "moral tragedy" though not in the
     classical manner, Kate Croy represents "the moral ambiguity
     of a diplomatic approach to life," a typical Jamesian
     theme.

39   ROBERTS, MORRIS. "Introduction," in Henry James: The Art of
     Fiction and Other Essays. Edited by Morris Roberts. New
     York: Oxford University Press, pp. ix-xxiv.
        Examination of James' approach to the art of the novel,
     with reference to his views on other artists. The reviews
     "are often wrong, badly focused, or mistakenly emphasized,
     but they are never stupid or dull." Discusses James' re-
     lationship to French writers. Despite his appreciation
     for them, "James's appetite for realism was clearly limit-
     ed." Reviewed: Willard Thorp, New England Quarterly, 21
     (September 1948), 415-16; F. W. Dupee, New York Times Book
     Review (23 May 1948), p. 33; B. R. Redman, Saturday Review
     of Literature, 31 (15 May 1948), 29; John L. Stewart,
     Sewanee Review, 57 (Winter 1949), 135-41.

40   RODITI, EDOUARD. "Oscar Wilde and Henry James." University
     of Kansas City Review, 15 (Autumn), 52-56.
        Wilde's interest in James and appreciation of his im-
     portance represent "the attitude of one distinguished

1948

        hierophant of Beauty towards another." Cites remarks of
Wilde concerning James before 1890, when the two shared
many of the same ideas and frequented much the same artistic and intellectual circles. Notes examples of the
changes in James' Aestheticism during the evolution of a
"doctrine of ethics and aesthetics of his own."

41   SACKVILLE-WEST, EDWARD. "Books in General." New Statesman
       and Nation, 35 (28 February), 177-78.
          Nowell-Smith (see 1947.A2) has helped resolve "The
question of Henry James himself," which is "quite as complicated as that of his work...." Discusses the "feminine
streak" in James, and characterizes The Spoils of Poynton
as "a tragi-comic nouvelle" which shows James "on the
threshold of the Impressionist painter's technique."

42   SASSOON, SIEGFRIED. Meredith. New York: The Viking Press,
       pp. 232-33 and passim.
          James' visits with Meredith "were more in the nature of
witnessing a performance than occasions for reciprocal
communication." Presents Meredith's views of James as revealed to an American journalist.

43   SPECKER, HEIDI. "The Change of Emphasis in the Criticism of
       Henry James." English Studies (Amsterdam), 29 (April),
       33-47.
          A survey of critical trends which points out the con-
tradictory nature of Jamesian criticism. Suggests biases
which influenced the judgments of writers like Van Wyck
Brooks, Vernon Parrington, T. S. Eliot. Recent criticism
is raising questions about the psychological and technical
issues and reexamining James' view of the artist in society, which indicates increasing attention to and interest
in his writing. Reviews prominent critical opinions on
expatriation; summarizes a group of studies dealing with
James' craftsmanship.

44   STEEGMULLER, FRANCIS. "Flaubert's Sundays: Maupassant and
       Henry James." Cornhill Magazine, 163 (Spring), 124-30.
          Cites evidence that James' association with Maupassant,
which began at Flaubert's Sunday gatherings 1875-1876,
may have continued after that winter. Concludes that
whether or not there were further meetings, James exhibits
the influence, although not obvious, of Maupassant on his
own story-telling.

45 STOLL, E. E. "Symbolism in Coleridge." <u>Publications of the</u>
    <u>Modern Language Association</u>, 63 (March), 229-33.
        Sees tendency to look for "traps" in <u>The Turn of the</u>
    <u>Screw</u> (as do Kenton [1924.B10] and Wilson [1934.B37]) as
    confounding art and reality, a misreading of the Preface
    discredited by evidence in the tale.

46 SWAN, MICHAEL. "Introduction," in <u>Henry James: Ten Short</u>
    <u>Stories</u>. Edited by Michael Swan. Chiltern Library. Lon-
    don: John Lehmann, pp. 5-14.
        Although James' early novels display naturalistic plots
    and ideas, in the short stories, the naturalistic treat-
    ment is often at odds with the content. James' develop-
    ment was a "gradual resolution of this split." Describes
    James as an autobiographical fiction writer who made ref-
    erence to the events of his mental life, and notes exam-
    ples in the stories.

47 SWINNERTON, FRANK. "Introduction," in <u>The Ambassadors</u>.
    Edited by Frank Swinnerton. Everyman's Library. New
    York: E. P. Dutton and Co., pp. v-xii.
        <u>The Ambassadors is</u> the "fine flower" of the later meth-
    od, James at "his most distinguished, penetrating, and
    amusing." Views James as a romantic dramatist, whose vi-
    sion was ironic.

48 THOMPSON, FRANCIS. Review of <u>The American Scene,</u> in <u>Literary</u>
    <u>Criticism</u>. Edited by T. L. Connolly. New York: E. P.
    Dutton and Co., pp. 301-306.
        <u>The American Scene</u> possesses "no oasis in the level,
    unbroken expanse of Jacobean style," and the book is an
    "elaborated impression of America as it vibrates on the
    very conscious consciousness of Mr. Henry James...."
    Originally appeared in <u>Athenaeum</u>, 9 March 1907.

49 THOMPSON, FRANCIS. Review of <u>The Golden Bowl</u>, in <u>Literary</u>
    <u>Criticism</u>. Edited by T. L. Connolly. New York: E. P.
    Dutton and Co., pp. 298-301.
        In <u>The Golden Bowl</u>, "evolution of character" is fore-
    most, and James is outstanding at presenting nuances of
    psychological feeling. Originally appeared in <u>Academy</u>,
    11 February 1905.

50 TRILLING, LIONEL. "<u>The Princess Casamassima</u>: An Introductory
    Essay." <u>Horizon</u>, 17 (April), 267-95.
        Hyacinth is an example of a literary motif, The Young
    Man from the Provinces, and <u>The Princess Casamassima</u>,
    despite James' use of romantic elements, possesses striking

1948

literary accuracy as evident from comparison with the nature of radicals and the growth of Anarchism during James'
time. Views Hyacinth as an expression of James' personal
fantasy, of his dispute with his family concerning the
claims of art and moral action, and analyzes the meaning
of Hyacinth's suicide as an action which acknowledges both
his parents. The "informing spirit" of the novel is James'
"moral realism." Reprinted: 1948.B51; 1950.B71; in Naomi
Lebowitz, ed. Discussions of Henry James. Boston: D. C.
Heath and Co., 1962, pp. 31-48.

51 TRILLING, LIONEL. "Introduction," in The Princess Casamassima.
New York: The Macmillan Co., pp. v-xlviii.
Reprint of 1948.B50. Reviewed: Robert W. Flint, Hudson
Review, 1 (Autumn 1948), 418-20; Richard Chase, Nation, 166
(19 June 1948), 695; B. R. Redman, Saturday Review of Lit-
erature, 31 (12 June 1948), 25.

52 WADE, ALLAN. "Introduction," in The Scenic Art, Notes on
Acting and the Drama, 1872-1901. By Henry James. Edited
by Allan Wade. New Brunswick, N.J.: Rutgers University
Press, pp. xi-xxv. Reprinted: New York: Hill and Wang,
1957.
A reprint of 1943.B54 prefatory to essays and notes re-
lating to the drama which James contributed to newspapers
and periodicals, 1872-1901. Reviewed: Harold Clurman,
New Republic, 118 (28 June 1948), 26; A. S. Downer, New
York Times Book Review (23 May 1948), p. 33; H. S. Canby,
Saturday Review of Literature, 31 (29 May 1948), 15.

53 WAGENKNECHT, EDWARD. "Our Contemporary Henry James." College
English, 10 (December), 123-32.
James, the founder of the psychological novel, composed
from the point of view of an observer rather than a participant. Discusses values in James' works, and describes
him as the novelist of experience imaginatively apprehended.
See 1952.B65.

54 WARREN, AUSTIN. "Henry James: Symbolic Imagery in the Later
Novels," in Rage for Order: Essays in Criticism. Chicago:
University of Chicago Press, 142-61. Reprinted: 1959.
Reprint of 1943.B55.

55 WEBER, C. J. "A Unique Henry James Item." Colby Library
Quarterly, 2 (August), 123.

1949

Bibliographic description of a printing of "The Point of
View," published in The Century Magazine in 1882, which
takes precedence over the five subsequent publications of
the short story between 1883 and 1921.

56   WILSON, EDMUND. "The Ambiguity of Henry James," in Criticism:
     The Foundations of Modern Literary Judgment. Edited by
     Mark Schorer, Josephine Miles and Gordon McKenzie. New
     York: Harcourt, Brace and Co., pp. 147-62.
     Reprint of 1934.B37.

57   WILSON, EDMUND. "The Ambiguity of Henry James," in The Triple
     Thinkers: Ten Essays on Literature. Revised and enlarged
     edition. New York: Oxford University Press, pp. 88-132.
        Restatement of thesis in 1934.B37 in view of recent
     evidence in the notebooks. Suggests that James, emerging
     from his theatrical debacle and in a "relatively neurotic
     phase," unconsciously communicated his doubts about him-
     self in the ambiguity of the governess' story. In The Turn
     of the Screw, "not merely is the governess self-deceived,
     but...James is self-deceived about her." Reprinted: in
     Gerald Willen, ed. A Casebook on "The Turn of the Screw,"
     pp. 115-53.

1949 A BOOKS

1   STEVENSON, ELIZABETH. The Crooked Corridor: A Study of Henry
    James. New York: The Macmillan Co., 172 pp. Reprinted:
    1961.
       After a brief analysis of James the man, who "had no
    other function than as an observant, reflective, produc-
    tive imagination," examines the scope, thematic content
    and techniques of James' fiction. His works portray the
    tension between the sensitive individual and the raw mate-
    rial of existence: "...James sees life and reports it in
    terms of the intrusion of the strange element, the in-
    dividual, into the world," and both are ultimately changed
    by the encounter. James viewed this as a necessary con-
    flict, "both for the exercise of the individual's moral
    and aesthetic qualities, and for the leavening of soci-
    ety." Traces James' use of imagery, which becomes more
    concentrated in the later works. Concludes that "James
    is oblique, he is direct, he is difficult. But he is not
    difficult for nothing.... James' kind of complexity was...
    an effort of the mind to bring about a real and fruitful

1949

order.... This is his 'crooked corridor.' This is the
stumbling block to a just understanding of James." Includes "Bibliography," pp. 164-66. Reviewed: Leon Edel,
New England Quarterly, 23 (June 1950), 245-49; Gerald
Sykes, New York Times Book Review (20 November 1949), p. 3;
Robert Halsband, Saturday Review of Literature, 33 (18 February 1950), 17; Times Literary Supplement (28 July 1950),
p. 470.

1949 B SHORTER WRITINGS

1   ANON. "Henry James Reprints." Times Literary Supplement
    (5 February), p. 96.
        Considers whether James' late revision of early works
    improved or spoiled them, and remarks that, until recently,
    most of James' works were available only in the revised
    versions. Notes some exceptions. Concludes that the issue
    of whether one version is superior to another is endlessly
    debatable and that the real question is which will improve
    James' reputation. See 1949.B8, B18, B23, B32, B34, B38.

2   BARRETT, LAURENCE. "Young Henry James, Critic." American
    Literature, 20 (January), 385-400.
        Examination of James' criticism from his first published
    review in 1864 to publication of French Poets and Novelists
    in 1878 in order to discover James' basic critical prin-
    ciples. These early writings offer insight into James'
    later narrative technique, and Barrett discusses modifica-
    tion of James' principles in later practice, using Roderick
    Hudson as an example.

3   BERTOCCI, ANGELO. "The Labyrinthine Spirit: Henry James,"
    in Charles Du Bos and English Literature. New York:
    King's Crown Press, pp. 196-205.
        An analysis of Du Bos' criticism of James, with quotes
    from his journal and dialogue with André Gide. Character-
    izes James as the "labyrinthine genius," complex within
    himself, and concludes that his literature is not life but
    "parallel to life." Du Bos "seems to mourn what the
    artist, or the artist-nature, has done to man."

4   BEWLEY, MARIUS. "James's Debt to Hawthorne (I): The Blithe-
    dale Romance and The Bostonians." Scrutiny, 16 (Winter),
    178-95.
        The influence of Hawthorne on James was both stronger
    and longer lived than that of the French novelists, and he
    was the American predecessor through whom James confronted
    his native tradition. Suggests differences between James'

early and later methods of assimilating Hawthorne's influence; emphasizes the "essential Americanism" of James; and compares The Blithedale Romance and The Bostonians, which demonstrate a closer relationship in characterization and theme than any other Hawthorne and James novels. Reprinted: 1952.B4.

5   BEWLEY, MARIUS. "James's Debt to Hawthorne (II): The Marble Faun and The Wings of the Dove." Scrutiny, 16 (Winter), 301-17.
      Considers the influence of The Marble Faun on James' early story, "The Last of the Valerii"; offers an extended comparison of The Wings of the Dove and The Marble Faun, in both of which symbolism carries "moral values that shed nearly identical lustres over the two girls [Milly and Hilda]"; and discusses the relationship between Milly and Hilda from the point of view of Quentin Anderson's analysis of James' novel (1946.B1). Concludes that the heroines are "sisters under the symbol, and it is a symbol that fails to convince one that its value is valid in either novel." Reprinted: 1952.B7.

6   CLARK, EDWIN. "Henry James and the Actress." Pacific Spectator, 3 (Winter), 84-99.
      Consideration of three aspects of James' theatrical career: "his ambition to be a popular dramatist with a smash hit; his intimate friendship with the enchanting actress, Elizabeth Robins; and the part he played both in the Ibsen movement and the development of the modern theatre in Britain." James failed to see the defects of his dramas because of his confidence in the outmoded methods of Théâtre Francais.

7   CLARK, EDWIN. "An 'Idiosyncrasy' of the Master." Saturday Review of Literature, 32 (12 November), 16-17.
      With reference to Edel's edition of the plays (see 1949.B11), suggests that James' later "technical virtuosity...is derived from his experience with the theatre."

8   EDEL, LEON. "Henry James Reprints." Times Literary Supplement (12 March), p. 169.
      Suggests scholars should attend to the content of revisions as well as "verbal amplifications and stylistic elaborations," and concludes that different texts are "a good thing." See 1949.B1.

1949

9   EDEL, LEON. "Henry James and <u>The Outcry</u>." <u>University of
     Toronto Quarterly</u>, 18 (July), 340-46.
          In this expanded version of a portion of the prefatory
     material in 1949.B11, Edel examines James' play <u>The Outcry</u>,
     written for a London repertory season, 1909. Discusses
     James' choice of theme, the historical details of composi-
     tion, written with "intensity and anxiety," and the diffi-
     culty James experienced in cutting it.

10   EDEL, LEON. "The Text of Henry James's Unpublished Plays."
     <u>Harvard Library Bulletin</u>, 3 (Autumn), 395-406.
          Reprints a letter which demonstrates James' willingness
     to consider publishing his unpublished dramatic works.
     Describes the task of editing James' plays, the problem of
     arriving at a "definitive" text and form faithful to James'
     intentions. Includes a list and evaluation of typescripts
     and prompt-books of the unpublished plays.

11   EDEL, LEON. "Henry James: The Dramatic Years," in <u>The Com-
     plete Plays of Henry James</u>. Edited by Leon Edel. Phila-
     delphia: J. B. Lippincott Co., pp. 19-69.
          A concise history of James' experience with and approach
     to the theatre, illustrated with biographical details and
     anecdotes. James' adult biases and reactions to the thea-
     tre were influenced by his childhood experiences there,
     which Edel outlines. Analyzes the effect of James' dra-
     matic interlude on his later works, and concludes that the
     plays should be read "in the context of Henry James's
     creative life." In the scenic method, James found "salva-
     tion that enabled him to pursue his art and arrive at those
     discoveries which mark him out as one of the great archi-
     tects of the modern novel." Reviewed: John Lucas, <u>Furi-
     oso</u>, 5 (Winter 1950), 84-88; Edna Kenton, <u>Kenyon Review</u>,
     12 (Spring 1950), 352-57; Francis Fergusson, <u>Partisan Re-
     view</u>, 17 (July-August 1950), 623-26.

12   EDEL, LEON. "Introduction," in <u>The Ghostly Tales of Henry
     James</u>. Edited by Leon Edel. New Brunswick, N.J.: Rut-
     gers University Press, pp. v-xxxii.
          Enumerates elements in James' emotional and familial
     background which fed into the consciousness from which the
     ghostly tales were derived, and details "surface materials"
     which contributed to his composition of the supernatural
     stories. Describes their characteristics, emphasizing
     James' "refusal to <u>specify</u> the nature of the horror, the
     character of the evil...," and concludes that the tales
     offer the reader entertainment, psychological case his-
     tories, and a record of James' own emotional state.

Reviewed: F. W. Dupee, <u>Nation</u>, 169 (2 July 1949), 16;
B. R. Redman, <u>Saturday Review of Literature</u> (25 June 1949),
41; Morris Roberts, <u>Sewanee Review</u>, 57 (Summer 1949), 521-
25.

13   EVANS, OLIVER. "James's Air of Evil: <u>The Turn of the Screw</u>."
     <u>Partisan Review</u>, 16 (February), 175-87.
         The sensationalism of <u>The Turn of the Screw</u> results from
     James' preoccupation with the supernatural theme and with
     perverse sexuality. Considers the reality of the appari-
     tions, with reference to Wilson's (1934.B37) and Kenton's
     (1924.B10) theories, which he disputes as contradicting
     the story, Preface and letters. James sought to communi-
     cate an evil perceived primarily in sexual terms, although
     the real theme of the tale is appearance vs. reality, or,
     considered on an ethical level, good vs. evil, expressed
     in the form of a paradox. Reprinted: in Gerald Willen,
     ed. <u>A Casebook on "The Turn of the Screw</u>," pp. 200-11.

14   FAY, ELIOT G. "Henry James as a Critic of French Literatures."
     <u>French American Review</u>, 2 (September), 184-93.
         James' <u>French Poets and Novelists</u> marks him as "the
     earliest important American critic of French literature."
     Gives account of James' cosmopolitan background, and notes
     periodicals which published his French reviews and volumes
     of his essays which include such. Discusses James' essays
     on de Musset, Gautier, Baudelaire, Balzac and George Sand,
     and points out "the puritanical squeamishness of his ap-
     proach, and...the exquisite urbanity of his style."

15   FERGUSON, A. R. "Some Bibliographical Notes on the Short
     Stories of Henry James." <u>American Literature</u>, 21 (Novem-
     ber), 292-97.
         A record of publication in periodicals is lacking for
     only twelve of James' shorter fictions. On the basis of
     James' comments, "it seems probable that no identification
     with the magazines need be expected for 9 of these stor-
     ies." Provides facts of first publication on the remain-
     ing three stories, thus completing the record of James'
     contributions to periodicals.

16   FERGUSSON, FRANCIS. "The End of <u>Ghosts</u>: The Tasteless Par-
     lor and the Stage of Europe," in <u>The Idea of a Theatre</u>.
     Princeton, N.J.: Princeton University Press, p. 158.
         Notes James' criticism of the parlor scene in Ibsen's
     <u>Ghosts</u>, and suggests that James' "comments on Ibsen are at
     once the most sympathetic and the most objective that have
     been written" and that the artists are alike in their
     "artistry" and "moral exactitude."

1949

17 FLEET, SIMON. "The Nice American Gentleman." <u>Vogue</u> (1 Octo-
    ber), pp. 136, 183-85.
        Describes James' impressions of Rye, the inhabitants'
    reactions to his presence, and Lamb House (both exterior
    and interior); reports one of his secretary's recollections
    of working for James. At Rye, James "is remembered as a
    benevolent human being, the very nice American gentleman
    who had Lamb House."

18 GARNETT, DAVID. "Henry James Reprints." <u>Times Literary
    Supplement</u> (19 March), p. 185.
        Disputes a point Edel made (<u>see</u> 1949.B8) about James'
    revision of the last line of "Owen Wingrave."

19 HAMILTON, EUNICE C. "Biographical and Critical Studies of
    Henry James, 1941-1948." <u>American Literature</u>, 20 (Janu-
    ary), 424-35.
        Supplement to Lyon Richardson's bibliography in
    1941.B15. Bibliography, chronologically arranged, includes
    certain studies not included in Richardson, a brief list of
    doctoral dissertations, and an enumeration of reprints of
    James' works between 1930 and 1948. See 1950.B30.

20 HARLOW, VIRGINIA. "Thomas Sergeant Perry and Henry James."
    <u>Boston Public Library Quarterly</u>, 1 (July), 43-60.
        A consideration of the friendship and literary associa-
    tion between James and Perry, author and editor. With
    Howells, "Their enthusiasm for contemporary novelists of
    Europe, particularly for the Russians, their steady pio-
    neering for the cause of realism in America, and the gen-
    erous affection which they had for one another bound them
    together with the strongest of ties." The concern which
    Perry and James shared for each other's literary success
    is repeatedly reflected in their correspondence, and Har-
    low suggests similarities in their critical attitudes.

21 HEMPHILL, GEORGE. "Hemingway and James." <u>Kenyon Review</u>, 11
    (Winter), 50-60.
        James and Hemingway represent the contemporary rift in
    fictional possibilities, the former putting poetic dramas
    into novelistic form and thereby sacrificing a great deal
    of the moral persuasive force available in prose narra-
    tive; the latter, "more purely novelist," writing moral
    tracts for modern times. Analyzes <u>In Our Time</u> as exempli-
    fying the strengths and limitations of Hemingway's non-
    Jamesian moral vision.

22   HONIG, EDWIN. "The Merciful Fraud in Three Stories by James."
      Tiger's Eye, 1 (15 October), 83-96.
          Notes similarity between Dionysus myth, in which the
      sacrifice of an animal may be substituted for a human being
      as "'part of a pious and merciful fraud,'" and the moral
      situation in at least three Jamesian tales, "The Jolly Cor-
      ner," "The Beast in the Jungle," and "The Altar of the
      Dead." James framed the problem in terms of discovery of
      total selfhood by rediscovering the importance of self in
      another form. Traces the motif in each of the stories,
      then formulates the "hypothetical terms of James's ritual
      romance," which "invests with a new relevance the culture
      myths of man's beginnings." Partially reprinted:
      1959.B42.

23   HOPPE, A. J. "Henry James Reprints." Times Literary Supple-
      ment (26 February), p. 137.
          The Everyman's Library edition of The Ambassadors should
      be added to the list in 1949.B1.

24   HOUGH, GRAHAM. "Books in General." New Statesman and Nation,
      37 (16 April), 382.
          Comments in general about novel writing and notes James'
      "technical distinction," but suggests that he lacked
      knowledge of even one small area of life. Gives examples
      of what he views as unfit foundations of novels: false
      picture of civilization, unconsciousness of norms. Con-
      cludes that he feels "an almost awestruck admiration for
      the consummate technical achievement, and a quite unsilence-
      able hate for the code in whose service it is employed."

25   HOUGH, GRAHAM. "Henry James." New Statesman and Nation, 37
      (14 May), 503.
          Rejoinder to Leavis' criticism (see 1949.B33): "What
      continues to surprise me is that critics who point out
      this moral obliquity in parts of James's work do not find
      a similar element all-pervading; and that they do not find
      it more damaging."

26   HOUSER, Z. L. "Early Years of Henry James." Mark Twain
      Quarterly, 8 (Winter-Spring), 9-10.
          James' childhood "undoubtedly was of great import in
      the shaping of his plots and in the formation of his
      opinions." Mentions the "peculiar restlessness" of his
      parents, the education both American and European, the
      atmosphere of literary discussion and intellectual recrea-
      tion. "As a spectator he lived and as a spectator he
      wrote."

1949

27   HOWE, M. DeWOLFE. "The Letters of Henry James to Mr. Justice
      Holmes." <u>Yale Review</u>, NS 38 (Spring), 410-33.
            Correspondence illuminates the "slightly unhappy story
      of the friendship of the two men." Despite initial enthu-
      siasm, they held divergent points of view, and their early
      sympathy cooled. Although only one letter from Holmes to
      James is extant, James' to Holmes have been preserved and
      are here reprinted.

28   KANE, R. J. "<u>Virgin Soil</u> and <u>The Princess Casamassima</u>."
      <u>Gifthorse</u> (Ohio State), pp. 25-29.
            Views <u>Virgin Soil</u> and <u>The Princess Casamassima</u> as "in-
      teresting and not always perfect analogues" in his com-
      parison of the works, especially their protagonists. Con-
      cludes that "James's is the better constructed, the more
      completely done" of the two novels. Apparently Turgenev's
      influence on James was unrealized.

29   KIRK, RUDOLF. "Five Letters of Henry James." <u>Journal of the</u>
      <u>Rutgers University Library</u>, 12 (June), 54-58.
            Reprints five letters in Rutgers Library, written by
      James to four different people over a 28 year period on
      unrelated topics. Includes an introduction to each letter
      with details concerning recipients. <u>See</u> 1953.B36.

30   LaFARGE, JOHN. "Henry James's Letters to the LaFarges." <u>New</u>
      <u>England Quarterly</u>, 22 (June), 173-92.
            Describes James' relationship with his parents, John
      and Margaret Mason Perry LaFarge, both in Newport and much
      later in Rye, where the author of the article, his mother
      and his sister visited Lamb House. Reprints six letters
      written by James shortly before and after this visit, two
      letters to his father, John LaFarge, Sr., and one to
      James' nephew following Henry's trip to the United States.

31   LeCLAIR, R. C. "Henry James and Minny Temple." <u>American</u>
      <u>Literature</u>, 21 (March), 35-48.
            Considers question of relationship between James and
      his cousin, Mary Temple, in light of new material concern-
      ing her. A study of unpublished documents shows that James
      consciously excluded from <u>Notes of a Son and Brother</u> any
      material which might have revealed his actual connections
      with her. Reprints several of Minny's letters to James
      which suggest a sympathetic, affectionate response on her
      part, and that this association was what James later called
      "'the starved romance of my life.'"

32   LEAVIS, F. R. "Henry James Reprints." <u>Times Literary Supple-</u>
      <u>ment</u> (12 February), p. 105.
           Remarks that the early edition of <u>Roderick Hudson</u> makes
      relation to Dickens plainer than the revised version. <u>See</u>
      1949.B1.

33   LEAVIS, F. R. "Henry James." <u>New Statesman and Nation</u>, 37
      (23 April), 406.
           Claims Hough misrepresented him (see 1949.B24), and
      calls him "another critic who shows a patent indisposition
      to be interested in James...." <u>See</u> Hough's reply,
      1949.B25.

34   LEHMANN, JOHN. "Henry James Reprints." <u>Times Literary Sup-</u>
      <u>plement</u> (12 February), p. 105.
           Used the New York edition texts in his reprinting of
      James' works so he could include the "incomparable intro-
      ductions." <u>See</u> 1949.B1.

*35   MacCARTHY, DESMOND. "Otherness." <u>Sun Times</u> (27 February),
      p. 3. Cited in Beatrice Ricks, comp. <u>Henry James: A</u>
      <u>Bibliography of Secondary Works</u>, #2869.1.

36   McELDERRY, B. R., JR. "The Uncollected Stories of Henry
      James." <u>American Literature</u>, 21 (November), 279-91.
           Proposes to make "a concise statement of the whole
      corpus of James's shorter fiction, with an indication of
      just what was excluded from the chief collected editions,"
      and give a brief evaluation of the excluded material. Of
      the eight stories never reprinted from the periodical
      files, all deal with the American scene and all, with one
      possible exception, "fail to cut through the surface of
      life to something of solid interest." Discusses these
      "neglected" works. <u>See</u> 1951.B39.

37   MARQUARDT, WILLIAM F. "A Practical Approach to 'The Real
      Thing.'" <u>English "A" Analyst</u> (Northwestern University),
      no. 14, pp. 1-8.
           Suggests use of class participation through the Socratic
      method in analysis of "The Real Thing," including questions
      and answers about technique as well as "philosophical and
      aesthetic implications." Provides a statement of funda-
      mental problems in the story, which deals with the nature
      of the artist, art and society. Lists thirty-two ques-
      tions and answers for discussion.

1949

38 MAXWELL, J. C. "Henry James Reprints." <u>Times Literary Sup-</u>
    <u>plement</u> (19 February), p. 121.
       The publishers of the English collected edition of
    James should reprint it, and other publishers should cater
    to those who want to study revisions or approach James
    through the original form of the earlier works. <u>See</u>
    1949.B1.

39 MENCKEN, H. L. "Henry James," in <u>Mencken Chrestomathy</u>. New
    York: Alfred A. Knopf, pp. 500-501.
       Restatement of 1920.B23. Describes James' works as
    "hollow" and James himself as a "superb technician" with
    "timorous ideas" who suffered from lack of contact with
    his native country.

40 MILLER, BETTY.   "Two Fathers and their Sons." <u>The Nine-</u>
    <u>teenth Century and After</u>, 146 (October), 251-60.
       James and Samuel Butler, although recipients of sub-
    stantially different "parental legacies," acquired from
    their fathers "a disposition, an attitude to life that
    subsequent events served...to reinforce, producing, in
    Henry James and in Samuel Butler, personalities so diverse
    that they appear...to complement each other in their very
    antipathy." Comparison/contrast of James and Butler
    households and fathers, with discussion of effect on
    writer-sons.

41 MILLER, WARREN. "Henry James in Hollywood." <u>Masses and</u>
    <u>Mainstream</u>, 2 (December), 81-83.
       Reviews film version of <u>The Heiress</u>, based on <u>Washing-</u>
    <u>ton Square</u>, "faithful to James in atmosphere, language,
    and meaning." The story "has a richness of meaning and
    insight that transforms a trivial situation into a signi-
    ficant drama."

42 POCHMANN, HENRY A. and GAY WILSON ALLEN. "Henry James," in
    <u>Masters of American Literature</u>. Edited by Henry A. Poch-
    mann and Gay Wilson Allen. Vol. 2. New York: The Mac-
    millan Co., pp. 541-47.
       Biocritical sketch of James which considers the con-
    sequences of expatriation, the "duality of American char-
    acter" seen in books of the 1870's, his tales of the
    artist during the dramatic years followed by the "'major
    phase.'" Notes James' "clinical interest in human mo-
    tives" which made him a "social prophet" who "disclosed the
    stresses and the weaknesses of the social structure of his
    generation." Includes "Selected James Bibliography."
    <u>See</u> 1959.B27.

43 POPKIN, HENRY. "Pretender to the Drama." Theatre Arts, 33
    (December), 32-35, 91.
        Traces James' "career" as a playwright, after which he
    viewed novels as drama. James' two biggest problems in
    writing plays were subject and language, and his works are
    unsatisfactory because they were written for "the theatre
    of his reader's imagination."

44 RAETH, CLAIRE. "The Real Approach to The Real Thing."
    English "A" Analyst (Northwestern University), no. 15,
    pp. 1-5.
        Disputes Marquardt's explication (see 1949.B37) as
    "superficial," and examines action of "The Real Thing"
    "in relation to the point of view from which the couple is
    regarded, and in relation to the complex meaning of the
    title." The narrator-artist becomes aware in his "process
    of learning" that the Monarchs "have no power to represent
    for him the society which he is to produce in his drawings."
    Rather, they are "intellectually dead and spiritually
    bankrupt," failures as models and as individuals, judged
    by the values of the artist-narrator's world.

45 RAETH, CLAIRE. "Henry James's Rejection of The Sacred Fount."
    English Literary History, 16 (December), 308-24.
        James' decision to omit The Sacred Fount from the col-
    lected edition marks it as an important commentary upon
    his final concept of the art of the novel. Analyzes the
    faults of this work to determine what James considered to
    be the valid form of the short story and novel, "what de-
    vices of presentation and point of view he held to be
    proper to each form, and what expression and meaning could
    be fitted into these forms." Also suggests the meaning of
    the novel.

46 RAHV, PHILIP. "Attitudes to Henry James," in Image and Idea:
    Fourteen Essays on Literary Themes. A New Directions Book.
    Norfolk, Conn.: New Directions Press, pp. 63-70. Re-
    printed: 1952; 1957; 1959.
        Reprint of 1943.B39.

47 RAHV, PHILIP. "The Heiress of All the Ages," in Image and
    Idea: Fourteen Essays on Literary Themes. A New Direc-
    tions Book. Norfolk, Conn.: New Directions Press,
    pp. 42-70. Reprinted: 1952; 1957; 1959.
        Reprint of 1943.B40.

48 REED, GLENN A. "Another Turn of James's 'The Turn of the
    Screw.'" American Literature, 20 (January), 413-23.

1949

Summarizes two currents of thought in interpreting The
Turn of the Screw, and suggests that James' stated intentions indicate no ambiguity and that the tale is a "haunted and haunting ghost story replete with all imaginable
intangible horrors," purely a "fairy tale," with demons
and spirits and unexplained actions. Reprinted: in
Gerald Willen, ed. A Casebook on "The Turn of the Screw,"
pp. 189-99.

49   ROBERTS, MORRIS. "Henry James." Sewanee Review, 57 (Summer),
        521-25.
        Reviews Smith's volume on James and Stevenson (see
1948.A3). Considers the personal appeal of James, who was
"interested only in the fate that befalls people as individuals, never in their collective life; in their private
rather than their public relations." Calls "The Art of
Fiction" "the best essay on the subject in English."

50   ROELLINGER, F. X., JR. "Psychical Research and 'The Turn of
        the Screw.'" American Literature, 20 (January), 401-12.
        The publication of the Society for Psychical Research
might be a logical source of suggestion for development
of Benson's anecdote, of which the January 12, 1895 notebook entry gives the most accurate account. James was
interested in psychical phenomena and had friends and a
brother in the society. Points out resemblances in details, parallels in story line and type of ghosts in the
Proceedings of the Society for Psychical Research, and
concludes that if such evidence doesn't prove a direct indebtedness, it shows James constructed his apparitions in
terms of modern psychical cases.

51   SACKVILLE-WEST, EDWARD. "Books in General." New Statesman
        and Nation, 25 (17 April), 259.
        Isabel Archer in The Portrait of a Lady represents
a "standard of conduct" in the code of social behavior for
a lady, and the novel is "a typically Cornelian tragedy,"
its "conception of duty being to embrace danger and unhappiness in the aesthetic fulfillment of personality." See
1949.B53.

52   SACKVILLE-WEST, EDWARD. "Books in General." New Statesman
        and Nation, 34 (4 October), 273.
        The Sacred Fount has as its theme "life-givers and
spiritual vampires" and is a "detective story" which
fuses theatrical construction and discursive characteristics of nineteenth-century fiction. The novel is "a
supreme exercise in the spirit of poetic analysis." See
1949.B53.

53   SACKVILLE-WEST, EDWARD. "The Personality of Henry James," in
      Inclinations. New York: Charles Scribner's Sons, pp. 42-
      71. Reprinted: New York: Kennikat Press, 1967.
          A revision and expansion of essays previously printed on
      James, including 1948.B41 and 1949.B51-52. James' "femi-
      nine streak" caused features in works that critics found
      disturbing: "detachment, vagueness about practical de-
      tails, squeamishness, and an over-developed taste for
      renunciation."

54   SAVELLI, GIOVANNI. "Posizione di Henry James." Humanitas, 4
      (March), 322-25. (Italian)
          Considers the significance of Europe for the nineteenth-
      century wealthy as portrayed in the works of "the transcen-
      dentalist and rationalist James," who "turns vision into
      breath." He "probes the situations, the conflicts between
      people and creates a mosaic that reflects their reactions,
      intersecting or diverging."

55   SEZNEC, JEAN. "Lettres de Tourguéneff à Henry James." Com-
      parative Literature, 1 (Summer), 193-209. (French)
          Discusses James' discovery of Turgenev in 1873, their
      acquaintance in Paris, their respective attitudes towards
      the French realists, the tone of Turgenev's correspondence;
      reprints several of Turgenev's letters to James, who
      viewed the Russian as an ideal artist.

*56   SIMON, IRÈNE. Les formes du roman anglais de Dickens à
      Joyce. Liège: Faculté de philosophie et lettres. Cited
      in 1956.B70, p. 406.

57   SIMON, JEAN. "Les exilés," in Le roman américain aux xxe
      siècle. Paris: Boivin and Cie, pp. 45-51. (French)
          Considers place of an exile like James in a study of the
      twentieth-century American novel. Points out the psycholo-
      gical repercussions of James' first period, 1871-1890,
      discusses characteristics of the middle manner, and sug-
      gests comparison to Proust in the late period. Analyzes
      "The Jolly Corner" and The Ambassadors, in which Strether
      is "clearly still Henry James," and calls the latter work
      "the supreme product of a perfect art."

58   SMITH, ROLAND M. "Anglo-Saxon Spinsters and Anglo-Saxon
      Archers (Two Steps Towards A Study in Extension)." Modern
      Language Notes, 64 (May), 312-15.
          Reference to A. J. A. Waldock's use of the term "Anglo-
      Saxon spinster" in describing the governess in The Turn of
      the Screw. Notes James' limited use of the term "Anglo-

1949

Saxon," and concludes that "...recent critics of the novelist appear to have taken over the term more completely than the novelist himself."

59   STONE, GEOFFREY. <u>Melville</u>. London: Sheed and Ward, p. 290. New York: William Sloane, 1950. Reprinted: Toronto: The Macmillan Co., 1957; Viking Compass Books. New York: The Viking Press, 1957.
      Suggests similarity between Ungar of <u>Clarel</u> and Basil Ransom of <u>The Bostonians</u>.

60   SWAN, MICHAEL. "Introductory Note," in <u>The American</u>. Edited by Michael Swan. London: John Lehmann, pp. 5-6.
      Points out realism of the novel, suggests that Newman "is an embryo of Strether," and discusses dramatization of the novel.

61   THERSITES. "Talk on Parnassus." <u>New York Times Book Review</u> (22 May), pp. 7, 27.
      Conversation among souls of authors on Mt. Parnussus, including James, Melville, Kafka. According to Melville, "America wants the world to judge her by her flossy exiles" like James. Kafka tells James, "Your sentences are like my plots."

62   TINDALL, WILLIAM YORK. "Stream of Consciousness," in <u>Forces in Modern British Literature, 1885-1946</u>. New York: Alfred A. Knopf, pp. 283-317.
      James sought to present minds in moral and social situations and adjusted his "techniques to the demands of the flux." He used "impressionism," the "method whereby an observer's mind is the stage upon which all action occurs," in his novels and anticipated Proust both in his analysis of decaying society and in his method.

63   VAN DOREN, CARL. "Introduction," in <u>The Turn of the Screw</u>. Edited by Carl Van Doren. New York: Heritage Press, pp. ix-xiv.
      Critics "have read so hotly between the lines of the story that they have missed the whole of it, including the point." James kept the story "pure mystery," allowing Quint and Jessel to remain matters of speculation and imagination and represent "essential malevolence." Describes <u>The Turn of the Screw</u> as "the blackest of all nursery tales, the most terrifying of all ghost stories, the most pathetic of all the chronicles of damnation."

64   WEST, KATHARINE. "The Turn of the Screw," in Chapter of Gov-
      ernesses: A Study of the Governess in English Fiction,
      1800-1949. London: Cohen and West, pp. 179-86.
          Considers The Turn of the Screw in light of information
      it provides on the governess' life, and describes the
      narrator-governess as displaying "intelligence and cour-
      age." In What Maisie Knew, again two governesses struggle
      for a child's soul on the sides of good and evil.

65   WEST, RAY B., JR. and R. W. STALLMAN. "The American," in The
      Art of Modern Fiction. New York: Rinehart and Co.,
      pp. 583-93.
          Newman's name suggests his qualities and function. He
      is an "outgrowth of the typical Yankee character, a figure
      in a long line of American mythical and fictional charac-
      ters...." The structure of The American is similar to that
      of popular romances which lead to expectations of trium-
      phant virtue and love, and James had problems in this re-
      gard. Examines allegory in the novel on three levels:
      social (the theme of the American in Europe); artistic
      (contrast between spiritual and natural beauty); and moral
      (Newman's moral innocence vs. knowledge and evil of Belle-
      gardes).

66   WEST, RAY B., JR. and R. W. STALLMAN. "Analysis [of "The
      Liar"], in The Art of Modern Fiction. New York: Rinehart
      and Co., pp. 209-16.
          Study of "The Liar," in which the central intelligence
      of Lyon unifies the story of Love vs. Honor. Demonstrates
      how the story is dramatized in scenes approximating those
      of a play; discusses the ironic focus and moral problem of
      the tale.

67   WILLIAMS, OWEN P. D. "The Three 'R's.'" Times Literary Sup-
      plement (5 February), p. 89.
          Reference to the account of James' opinion of emotions
      of George Eliot's husband as recounted in The Legend of
      the Master, 1947.A2.

1950 A BOOKS

1   EMERSON, DONALD C. "Henry James and the Life of the Imagina-
     tion." Ph.D. dissertation, University of Wisconsin.
     (Abstracted in University of Wisconsin Summaries of Doc-
     toral Dissertations, 12 [1952], 445-47.)
         Examination of the theme of imagination in James' fic-
     tion, autobiography, travel writings and criticism, and of

1950

the characteristics and development of the "'man of imagination'" in James' novels reveals that the theme is a
primary one in James, and that he "is the very type of the
richly imaginative characters he draws."

2   SWAN, MICHAEL. <u>Henry James</u>. Bibliographical Series of Supplements to <u>British Book News</u>, edited by T. O. Beachcroft.
London: Longmans, Green and Co., 43 pp. Reprinted:
1957; as <u>British Writers and Their Work: No. 10</u>, edited
by T. O. Beachcroft. American editor, J. W. Robinson.
Lincoln: University of Nebraska Press, 1966.
       Biographical sketch followed by examination of represen-
tative novels of three periods in James' career. <u>Roderick
Hudson</u>, <u>The Portrait of a Lady</u> and <u>The Golden Bowl</u> mark a
"progression in subject matter, in style, and, above all,
in technique..." from simple statement of thought and
feeling to subtle tenuous expression of states of mind.
Chronological review of selected short stories and brief
discussion of "non-fictional" output included. In "psychological content" of James' works is the virtue of the modern novel. Select bibliography of James' works and criti-
cal/biographical studies and index of short stories
appended.

1950 B SHORTER WRITINGS

1   ÄHNEBRINK, LARS. "Literary Credos: I. Henry James and 'The
Art of Fiction.' 1884," in <u>The Beginnings of Naturalism in
American Fiction</u>. Essays and Studies on American Language
and Literature, No. 9, edited by S. B. Liljegren. Upsala:
A. -B. Lundequistska Bokhandelin; Cambridge, Mass.: Harvard University Press, pp. 128-29.
       In "The Art of Fiction," James "pleaded for realism and
freedom for the artist to paint all life." Categorizes
and discusses themes in essay under the headings "A Definition," "The Importance of Reality," "The Sphere of the
Novel," "The Question of Morality," and "Advocacy of Ob-
jectivity and Sincerity."

2   ANDERSON, QUENTIN.   "Introduction," in <u>Henry James: Selected
Short Stories</u>. Edited by Quentin Anderson. New York:
Rinehart and Co., pp. v-xix. Reprinted: 1957.
       James consciously defeats the reader's expectations
"and drives you toward his conclusions...and this covert
struggle with his reader is the central fact about his
fiction." The conclusion of the story occurs when author's
and reader's positions coincide. Analyzes "The Real Thing"
and "A Bundle of Letters," as dealing "with the materials

of fiction and their use," and "The Birthplace," with its
theme of "the splendid mystery of creation." Discusses
importance of James' moral intention, and concludes that
"our accountability for our experience" is the crux of his
moral convention.

3 ANON. "James the Dramatist." Times Literary Supplement
    (6 January), p. 8.
        Examines James' lifelong interest in the theatre, his
    "orderly and traceable development from the stage-struck
    child...to the elderly novelist" and the influence of his
    preoccupation with the drama. Suggests that James' failure
    was due to his lack of understanding of his own limita-
    tions, which are described with reference to The High Bid
    and Guy Domville.

4 ARVIN, NEWTON. Herman Melville. The American Men of Letters
    Series. New York: William Sloan Associates, pp. 103, 275.
    Reprinted: Viking Compass Books. New York: Viking
    Press, 1957.
        Alludes to James' use of the initiation theme in dis-
    cussing Redburn, and suggests comparison between Basil
    Ranson of The Bostonians and Ungar of Clarel.

5 ATKINSON, BROOKS. "At the Theatre." New York Theatre Crit-
    ics' Reviews, 11 (6 February), 360.
        In a review of The Innocents, an adaptation of James'
    The Turn of the Screw, remarks that "none of his plays was
    as dramatic as these novels have turned out to be," and
    suggests that the drama "retained the baleful candor of
    the writing."

6 BARRETT, CLIFTON WALLER. "Some Bibliographical Adventures in
    Americana." Papers of the Bibliographical Society of
    America, 44 (1st quarter), 21, 24.
        "An exhaustive gathering of the first editions, English
    and American, of the old master Henry James, is apt to
    exhaust the collector."

7 BERLAND, ALWYN. "Henry James." University of Kansas City
    Review, 17 (Winter), 94-108.
        Surveys criticism of James which, "with its different
    assumptions and conclusions, provides if not a consistent
    critical evaluation of James, at least an insight into
    contemporary cultural history." Points out need for study
    of the precise manner in which James worked, and analyzes
    The Princess Casamassima to demonstrate James' "actual
    practice in the 'middle period,'" and The Ambassadors to
    show his method "at its highest point."

1950

8   BERRYMAN, JOHN. Stephen Crane. The American Men of Letters
     Series. New York: William Sloane Associates, pp. 55,
     103-104, 187-88, 237-38, 251-52.
         Notes Crane's association with other realists like Gar-
     land, Howells and James, his response to James' critical
     works, and the motives for expatriation of both James and
     Crane. Considers James' dislike of Cora, Stephen's wife,
     and his friendship with Crane. "Nothing could be stranger
     than this close relation...of the two Americans who were
     making ready Twentieth Century prose in English, with
     nearby in Essex a Pole the friend of both, who learned
     from both, their solitary peer in Art though not in orig-
     inality."

9   BEWLEY, MARIUS. "James' Debt to Hawthorne (III): The Ameri-
     can Problem." Scrutiny, 17 (Spring), 14-37.
         Analyzes the affinity between James and Hawthorne re-
     sulting from like problems faced in similar ways. Discuss-
     es problem of Europe vs. America, past vs. present vs.
     future. "...Conflict between their native allegiances and
     the centrifugal compulsions of temperament lie at the basis
     of their resemblance." Suggests influence of The Scarlet
     Letter and The House of the Seven Gables on James' style.
     Uses The Sense of the Past in illustrating James' working
     shoulder to shoulder with Hawthorne, and concludes that
     Hawthorne helped make James an American novelist, concerned
     at a serious moral level with national and social problems.
     Reprinted: 1952.B2.

10   BEWLEY, MARIUS. "Appearance and Reality in Henry James."
     Scrutiny, 17 (Summer), 90-114.
         Notes predominance in American literature of the con-
     flict of appearance and reality, which occupies a central
     position in James' work. Examines James' use of this theme
     in the short stories and The Golden Bowl. Analyzes What
     Maisie Knew, in which "appearance and reality co-exist
     without violence to each other," and The Turn of the Screw,
     its companion piece in certain respects, "a metaphysic
     demonstrating the enmity of appearance and reality...."
     Relates the conflict between appearance and reality to that
     between America and Europe, past and present. Reprinted:
     1952.B3.

11   BEWLEY, MARIUS. "Maisie, Miles and Flora, the Jamesian Inno-
     cents." Scrutiny, 17 (Summer), 255-63.
         Examines areas of dispute with Leavis (see 1950.B52);
     asserts that his purpose was to isolate and consider a
     preoccupation of James, appearance and reality, and

demonstrate its effect on his art (see 1950.B10). Con-
tests three points made by Leavis, supports his point that
comedy and horror can exist simultaneously in What Maisie
Knew, and notes the ambiguous nature of the lie in James'
works. Reprinted: 1952.B6.

12 BEYER, WILLIAM. "The State of the Theatre: Actors Take the
Honors." School and Society, 71 (8 April), 213-17.
In a review of The Innocents, points out the "psychological discernment and the eerie impact derived from man-
ipulating the mounting tensions" in The Turn of the Screw.

13 BOOTH, BRADFORD A. "Form and Technique in the Novel," in The
Reinterpretation of Victorian Literature. Edited by Joseph
E. Baker. Princeton, N.J.: Princeton University Press,
pp. 94-95.
In a survey of the Victorian novel, sees James' achievement as that of maintaining a stationary and restricted
point of view. "James opened as great a chasm between himself and the great Victorians as he did between himself and
the average reader."

14 BOTTKOL, JOSEPH M. "Introduction," in "The Aspern Papers"
and "The Europeans." Norfolk, Conn.: New Directions
Press, pp. vii-xxi.
Considers the source of The Aspern Papers, which attracted James with "the evocation of a continuity with an
illustrious past...," and discusses Jamesian transformation
of the germinal idea. Notes connections with the Orpheus
myth and similarities between the narrator of the tale and
Fleda of The Spoils of Poynton, both of whom "arouse and
frustrate love---" and both of whom are "excluded from the
tabernacle by fire." In The Europeans, James summons "a
vision of a Puritan Phaecia, a Unitarian Eden...." Describes the Baroness as "an unintentional Aphrodite" who
brings "joy even against her will."

15 BROWN, E. K. "Phrase, Character, Incident," in Rhythm in the
Novel. Toronto: University of Toronto Press, pp. 24-27.
From Turgenev, James "learned the art of arranging
characters by gradation and combining with it surprise."
Looks at the "gradations" between characters, each of whom
"irradiates the others, and...becomes clearer by irradia-
tion" in The Ambassadors, in which James draws strength
from "complementary use of antithesis."

1950

16   BROWN, JOHN MASON. "Seeing Things." Saturday Review of Lit-
      erature, 33 (25 February), 32, 34-36.
          Suggests what James' attitude might have been to the
      adaptation of The Turn of the Screw: "...Henry James was
      always stagestruck...." Recounts the Guy Domville inci-
      dent, discusses connection between James' theatrical writ-
      ing and The Turn of the Screw, and presents a psychoana-
      lytic interpretation of the tale, which is not the view
      shared by the author of The Innocents.

17   BURKE, KENNETH. "Carlyle on 'Mystery,'" in A Rhetoric of Mo-
      tives. New York: Prentice-Hall, pp. 116-17.
          James appears to have a "special fondness for the am-
      biguities of that word, 'intercourse,'" related to "sexual
      and homosexual analogies in courtship between classes."
      Views governess' struggle with ghosts for possession of the
      children in The Turn of the Screw as "one class struggling
      to possess the soul of another class."

18   BURKE, KENNETH. "Rhetorical Radiance of the 'Divine,'" in
      A Rhetoric of Motives. New York: Prentice-Hall, pp. 294-
      98.
          In "Henry James on the Deity of 'Things,'" discusses
      germination of The Spoils of Poynton with reference to the
      Preface. "...Clearly these household Things are also
      Spirits, or they are charismatic vessels of some sort."
      In "'Social Ratings' of Images in James," applies passages
      from Warren's Rage for Order (1948.B54) to James to demon-
      strate how the latter unites "moral and social hierarchies
      with the natural and artificial objects that James treats
      as their equivalents," thus having the "hierarchical judg-
      ment implicit...in a given image."

*19   CAHEN, J. G. La littérature américaine. Paris: Presses
      universitaires de France. Cited in 1956.B70, p. 406.

20   CANBY, HENRY SEIDEL. "Henry James and the Observant Profes-
      sion." Saturday Review of Literature, 33 (2 December),
      11-12, 70-71.
          James made observing a profession, avoiding too com-
      plete an identification with the personalities of his
      characters.

21   CARTER, EVERETT S. "The Palpitating Divan." English Journal,
      39 (May), 237-42.
          In discussion of authors working within the "range and
      the taste and the tolerance of their readers," notes

extreme reticence in the late nineteenth century. James
treated sex in his works in an acceptably delicate and indirect way, thereby adjusting himself to his audience.
Concludes that writers like Howells, Twain and James worked
"honestly and effectively" within a limited spectrum.

22 CHESTERTON, G. K. "Henry James," in The Common Man. New
    York: Sheed and Ward, pp. 144-48.
         Contradicts view of James' art as slight or thin by
    enumerating characteristics shared with other outstanding
    writers, and disputes attack against James for making too
    much out of small things: "...He never wrote about noth-
    ing." Notes James' fastidiousness, his American character-
    istic of idealism, his sense of wonder, and concludes that
    "The books of Henry James will always be beautiful."

23 CLURMAN, HAROLD. "Theatre: Change of Mood." New Republic,
    122 (27 February), 20-21.
         The Turn of the Screw represents "a phase of James'
    work in which a preternatural psychological tension is
    converted into a spooky stylization halfway between reality
    and nightmare." The tale suggests James' "horror at his
    own lacks," especially sexually related ones.

24 COMMAGER, HENRY STEELE. "The Literature of Revolt," in The
    American Mind: An Interpretation of American Thought and
    Character Since the 1880's. New Haven, Conn.: Yale Uni-
    versity Press, pp. 258-60.
         James apprehended the "pervasive corruptions" of wealth
    and "pictured the acquisitive society" in The Ivory Tower.

25 COMMAGER, HENRY STEELE. "Transition Years in Literature," in
    The American Mind: An Interpretation of American Thought
    and Character Since the 1880's. New Haven, Conn.: Yale
    University Press, pp. 64-66.
         James' expatriation "was physical rather than intellec-
    tual...."

26 CONNOLLY, FRANCIS X. "Literary Consciousness and the Literary
    Conscience." Thought, 25 (December), 663-80.
         James' The Spoils of Poynton is a "kind of parable on
    the unity in criticism of fine consciousness and fine con-
    science, of the use of technique to determine values."
    Analyzes the structure of the novel and the contrast of
    characters, Fleda representing the "union of consciousness
    and conscience." This duality in the novel parallels the
    double function of literature, "the intrinsic literary
    function and the complementary philosophical one."

1950

27   D'ARZO, SILVIO. "Henry James (Di società, di uominie fantas-
        mi)." Paragone (1 December), 13-21. (Italian)
            In the best parts of James' works, nothing happens: He
        is a master of subtle complications and obstacles and be-
        lieves in a depth which has been replaced in modern society
        by shallowness and fast action. Deplores Italians' ignor-
        ance of James because there are no editions of his best
        works. Discusses James' heroes, inactive, "ghosts," trans-
        parent symbols of their class, and suggests that his char-
        acters are real people because James picks out the most
        intimate and daily banalities, thereby having a sense of
        society and its directions.

28   DELÉTANG-TARDIF, YANETTE. "Henry James." Vie Art Cité, 14
        (1950), 50-51. (French)
            "Among the novelists of all countries and all times,
        Henry James is probably the one who makes the entire estab-
        lished structure of human relations the most unsteady."
        Distinguishes between James and Proust; discusses James'
        style and its effect on readers, especially in The Ambassa-
        dors.

29   DE VOTO, BERNARD. "The Invisible Novelist," in The World of
        Fiction. Boston: Houghton Mifflin Co., pp. 213-14
            In considering the problem of the novelist presenting
        his world without being present in it, remarks that the
        narrator of The Turn of the Screw provides "a point of
        orientation that makes the desired uncertainty inevitable
        as soon as the governess, a second 'I,' begins to tell her
        story." James' method allowed for finely discriminating
        feelings.

30   DUNBAR, VIOLA R. "Addenda to 'Biographical and Critical
        Studies of Henry James, 1941-1948,' American Literature,
        20, 424-435 (January, 1949)." American Literature, 22
        (March), 56-61.
            Update of 1949.B19. Lists books and articles on James
        alphabetically, according to author, and reprints of James'
        works between 1930 and 1948, arranged chronologically.

31   DUNBAR, VIOLA R. "The Revision of Daisy Miller." Modern
        Language Notes, 65 (May), 311-17.
            In his revision of Daisy Miller for the New York edi-
        tion, James used "'the helpful imagination'" to "emphasize
        Daisy's charm, the disagreeableness of her critics, and
        the innocence of her conduct." The result is "to make
        plainer the meaning of the story."

1950

32   DUPEE, F. W. "Henry James and the Play." <u>Nation</u>, 171
          (8 July), 40-42.
              Discusses James' knowledge of the theatre and the rea-
          sons for his failure as a dramatist. Sees the dramatic
          interlude as "a token of power and rejuvenation and re-
          union with the tribe," which eventuated in a crisis, "both
          for ego and for career," but "did not involve a collapse,
          a 'crack-up.'"

33   FADIMAN, CLIFTON. "Foreword: The 'Meaning' of <u>The Innocents</u>,"
          in <u>The Innocents: A New Play by William Archibald. Based
          on The Turn of the Screw by Henry James</u>. New York:
          Coward-McCann, pp. ix-x.
              Notes that the "meaning" of James' tale <u>The Turn of the
          Screw</u> is more difficult to define than that in Archibald's
          adaptation, in which "the original Jamesian movement and
          motives" are simplified.

34   FADIMAN, CLIFTON. "Introduction," in <u>Washington Square</u>.
          Edited by Clifton Fadiman. Modern Library. New York:
          Random House, pp. v-xii.
              <u>Washington Square</u> is a realistic picture of American
          manners and reveals much about national character. Dis-
          cusses genesis of the novel, and examines it as "an acute
          study of a small segment of American culture," but more
          importantly an investigation of the relationships between
          individuals. Reprinted: 1955.B30.

35   FALK, ROBERT P. "Henry James's Romantic 'Vision of the Real'
          in the 1870's," in <u>Essays Critical and Historical Dedi-
          cated to Lily B. Campbell</u>. Berkeley and Los Angeles:
          University of California Press, pp. 235-55.
              Whereas most studies consider James apart from his age,
          Falk looks at his early career against the background of
          the Gilded Age and the rise of realism in the late 1860's
          and 1870's, emphasizing James' effort in "his formative
          years to work out, in critical and artistic terms, a syn-
          thesis of the two underlying intellectual currents of his
          time." James sought "a new kind of realism" combining
          "ethical and idealistic elements of a pre-Darwinian psy-
          chology, without becoming didactic, and which would also
          include the deterministic elements of the new Science...."

36   FIOCCO, A. "Un romanzo di James sul palcoscenio." <u>La Fiera
          Letteraria</u>, no. 38 (24 September), p. 8. (Italian)
              Description of the theatrical production in Rome of <u>The
          Heiress</u>, with a synopsis of <u>Washington Square</u>, the novel
          from which it was adapted.

177

1950

37 FITZPATRICK, KATHLEEN ELIZABETH. "Notes on Henry James and
    The Turn of the Screw." Meanjin, 9 (Summer), 275-78.
        Argues against the Freudian interpretation of The Turn
    of the Screw (see 1924.B10, 1934.B37) from the standpoint
    of "the text of the story and the technique of Henry James
    as a story-teller," and interprets the tale as revelations
    on a characteristic Jamesian theme of innocence betrayed,
    based on James' belief in the presence of evil. "If The
    Turn of the Screw is really the story of the governess and
    not of the children, Henry James did not know it."

38 GARLAND, ROBERT. "Eerie and Arresting--Truly Spellbinding."
    New York Theatre Critics' Reviews, 11 (6 February), 361.
        Describes The Turn of the Screw as "one of the most
    sinister and obscure of modern fictions."

39 GIBBS, WOLCOTT. "Black Magic and Bundling." New Yorker, 25
    (11 February), 44, 46.
        Supports psychoanalytic interpretation of The Turn of
    the Screw, contrary to Archibald's view in The Innocents,
    and discusses differences between the drama and the nou-
    velle.

40 GREENE, GRAHAM. "Books in General." New Statesman and Na-
    tion, 39 (28 January), 101-102.
        James began writing for the theatre because he was
    "challenged by a new method of expression," and the recent
    publication of the plays (see 1949.B11) shows how com-
    pletely he failed. Reprinted: 1951.B30.

41 GREENE, GRAHAM. "Henry James." La Table Ronde, 29 (May),
    9-22.
        French translation by Marcelle Sibon of 1936.B8.

42 HARLOW, VIRGINIA. Thomas Sergeant Perry: A Biography, and
    Letters to Perry from William, Henry and Garth Wilkinson
    James. Durham, N.C.: Duke University Press, passim.
        Biography of Perry which includes an account of his
    lifelong association with the James family, especially
    "Willie and Harry," with whom he carried on "voluminous
    correspondence." The letters provide "evidence not only
    of the help that James was able to give to Perry in his
    literary work but of the affection between the two men
    even when they had little opportunity to see each other."
    Reprints over 80 letters from James to Perry.

1950

43   HAVENS, RAYMOND D.   "Henry James' 'The Impressions of a Cous-
         in.'"   Modern Language Notes, 65 (May), 317-19.
         Preliminary sketches in James' notebooks have a differ-
     ent "center of interest" from the published version of "The
     Impressions of a Cousin."

44   HAWKINS, WILLIAM.   "'The Innocents' Is Splendidly Cast."   New
         York Theatre Critics' Reviews, 11 (6 February), 361.
         The Turn of the Screw is "notoriously ambiguous among
     scholars.   They like to read into it a deep truth that
     conflicts with the surface reality."

*45 HENNECKE, H.   "Henry James."   Süddeutsche Zeitung (21 Janu-
         ary).   Cited in 1959.B5.   (German)
         James "is the first 'consistent psychologist'" among
     nineteenth-century American novelists "and has remained to
     this day one of the greatest and most epoch-making, next to
     Dostoevsky and Proust."   The only counterparts to the
     Jamesian conflicts, "his 'casuistry of the heart'...are
     those of Adalbert Stifter."   James' "ultimate objective is
     not theology or metaphysics, but is of a moral nature."
     (Quotations from 1959.B5.)

46   HOWE, IRVING.   "Henry James and the Millionaire."   Tomorrow,
         9 (January), 53-55.
         Characterizes The American as one of the first efforts
     by an American novelist to represent "the American who,
     because of the country's geographical and cultural isola-
     tion, is taken to be radically different from Europeans...."
     Because this country lacks a homogeneous culture and there-
     fore a truly "national character," Newman exhibits "a con-
     fusing pastiche of standardized sectional traits," and
     "Newman as a type conflicts with Newman as a character."
     Points out "several layers of disharmony in the novel,"
     which is described as "transitional" and lacking full
     "dramatic realization."

47   JONES, M.   "Balzac aux États-Unis."   Revue de Littérature
         Comparée, 24 (April), 228-30.   (French)
         James and Dreiser reveal the influence of Balzac on
     American writers.   Examines similarities between James'
     work and that of Balzac in selected stories.   In Washing-
     ton Square and Eugenie Grandet, not only are subject and
     characters comparable, but James' treatment of theme is
     similar to Balzac's.   James' later works, less heavily
     influenced by the French writer, show his determination
     to become more independent.

1950

48   KANE, ROBERT J.   "Hawthorne's 'The Prophetic Pictures' and
      James's 'The Liar.'"   Modern Language Notes, 65 (April),
      257-58.
           James' "The Liar" may owe an "unconscious and unac-
      knowledged debt" to Hawthorne's "The Prophetic Pictures."

49   KAYSER, VON RUDOLF.   "Henry James: Ein europäischer Ameri-
      kaner."   Neue Schweizer Rundschau, 18 (December), 480-84.
      (German)
           James' passion for art is what made him choose Europe
      over America, where the reality of searching souls who are
      divided in themselves was not yet of interest. Unlike the
      Europeans, however, James' psychology is generally linked
      to moral judgments.

50   KENTON, EDNA.   "Introduction," in Eight Uncollected Tales of
      Henry James.   Edited by Edna Kenton.   New Brunswick, N.J.:
      Rutgers University Press, pp. 3-20.   Reprinted: Freeport,
      New York;   Books for Libraries Press, 1971.
           Briefly surveys the short fictions of 1865-1876, of
      which fifteen remain uncollected. The volume reprints
      eight, five for the first time. Reviews these early tales,
      "far less as stories with 'plots' than as foreshadowings of
      ideas and techniques that are basic in all of his later
      work." Concludes with a chronological listing of 28 stor-
      ies of this period and bibliographical information concern-
      ing them. Reviewed: Leon Edel, New York Times Book Re-
      view (10 September 1950), p. 5.

51   KERNER, DAVID.   "A Note on The Beast in the Jungle."   Univer-
      sity of Kansas City Review, 17 (Winter), 109-18.
           Summarizes the puzzling opening of "The Beast in the
      Jungle" and the questions it raises. Analyzes character
      of Marcher, "founded on self-deception," and suggests that
      May "is Marcher," that she plays two roles which are "pro-
      jections of different parts of Marcher's mind" by which
      "he can judge his failure to live.... The reader is
      twitted by her name: May is may-be." Views short story
      as a parable, "an illustration of a law of human conduct"
      which in this case is "'It is not good for man to live
      alone.'" May represents love, Marcher represents fear.
      "By isolating ingrownness James wishes to terrify the read-
      er out of wasting his humanity." See 1954.B41.

52   LEAVIS, F. R.   "James's 'What Maisie Knew': A Disagreement."
      Scrutiny, 17 (Summer), 115-27.
           Protests Bewley's view of What Maisie Knew, disputes
      the parallel with The Turn of the Screw, and contests the

"ambiguity" interpretation of the latter tale in which
"evil" had no particular significance for James. (See
1950.B10.) Describes the tone and mode of What Maisie
Knew as one of "extraordinarily high-spirited comedy,"
which includes pathos, but not that of "innocence as-
sailed." Suggests similarities to David Copperfield. Reprinted: 1952.B30; also in Anna Karenina and Other Essays. Pantheon Books. New York: Random House, 1967,
pp. 75-91.

53   McELDERRY, B. R., JR. "Henry James and The Whole Family."
     Pacific Spectator, 4 (Summer), 352-60.
         An examination of James' chapter, "The Married Son," in
     the collaborative work The Whole Family, written for Har-
     per's Bazaar, 1906-1907. Gives background of the "novel,"
     suggested by Howells; discusses how James became involved;
     summarizes his contribution, of which "warp and woof are
     sentiment and surprise"; and concludes that Howells' and
     James' chapters "stand out from the others with their
     primary interest in character."

54   McFARLANE, I. D. "A Literary Friendship--Henry James and Paul
     Bourget." Cambridge Journal, 4 (December), 144-61.
         A study of the friendship between James and Paul Bour-
     get, French novelist and critic, in view of information
     from the notebooks. Describes their meeting in 1884,
     points of commonality, respect for each other's work,
     views of technique, theory of fiction, and mutual assist-
     ance rendered, although "James...appeared to have given
     more than he got in the friendship." Concludes that "they
     were...closest in their general ideas of the novel: in
     their application of those principles they showed irrecon-
     cilable divergences" which probably helped them "to clarify
     their ideas on art," considered by both to be "a matter of
     great seriousness...."

55   MacKENZIE, COMPTON. "Memories of Henry James." Commonweal,
     51 (13 January), 394-97.
         Reprint of 1943.B30.

56   MARSHALL, MARGARET. "Drama." Nation (11 February), 140-41.
         The Turn of the Screw is "a great story of all-too-
     earthly human relationships" in which James uses the con-
     ventions of the ghost story "to enhance...the frightening
     human realities with which he is dealing."

1950

57   MILLETT, FRED B. Comment on "The Tone of the Time," in <u>Read-
     ing Fiction: A Method of Analysis with Selections for</u>
     <u>Study</u>. New York: Harper and Brothers, pp. 199-200.
         James' story "The Tone of the Time" is "characteristic
     of the art of Henry James at its ripest." Discusses James'
     choice of point of view, the nature of the "observer-
     narrator," and James' use of coincidence in the tale. The
     focal symbol of the story is the painting, which takes on
     increasingly complex significance for the characters. Of-
     fers questions dealing with structure, style, and "pattern
     of feelings and emotions" in the tale.

58   MUNSON, GORHAM. "'The Real Thing': A Parable for Writers of
     Fiction." <u>University of Kansas City Review</u>, 16 (Summer),
     261-64.
         "The Real Thing" can be viewed as a parable for profes-
     sional writers and is "about the preference that graphic
     artists and literary artists have for inventing characters
     rather than copying characters from actual life." Sees as
     "the figure in the carpet" the concept that "there is for
     each art-medium a special suitability of characters."

59   POUND, EZRA. <u>The Letters of Ezra Pound</u>. Edited by D. D.
     Paige. New York: Harcourt, Brace and Co., pp. 125, 137-
     38 and passim.
         Objects to treating Howells and James together: "You
     shouldn't treat a great man and a mutton-shank in one page
     as if there were no gulph between 'em." James "<u>HAS</u> writ-
     ten the <u>MOST</u> obscene book of our time...." Suggests that
     the primary purpose of his essay on James for <u>Little Re-</u>
     <u>view</u> (<u>see</u> 1918.B20-24) "is to get the really good stuff
     disentangled from the inferior...."

60   ROUSE, BLAIR. "Charles Dickens and Henry James: Two Ap-
     proaches to the Art of Fiction." <u>Nineteenth-Century Fic-</u>
     <u>tion</u>, 5 (September), 151-57.
         Considers work of Dickens and James with regard to
     factors which affect their appeal. Both were concerned
     with human character, understood the necessity of drama-
     tizing their material, but Dickens saw humanity panoramic-
     ally, whereas James investigated it microscopically.
     Dickens, a nineteenth-century artist in his use of mate-
     rial, had great popular appeal, while James, whose treat-
     ment of moral and aesthetic problems was timeless, was
     not understood in his time.

1950

61   SCHORER, MARK. "Introductory Comment," in The Story: A
      Critical Anthology. Englewood Cliffs, N.J.: Prentice-
      Hall, pp. 329-32.
           Defines the novelette, in which form James "showed later
      writers the full potentialities." Describes The Turn of
      the Screw as "a ghost story in the demonic tradition,"
      which has also been interpreted as a "drama of hysterical
      obsession."

62   SHORT, R. W. "Some Critical Terms of Henry James." Publica-
      tions of the Modern Language Association, 65 (September),
      667-80.
           An analysis of "3 pairs of James' key critical words:
      action and character, register and centre, and scene and
      picture," using the critical prefaces and later fiction
      as sources of his "mature theory and practice."

63   SIGAUX, GILBERT. "'Les Ambassadeurs.'" La Nef, no. 71-72
      (December 1950; January 1951), pp. 197-99. (French)
           Considers the significance of the James revival, in
      America "one sign among others of an aesthetic evolution,"
      and surveys the history of Jamesian translations in France.
      The Ambassadors possesses "unique qualities, the mark of
      his [James'] own genius, his familiar themes, the concerns
      of his writing." Concludes that "In each Jamesian novel,
      there is a secret that the characters attempt to pene-
      trate, an invisible barrier that they attempt to clear."

*64   STOKES, DONALD HUBERT. "Honors for Henry James." Christian
      Science Monitor Magazine (June 17), p. 14.
           Cited in Beatrice Ricks, comp. Henry James: A Bib-
      liography of Secondary Works, #3425.

65   STONE, EDWARD. "A Further Note on Daisy Miller and Cherbuli-
      ez." Philological Quarterly, 29 (April), 213-16.
           Dunbar's article on the source of Daisy Miller (see
      1948.B13) understates "the evidence of indebtedness to
      Victor Cherbuliez." Points out similarities of character-
      ization, theme and plot in Daisy Miller and Paul Méré, and
      suggests that James expected his readers to recognize his
      source, "almost led them to it...."

66   STONE, EDWARD. "Henry James's First Novel." Boston Public
      Library Quarterly, 2 (April), 167-71.
           James' early works should be examined to discover what
      hints of later characteristics they reveal. Summarizes
      plot of Watch and Ward, which demonstrates "The familiar
      Jamesian vagueness about facts," and describes the style

1950

as "surprisingly straightforward." The outstanding features of the novel are James' "infinite care for characterization, manifested as the hero's personality unfolds,"
and his "'historic sense.'"

67   STONE, EDWARD. "Henry James's Last Novel." Boston Public
      Library Quarterly, 2 (October), 348-53.
          The Sense of the Past provides as much autobiographical
      commentary as any of the prefaces. Discusses the history
      of composition of the novel and reasons for altering the
      original sketch. James probably "extended the boundaries
      of the past forward in time" in 1914, due to the impact
      of the war, rather than abjuring his lifelong devotion to
      the past, thereby asserting his allegiance to his own
      time both fictionally and personally.

68   TATE, ALLEN. "Three Commentaries: Poe, James, and Joyce."
      Sewanee Review, 58 (Winter), 5-10.
          Compares "The Beast in the Jungle" to Joyce's "The
      Dead," both of which "hinge upon climaxes of self-
      revelation, and both limit the reader's access to the sub-
      ject to a central intelligence; both end with a powerful
      irony...." The subject of James' tale is "the isolation
      and frustration of personality." Distinguishes certain
      technical features, such as "Indirect Approach" and "Op-
      erative Irony." Concludes that "The Beast in the Jungle"
      is "one of the great stories in the language," the effect
      being "that of tone, even of lyric meditation." Re-
      printed: 1950.B69.

69   TATE, ALLEN. "Three Commentaries: Poe, James, and Joyce,"
      in The House of Fiction. Edited by Caroline Gordon and
      Allen Tate. New York: Charles Scribner's Sons, pp. 228-
      31. Reprinted: 1960.
          Reprint of 1950.B68.

70   THORP, MARGARET FARRAND. "James as Script Writer." Furioso,
      5 (Spring), 72-75.
          The success of The Heiress, adapted from Washington
      Square, suggests that James might have been a successful
      screen writer. "The play was James and the movie is
      James."

71   TRILLING, LIONEL. "The Princess Casamassima," in The Liberal
      Imagination: Essays on Literature and Society. New York:
      The Viking Press, pp. 58-92.
          Reprint of 1948.B50.

72 WATTS, RICHARD, JR. "The Case of the Haunted Children." New
    York Theatre Critics' Reviews, 11 (6 February), 359.
        The Innocents "makes no compromise with the theory that
    James intended to suggest that the cruel phantoms of his
    novel were but figments of the unhappy heroine's diseased
    imagination."

73 WILLIAMS, STANLEY THOMAS. "Cosmopolitanism in American Lit-
    erature before 1880," in The American Writer and the Eu-
    ropean Tradition. Edited by Margaret Denny and William H.
    Gilman. Minneapolis: University of Minnesota Press,
    pp. 45-62.
        A study of literary cosmopolitanism in American litera-
    ture, the "facing toward Europe," which suggests that
    James turned to the Old World "for its society and the
    mind of its society."

74 YOUNG, ROBERT E. "An Error in The Ambassadors." American
    Literature, 22 (November), 245-53.
        In all available editions since first published in
    1903, Chapters 28 and 29 of The Ambassadors are reversed,
    causing several discrepancies in facts and time. Explains
    what makes the error evident, and theorizes why it was
    propogated. Remarks on the curiosity of the feature re-
    maining unnoticed by critics. See 1951.B15; 1952.B18,
    B71.

75 ZABEL, MORTON DAUWEN. "Henry James," in Historia de la lit-
    eratura norteamericana. Buenos Aires: Losada, pp. 282-
    312. (Spanish)
        Exposition of the life and works of James focusing on
    the international theme and the problem of art. Analyzes
    The Portrait of a Lady as "one of the best novels and one
    of the most beautiful of modern literature," and as dem-
    onstrating the diverse effects that Europe produces on the
    American character. Examines James' presentation of the
    theme of the seduction of innocence by the world, and
    studies The Ambassadors, James' major tribute to European
    civilization, and The Wings of the Dove. James' world,
    however specialized, is a "microcosm of the life and des-
    tiny of man."

1951 A BOOKS

1 CANBY, HENRY SEIDEL. Turn West, Turn East: Mark Twain and
   Henry James. Boston: Houghton Mifflin Co., 330 pp.

1951

A biography of James and Twain, using the technique of
counterpoint, based on the hypothesis that members of every
progressive American family have at some time turned West
or East, becoming new men and women through the Western
experience or more civilized individuals by returning to
the sources of our culture in Europe. James and Twain are
viewed as representatives of these two movements, articu-
late observers who "were violently in contrast in temperament; in their art, in their strengths, in their weaknesses,
and in their excesses...," yet both of whom described
"American innocence." Emphasizes the two men's personalities, art, and the native impulses behind them. Uses
parallel chapters to point out the similarities and differences and the significance of both writers. Concludes
that both were "Innocents, James as regards morals, Twain
in culture and morals...." Yet they came from two different Americas of the same time and reveal important contrasts in the qualities of their work, both in subject and
art. James founded the "cult of awareness," Twain, the
"cult of youth." Reviewed: William M. Gibson, American
Literature, 24 (May 1952), 253-54; Howard Doughty, Nation,
173 (8 December 1951), 505; Leon Edel, New York Times Book
Review (11 November 1951), p. 8.

2   DUPEE, FREDERICK WILCOX. Henry James. American Men of Let-
    ters Series. New York: William Sloane Associates, 309
    pp. Partially reprinted: 1951.B14. Revised: 1956.A2.
       A critical biography of James which attempts "to por-
    tray him in the wholeness of his life, mind, and work...,"
    to present his thoughts and feelings as well as study his
    artistic development. Includes plot synopses and discus-
    sions of works against the background which generated
    them, and deals with such topics as James' unconventional
    childhood, bachelorhood, disappointment over dramatic
    career, life at Lamb House, friendships, and later years.
    Reviewed: Cornelia P. Kelley, American Literature, 24
    (May 1952), 251-53; Joseph Frank, Hudson Review, 4 (Winter
    1952), 612-19; Arthur Mizener, Partisan Review, 18 (May-
    June 1951), 361-64; Granville Hicks, Sewanee Review, 60
    (Winter 1952), 149-56; Kenneth B. Murdock, Yale Review,
    NS 41 (Autumn 1951), 115.

1951 B SHORTER WRITINGS

1   ARNAVON, CYRILLE. "Henry James," in Les lettres américaines
    devant la critique française. Paris: Societe d'Edition
    Les Belles Lettres, pp. 87-94. (French)

1951

Discusses French critical attitudes towards James, especially those of Régis Michaud, Marie-Anne de Bovet, Davray. At James' death, his work had still not been "penetrated" in France.

2   BEWLEY, MARIUS. "Correspondence: The Relation Between William and Henry James." Scrutiny, 17 (March), 331-34.
      Letter to Leavis in response to his remarks on The Turn of the Screw (see 1950.B52). For James, "the universe was pragmatically plastic, both for good and for evil." Suggests development between William and Henry was frequently parallel, discusses tension between appearance and reality in terms of William's pragmatism, and describes Maggie Verver of The Golden Bowl as the "greatest pragmatist in literature." The Turn of the Screw is a credo of pragmatism read backwards. The governess constructs an Evil out of truth that resides in the children's innocence. Reprinted: 1952.B8.

3   BLACKMUR, RICHARD P. "The Loose and Baggy Monsters of Henry James: Notes on the Underlying Classic Form in the Novel." Accent, 11 (Summer), 129-46.
      Technical form has as its major purpose bringing to the writer and reader "the feeling of what life is about." James' technical forms have been "misunderstood both with regard to themselves and...to their mutual relations with other forms." The ideal and substantial origin of classic form has been ignored, and the poetic aspects of his language and conventions of his forms minimized. Suggests that James' superior art is a result of "'organic form.'" The later novels demonstrate the well-made play structure, presenting the journey of a searcher or pilgrim in the Christian pattern of rebirth, ending in a "living analogue of death, sacrifice and renunciation." The Ambassadors deals with life of the senses; Kate Croy in The Wings of the Dove is the lady of philosophy or practical wisdom; Maggie Verver in The Golden Bowl is the lady of theology or divine wisdom. James creates "heaving motion of a conscience out of consciousness." Questions with what ideas James' imaginative response to life is related, perhaps those concerned with his whole work, and concludes that the "burden" is on "the pure individual consciousness." Reprinted: 1955.B11.

4   BROWER, REUBEN. The Fields of Light: An Experiment in Critical Reading. New York: Oxford University Press, passim.

1951

> Reference to the values behind irony in James' works
> as being "so subtle as to defy satisfactory analysis."

5 C., R. W. "James and Kipling." <u>Notes and Queries</u>, 196
   (9 June), 260.
   Questions whether the reference in Kipling's <u>The Jane-</u>
   <u>ites</u> to "'Enery James'" is "the dramatic method of which
   <u>Emma</u> is the first example."

6 CANBY, HENRY SEIDEL. "Hero of the Great Know-How: Mark
   Twain's Machine-Age 'Yankee.'" <u>Saturday Review of Litera-</u>
   <u>ture</u>, 34 (20 October), 7-8, 40-41.
   In a consideration of Twain's <u>A Connecticut Yankee in</u>
   <u>King Arthur's Court</u>, mentions James' "passion for the
   'refinement' of culture (and religion)...." Reprinted:
   1959.B18.

7 CANBY, HENRY SEIDEL. "He Knew His Women." <u>Saturday Review</u>
   <u>of Literature</u>, 34 (10 November), 9-10, 34-35.
   James was the first writer to present "feminine obses-
   sions" powerfully in English. For this reason, <u>The Boston-</u>
   <u>ians</u> and <u>The Princess Casamassima</u> were poorly received and
   ranked as minor works.

8 CONNELL, JOHN. "Unpublished Letters." <u>National and English</u>
   <u>Review</u>, 136 (January), 29-32.
   An account of how the author procured letters to and
   from W. E. Henley, including ten letters from James "discussing the theatre with lucidity and vigour."

9 CROMWELL, AGNES WHITNEY. "Innocent Among the Lions." <u>Vogue</u>,
   15 (November), 158.
   Recalls conversation at a dinner party with James, who
   "had taught me the value of words and their power to ex-
   press the finest shades of meaning." She suggested the
   "post-plot" for <u>The Ambassadors</u>.

*10 CUBE, H. von. "Ein vollkommener Roman." <u>Die Neue Zeitung</u>
   (21 July). Cited in 1959.B5. (German)
   James' "artistic precision makes him superior to Balzac." <u>The Portrait of a Lady</u> "is not James's best book
   since it was written by James the observer and portraitist
   rather than the creative analyst. However, precisely for
   this reason it is one of his most accessible and least
   complicated books for the reader." (Quotations from
   1959.B5.)

11   DOLMATCH, THEODORE B. "Edmund Wilson as Literary Critic."
      University of Kansas City Review, 17 (Spring), 213-19.
            Wilson's "The Ambiguity of Henry James" (see 1934.B37),
      modified in light of the notebooks and closer critical
      examination, treats "James as a case history (rather than
      the story [The Turn of the Screw] as a case history)."

12   DORT, B. "Un roman de la connaissance: 'Les Ambassadeurs'
      d'Henry James." Cahiers du Sud, 38 (Summer), 329-33.
      (French)
            The Ambassadors motivates us to question the direction
      and capacities of contemporary literature, which is above
      all a romantic literature. Summarizes James' novel, which
      is generally interpreted as a history of an American in
      Paris, discusses effect of novel taking place in Strether's
      consciousness, compares James' method with Faulkner's.
      Analyzes novel as an interplay between the actions and
      thoughts of Strether, "the drama of the witness of his
      consciousness." The stream of consciousness technique
      reconciles the opposition between the subjective novel and
      the objective novel.

13   DOWNING, F. "The Art of Fiction." Commonweal, 55 (28 Decem-
      ber), 297-99.
            Disputes view of James as an artist remote from life,
      and sees him as a writer who was confident about his power
      to command the reader's attention. Describes James' pic-
      ture of Isabel meditating about her life in The Portrait
      of a Lady as "one of the most convincing, felt, and beau-
      tiful chapters...in all of literature."

14   DUPEE, FREDERICK WILCOX. "Henry James in the Great Grey
      Babylon." Partisan Review, 18 (March-April), 183-90.
            A section from 1951.A2. Discussion of James' life in
      England, his practice of defining "his limits in propor-
      tion as he extended them...." Details his double life as
      artist and "perpetual guest" in London, which resulted in
      his becoming "the extremely critical champion of luxury
      and privilege," though he never questioned the "aristo-
      cratic ideal itself." He reconciled the American ideals
      of "talents and money."

15   EDEL, LEON. "A Further Note on 'An Error in The Ambassadors.'"
      American Literature, 23 (March), 128-30.
            Response to 1950.B74. The reversal of chapter in The
      Ambassadors is not "as alarming" for the reputation of
      American critics or James as Young makes it seem, as the

error does not appear in the first English edition which
James saw through the press. Discusses reasons for per-
petuation of reversal in the New York edition, and labels
Young's as "hit and run" scholarship on a complex writer.
See 1952.B18, B71.

16 EDEL, LEON. "The Architecture of Henry James's 'New York
Edition.'" New England Quarterly, 24 (June), 169-78.
    The architecture of the New York edition "derived its
inspiration from Balzac and its subtlety from James's own
love of patterns and figures, secrecy, and mystification."
The entire edition is in its scope and organization "a
vast work of art."

17 EDEL, LEON. "The Versatile James." Nation, 173 (10 November), 406-408.
    Essay-review of Zabel's The Portable Henry James (see
1951.B58). "...Between the starched and stuffy James of
the legend and the creative artist there exists a marked
disparity."

18 EDEL, LEON. "Hugh Walpole and Henry James: The Fantasy of
the 'Killer and the Slain.'" American Imago, 8 (December),
351-69.
    Walpole's dedication of his 1941 The Killer and the
Slain to "'author of The Turning of the Screw'" is significant, and Edel examines Walpole's novel to discover the
relationship between its content and an association with
James' nouvelle. Walpole's story concerns a "personality
with a strongly homosexual component" in conflict, where
The Turn of the Screw concerns a governess in conflict
over "masculinity in the bud" (Miles) and "evil masculinity" (Quint). Suggests Walpole was, perhaps unconsciously,
putting "some of his feelings about James into the super-
masculine character," and that he identified James as a
surrogate father, the story representing "classical destruction of the father-image."

19 FAY, ELIOT G. "Balzac and Henry James." French Review, 24
(February), 325-30.
    Examination of James' ideas about Balzac based on his
five essays on the French writer which cover "every con-
ceivable aspect of Balzac's life, works, and literary
significance." First considers James' remarks on Balzac
as a man, then discusses his analysis of Balzac's literary
craftsmanship (his creation of characters, evocation of
atmosphere, documentation) and his view of Balzac's style
and philosophy.

20 FIREBAUGH, J. J. "Pragmatism of Henry James." <u>Virginia</u>
    <u>Quarterly Review</u>, 27 (Summer), 419-35.
       A study of <u>The Awkward Age</u>, "which begins as a state-
    ment of a rather slight social problem, and ends as a
    brilliant novel which implies a total view of human rela-
    tionships and a theory of truth." Shows how James' idea
    grew from its conception into expression in the novel,
    discusses the notebook entry and the "ultimate philosoph-
    ical problem" posed by the work. "Henry James expressed
    fictionally in 'The Awkward Age' what his brother William
    James was expressing in the pragmatic philosophy: the
    discovery of truth in the market place of human life:
    truth as process rather than truth as absolute...."

21 FURBANK, P. N. "Henry James: The Novelist as Actor."
    <u>Essays in Criticism</u>, 1 (October), 404-20.
       Singles out James' talent in "<u>expression</u>, in the actor's
    sense of the word...," and suggests that throughout his
    career James "takes a closer and closer look at the imme-
    diate performance of his characters" and "enlarges the
    scope of their acting...," as illustrated in <u>The Golden</u>
    <u>Bowl</u>.

22 GEGENHEIMER, ALBERT FRANK. "Early and Late Revision in Henry
    James's 'A Passionate Pilgrim.'" <u>American Literature</u>, 23
    (May), 233-42.
       James' revisions reveal the "method and purposes of his
    art." For example, the four versions (three revisions) of
    "A Passionate Pilgrim" show James in several periods and
    demonstrate that he "was a considerably more ornate and
    self-conscious author" than some critics recognize. De-
    scribes the general types of revisions, points out inter-
    esting sidelights on the development of James' personality
    and attitudes as seen in the revisions, and concludes that
    modern readers see better style in the revisions of the
    novels and tales than James' first readers.

23 GIBSON, WILLIAM M. "Metaphor in the Plot of <u>The Ambassadors</u>."
    <u>New England Quarterly</u>, 24 (September), 291-305.
       James employs metaphorical devices in <u>The Ambassadors</u>
    "to dramatize...key stages in the developing action" and
    to clarify "the moral significance of Strether's experi-
    ence to himself and to the reader." James' metaphors are
    "often sustained throughout a single novel," contributing
    greatly to its structure and effect.

1951

24   GOHDES, CLARENCE. "Escape from the Commonplace," in <u>The Lit</u>-
       <u>erature of the American People: An Historical and Critical</u>
       <u>Survey</u>. Edited by Arthur Hobson Quinn. New York: Apple-
       ton-Century-Crofts, pp. 688-700.
          James ranks with Hawthorne as "one of the two most dis-
       tinguished practitioners of the art of fiction whom Ameri-
       ca has so far produced." Discusses James' lack of
       popularity, provides a biographical sketch with correspond-
       ing survey of his works, reviews James' theory of fiction,
       and suggests that as a "practicing critic James, in his
       prime, was probably more like Sainte-Beuve than any other.
       ..." Concludes that James "was a humanist, convinced of
       moral responsibility; but consciousness rather than con-
       science was his theme."

25   GRAY, JAMES. "Interpreting Genius." <u>Saturday Review of Lit</u>-
       <u>erature</u>, 34 (1 December), 27.
          Canby (<u>see</u> 1951.A1) shows James was no trivial snob;
       "he was a wit who dropped into the boiling rapids of his
       rhetoric brilliant jewels of phrasemaking...."

26   GREENE, GRAHAM. "L'aspect religieux de Henry James." <u>Dieu</u>
       <u>Vivant</u>, no. 20, pp. 103-14.
          French translation of 1933.B8, formerly entitled "Henry
       James--An Aspect."

27   GREENE, GRAHAM. "Henry James: The Private Universe," in <u>The</u>
       <u>Lost Childhood and Other Essays</u>. London: William Heine-
       mann, pp. 21-30.
          Reprint of 1936.B8.

28   GREENE, GRAHAM. "Henry James: The Religious Aspect," in <u>The</u>
       <u>Lost Childhod and Other Essays</u>. London: William Heine-
       mann, pp. 31-39.
          Reprint of 1933.B8.

29   GREENE, GRAHAM. "The Lesson of the Master," in <u>The Lost</u>
       <u>Childhood and Other Essays</u>. London: William Heinemann,
       pp. 49-50.
          James has been the "victim of...misleading criticism,"
       examples of which are presented. Repudiates view of James
       as one who withdrew from life. He didn't avoid violence
       in his work, but the violence is of a subdued kind, draw-
       ing its "tone from all the rest of life." James' consid-
       eration of the rules of his art were liberating to his
       genius: "You cannot be a protestant before you have
       studied the dogmas of the old faith." The prefaces "have
       made future novelists conscious: that the planned effect
       has been substituted for the lucky stroke...."

1951

30 GREENE, GRAHAM. "The Plays of Henry James," in The Lost
    Childhood and Other Essays. London: William Heinemann,
    pp. 45-48.
        Reprint of 1950.B40.

31 GREENE, GRAHAM. "The Portrait of a Lady," in The Lost Child-
    hood and Other Essays. London: William Heinemann,
    pp. 40-44.
        Reprint of 1947.B14.

32 HARRIS, MARIE P. "Henry James, Lecturer." American Litera-
    ture, 23 (November), 302-14.
        A consideration of James as a public speaker during his
    American visit, 1904-1905, which provides a slightly dif-
    ferent picture of him. Describes James' manner and physi-
    cal appearance, the content of lectures and public recep-
    tion of them. "As a lecturer James had shown himself
    always modest, agreeable, even witty, and the farthest
    removed from pomposity...," yet the lectures brought him
    some misunderstanding and abuse.

33 HARTLEY, L. P. "Henry James," in Sixteen Portraits of People
    Whose Houses Have Been Preserved by The National Trust.
    Edited by L. A. G. Strong. London: The Naldrett Press,
    pp. 80-92.
        James' taking of Lamb House represented a "water-shed"
    in his career, which "intervened between two periods of
    his literary development...." It also marked "an important
    change in his method of composition." Discusses James'
    residence at Lamb House, and concludes that it was "the
    temple--the shrine in which he worshipped it [art]."

34 HAVENS, R. D. "Henry James on One of His Early Stories."
    American Literature, 23 (March), 131-33.
        Reprints a letter from James to J. A. Hammerton,
    July 23, 1914, objecting to the latter publishing "The Ro-
    mance of Certain Old Clothes" in his collection because
    the work is unrepresentative. Gives details of the story's
    various publications, notes minor revisions James made on
    it, and enumerates its problems.

35 HOFFMAN, FREDERICK J. "Henry James, W. D. Howells and the
    Art of Fiction," in The Modern Novel in America. Chicago:
    Henry Regnery Co., pp. 1-30. Reprinted: Gateway Edition,
    1956.
        "James set out to reveal the state of civilization, to
    study it in terms of the most highly conscious and dis-
    criminating intelligence he could bring to it." Views

193

1951

> James as a "link in the continuation of the traditional
> novel," discusses his belief that method is the controlling
> element in fiction, and his understanding of the moral
> purpose of the novel. "In his preoccupation with method,
> with point of view, and with the precise integration of
> every element of fiction, James gained a moderate following
> in his lifetime.... As a critic of fiction, he has gained
> enormously in following in recent years...."

36 HOWE, IRVING. "The Future of the Novel: The Political Novel."
     Tomorrow, 10 (May), 51-58.
       Describes the political novel in general terms as "pe-
     culiarly a work of internal tensions" incorporating repre-
     sentative action and ideology. The Princess Casamassima
     "presented...a purely objective problem in imaginative
     creation." Considers accuracy of surface realities in the
     novel, in which Paul Muniment is the "great triumph." The
     work "raises with unexcelled pathos and sensitivity the
     very problem of the political vocation itself."

37 LERNER, DANIEL and OSCAR CARGILL. "Henry James at the Grecian
     Urn." Publications of the Modern Language Association, 66
     (June), 316-31.
       An examination of The Bostonians and The Other House
     "to upset the theory of James's cultural limitations" and
     to provide evidence of his familiarity with ancient liter-
     ature. Points out multiple resemblances between The Bos-
     tonians and Antigone, and suggests the similarity to Greek
     drama in The Other House.

38 LIND, ILSE DUSOIR. "The Inadequate Vulgarity of Henry James."
     Publications of the Modern Language Association, 66 (Decem-
     ber), 886-910.
       James' brief experience as a Tribune correspondent, like
     his later association with the theatre, is an example of "a
     persistent literary problem, his inability to achieve
     'adequate vulgarity.'" Gives an account of James' associa-
     tion with the newspaper; reprints several of his letters
     in an effort to assess the significance of this period in
     his attitude towards the public, his art and himself; and
     investigates his recollections, especially those in "The
     Next Time," "to show how he confronted and interpreted a
     crucial problem which threatened the very basis of his
     artistic integrity."

39 LIND, S. E. "Some Comments on B. R. McElderry's 'The Uncol-
     lected Stories of Henry James.'" American Literature, 23
     (March), 130-31.

1951

McElderry (see 1949.B36) made some questionable statements and assumptions, especially in considering "playlets"
as uncollected short stories.

40   LIND, S. E. "James's 'The Private Life' and Browning."
     American Literature, 23 (November), 315-22.
          In "The Private Life," the character of Clare Vawdrey
     was inspired by Browning, and "F. L.," referred to in the
     notebooks, is the prototype for Lord Mellifont, Frederick,
     Lord Leighton, a Victorian painter. This tale of double
     personality, of the dichotomy between the social and crea-
     tive life, is viewed as "disguised autobiography," in which
     James transposed the general and specific aspects of his
     own life.

41   MARKOW, GEORGES. "Charles DuBos et Henry James." Revue de
     Littérature Comparée, 25 (October-December), 436-48.
     (French)
          Charles DuBos brought his thought and insight to an
     analysis of James. Discusses DuBos' association with
     James, his impressions of the American author, his role
     as the defender and promoter of James in France. Quotes
     some of DuBos' critical comments about James from his
     journal, which suggest his admiration for James' art.

42   MICHAELS, H. S. "An Unpublished Letter of Henry James."
     Colby Library Quarterly, 3 (May), 23-26.
          Reprints a letter written by James, probably during
     rehearsals in December, 1894, to praise actress Marion
     Terry for her "perfectly beautiful and right" performance
     in Guy Domville.

43   MILLETT, FRED B. "Introduction," in The Portrait of a Lady.
     Modern Library. New York: Random House, pp. v-xxxv.
          Biographical sketch and discussion of James' view of
     the purpose, nature and technique of the novel as outlined
     in "The Art of Fiction" and the prefaces. Compares The
     Portrait of a Lady to James' standards and considers how
     closely he came to meeting the demands he set forth for
     the novelist. Analyzes Isabel; remarks on consistency of
     the ending of the work.

44   MUSTANOJA, TAUNO F. "W. Somerset Maugham Portrays Henry
     James." Neuphilologische Mitteilungen, 52 (April), 99-
     103.
          "W. Somerset Maugham is one of those whose attitude
     towards Henry James remains on this side of idolatry."

1951

Looks at Maugham's remarks on James in <u>Teller of Tales</u>
(<u>see</u> 1939.B6) against the background of <u>The Razor's Edge</u>,
in which Elliott Templeton displays many Jamesian characteristics. "Maugham's use of Henry James as a model for...
Elliott Templeton is interesting because it shows that
Maugham was intrigued by the personality of the American
novelist...."

*45   NAEFE, ANNELIESE. <u>Bucherei und Bildung</u>, 3 (October). Cited
in 1959.B5. (German)
Criticizes <u>The Portrait of a Lady</u> as lacking life, containing excessive unimportant details and technical preoccupations which reduce the effectiveness of James' art.
"...Since the Jamesian conflicts are conditioned too much
by past ways and standards of life, plot and action do not
strike the modern reader sufficiently to outweigh long-
windedness" (quotation from 1959.B5).

46   NATHAN, MONIQUE. "Les 'Ambassadeurs' et les carnets de
James." <u>Critique</u>, 7 (June), 492-98. (French)
<u>The Ambassadors</u> and <u>The Notebooks of Henry James</u>
(1947.B32) are both important works as far as the growth
of the novel is concerned. Lists reasons for James' lack
of broad public appeal, and describes Madame de Vionnet
of <u>The Ambassadors</u>, the role she plays in that novel.

47   PIERHAL, ARMAND. "Henry James, le civilisé." <u>Hommes et</u>
<u>Mondes</u>, 6 (March), 413-20. (French)
A survey of critical attitudes towards James, with attention to views of James' expatriation, and description
of the emphases of the three periods of his career. Mentions opinions of Jacques-Émile Blanche, Edna Kenton,
Edmund Wilson, André Gide, T. S. Eliot, and Ford Madox
Hueffer (Ford).

48   POPKIN, HENRY. "The Two Theatres of Henry James." <u>New Eng-</u>
<u>land Quarterly</u>, 24 (March), 69-83.
"Henry James wrote for two theatres: for the commercial stage and for the theatre of his mind's eye." After
little success in the London theatres, James emphasized
the dramatic in later novels, creating in these the "perfect audience that existed only in James' imagination."
His "divergent techniques" employed for each of these two
theatres are illustrated in the several versions of <u>The</u>
<u>American</u>.

49   RALEIGH, J. H. "Henry James: The Poetics of Empiricism."
      Publications of the Modern Language Association, 66
      (March), 107-23.
          Defines and examines the nature of "consciousness," the
      subject of James' later works, and sees a relationship be-
      tween his conception of consciousness and the psychological
      premises of Lockean empiricism. "James's beloved con-
      sciousness...was nothing more than an artistic presentation
      of the idea of the tabula rasa being written upon by expe-
      rience, or sense impressions." Points out other implica-
      tions of empirical psychology in James' works, especially
      "passivity of the individual mind and ambiguity in human
      relations." Compares James' handling of the psychological
      process at three different stages, and concludes that he
      reached out "to a more complex view of personality."

50   REDMAN, BEN RAY. "New Editions." Saturday Review of Litera-
      ture, 34 (29 September), 15.
          Reviews Zabel's The Portable Henry James (see 1951.B58),
      which reveals "James's thematic range and stylistic evolu-
      tion."

51   SACKVILLE-WEST, EDWARD. "James: An American in Europe."
      Saturday Review of Literature, 34 (20 January), 24-25.
          The theme of the destruction of innocence runs through
      James' work. A "historian of civilized private life,"
      James deals with the problem of "how to gain the world
      without losing one's soul."

52   SCOTT-JAMES, ROLFE ARNOLD. "Above the Battle," in Fifty
      Years of English Literature, 1900-1950. New York: Long-
      mans, Green and Co., pp. 56-58. Reprinted: 1956.
          Discusses James' development of his themes, his method
      of "letting the life of his story speak for itself," and
      his style, which "reaches the height of its obscurity"
      with The Golden Bowl. "With him English fiction starts
      again."

53   SHROEDER, J. W. "The Mothers of Henry James." American Lit-
      erature, 22 (January), 424-31.
          "The Beast in the Jungle," "The Jolly Corner," and
      "Crapy Cornelia" reveal the stereotyped relation of a male
      protagonist (mature, sensitive gentleman) to a principle
      female protagonist (mature, sensitive woman), and suggest
      the return to the mother, the symbolized quest for release
      and security. Examines "The Great Good Place" as showing
      Dane returning to maternal depths to shed his burden, both
      by transferring it to a young visitor and relapsing into

1951

foetal dependency, and hypothesizes that James placed this
symbolic component in the tale consciously. Dane's,
White-Mason's and Brydon's are "three definite examples of
the archetypal mother-quest as an integrative symbolic
element in the work of Henry James."

54   SMITH, JAMES HARRY and EDD WINFIELD PARKS. "Henry James," in
      Great Critics. Edited by James Harry Smith and Edd Win-
      field Parks. Third edition, revised and enlarged. New
      York: W. W. Norton and Co., pp. 648-51.
          Biographical sketch and summary of James' criticism of
      prose fiction, which he preferred "be considered simply as
      one inclusive genre." Suggests that James viewed the
      problem of modern criticism as synthesizing the real and
      the aesthetic, life and art. "The Art of Fiction" stresses
      the "freedom of the novel, and its correspondence with
      life."

55   STONE, EDWARD. "Henry James and Rome." Boston Public Li-
      brary Quarterly, 3 (April), 143-45.
          "The Last of the Valerii," with a theme presumably bor-
      rowed from Mérimée, and other fiction of this period are
      "as 'highly documentary' of the enchantment which the an-
      tiquity of the Italian capital worked on Henry James as
      they are of an early artistic indebtedness," and reveal
      his ambivalence about Rome, with its antiquity both
      dazzling and oppressive.

56   THURBER, JAMES, MARK VAN DOREN and LYMAN BRYSON. "The Ambas-
      sadors." Invitation to Learning, I (Winter), 364-71.
          A discussion of the drama of The Ambassadors as Streth-
      er's moral decision. Thurber views the hero as "a man who
      does the saving, a man whose final word sets free a spirit,
      who has also saved himself." Van Doren describes James'
      interest "in the effects of experiences...on the persons
      who have them, and on others, too." Bryson suggests that
      readers "haven't been willing to make the effort" with the
      novel, which "like most precious things" is "very deep and
      you have to dig to get it." Reprinted: in George D.
      Crothers, ed. Invitation to Learning: English and Ameri-
      can Novels. New York and London: Basic Books, 1966,
      pp. 262-71.

57   YOUNG, FREDERIC HAROLD. "The Doctrine of Spiritual Man," in
      The Philosophy of Henry James, Sr. New York: Bookman
      Associates, p. 219 and passim.
          Notes how Quentin Anderson (see 1946.B1) has "explored
      the use to which Henry James, Jr. put the implications of

his father's spiritual psychology in the creation of literary 'individuals' in his novels."

58   ZABEL, MORTON D. "Introduction," in The Portable Henry James.
Edited by Morton D. Zabel. New York: The Viking Press,
pp. 1-29. Reprinted: 1956.
     Considers James a major exponent of "dialectic intelli-
gence," as presenting the oppositions in morality and culture, and discusses his presentation of the American/
European conflict. Assesses the James revival: "When
controversy, enthusiasm, personal legend, and historic oc-
casion combine in the rediscovery of a writer," he is
clearly "marked by circumstances as well as genius to play
a significant role in the drama of culture." Surveys
James' career as "a major instance of the persistence and
integrity of the writer's vocation." The clue to James
is in the words "life" and "freedom," and the "ideal of
consciousness" he implies is the basis of his "morality as
an artist." His is "the vision of human and moral truth."
Revised: 1957.B78; 1968, by Lyall H. P. Powers. Reviewed:
G. F. Whicher, New York Herald Tribune Book Review (30 September 1951), p. 16; F. W. Dupee, New York Times Book Review (2 September 1951), p. 5; New Yorker, 27 (22 September 1951), 119.

1952 A BOOKS

1   GALE, ROBERT L. "The Caught Image: A Study of Figurative
Language in the Fiction of Henry James." Ph.D. dissertation, Columbia University. Published as The Caught Image:
Figurative Language in the Fiction of Henry James. Chapel
Hill: University of North Carolina Press, 1964, 266 pp.
     A study of the images in James' works, which "reveal
character and move the plot." Divides figures into six
major groups and examines each: water, flower, animal,
religion, war and art. Includes appendices charting
James' imagery "with respect to time of writing, length of
fictional piece, and setting."

2   SWAN, MICHAEL. Henry James. European Novelists Series.
London: Arthur Barker, 96 pp.
     "Life and Works" relates James' life to his literary
output, with reference to journals, letters and fiction.
Attempts to discover major preoccupations of his interior
life during various periods of his career. "Various Aspects" provides analyses of novels and stories according
to theme (e.g., international situation; innocence/

1952

corruption). In "The Figure in the Carpet," seeks to de-
tect James' attitude toward life and art, and concludes
that morality is closely linked to artistic effect in
James' work. Reviewed: Robert Halsband, Saturday Review
of Literature, 36 (8 August 1953), 40; Times Literary
Supplement (9 January 1953), p. 23.

3   TRASCHEN, ISADORE. "Henry James: The Art of Revision, a
     Comparison of the Original and Revised Versions of The
     American." Ph.D. dissertation, Columbia University.
        James' revisions are a significant element of his final
     period, and The American was most extensively revised.
     Examines revisions in this novel, which "were organized
     into a narrative sequence roughly corresponding to the
     principal actions, and around the several characters," and
     which suggest James' idea of form. James both heightened
     the illusion of realism and touched up the romantic aspects
     of The American.

1952 B SHORTER WRITINGS

1   BEEBE, MAURICE. "Henry James and the Sophomore." College
     English, 13 (May), 455-57.
        Considers whether the novels of James are suitable
     teaching material; questions the standard of greatness in
     literature applied by Scott (see 1952.B60), the "literature-
     as-communication pattern" which fails to take into account
     all the possible virtues. Suggests that the value of
     "awareness" advocated by James is part of the importance
     of liberal education, and defends the idea of exposing
     undergraduates to James in an effort to counteract the
     popular arts as a main criterion of literature.

2   BEWLEY, MARIUS. "The American Problem," in The Complex Fate:
     Hawthorne, Henry James and Some Other American Writers.
     London: Chatto and Windus, pp. 55-78; New York: Grove
     Press, 1954. Reprinted: New York: Gordian Press, 1967.
        Reprint of 1950.B9. Reviewed: Randall Stewart, Ameri-
     can Literature, 26 (January 1955), 580-83; E. A. Bloom,
     Saturday Review of Literature, 37 (4 September 1954), 31.

3   BEWLEY, MARIUS. "Appearance and Reality in Henry James," in
     The Complex Fate: Hawthorne, Henry James, and Some Other
     American Writers. London: Chatto and Windus, pp. 79-113;
     New York: Grove Press, 1954. Reprinted: New York:
     Gordian Press, 1967.
        Reprint of 1950.B10.

1952

4   BEWLEY, MARIUS. "'The Blithedale Romance' and 'The Bostoni-
     ans,'" in The Complex Fate: Hawthorne, Henry James, and
     Some Other American Writers. London: Chatto and Windus,
     pp. 11-30; New York: Grove Press, 1954. Reprinted:
     New York: Gordian Press, 1967.
          Reprint of 1949.B4.

5   BEWLEY, MARIUS. "Hawthorne, Henry James, and the American
     Novel," in The Complex Fate: Hawthorne, Henry James, and
     Some Other American Writers. London: Chatto and Windus,
     pp. 1-10; New York: Grove Press, 1954. Reprinted: New
     York: Gordian Press, 1967.
          Considers Cooper, Melville, Hawthorne and James as
     forming a tradition in the American novel, separate from
     the frontier colloquial tradition, based on the problem
     of the "nature of his [writer's] separateness, and the
     nature of his connection with Europe, and particularly
     with English culture." Asserts influence of Hawthorne on
     James' artistic development as part of a literary tradi-
     tion."

6   BEWLEY, MARIUS. "Maisie, Miles and Flora, the Jamesian Inno-
     cents: A Rejoinder," in The Complex Fate: Hawthorne,
     Henry James, and Some Other American Writers. London:
     Chatto and Windus, pp. 132-43; New York: Grove Press,
     1954. Reprinted: New York: Gordian Press, 1967.
          Reprint of 1950.B11.

7   BEWLEY, MARIUS. "'The Marble Faun' and 'The Wings of the
     Dove,'" in The Complex Fate: Hawthorne, Henry James, and
     Some Other American Writers. London: Chatto and Windus,
     pp. 31-54; New York: Grove Press, 1954. Reprinted: New
     York: Gordian Press, 1967.
          Reprint of 1949.B5.

8   BEWLEY, MARIUS. "The Relation Between William and Henry
     James," in The Complex Fate: Hawthorne, Henry James, and
     Some Other American Writers. London: Chatto and Windus,
     pp. 145-59; New York: Grove Press, 1954. Reprinted: New
     York: Gordian Press, 1967.
          Reprint of 1951.B2.

9   BLACKMUR, RICHARD P. "Introduction," in The Golden Bowl.
     Edited by Richard P. Blackmur. New York: Grove Press,
     pp. v-xxi.
          The Ambassadors, The Wings of the Dove, and The Golden
     Bowl form a spiritual trilogy, an account of the soul
     struggling with the outer world which it must deny,

1952

renounce or accept. Each of the three novels is a tale of
adultery with similarities in character and theme. Illustrates with The Golden Bowl how a novel involving "shabby
adultery" is also "a poetic drama of the soul's action."

10   BLAND, D. S. "The Bostonians." Times Literary Supplement
      (18 April), p. 265.
          Comments on a remark by Trilling in his edition of The
      Bostonians (see 1952.B63) in reference to an "incomplete"
      quotation concerning James' intentions found in his note-
      books.

11   BOMPARD, PAOLA. "Henry James e il problema del male." La
      Fiera Letteraria, 11 (16 March), 4. (Italian)
          For James, "The reality of evil became the decisive
      element of his judgment and the world of his imagination."
      Recounts how the other members of the James family had
      encounters with personifications of evil, which in James'
      work is defined as "egoism, the violation of integrity,
      infidelity, lies, that which alienates and isolates the
      individual..." as opposed to the "ability to enter into
      the lives of others, to receive them and understand them."
      Reaffirms the link between Hawthorne and James in their
      concern about the nature of evil.

12   CRAIG, G. ARMOUR. "A Series of Exercises on The Education of
      Henry Adams and The Portrait of a Lady." Exercise Ex-
      change, 1: 1-6.
          A series of exercises for a sophomore course in "Intro-
      duction to Literature." Three exercises on The Portrait
      of a Lady, for use as part of a continuing study of the
      novel, are designed to make the student see Osmond as evil
      and to address the problem of the "unsatisfactory" ending
      of the work through analysis of it. Discusses relation of
      "moral structure to a society assumed by a novel."

13   DAUNER, LOUISE. "Henry James and the Garden of Death."
      University of Kansas City Review, 19 (Winter), 137-43.
          Examination of the consistent recurrence of the garden
      symbol in James' work, with reference to metaphysical as
      well as physical value. Just as the "garden is an act of
      cultivation," so "in the human being, the act of spiritual
      and intellectual cultivation creates...culture." Focuses
      upon "several characteristic garden situations, attempting
      thus to suggest the relationship...between the symbol, the
      thing, and the perhaps paramount Jamesian theme." Con-
      cludes that the symbol constantly recurs with its "ambiva-
      lence, its paradox, its thickness of association. It

reinforces the psychological and emotional overtones of
characters and situations. It is highly suggestive of the
Jamesian ethic...And it contributes tonally as irony to
James' many-faceted representation of the human drama."

14   DECKER, CLARENCE R. The Victorian Conscience. New York:
        Twayne Publishers, passim.
        References to James in relation to his views of the
     French realists and their influence on him, and to his
     association with Robert Louis Stevenson.

*15 DOMKE, H. Frankfurter Allgemeine Zeitung (16 February).
        Cited in 1959.B5. (German)
        "In the last analysis his [James'] characters strike us
     as purely literary ones" (quotation from 1959.B5).

16   DUNBAR, VIOLA R. "The Problem in Roderick Hudson." Modern
        Language Notes, 67 (February), 109-13.
        Roderick Hudson makes the point that man is responsible
     for his own destiny. Emphasis on the problem of freedom
     of will and exposure of "the fallacy of Roderick's theory
     of determinism" help James avoid a "depressing effect in a
     story of tragic events."

17   EDEL, LEON. "The Aspern Papers: Great-Aunt Wyckoff and
        Juliana Bordereau." Modern Language Notes, 67 (June),
        392-95.
        Juliana Bordereau was modeled after James' Great-Aunt
     Wycoff.

18   EDEL, LEON. "A Letter to the Editors." American Literature,
        24 (November), 370-72.
        Another rejoinder to Young's article on the order of
     chapters in The Ambassadors (see 1950.B74; 1951.B15).
     Young's reply (see 1952.B71) "contains certain serious
     bibliographical errors." Challenges Young's questioning
     of Edel's initial response to the hypothesis of reversal,
     and discusses his failure to examine all editions of The
     Ambassadors. It is impossible to deduce that something
     was wrong with James as a writer because of the reversal.

19   EDWARDS, HERBERT. "Henry James and Ibsen." American Litera-
        ture, 24 (May), 208-23.
        Reviews recent critical opinions on probable influence
     of Ibsen on technique of James' later period, and seeks to
     extend previous conclusions by suggesting that Ibsen's
     influence was greater than previously recognized. James
     admired the playwright's objectivity, precedence of

1952

character over plot, retrospective analysis, and tightly
woven artistry. The naturalistic technique of Ibsen had a
greater effect on James' later novels than on his dramas.

20 FALK, ROBERT P. "Henry James and the 'Age of Innocence.'"
Nineteenth-Century Fiction, 7 (December), 171-88.
James remained within the contemporary moral code without wholly excluding tabooed areas of experience by using
suggestion and ambiguity to reveal undercurrents of social
conduct. "Outwardly, he had the manner of Victorian pro-
priety; inwardly, he burned with the aesthetic license of
the fin de siècle." Points out plots and selected scenes
in selected novels to illustrate James' "yawning reali-
ties," the "forms of human depravity" portrayed under the
surface in his works. His canon "may be taken as a kind
of projected symbol of the social trend of the late nineteenth century when more and more an outward disguise of
manner and display concealed an inward decay."

21 FAY, GERARD. "The Innocents." Spectator (11 July), p. 65.
Calls The Turn of the Screw a "unique story" in which
"James was wise and artful to leave the evil in the boy's
life un-named."

22 FORSTER, E. M. "Pattern and Rhythm," in Essays in Modern
Literary Criticism. Edited by Ray B. West. New York:
Rinehart and Co., pp. 431-42.
Reprint of 1927.B5.

23 FOX, ADAM. "James for Americans." Spectator (18 January),
p. 84.
Review of Dupee's biography (see 1951.A2), which notes
the distinction between English and American literary
criticism, suggests the work is "meant mainly for Americans," and judges it to be "very well done." "Henry James
was one of those all too rare authors who, having an unusual mind, have managed to create a style to match it."

24 GEIST, STANLEY. "Fictitious Americans: 2. Portraits From a
Family Album." Hudson Review, 5 (Summer), 203-206.
"The heroine of this fragile, glittering little narrative [Daisy Miller]...is surpassed only by other personages
of James as a study in the most elusive singularities of
an American mind." Analyzes Daisy's character: "Pene-
trating nothing, penetrated by nothing, she moves over the
surface of human life like a fly on an infinite sheet of
glass; and it is the absolute detachment, this absolute

freedom to 'see' everything and be contaminated by nothing,
that constitutes her moral honor." Reprinted: in William
T. Stafford, ed. James's Daisy Miller: The Story, The
Play, The Critics. Scribner Research Anthologies. New
York: Charles Scribner's Sons, 1963, pp. 203-206.

25 GHISELIN, BREWSTER. "Introduction," in The Creative Process:
    A Symposium. Edited by Brewster Ghiselin. Berkeley and
    Los Angeles: University of California Press, pp. 1-21.
        Reference to James' writing on the creative process in
    his "monumental work," the prefaces to the New York edi-
    tion, "perhaps the greatest body of such writing." In The
    Ambassadors, James recorded "observations of automatic
    production going on under the fully wakeful eye of con-
    sciousness."

26 GORDON, JOHN D. "The Ghost at Brede Place." Bulletin of the
    New York Public Library, 56 (December), 591-96.
        Discussion of the play, The Ghost, produced by the
    guests as part of the entertainment at a Christmas gather-
    ing, 1899, at Brede Place, hosted by Stephen Crane and his
    wife. Reprints reminiscences about the occasion, includ-
    ing comments by Charles Lewis Hind and H. G. Wells. No
    manuscript of this "curiosity," in which James had a part,
    has yet been discovered.

27 HOFFMANN, CHARLES G. "The Development toward the Short Novel
    Form in American Literature, with Special Reference to
    Hawthorne, Melville and James." Ph.D. dissertation, Uni-
    versity of Wisconsin. (Abstracted in University of Wis-
    consin Summaries of Doctoral Dissertations, 13 [1952-1954],
    380-81.
        James "turned to the short-novel form as a way of de-
    veloping the story's idea without sacrificing economy of
    structure and compactness of form." Examines representa-
    tive short novels from each of James' three periods to
    illustrate his artistic development.

28 JONES, HOWARD MUMFORD and ERNEST E. LEISY. Supplementary
    material to Daisy Miller: A Study and "The Art of Fic-
    tion," in Major American Writers. New York: Harcourt,
    Brace and Co., p. 1443.
        Present chronology, brief bibliography including "biog-
    raphies," "criticism," "bibliography and editions," and
    short discussion of James as one who "finds in the con-
    templation of contrasting national cultures a new integra-
    tion," and one for whom "morality lies partially in
    esthetic truth...."

1952

29   KEOWN, ERIC. "At the Play." <u>Punch</u> (16 July), p. 127.
          Views London production of <u>The Innocents</u> as truer to
      the spirit of James' <u>The Turn of the Screw</u> than Archibald's,
      which electrifies "the spine rather than the imagination."

30   LEAVIS, F. R. "Comment by F. R. Leavis," in <u>The Complex Fate:</u>
      <u>Hawthorne, Henry James, and Some Other American Writers</u>.
      London: Chatto and Windus, p. 144; New York: Grove
      Press, 1954. Reprinted: New York: Gordian Press, 1967.
      Reprint of 1950.B52.

31   LEAVIS, F. R. "Henry James and the Function of Criticism,"
      in <u>The Common Pursuit</u>. London: Chatto and Windus,
      pp. 223-32. Reprinted: 1962; Harmondsworth: Penguin
      Books, 1963.
          Reprint of 1948.B25.

32   LEHMANN, JOHN. "A Question of Covering One's Tracks," in <u>The</u>
      <u>Open Night</u>. London: Longmans, Green and Co., pp. 45-53.
          Suggests that the tracks James was covering up in <u>The</u>
      <u>Aspern Papers</u> involved projection of himself into Aspern.
      "I find...a symbolic presentation of the glamour and decay
      of Europe's culture more richly and interestingly worked
      out than anywhere else in the work of an author who was
      particularly susceptible to such impressions." Describes
      the tale as "a poem about Venice," "a new invention, a
      sonnet of the novel."

33   LUBBOCK, PERCY. "Strategy of Point of View," in <u>Critiques</u>
      <u>and Essays on Modern Fiction, 1920-1951</u>. Edited by J. W.
      Aldridge. New York: The Ronald Press Co., pp. 9-30.
          Originally appeared as Chapters XI, XIII, XVII in <u>The</u>
      <u>Craft of Fiction</u>, 1921.B13, here in rearranged and slightly
      emended form.

34   LÜDEKE, HENRY. "Henry James." <u>Neue Schweitzer Rundshau</u>, 1
      (May), 34-42. (German)
          Sketches James' life and works, and mentions such topics
      as art vs. social and political life, James as an observer,
      his refusal to capitulate to art for art's sake, his tragic
      undertone, the new novel with a perceptive center in one
      hero, and his lasting contribution in the area of style.

35   LUDWIG, RICHARD and MARVIN B. PERRY, JR. "Introduction," in
      <u>Nine Short Novels</u>. Edited by Richard Ludwig and Marvin B.
      Perry, Jr. Boston: D. C. Heath and Co., pp. xxiii-xxix.
          Discusses variance in critical opinion concerning
      James, both in this century and during his lifetime. "The

Jamesian magic has been recognized, thoroughly analyzed, and properly praised by now through several generations of eminent critics...." Describes James' focus as "the world of art, of the theatre, of the wealthy leisured class" in which he sought "essences of a high moral order." Analyzes <u>Madame de Mauves</u>, which unfolds through Bernard Longmore's eyes, and judges it to be "a little masterpiece of the nouvella form," "an immensely illuminating study of feminine psychology, cultural variations, moral dissipation, and marital unhappiness."

36 LYND, ROBERT. "The Literary Life," in <u>Books and Writers</u>. New York: The Macmillan Co., pp. 113-17.
       Comments on how infrequently novelists present characters in their own profession; examines "The Figure in the Carpet," in which an author is the principal character; and concludes that "I should agree with any one who described" the tale "not as a literary masterpiece but as a first-rate magazine story for the intellectuals." James "fails to persuade us...that literary figures are such as he depicts them."

37 LYND, ROBERT. "The Return of Henry James," in <u>Books and Writers</u>. New York: The Macmillan Co., pp. 8-12.
       In the James revival, the period of "James I" will probably be preeminent. Notes tendency of critics to look for meanings below the surface of James' works, even when they're absent. Suggests that the "obscure prose" of the later period may be the effect of a suppressed stammer which apparently affected James' conversation.

38 LYNSKEY, WINIFRED. Comment on "The Bench of Desolation," in <u>Reading Modern Fiction</u>. New York: Charles Scribner's Sons, pp. 306-10.
       Discussion and questions on "The Bench of Desolation," dealing with topics such as "the story," James' "intent" in the tale of "a man's moral growth and of his self-fulfillment...the story of love itself," the life of Dodds, the life of Kate, metaphors, theme and style.

39 McELDERRY, B. R., JR. "Hamlin Garland and Henry James." <u>American Literature</u>, 23 (January), 433-46.
       Regarding the controversy concerning the effect of James' residence abroad on his career, Garland was a witness. Surveys references on this matter in Garland's published writings, his notebook, and unpublished correspondence between the two writers in an effort to define

1952

the relationship between Garland and James and to place
the latter's reported statements about his expatriation in
their proper perspective.

40   McELDERRY, B. R., JR. "The Published Letters of Henry James:
A Survey." Bulletin of Bibliography and Dramatic Index,
20 (January-April), 165-71.
In addition to Lubbock's volume (see 1920.B20) containing four hundred and three of James' letters, McElderry
uncovered about seven hundred letters in over one hundred
sources. Includes chronological listing of various publications in which letters have been located, indicating
number of letters, recipients, dates, and principal topics,
and suggests uses of his survey. See 1952.B41.

41   McELDERRY, B. R., JR. "The Published Letters of Henry James:
A Survey. Part II." Bulletin of Bibliography and Dramatic Index, 20 (May-August), 187.
An addendum to 1952.B40, listing six further sources
of James' letters.

42   McELDERRY, B. R., JR. "Henry James's Revision of Watch and
Ward." Modern Language Notes, 67 (November), 457-61.
Revisions of Watch and Ward improved the original text
by making it "simpler and more precise," but "no merely
literary labor" could eliminate the deficiencies of the
novel.

43   McELDERRY, B. R., JR. "Henry James's Neglected Thriller:
The Other House." Arizona Quarterly, 8 (Winter), 328-32.
James' "only murder story" is a gripping, suspenseful
melodrama and should be adapted for the stage. Provides
synopsis of the play, and discusses the subtlety with
which James develops it.

44   McMAHON, HELEN. "Patterns of Realism in the Atlantic," in
Criticism of Fiction: A Study of Trends in "The Atlantic
Monthly," 1857-1898. New York: Bookman Associates,
pp. 34-35.
As an illustration of "distinction between content, the
actual, and what Mark Schorer has called 'achieved content' of art," McMahon quotes Horace Scudder's comments
on James' "The Real Thing" which appeared in The Atlantic
Monthly.

1952

45   MATTHIESSEN, F. O. "Henry James," in <u>Responsibilities of the</u>
      <u>Critic: Essays and Reviews</u>. New York: Oxford University
      Press, pp. 230-33.
         Reprint of 1945.B34, previously entitled "Not Quite the
      Real Thing."

46   MAUGHAM, SOMERSET. "Some Novelists I Have Known," in <u>The</u>
      <u>Vagrant Mood</u>. London: William Heinemann, pp. 199-209;
      New York: Doubleday and Co., 1953, pp. 205-17.
         Revised and expanded version of 1939.B6. A not alto-
      gether flattering portrait of James: "...I have made
      Henry James...a trifle absurd...because that is what I
      found him." Suggests that James remained an alien in
      England, that he lacked empathy, that "the author absorbed
      the man." "...You accept...the abominable style of his
      later work, with its ugly Gallicisms, its abuse of adverbs,
      its too elaborate metaphors, the tortuosity of ·its long
      sentences, because they are part and parcel of the charm,
      benignity and amusing pomposity of the man you remember."

47   MENDILOW, A. A. <u>Time and the Novel</u>. London: Peter Nevill;
      New York: Humanities Press, passim.
         James and Proust "expand small blocks of time, so as to
      give an impression of fullness and continuity within the
      limits of the unit of time chosen." Mentions James' limit-
      ation of point of view and his need for concealed art in
      the novel, and describes him, along with Richardson and
      Flaubert, as "masters of slow motion."

48   MILLETT, FRED B. "Henry James and the Undergraduate." <u>Col-</u>
      <u>lege English</u>, 14 (December), 167-68.
         Rebuttal of A. L. Scott's discussion of the effect of
      James on underclassmen (<u>see</u> 1952.B60). Millett gives a
      sampling of students' positive reactions to James.

*49   MOROOKA, HIRASHI. "On Henry James's <u>Roderick Hudson</u>."
      <u>Rikkyo Review</u>, no. 14, pp. 95-113.
         Cited in Lewis G. Leary, comp. <u>Articles on American</u>
      <u>Literature, 1950-1967</u>, p. 314.

50   MURRAY, DONALD M. "Henry James and the English Reviewers,
      1882-1890." <u>American Literature</u>, 24 (March), 1-20.
         Examination of views of English reviewers to clarify
      why James never achieved either financial rewards or wide
      public appeal, his goals. Sketches attitude of English
      periodical critics towards James up to 1890, with emphasis
      on the 1880's. After "the early generous if sometimes

1952

patronizing attitude of encouragement toward a beginner,
the reviewers steadily cooled toward James."

51 MURRAY, DONALD M. "James and Whistler at the Grosvenor Gallery." American Quarterly, 4 (Spring), 49-65.
Considers relationship between James and Whistler in
view of the cultural currents of their time. Discusses
Whistler's background and theory of art, compares and contrasts his "Ten O'Clock" lecture with James' "The Art of
Fiction." Concludes that "...although James and Whistler,
as creative artists, both took new and similar directions
in the eighties, there was no meeting of minds between
them." James as a critic was too conservative and viewed
Whistler as the buffoon of the Grosvenor Gallery.

52 OCHSHORN, MYRON. "Henry James: The Golden Bowl." New Mexico
Quarterly, 22 (Autumn), 340-42.
Isolates James' "essential territory" as "the fine conscience in action," and considers The Golden Bowl as "the
most elaborately exfoliated representation of his mature
vision," a retelling of "the legend of Adam (Verver) and
Eve (Maggie) in the Garden (Fawns)," and as dealing with
"the reciprocity of evil and good, of appearance and
reality."

53 O'CONNOR, WILLIAM VAN. An Age of Criticism, 1900-1950.
Chicago: Henry Regnery Co., pp. 58-63 and passim.
James, more than his contemporaries, "understood the
issues criticism was facing" and considered "the elements
of the real, of documentation, and of scientific and moral
determinism." Presents James' definition of critical
function: He "implied that opposing the real and the true
or the beautiful and the useful was a fallacious view of
the literary object, the work of art."

54 PÉCNIK, B. "Henry James." Republika, 8 (May), 329-30.
(Serbo-Croatian)
Biocritical sketch of James, and discussion of Ruth and
Augustus Goetz's theatrical adaptation of Washington
Square, of which novel Pécnik provides a plot synopsis.

55 PENZOLDT, PETER. "Comparisons and Affinities (Henry James,
Conrad Aiken, W. F. Harvey)," in The Supernatural in Fiction. London: Peter Nevill, pp. 218-23.
Discusses similarities and differences between Walter
de la Mare's "Out of the Deep" and The Turn of the Screw,
and proclaims the former to have "dramatic superiority."
James' interest was in "psychoanalysis of the human beings
confronted with the supernatural powers."

56   PORTER, KATHERINE ANNE. "The Days Before," in The Days Be-
      fore. New York: Harcourt, Brace and Co., pp. 3-22.
           Revised version of 1943.B38. "...Though no writer ever
      'grew up' more completely than Henry James, and 'saw
      through' his own illusions with more sobriety and pure in-
      telligence, still there lay in the depths of his being the
      memory of a lost paradise...."

57   RAY, GORDON. "The Importance of Original Editions," in Nine-
      teenth Century English Books. Edited by Gordon N. Ray,
      Carl J. Weber and John Carter. Urbana: University of
      Illinois Press, p. 22.
           In pointing out a "hazard to which Mr. Leavis' exclu-
      sive preoccupation with contemporary relevance has exposed
      him," notes that he fails to give information concerning
      texts he is quoting, a failure which "leads him into some-
      thing like absurdity" as when he quoted the revised edi-
      tion of Roderick Hudson as substantiation of James' early
      manner.

58   ROBINSON, JEAN JOSEPH. "Henry James and Schulberg's The Dis-
      enchanted." Modern Language Notes, 67 (November), 472-73.
           James had "a pronounced influence" on Schulberg's novel
      The Disenchanted as illustrated by an example from "The
      Middle Years."

59   SCHERMAN, DAVID E. and ROSEMARIE REDLICH. "Henry James," in
      Literary America: A Chronicle of American Writers from
      1607-1952 with 173 Photographs of the American Scene That
      Inspired Them. New York: Dodd, Mead and Co., pp. 96-97.
           Describes James as "the last Victorian romantic" and
      "an all-important forerunner of the modern psychological
      novel." Includes picture of a Washington Square mansion
      with excerpts from Washington Square and The American
      Scene.

60   SCOTT, ARTHUR L. "A Protest against the James Vogue." Col-
      lege English, 13 (January), 194-201.
           "Henry James is nothing short of a disaster to the
      underclass course in American literature.... He continues
      to breed in the normal student an active distaste for
      literature." Suggests that James lacks "those prerequi-
      sites of a great writer: passion, energy, gusto, love of
      life," and criticizes James' characters and situations,
      style, dialogue, lack of sense of humor, falsification of
      reality. Uses The Portrait of a Lady and The Spoils of
      Poynton to illustrate his point. See 1952.B1, B48.

1952

61 SHAW, GEORGE BERNARD. "Two New Plays," in <u>Plays and Players:</u>
    <u>Essays on the Theatre</u>. Selected with an introduction by
    A. C. Ward. London and New York: Oxford University Press,
    pp. 1-9.
        Reprints an essay-review by Shaw on <u>Guy Domville</u>, which
    originally appeared in <u>Saturday Review</u> (London), 12 Janu-
    ary 1895.

62 TILLOTSON, GEOFFREY. "Henry James and His Limitations," in
    <u>Criticism and the Nineteenth Century</u>. New York: Barnes
    and Noble, 244-69.
        Refutes charges that James treated only the wealthy
    class and that his characters lack carnality. "If James
    the novelist is not so great as George Eliot or Tolstoy it
    is because he is too much himself," and his "limitations
    are ones he has chosen for himself." He is "as construc-
    tive a moralist as he is a searching psychologist."

63 TRILLING, LIONEL. "Introduction," in <u>The Bostonians</u>. Edited
    by Lionel Trilling. The Chiltern Library. London: John
    Lehmann, pp. vii-xv.
        Details relationship between <u>The Bostonians</u> and <u>The</u>
    <u>Princess Casamassima</u>, and describes the former as "marked
    by a comicality which has rather more kinship with Ameri-
    can humour than with British humour...." Analyzes <u>The</u>
    <u>Bostonians</u>, a "doctrinaire demand for an equality of the
    sexes," a "sign of a general diversion of the culture from
    the course of nature." Discusses the characterization of
    Basil Ransom, a "proto-martyr" of Southern men with a
    "distrust of theory, an attachment to tradition, and...the
    tragic awareness of the intractability of the human cir-
    cumstance." Concludes that the novel, written "when the
    parental family had come to an end" for James, is a "story
    of the parental house divided against itself...." Re-
    printed: 1955.B68.

64 VALLETT, JACQUES. "Petite bibliographe de Henry James depuis
    la guerre." <u>Mercure de France</u>, 315 (July), 528-31.
    (French)
        Account of works by or about James issued since World
    War II. "Let us say only that the person and his work,
    in their complexity," suggest contradictions and conflicts.
    "James is not exclusively an egotist or altruist; an es-
    thete or moralist...a romancer of the heart or the sym-
    bolic inhabitant of an ivory tower."

65 WAGENKNECHT, EDWARD. "The American as Artist: Henry James,"
    in Calvalcade of the American Novel, from the Birth of the
    Nation to the Middle of the Twentieth Century. New York:
    Henry Holt and Co., pp. 145-65.
        In "Our Contemporary Henry James," includes portions of
    1948.B53. Views important influences on James and his at-
    titude toward the relationship between art and morality
    in "Some Technical Considerations," and discusses James as
    an observer of life in "The Figure in the Carpet." De-
    scribes James as a "novelist of personal relationships,"
    basically a pragmatist who examines manners as an outward
    manifestation of "inward spiritual grace."

66 WEST, RAY B., JR. The Short Story in America, 1900-1950.
    Chicago: Henry Regnery Co., pp. 1-27.
        Surveys history of the short story as a literary form,
    placing James in the "pre-World War I" period. James saw
    "that the American story was a story of initiation, a rec-
    ognition of the significance of evil, a pessimistic rather
    than an optimistic view of man." Describes James as a
    traditionalist, and suggests that his attitude toward his
    craft and awareness of its problems has had influence on
    later writers. Concludes that James' view of the short
    story was a modern one, "as an organic whole in which none
    of the parts may be considered in isolation...."

67 WILSON, EDMUND. "The Pilgrimage of Henry James," in The
    Shores of Light: A Literary Chronicle of the Twenties and
    Thirties. New York: Farrar, Straus, and Young, pp. 217-
    28.
        Praises Van Wyck Brooks' The Pilgrimage of Henry James
    (see 1925.A1) from the standpoint of literary form, but
    objects to its "failure to recognize the real nature and
    development of James' art." James' work has been dis-
    torted "to make it fit the Procrustes bed of a thesis."
    Divides James' works during his English residence into
    three periods, the second of which demonstrates "his com-
    pletest artistic maturity," the later characterized by
    "deterioration." James' basic theme is opposition between
    "good conscience" and "doing what one likes." Reprinted:
    in Leon Edel, ed. Henry James: A Collection of Critical
    Essays, pp. 63-71.

68 WOODCOCK, GEORGE. "Henry James and the Conspirators." Sew-
    anee Review, 60 (Spring), 219-29.
        The Princess Casamassima is significant in demonstrating
    James' "sense of the doom that is approaching the world of
    moneyed ease and aristocratic values..." and his "sense of

1952

personal isolation as a devotee of dying values." Suggests
that the "international organization of the conspirators"
resembles "more or less authoritarian groups as the Italian
Carbonari or the Blanquists of France" rather than anarch-
ist organizations which played an important part in European revolutionary activity.

69   WOODRESS, JAMES L., JR. Howells and Italy. Durham, N.C.:
     Duke University Press, passim.
        Passing references to James in examination of Howells
     during his four years as American consul at Venice and the
     effect of residence in Italy on his work.

70   WORSLEY, T. C. "The Massacre of the Innocents." New States-
     man and Nation, 44 (12 July), 39-40.
        Review of The Innocents: "...To the unaddicted, the
     name Henry James...would have spelled boredom unmitigated,
     while to addicts the ominous words 'based on' must spell
     the inevitable debasement of the novelist's beloved val-
     ues."

71   YOUNG, ROBERT. "A Final Note on The Ambassadors." American
     Literature, 23 (January), 487-90.
        Reaffirms his position in 1950.B74, and responds to
     Edel's comments (1951.B15), which contain inaccuracies and
     "misleading" statements. The Methuen edition is a "rar-
     ity," a neglibible factor in evaluating the significance
     of a long undetected error. The salient point is perpetu-
     ation of the reversed chapters, and the error might well
     have been James'. It appears that he had several oppor-
     tunities to correct the reversal. (See also 1952.B18.)

1953 A BOOKS

1   ANDERSON, QUENTIN. "The American Henry James: A Study of
     the Novelist as a Moralist." Ph.D. dissertation, Columbia
     University.
        "An examination of the relation between his father's
     work and his own leads to the conclusion that he [James]
     was deeply influenced by his father." His "employment of
     his father's symbols may be demonstrated in both early and
     late work," and the final three completed novels form a
     trilogy detailing the "process of universal salvation."
     See 1957.A1.

2 EDEL, LEON. Henry James: The Untried Years, 1843-1870.
   Philadelphia: J. B. Lippincott Co.; Toronto: Longmans;
   London: Hart-Davis, 350 pp.
      A psychological and literary biography of James, dealing
   with his childhood and youth, which attempts a more bal-
   anced view, correcting the distortions and caricatures of
   legend. "To untangle his life, to bring order out of the
   web of his many friendships, to throw light on the much-
   discussed 'ambiguities,' to see Henry James in that late
   nineteenth-century world laying 'siege' to Rome, to Paris
   and finally to London, to catch the life that throbbed behind the work, this is our task." Discusses James in his
   home environment and relationship with his siblings, his
   non-participation in the Civil War, his "obscure hurt," his
   association with Minny Temple, and his early periods in
   Europe. With James, "the novel in English achieved its
   greatest perfection." Reviewed: Elmer Borklund, Chicago
   Review, 7 (Fall-Winter 1953), 72-79; Jacob Cleaver Levenson, New England Quarterly, 26 (December 1953), 533-37;
   Carlos Baker, New York Times Book Review (3 May 1953),
   p. 4; Joseph Frank, Sewanee Review, 63 (Winter 1955), 168-
   74; Charles Feidelson, Yale Review, NS 43 (Autumn 1953),
   128.

3 HENDRICK, LEO T. "Henry James: The Late and Early Styles."
   Ph.D. dissertation, University of Michigan.
      A study describing "the unique 'later prose style' of
   Henry James" and explaining "what caused the Jamesian later
   style." James' later nondialogue style "is characterized
   by density..., by complexity..., and by irregularity..."
   The dialogue style is "intellective," "stichomythic,"
   "tentative" and "non-constructive." Accounts for stylistic
   characteristics with reference to James' subject matter,
   narrative method, and personality.

1953 B SHORTER WRITINGS

1 ALLOTT, MIRIAM. "The Bronzino Portrait in Henry James's The
   Wings of the Dove." Modern Language Notes, 68 (January),
   23-25.
      Bronzino's portrait of Lucrezia Panciatichi in the
   Uffizi gallery helps reveal "the working of James's...
   imagination" in The Wings of the Dove.

2 ALLOTT, MIRIAM. "'Romola' and 'The Golden Bowl.'" Notes and
   Queries, 198 (March), 124-25.
      The Golden Bowl has echoes of George Eliot's Romola,
   with evident similarities between Maggie Verver and Romola,
   and between Prince Amerigo and Tito Melema. See 1953.B60.

1953

3 ALLOTT, MIRIAM. "Symbol and Image in the Later Work of Henry
James." Essays in Criticism, 3 (July), 321-36.
A "vein of poetic symbolism and imagery" deserves attention as the most important aspect of James' later style.
Animal, money and objet d'art images emerge as sustained
metaphors of the major phase, and some elements acquire a
symbolic force they did not originally possess. Uses The
Golden Bowl as an example of "James' use of a concrete symbol to reinforce his theme," and attempts to connect the
symbol of the bowl with James' use of the portrait symbol,
an analogous device for exploring the relationship between
appearance and reality, seen in The Sacred Fount, The Wings
of the Dove, and The Sense of the Past. James' later vision resulted from a "strongly developed 'religious' sense,
a heightened sensitivity to the existence of evil, a habit
of rendering experience in terms of universal moral conflict." See 1953.B4, B61.

4 ALLOTT, MIRIAM. "Symbol and Image in the Later Works of Henry
James: A Correction." Essays in Criticism, 3 (October),
476.
Acknowledges error pointed out by Tillotson, 1953.B61.

5 ALLOTT, MIRIAM. "Henry James and the Fantastical Conceits:
The Sacred Fount," in The Northern Miscellany of Literary
Criticism. Edited by D. W. Jefferson. No. 1. Hull:
Hull Printers, pp. 76-86.
Even in James' relatively early stories, "a tenuous
element of the fantastic" exists, while in the later works
this element "conditions the whole atmosphere of their
fabulous world," becoming a means of investigating the
more difficult or unusual aspects of experience. Examines
The Sacred Fount as representing an important stage in
James' treatment of fantasy in its use of the fantastic
conceit and its thematic implications.

6 AMACHER, RICHARD E. "James's 'The Two Faces.'" Explicator,
12 (December), Item 20.
Sutton makes a correct moral choice in "The Two Faces"
in admiring the pathetic Lady Gwyther and loathing Mrs.
Grantham. By refusing to suffer, as Sutton had advised,
Mrs. Grantham makes the wrong choice. James expressed the
theme of "the moral superiority of suffering innocence to
heartless sophistication." See 1956.B60.

7 ANDERSON, SHERWOOD. "Letter to Van Wyck Brooks," in Letters
of Sherwood Anderson. Edited by Howard Mumford Jones and
Walter B. Rideout. Boston: Little, Brown and Co.,
pp. 102-103.

Describes James as "a man who never found anyone to
love...he, in short, takes my love from me too." James
carried "the thing...far into the field of intellectuality,
as skillful haters find out how to do."

8 ARADER, HARRY F. "American Novelists in Italy: Nathaniel
   Hawthorne, Howells, James, and F. Marion Crawford." Ph.D.
   dissertation, University of Pennsylvania.
       In discussing Italian experiences as an influence on
   four novelists, asserts that "Hawthorne and James found
   motivation and theme for major works; in the expatriates
   they found material for character development."

9 ARMS, GEORGE and WILLIAM M. GIBSON. "'Silas Lapham,' 'Daisy
   Miller,' and the Jews." New England Quarterly, 16 (March),
   118-22.
       Referring to Howells' reputation for yielding to his
   editor or his public, gives example of refusal to delete
   phrase "Daisy Millerism" from The Rise of Silas Lapham,
   despite the fact that the term was anachronistic, the
   novel being set a year before Daisy Miller appeared in
   print.

*10 ARNOLD, F. Radio Broadcast. Hessicher Rundfunk (7 April).
   Cited in 1959.B5. (German)
       James' "particular themes and difficult style...permit
   a comparison with Marcel Proust, who met with an equally
   retarded and restricted success in Germany." Appreciation
   of James is based on "the lasting pleasure derived from
   'stylistic beauty and elegance, from the nobility in
   thought, feeling, and ethical obligation.'" Criticizes
   James for his "'indiscreet' meddling in other people's
   innermost and private sanctuaries," with reference to The
   Turn of the Screw and The Aspern Papers. (Quotations from
   1959.B5.)

11 BANTOCK, G. H. "Morals and Civilization in Henry James,"
   Cambridge Journal, 7 (December), 159-81.
       Considers James a moralist concerned with problems of
   good and evil, in whose works civilization plays a role in
   the resolution of moral conflicts. "The play of a certain
   consciousness of moral sensibility on the 'experience'
   afforded by a particular set of social groupings provides
   James' contribution to our awareness of the human condition." Examines Roderick Hudson ("interplay of experience
   and moral consciousness"), discusses Madame de Mauves, The
   Portrait of a Lady, The Spoils of Poynton and The Ambassadors.

1953

12　BERLAND, ALWYN.　"James and Forster:　The Morality of Class."
　　　<u>Cambridge Journal</u>, 6 (February), 259-80.
　　　　Discussion of similarities in <u>The Princess Casamassima</u>
　　　and Forster's <u>Howards End</u>, both of which deal with problems
　　　of "class," although from different points of view.　James'
　　　novel "proposes the violent dichotomy between revolution
　　　and civilization; <u>Howards End</u>, the possibility of bridging
　　　the worlds of commercial civilization and of culture."
　　　Analyzes differences in the two writers' attitudes towards
　　　art and the novel, relative merits of the two novels, and
　　　"the life and the art, the ideas and the form" in them.
　　　Assigns to James the vision of civilization as a positive
　　　good, and to Forster the beatific vision of bypassing or
　　　renouncing civilization, returning to the earth.

13　BOOTH, BRADFORD A.　"Henry James and the Economic Motif."
　　　<u>Nineteenth-Century Fiction</u>, 8 (September), 141-50.
　　　　Disputes critical idea that James had no conception of
　　　the influence of economics on individuals, and proposes
　　　that "the heart of virtually every James novel and of many
　　　short stories is a squabble over money."　Labels James an
　　　"economic determinist," and illustrates his thesis with
　　　reference to James' major novels.

14　BOWDEN, EDWIN T.　"Henry James and the Struggle for Interna-
　　　tional Copyright:　An Unnoticed Item in the James Bibliog-
　　　raphy."　<u>American Literature</u>, 24 (January), 537-39.
　　　　In the struggle for protection of foreign books on the
　　　American market and for protection of American books,
　　　James took part by sending an open letter to the Executive
　　　Committee for a series of meetings of the American Copy-
　　　right League, 1887; this was subsequently printed in
　　　<u>Critic</u>, December 10, 1887, and partially reprinted in a
　　　League pamphlet.　James also included to the Treasurer of
　　　the League a personal letter, "predominantly moralistic,"
　　　with rational argument and impassioned appeal for "inter-
　　　national morality and good faith."　<u>See</u> 1954.B8.

15　COOK, DOROTHY and ISABEL S. MONRO, comps.　"Henry James," in
　　　<u>Short Story Index:　An Index to 60,000 Stories in 4,320</u>
　　　<u>Collections</u>.　New York:　H. W. Wilson Co., pp. 693-95.
　　　　Lists collections of short stories published in 1949
　　　or earlier, giving author, birth and death dates, title of
　　　story and of collection(s) in which story is found.　"...
　　　The majority of the stories are entered under at least one
　　　subject" as used in the Fiction Catalogue.　Supplements
　　　have appeared covering 1950-1954, published in 1956, com-
　　　piled by Dorothy Cook and Estelle A. Fidell, and covering

1955-1958, published in 1960, compiled by Estelle A.
Fidell and Esther V. Flory. Supercedes Ina Ten Eyck Fir-
kins' compilation covering 1923-1936, entitled Short Story
Index.

*16   D., J. Frankfurter Neue Presse (27 March). Cited in 1959.B5.
(German)
      Praises "subtlety with which James depicts his charac-
ters through the responses of their fellows," and suggests
that in James "We get...the clear separation of genuine
tradition from the false, stagnant and rigid conventions
of social life. 'The scenery of the time has changed.
But so much (of what was false) already appears as danger-
ously contemporary again,' and, in James' rendering, as
valid today." The Siege of London is described as a remarkably modern psychological masterpiece. (Quotations
from 1959.B5.)

17   EDEL, LEON. "Jonathan Sturges." Princeton University Library Chronicle, 15 (Autumn), 1-9.
      Quotes letter from James to Howells, notebook entry,
and outline of the novel The Ambassadors for the publisher
concerning an incident in the Whistler garden between
Jonathan Sturges and Howells which was the source for the
encounter between Strether and little Bilham in Gloriani's
garden in The Ambassadors. Gives biographical account of
Sturges, a journalist: "...It is perhaps appropriate to
think of the book [The Ambassadors] itself as a kind of
memorial to the 'dauntless' side of Jonathan Sturges, his
devotion to art and to his friends, and his particular
role in touching off the creation of an American masterpiece."

*18   EDEL, LEON. "Introduction," in The Sacred Fount. New York:
Grove Press. Cited in 1957.B2.
      Reissued in 1959 by Hart-Davis: see 1959.B26.

19   EDEL, LEON. "Introduction," in Selected Fiction. By Henry
James. Edited by Leon Edel. Everyman's Library. New
York: E. P. Dutton and Co., pp. ix-xix. Reprinted: 1964.
      The stories and short novel in the volume, composed
between 1879 and 1909, show the "artist's progression from
a narrative of crystal simplicity to one of rich and elaborate complexity...." Classifies types of stories exem-
plified, such as "international tale," "ghostly tale,"
"story about the 'sense of the past,'" "a story of childhood." Points out some links between tales, and "profound
differences." Includes a bibliography, pp. xxi-xxiv, and

1953

after each tale appends a portion of the preface in the
New York edition which refers to it, as well as notebook
entries of story germs and relevant editorial notes.

20   FALK, ROBERT P. "The Rise of Realism, 1871-1891," in <u>Transi-
     tions in American Literary History</u>. Edited by Harry Hayden
     Clark. Durham, N.C.: Duke University Press, pp. 381-442.
        Discussion of the literary period following the Civil
     War: "James...was clearly a product of the sixties and
     seventies in his efforts to reconcile the conflicting ten-
     dencies of the time" and "in his emphasis on the individ-
     ual rather than the social or the critical in literature."
     Also mentions James' eclecticism as a critic, distaste for
     conventional romance, psychological depiction of the in-
     tellectual tone of the 70's, interest in characters in the
     80's, and later subjectivity.

21   FEIDELSON, CHARLES, JR. "The Symbolistic Imagination," in
     <u>Symbolism and American Literature</u>. Chicago: University
     of Chicago Press, pp. 47-49.
        In considering the reality which a writer "at once
     makes and finds in language," looks at James as taking a
     position similar to that of T. S. Eliot. "The Jamesian
     technique is discovery as well as construction...James
     clearly assumed that his work lay in a realm of meaning
     equally distinct from his own ego and from the world of
     objective experience. His work <u>presented itself</u> to him."

22   FIREBAUGH, JOSEPH J. "The Relativism of Henry James." <u>Jour-
     nal of Aesthetics and Art Criticism</u>, 12 (December), 237-42.
        James favored a relativistic rather than an absolute
     aesthetic, "an art concerned with...a pluralistic...world
     rather than with a world of absolute formal perfection."
     Those characters who perceive art in relationship to life
     are portrayed sympathetically.

23   GABRIELSON, THOR. "Henry James' gjenkomst." <u>Edda</u>, 53: 131-44.
     (Norwegian)
        Henry James criticism has become a fad. Describes
     James' life and career, in the last period of which he is
     unequalled for his subtle style and consistent composition.

24   GARDNER, BURDETT. "An Apology for Henry James's 'Tiger-Cat.'"
     <u>Publications of the Modern Language Association</u>, 68 (Sep-
     tember), 688-95.
        A response to 1953.B64, based on five unpublished let-
     ters from James to Paget. Proposes that James' relation-
     ship to Violet, his response to <u>Miss Brown</u> and "Lady Tal,"

were a result of his discovery of "the core conception for
the genesis of the character 'Christina Light' [in Roderick
Hudson] through his observation of what a fantastically
strenuous educational programme motivated by an abnormal
attachment to her mother had brought about in the personality of Violet Paget." Violet, in "Lady Tal," is "merely
paying off a very old score." See 1954.B12.

25 GARNETT, DAVID. The Golden Echo. London: Chatto and Windus,
    passim; New York: Harcourt, Brace and Co., 1954.
        Autobiography in which Garnett tells of his childhood
    and association with James. Recalls visit at Rye, where
    James was "dressed in an extremely tight-fitting pair of
    knickerbockers and an equally exiguous jacket of black-and-
    white checks."

26 GEISMAR, MAXWELL. "The Literary Orphan." Nation, 176 (2 May),
    374-75.
        In reviewing Edel's biography (1953.A2), says of James
    that "The life of art to which he had dedicated himself
    with utter and complete passion, and which apparently had
    prohibited, or become a substitute for, the rich and tor-
    mented human relationships of ordinary life" was for him
    the "single great experience."

27 GERARD, ALBERT. "Introduction à Henry James." Revue Nouvelle
    (June), 651-58. (French)
        A "double hiatus" existed "between James and his time,
    between James and the American public: the delicately-
    shaded pessimism of the writer, his keen sense of the tan-
    gle of good and evil, as justified as they were, came too
    soon, and isolated him in his perspicacity." Considers
    the "romantic inner principle," the international novel,
    and characterization of Isabel and depiction of manners in
    The Portrait of a Lady, and analyzes The Golden Bowl as
    the reduction of the "focal antithesis of his work, knowl-
    edge of evil yet maintainance of innocence."

28 GORDON, CAROLINE. "Some Readings and Misreadings." Sewanee
    Review, 61 (Summer), 386-88.
        Discusses pattern of Christian symbolism and Christian
    elements in selected novels. Despite James' ignorance of
    religious dogma and rites, "all his novels have one theme:
    caritas, Christian charity." Analyzes The Ambassadors, in
    which Strether helps Madame de Vionnet arrive at a "pro-
    fession of faith," having sacrificed "Eros, or pagan love,
    that Agape, Christian love, may be born."

1953

*29 HAERDTER, R. "Henry James." Die Gegenwart, 8 (14 February),
     117 ff. Cited in 1959.B5. (German)
         James is associated with T. S. Eliot, another expatri-
     ate. In Europe, James sought "'those stimulating contacts'
     from which Americans were about to sever themselves in
     order to become a nation with nothing but a future. James
     admired Europe for its historic consciousness as a life
     source, and his exodus was a matter of moral responsibility
     toward the American future" (quotation from 1959.B5).

30   HARRIER, R. C. "Letters of Henry James." Colby Library
     Quarterly, series 3, no. 10 (May), 153-64.
         Transcription of ten letters from James to Edmund Gosse
     and Mrs. Gosse, and one to James R. Osgood concerning pro-
     posal of two volumes of essays, with explanatory notes.

31   HIGHET, GILBERT. "The Making of Literature," in People,
     Places, and Books. New York: Oxford University Press,
     pp. 187-90.
         Discusses the notebooks in view of what they reveal of
     the creative process, James' life and work, and his inter-
     est in "the world of social and family relationships."
     The idea of "Paste" reverses Maupassant's idea in "The
     Necklace," and it has a plot similar to that in Maugham's
     later "Mr. Knowall."

32   HOFFMANN, CHARLES G. "Innocence and Evil in James' The Turn
     of the Screw." University of Kansas City Review, 20 (Win-
     ter), 97-105.
         The central conflict in The Turn of the Screw is that
     of innocence and evil, and since James presents innocence
     as a lack of knowledge of evil, it is the governess, not
     the children, who are innocent. Views ghosts as the agents
     rather than personifications of evil. Reprinted: in
     Gerald Willen, ed. A Casebook on "The Turn of the Screw,"
     pp. 212-22.

33   JONES-EVANS, MERVYN. "Henry James's Year in France," in
     Golden Horizon. Edited by Cyril Connolly. London:
     British Book Centre, pp. 571-79.
         Reprint of 1946.B16.

34   KAR, ANNETTE. "Archetypes of American Innocence: Lydia
     Blood and Daisy Miller." American Quarterly, 5 (Spring),
     31-38.
         Howells and James shared "a common impulse to examine
     the European vs. the American solutions to a major problem

of social morality...." <u>Lady of the Aroostook</u> and <u>Daisy Miller</u> possess fictional counterparts in their heroines, whom Kar compares.

35   KETTLE, ARNOLD. "Henry James: <u>The Portrait of a Lady</u> (1880-81)," in <u>An Introduction to the English Novel</u>. Vol. 2 London and New York: Hutchinson Publishing Group, pp. 13-34.
Analysis of The Portrait of a Lady as "a novel about destiny," a "novel about freedom." Defines two types of characters in the work, "those whom we know from straight-forward, though not unsubtle, description by the author and those who reveal themselves in the course of the book," and discusses main themes, including the importance of wealth and the problem of freedom and independence. Isabel's final choice is a "sacrificial tribute to her own ruined conception of freedom." Reprinted: in William Stafford, ed. <u>Perspectives on James's "The Portrait of a Lady</u>," pp. 91-112; also in Lyall Powers, ed. <u>Studies in "The Portrait of a Lady</u>," pp. 46-66.

36   KIRK, RUDOLF. "Henry James: Correction." <u>Journal of the Rutgers University Library</u>, 16 (June), 63.
A letter erroneously attributed to James in 1949.B29 was actually written by Sir Henry James, "'the eminent Victorian barrister and social light.'"

37   LAURENCE, DAN H. "Henry James and Stevenson Discuss 'Vile' Tess." <u>Colby Library Quarterly</u>, series 3, no. 10 (May), 164-68.
Full text of remarks of James and Stevenson on Hardy's novel, <u>Tess of the D'Urbervilles</u>. James saw "faults and falsity" in the work, whereas Stevenson was more sympathetic.

38   LIDDELL, ROBERT. "Dialogue," in <u>Some Principles of Fiction</u>. London: Jonathan Cape, pp. 73-75, 83-86. Reprinted: 1969.
Notes James' use of "the highly polished conversation of very sophisticated and clever people," suggests that opening dialogue between Kate and Densher in <u>The Wings of the Dove</u> is "proof of the superiority of fiction over the drama," and discusses James' use of "verbal flux" in order to "get to the bottom of everything."

1953

39 LIDDELL, ROBERT. "Summary," in <u>Some Principles of Fiction</u>.
    London: Jonathan Cape, pp. 58-59, 61, 64-67. Reprinted:
    1969.
        In a discussion of fictional techniques, including the
    use of "Summary to guide the reader down the crooked corri-
    dor, or to entertain him in the ante-chambers...," refers
    to James' theory of the novel, especially his use of
    "representation" rather than just "bare summary." Dis-
    tinguishes scene as "that part of a novel in which the
    novelist makes things happen under the reader's eyes," and
    illustrates using <u>The Spoils of Poynton</u>.

40 LUCKE, JESSIE RYON. "The Inception of 'The Beast in the
    Jungle.'" <u>New England Quarterly</u>, 26 (December), 529-32.
        A passage from <u>The Blithedale Romance</u> provided the
    original inspiration for "The Beast in the Jungle."

41 MacCARTHY, DESMOND. "Two Short Reminiscences: Henry James
    and Rupert Brooke," in <u>Memories</u>. New York: Oxford Uni-
    versity Press, pp. 202-204.
        Recalls meeting with James in which the latter encoun-
    tered Rupert Brooke, inquired of MacCarthy if he had talent,
    later talked with Brooke and gave him advice.

42 MELCHIORI, GIORGIO. "Due manieristi: Henry James e G. M.
    Hopkins." <u>Lo Spettatore Italiano</u>, 6 (January), 20-27.
    (Italian)
        The peculiar features, "almost personal idiosyncrasies,"
    which distinguish James and G. M. Hopkins from their con-
    temporaries, are common to both. Examines characteristics
    of Jamesian syntax and of Hopkinsian poetic language:
    "The same preoccupation [seen in Hopkins] with the 'height-
    ening' of current language and expression seems responsible
    for the peculiarities of James's style, especailly in his
    later...phase." Possibly the link between the two writers
    was Walter Pater and the influence of the aesthetic move-
    ment. Both James and Hopkins used "euphuistic" style, one
    stage of mannerism, to penetrate deeper levels of con-
    sciousness. "Hopkins explored in the habit of a priest
    searching for the secrets of a soul; James in that of a
    man of the world who inquires into the confused motives
    behind human action." English translation: 1956.B48.

43 MOELLER, CHARLES. "Henry James et l'athéisme mondain."
    <u>Revue Génerale Belge</u> (April), pp. 907-23. (French)
        Consideration of the art of James reveals that the dif-
    ficulties encountered in reading his works are worthwhile.

His novels are "documents of the first order of a dead society...." Discusses James' fictional technique, including
his lack of authorial intervention and his close examination of characters, with reference to the criticism of Du
Bos; and then looks at the "religious significance" of
James' works, to be found "in the artistic techniques themselves of the novels."

44   NEVIUS, BLAKE. Edith Wharton: A Study of Her Fiction.
      Berkeley and Los Angeles: University of California Press,
      passim.
          Examines influence of James on Wharton, between whom
      there was a "striking affinity," noting her adherence to
      James' view of the short story as presenting what he called
      "'a personal, a direct impression of life.'" Suggests that
      "somewhere around 1900 they separated--with James taking a
      high road where the atmosphere, for Edith Wharton, proved
      too rare."

45   ORAGE, A. R. "Henry James and the Ghostly," in The Little
      Review Anthology. Edited by Margaret Anderson. New York:
      Hermitage House, pp. 230-32.
          Reprint of 1918.B18.

46   PATTERSON, DAVID. "James and Jewett." Colby Library Quar-
      terly, series 3, no. 9 (February), 152.
          Suggests that two passages referring to "Flickerbridge"
      in James' notebooks be included in the "Biographical and
      Critical Comment" section of A Bibliography of the Pub-
      lished Writings of Sarah Orne Jewett, by Weber and Weber,
      1949.

47   POUILLON, JEAN. "Henry James." Les Temps Modernes, 118
      (October), 549-60. (French)
          James is a Puritan not only in the sexual sense but in
      every area. Compares James and Proust, describing the
      American as a painter of society, whose characters are
      simple but never positively defined.

48   POWYS, JOHN COWPER. "John Cowper Powys on Henry James," in
      The Little Review Anthology. Edited by Margaret Anderson.
      New York: Hermitage House, pp. 28-30.
          "Henry James is a revealer of secrets, but never does
      he entirely draw the veil." Praises James' character de-
      lineation, and views "1900 as the climacteric period."
      For James, "nothing exists but civilization." Describes
      him as a "grand, massive, unflinching, shrewd old realist."

1953

49 PRITCHETT, V. S. "The Notebooks of Henry James," in Books in
    General. New York: Harcourt, Brace and Co., pp. 43-49.
    Reprint of 1948.B36.

50 RYPINS, H. L. "Henry James in Harley Street." Edited by
    Leon Edel. American Literature, 24 (January), 481-92.
    Edel reprints a paper, written by Rypins, an M.D., 25
    years earlier, that attempts to identify the original of
    Sir Luke Strett of The Wings of the Dove as Sir James
    Mackenzie. Suggests that the value of Rypins' study is
    that "his researches enable us to enter a Harley Street
    consulting room and catch a highly contemporaneous glimpse
    of Henry James himself, face to face with a great healer."

51 SHARP, ROBERT L. "Stevenson and James's Childhood." Nine-
    teenth-Century Fiction, 8 (December), 236-37.
    Points out "amusing emendation" in revision of "The
    Art of Fiction" for Partial Portraits, based on Robert
    Louis Stevenson's objection to a point James made in the
    original version in reference to Treasure Island.

52 SHORT, R. W. "Henry James's World of Images." Publications
    of the Modern Language Association, 68 (December), 943-60.
    Generalizations about James' imagery, followed by an
    investigation of "the areas of existence or experience
    most used by James as sources for his imagery," of the
    "image areas" in the latter works generally, and of the
    "image-areas found usually concentrated within given
    works." Classifies images into areas such as "flowers,"
    "birds," "art," the "East," and "light/dark," and dis-
    cusses three image-areas (machinery, cage-beast, travel-
    water) "for the way they work with each other, or with
    previously discussed image-areas, either contrapuntally
    or actually blurred together," especially in The Golden
    Bowl and The Wings of the Dove.

53 SNOW, LOTUS. "The Pattern of Innocence through Experience
    in the Characters of Henry James." University of Toronto
    Quarterly, 22 (April), 230-36.
    Asserts that "In the passage of characters from inno-
    cence to experience James displayed a consistent interest"
    throughout his career. Considers the nature of the inno-
    cence of his characters, the quality of their experience,
    and concludes that James' characters "lack the principle
    of growth" and journey "not from innocence to experience"
    but from "innocence through experience."

54   SPILLER, ROBERT. "Seer of the Gem-like Flame." <u>Saturday Review of Literature</u>, 36 (9 May), 13-14.
     Reviews James' attitude towards biographical studies.
In <u>Henry James: The Untried Years</u> (1953.A2), Edel applies
"the techniques of analysis of the inner life" in his
"psychological biography."

55   STAFFORD, W. T. "Emerson and the James Family." <u>American Literature</u>, 24 (January), 433-61.
     The Jameses' views of Emerson anticipated conclusions
which scholarship has only recently reached. Although
Henry James, Sr., William and Henry James each saw Emerson
only partially, they "saw him whole--according to Emerson's
own definition of a whole man." Relates opinions of Emerson of the three Jameses, contemporaries and personal acquaintances.

56   STOVALL, FLOYD. "The Decline of Romantic Idealism, 1855-1871," in <u>Transitions in American Literary History</u>. Edited by Harry Hayden Clark. Durham, N.C.: Duke University Press, pp. 352-53.
     In examination of changes in American literature between
1855 and 1871, and discussion of causes of changes, refers
to James as writing short stories which "illustrate his
characteristic absorption in the personal lives of people...."

57   STRONG, L. A. G. "James and Joyce," in <u>Personal Remarks</u>.
New York: Liveright Publishing Corporation, 184-89.
     Considers whether Joyce and James stood for opposing
principles, noting James' quest for form and order, and
his views of their importance for the work of art which
must also have the quality of life. "...Joyce's work,
with all its faults, transcends the rules of the game as
understood by Henry James."

*58 S.[ÜSSKIND], W. E. <u>Süddeutsche Zeitung</u> (14 February). Cited in 1959.B5. (German)
     James chose Europe. "As 'the first and most important
homecomer from the New World' in the history of literature,
he became Europeanized--that is, he acquired and developed
conservative European forms, almost to the point of exaggeration." James' "somewhat snobbish passion for high
society makes him a forerunner of Proust." With reference
to the relationship between America and Europe, describes
Nancy Headway of <u>The Siege of London</u> as "'amazingly contemporary,' equally convincing as an individual person and
representative of her nation...doing with the European

1953

cultural heritage something quite different from what
Europeans do with it." (Quotations from 1959.B5.)

59   SWAN, MICHAEL. "Henry James and H. G. Wells: A Study of
     Their Friendship Based on Their Unpublished Correspond-
     ence." Cornhill Magazine, 167 (Autumn), 43-65.
        A study of eleven letters from Wells to James and about
     50 letters from James to Wells, which suggest that the re-
     lationship between the two writers was one of "Father and
     Son," in four "acts": (1) "James the admiring father,
     Wells the delighted son"; (2) "State of quiescence, with
     more than a touch of fear in James's praise"; (3) James's
     recognition that Wells and others "held the day," culmi-
     nating after 1910 in the idea that his own work would not
     survive. Hereafter, the father attacks "errant sons" in
     the Times Literary Supplement; (4) Son turns against father
     and publishes Boon. Reprinted: 1958.B75.

60   TILLOTSON, GEOFFREY. "'Romola' and 'The Golden Bowl.'"
     Notes and Queries, 198 (May), 223.
        With reference to 1953.B2, points out parallel between
     The Golden Bowl and a scene in The Virginian, Chapter Five,
     further "evidence of the debt" of James' novel "to earlier
     nineteenth-century novels."

61   TILLOTSON, GEOFFREY. "Symbol and Image in the Later Work of
     Henry James: A Correction." Essays in Criticism, 3 (Oc-
     tober), 476.
        Corrects Allott's use of term "New Englander" for Basil
     Ransom in 1953.B3. See also 1953.B4.

62   VALLETT, JACQUES. "Du nouveau sur Henry James." Mercure de
     France, 319 (October), 333-34. (French)
        Essay-review of Edel's Henry James: The Untried Years
     (see 1953.A2): "Behind the cerebral James, Edel begins to
     reveal to us the total James, and above all the history of
     his sensibility in his relationship with the sensual life."

63   VAN GHENT, DOROTHY. "On The Portrait of a Lady," in The Eng-
     lish Novel: Form and Content. New York: Rinehart and
     Co., pp. 211-28. Reprinted: Harper Torchbooks. New York:
     Harper and Brothers, 1961.
        The theme of The Portrait of a Lady is "The informing
     and strengthening of the eye of the mind...." Views novel
     in terms of basic metaphor of sight, with emphasis on modu-
     lations of perception of the observer. The moral question
     raised by each character is that of the "'amount of felt
     life'" that each is able to experience. Includes a list
     of "Problems for Study and Discussion" on the novel,

pp. 428-39. Reprinted: 1959.B89; also in Lyall A. Powers, ed. Studies in "The Portrait of a Lady," pp. 28-45; and in William Stafford, ed. Perspectives on James's "The Portrait of a Lady," pp. 113-31.

64   WEBER, C. J. "Henry James and His Tiger-Cat." Publications of the Modern Language Association, 68 (September), 672-87.
      Relates James' reaction to the unsympathetic presentation of himself in Violet Paget's (pseud. Vernon Lee) "Lady Tal." Publically presents James' side of the story, and William's "gallant part in the episode." Reviews several years of friendship between James and Violet preceding the rupture. "After all his numerous acts of kindness and of friendship, after all his gifts of tickets and books and meals, she decided to make callous use of him in a piece of fiction of her own." See 1953.B24.

65   WESTBROOK, PERRY D. "The Supersubtle Fry." Nineteenth-Century Fiction, 8 (September), 134-40.
      Discusses "The Middle Years" not simply as another statement of artistic perfectionism, but as a satire against the perfectionist's egotism, and "The Figure in the Carpet" as another ironical treatment of the would-be supersubtle novelist, showing the results of pretense and pomposity. The critics in the tale "are merely dupes; the novelist is a poseur, a fraud."

66   WHALLEY, GEORGE. "Imagination: Image-Making," in Poetic Process. London: Routledge and Kegan Paul, 85-86.
      Uses James' explanation of the source for The Spoils of Poynton as illustration of the recognition and growth of the "poetic germ."

67   WORDEN, WARD S. "A Cut Version of What Maisie Knew." American Literature, 24 (January), 493-504.
      In the serial publication of What Maisie Knew for the New Review, February-September 1897, the full text of the novel was severely cut in numbers beginning with July. Judges that exclusions are not more of James' stylistic revisions, and theorizes that perhaps the excisions were imposed on James by the periodical. Discusses the omissions themselves and effect on full version of the novel: "In comparison with the full text the cut version is not remarkable as an artistic success."

68   WORDEN, WARD S. "Henry James's What Maisie Knew: A Comparison with the Plans in The Notebooks." Publications of the Modern Language Association, 68 (June), 371-83.

1953

Six notebook entries on <u>What Maisie Knew</u> show that
"there is much in the book that is scarcely hinted at,
much less planned, in the preparatory write-ups." Lists
six important differences, suggests that "a structural
extension of considerable interest was worked out" for
the novel, and concludes that "an interesting story of a
realistic incident becomes a serious moral study, and
Maisie changes from a helpless child to a superior spirit...."

<u>1954 A BOOKS</u>

1   BEACH, JOSEPH WARREN. <u>The Method of Henry James</u>. Revised
        and enlarged. Philadelphia: Alfred Saifer, 403 pp. Re-
        printed: 1964.
            <u>See</u> 1918.A1. "Introduction: 1954," pp. vii-cxiv, in-
        cludes remarks on how Beach became interested in the story
        of the "mechanics of technique" in James, and reviews bio-
        graphical studies, critical works examining the relation-
        ship between James' art and personality, purely critical
        studies which evaluate works aesthetically and distinguish
        degrees of excellence, and comprehensive, informative in-
        troductions to James and his work. Examines <u>The Wings of</u>
        <u>the Dove</u> as the "best example of his ultimate story-telling
        method," attempts to classify James with reference to his-
        torical trends, and characterizes his concern as "<u>the fine</u>
        <u>art of living</u>." The text contains corrections, additional
        bibliography and notes.

2   BOCKES, DOUGLAS. "The Late Method of Henry James." Ph.D.
        dissertation, Syracuse University.
            Examination of key novels and tales of the New York
        edition "shows that the chief technical elements of 'the
        major phase'--the scenic method and the fine consciousness
        --can be found in his earlier work...." The method of
        James' later works "is an organic form, suited to his
        temperament and vision of life, developed over a period of
        forty years."

3   HART, JAMES S. "Henry James's Later Novels: The Objectifying
        of Moral Life." Ph.D. dissertation, Stanford University.
            James' intention in the later works was to express, in
        objective terms, the "nature of moral life," the influences
        of moral conflict on character development, and the "ex-
        altation of moral consciousness." James' solution to the
        objectifying of moral life is seen in three elements of the
        later fiction: "The exploitation of dramatic structures;

the use of a newly contrived dialogic prose that compro-
mises with dramatic dialogue; and extension of the interpretive range of the symbol and a rich development of the
symbolic method."

4   VOLPE, EDMOND L.   "Henry James and the Conduct of Life: A
     Study of the Novelists' Moral Values." Ph.D. dissertation,
     Columbia University.
        Analysis of Roderick Hudson, The American, The Portrait
     of a Lady, The Spoils of Poynton, The Ambassadors, The
     Wings of the Dove, and The Golden Bowl reveals James' views
     about the "conduct of life." "...Live as fully as possible
     without hurting another person. To live consciously, to
     utilize one's highest attributes, was for Henry James the
     art of life."

1954 B SHORTER WRITINGS

1   ALLEN, WALTER.   "The Novel from 1881 to 1914," in The English
     Novel: A Short Critical History. London: Phoenix House;
     New York: E. P. Dutton and Co., pp. 251-68.
        Views James in history of English novel as analogous to
     Flaubert for the French. Distinguishes James' dominant
     themes as the corruption of innocence and the international
     subject, looks at The Portrait of a Lady as dealing with
     the notion of honor, points out influence of Balzac on The
     Bostonians and The Princess Casamassima, deals with What
     Maisie Knew as a non-traditional, landmark novel, and ex-
     amines The Wings of the Dove, which has the "true heroic
     stature of tragedy." Briefly describes James' style.
     Partially reprinted: in William Stafford, ed. Perspec-
     tives on James's "The Portrait of a Lady," pp. 132-35.

*2   ARNOLD, F.   "Die sündigen Engel." Süddeutsche Zeitung (29
     May). Cited in 1959.B5. (German)
        James deals with evil in a way that transcends his age.
     His "classical wisdom makes us appreciate the palpitation,
     the tension, and the hidden crevasse in life and the human
     soul" (quotation from 1959.B5).

3   BEEBE, MAURICE L.   "The Turned Back of Henry James." South
     Atlantic Quarterly, 53 (October), 521-39.
        The "detached observer is both a technical device and a
     point of view towards life" in James. Discusses James'
     view of the artist, and notes his use of the turned-back
     image which is illustrative of the Jamesian theme: When
     the artist creates, "he inevitably withdraws to a private
     realm." Hence, "...there were two Jameses, just as there
     are two selves of any creative artist."

1954

4   BENNETT, JOAN. "The Mill on the Floss," in <u>George Eliot:</u>
     <u>Her Mind and Her Art</u>. Cambridge, England: At the Univer-
     sity Press, pp. 128–30.
         Suggests Eliot's similarity to James and Conrad in
     "embryonic" use "of a wise, disinterested spectator as a
     commentator on the action and...a lens through which the
     reader may see it in a new perspective..." in her charac-
     ter Dr. Kenn in <u>The Mill on the Floss</u>.

5   BODE, CARL. "Henry James and Owen Wister." <u>American Litera-</u>
     <u>ture</u>, 26 (May), 250–52.
         James, when dealing with the works of friends, allowed
     his feelings to overwhelm his critical skills. An example
     can be seen in the case of Wister's <u>The Virginian.</u> Re-
     prints James' enthusiastic letter to Wister, 7 August 1902.

6   BOSANQUET, THEODORA. "As I Remember Henry James." <u>Time and</u>
     <u>Tide</u>, 35 (3 July), 875–76.
         Retrospective account of Bosanquet's association with
     James, a restatement of 1924.A1. <u>See</u> 1954.B7.

7   BOSANQUET, THEODORA. "As I Remember Henry James." <u>Time and</u>
     <u>Tide</u>, 35 (10 July), 913–14.
         Continuation of 1954.B6.

8   BOWDEN, EDWIN T. "Henry James and International Copyright
     Again." <u>American Literature</u>, 25 (January), 499–500.
         Corrects 1953.B14: The first and longer printing of
     James' letter on international copyright in <u>Critic</u> was
     noted by Edna Kenton in 1934.B18.

9   BROWN, CLARENCE ARTHUR. "Realism ind Aestheticism: Introduc-
     tion," in <u>The Achievement of American Criticism: Represen-</u>
     <u>tative Selections from Three Hundred Years of American</u>
     <u>Criticism</u>. New York: The Ronald Press Co., pp. 386–90.
         Points out contrast between James' literary criticism
     and that of his contemporaries in "emphasis on the artis-
     tic, upon problems of technique...." Surveys James' career
     as a critic and presents some of his critical principles.
     Concludes that "James developed gradually from evaluation
     in the light of rigid moral standards to inductive inquiry
     and a subtle perception of aesthetic nuances...."

10   CUNLIFFE, MARCUS. "The Expatriates: Henry James, Edith
     Wharton, Henry Adams, Gertrude Stein," in <u>The Literature</u>
     <u>of the United States</u>. A Pelican Book. Harmondsworth:
     Penguin Books, pp. 213–25.

Discusses James' family environment, his idea of realism, his decision that "his writings had to be anchored in
Europe." Considers the thematic conjunction of the Old
and New World: He "depended on America for one element of
his dialectic." Suggests that "James searched throughout
his life for a literary equivalent to the James Family."

*11 DIXSON, ROBERT J. The Portrait of a Lady. Simplified and
      Adapted with Exercises for Study and Vocabulary Drill.
      New York: Regents Publishing Co. Cited in Beatrice Ricks,
      comp. Henry James: A Bibliography of Secondary Works,
      #756.

12   EDEL, LEON. "Henry James and Vernon Lee." Publications of
      the Modern Language Association, 69 (June), 677-78.
           There is insufficient evidence to suggest that Christina
      Light was modelled on Violet Paget [pseud. Vernon Lee]
      (see 1953.B24). The "reason for James's embarrased epis-
      tolary tone" was his opinion that Violet's novel, Miss
      Brown, dedicated to James, was "'very bad.'"

13   EDMONDSON, ELSIE. "The Writer as Hero in Important American
      Fiction Since Howells (Howells, James, Norris, London,
      Farrell, Cabell)." Ph.D. dissertation, University of
      Michigan.
           "Howells and James posit a moral universe, in which the
      protagonists have freedom of choice, and may achieve and
      maintain integrity.... James probes the souls of his pro-
      tagonists, makes it clear that the artist must make su-
      preme sacrifices for his art."

14   FIREBAUGH, JOSEPH J. "The Ververs." Essays in Criticism, 4
      (October), 400-10.
           Disputes interpretations of the Ververs in The Golden
      Bowl as deserving of reader sympathy, and proposes rein-
      terpretation of the novel as a "horrified protest" against
      absolutism, with Maggie as an unsympathetic, "monstrous"
      representative of the Absolute. She may even be seen as a
      symbol of a "cartelized totalitarian state." Adam repudi-
      ates passion for an aesthetic absolute, Maggie for a legal-
      istic, moral one. See 1955.B21, B56.

15   FRIEND, ALBERT C. "A Forgotten Story by Henry James." South
      Atlantic Quarterly, 53 (January), 100-108.
           Analysis of In the Cage, James' "attempt to render a
      modern story in terms of a classical myth," the legend of
      Danae. The theme is "the awakening of an intelligent, but

1954

inexperienced, young woman...." Considers the story, a
"social comedy," as an account of "rebirth recounted in
symbols," which heralded a new period in James' career.

16 GALE, ROBERT L. "Freudian Imagery in James' Fiction."
    <u>American Imago</u>, 11 (Summer), 181-90.
        James' major categories of imagery can be interpreted
    in Freudian terms as sexually symbolic. Analyzes images
    in James' fiction descriptive "of men and women, and their
    relationships, when not only the terms but also the con-
    texts appear sexual or at any rate suggestive." Concludes
    that James used "unconscious sexual symbols in many of his
    figurative comparisons," and that they can aid in inter-
    pretation of male/female interplay.

17 GIBSON, PRISCILLA. "The Uses of James's Imagery: Drama
    through Metaphor." <u>Publications of the Modern Language
    Association</u>, 69 (December), 1076-84.
        Examination of the ways in which images function, the
    contexts in which they are used. "The changing conditions
    under which he applies certain figures in part explain
    why James's later fiction becomes more dramatic, at the
    same time that it remains realistic and more exclusively
    concerns itself with subjective events." Studies function
    of imagery within the context of "'picture' and 'scene,'"
    especially in the last three completed novels.

18 HARRIER, RICHARD C. "'Very Modern Rome'--An Unpublished Essay
    of Henry James." <u>Harvard Library Bulletin</u>, 8 (Spring),
    125-40.
        Reprints essay which resulted from James' fourth visit
    to Rome, in which is developed "the note of change perme-
    ated by an old enchantment," and which resolves a paradox
    about Rome. Gives background and bibliographical informa-
    tion about the essay.

19 HOFFMANN, CHARLES G. "The Art of Reflection in James's <u>The
    Sacred Fount</u>." <u>Modern Language Notes</u>, 69 (November),
    507-508.
        The "art of reflection" is employed by James in <u>The
    Sacred Fount</u> to such a degree of abstractness that it is
    "an almost exclusively intellectual experience" for the
    reader.

20 HOWE, IRVING. "Henry James and the Political Vocation."
    <u>Western Review</u>, 18 (Spring), 199-208.
        Examines <u>The Princess Casamassima</u>, a "virtuoso flight,"
    an "experiment in craft and imagination" which investigates

an unfamiliar subject. Describes novel as a "bewildering
mixture of excellence and badness" with three lines of action: the personal faith of Robinson, the career of the
Princess, and the activities of the revolutionists. Analyzes characters of Princess and Hyacinth, and concludes
that "Remarkable as was James's insight into political
personality, I think it reasonable to say that it [the
novel] does not quite come to a commanding vision of the
political life." Reprinted: 1957.B39; also in Leon Edel,
ed. Henry James: A Collection of Critical Essays,
pp. 156-71.

*21 HÜHNERFELD, P. "Die sündigen Engel." Die Zeit (29 April).
     Cited in 1959.B5. (German)
        Because James is "so European," we may "miss in him 'das
     barbarische Element' which Europeans admire so much about
     other American writers." "James has the fine perception
     of Dickens and the density of the French realists, espe-
     cially of Balzac." In The Turn of the Screw, he deals
     "with man's 'real original sin,' with the fact that man in
     his very state of innocence is tempted by evil even in the
     presence of good which lacks any attraction or splendor."
     James "located the problem of life in the human soul rather
     than in the alley." (Quotations from 1959.B5.)

22 HUMPHREY, ROBERT. "The Functions," in Stream of Consciousness
    in the Modern Novel. Berkeley and Los Angeles: University
    of California Press, pp. 3-4.
       Distinguishes James' technique from stream of conscious-
    ness: "...James has written novels which reveal psycho-
    logical processes in which a single point of view is main-
    tained so that the entire novel is presented through the
    intelligence of a character," rather than making use of
    "prespeech levels of consciousness" or stream of conscious-
    ness.

23 HUMPHREYS, SUSAN M. "Henry James's Revisions for The Ambassa-
    dors." Notes and Queries, NS 1 (September), 397-99.
       James made many verbal revisions and "interpolated whole
    sections" in preparing The Ambassadors for the New York
    edition. This is evident when the original serialized ver-
    sion in The North American Review is examined.

*24 KÄSTNER, E. "Henry James. Die sündigen Engel." Das kleine
     Buch der hundert Bücher, 2. Cited in 1959.B5. (German)
        "Since our experience of Kafka we have become more per-
     ceptive about James" (quotation from 1959.B5).

1954

25 KNIGHT, GRANT C. "Henry James and the Direct Impression,"
    in The Strenuous Age in American Literature. Chapel Hill:
    University of North Carolina Press, pp. 101-22.
       James questioned "the rationality of the sentimental,
    the romantic idealization of love...." Examines James'
    departure from Victorian conventions and morality, and
    considers his view of the novel and what his public wished
    it to be. He "returned to the mythopoeic tradition in
    American literature which he inherited from Hawthorne and
    Melville and Poe and sought to give by way of ambiguities
    a direct impression of life, only his allegories had for
    hero not the pilgrim soul but the pilgrim conscience."

26 KROOK, DOROTHEA. "The Method of the Later Works of Henry
    James." London Mercury, 1 (July), 55-70.
       An examination of the significance of a "curious fea-
    ture" of James' later style, the frequent occurrence of
    "'logical' terms, expressions and images" which help create
    the abstract quality, focusing on The Golden Bowl. Con-
    siders "the sources of James' view of reality and its es-
    sential logic...," and concludes that "it is...the percep-
    tion of the logical structure, the logical properties, of
    his own responses to the world, that James records in those
    curious terms and images...." Revised: 1959.B51.

27 KROOK, DOROTHEA. "The Wings of the Dove." Cambridge Journal,
    7 (August), 671-89.
       Exposes the "melodramatic" foundation of The Wings of
    the Dove, and explains the peculiarity of the novel in
    terms of "the intense generality of the picture...with the
    intense concreteness." Analyzes portrayal of Milly, a re-
    handling of the "Poor Little Rich Girl" theme, whose "fatal
    flaw" is pride. James' purpose in the novel was "to ex-
    hibit the world...in the fulness of its glory and horror;
    and to exhibit it, therefore, as a world prepared for the
    descent of the Dove."

28 KROOK, DOROTHEA. "The Golden Bowl." Cambridge Journal, 7
    (September), 716-37.
       Discusses Maggie's struggle "to restore what has been
    lost and to glorify by her suffering the three lives
    linked with hers in the loss and the restoration," and
    views her as an "emblem of love triumphant," the "image of
    the resurrected God." The Golden Bowl "is a drama about
    the tragic condition of man, in particular about the funda-
    mental and perennial experiences of sin, expiation, and
    redemption."

1954

29   LAS VERGNAS, RAYMOND. "Lettres anglo-américaines: Henry
     James." Hommes et Mondes, 9 (February), 445-47. (French)
        1953 was an important year for translations of James'
     works into French, in particular The Wings of the Dove and
     Washington Square. "It has become a truism in literary
     criticism to see James as one of the people responsible
     for the evolution of fictional technique."

30   LEARY, LEWIS, comp. Articles on American Literature, 1900-
     1950. Durham, N.C.: Duke University Press, pp. 155-65.
        Alphabetical listing by author of articles on James
     written in English which appeared in periodicals between
     1900 and 1950. Includes some foreign language articles.

31   McELDERRY, B. R., JR. "Gertrude Atherton and Henry James."
     Colby Library Quarterly, series 3, no. 16 (November),
     269-72.
        "The Bell in the Fog," a short story written by Atherton
     in 1904, "records in cryptic fashion her impressions of
     James." Summarizes the tale, which contains "several ob-
     vious Jamesian themes," and examines the significance of
     the story, "a warning to James of his isolation from his
     old reading public, and from his native country."

32   MALE, ROY R., JR. "The Dual Aspects of Evil in 'Rappaccini's
     Daughter.'" Publications of the Modern Language Associa-
     tion, 69 (March), 101.
        Reference to children in The Turn of the Screw who are,
     according to the governess, "'blameless and foredoomed,'"
     like Beatrice in "Rappaccini's Daughter."

33   MAYOUX, JEAN-JACQUES. "L'homme sans présent." Lettres
     Nouvelles, 2 (October), 547-58. (French)
        The notebooks of James are so personal that the reader
     feels uninvited. James' definition of beauty is closer to
     Cardinal Newman's than Flaubert's, and for him art is a
     means of communication and not an end in itself. Uses ex-
     amples from several stories to elucidate James' point of
     view.

34   MINER, EARL R. "Henry James's Metaphysical Romances."
     Nineteenth-Century Fiction, 9 (June), 1-21.
        Categorizes 18 of James' stories as "metaphysical ro-
     mances," "the fruit of a vast and varied tradition of
     supernaturalism in literature" and the romance tradition.
     Discusses background of this type, and suggests that James'
     works in this genre provide a "microcosm of the various

1954

styles and moods" of his longer fiction. In the metaphysical romance, James combined moral intensity and psychological insight in a supernatural context.

35   MUECKE, D. C. "The Dove's Flight." Nineteenth-Century Fic-
      tion, 9 (June), 76-78.
          The Wings of the Dove has a pattern, a two-dimensional
      symmetrical form, in which the second half, with chiefly
      psychological movements and situations, is a reverse of
      the first, with primarily physical movements and situa-
      tions. Presents the pattern in diagram.

36   PICON, GAËTAN. "Lecture d'Henry James." La Nouvelle Nouvelle
      Revue Française, 3 (June), 1080-86. (French)
          James is the first truly boring novelist in history,
      representative of an expanded naturalism, precursor of the
      modern novel. James opposed the "logic of art" to the
      "logic of existence."

37   QUINN, PATRICK F. "Morals and Motives in The Spoils of Poyn-
      ton." Sewanee Review, 62 (Autumn), 563-77.
          The subject of The Spoils of Poynton is an ethical
      question, "the difficulty of arriving at intelligent moral
      decisions. Its theme is that a lofty moral idealism may
      be humanly disastrous." Considers the focus of the novel
      the "character and conduct of Fleda Vetch," in whom is
      studied "the psychology of ethical absolutism."

*38   RAUCH, K. "Unlautere Unschuld." Stuttgarter Zeitung (8 May).
      Cited in 1959.B5. (German)
          Rejects Freudian interpretation of James' works as old-
      fashioned. The Turn of the Screw is "a 'modern fairy-tale
      for adults and an excursion into chaos.'" James was aware
      of "the daemonic powers that pervade human life...and no
      more explicit definition by the author could have rendered
      it more effectively." (Quotations from 1959.B5.)

39   ROBSON, W. W. "Henry James's 'The Tragic Muse.'" Mandrake,
      2 (Autumn-Winter), 281-95.
          The Tragic Muse is "a comedy of manners and a piece of
      social history...." Suggests that James was concerned with
      "the relation between Art and Life, or the relation between
      the 'aesthetic' and the 'moral' judgment...." Analyzes
      the characters, and concludes that the work remains an
      "experiment in a kind of novel (the roman à thèse which is
      also something else) and a kind of subject-matter (a real-
      istic handling of English upper- and upper-middle-class
      society) which James never repeated."

1954

40   SANDEEN, ERNEST.   "The Wings of the Dove and The Portrait of
       a Lady: A Study of Henry James's Later Phase."   Publica-
       tions of the Modern Language Association, 69 (December),
       1060-75.
            Compares The Wings of the Dove and The Portrait of a
       Lady, both influenced by the image of Minny Temple, both
       informed by the ironic disparity between the great endow-
       ment of the heroine and the defeat she suffers.   Mentions
       similarities among supporting characters in the two novels,
       and judges the later work to possess greater economy and
       refinement, more sustained metaphors.   Reprinted: in
       William Stafford, ed.   Perspectives on James's "The Por-
       trait of a Lady," pp. 187-205.

41   STONE, EDWARD.   "James's 'Jungle':   The Seasons."   University
       of Kansas City Review, 21 (Winter), 142-44.
            Considers the imagery of the months and seasons in "The
       Beast in the Jungle," including that implicit in the names
       of the characters and in the meeting at Weatherend.   Views
       "calendar in James's tale" as "a backdrop to James's little
       play."   See 1950.B51.

42   TRASCHEN, ISADORE.   "An American in Paris."   American Litera-
       ture, 26 (March), 67-77.
            The revisions of The American for the New York edition
       which develop Newman's innocence are of special interest,
       revealing James' intensity in the theme of the American
       journey from innocence to experience.   Shows how James
       emphasized and elaborated on certain aspects of the pro-
       tagonist's innocence, and concludes that "his innocence is
       a kind of flaw in his character," which caused him to learn
       "a more affecting lesson in evil, made his loss severer,
       and his final relinquishment of power morally greater."

*43   WASNER, E.   "Das Pandämonium der Kinder."   Frankfurter Allge-
       meine Zeitung (5 June).   Cited in 1959.B5.   (German)
            Rejects psychoanalytic approach to James, and views the
       children in The Turn of the Screw as "under the spell of
       darkness to which they have been exposed early," a thesis
       supported by "the fading genius of the boy who is ready to
       confess" and by "the fact that the governess perceives in
       the housekeeper's lack of imagination a help against her
       own terror rather than a threat to credibility."   (Quota-
       tions from 1959.B5.)

1955

<u>1955 A BOOKS</u>

1   KAUFMAN, MARJORIE R.   "Henry James's Comic Discipline: The
     Use of the Comic in the Structure of His Early Fiction."
     Ph.D. dissertation, University of Minnesota.
         In his early fiction, "...James's comic technique is a
     means, both of disciplining the nature of his material and
     of creating the overlay of complexity necessary to the
     realization of his intention," revealing James' view of
     reality through "the multiplicity of man's subliminal so-
     cial relationships."

2   KRICKEL, EDWIN F., JR.   "Henry James and America." Ph.D.
     dissertation, Vanderbilt University.
         Examination of James' nonfictional works to determine
     the significance America had for him reveals that his mature
     "ideal was a union of American moral qualities with Euro-
     pean social forms."

3   LeCLAIR, ROBERT C.   <u>Young Henry James: 1843-1870</u>. New York:
     Bookman Associates, 469 pp.
         A study of James' "formative" first 27 years, from birth
     to what he called "'the end of youth.'" Views James as a
     "detached observer of life," which influenced his philoso-
     phy of art and fiction. Also treats influence of James'
     father and brother. LeClair considers documents of this
     period of James' life, in addition to letting "James speak
     for himself" through his fiction, letters and reminiscences.
     Divides work into three chronological segments, "Book I:
     1843-1855," "Book II: 1855-1858," and Book III: 1858-
     1870." James possessed an "instinctive response to and
     consuming interest in whatever he observed or experienced,"
     and "was deeply, keenly a feeling person." Reviewed: Lyon
     N. Richardson, <u>American Literature</u>, 28 (November 1956),
     385-86; <u>Modern Fiction Studies</u>, 1 (November 1955), 41;
     Carlos Baker, <u>New York Times Book Review</u> (25 September
     1955), p. 7; William T. Stafford, <u>Western Review</u>, 20 (Sum-
     mer 1956), 321-25.

4   POWERS, LYALL H.   "Henry James and French Naturalism." Ph.D.
     dissertation, University of Indiana.
         <u>The Bostonians</u>, <u>The Princess Casamassima</u> and <u>The Tragic
     Muse</u> show evidence of French naturalist influence in the
     importance given to forces of heredity and environment and
     in James' efforts to achieve objectivity. Notably, James
     is as interested "in the character's awareness of the
     heredity and environment factors as in their determining
     force," which foreshadows later preoccupation with

240

characters' awareness. "The dramatic and the Naturalist experiments were supremely important in developing James's final style."

5   TAYLOR, CHRISTY M. "The Pictorial Element in the Theory and Practice of Henry James." Ph.D. dissertation, Stanford University.
        Investigation of "the influence of pictorial composition as central to the theory and practice of Henry James." A study of James' criticism and application of his theories to his works reveals that he "aimed always to integrate the various ideas of pictorial representation and to apply them in his work." Discusses the merits and flaws in James' "pictorial preoccupation."

6   TERRIE, HENRY L., JR. "Pictorial Method in the Novels of Henry James." Ph.D. dissertation, Princeton University.
        "James had a remarkably visual imagination" which he used "to achieve significant pictorial effects in his novels." Studies James' pictorial imagination, demonstrates his use of it in writing novels, and examines four major aspects of the pictorial method, "one of his principal means for rendering that 'direct impression of life'...."

1955 B SHORTER WRITINGS

1   ALLOTT, MIRIAM. "'The Lord of Burleigh' and Henry James's 'A Landscape Painter.'" Notes and Queries, NS 2 (May), 220-21.
        James reacted to Tennyson's naïve fable "The Lord of Burleigh" with a "youthfully dry sophistication," and "A Landscape Painter" is a reply to Tennyson's narrative poem.

2   ALLOTT, MIRIAM. "James Russell Lowell: A Link between Tennyson and HJ." Review of English Studies, NS 6 (October), 399-401.
        The real source of James' "The Romance of Certain Old Clothes" and a partial source for The Sense of the Past is a legend told by Lowell.

3   ANDERSON, CHARLES R. "Henry James's Fable of Carolina." South Atlantic Quarterly, 54 (April), 249-57.
        Analysis of The Reverberator, James' "fable of the South," his "rendering of an expatriated Carolina family." James conceived of the "Carolinian as a formalist, a conservative, deeply wedded to privacy and the traditional manners." In The American Scene, "we find...practically every thread of the fable of Carolina he [James] had woven into his novel The Reverberator two decades earlier."

1955

4   ANDERSON, CHARLES R. "James's Portrait of the Southerner."
      <u>American Literature</u>, 27 (November), 309-31.
          Basil Ransom is one of James' most complex male charac-
      terizations, and <u>The Bostonians</u> is "a fable championing
      the institution of marriage and reaffirming the values of
      a traditional society in which the family is central."
      Analyzes the character of Basil, emphasizing his chivalry
      and his conservatism, and concludes that James didn't know
      enough of the reality of the South to create a hero "in
      whom he could altogether believe nor an entirely credible
      fable of the traditional society that produced him."

5   ANON. "L'atene dei James." <u>La Fiera Letteraria</u>, no. 52
      (18 December), p. 7. (Italian)
          In a letter sent by the Boston Chamber of Commerce con-
      gratulating Italy on the centenary of its Unification of
      the Republic, notes that James' only two novels which take
      place in the United States, <u>Washington Square</u> and <u>The
      Bostonians</u>, are set in Boston.

6   BANGS, JOHN KENDRICK. "The Involvular Club; or, the Return
      of the Screw," in <u>The Antic Muse: American Writers in
      Parody</u>. Edited by R. P. Falk. New York: Grove Press,
      136-41.
          In recital of ghost story by "Jones" to his Involvular
      Club, parodies James, especially the "intricacies" of
      style and long sentences.

7   BAXTER, ANNETTE K. "Independence vs. Isolation: Hawthorne
      and James on the Problem of the Artist." <u>Nineteenth-
      Century Fiction</u>, 10 (December), 225-31.
          A pivotal difference exists between James' and Haw-
      thorne's views of the artist. James questioned how to use
      society without being used by it, whereas Hawthorne foresaw
      the artist's necessary detachment from imperfection, human-
      ity. James asked his artist to be but partially a man, and
      Hawthorne that he be more than a man.

8   BISHOP, FERMAN. "Henry James Criticizes <u>The Tory Lover</u>."
      <u>American Literature</u>, 27 (May), 262-64.
          Reprints unpublished letter from James to Sarah Orne
      Jewett, with whom he was friends and who apparently pro-
      vided him with the germ of an idea for a story in "A Lost
      Lover," in which he criticizes her novel, <u>The Tory Lover</u>.

9   BLACKMUR, RICHARD P. "The American Literary Expatriate," in
      <u>The Lion and the Honeycomb: Essays in Solicitude and Cri-
      tique</u>. New York: Harcourt, Brace and World, pp. 61-78.

1955

Defines expatriate as one who chooses to live in a
country not his own because he can't do his serious work
as well at home, and examines James' passage in Hawthorne
in which he catalogues the elements necessary for the
artist and lacking in America, in studying reasons for
expatriation.

10   BLACKMUR, RICHARD P.   "The Critical Prefaces," in The Lion
     and the Honeycomb: Essays in Solicitude and Critique.
     New York: Harcourt, Brace and World, pp. 240-88.
         Reprint of 1934.B2.

11   BLACKMUR, RICHARD P.   "The Loose and Baggy Monsters of Henry
     James," in The Lion and the Honeycomb: Essays in Solici-
     tude and Critique. New York: Harcourt, Brace and World,
     pp. 276-88.
         Reprint of 1951.B3.

*12 BLÖCKER, G. Der Tagesspiegel (6 February). Cited in 1959.B5.
     (German)
         "'In our world of plump straight-forwardness the master
     of narrative discretion, of subtle circumscription, and of
     artful suspense no longer meets appreciation. If James
     can be accessible across this barrier at all,'" it would
     have to be by way of The Princess Casamassima (quotation
     from 1959.B5).

13   BLOTNER, JOSEPH L. "Henry James: The Breakup of Victorian
     Tranquillity," in The Political Novel. Garden City, N.J.:
     Doubleday and Co., pp. 20-21.
         The Princess Casamassima "focused upon the revolutionary
     currents beginning to stir beneath the surface of English
     political life." Summarizes the novel, notes "gallery of
     types," James' concern with "personal relationships, back-
     grounds and motivations," and his presentation of "an en-
     vironment out of which political violence can explode."

14   BOGAN, LOUISE. "James on a Revolutionary Theme," in Selected
     Criticism: Prose, Poetry. New York: Noonday Press,
     pp. 112-21.
         Reprint of 1938.B5.

15   BOGAN, LOUISE. "The Portrait of New England," in Selected
     Criticism: Prose, Poetry. New York: Noonday Press,
     pp. 295-301.
         Reprint of 1948.B7.

1955

16 BOGAN, LOUISE. "The Silver Clue," in <u>Selected Criticism:</u>
    <u>Prose, Poetry</u>. New York: Noonday Press, pp. 267-68.
        Reprint of 1944.B2.

17 BRADBROOK, FRANK W. "James's 'Woman of Genius.'" <u>Times Lit-</u>
    <u>erary Supplement</u> (29 July), p. 429.
        In reference to McElderry's query concerning the "woman
    of genius" (<u>see</u> 1955.B49), suggests that "there appear to
    be two possible literary reminiscences" in James' anecdote.

18 BRADBROOK, FRANK W. "James's 'Woman of Genius.'" <u>Times</u>
    <u>Literary Supplement</u> (12 August), p. 461.
        Points out James' reference to Anne Thackeray's <u>The</u>
    <u>Story of Elizabeth</u> in a note to T. S. Perry. (<u>See</u>
    1955.B49.)

19 BREIT, HARVEY. "Repeat Performances." <u>New York Times Book</u>
    <u>Review</u> (8 May), p. 15.
        Notes recent less expensive issue of James' notebooks
    by George Braziller, edited by Matthiessen and Murdock
    (<u>see</u> 1947.B32). "Mr. James, it turns out unsurprisingly,
    is a fantastic keeper of the Notebooks...."

20 COLLINS, CARVEL. "James's 'The Turn of the Screw.'" <u>Expli-</u>
    <u>cator</u>, 13 (June), Item 49.
        James wanted the introductory section of <u>The Turn of the</u>
    <u>Screw</u> "to make the reader puzzle over the <u>possibility</u> that
    Douglas...is little Miles grown up." This makes the reader
    doubt even more the accuracy of the governess as a witness.

21 COX, C. B. "<u>The Golden Bowl</u>, II." <u>Essays in Criticism</u>, 5
    (April), 190-93.
        Firebaugh's argument concerning <u>The Golden Bowl</u> (<u>see</u>
    1954.B14) is an untenable one. James proposed "to show
    how her [Maggie's] character develops from weakness into
    strength," rather than to attack her selfishness. "Maggie
    is not...a Machiavellian schemer, but a woman battling for
    her rights as an individual."

22 COX, C. B. "Henry James and Stoicism." <u>Essays and Studies</u>,
    NS 8: 76-88.
        A consideration of James' review of <u>The Works of Epic-</u>
    <u>tetus</u>, in which he summarized his attitude toward Stoic
    philosophy, of interest "because James so rarely committed
    himself to direct statement of his own moral ideals." The
    review also provides a guide to the significance of many
    references to stoicism in James' later works. Concludes
    that for James, "The nature of each individual's

consciousness is determined by the type of environment in which he has lived, and by the quality of his mind; but in this apparently determined tin mould a man retains a sense of freedom. He feels that he can choose to live to the full within the determined conditions of his life."

23   EDEL, LEON. "Henry James's Revisions for The Ambassadors."
      Notes and Queries, NS 2 (January), 37-38.
            The first English edition of The Ambassadors is "the
      only accurate edition" of the novel extant. The work was
      extensively revised from serial to first edition, but
      "there was little revision in the incorporation of the
      first edition (American) into the New York edition."
      James did not interpolate passages in his New York text,
      but rather restored portions he had been forced to remove
      for the purpose of abridging serial installments.

24   EDEL, LEON. "The Choice So Freely Made." New Republic, 133
      (26 September), 26-28.
            Isabel Archer, for James, "occupied the entire canvas."
      She was "the first modern American woman" in "the great
      gallery of the world's fiction." Analyzes Isabel as a
      heroine, suggests comparisons with Portia, and notes "sin-
      gular beauty of the writing, the inner harmonies of struc-
      ture, the rhythm within the drama and the strength of
      characterizations." See 1956.B25.

25   EDEL, LEON. "Time and the Biographer: Leon Edel on Writing
      about Henry James." Listener, 54 (September), 461-62.
            Describes his work on the James biography covering the
      middle years, his attempt to sift through a mass of mate-
      rial and "arrive at the quality...of the lived life."
      Demonstrates how he will write one chapter of this second
      volume of biography to "illustrate what I mean by the
      problem of time in modern literary biography." See
      1957.B21.

26   EDEL, LEON. "Introduction," in The Selected Letters of Henry
      James. Edited by Leon Edel. The Great Letters Series.
      New York: Farrar, Straus and Cudahy, pp. xiii-xxx. Re-
      printed: Garden City, N.Y.: Doubleday and Co., 1960.
            Describes the basis of his choice of James' letters,
      suggests general facts which can be deduced from them,
      discusses characteristics of correspondence in various
      periods, advises how the letters, of "social," "business"
      and "working" types, should be read. James' correspondence
      displays "the complexities of his personality and all the
      refinements of his relationships with his fellow-men."

1955

        Provides annotated list of recipients of letters reprinted.
Reviewed: <u>Modern Fiction Studies</u>, 1 (November 1955), 41;
F. W. Dupee, <u>New York Times Book Review</u> (27 November 1955),
p. 32; Morton D. Zabel, <u>New Republic</u>, 135 (30 April 1956),
25; William T. Stafford, <u>Western Review</u>, 20 (Summer 1956),
321-25.

27   EDEL, LEON. "The Point of View," in <u>The Psychological Novel,
        1900-1950</u>. Philadelphia: J. B. Lippincott Co., pp. 53-75
        and passim.
           <u>The Turn of the Screw</u> and <u>The Sacred Fount</u> "admirably
illustrate the novelist's cunning experiments with the
point of view," and Edel examines the technique of story-
telling in these two works. "In locating his angle of
vision in one specific consciousness, or in a series of
reflecting minds, James anticipated most of the problems
of the stream-of-consciousness writers."

28   EPSEY, JOHN J. "The Major James," in <u>Ezra Pound's Mauberley</u>.
        Berkeley: University of California Press, pp. 49-61.
           Views <u>Mauberley</u> as Pound's "condensation of the James
novel," <u>The Ambassadors</u>. In order to understand Pound's
work, it is important to recognize his "perception of James
as a fighter against pressures": One of <u>Mauberley's</u> main
themes is that of the "pressure of society exerted upon the
the individual." <u>Mauberley</u> is Pound's rehandling of James'
Strether and "enjoys a structural relation with the novels
of James as seen by Pound."

29   EVANS, PATRICIA. "The Meaning of the Match Image in James's
        <u>The Ambassadors</u>." <u>Modern Language Notes</u>, 70 (January),
        36-37.
           Woollett's "chief product of manufacture" was matches,
as suggested by the image in Part Eighth.

30   FADIMAN, CLIFTON. "Three Notes on Henry James," in <u>Party of
        One</u>. Cleveland, Ohio: World Publishing Co., pp. 154-75.
           Reprints versions, with minor revisions, of 1945.B10,
B18; 1950.B34.

31   FALK, ROBERT P. "The Literary Criticism of the Genteel Dec-
        ades, 1870-1900," in <u>The Development of American Literary
        Criticism</u>. Edited by Floyd Stovall. Chapel Hill: Uni-
        versity of North Carolina Press, pp. 113-57.
           Surveys development of American criticism between 1870
and 1900, when James was the leading practitioner of the
art, and during which time realism was attempting to har-
monize the literary ideals of New England renaissance

with the claims of Darwinism and industrial democracy.
Discusses James as demonstrating "sharp fluctuations of
taste and a certain unevenness of tone" typical of "intellectual vacillation of the 1870's," and views the 1880's
as "the epoch of Howells and James."

32   FERGUSSON, FRANCIS. "The Golden Bowl Revisited." Sewanee
       Review, 63 (Winter), 13-28.
           With reference to Quentin Anderson's thesis concerning
       the allegorical meaning of the trilogy of late novels (see
       1946.B1), questions relationship between allegory and the
       "meaning" of The Golden Bowl, "the saving power of love."
       In the novel, "action moves from reason and the moral will
       to a kind of religious humanism in which love is supposed
       to transcend the paradoxes of rationality." Concludes that
       "James was...suggesting a meaning in western history and
       in human life without benefit of an objectified system of
       philosophy or religion." See 1934.B11.

33   FIREBAUGH, JOSEPH J. "Coburn: Henry James's Photographer."
       American Quarterly, 7 (Fall), 215-33.
           Consideration of the friendship and artistic collabora-
       tion between James and Coburn, the photographer for whom
       James sat during his 1905-1906 American visit. Presents
       biographical data on Coburn, and suggests similarities to
       James: Both respected craftsmanship, were dedicated to
       art, and were interested in the origins of creative genius.

34   FOGLE, RICHARD H. "Organic Form in American Criticism, 1840-
       1870," in The Development of American Literary Criticism.
       Edited by Floyd Stovall. Chapel Hill: University of North
       Carolina Press, pp. 82, 86.
           Considers James "a thorough going organicist," who "re-
       trogressed from as much as he advanced upon his predecessor
       Hawthorne." The "gain in technique is balanced...by his
       loss in vigor."

35   FULLER, HESTER THACKERAY. "James's 'Woman of Genius.'" Times
       Literary Supplement (5 August), p. 445.
           The woman mentioned by James in "The Art of Fiction"
       (see 1955.B49) is her mother, Anne Thackeray Ritchie; the
       novel, The Story of Elizabeth.

36   GETTMAN, ROYAL A. and BRUCE HARKNESS. Commentary on "Europe,"
       in Teacher's Manual for "A Book of Stories." New York:
       Rinehart and Co., pp. 36-39.
           "Europe" is concerned with the problems of living life
       to the fullest, Europe versus America, and the evil of
       personal tyranny, of using another individual.

1955

37 GOLDSMITH, ARNOLD LOUIS. "Free Will, Determinism, and Social
    Responsibility in the Writings of Oliver Wendell Holmes,
    Sr., Frank Norris, and Henry James." Ph.D. dissertation,
    University of Wisconsin. (Abstracted in University of Wis-
    consin Summaries of Doctoral Dissertations, 15, 610-12.)
        Views James as "an avowed sharer of his brother's prag-
    matism." An investigation of his outlook in his non-fiction
    finds James "mainly favoring free will." Despite his be-
    lief that men could be victimized by fate, he still "ex-
    alted the aristocrats of consciousness who used their
    wills...to liberate themselves...and to develop nobility
    of character...."

38 GORDON, CAROLINE. "Mr. Verver, Our National Hero." Sewanee
    Review, 63 (Winter), 29-47.
        The Golden Bowl is "the story of the triumph of virtue
    over vice." Adam is presented "not as a businessman but
    as a hero" who must "save his country from a menace." He
    subdues Charlotte, whose "evil practices have turned her
    into a monster." James' secret is "caritas, Christian
    charity." Only "in Adam Verver, whose Christian name is
    that of the first man and whose last name signifies rejuve-
    nation," is James "able to realize his ideal."

*39 H., R. "Hamlet 1886." Die Gegenwart, 10 (12 February), 119.
    Cited in 1959.B5. (German)
        Possibly authored by Robert Haerdter.

*40 HANSEN-LÖVE, F. Wort und Wahrheit, 3. Cited in 1959.B5.
    (German)
        The Princess Casamassima provides "a variation of the
    father and son theme which means the problem of legitimate
    existence as we find it in Stendhal, Kierkegaard, Turgenev,
    Dostoevsky, and Kafka." The novel is viewed as a "'key'"
    of "the leftist intellectual who, misled by false prophets
    remains isolated and directs against himself the weapon
    which 'the black and merciless things,' as James puts it,
    place in his hand." (Quotations from 1959.B5.)

41 HAVENS, RAYMOND D. "Henry James on 'The Outcry.'" Modern
    Language Notes, 70 (February), 105-106.
        Letter from Granville-Barker to James concerning dis-
    cussion of The Outcry in Moscow, and James' reply concern-
    ing the Moscow Theatre.

*42 HERMANOWSKI, G. Die Begegnung, 10 (June). Cited in 1959.B5.
    (German)
        "...With the advent of Henry James we must revise our
    idea that the literary nineteenth century was primarily the
    domain of Russia and France" (quotation from 1959.B5).

43   HYMAN, STANLEY EDGAR. The Armed Vision: A Study in the
      Methods of Modern Literary Criticism. Revised edition.
      Vintage Books. New York: Alfred A. Knopf, passim.
          In a survey of modern critical "schools" and trends,
      discusses views of James by such critics as Yvor Winters,
      T. S. Eliot, Van Wyck Brooks, Constance Rourke, Saul Rosenz-
      weig and R. P. Blackmur.

44   KAZIN, ALFRED. "William and Henry James: 'Our Passion is Our
      Task,'" in The Inmost Leaf: A Selection of Essays. New
      York: Harcourt, Brace and Co., pp. 9-20.
          Reprint of 1943.B25.

*45   KRAUSS, W. "Hinweis auf Henry James." Neue Zürcher Zeitung
      (5 April). Cited in 1959.B5. (German)
          Questions why in The Princess Casamassima "Robinson,
      virtually seduced by the Princess, would not take posses-
      sion of her; why the Princess would not recognize happi-
      ness when it is closest to her, while she is in constant
      search of it--and remains unsatisfied until the end...."
      Suggests that "James's idea of the revolutionary action as
      'the boiling pot with the rich dancing on the surface' im-
      presses modern readers as slightly antiquated. The dis-
      tinction between suppressor and suppressed has long since
      ceased to be so clear as that...." Although the novel "is
      a first-rate study of the mind and soul," it falls short
      of Dostoevsky's Daemons as a novel of revolutionary activ-
      ity. (Quotations from 1959.B5.)

*46   LANG, H. -J. "Der unsichtbare Schatten." Hamburger Echo
      (12 March). Cited in 1959.B5. (German)
          Notes parallel between the way "in which Hyacinth Rob-
      inson remains 'between the classes' very much as does Tonio
      Kroger." Questions whether "the central moral problem [of
      The Princess Casamassima] has been stated and treated
      justly...": "'It is not right that James should have used
      envy as the psychological moving force of social dissatis-
      faction. And making his hero fall in love with all of cul-
      tural accomplishment indiscriminately strikes us as poor--
      so much so that Hyacinth Robinson and with him his author
      at last do impress us as vulgar.'" (Quotation from
      1959.B5.)

47   LEAVIS, QUEENIE D. "A Note on Literary Indebtedness: Dickens,
      George Eliot, Henry James." Hudson Review, 8 (Autumn),
      423-28.
          Quotes parallel passages in Little Dorrit, Middlemarch
      and The Portrait of a Lady treating the theme of the

1955

lovelorn or heartbroken discovering in Rome a "sympathetic
literary background...." Eliot used Dickens constructively
"by extending and deepening, an invention of a less profound artist"; James, in relation to Dickens and Eliot, is
"an example, however engaging and accomplished, of the
parasitic." His passage is largely "insignificant and dis-
appointing, betraying its derivativeness everywhere...."

48 LUBBOCK, PERCY. "James's 'Woman of Genius.'" Times Literary
Supplement (12 August), p. 461.
    The woman in question (see 1955.B49) was Anne Thackeray.
Gives evidence for this assertion.

49 McELDERRY, B. R., JR. "James's 'Woman of Genius.'" Times
Literary Supplement (22 July), p. 413.
    Questions who the person referred to in "The Art of
Fiction" as "'an English novelist, a woman of genius'"
might be, and what was the title of the novel. See
1955.B17-18, B35, B48, B54.

50 McELDERRY, B. R., JR. "The 'Shy Incongruous Charm' of Daisy
Miller." Nineteenth-Century Fiction, 10 (September),
162-65.
    Reprints letter from James to Mrs. Lynn Linton, English
novelist and journalist, concerning the character of Daisy
Miller and why she went with Giovanelli, which affirms her
innocence.

51 MAUGHAM, W. SOMERSET. "The Art of Fiction," in The Art of
Fiction: An Introduction to Ten Novels and Their Authors.
Garden City, N.Y.: Doubleday and Co., pp. 21-22 and passim.
Reprinted: New York: Greenwood Press, 1968.
    Uses James' The Ambassadors to illustrate the technique
of omniscience "concentrated in a single character" in a
description of two main types of novels--first person and
omniscient--telling the story from the inside or outside.

52 MAURIAC, FRANÇOIS. "En marge des 'Bostoniennes.'" Figaro
Littéraire, 10 (6 August), 1, 9. (French)
    On the occasion of a French translation of The Boston-
ians, considers Freudian implications of James' novel and
the effect of the emphasis on sexuality in the contemporary
novel. "The Bostonians, aside from all physiology, presents the deepest study that I know of the scabrous struggle between a man and an amazon, in which a young woman is
the prize." The example of the novel suggests that "in
the plan of the carefully contrived psychological novel,
in which the human being is described from without and

within by a novelist who delineates his models with a clean
stroke, who defines and arbitraily fixes character, the
considerations of the sexual order are the things in the
world which he could best omit."

53 MOORE, MARIANNE. "Henry James as a Characteristic American,"
      in Predilections. New York: The Viking Press, pp. 21-31.
      Reprint of 1934.B21.

54 NOBBE, SUSANNE H. "James's 'Woman of Genius.'" Times Liter-
      ary Supplement (26 August), p. 493.
          In reference to 1955.B49, points out that H. T. Fuller
      and Violet Hammersley print "spirited letters from Henry
      James to Annie" in Thackeray's Daughter, 1951.

55 PARKES, HENRY BAMFORD. "The Industrial Mind," in The American
      Experience: An Interpretation of the History and Civiliza-
      tion of the American People. Second edition, revised.
      New York: Alfred A. Knopf, pp. 261-65.
          James "saved himself by looking for his subject matter...
      in Europe," yet he remained "more profoundly American than
      the Anglophiles of the Genteel Tradition...." Sees James'
      deficiency as "lack of sensuous awareness and participa-
      tion."

56 PERRIN, EDWIN N. "The Golden Bowl, I." Essays in Criticism,
      5 (April), 189-90.
          Refutation of 1954.B14. Maggie is "simply a Jamesian
      heroine of considerable complexity," and the Ververs "con-
      stitute something of a Jamesian ideal of behaviour for rich
      Americans."

*57 SCHNEDITZ, W. "Ein Grandseigneur des menschlichen Herzens."
      Salzburger Nachrichten (18 May). Cited in 1959.B5. (German)
          James is a "'grandseigneur of the heart,'" and "during
      the last hundred years no one has written with more refine-
      ment and insight about the human heart and its ways..."
      (quotations from 1959.B5).

58 SCHULZ, MAX F. "The Bellegardes' Feud with Christopher New-
      man: A Study of Henry James's Revision of The American."
      American Literature, 27 (March), 42-55.
          James tried to disguise the artistic problem in The
      American, "a falsely romantic conception of denoument...."
      Demonstrates how James attempted to make the unreality
      acceptable. Revisions were aimed at deepening the feud
      between Newman and the Bellegardes by presenting it on
      different levels, which Schulz enumerates.

1955

59   SPILLER, ROBERT E. "Art and the Inner Life: Dickinson,
      James," in The Cycle of American Literature: An Essay in
      Historical Criticism. New York: The Macmillan Co.,
      pp. 163-83.
           Views James as a pioneer of "exploration of the con-
      sciousness" in order to reveal inner reality, in contrast
      to the exponents of the outer world, the West, expansion.
      Provides biographical/critical survey of James, concluding
      that "The most self-centered and subjective of all Ameri-
      can writers of fiction had...succeeded in an art of total
      revelation through perfect workmanship."

60   STAFFORD, WILLIAM T. "The Two Henry Jameses and Howells: A
      Bibliographical Mix-up." Bulletin of Bibliography, 21
      (January-April), 135.
           Three bibliographies of Henry James erroneously list an
      item by Austin Warren, 1932, entitled "James and his Se-
      cret," which should be listed in bibliographies of Henry
      James, Sr. and Howells.

61   STAFFORD, WILLIAM T. "Henry James the American: Some Views
      of His Contemporaries." Twentieth-Century Literature, 1
      (July), 69-76.
           Surveys the issue of James' expatriation, mentions de-
      fenses of James' internationalism, especially by American
      writers, and suggests three approaches to James' expatria-
      tion: "that which would attack James for supposed nation-
      alistic deficiencies; that which would find fault in such
      judgments; and that which would extract and elucidate the
      peculair [sic] American qualities in his work and in the
      man."

62   STEVENS, A. W. "Henry James' The American Scene: The Vision
      of Value." Twentieth-Century Literature, 1 (April), 27-33.
           James attempted "to evoke moral value from the American
      scene," and The American Scene is "a painfully complex
      picture of James' struggle between the internal man and the
      external observer," an effort to reappraise the reasons for
      his expatriation. The book possesses "all the signs of a
      moral purgative," dealing with the themes of alienation
      and hierarchy, and prophesying the "deterioration of the
      heroic values in American life and the assumption of power
      in terms of units rather than individuals."

63   STONE, EDWARD. "From Henry James to John Balderston: Rela-
      tivity and the '20's." Modern Fiction Studies, 1 (May),
      2-11.

252

"James received a kind of posthumous fame" for <u>The Sense of the Past</u>, "an arresting bit of time phantasy," through John L. Balderston's play <u>Berkeley Square</u>, and the fame was attributable to the popularity of Einstein's theory of relativity of time about which James "must have been completely unaware." Discusses James' novel, which documents his favorite proposition, "that the only true adventures are those of the mind."

*64 STURM, VILMA. <u>Schwäbische Landeszeitung</u> (2 July). Cited in 1959.B5. (German)
Ambiguity and lack of determinism make James' characters realistic. "On the whole, 'James worked the miracle of providing just as much clarity as there is in real life. The fascinating thing is "that residue" which we can never track down. It is exactly like that which sets the reader wondering in his own life.'" With reference to <u>The Princess Casamassima</u>, "'The story of the man between social levels has probably never been told more impressively and terribly.'" (Quotations from 1959.B5.)

*65 SÜSSKIND, W. E. <u>Süddeutsche Zeitung</u> (26 February). Cited in 1959.B5. (German)
"Not until we have removed 'many a layer of dust' do we retain from the novel [...<u>The Princess Casamassina</u>] the strong and lasting impression of scenes and characters. As an inventor of stories James is not very resourceful" (quotation from 1959.B5).

66 SWAN, MICHAEL. "Henry James and the Heroic Young Master." <u>London Mercury</u>, 2 (May), 78-86.
Details James' relationship with Hendrik Christian Anderson, sculptor, which began in Rome in 1899 and lasted until James' death, based on 77 letters written by James to Anderson. Anderson became "one of the family of 'son-figures' which James gathered around him during the remaining years of his life." Includes two 1907 photographs of the men and several letters from James, who was "worried by his friend's insistence on the monumental...." Reprinted: 1958.B76.

67 TINDALL, WILLIAM YORK. <u>The Literary Symbol</u>. New York: Columbia University Press, passim. Reprinted: Bloomington: University of Indiana Press, 1960.
Uses Forster's description of the hourglass pattern in <u>The Ambassadors</u> (<u>see</u> 1927.B5) to illustrate structure as opposed to form.

1955

68 TRILLING, LIONEL. "The Bostonians," in The Opposing Self:
    Nine Essays in Criticism. New York: The Viking Press,
    pp. 104-17.
        Reprint of 1952.B63.

69 UHLIG, HELMUT. "Henry James deutsch." Texte und Zeichen, 2
    (Spring), 262-66. (German)
        As a sensitive observer of his era, James had "an im-
    mense ability to make the surface of life transparent
    without analyzing." He is as important to the development
    of the modern novel as Melville or Kafka. Notes James'
    increasing influence in Germany as a result of better
    translations.

70 VIVAS, ELISEO. "Henry and William (Two Notes)," in Creation
    and Discovery: Essays in Criticism and Aesthetics. New
    York: Noonday Press, pp. 15-28.
        Reprint of 1943.B53.

71 VOLPE, EDMOND L. "The Prefaces of George Sand and Henry
    James." Modern Language Notes, 70 (February), 107-108.
        James' essay on George Sand published in 1877 reveals
    her prefaces as possible inspiration for the prefaces in
    the New York edition.

72 WEGELIN, CHRISTOF. "Henry James: The Expatriate as Ameri-
    can." Symposium, 9 (Spring), 46-55.
        Notes motives for resentment of James' expatriation,
    and asserts that "only an American could have portrayed
    Americans as he did." Although his point of view remained
    American, he was "an Anglophile." Examines the founda-
    tions of James' cosmopolitanism and suggests that its
    origins were, paradoxically, "in his American conscious-
    ness," based on his devotion to "the cause of civilization"
    rather than to a state and on his "sense of the sovereignty
    of the individual conscience."

73 WILCOX, THOMAS W. "A Way into The Aspern Papers." Exercise
    Exchange, 3 (December), 5-6.
        Poses the question whether the narrator in The Aspern
    Papers is James himself or a participant in the action of
    the story, in an attempt "To define a large part of the
    meaning of the story by defining the strategy by which that
    meaning is expressed."

74   WOODRESS, JAMES. "Henry James." Publications of the <u>Modern</u>
     <u>Language Association</u>, 70 (April), 170-71.
         Bibliography of books and articles on James which ap-
     peared in American periodicals during the previous year.

<u>1956 A BOOKS</u>

  1   BOWDEN, EDWIN T. <u>The Themes of Henry James: A System of Ob-</u>
      <u>servation through the Visual Arts</u>. Yale Studies in Eng-
      lish. Vol. 132. New Haven, Conn.: Yale University
      Press, 130 pp. Reprinted: 1960.
          Originally a dissertation (Yale University, 1952). The
      visual arts offer a critically valid method of interpreta-
      tion as well as a means of analyzing the central themes of
      James' works. The European-American theme and the theme
      of moral decision are synthesized in the novels of the
      major phase, which "provide the natural summary of James'
      development and presentation of theme, and by implication
      the development of his own aesthetic consciousness." Pro-
      vides biographical account of James' "personal relationship
      with the visual arts." Chapters include "The Man and the
      Arts," "The European-American Theme: Europe," "The Euro-
      pean-American Theme: America," "The Theme of Moral Deci-
      sion," "The Experiment and The Conjunction of Themes," and
      "The Final Synthesis of Themes." Reviewed: Elaine Coul-
      ter, <u>Modern Fiction Studies</u>, 2 (Winter 1956-1957), 248;
      <u>New England Quarterly</u>, 30 (September 1957), 413-17; Lewis
      Leary, <u>Saturday Review of Literature</u>, 40 (23 February
      1957), 35.

  2   DUPEE, FREDERICK W. <u>Henry James</u>. Second edition, revised
      and enlarged. Doubleday Anchor Books. Garden City, N.Y.:
      Doubleday and Co., 272 pp.
          <u>See</u> 1951.A2.

  3   KRAUSE, SYDNEY J. "Henry James's Revisions of <u>The Portrait of</u>
      <u>a Lady</u>: A Study of Literary Portraiture and Perfection-
      ism." Ph.D. dissertation, Columbia University.
          An examination of James' revisions for <u>The Portrait of</u>
      <u>a Lady</u> reveals his "insistent drive for artistic perfec-
      tion" and his enhancement of the method of literary por-
      traiture "which involves the depiction of moral and mental
      states by the tangible analogues that symbolize them, and
      the framing of characters and scenes for the effect of
      rendering them as symbolic pictures."

1956

4   VIENTÓS GASTÓN, NILITA. Introducción a Henry James. Rió
    Piedras: Universidad de Puerto Rico, 98 pp. Reprinted:
    Ediciones de la Torre. Puerto Rico: Universidad de
    Puerto Rico, 1964. (Spanish)
        Consideration of James the man and the Jamesian con-
    ception of the novel, which involves the author viewing
    his works objectively and candidly and realizing the "di-
    rect, personal, intense, and free" impressions of life.
    Examines The Ambassadors as an example of a Jamesian novel,
    traces the evolution in five novels of the "personage of
    the heiress, key to Jamesian work," and studies James'
    presentation of the artist. Looks at James' exaltation of
    the values of individualism and art, and compares his
    theory of the novel as an art form with that of Ortega y
    Gasset in Ideas sobre la novela. Includes bibliography of
    James' works, listing Spanish translations and critical
    studies in Spanish of James' works.

1956 B SHORTER WRITINGS

1   ALLOTT, MIRIAM. "A Ruskin Echo in The Wings of the Dove."
    Notes and Queries, 201 (February), 87.
        "Brittania of the Market Place" imagery used for Mrs.
    Lowder in The Wings of the Dove recalls Ruskin's "Goddess
    of Getting-on" or "Brittania of the Market" in The Crown
    of Wild Olive.

*2 ANON. "Eine Phrase wird angeklagt. Henry James schreibt
    gegen das Jahrhundert des Kindes." Hohenloher Tagblatt
    (10 February). Cited in 1959.B5. (German)
        "What Maisie Knew is a piece of social psychology anti-
    cipating our most modern insights, and appeals to us as a
    protest in the name of all the children of divorced par-
    ents" (quotation from 1959.B5).

3   ANON. "James the Obscure." Newsweek, 47 (7 May), 110-11.
        Describes James as "a literary man in full dress," and
    his autobiography (see 1956.B20) as "great literary fili-
    gree." James "gives...a powerful picture of his own growth
    into what deserves to be called a priestlike dedication to
    the art of letters."

4   ANON. "Memories of a Mandarin." Time, 67 (7 May), 114-15.
        The James revival has deservedly placed him "at the hard
    core of great American novel writing," acting as "an en-
    lightening bridge to the greatest of twentieth-century
    writing." Surveys James' early life, from which he emerged

"a staunch culture hero," and defines his autobiography
(see 1956.B20) as a writer "sinking roots in the soil of
his creative imagination...."

*5   ANON. Die Tat (8 December). Cited in 1959.B5. (German)
James' "never-ending and uncompromising effort toward
artistic perfection and the rigid defense of ethics as the
purpose of literary art" may account for his lack of public
popularity. "This 'aristocrat of literature' may well re-
mind Europeans of their obligations." Revived interest in
James is due in part to disappointment in "'the casual and
careless manner'" of contemporaries. (Quotations from
1959.B5.)

6   ARVIN, NEWTON. "Looking Backward with Henry James." New York
Times Book Review (29 April), p. 1.
James' is the "richest, warmest and most luminous of
American literary biographies." (See 1956.B20.) Sketches
the background of its writing, the style of the work, and
suggests that its value resides in the fact of its "revelation of the process by which the mind of a deeply im-
pressionable but sedate and not obviously gifted child
becomes...the mind of an actively and tirelessly produc-
tive artist."

*7   BARZUN, JACQUES. "'The Blest Group of Us.'" Griffin, 5
(June), 4-13. Cited in Lewis G. Leary, comp. Articles on
American Literature, 1950-1967, p. 297.

8   BARZUN, JACQUES. "Henry James, Melodramatist," in The Ener-
gies of Art: Studies of Authors Classic and Modern. New
York: Harper and Brothers, pp. 227-44. Reprinted: Vin-
tage Books. New York: Alfred A. Knopf, 1962.
Reprint of 1943.B8.

9   BENNETT, JOAN. "The Art of Henry James: The Ambassadors."
Chicago Review, 9 (Winter), 12-26.
In The Ambassadors, "life" is a key word, and the major
theme can be accentuated by isolating a number of points
in the action where Strether considers the content of that
word. Examines four such examples which demonstrate the
hero's gradual discovery of new meaning of the term, and
analyzes the scene in which Strether wanders into Notre
Dame to dispel the view that the novel is concerned with
politics, economics or religion, except as they influence
human beings. Reprinted: in Albert E. Stone, ed. Twentieth Century Interpretations of "The Ambassadors," pp. 57-
65.

1956

10   BLANKE, G. H. "Henry James als Schriftsteller zwischen Ameri-
         ka und Europe." <u>Die Neueren Sprachen</u>, 2: 59-71. (German)
            For James, Europe symbolizes experience, America sym-
         bolizes innocence, and each should learn from the other.
         James' message supported the "Atlantic Community."

11   BOMPARD, PAOLA. "Una nota su <u>The Golden Bowl</u>." <u>Studi Ameri-
         cani</u>, no. 2, pp. 143-62. (Italian)
            After explaining the intricacies of plot of <u>The Golden
         Bowl</u>, focuses on the dramatic and psychological development
         of Maggie. Unlike other Jamesian heroines, she is unwill-
         ing to sacrifice her adolescent innocence and Electral link
         to her father until she realizes she has pushed Amerigo and
         Charlotte together; and she develops from a useless, in-
         sipid character into a responsible woman, capable of love.
         Mentions previous interpretations of the novel, discusses
         the symbolism of the golden bowl. Concludes by noting
         that "James wrote at a time when Freud's theories had yet
         to become part of [literature]...and it is because of his
         intuition if he, in his passionate examining of the con-
         science, has broken into the realms of the subconscious...."

12   BREBNER, ADELE. "How to Know Maisie." <u>College English</u>, 17
         (February), 283-85.
            Describes her techniques for teaching <u>What Maisie Knew</u>.
         Students who consider "What <u>does</u> Maisie know?" ultimately
         discover that James made that question unanswerable, and
         find that "the story of a sensitive child, if well enough
         told, can have both pathos and humor."

*13   BUTLER, JOHN F. <u>Exercises in Literary Understanding</u>. Chi-
         cago: Scott-Foresman, pp. 34-38. Cited in 1957.B2, p. 93.

14   CARGILL, OSCAR. "<u>The Princess Casamamassima</u>: A Critical Re-
         appraisal." <u>Publications of the Modern Language Associa-
         tion</u>, 71 (March), 97-117.
            A survey of critical interpretations of <u>The Princess
         Casamassima</u>, with discussion of James' debt to Dickens,
         his familiarity with the revolutionary movement, delinea-
         tion of characters, and the point of Hyacinth's tragedy.
         Considers references to and use of the Hamlet story, and
         concludes that Hyacinth is "pitiable and small" as in
         Turgenev's rendering, but also a "tragic figure" as is
         Shakespeare's hero.

15   CARGILL, OSCAR. "Henry James as Freudian Pioneer." <u>Chicago
         Review</u>, 10 (Summer), 13-29.

Hypothesizes that James may have had reason to disguise his purpose in <u>The Turn of the Screw</u>, since Alice James' tragic story "provides an explanation for the 'ambiguity' of both the commentary and the tale itself." Suggests that an early Freudian case study, "The Case of Miss Lucy R.," supplied relevant elements for James' tale, that James could have become familiar with the methods of Freud and the details of this particular study through Alice's condition of hysteria and the associations it produced, and with the delusions and fantasies of her illness. Hence, the ghosts are hallucinations, and in the Preface James was protecting Alice's memory and establishing a legal shield. Reprinted: in Gerald Willen, ed. <u>A Casebook on "The Turn of the Screw</u>," pp. 223-38.

16   CARGILL, OSCAR. "Introduction," in <u>Washington Square and Daisy Miller</u>. Edited by Oscar Cargill. New York: Harper and Brothers, pp. vii-xxv.
      "...The 'American Girl'...found her best appreciator and recorder in...Henry James," who "possessed an acute understanding of the feminine character...." Discusses influence of Turgenev and French naturalists, describes circumstances of composition of <u>Daisy Miller</u>, and compares it to <u>Washington Square</u> to illustrate the superiority of James' work.

17   COHEN, B. BERNARD. "Henry James and the Hawthorne Centennial." <u>Essex Institute Historical Collection</u>, 92 (July), 279-83.
      Reprints four unpublished Henry James letters to R. S. Rantoul concerning commemoration of the one-hundredth anniversary of Hawthorne's birth.

18   D'AGOSTINO, NEMI. "Sul teatro di Henry James." <u>Studi Americani</u>, no. 2, pp. 163-77. (Italian)
      James failed to produce a play of great significance, one "that adds to his poetic stature or to the living inheritance of the English language." The social and collective experiences of the theatre, especially the quality of oral communication, escaped him.

19   DEURBERGUE, JEAN. "Un romancier en porte-à-faux: Henry James." <u>Critique</u>, 14 (June), 501-11. (French)
      An exposition on the international theme in James' work, with reference to his expatriation, concluding that James' drama has roots in both continents simultaneously, and that he was unable to choose one or the other decisively.

1956

20   DUPEE, FREDERICK W. "Introduction," in Autobiography. By
     Henry James. Edited by Frederick W. Dupee. New York:
     Criterion Books, pp. vii-xiv.
        This first reprint of A Small Boy and Others, Notes of
     a Son and Brother and The Middle Years provides an "ex-
     tended account of his [James'] development," of his moral
     and professional growth and search for a vocation. De-
     scribes conditions under which the work was written, dis-
     cusses material dealt with in each of the three volumes,
     and concludes that "The growth of a mind from a state of
     relative moral freedom was James' subject in his autobiog-
     raphy as in much of his fiction." Reviewed: Modern Fic-
     tion Studies, 2 (May 1956), 88; Elizabeth Stevenson, New
     England Quarterly, 29 (December 1956), 541-43.

21   DURR, R. A. "The Night Journey in The Ambassadors." Philo-
     logical Quarterly, 35 (January), 24-38.
        James wished to excite the reader's sense of mystery in
     The Ambassadors through use of the occult and the violent,
     "the night journey--that mythical adventure into the re-
     gions of mystery, terror, and apotheosis." In the novel,
     because events are experienced through Strether, "the
     structure and meaning of the adventure become comparable"
     to those of "ancient and contemporary rites de passage
     and to the many myths and folk tales embodying the rhythm
     of death and rebirth." Details the archetypal pattern in
     the novel.

22   EDEL, LEON. "Prefatory Note. 'A Tragedy of Error': James's
     First Story." New England Quarterly, 29 (September),
     291-95.
        Presents evidence authenticating "A Tragedy of Error"
     as James'. A letter written by "an unobstrusive bystander"
     revealed the location of James' first story in The Conti-
     nental Monthly.

23   EDEL, LEON. "Introduction," in The American Essays of Henry
     James. Edited by Leon Edel. Vintage Books. New York:
     Alfred A. Knopf, pp. v-xvii.
        The essays on American subjects included in the volume
     "constitute a vivid store of American observations, impres-
     sions, and memories," written in an informal way. Con-
     siders material covered in the essays, and suggests that
     James' artist life was devoted to the problem of America's
     relations with the rest of the world. The essays demon-
     strate "the exploratory reach of James's mind--and this
     mind, and the pen it guided, were ever concerned with the
     American consciousness and the American character."

1956

24   EDEL, LEON. "Introduction," in <u>Henry James: The Future of</u>
      <u>the Novel: Essays on the Art of Fiction</u>. Edited by Leon
      Edel. Vintage Books. New York: Alfred A. Knopf, pp. v-
      xvi.
           The collection includes essays in which James expresses
      his views on fiction and makes "pronouncements about the
      art he practiced with such highly professional devotion."
      Edel considers some of James' assumptions about the novel
      as an art form, his fictional theories; discusses James'
      hope that writers be "relieved of the burden of subterfuge
      and indirection" and allowed to treat subject matter hon-
      estly. Concludes with consideration of James' "humane
      approach to his material."

25   EDEL, LEON. "Introduction," in <u>The Portrait of a Lady</u>.
      Edited by Leon Edel. Riverside Editions. Boston: Hough-
      ton Mifflin Co., pp. v-xx.
           Restatement of material in 1955.B24. In <u>The Portrait</u>
      <u>of a Lady</u>, James "opened a new window for the novel...."

26   EDWARDS, OLIVER. "Christina Light." <u>The Times</u> (1 March),
      p. 11.
           Christina Light in <u>Roderick Hudson</u> and <u>The Princess</u>
      <u>Casamassima</u> is "enigmatic," "challengingly alive all the
      time." One aspect of her "quality was that no two people
      saw it alike."

27   EDWARDS, OLIVER. "Truthful James." <u>The Times</u> (1 November),
      p. 13.
           Describes sixteen pages of "The Letters of Henry James"
      in a volume of William Roughead's <u>The Tales of the Cri-</u>
      <u>minous</u>. Questions James' style in the correspondence,
      which Edwards reads in light of the author's old-fashioned
      New England origins. "The septuagenarian was being true
      to the stripling. There had, indeed, been only one James
      all through, with his spiritual home in these shades."

28   ENKVIST, NILS ENK. "Henry James and Julio Reuter: Two
      Notes." <u>Neuphilologische Mitteilungen</u>, 57 (December),
      318-24.
           In "Henry James's Finnish Governess: An Unpublished
      Letter," reprints letter from James to Reuter answering a
      question about a Finnish <u>bonne</u> employed by the James fam-
      ily in the '50's. "Henry James and the Nobel Prize" in-
      cludes the translation of a proposal of Reuter that James
      be awarded the Nobel Prize, Reuter being "much ahead of
      many of his Scandinavian colleagues in realizing the great-
      ness of Henry James."

1956

29   FERGUSON, A. R.   "The Triple Quest of Henry James: Fame, Art,
     and Fortune."   American Literature, 27 (January), 475-98.
       A rebuttal of the interpretation of James as an absorbed
     artist, unconcerned with money and popularity. The triple
     quest for fame, art, and fortune was part of James' per-
     sonal life and artistic creativity, and when fame and for-
     tune eluded him, he turned to the technique of art. Ex-
     amines the importance of wealth for James, and views his
     trip to America and the definitive edition as experiences
     in his later career which represented the triple motiva-
     tions behind his creative activity. "To the last, fame,
     art, and fortune were the challenge, the lure, and the
     complication of the writer."

30   FORSTER, E. M.   "Henry James in the Galleries,"   New Republic
     135 (17 December), 24-25.
       With reference to The Painter's Eye (see 1956.B74),
     suggests that James' standards "were in theory aesthetic,
     and indeed hedonistic," and his essays on art contain "much
     good entertainment and good sense."

31   GIRLING, H. K.   "The Function of Slang in the Dramatic Poetry
     of 'The Golden Bowl.'"   Nineteenth-Century Fiction, 11
     (September), 130-47.
       In The Golden Bowl, James frequently, at critical points,
     required simplicity; he used slang, the words of daily
     speech, to achieve it. To demonstrate the part played by
     slang in the novel, considers some of its general problems,
     which are associated with comprehension, and illustrates
     James' two approaches to slang expression, either as a
     rich metaphor or an extremely comprehensive phrase. The
     use of slang represents part of James' technique of dra-
     matic representation, and slang phrases are "nodal points
     in his task of exhibiting through words his profound and
     delicate analysis."

32   GRANA, GIANNI.   "Henry James e la grande arte narrativa."
     La Fiera Letteraria, no. 5 (4 March), pp. 4-6. (Italian)
       James was a spokesman for the aristocracy and a product
     of his times. Considers his reasons for leaving America.

33   HALL, JAMES B. and JOSEPH LANGLAND. Comment on "Greville
     Fane," in The Short Story. New York: The Macmillan Co.,
     pp. 346-47.
       Suggests, by means of comment and question, some of
     James' fictional techniques, such as use of "reflectors"
     and central intelligence, and notes the "frequent occur-
     rence of wit" in "Greville Fane."

34 HOWE, IRVING. "Introduction," in The Bostonians. Edited by
    Irving Howe. Modern Library. New York: Random House,
    pp. v-xxviii.
        Compares The Bostonians and The Princess Casamassima,
    which "share a community of subject matter and literary
    method..." and which failed as a result of "the quality
    of American culture during the 1880's." Suggests influ-
    ence of Hawthorne on The Bostonians, and analyzes the nov-
    el's characters and theme, "dramatizing a parallel disar-
    rangment of social and sexual life...." The struggle
    presented in the novel is on the surface concerned with
    love "but in its depths a struggle of politics."

35 HYDE, H. MONTGOMERY. "An Afternoon with Max." Spectator
    (5 October), pp. 445-47.
        Records impressions of a conversation with Sir Max
    Beerbohm, who relates an anecdote involving James. See
    1946.B5.

36 IZZO, CARLO. "Henry James scrittore sintattico." Studi
    Americani, no. 2, pp. 127-42. (Italian)
        Attempts to prove the metaphysical nature of James'
    writing--the interrelationship of the abstract mental form
    with the artful matter of his narration. The crux of
    James' work is his establishment of artistic relations
    between America and Europe, his "pilgrim's progress" back
    to the continent.

37 KIMBALL, JEAN. "The Abyss and The Wings of the Dove: The
    Image as a Revelation." Nineteenth-Century Fiction, 10
    (March), 281-300.
        The central situation in The Wings of the Dove is
    Milly's struggle to live, even beyond death. Kimball ex-
    amines the novel's action from her point of view, and
    discusses the use and meaning of the image of the abyss
    and the dove symbol to portray the struggle of Milly's
    soul to rise above annihilation, to strengthen itself for
    a life beyond death. Her existence is justified by her
    inward self-development, and only as the other characters
    are aware of Milly's consciousness of death and of the
    universal abyss do they benefit from her life.

38 KNOX, GEORGE. "James's Rhetoric of 'Quotes.'" College Eng-
    lish, 17 (February), 293-97.
        Demonstrates in The Ambassadors a "rhetoric of 'quotes.'"
    Divides James' use of quotation marks into five categories,
    according to function, which provide evidence of the stress
    James placed on language during the later period.

1956

39 KOSKIMIES, RAFAEL. "Novelists' Thoughts About Their Art. I.
    Anthony Trollope and Henry James." Neuphilologische
    Mitteilungen, 57: 148-59.
        Examines James' criticism of authorial digressions, his
    view of Trollope as deviating from the writer's duty to be
    "a historian" and to provide the reader with an illusion
    of reality.

40 LAINOFF, SEYMOUR. "A Note on Henry James's 'The Real Thing.'"
    Modern Language Notes, 71 (March), 192-93.
        In his depiction of the Monarchs in "The Real Thing,"
    James attacks "a theory of literal imitation in the arts"
    and the theory of the beau idéal. The artist instead
    seeks "a more expressive and imaginative realism than that
    suggested by the Monarchs."

41 LEARY, LEWIS. "Over Henry's Shoulder." Saturday Review of
    Literature, 39 (7 April), 19.
        In review of Edel's edition of James' letters (see
    1955.B26), describes correspondence as "very charming,"
    and suggests that "his residue seems often quite as good
    as another man's granite."

42 LEISI, ERNST. "Der Erzählstandpunkt in der neueren englischen
    Prosa." Germanischromanische Monatsschrift, Neue Folge,
    6: 40-51. (German)
        The founder of a new style in the English language,
    James puts the center of perception into the hero instead
    of the author and preserves the mystery of the psyche.

43 LEVIN, HARRY. Symbolism and Fiction. Charlottesville:
    University of Virginia Press, pp. 12-13.
        Reference to Wilson's interpretation of The Turn of the
    Screw (see 1934.B37) as an example of "isolating text from
    context in the name of 'close reading'...."

44 LEVY, LEO B. "The Turn of the Screw as Retaliation." College
    English, 17 (February), 286-88.
        The Turn of the Screw, rather than displaying James'
    frustrations of the dramatic years, is a "celebration of a
    self once more in possession of its powers," an act of
    retaliation on the "'vulgar'" spectators of Guy Domville
    by confusing the reader with ambiguity and unpredictability.
    "As a complex resolution, in literary terms, of the be-
    setting conflicts of the dramatic years, The Turn of the
    Screw is at once a retaliatory gesture toward the immediate
    past and the achievement of a creative spirit which had
    rediscovered itself."

1956

45 LEVY, LEO B. "Henry James's <u>Confidence</u> and the Development of
    the Idea of the Unconscious." <u>American Literature</u>, 28
    (November), 347-58.
        Deals with the way in which James' understanding of the
    unconscious motivation grew intuitively and experimentally
    out of his early writings. With <u>Confidence</u> in 1880, James
    developed the idea that character and motivation are
    shaped unconsciously, and the novel represents an important
    attempt to construct hypotheses about unconscious behavior
    and to present motives to the readers by means of technique.
    The work also displays two previously established interests
    in a new combination, that is, a description of the path-
    ological joined with the device of reversal as it existed
    in the well-made play. Thus, <u>Confidence</u> is "a landmark in
    the history of James's long and rewarding study of human
    consciousness."

46 McCARTHY, HAROLD T. "Henry James and 'The Personal Equation.'"
    <u>College English</u>, 17 (February), 272-78.
        James deliberately cultivated a personal expression of
    things, viewing human situations as problems to which no
    conventional moral system could be applied. Points out
    James' belief in the importance of the individual, examines
    some of his views of his art, and discusses his personal
    style, another aspect of his individual rendering of mate-
    rial.

47 MELCHIORI, GIORGIO. "Un personaggio di Henry James." <u>Studi</u>
    <u>Americani</u>, no. 2, pp. 179-93. (Italian)
        An analysis of the character Eugenio, the indispensable
    courier who accompanies Daisy Miller on her European visit.
    James paints him as "that type of Italian servant sour and
    compassionately insolent, yet extremely competent," shrewd,
    cultured, and intelligent, almost typical of that part of
    the Italian mind that gave birth to Niccolo Machiavelli.
    Describes Eugenio in the dramatic version of <u>Daisy Miller</u>,
    in which he is simplified for commercialism, and concludes
    by affirming James' fascination for the character, "sus-
    pended between two worlds, this dishonest but extremely
    competent mediator between the two civilizations which
    James himself was torn between."

48 MELCHIORI, GIORGIO. "Two Mannerists: James and Hopkins," in
    <u>The Tightrope Walkers: Studies of Mannerism in Modern</u>
    <u>English Literature</u>. London: Routledge and Kegan Paul,
    pp. 13-33.
        English translation of 1953.B42.

1956

49 MONROE, ELIZABETH N. "Other Books." America, 95 (19 May),
    207.
        Notes James' "habit of making a mystery of things where
    no mystery inheres" and his inability to accept criticism,
    and suggests that Edel's selection of letters (1955.B26)
    is helpful "in checking the legend against the fact."

50 NIESS, R. J. "Henry James and Emile Zola: A Parallel."
    Revue de Littérature Comparée, 30 (January-March), 93-98.
        Suggests the source of Zola's L'Oeuvre is possibly
    James' The Madonna of the Future rather than Balzac's Le
    Chef-d'oeuvre inconnu. "With infinite pity, but with the
    clearest judgment," James and Zola "wrote the tragedy of
    the incomplete artist, living in his own special circle of
    the human Inferno." They also "depicted in the highest
    symbolic terms the whole tragedy of man, our stubborn will
    to transcend our condition, our endless wish to play God."

51 O'CONNOR, FRANK [pseud.]. "Transition: Henry James," in The
    Mirror in the Roadway: A Study of the Modern Novel. New
    York: Alfred A. Knopf, pp. 223-36.
        See 1956.B52.

52 O'DONOVAN, MICHAEL. "Transition: Henry James," in The Mirror
    in the Roadway: A Study of the Modern Novel. New York:
    Alfred A. Knopf, pp. 223-36.
        Views James as a transitional figure between the classi-
    cal and modern novelists, the change taking place somewhere
    in his works. Describes James' major theme as "innocence
    and corruption, and it formed an antithesis about which his
    whole literary personality shaped itself." James' novels
    tended "to become more and more disembodied," until in The
    Wings of the Dove "he reaches the climax of evasiveness."
    See 1956.B51.

53 PAULDING, GOUVERNEUR. "Henry James Came Home at Last." Re-
    porter, 15 (4 October), 40-42, 44.
        In his autobiography (see 1956.B20), James recorded "the
    awakening of an artist's mind." Discusses appropriateness
    of style, which compels "slow reading...," and James'
    treatment of the international problem, which he was "never
    to solve...."

54 PHELPS, GILBERT. "The Beautiful Genius: Turgenev's Influence
    in the Novels and Short Stories of Henry James," in The
    Russian Novel in English Fiction. London: Hutchinson and
    Co., pp. 71-87.

Examines similarities between characters of James and
Turgenev, and suggests that the American writer found in
the Russian a "synthesis which he was now convinced was
the real aim of the serious novelist," duty and conscience
fused with elements of plot, situation and style. Concludes that "Turgenev's influence was a matter of the heart
and the emotions as much as of the intellect."

55   PHELPS, GILBERT. "A Nest of Gentlefolk at Cambridge, Massa-
     chusetts: Turgenev's American Reputation in the Nineteenth
     Century--His Impact on the Youthful Henry James," in The
     Russian Novel in English Fiction. London: Hutchinson and
     Co., pp. 59-70.
        After reviewing the circumstances leading up to the
     meeting between Turgenev and James, considers its implica-
     tions, the impact of the Russian on James' works, "effects
     that the pressure of the times had upon his creative im-
     agination in its most fluid and impressionable stages."

56   POULET, GEORGES. "Appendix: Time and American Writers," in
     Studies in Human Time. Translated by Elliott Coleman.
     Baltimore, Md.: Johns Hopkins Press, pp. 350-54.
        An exploration of James' relationship to time and the
     past. Suggests that for James the past is always present,
     and that the "loss of the self in the multiplicity of its
     memories" is characteristic of the author. James invented
     a "new kind of time...aesthetic time," in which "a moving
     circle of points of view" are situated around a center,
     "from one to the other of which the novelist proceeds."

57   PRITCHARD, JOHN PAUL. "The Realists: Henry James," in
     Criticism in America: An Account of the Development of
     Critical Techniques from the Early Period of the Republic
     to the Middle Years of the Twentieth Century. Norman:
     University of Oklahoma Press, pp. 175-84, 275.
        Consideration of James as a realist, including remarks
     on his distinction between realism and romance, his view
     of the novel as "an organism," and his traditional concept
     of art, which accepts "that art is method."

58   READ, HERBERT. "Particular Studies: Henry James," in Col-
     lected Essays in Literary Criticism. Second edition, re-
     vised. London: Faber and Faber, pp. 354-68. American
     edition entitled The Nature of Literature. New York:
     Horizon Press.
        Reprint of 1927.B8, which restores the final paragraph
     omitted in 1938.B13.

1956

59   ROGERS, ROBERT. "The Beast in Henry James." <u>American Imago</u>,
     13 (Winter), 427-54.
         A Freudian interpretation of "The Jolly Corner," which
     represents "a tragic lament for a life unlived, for deeds
     undone." Concerns James' "orientation to life...his in-
     stinctual drives as modified by his life experience." The
     "'mark of the beast'" on Henry James symbolized his "sense
     of guilt," an archetypal figure against whom "the passive,
     powerless Futile Man was set."

60   RUPP, HENRY R. "James's <u>The Two Faces</u>." <u>Explicator</u>, 14
     (February), Item 30.
         Amacher, in his commentary on "The Two Faces" (<u>see</u>
     1953.B6), did not "completely cover all aspects of this
     story." His reference to the "impairment" of Mrs. Gran-
     tham's beauty was not "hitherto unnoticed"; rather, it was
     "previously noticed but not understood." What ultimately
     repels Sutton "is not that Mrs. Grantham has refused to
     suffer but rather...that she is incapable of suffering."

61   RUSSELL, JOHN R. "The Henry James Collection." <u>University
     of Rochester Library Bulletin</u>, 11 (Spring), 50-52.
         Description of the Henry James collection at the Uni-
     versity of Rochester Library, which contains "practically
     all the first editions of Henry James's books," in an ef-
     fort to "indicate its scope and importance to scholars...."

*62 S., C. <u>Das Bücherblatt</u>, 20 (16 March). Cited in 1959.B5.
     (German)
         Although James "does meet our generation's interest in
     psychological analysis, his indifference toward social
     problems, his dependence on a past upper class society,
     and his difficult style necessarily diminish his success.
     He impresses the modern reader as a representative of <u>l'art
     pour l'art</u> for which our more robust generation has lost
     the taste" (quotation from 1959.B5).

*63 SAMOKHVALOV, N. I. "Genri Dzheims [Henry James]." Uchenye
     zapiski Krasnodarskogo pedagogicheskogo instituta, vyp. 18.
     <u>Filologiia</u>, pp. 106-29.
         Cited in Beatrice Ricks, comp. <u>Henry James: A Bibliog-
     raphy of Secondary Works</u>, #3291.

*64 SIEDLER, W. J. "Das Kind bei Henry James." <u>Bucher-Kommentare</u>
     (15 June). Cited in 1959.B5.
         James lacks the "vitality and 'richness'" of Tolstoi,
     "his scope of subject matter being limited, more exclusive,
     less universal, and his inventive power considerably
     smaller." In James, conflicts and complications are

"significant" only as "comprehended by and reflected in the
child's mind." Suspense in What Maisie Knew "develops only
from the author's intelligent curiosity as he traces the
tenderest moves in Maisie's mind." (Quotations from
1959.B5.)

*65 SIEDLER, W. J. "Sehnsucht nach Wirklichkeit." Der Tagess-
     piegel (2 December). Cited in 1959.B5. (German)
         Strether is too clearly a product of the old age, and
     The Ambassadors lacks naturalness and life.

*66 SIEDLER, W. J. "Henry James. Die Gesandten." Das kleine
     Buch der hundert Bücher, 4. Cited in 1959.B5.

 67 SINCLAIR, UPTON. "Letter: [Henry James]." Chicago Review,
     10 (Spring), 131.
         Letter to the editor in which Sinclair describes his
     reading of The Ambassadors, concerned with "a conflict
     between French civilization and that of New England. It is
     Paris confronted by Boston, and Boston getting the worst of
     it." Suggests as a subtitle to the novel, "'Defensio Meae
     Vitae; or Why I Live Abroad.'"

 68 SMITH, JANET ADAM. "That One Talent." New Statesman and
     Nation, 52 (13 October), 455-56.
         Essay-review of Sweeney's The Painter's Eye (see
     1956.B74), including remarks on James as a reporter of
     specific works, the lack of technical criticism, the
     changes in his taste, and the "odd particular judgments."
     The value of the collection is in seeing develop "those
     attitudes and beliefs that provided the firm framework"
     for James' novels about the "life of art and how, in dis-
     cipline, in effort, in intensity, that life must be paid
     for."

 69 SPILLER, ROBERT E. "Artist of Fiction." Saturday Review of
     Literature, 39 (9 June), 19-20.
         The "...sensibility of James" is more "objective" than
     that of Proust. Discusses James' transformation from man
     to artist and the "alienation of the artist from his right
     to live for himself," as seen in the autobiography
     (1956.B20). "All that is important of this story of the
     birth of an artist has been told...."

 70 SPILLER, ROBERT E. "Henry James," in Eight American Authors:
     A Review of Research and Criticism. Edited by Floyd Stov-
     all. New York: Modern Language Association of America,
     pp. 364-418.

1956

A survey of relevant scholarship on James, with reference to selected titles and essential bibliographical facts
in the following areas: (1) Bibliography, Text, Manu-
scripts; (2) Biography; (3) Criticism, including "Contemporary Comment (1865-1916)," "Alienation (1916-1934)," and
"The James Revival (1934-1954)."

71 STANZEL, FRANZ. Die typischen Erzählsituationen im Roman:
Darge stellt an Tom Jones, Moby-Dick, The Ambassadors,
Ulysses u.a. (Wiener Beiträge zur engl. Phil., Bd. 63.)
Wien: W. Braumüller. (German) Translated as "The Figural
Novel," in Narrative Situations in the Novel: "Tom Jones,"
"Moby-Dick," "The Ambassadors," "Ulysses." Translated by
James P. Pusack. Bloomington: University of Indiana
Press, 1971, pp. 92-120.
Gives characteristics of the figural novel and its
variant, the neutral narrative situation; defends the
figural novel as a consistent possible type-form; and discusses objections to it. Interprets The Ambassadors,
which, although not a strictly consistent realization of
the form, shows James' selection of narrative situation by
considering various possibilities in his composition of a
novel of consciousness with objective, scenic presentation
of external events.

72 STEIN, WILLIAM BYSSHE. "The Ambassadors: The Crucifixion of
Sensibility." College English, 17 (February), 289-92.
Suggests that the metaphor of "'the golden nail'" "con-
trols and defines, organizes and unifies" structure and
theme in The Ambassadors. Structurally, the image follows
the progression of Strether's sensibility adjusting itself
to a set of values which conflict with his innate Puritanism. Thematically, the metaphor acts as symbol related to
the idea of crucifixion, although the implications are
aesthetic rather than religious. Strether is, essentially,
crucified on a "cross of sensibility."

73 SWAN, MICHAEL. "Introduction," in Henry James: The Turn of
the Screw, The Aspern Papers, and Other Stories. Edited
by Michael Swan. London: William Collins Sons and Co.,
pp. 13-17.
Discusses James' credo of art in relation to his short
stories, the germs of which usually came from some actual
event. Includes brief analyses of each story in the collection.

1956

74 SWEENEY, JOHN L. "Introduction," in The Painter's Eye: Notes
and Essays on the Pictorial Arts by Henry James. London:
Rupert Hart-Davis; Cambridge, Mass.: Harvard University
Press, pp. 9-31.
Selections in the volume present James' published comments on the painter's arts, including sculpture, with the
purpose of providing "a convenient means of observing a
significant tributary of his talent." Notes James' claims
for artistic value of such criticism and his use of the
arts in "background, manner and metaphor...," and provides
a chronological sketch of James' interest in and reaction
to the pictorial arts, with reference to his comments in
essays and reviews. Reviewed: F. W. Dupee, New England
Quarterly, 30 (December 1957), 529-32.

75 SWINNERTON, FRANK. "From Henry James to Gissing," in Background with Chorus: A Footnote to Changes in English Literary Fashion Between 1901 and 1917. New York: Farrar,
Straus and Cudahy, pp. 120-25.
Discusses James' "devotion to the finesses of novel-
writing as supreme art...," and describes "the secret of
James's craft" as "The fusion and synthesis of picture...."

76 SWINNERTON, FRANK. "Henry James," in Authors I Never Met.
London: Allen and Unwin, pp. 17-24.
James "taught perfection in the art of writing novels."
However, the style of the letters is "positively bloated."
Further, "James had to run, to test, to question, to listen
to every word vouchsafed to him by other intelligences,
because without the gossip, the anecdote, the report of
other men, he would have had nothing to write about."

77 TILLEY, WINTHROP. "Fleda Vetch and Ellen Brown, or, Henry
James and the Soap Opera." Western Humanities Review, 10
(Spring), 175-80.
Examines parallels between James' The Spoils of Poynton
and a radio serial, Young Widder Brown, to show how much
they have in common. Points out such similarities as the
fact that both "are dominated by woman characters"; both
"go forward primarily by means of dialogue or stream of
consciousness monologue..."; "attention to personal, private, emotional problems goes forward in both...in a milieu
which has a dreamy and unreal quality about it"; and both
have heroines capable of "Gallant Suffering." Concludes
that "Jamesland and Soapland being so much alike, the appeal of soap opera is doubtless to the same type."

1956

78 TRASCHEN, ISADORE. "Henry James and the Art of Revision."
   Philological Quarterly, 35 (January), 39-47.
   The primary motivation of James' revisions is an attempt
   to change meaning rather than merely style. Seeks to demonstrate, by using The American, that "the bulk of the revisions is informed by a single and continuous act of
   James's imagination." Focuses on James' imagery, especially "the symbolic recurrence of images to emphasize character and theme," which had the effect of making Newman more
   strongly affirm the values he temporarily abjured.

79 TRASCHEN, ISADORE. "James's Revisions of the Love Affair in
   The American." New England Quarterly, 29 (March), 43-62.
   James' revisions represent an attempt to make his
   lovers' intimacy more realistic. Revisions are dominated
   by Newman's "violent embraces and passive imaginings."
   James' interest is in "the ethical problems love created,
   rather than in love itself." James knows little about
   "the more intense moments of love," and in compensating
   for his "deficient masculinity" he overdoes it.

80 VOLPE, EDMOND L. "The Childhood of James's American Innocents." Modern Language Notes, 71 (May), 345-47.
   The Americans in James' novels who are susceptible to
   the "complicated web of European social and moral intrigue"
   are those whose moral characters are natural and innocent.
   These "American Innocents" often resemble James' cousins.

81 WALLACE, IRVING. "The Real Juliana Bordereau," in The Fabulous Originals. New York: Alfred A. Knopf, pp. 46-80.
   Identifies the historical counterparts to characters
   in The Aspern Papers: Captain Silsbee, a "'Shelley-
   worshipper,'" and Claire Clairmont, a mistress of Byron
   and a friend of Shelley. James' fictionalized account
   "hewed close to the facts," and "James publicly, if cau-
   tiously, admitted the precise source of inspiration in a
   detailed preface." Presents a biographical sketch of
   Clairmont, who, during her 24 years, "lived tremendously
   and among giants."

82 WEGELIN, CHRISTOF. "The 'Internationalism' of The Golden
   Bowl." Nineteenth-Century Fiction, 11 (December), 161-81.
   The Ambassadors, The Wings of the Dove and The Golden
   Bowl form a "trilogy explaining the possibilities of two
   radically different systems of morality--one idealistic,
   the other empirical--represented by America and Europe."
   Views marriage of Maggie and the Prince in The Golden Bowl
   as a union of Europe and America which must be purged of

the irresponsibility represented by Adam Verver. The novel
stands as a prophetic fable of the fusion of two points of
view.

83   WELLEK, RENÉ and AUSTIN WARREN. Theory of Literature. Third
     edition. A Harvest Book. New York: Harcourt, Brace and
     World, passim.
        James is an exponent of the "objective" or "dramatic"
     method, which makes use of a "controlled 'point of view'"
     and emphasizes "the self-consistent objectivity of the
     novel" through "picture" or "drama."

84   WILSON, HARRIS W. "What Did Maisie Know?" College English,
     17 (February), 279-82.
        Submits that the theme of What Maisie Knew is the cor-
     ruption of a sensitive child by her own parents, represen-
     tatives of a frivolous and vicious segment of London soci-
     ety. Presents a detailed analysis of the novel in support
     of his claim. Maisie represents the inevitable product of
     her sordid, irresponsible rearing, though there is perverse
     innocence and directness in her degeneration.

85   WOODRESS, JAMES. "Henry James." Publications of the Modern
     Language Association, 71 (April), 174-75.
        A list of books and articles which appeared in periodi-
     cals during the previous year, including those written in
     English, French, German, Spanish, Italian, Portuguese,
     Scandinavian and Dutch.

86   WRIGHT, AUSTIN. "Henry James," in Bibliographies of Studies
     in Victorian Literature for the Ten Years, 1945-1954.
     Urbana: University of Illinois Press, passim.
        A reprint of annual Victorian Bibliographies for 1945-
     1954, published in Modern Philology. Entries listed under
     categories such as "Bibliographic Material" and "Movements
     of Ideas and Literary Forms, Anthologies."

1957 A BOOKS

1   ANDERSON, QUENTIN. The American Henry James. New Brunswick,
     N.J.: Rutgers University Press, 382 pp.
        An examination of James' relationship to his father's
     psychological and philosophical views (Swedenborgianism),
     which proclaimed a religion of consciousness, hypothesizing
     that James continued to employ in elaborate allegory the
     mode of vision that had colored his childhood. Anderson
     seeks to identify the emblems, such as the bowl, the house

of life, the portraits, the river, the sea, derived or bor-
rowed by James from his father's system of universal
analogues, emblems which stand for principles believed to
order consciousness itself. Suggests that this thesis explains many of the difficulties in James' works, such as
the end of <u>The Portrait of a Lady</u>, the later prose style,
the moral authority of Milly Theale. Anderson draws analogues from Dante in interpreting <u>The Ambassadors</u>, <u>The Wings</u>
<u>of the Dove</u> and <u>The Golden Bowl</u> as a "divine novel." <u>See</u>
1946.B1, 1947.B1-2, 1953.A1 for earlier statements of these
ideas. Partially reprinted: as "News of Life," in Lyall
Powers, ed. <u>Studies in "The Portrait of a Lady</u>," pp. 67-
79; also in Peter Buitenhuis, ed. <u>Twentieth Century Inter-</u>
<u>pretations of "The Portrait of a Lady</u>," pp. 51-54. Re-
viewed: Charles Feidelson, <u>Kenyon Review</u>, 19 (Autumn
1957), 626-36; <u>Modern Fiction Studies</u>, 3 (Summer 1957),
181-82; Jacob Cleaver Levenson, <u>New England Quarterly</u>, 30
(Summer 1957), 422-26; Irving Howe, <u>Partisan Review</u>, 24
(Spring 1957), 282-90; William T. Stafford, <u>Western Review</u>,
22 (Winter 1958), 155-60; R. W. B. Lewis, <u>Yale Review</u>, NS
NS 47 (December 1957), 268.

2   CREWS, FREDERICK C. <u>The Tragedy of Manners: Moral Drama in</u>
the Later Novels of Henry James. Yale University Undergraduate Prize Essays. Vol. 10. New Haven, Conn.: Yale
University Press, 114 pp. Reprinted: Hamden, Conn.:
Anchor Books, 1971.
     An explication of <u>The Ambassadors</u>, <u>The Wings of the Dove</u>
and <u>The Golden Bowl</u> in view of "the dramatic opposition of
certain moral and social values." The action in these
novels arises from "philosophical differences of opinion
among the principal characters," caused by "differing social
backgrounds." Develops the method of analysis for interpreting both social and moral concepts, and attempts to
distinguish between the early and later James. His characters became increasingly "less susceptible to moral cate-
gorization." Near the end of <u>The Golden Bowl</u>, James
"ceases to be a moral critic of his characters," despite
the fact that his awareness of evil is as strong as ever,
and "a new and better morality" is introduced. Reviewed:
Lewis Leary, <u>English Studies</u>, 39 (1958), 42-43; <u>Modern</u>
<u>Fiction Studies</u>, 4 (Summer 1958), 188; Joseph Aub, <u>New</u>
<u>England Quarterly</u>, 31 (March 1958), 123-29.

3   EDEL, LEON and DAN H. LAURENCE. <u>A Bibliography of Henry</u>
James. Soho Bibliographies. London: Rupert Hart-Davis,
411 pp. Second edition, revised, 1961.

A bibliography of the works of James, including collations of first editions, which "tells the story of what
happened to the writings...after they left his busy work-
table to be set up in type and published in magazine and
book." In the "Introduction" (pp. 11-21), Edel and Laurence discuss their bibliographical method and the basis
of their descriptions. Includes a non-exhaustive checklist of letters and fragments of letters, and a section on
foreign translations. The contents are divided into "Original Works," "Contributions to Books, including prefaces,
introductions, translations, unauthorized and posthumous
fugitive writings," "Published Letters," "Contributions to
Periodicals," "Translations," and "Miscellanea" (which includes such areas as English language foreign editions,
Times Book Club issues, Braille editions). Reviewed: <u>Mod-
ern Fiction Studies</u>, 4 (Summer 1958), 187.

4   HOFFMANN, CHARLES G. <u>The Short Novels of Henry James</u>. New
York: Bookman Associates, 143 pp.
A critical analysis of James' use of the <u>nouvelle</u>, which
had greater scope than the short story, thus allowing adequate space for him to fully develop his ideas. Suggests
that the short novels are significant as a mirror of James'
literary development because James evolved artistically
more rapidly in the <u>nouvelle</u> form, because they provided a
medium for experimentation with theme and technique, and
because they demonstrate, with the major works, a continuity in artistic evolution. Selects and analyzes representative short novels from each of three periods "to show
the continuity of James' literary development, to explore
all the aspects of James' art, and discover the limits of
the short novel form." Concludes that the short novel "as
a distinct art form" began in America with James, "ap-
proached consciously as a literary form." Reviewed: <u>Modern
Fiction Studies</u>, 3 (Winter 1957-1958), 375; Lewis Leary,
<u>Saturday Review of Literature</u>, 40 (21 September 1957), 33.

5   JOHNSON, ALICE E. "A Critical Analysis of the Dislocated
Character as Developed in the Major Novels of Henry James."
Ph.D. dissertation, University of Wisconsin.
An analysis of the development of "James's social vision
as seen through his treatment of dislocated characters" in
major novels. "...The theme of dislocation was an important element in shaping the kinds of novels he progressive-
ly wrote and...his early concern over the commitment of the
United States to materialistic values gradually broadened
until the vision came to include Western civilization."
The theme also reveals James' "concern with the loss of

moral values, with materialism as the chief corrupter, and
with the increasing confusion of money and morality...."

6   LEVY, LEO B. <u>Versions of Melodrama: A Study of the Fiction
and Drama of Henry James, 1865-1897.</u> Berkeley and Los
Angeles: University of California Press, 130 pp.
    Originally a dissertation (University of California at
Berkeley, 1954). A description and analysis of melodra-
matic qualities in James' work. Calls James a "civilized
melodramatist," and suggests that melodrama "is an essential Jamesian mode of perceiving and organizing moral experience—the crystallization of thought and feeling into
a particular kind of dramatic pattern." Just as melodrama
is concerned with the ultimate goodness of man, with the
triumph of good over evil, so James' themes deal with good
and evil, moral issues. Examines the way in which melodrama is a part of James' moral and aesthetic world in
chapters which include "James and the Tradition of Melodrama," "Melodrama and the Imagination of Disaster," "The
Melodramatist in the Theatre," and "Melodrama as a Technique of the Novel." Reviewed: Leon Edel, <u>American Lit-
erature</u>, 30 (May 1958), 251-52.

7   WARD, JOSEPH A., JR. "Evil in the Fiction of Henry James."
Ph.D. dissertation, Tulane University.
    Although James' conception of evil as "the violation of
another individual's soul" remains unchanged throughout
his writings, he gradually lessens the distance between
good and evil, and his protagonists' attitudes towards evil
change. He stresses the omnipresence of evil, an inevit-
able component of reality.

1957 B SHORTER WRITINGS

1   ABEL, DARREL. "'Howells or James?'—An Essay by Henry Blake
Fuller." <u>Modern Fiction Studies</u>, 3 (Summer), 159-64.
    Reprints an essay by Henry Blake Fuller in which he
labels Howells a realist, James an idealist, and asserts
that Howells' Americanism was more American than James'.
Abel explains the background of the paper, and suggests
its importance as pioneer comparative criticism.

2   BEEBE, MAURICE and WILLIAM T. STAFFORD. "Criticism of Henry
James: A Selected Checklist with an Index to Studies of
Separate Works." <u>Modern Fiction Studies</u>, 3 (Spring),
73-96.
    A bibliography of general studies and studies of sepa-
rate works on James, with emphasis on post-1950 scholarship.

Retains earlier studies not covered in previous bibliographies, but omits reviews, unpublished dissertations,
foreign language criticism, items of slight importance,
and notes of a bibliographical nature. Discusses arrange-
ments of items, includes list of abbreviations.

3   BELL, MILLICENT. "A James 'Gift' to Edith Wharton." Modern
     Language Notes, 72 (March), 182-85.
         Wharton's short story "The Pretext" owes its origin to a
     suggestion made by James in a letter dated January 7, 1908.

4   BIELENSTEIN, GABRIELLE MAUPIN. "Affinities for Henry James?"
     Meanjin, 16 (June), 196-99.
         Notes "conspicuous identity of plot and character" be-
     tween James' The Portrait of a Lady and Rosa Praed's Affi-
     nities (1886), and suggests possible explanations for the
     similarities. Adopts the plagiarism theory, although Ms.
     Praed probably "bowdlerized her version" somewhat uncon-
     sciously. Discusses differences in "talents and outlook"
     between James and Praed, and concludes that a comparison
     of the two novels "shows to what extent material that has
     become available to two minds of vastly different calibre
     and outlook can be used to serve divergent purposes."

5   BLÖCKER, GÜNTER. "Henry James." Merkur, 11 (August), 730-43.
     (German)
         James perceived the flowers of hell below the glass
     floor, the discrepancy between the inner and outer world,
     yet his stories remain anecdotal, since he was no man of
     ideas.

6   BREWSTER, HENRY. "Henry James and the Gallo-American."
     Botteghe Oscure, 19 (Spring), 170-81.
         Brewster discovered 20 letters from James among family
     documents, covering about seven years beginning in the
     early 1890's, addressed to his paternal grandfather. Re-
     marks on the circumstances of the meeting and friendship
     of James and Henry B. Brewster, and provides a biographical
     sketch of Brewster with emphasis on his life in Rome.
     Hypothesizes that external facts and his grandfather's
     features suggest he may have been the source of Gilbert
     Osmond in The Portrait of a Lady. Considers the letters
     in three groups, and concludes that "...a world of European-
     wide culture, and with it the very essence of the James-
     Brewster relationship, is to be found reflected in these
     letters." See 1957.B7.

1957

7   BREWSTER, HENRY. "Henry James: Fourteen Letters." <u>Botteghe Oscure</u>, 19 (Spring), 182-94.
        Text of letters described in 1957.B6.

8   BROOKS, VAN WYCK. "The Pilgrimage," in <u>Days of the Phoenix</u>. New York: E. P. Dutton and Co., pp. 175-82.
        The thesis of Brooks' earlier work, that something went wrong in James' development (see 1925.A1), was corroborated by F. R. Leavis, although he disagreed with the cause Brooks defined, that James lost touch with the people he understood. Reviews the reception of his thesis, insists that "people of ripe heart and mind who know the world as they know life" agree with him. Despite interval in which he (Brooks) questioned his explanation of James' problem, he resolved the issue in a "certain notion of literary values—that there is a gulf between those who see literature in terms of itself and those who see it in terms of a wider connection." Reprinted: in Leon Edel, ed. <u>Henry James: A Collection of Critical Essays</u>, pp. 57-62.

9   BUITENHUIS, PETER. "Aesthetics of the Skyscraper: The Views of Sullivan, James and Wright." <u>American Quarterly</u>, 9 (Fall), 316-24.
        Discusses the views of Louis Sullivan, Frank Lloyd Wright and James on the skyscraper, which demonstrate how men of different generations, backgrounds and temperaments can agree on aesthetic judgments. In their comments one can see the spectrum of architectural criticism.

10   CARGILL, OSCAR. "<u>The Portrait of a Lady</u>: A Critical Reappraisal." <u>Modern Fiction Studies</u>, 3 (Spring), 11-32.
        Questions identification of Isabel with Minny Temple or Gwendolyn Harleth, and suggests that she is a "<u>limited</u>" heroine, "cautious, theoretical, and inhibited; and the touch is satiric"; and that she is "a rich, synthesized figure about which the novelist has reflected a long time, gathering material." Reviews critical conjectures concerning Isabel's motives in returning to Osmond at the conclusion of the novel, and concludes that her growth is established by the human markers the novelist has posted on her way.

11   CARGILL, OSCAR. "Mr. James's Aesthetic Mr. Nash." <u>Nineteenth-Century Fiction</u>, 12 (December), 177-87.
        Identifies James' aesthete Gabriel Nash in <u>The Tragic Muse</u> as Oscar Wilde. Points out internal evidence which connects Nash and Wilde, and suggests that the name is a combination of Gabriel [Harvey] and [Thomas] Nash, famous

Elizabethan controversialists and wits. The mildness of
James' treatment further indicates that the portrait is of
Wilde. See 1959.B71.

12   CHASE, RICHARD. "The Lesson of the Master," in The American
      Novel and its Tradition. Doubleday Anchor Books. Garden
      City, N.Y.: Doubleday and Co., pp. 117-37.
          James' The Portrait of a Lady was the first American
      novel to make full use of the form, by transmuting romantic
      elements for novelistic purposes: the romance is assimi-
      lated into the language of the work and into the character
      of Isabel, who sees things as a romancer does and who final-
      ly affirms the primacy of the novelist's imagination. Re-
      printed: in Naomi Lebowitz, ed. Discussions of Henry
      James. Boston: D. C. Heath and Co., pp. 60-70; also in
      Peter Buitenhuis, ed. Twentieth Century Interpretations
      of "The Portrait of a Lady," pp. 15-28; and in William
      Stafford, ed. Perspectives on James's "The Portrait of a
      Lady," pp. 148-65.

13   CHASE, RICHARD. "Sanctuary vs. The Turn of the Screw," in
      The American Novel and its Tradition. Doubleday Anchor
      Books. Garden City, N.Y.: Doubleday and Co., pp. 237-41.
          A comparison of Faulkner's Sanctuary and The Turn of the
      Screw to illustrate the difference between allegory and
      symbolism. Both use Gothic conventions, the former for
      sociological purposes, the latter for psychological pur-
      poses.

*14   COVENEY, PETER. Poor Monkey: The Child in Literature.
      Rockliff, pp. 164-68. Cited in Jarvis Thurston et al.,
      Short Fiction Criticism, p. 112. Stylistically revised:
      as "Innocence in Henry James," in The Image of Childhood.
      The Individual and Society: A Study of the Theme in Eng-
      lish Literature. Revised edition. Baltimore, Md.: Pen-
      guin Books, 1967, pp. 194-214.
          James created a literary tradition in regard to child-
      hood and innocence: his is "the child of an expatriate
      American, ultimately concerned with the problems of the
      influence of an 'old' culture upon the 'innocent' new, the
      product of a sensibility functioning in the society of a
      wealthy expatriate." James deals with the "dramatic and
      moral possibilities of innocence confronted with life."
      Examines What Maisie Knew and The Awkward Age, novels of
      "moral conflict" and the "development of innocent conscious-
      ness," and The Turn of the Screw, which suggests "a neu-
      rotic complication in James's sensibility."

1957

15   COWSER, JOHN. "Henry James's Ancestry." <u>Times Literary Sup-</u>
      <u>plement</u> (25 January), p. 49.
          A note on the name of the Irish community from which
      James' maternal grandfather on his father's side originated,
      which Cowser suggests is Killinchy, rather than Killings-
      ley, County Down as identified by Edel. <u>See</u> 1957.B18 for
      Edel's reply.

16   DUPEE, FREDERICK W. "Approaches to Henry James," in <u>Litera-</u>
      <u>ture in America</u>. Edited by Philip Rahv. Meridian Books.
      New York: The World Publishing Co., pp. 242-46.
          Reprints selections from Dupee's biography (1951.A2),
      from T. S. Eliot's <u>Little Review</u> essay (1918.B5-6), and from
      Pound's remarks in the same periodical (1918.B21, B24).

17   EDEL, LEON. "Autobiography in Fiction: An Unpublished Review
      by Henry James." <u>Harvard Library Bulletin</u>, 11 (Spring),
      245-57.
          Discussion of a review of Bayard Taylor's <u>John Godfrey's</u>
      <u>Fortunes</u>, 1865, found with three other reviews by James
      among a mass of essays written for <u>The North American Re-</u>
      <u>view</u>. As the earliest extant James manuscript, it "hints
      at the future cosmopolitan novelist, and it discloses cer-
      tain valuable primitive utterances on the craft of fiction."
      Remarks on self-confident tone of essay, precocity of pre-
      liminary literary steps. In the review, "the young man
      looks to the future novelist...."

18   EDEL, LEON. "Henry James's Ancestry." <u>Times Literary Supple-</u>
      <u>ment</u> (8 March), p. 145.
          Reply to 1957.B15, in which Edel reveals his source of
      the variant name as Rev. William Walsh's <u>A Record and</u>
      <u>Sketch of Hugh Walsh's Family, 1903</u>.

19   EDEL, LEON. "The Literary Convictions of Henry James." <u>Mod-</u>
      <u>ern Fiction Studies</u>, 3 (Spring), 3-10.
          Abridged version of 1957.B20.

20   EDEL, LEON. "Introduction," in <u>The House of Fiction: Essays</u>
      <u>on the Novel</u>. By Henry James. Edited by Leon Edel. Lon-
      don: Rupert Hart-Davis, pp. 9-19. Reprinted: Westport,
      Conn.: Greenwood Press, 1973.
          This collection of James' critical papers on novels and
      novelists displays the "happy coalescence of critic and
      creator." The essays "offer us the vision of a theorist
      of fiction approaching, in the light of his aesthetic, the
      work of certain of his compeers." Examines James' views
      in his essay "The Science of Criticism," reprinted as

"Criticism," and reviews rationale of selection in the
volume, which shows "James at large in his 'House of Fiction,'" pondering novels and novelists, seeking to place
himself at their particular windows and to glimpse the
world through their eyes. See 1957.B19. Reviewed: Times
Literary Supplement (10 January 1958), p. 17.

21   EDEL, LEON. Literary Biography: The Alexander Lectures,
        1955-1956. London: Rupert Hart-Davis, passim.
        Reprints remarks in 1955.B25. Also discusses James'
     view that time summarizes and makes remote the dead, and
     uses James to illustrate how "biography can violate chron-
     ology without doing violence to truth."

22   EDEL, LEON and ILSE DUSOIR LIND. "Introduction," in Parisian
        Sketches: Letters to the New York Tribune, 1875-1876.
     New York: New York University Press, pp. ix-xxxvii.
        This volume contains James' Paris letters to the New
     York Tribune, his only newspaper writing. Introduction
     remarks on the uniqueness of the experience, James' atti-
     tude towards the assignment, and the circumstances of his
     being offered the position. Examines James' problems in
     writing the letters, particularly that he "did not know
     how to exploit...material in a newspaper column..." and
     found the task irksome. Details the history of James'
     association with the newspaper, and comments on the impact
     of the experience on his later work. Concludes that "The
     Parisian sketches may be too literary, too reflective, as
     journalism, but they possess intelligence and suavity,
     they speak for good manners, refined taste, high civiliza-
     tion," and raise fundamental issues. Reviewed: Parker
     Tyler, Chicago Review, 12 (Spring 1958), 67-73; Modern
     Fiction Studies, 3 (Winter 1957-1958), 374-75; John L.
     Sweeney, New England Quarterly, 31 (June 1958), 259-63.

23   ELLISON, RALPH. "Society, Morality and the Novel," in The
        Living Novel: A Symposium. Edited by Granville Hicks.
     New York: The Macmillan Co., pp. 58-91.
        In a theoretical discussion of the novel's form and
     function, looks at Hawthorne and James as providing "a
     definition of American fiction...."

24   FAISON, S. LANE, JR. "The Novelist as Art Critic." Saturday
        Review of Literature, 40 (1 June), 28.
        In reference to Sweeney's The Painter's Eye (see
     1956.B74), describes James' attitude in writing about art
     as "joyless," identifies two "barriers" between the reader
     and the essays, "the barrier of another era and the barrier

1957

of the littérateur's approach to painting," and concludes
that "there is much good writing in these pages, though
the eye of this fine mind suffered from atrophy."

25 FIREBAUGH, JOSEPH J. "Inadequacy in Eden: Knowledge and The
Turn of the Screw." Modern Fiction Studies, 3 (Spring),
57-63.
    The Turn of the Screw is concerned with personal free-
dom, educational questions, and the problems of knowledge,
and deals with the dilemma in the early years of helpless
immaturity met with inadequacy and irresponsibility.
Looks at the inadequacies of the various characters, in
particular the governess, and suggests that the major theme
of the story is the denial of knowledge. The governess "is
the inadequate priestess of an irresponsible deity--the
Harley Street uncle..." and imposes Original Sin on the
innocent children (i.e., the human race), thereby causing
their destruction. Reprinted: in Gerald Willen, ed.
A Casebook on "The Turn of the Screw," pp. 291-97.

26 FRYE, NORTHROP. Anatomy of Criticism: Four Essays. Princeton, N.J.: Princeton University Press, passim.
    Describes long sentences in later James as "containing
sentences: all the qualifications and parentheses are
fitted in to a pattern..." from which "emerges...a simul-
taneous comprehension." Illustrates his modes and describes kinds of symbols with reference to James' works.

27 GALE, ROBERT L. "A Note on Henry James's First Short Story."
Modern Language Notes, 72 (February), 103-107.
    The figurative and near-figurative language of "A Trag-
edy of Error" provides added proof that Henry James was
its author.

28 GALE, ROBERT L. "Art Imagery in Henry James's Fiction."
American Literature, 29 (March), 47-63.
    James' imagery provides subtle proof of his interest in
art, the largest proportion of which relates to literature,
painting or music in some form. Gives examples of each of
these kinds of imagery, and concludes that James "used his
knowledge of many of the arts...in elaborating a large
proportion of his metaphors and similes which add glints of
color to his celebrated texture and throw added light upon
his absorbing characters."

29 GALE, ROBERT L. "Religious Imagery in Henry James's Fiction."
Modern Fiction Studies, 3 (Spring), 64-72.

1957

Analysis of figures of speech in James' fiction proves
that he was aware of dramatic impact of religion throughout the ages and used religious imagery frequently and
excellently. Illustrates James' use of religious similes
and metaphors. States that James used the images to gain
pictorial and dramatic effect and for personality development; that he finds women the more suitable subjects for
such images; that he used religious imagery more frequently
in the later and revised works; and that despite his awareness of spiritual matters, he adhered to no specific creed.

30 GALE, ROBERT L. "Henry James and Italy." Studi Americani,
     no. 3, pp. 189-203.
        Describes James' several visits in Italy, where he
     "found rest, spiritual refreshment, and artistic inspira-
     tion...." Suggests that "Italy served Henry James best
     not by providing him subjects for travel sketches...but
     instead by aiding his literary art in two subtle ways:
     Italy laid before James's vision scene after scene upon
     which to cast his fictional actions, and Italy filled his
     mind with clustered images which he frequently drew upon
     for figurative descriptions." Identifies and discusses
     examples of James' use of Italian setting, characters, and
     imagery in his works.

31 GODDARD, HAROLD C. and LEON EDEL. "A Pre-Freudian Reading of
     The Turn of the Screw." Nineteenth-Century Fiction, 12
     (June), 1-36.
        Edel explains about the manuscript of Goddard's article,
     found among his posthumous papers, which stands as the
     first presentation of a hallucination theory of The Turn
     of the Screw based on a close textual study. Goddard ex-
     amines in detail the facts of the tale, which substantiate
     the idea that the tragedy is caused by the governess' in-
     sanity. Relates the story to his early experience with an
     insane servant, and suggests that his thesis is corrobor-
     ated by the introduction to the New York edition and by
     published letters of James referring to the story. Re-
     printed: in Gerald Willen, ed. A Casebook on "The Turn
     of the Screw," pp. 244-72; also in Jane P. Tompkins, ed.
     Twentieth Century Interpretations of "The Turn of the
     Screw" and Other Stories," pp. 60-87.

32 GOLDBERG, M. A. "'Things' and Values in Henry James's Uni-
     verse." Western Humanities Review, 11 (Autumn), 377-85.
        James objected to the way in which "Things," objects,
     details and places, are presented, "to the proportion they
     assume in the whole that is the novel...." Examines the

1957

"detailed setting into which he thrusts his characters" to
determine James' "'measure of reality.'" For James, reality is in "the awareness and consciousness of the individual," and his technique is part of an innovative conception
of reality, which is "isolated, personal, and highly at-
tenuated."

33 GORDON, CAROLINE. "The Central Intelligence," in How to Read
    a Novel. New York: The Viking Press, pp. 120-44.
        Discussion of James' technique, especially the charac-
    teristics of the "central intelligence," which is "perhaps
    the greatest technical triumph...the novel has known in
    its short history." Suggests implications of James' "fig-
    ure at the window" metaphor for the novel reader.

34 GORDON, CAROLINE. "Henry James and His Critics," in How to
    Read a Novel. New York: The Viking Press, pp. 111-19.
        Some of James' critics have been "blinded by their own
    preconceptions," among them H. G. Wells, E. M. Forster,
    F. R. Leavis, Rebecca West and Van Wyck Brooks.

35 GORDON, CAROLINE. "Tone, Style, and Controlling Metaphor,"
    in How to Read a Novel. New York: The Viking Press,
    pp. 148-55.
        Consideration of the effect of James' exposure to his
    father's prose style. James was "deeply influenced by his
    father's example of saintliness and lifelong dedication to
    an ideal so high that it seemed almost impossible of real-
    ization," and his prose "echoed the cadences which recorded
    his father's agonized...search for the eternal verities."

36 HAMBLEN, ABIGAIL A. "Henry James and the Press: A Study of
    Protest." Western Humanities Review, 11 (Spring), 169-75.
        James' "distaste for popular journalism" demonstrates
    that "so far as...the impersonal artist, is capable of
    hate, he hates the popular press." Considers the causes
    of James' revulsion, and reviews the history of "'intimate
    revelations'" in journalism, especially the "'penny press.'"
    Discusses the journalistic types which James characterized
    in his novels and stories, and concludes that although
    James dealt with "the sordidness, the sorrows and despair"
    of humanity, he presented them as "a matter of art," and
    placed them in perspective. "They are not to be smeared
    over penny sheets, shouted into the common air to arouse
    mere surface feelings. In short, they are to be handled
    with good taste."

1957

*37   HENZE, HELENE. "Den Leser zu unterhalten." <u>Frankfurter</u>
      <u>Allgemeine Zeitung</u> (6 July). Cited in 1959.B5. (German)
         "James provides again a valid standard for the art of
      the novel at a time of drought." In addition, he can
      "entertain and please his reader--something which our con-
      temporary novelists have almost made us forget." (Quota-
      tions from 1959.B5.)

38   HOPKINS, GERARD. "Introduction," in <u>Selected Stories</u>. By
      Henry James. Edited by Gerard Hopkins. The World's Clas-
      sic Series. London: Oxford University Press, pp. vii-x.
         Describes the principle of arrangement in this selection
      of shorter pieces by James. On his later style, asserts
      that "if, as he grew older and more experienced in his
      art, he came to prefer indirection to the bull-headed ap-
      proach, the reason was technical rather than moral," and
      remarks on James' "wide understanding of human nature and
      compassion for the human situation...." Reviewed: <u>Times</u>
      <u>Literary Supplement</u> (10 January 1958), p. 17.

39   HOWE, IRVING. "Henry James: The Political Vocation," in
      <u>Politics and the Novel</u>. New York: Horizon Press, pp. 139-
      56.
         Reprint of 1954.B20.

40   JENKINS, IREDELL. "The Aesthetic Object." <u>The Review of</u>
      <u>Metaphysics</u> (New Haven), 11 (September), 3-11.
         In a consideration of "What sort of symbol is the work
      of art?," refers to James in illustrating that the artist
      "expresses and presents his matured grasp--his prolonged
      and repeated experiences--of numerous similar things on
      occasions." James, in <u>Daisy Miller</u>, <u>The Portrait of a</u>
      <u>Lady</u> and <u>The Wings of the Dove</u> depicted three distinctive
      women and the "general situation of the 'simple' American
      girl" in Europe.

41   KIMBALL, JEAN. "Henry James's Last Portrait of a Lady:
      Charlotte Stant in <u>The Golden Bowl</u>." <u>American Literature</u>,
      28 (January), 449-68.
         Considers evidence in <u>The Golden Bowl</u> and its preface
      that James intended that Charlotte's predicament, the drama
      of her struggle, be the focal point in the novel, which is
      analyzed in terms of Charlotte as heroine. The bowl is
      interpreted as a receptacle which encloses characters in
      the false security of their "'see-no-evil'" world, their
      ironic Eden. Charlotte is derived from James' archetype of
      the heroic woman, Minny Temple, and the novel is the working
      out of the question of Minny's fate, had she lived.

1957

42   KUHN, BERTHA M. "Study Questions and Theme Assignment on
     Henry James's 'Paste.'" Exercise Exchange, 4 (April), 4-5.
        For a composition course, Kuhn suggests a series of
     fourteen questions about "Paste" in an attempt to "help the
     freshman to understand the symbolism and underlying meaning
     of the story," and offers a four point theme assignment.

43   LEWIS, R. W. B. "The Vision of Grace: James's The Wings of
     the Dove." Modern Fiction Studies, 3 (Spring), 33-40.
        The Wings of the Dove is a novel "about senselessness
     and collapse, about dissociation and confusion, and it is
     a triumph over them." Out of the battle of spirit which
     takes place in the work, James recovered "a sacramental
     sensibility," and prophetically suggested that a new soci-
     ety might be emerging. The novel also incorporates an
     evolving definition of marriage and passion, and their
     relationship to money.

44   LYDENBERG, JOHN. "The Governess Turns the Screws."
     Nineteenth-Century Fiction, 12 (June), 37-58.
        The Turn of the Screw is a story of horror for horror's
     sake, in which James tried to leave the governess' person-
     ality, as he left the nature of evil, undefined. Theorizes
     that the governess is ever tightening the screws, and in
     her overprotective way harries the children "to distraction
     and death...." Considers her personality traits, typical
     of the authoritarian character described by Erich Fromm,
     and suggests that the ghosts are of a symbolic sort, rep-
     resenting a generalized evil that is part of mankind. The
     governess, a "hysterical woman," "turns the screws of
     Puritan discipline and suspicion until the children finally
     crack under the strain." Reprinted: in Gerald Willen, ed.
     A Casebook on "The Turn of the Screw," pp. 273-90.

45   McCORMICK, JOHN O. "The Rough and Lurid Vision: Henry James,
     Graham Greene and the International Theme." Jahrbuch für
     Amerikastudien, 2: 158-67.
        Examines Graham Greene's The Quiet American as "a curi-
     ous analogue to James's most basic propositions" relating
     to the international theme and its moral implications.
     Shows dominance of theme in James' work; analyses Madame
     de Mauves as the encounter of innocent Americans reacting
     to an alien world; and suggests that James' "'rough and
     lurid vision'" of oversimplified thesis of innocence "seems
     prophetic of fifty years to come" and is expanded upon by
     a "resentful Englishman" in The Quiet American, a reversal
     of the Jamesian situation. Both James and Greene "attempt-
     ed to cope with the American scene."

46   MELCHIORI, BARBARA. "The Taste of Henry James." Studi
      Americani, no. 3, pp. 171-87.
          If followed through his novels and tales, James the art
      critic reveals two characteristics: "an indication of the
      best taste of the time, with generous diversions on behalf
      of his friends, and secondly, an excess of caution...."
      Melchiori concentrates on the second aspect in an effort
      "to see some of the reasons and results of this caution,"
      which "strengthened" James "as an artist. The fear of
      vulgarity, or error, in taste, led him to produce more and
      more perfect work up to the final achievement of The Golden
      Bowl."

47   MELLOW, JAMES R. "James as Journalistic Critic." Commonweal,
      65 (1 February), 469-70.
          In essay-review of Sweeney's The Painter's Eye (see
      1956.B74), notes the "energy and interest of his own
      [James'] observations, style, and wry humor" of topical
      pieces, despite occasional "critical blindness." James
      kept "his critical judgment and personal taste as discrete
      as anyone could want or expect...."

*48   MENNEMEIER, F. N. "Das Drama der differenzierten Sicht."
      Rheinische Post (16 March). Cited in 1959.B5. (German)
          Dissatisfaction with much contemporary writing has pro-
      voked new interest in James, who is praised for his "dis-
      gust with 'the rough manners and uncultured materialism in
      our present-day society. He is our companion in a clan-
      destine aristocratic longing, in veritable hallucinations
      of a refined and harmonious life.'" Appreciates James'
      "'almost hellenistic objective': life as 'freedom chosen
      for the perfection of the human soul and form.'" However,
      perhaps James idealizes existence "to the point of falsi-
      fication." (Quotations from 1959.B5.)

49   MILLER, RAYMOND A., JR. "Representative Tragic Heroines in
      the Work of Brown, Hawthorne, Howells, James, and Dreiser."
      Ph.D. dissertation, University of Wisconsin.
          "From Christina Light to Mme. de Vionnet, the tragic
      heroines exercise painstaking self-examination to promote
      internal reform" in James' works. "...Their high goal is
      perfection." James, of the five novelists considered, has
      the "highest tragic sense."

50   MORDELL, ALBERT. "Introduction," in Literary Reviews and Es-
      says by Henry James on American, English, and French Lit-
      erature. New York: Twayne Publishers, pp. 9-27. Re-
      printed: New Haven, Conn.: College and University Press,
      1962.

1957

The volume, which contains over sixty previously uncollected items from the first twenty years of James' literary
career, provides a means of evaluating his early fiction.
As a critic, James looked "for the ideas at the base of an
author's writings." Assesses James' reputation and the
"magnificent" Jamesian scholarship, concluding that "To
some extent features of literary criticism entered into his
fiction, and his imaginative novelist's mind characterized
his literary criticism." Reviewed: Modern Fiction Studies,
4 (Summer 1958), 187; Morton D. Zabel, Victorian Studies, 2
(March 1959), 268-73.

51 MURDOCK, KENNETH B. "Introduction," in The Turn of the Screw
--The Aspern Papers. London: J. M. Dent and Sons; New
York: E. P. Dutton and Co., pp. v-xi. Reprinted: 1960.
Remarks on the way in which James transformed the germ
of The Aspern Papers into "a piece of high comedy with
pathetic overtones" which reveals a "feeling for the past"
and treats the international theme. Describes the source
of The Turn of the Screw, which appealed to James' "sense
of the pervasive reality of evil." However the work is
interpreted, its "enchantment remains."

52 NOWELL-SMITH, SIMON. "Introductory Note," in The Reverberator. New York: Grove Press, pp. v-x.
Discusses James' use of the "New Journalism types" for
the sake of liveliness or local color, and his "transmuta-
tion of two squalid little journalistic discourtesies of
real life into the gem of comedy...." Mentions bibliographical considerations, variant editions.

53 PHILLIPS, J. NOVA. "A Twaddle of Graciousness." Botteghe
Oscure, 19 (Spring), 195-202.
Describes his effort to have twelve letters from James
to the founder of a New England boys school published, and
James' nephew's refusal as literary executor to allow re-
printing on the basis that the letters generally lacked
interest and were examples of what James termed "'twaddle
of graciousness.'"

54 POCHMANN, HENRY A. "Henry James," in German Culture in
America: Philosophical and Literary Influences, 1600-
1900. Madison: University of Wisconsin Press, p. 477.
"Germany was largely irrelevant for Henry James."
Notes his two trips to Germany, his "occasional references
to Goethe and other Germans," and the inclusion of a few
German characters in his works. "...Fundamentally, he
remained antipathetic toward Germany...."

55   POWERS, LYALL H. "Preoccupations of Henry James." <u>Nation</u>,
      184 (29 June), 571-72.
          Anderson's thesis (in 1957.A1) appears to be "eminently
      useful in providing a substantial and extensive basis for
      understanding the meaning of his work," and, like the essay
      on Hawthorne, the Story biography, reissued in 1957, deals
      "indirectly with the problem of expatriation for the Ameri-
      can artist...."

56   PRATT, WILLIAM C. "Henry James: The Sublime Consensus of
      the Educated," in <u>Revolution without Betrayal: James,</u>
      <u>Pound, Eliot and the European Tradition</u>. Nashville, Tenn.:
      Vanderbilt University Press, pp. 211-63.
          "James, Pound, and Eliot are Americans by birth and tem-
      perament, but Europeans by intent and achievement." Con-
      siders the "moral discipline" of James' work and his vision
      of an ideal society. The "character of James's ideal
      civilization" is revealed in a comparison of common quali-
      ties in his last three completed novels.

57   RALEIGH, JOHN HENRY. "Henry James," in <u>Matthew Arnold and</u>
      <u>American Culture</u>. University of California English Studies,
      No. 17. Berkeley and Los Angeles: University of California
      Press, pp. 17-46.
          Citing James' review of Arnold's <u>Essays in Criticism</u>,
      discusses James' views of the English writer's theories of
      criticism and describes him as "'Arnoldian.'" "Arnold was
      for James a kind of archetypal angel...." Points out simi-
      larities in their points of view and attitudes towards
      literature, and the influence of Arnold on James in "mat-
      ters of practical criticism...." Concludes that there
      exists "a commonality of purposes and values in the total
      work of Arnold and James."

58   READ, HERBERT. "Two Notes on a Trilogy," in <u>Tenth Muse:</u>
      <u>Essays in Criticism</u>. New York: Horizon Press; London:
      Routledge and Kegan Paul, pp. 189-97. Reprinted: Free-
      port, N.Y.: Books for Libraries Press, 1969.
          Examines the last three completed novels in view of
      James' evolution, suggesting that they "represent--a per-
      fection at once intellectually formal and deeply moving."
      Presents James' self-proclaimed idea for <u>The Golden Bowl</u>,
      his "carrying over into the novel of the formal demands
      that are implicit in the drama." The novel embodies the
      "subtlest ethical intelligence of our time," and the tril-
      ogy contains "the greatest poetry of our time."

1957

59   SCHIEBER, ALOIS J. "Autobiographies of American Novelists:
Twain, Howells, James, Adams, and Garland." Ph.D. dissertation, University of Wisconsin.
"Henry James remained a wealthy socialite, an affection-
ate person aloof to close attachments.... His introspec-
tiveness contributed to the complexity of his thought and
expression and to his hypochondria." Views all the writers
considered as essentially romantic.

*60   SCHÜRENBERG, W. "Das versäumte Leben." <u>Neue Deutsche Hefte</u>,
no. 31 (January), p. 590 ff. Cited in 1959.B5. (German)
Suggests that "Strether appears to be a betrayed trait-
or," and that in <u>The Ambassadors</u> art replaces life, making
it James' most artificial work (quotation from 1959.B5).

61   SHAPIRA, MORRIS. "The Artist and the Artistic." <u>Cambridge
Review</u>, 78 (15 June), 711-12.
James' autobiography (<u>see</u> 1956.B20) "communicates the
essential feel, particularly the growing child's rich but
vague sense of the world around him."

62   SILVER, JOHN. "A Note on the Freudian Reading of 'The Turn of
the Screw.'" <u>American Literature</u>, 29 (May), 207-11.
Supports Edmund Wilson's Freudian interpretation of <u>The
Turn of the Screw</u> (<u>see</u> 1934.B37), and dissipates "the major
objection to it." The tale is the governess' story "as
told by the governess," her apologia, her justification
of behavior. Theorizes that the governess had already
learned about Peter Quint before her seemingly astounding
description of the dead man and skillfully disguises her
knowledge in order to maneuver Mrs. Grose and the reader
into believing in the reality of the ghosts. Reprinted:
in Gerald Willen, ed. <u>A Casebook on "The Turn of the
Screw</u>," pp. 239-43.

63   SPENCER, BENJAMIN T. "The Jamesian Resolution," in <u>The Quest
for Nationality: An American Literary Campaign</u>. Syracuse,
N.Y.: Syracuse University Press, pp. 308-12.
Ambiguity not only marked James' writings but "also
characterized his reflections on the artist in America.
Discusses James' use of American locale, American characters in his fiction. "Through this paradox of the New
World heiress who in the Old World uniquely incarnated the
flowering of Western civilization, James apparently found
his own solution for an old problem: the absence in America of a settled culture which would allow the novelist a
suitably firm frame of reference."

1957

64   SPENCER, JAMES L.   "Symbolism in James's The Golden Bowl."
      Modern Fiction Studies, 3 (Winter), 333-44.
          Examines the symbol of the golden bowl at work in The
      Golden Bowl, and asserts that "James was writing not a
      fable or an allegory, but a novel about real life.... The
      ambiguities help the central symbol to resist oversimpli-
      fication and to remain true to the richness and complexity
      and irony of human life." Maggie must accept the golden
      bowl "with its flaw--Amerigo's lack of moral consciousness
      as distinguished from his traditional sense of form."

65   STALLMAN, R. W.   "Time and the Unnamed Article in The Ambas-
      sadors." Modern Language Notes, 72 (January), 27-32.
          The "unnamed article" in The Ambassadors is a clock,
      which object "informs the meaning of the whole novel" in
      which time is "the all-consuming theme." See 1958.B27.

66   STALLMAN, R. W.   "'The Sacred Rage': The Time-Theme in 'The
      Ambassadors.'" Modern Fiction Studies, 3 (Spring), 41-56.
          The theme of The Ambassadors is "Time--How to Live It."
      Gives examples of the pervasive concern with time,
      "Woollett versus Paris--represents conventional time and
      conventional morality." The "Sacred Rage" is two-fold,
      like Strether's double consciousness, both a rage for free-
      dom from fixed temporal and moral impingements and "the
      rage for life moulded into the ordered forms of convention-
      al morality and conventional time." The progress of the
      novel consists of alternation between these two poles of
      his consciousness, from present to future. Reprinted:
      in The Houses that James Built and Other Literary Studies.
      East Lansing: Michigan State University Press, 1961,
      pp. 34-50.

67   STOVALL, FLOYD.   "Henry James's 'The Jolly Corner.'"
      Nineteenth-Century Fiction, 12 (June), 72-84.
          Hypothesizes that Brydon has a double consciousness,
      that the apparition which comes from without through ves-
      tibule doors is Brydon as he actually is: For 33 years
      he has been false to his true self without realizing it.
      Alice's love releases his real self. Refers to internal
      evidence in "The Jolly Corner" and looks briefly at some
      corroborative parallels in other tales.

68   THEOBALD, J. R.   "New Reflections on The Golden Bowl."
      Twentieth-Century Literature, 3 (April), 2-26.
          Considers The Golden Bowl "with special attention to...
      prodigious concern with motive." Discusses "wavering
      identity" of Charlotte, the "virtual monopoly of conscious

291

1957

motives," and James' "ogling" of the theatre "in a technique that marks both a concentration and a constriction."
Mentions Jamesian "detachment" which "fails of true objec-
tivity." James is "never for a single second out of ear-
shot."

69 VALLETT, JACQUES. "Croissance de Henry James." Mercure de
France, 329 (April), 706-709. (French)
    Review of 1956.B20, James' "intellectual and moral"
autobiography. Discusses James' early environment, the
major role art played in his development, the question of
his expatriation. "It is not possible to skim the autobiography without having a presentiment of all its riches."

70 WALTER, EUGENE. "A Rainy Afternoon with Truman Capote."
Intro Bulletin, 2 (December), 1-2.
    Capote, in response to an interview question about which
writers were most meaningful to him, mentions Flaubert,
James and Proust.

71 WATKINS, FLOYD C. "Christopher Newman's Final Instinct."
Nineteenth-Century Fiction, 12 (June), 85-88.
    Examination of Newman's final instinctive turning to
see if the note he chose to burn is consumed, which James
altered in the revision of The American, thus making his
hero better but perhaps less human.

72 WEST, REBECCA. "Nonconformist Assenters and Independent In-
troverts," in The Court and the Castle: Some Treatments
of a Recurrent Theme. New Haven, Conn.: Yale University
Press, pp. 203-207.
    James is one of the "resistant personalities unaffected
by the Rousseauist influences of their time." Describes
him as apolitical, one who identified evil with vulgarity
in an extreme way. "Henry James could not have been more
earnest regarding the salvation of the soul, but he was
historically unfortunate, as appears if his prefaces to the
collected editions of his novels...are compared with Field-
ing's essays on the same subject in Tom Jones."

73 WILKINS, M. S. "A Note on The Princess Casamassima."
Nineteenth-Century Fiction, 12 (June), 88.
    Identifies a possible source for The Princess Casamas-
sima, an international secret society in Naples, centering
around a Princess Oblensky who moved in 1866 to an island
off the southwest coast of Italy, Casamicciola.

74 WOODRESS, JAMES. "Henry James." <u>Publications of the Modern Language Association</u>, 72 (April), 254-55.
     International listing of books and articles on Henry James which appeared in the previous year.

75 WRIGHT, WALTER. "'The Real Thing.'" <u>Research Studies of the State College of Washington</u>, 25 (March), 85-90.
     "The Real Thing" is often misinterpreted as demonstrating in James the dichotomy between art and life. The title of the story "deepens in meaning as the story progresses." The Monarchs' "resignation to life has about it the very highest social value." They live with intensity and "never cease to be the real thing."

76 WRIGHT, WALTER. "Maggie Verver: Neither Saint nor Witch." <u>Nineteenth-Century Fiction</u>, 12 (June), 59-71.
     Disputes the view of Maggie as either a creature of virtue or of evil, presents evidence against these two positions, and suggests that Maggie needs the other characters "because she is also imperfect, because she lacks understanding and must come of age." She is a "wholesome, sensitive" girl with the flaw of ignorance, who, with the Prince, moves out of a "Garden of Eden of illusion" and the "wilderness of doubt," accepting the truth about herself and others. The novel achieves the "spiritual purification of tragedy."

77 WYLD, L. D. "Drama Vs. the Theatre in Henry James." <u>Four Quarters</u>, 7 (May), 17-23.
     Surveys James' dramatic output, discusses him as "an artist...resolved to master his chosen form," and points out his weaknesses. "As a novelist dramatizing, James could not relinquish his precious desire for character delineation or social situation." He "was essentially a novelist and a recognition of his complete 'at homeness' and pre-eminence in his major <u>genre</u> is basic to a full understanding of James as a playwright."

78 ZABEL, MORTON D. "Henry James: The Act of Life," in <u>Craft and Character in Modern Fiction: Texts, Method, and Vocation</u>. New York: The Viking Press, pp. 114-43.
     Slightly revised version of 1951.B58.

79 ZAULI-NALDI, CAMILLA. "James e Trollope." <u>Studi Americani</u>, no. 3, pp. 205-19. (Italian)
     A comparative study of James and Trollope. Both were "faithful interpreters of the surrounding world, intent on discovering the interior beauty of a character or

1957

environment, ready to create in each successive novel characters dear to them...pondering the doubts or uncertainties
in the conduct of individuals...lacking material difficulties." Both provide accounts of the craft of writing,
both deal with Anglo-American rapport. Their closest point
of contact is their attitudes towards their female characters, whom they portray as possessing femininity, strength,
health, and a moral outlook, and the closest thematic contact between the two writers is their mutual attention to
the dilemmas of conscience.

1958 A BOOKS

1   BLACK, JAMES O. "A Novel as a 'Work of Art': A Reading of
    The Ambassadors." Ph.D. dissertation, University of Ar-
    kansas.
        An attempt to demonstrate that "criticism of the novel...
    is careless and inadequate," and, with emphasis on The Am-
    bassadors, to propose a viable critical system based on
    "close textual reading of the novel," which should be ap-
    proached as a work of art.

2   EDEL, LEON and GORDON N. RAY. "Introduction," in Henry James
    and H. G. Wells: A Record of Their Friendship, Their De-
    bate on the Art of Fiction, and Their Quarrel. Edited by
    Leon Edel and Gordon N. Ray. Urbana: University of Illi-
    nois Press; London: Rupert Hart-Davis, 272 pp.
        A record of the disagreement between James and H. G.
    Wells about the purpose and practice of their art, which
    includes all extant letters exchanged between them, arti-
    cles by each, and passages from Wells' autobiography after
    James' death. In the introduction, the editors provide a
    chronological record of the troubled relationship between
    James and Wells, with reference to their personality and
    temperamental differences and differing attitudes towards
    art. Wells subordinated life to a social message, and
    James saw art as the only valid method of encompassing and
    preserving human experience, as the voice of the individ-
    ual. Reviewed: Modern Fiction Studies, 4 (Summer 1958),
    187; Kenneth Murdock, New England Quarterly, 31 (December
    1958), 554-56; Morton D. Zabel, Victorian Studies, 2
    (March 1959), 268-72.

3   McCARTHY, HAROLD T. Henry James: The Creative Process. New
    York: Thomas Yoseloff, 172 pp. Reprinted: Rutherford,
    N.J.: Fairleigh-Dickinson University Press, 1968.

A study of various aspects of James' aesthetics, with
emphasis on his concern with understanding the nature and
function of the creative process, his preoccupation with
the relationship of art to experience, the importance of
aesthetic perceptions for art, and the role of feeling in
the creative process and the work of art. Also considers
other aesthetic matters related to expression, such as
dramatic development and organic form, relates James'
method to his aesthetic theories, discusses his concept of
prose as an aesthetic medium, and points out aesthetic
considerations of his concern with the relation of the
artist to his work and to society. Reviewed: Modern Fiction Studies, 4 (Winter, 1958-1959), 372.

4   MARKOW-TOTEVY, GEORGES. Henry James. Introduction by André
    Maurois. Paris: Éditions Universitaires, 159 pp. Trans-
    lated by John Griffeths. London: The Merlin Press.
    Translated by John Cumming. New York: Funk and Wagnalls,
    1969.
       Following a biographical sketch, attempts to draw a
    psychological portrait of James, describes three periods
    of his career, and labels his work as an effort "to de-
    scribe man's conflict with himself and with the world."
    Treats such topics as the international theme; the por-
    trayal of places and characters in realistic manner; James'
    "constant preoccupation with life...as a confrontation
    with meaningful stresses"; love "as a probability of the
    future" and "denied love" as the "basis of transcendence";
    the world of fine arts and letters and the problems of the
    artist; James' literary theory and method of composition.
    Appendix includes previously unpublished letter by James,
    selected bibliography, chronological summary.

*5 OKITA, HAJIME. Henry James Bibliography in Japan. Kyoto:
    Showado, Apollon-sha. Cited in Beatrice Ricks, comp.
    Henry James: A Bibliography of Secondary Works, #3812.

6   TALLMAN, WARREN E. "Drama of a High Civilization. Prelimi-
    nary Studies in Henry James's Fiction." Ph.D. disserta-
    tion, University of Washington.
       "James' main achievement was to create a 'high civiliza-
    tion' presided over by his 'princess,'" who evolved from
    early partial portraits "to the final full portraits in
    The Ambassadors, The Wings of the Dove, and The Golden
    Bowl." Studies the gradual evolution of the princess
    type.

1958

7 WEGELIN, CHRISTOF. <u>The Image of Europe in Henry James</u>.
  Dallas, Texas: Southern Methodist University Press,
  200 pp.
      James is a representative of those writers who needed to
  "define their own and their country's relation to Europe...."
  Points out conflict "between the native and the European
  components of the American tradition," and suggests that the
  international situation helped James come to terms both with
  American character and with "the nature of morality, its relation to manners and to civilization." Traces "James's relation to traditional American attitudes toward Europe and
  the development of his treatment of the 'international situation'" throughout his career. Partially reprinted: as
  "The American as a Young Lady," in Peter Buitenhuis, ed.
  <u>Twentieth Century Interpretations of "The Portrait of a
  Lady</u>," pp. 55-59. Reviewed: <u>Modern Fiction Studies</u>, 4
  (Winter 1958-1959), 372; Edwin Cady, <u>Modern Language Notes</u>,
  74 (November 1959), 654-57; Robert E. Spiller, <u>Modern Phil-
  ology</u>, 56 (May 1959), 283-84; Leon Edel, <u>New York Times
  Book Review</u> (17 August, 1958), p. 4.

1958 B SHORTER WRITINGS

  1 AIKEN, CONRAD. "Henry James (1925)," in <u>A Reviewer's ABC:
     Collected Criticism of Conrad Aiken from 1916 to the Pres-
     ent</u>. New York: Meridian Books, pp. 230-33.
        Reprint of 1925.B1.

  2 AIKEN, CONRAD. "Henry James (1935)," in <u>A Reviewer's ABC:
     Collected Criticism of Conrad Aiken from 1916 to the Pres-
     ent</u>. New York: Meridian Books, pp. 233-36.
        Reprint of 1935.B1.

  3 AIKEN, CONRAD. "Henry James (1935)," in <u>A Reviewer's ABC:
     Collected Criticism of Conrad Aiken from 1916 to the Pres-
     ent</u>. New York: Meridian Books, pp. 236-38.
        Reprint of 1935.B2.

  4 ANON. "Wells vs. James." <u>Newsweek</u>, 51 (28 April), 99.
        "There has seldom if ever been a literary quarrel of
     more fascination," and this one "produced witty lightning
     on one side and polite thunder on the other." Summarizes
     James' and Wells' relationship.

  5 ANON. "The Soho Bibliography of Henry James." <u>Colby Library
     Quarterly</u>, series 4 (August), 277-79.

1958

Notes errors in the index of the Edel and Laurence bibliography (<u>see</u> 1957.A3), but otherwise praises "the completeness and the accuracy of the work."

6   BERGONZI, BERNARD. "An Early Wells Review of Henry James."
    <u>Times Literary Supplement</u> (18 April), p. 216.
        Discussion of an "early and previously undetected re-
    view by Wells of a book of James's short stories." Sup-
    plies background of the review, and concludes that Wells'
    remarks are generally "unsympathetic" but "by no means
    imperceptive" and reveal his "mounting irritation with
    James."

7   BERGONZI, BERNARD. "The Novelist and his Subject-Matter:
    Reflections on Henry James and H. G. Wells." <u>Listener</u>,
    60 (18 September), 426-27.
        Deals with the critical issues involved in the relation-
    ship between Wells and James, particularly on the question
    of art and life. "For Wells, art was something secondary
    and subservient to life." For James, "'life' was, pre-
    cisely, what one chose to make of it," needing "the dis-
    criminating and composing power of art" to eliminate the
    chaos or void.

8   BERLAND, ALWYN. "Henry James and the Grand Renunciation."
    <u>Kansas Magazine</u>, 4: 82-90.
        The theme of renunciation is a prevalent one in James'
    work, and Berland relates it to the idea of civilization
    in James, the "major theme: the pursuit, the definition,
    the defense of an Ideal Civilization wherein man may
    achieve and express the highest measure of his ethical-
    aesthetic wholeness." It is against this framework--
    "significantly related to his central theme of an ideal
    civilization, conditioned by a tendency to non-involvement
    in his lesser characters and by a strong exercise of stoi-
    cism in others--that the theme of renunciation must be
    seen."

9   BEWLEY, MARIUS. "Henry James and 'Life.'" <u>Hudson Review</u>, 11
    (Summer), 167-85.
        An investigation of the international theme in James,
    which is an attempt to resolve conflicts of "divergent
    national manners and attitudes." Shows how "James used
    the international theme to probe under the appearances of
    life towards a moral reality that remained essentially
    uncommitted to any national pattern or allegiance." Ana-
    lyzes <u>Madame de Mauves</u> as a "paradigm of Henry James's

1958

technique and intentions in dealing with the international
theme." Reprinted: 1959.B11.

10   BOWMAN, S. E. "Les héroines d'Henry James dans The Portrait
of a Lady et d'Yvan Tourguéniev dans A la Veille." Etudes
Anglaises, 11 (April-June), 136-49. (French)
        Compares Hélène, the heroine of A la Veille (On the
Eve), with Isabel, in The Portrait of a Lady. The techniques of presentation are similar. Concludes that both
novels offer a moral and an idealistic renunciation that
renders Hélène and Isabel heroic, that the heroines have
common traits which are determining factors in their his-
tories, and that both are exposed in dramatic fashion.

11   BROGAN, D. W. "No Innocents Abroad." Harper's Bazaar
(July), pp. 86-87, 98.
        Considers the "changing image of the American abroad,"
with reference to The Ambassadors as "a profound study of
a foreign society's impact on a mature American...."

12   BROME, VINCENT. "Henry James versus H. G. Wells," in Six
Studies in Quarrelling. London: Cresset Press, pp. 75-
102.
        Chronological examination of the complicated relation-
ship between James and H. G. Wells: "No two men differed
so much in outlook, temperament and manners, and had such
wonderful equipment to deal with one another's short-
comings."

13   BROOKS, VAN WYCK. "Henry James and Others," in The Dream of
Arcadia: American Writers and Artists in Italy. New
York: E. P. Dutton and Co., pp. 155-63.
        Discussion of James' first visit to Italy in 1869 and
his reactions to Rome. Describes James' circle of acquaintances, including the Sargents and F. Marion Crawford.

14   BROOKS, VAN WYCK. "The Jameses," in The Dream of Arcadia:
American Writers and Artists in Italy. New York: E. P.
Dutton and Co., pp. 164-75.
        When James returned to Italy after he began writing, he
"was startled by the change that had taken place since the
new Italy had triumphed...." Remarks on James' response
to painters, notes Italian settings in the early fiction,
discusses James' feelings about travelling Americans, mentions influence of Italy on his works.

15 BRUMM, URSULA. "Symbolism and the Novel." <u>Partisan Review</u>,
    25 (Summer), 327-42.
        In examining the "nature and function of symbols in the
    novel," describes the golden bowl in James' <u>The Golden Bowl</u>
    as "image, expressing the meaning it is meant to convey in
    image and not in a causal nexus." Labels this a "'trans-
    cendent'" symbol, because it "embodies a meaning with which
    it has no direct connection." Points out fairy tale ele-
    ments in the novel, suggesting a "connection between modern
    symbolism and its mythological origins...." Reprinted: in
    Philip Stevick, ed. <u>The Theory of the Novel</u>. New York:
    Free Press, 1967, pp. 354-68.

16 BURT, NATHANIEL. "Struthers Burt '04: The Literary Career of
    a Princetonian." <u>Princeton University Library Chronicle</u>,
    19 (Spring-Summer), 109-22.
        Discussion of the career of professional writer Struth-
    ers Burt, who was influenced stylistically by Conrad and
    James, "who cultivated respectively the ideals of gentleman
    adventurer and refined worldly wisdom."

17 CADY, EDWIN. "The Realism War," in <u>The Realist at War: The
    Mature Years 1885-1920 of William Dean Howells</u>. Syracuse,
    N.Y.: Syracuse University Press, pp. 40-48 and passim.
        James' "reputation became the objective of Howells'
    first, unpremeditated battle for realism" in the "melee"
    of the movement, and James was largely "responsible for
    the growth of the convictions Howells expressed." James'
    and Howells' "work and criticism would never coincide so
    meaningfully again as it did in the early stages of the
    Realism War."

18 CARGILL, OSCAR. "Henry James's 'Moral Policeman': William
    Dean Howells." <u>American Literature</u>, 29 (January), 371-98.
        Despite Howells' generous reception of James' work, he
    annoyed James "by persistent criticism of the 'immoral'
    implications of his tales." Reviews Howells' and James'
    assessments of each other, and concludes that during their
    lives "Howells and James had inflicted hurts on each other,
    but not more so than is common with persons closely asso-
    ciated, a fact which each seemed to appreciate, and their
    double striving, with Howells perhaps making the greater
    concession, made it a path of amity at the end, as it was
    in the beginning." Reprinted: in <u>Toward a Pluralistic
    Criticism</u>. Carbondale and Edwardsville: Southern Illi-
    nois University Press, 1965, pp. 69-94.

1958

19   CARGILL, OSCAR. "The First International Novel." Publica-
     tions of the Modern Language Association, 73 (September),
     418-25.
          A consideration of whether James "invented" the inter-
     national novel. Examines early prototypes of international
     fiction, and defines the type, applying the definition to
     James' work and asserting that "by the mid-seventies James
     had not seen or realized the possibilities of international
     fiction...." Traces the evolution of the international
     type of narrative in James; the place of Howells' A Fore-
     gone Conclusion and James' reviews of that work, an uncon-
     scious creation in the genre; and labels The American as
     "the first really conscious production of the type," the
     "true clash of characters based upon mores."

20   CARY, JOYCE. "Experience and Word," in Art and Reality: Ways
     of the Creative Process. New York: Harper and Brothers,
     pp. 94-98.
          Uses James' account of his getting the idea for The
     Spoils of Poynton as an example of the "problem of the
     artist...to preserve the force of his intuition...through-
     out the long process of technical construction."

21   CHASE, RICHARD. "James' Ambassadors," in Twelve Original Es-
     says on Great American Novels. Edited by Charles Shapiro.
     Detroit, Mich.: Wayne State University Press, pp. 124-47.
          The Ambassadors, a "notoriously great novel," presents
     the theme of Americans and Europeans and initiation. Dis-
     cusses James' humor, the "significant levity" in the work,
     the three great recognition scenes, and the leading images.
     The Ambassadors represents "a sort of handbook of manners
     and morals by a new Castiglione, an exposition and por-
     trait of the ideal gentleman of the late 19th-century
     Anglo-Saxon upper middle class."

22   CHASE, RICHARD. "Saturday Morning: The Illusion of the
     Middle Way," in The Democratic Vista: A Dialogue on Life
     and Letters in Contemporary America. Garden City, N.Y.:
     Doubleday and Co., p. 65.
          George, "a professor, middle-aging," debates George,
     "solid citizen of the new generation," concerning whether
     James was "ignorant of life."

23   COFFIN, TRISTRAM P. "Daisy Miller, Western Hero." Western
     Folklore, 17 (October), 273-75.
          "Daisy Miller, who is pretty typical of Henry James's
     American in Europe, is really little more than a western
     hero with parasol and bank account." Enumerates traits of

Daisy which correspond to those of the western hero, with
"simpler, more effective, and more moral ways" than society
at large. That James "sensed her essentially western na-
ture so early in the game," was aware of the backwash of
West on East, is remarkable. Reprinted: in William T.
Stafford, ed. James's Daisy Miller: The Story, The Play,
The Critics. Scribner Research Anthologies. New York:
Charles Scribner's Sons, 1963, pp. 136-37.

24 CROW, CHARLES R. "The Style of Henry James: The Wings of the
Dove." English Institute Essays, 4: 172-89.
    Inspects the style of The Wings of the Dove, questioning
its flexibility for expressing nuances in movement and tone.
Judges the later style to be elaborate but not monotonous.
In James, there is a "gravity brought partly by tightening
rhythm and by compression" and "a dryness that works to
keep solemnity away." Concludes that James strove to be
readable, that "The Wings of the Dove is not an indulgence
of private vision. It releases the notions and the tones
of its meanings to the reader." Reprinted: 1959.B22.

25 DeFALCO, J. M. "The Great Good Place: A Journey into the
Psyche." Literature and Psychology, 8 (Spring), 18-20.
    James uses a dream sequence in "The Great Good Place"
"to project the protagonist into a journey through the unconscious," into the recesses of the psyche "where the ego,
overwhelmed by the pressures of the conscious world, is
healed by the tender care of the Great Mother archetype and
emerges reborn." Points out the unifying images of rain,
water and bell, and describes the cycle.

26 DOVE, GEORGE N. "The 'Haunted Personality' in Henry James."
Tennessee Studies in Literature, 3: 99-106.
    Surveys the interpretations of the governess' haunted
state in The Turn of the Screw, and explains the character
in terms of James' other "'haunted personalities,'" created
in the years immediately preceding that tale. Proposes
three consistent qualities of the "haunted personality":
"anxiety over the security of one's own position, anxiety
for the security of other persons, and curiosity."

27 EDEL, LEON. "Time and The Ambassadors." Modern Language
Notes, 73 (March), 177-79.
    Time is not the "'all-consuming theme'" in The Ambassa-
dors, as suggested by Stallman (see 1957.B65). The "un-
named object" is whatever the reader, as participant in
the novel, makes it.

1958

28   EDEL, LEON and LYALL H. POWERS. "Henry James and the <u>Bazar</u>
     Letters." <u>Bulletin of the New York Public Library</u>, 62
     (February), 75-103.
          Reprints 30 letters from James to Elizabeth Jordan,
     editor of <u>Harper's Bazar</u>, 1900-1912, relating primarily
     to James' American lecture tour and his contributions to
     <u>Bazar</u> between 1904 and 1909. The correspondence can be
     categorized as "of the market-place," and demonstrates
     James' "professional realism." Provides brief biographical
     sketch of Jordan. The letters "enable us to understand...
     the full story of his [James'] strange collaboration with
     the <u>Bazar</u> in a composite novel; they offer the genesis of
     his article on 'Is There a Life After Death?' and his
     articles on the speech and manners of American women. They
     give us also his choice of his favorite fairy tale." Re-
     printed: 1958.B29.

29   EDEL, LEON and LYALL H. POWERS. "Henry James and the <u>Bazar</u>
     Letters," in <u>Howells and James: A Double Billing</u>. New
     York: New York Public Library.
          Reprint of 1958.B28.

30   ENCK, J. J. "Wholeness of Effect in <u>The Golden Bowl</u>."
     <u>Transactions of the Wisconsin Academy of Sciences, Arts,
     and Letters</u>, 47: 227-40.
          Summarizes the central conflicts, structure and style
     of <u>The Golden Bowl</u>, and surveys critical views with atten-
     tion to the "reliability of observers and details which
     they suppress or ignore." Examines tourist and museum
     imagery in the novel, and concludes that <u>The Golden Bowl</u>
     possesses a "wholeness" which "consists, ultimately, in
     a partial wholeness, in seeing things as they exist,
     evaluating them, and, then, accepting or transforming them
     for their moment but not eternity."

31   ESPEY, JOHN J. "The Epigraph to T. S. Eliot's 'Burbank with
     a Baedeker: Bleistein with a Cigar.'" <u>American Litera-
     ture</u>, 29 (January), 483-84.
          Reference to a passage from James' <u>The Aspern Papers</u>
     altered from the original in Eliot's epigraph, "Burbank
     with a Baedeker: Bleistein with a Cigar." Compression
     of James' passage suggests that Eliot may have drawn it
     from an intermediate source, perhaps Ford Madox Ford's
     <u>Henry James, A Critical Study</u> (1916).

1958

32 FIEDLER, LESLIE A. "From Redemption to Initiation." New
      Leader, 41 (26 May), 20-23.
         "In the modern version of the Fall of Man, there are
      four participants not three: the man, the woman, the
      serpent, and the child (presumably watching everything
      from behind the tree). It is Henry James who sets the
      pattern once and for all in What Maisie Knew...."

33 FIEDLER, LESLIE A. "The Profanation of the Child." New
      Leader, 41 (23 June), 26-29.
         The Turn of the Screw is the prototype of stories of
      "children possessed, children through whom the satanic
      attempts to enter the adult world."

34 FIREBAUGH, JOSEPH J. "The Idealism of Merton Densher."
      University of Texas Studies in English, 37: 41-54.
         Considers justification for viewing Milly as saviour,
      analyzes her motives, and describes Merton as a "passive
      modern man...possessing no sure identity." He will "force
      actuality to conform to the ideal even after events have
      made the ideal eternally impossible." He is, then,
      "solipsistic modern man," who "would keep life at a dis-
      tance, and satisfy himself with his own speculations."

35 FIREBAUGH, JOSEPH J. "A Schopenhauerian Novel: James's The
      Princess Casamassima." Nineteenth-Century Fiction, 13
      (December), 177-97.
         James felt sympathy with Schopenhauer's ideas "as af-
      fording possibilities of artistic development" and "enter-
      tained the Schopenhauerian world view," especially in The
      Princess Casamassima, in which Hyacinth alludes to that
      philosopher. Examines the extent to which the novel may
      have been influenced by Schopenhauer and the view that
      "within an ugly and deterministic universe may arise the
      freedom of art."

36 FRICKER, ROBERT. "Henry James," in Der moderne englische
      Roman. Gottingen: Vanderhoeck and Ruprecht, pp. 37-54.
      (German)
         Describes James as a "writer's writer," and views his
      subject as the conflict between social and cultural tradi-
      tions in opposition with ethical decisions of the individ-
      ual.

37 FRYCKSTEDT, O. W. In Quest of America: A Study of Howells'
      Early Development as a Novelist. Cambridge, Mass.:
      Harvard University Press, passim.

1958

James had considerable influence on Howells, causing
him to "organize his literary opinions more consistently
for the first time." Discusses the James-Howells relationship of the 1870's and the two writers' approaches to
the international novel.

38   FUSSELL, EDWIN. "Hawthorne, James and 'The Common Doom.'"
    American Quarterly, 10 (Winter), 438-53.
       Considers the theme of "the common doom" as a means of
tracing aspects of the complex relationship between James
and Hawthorne. The theme arose from "roughly analogous
conditions in their lives, predispositions in temperaments,"
and relates to Hawthorne's influence on James and James'
critical treatment of Hawthorne. Sources of the theme in
James' work include his "obscure hurt" and his non-involve-
ment in the Civil War, his encounter with Hawthorne's
writings, his emancipation from "the James family" and
dedication to the writing of fiction.

39   GALE, ROBERT L. "Evil and the American Short Story." Annali
    Istituto Universitario Orientale, Napoli, Sezione Germanica,
    1: 183-202.
       Examination of the "changing treatment of the element
of evil by American short story writers." For James, "the
most evil act one can commit is the deadening of sensitive,
creative awareness, whether in oneself through grossness,
lack of imagination, timidity in welcoming life, or in
others through being domineering or unsympathetic," a position similar to Hawthorne's.

40   GALE, ROBERT L. "A Letter from Henry James to Francis Marion
    Crawford." Studi Americani, no. 4, pp. 415-19.
       Reprints a letter from James to Francis Marion Crawford.
Gale points out differences and similarities between the
two writers, who were "firm friends," reviews the historical background of the letter, and presents further biographical data on this "unique item."

41   GASS, WILLIAM H. "The High Brutality of Good Intentions."
    Accent, 18 (Winter), 62-71.
       James viewed art and morality as interrelated, and his
major theme was "the evil of human manipulation," of which
The Portrait of a Lady was his first fully exposed example.
The best world is that observed from the most sensitive,
universal yet discriminating viewpoint, and "The value of
life lies ultimately in the experienced quality of it, in
the integrity of the given not in the usefulness of the
taken." Reprinted: in William Stafford, ed. Perspectives

1958

on James's "The Portrait of a Lady," pp. 206-16; and in
Naomi Lebowitz. Discussions of Henry James. Boston:
D. C. Heath and Co., 1962, pp. 89-95.

42   GIRLING, H. K.   "'Wonder' and 'Beauty' in The Awkward Age."
     Essays in Criticism, 8 (October), 370-80.
        "...The idea of the 'beautiful' is an important part of
     James's view of life and art; indeed the whole of his work
     could be taken as a commentary on it." Analyzes the mean-
     ing of the epithets "wonderful" and "beautiful" in The
     Awkward Age, which "come to be regarded as opposite poles,
     although their primary meanings are contiguous...."
     "'Wonderful'...nearly always carries some irony," and can
     suggest the "essence of ordinariness." "'Beautiful'...
     rarely sheds all its dignity." Concludes that "in this
     study of souls separated from each other by a torrent of
     talk, James allows his actors to communicate in a word
     gestures; 'beautiful,' like a gesture in a tragic mime,
     assumes symbolic significance."

43   GLECKNER, ROBERT F.   "James's Madame de Mauves and Hawthorne's
     The Scarlet Letter." Modern Language Notes, 73 (December),
     580-86.
        A comparison of Madame de Mauves and The Scarlet Letter
     reveals some similarities and also "James's implicit
     criticism of Howthorne's allegorical method," James' use
     of this method in Longmore's dream, and the relationship
     between James' presentation of certain scenes and his ex-
     plicit criticism of similar scenes in The Scarlet Letter.

44   GOLDSMITH, ARNOLD L.   "Henry James's Reconciliation of Free
     Will and Fatalism." Nineteenth-Century Fiction, 13 (Sep-
     tember), 109-26.
        With reference to James' works, especially The Awkward
     Age and The Spoils of Poynton, attempts to relate James to
     the nineteenth-century "climate of opinion." Examines his
     reconciliation of free will and fate, discusses his rela-
     tionship to the naturalistic movement. James believed that
     in a "hostile universe," stoicism and will power are
     necessary qualities. "Everybody in this world suffers, but
     decent people bear it if they are to get anything from
     life."

45   HAMALIAN, L. and E. L. VOLPE.   "Now that you've read James'
     'The Beast in the Jungle,'" in Ten Modern Short Novels.
     New York: G. P. Putnam's Sons, pp. 103-107.
        Marcher is a unique character in that nothing has hap-
     pened to him in "The Beast in the Jungle," the theme of

1958

which is "the opportunity to live being wasted...." Remarks on revelations of Marcher's inner life and the techniques necessary for such revelations which ultimately
"transformed the sprawling, nineteenth-century English
language novel into a carefully constructed work of art."

46   HARKNESS, BRUCE. "The Lucky Crowd--Contemporary British
       Fiction." English Journal, 47 (October), 387-97.
            In Kingsley Amis' I Like It Here, Strether "is probably
       taken by the reader as a comic protrait of Henry James...."

47   HICKS, GRANVILLE. "Henry James as Traveler." Saturday Review
       of Literature, 41 (19 July), 22,42.
            Discusses James' attitude towards European and American
       cultures in a review of Zabel's collection (1958.B91).
       James preferred an "ordered" society, despite his non-
       condescending view of America. "To travel with him rewards
       the senses and stretches the mind."

48   HICKS, GRANVILLE. "The Shape of a Career." Saturday Review
       of Literature, 41 (13 December), 16, 38.
            Brief discussion of the literary career of James, How-
       ells, Faulkner, and Hemingway with emphasis on the quantity
       of books written by each.

49   HØLMEBAKK, GORDON. "Romanen som redskap eller erkjennelse.
       Noen notater om forholdet mellom Henry James og H. G.
       Wells." Vinduet, 12, 170-78. (Norwegian)
            Contrasts James and H. G. Wells: James believed in art
       for art's sake, Wells, art for man's sake; James insists
       on including the whole field of reality, Wells is content
       with journalism, polemics, with the hope of reforming the
       world. James sought artistic perfection, and was skepti-
       cal towards conventional, superficial language.

50   HONIG, EDWIN. "In Defense of Allegory." Kenyon Review, 20
       (Winter), 1-19.
            Although James, Coleridge, Melville and Poe opposed
       the "debased view of allegory as didactic personifica-
       tion," their novels and poetry "seem often to hide behind
       the fanciful." Reprinted: 1959.B42.

51   KINNAIRD, JOHN. "The Paradox of an American 'Identity.'"
       Partisan Review, 25 (Summer), 380-405.
            Discusses a scene in Roderick Hudson "that might well
       be called a Whitmanesque occasion," and considers affini-
       ties between Whitman and James, who both possessed the
       "characteristic idealism" of nineteenth-century America

and were obsessed with the "manifold paradox of our American self-consciousness.... In James that paradox became
refined into the multiple ironies of our moral sensibility,
while in Whitman it remained the native paradox of democracy...."

52 KRAUSE, S. J. "James's Revisions of the Style of The Portrait
of a Lady." American Literature, 30 (March), 67-88.
James revised in two directions: he made corrections
in style and intensified the symbolic texture of his language for the purposes of thematic motivation. With emphasis on style, Krause discusses some representative
passages in James' early and late revision of The Portrait
of a Lady to show there is as much similarity as there is
difference, and to demonstrate that the late revisions are
aimed at greater clarity, economy and informality.

53 LAURENCE, D. H. "A Bibliographical Novitiate: In Search of
Henry James." Papers of the Bibliographical Society of
America, 52 (January-March), 23-33.
A report of his "personal bibliographical novitiate"
while working on the James bibliography with Edel (see
1957.A3). Provides caveats and recommendations for the
bibliographer, mentions examples of following his intui-
tion to a logical conclusion, and remarks on valuable
sources of bibliographic information. See 1958.B73.

54 LEVY, LEO B. "Henry James and the Jews: A Critical Study."
Commentary, 26 (September), 243-49.
Examines James' treatment of Jewish figures in his
works. "James's reactions to the Jew whom he perceived as
the mythical figure of anti-Semitic lore--and to the alien
--whose presence on American soil aroused acute distrust--
reveal a general uneasiness." James' "upper-class attitude" is one of "carefully regulated disdain...," which
displays "well-established New England feelings about the
alien and show him to be a member of a literary tradition
in which the Jew had long been suspiciously regarded."

55 LEWIS, NAOMI. "In Spite of Lit." Twentieth Century (August),
pp. 114-25.
Refers to Daisy Miller in a discussion of women and
literature. James "was never...unfair to women in the way
in which women are to themselves."

1958

56   McELDERRY, B. R., JR. "Henry James's 'The Art of Fiction.'"
      <u>Research Studies of the State College of Washington</u>, 25
      (March), 91-100.
            In "The Art of Fiction," James "defines his conception
      of fiction." Discusses the circumstances of the essay's
      publication and "its relation to the international discus-
      sion of fiction in the late 19th century." Suggests that
      "despite the excellence of James's essay, and his promi-
      nence as a novelist, little attention was paid to it for
      more than forty years after its publication. James's
      theoretical interest was apparently ahead of his time."

57   MARSDEN, MALCOLM M. "Discriminating Sympathy: Charles Eliot
      Norton's Unique Gift." <u>New England Quarterly</u>, 31 (Decem-
      ber), 463-83.
            Charles Eliot Norton attempted "to induce James to be-
      come a man of letters," and offered "an example of culture
      for him to emulate," influencing some of his important
      attitudes.

58   MARTIN, TERENCE J. "James's 'The Pupil': The Art of Seeing
      Through." <u>Modern Fiction Studies</u>, 4 (Winter), 335-45.
            "The Pupil" provides an example of what James termed
      "'seeing through,'" in that the structure is composed of a
      group of interdependent revelations which define characters
      and dramatic situation. Through Pemberton, we see Morgan;
      through Morgan, the rest of the family; through both, we
      see through the Moreens and even Pemberton himself. Morgan
      sees into "the chaos of self," achieves the supreme vision
      and is destroyed by it." He "mastered the art and paid the
      price of seeing through." <u>See</u> 1959.B39. Reprinted: in
      Jane P. Tompkins, ed. <u>Twentieth Century Interpretations</u>
      <u>of "The Turn of the Screw" and Other Tales</u>, pp. 11-21.

*59   MATSUHARA, IWAO. "Introduction and Notes," in <u>The Real Thing</u>.
      Tokyo: Yamaguchi Shoten. Cited in Beatrice Ricks, comp.
      <u>Henry James: A Bibliography of Secondary Works</u>, #955.

60   MORRIS, WRIGHT. "Henry James's <u>The American Scene</u>." <u>Texas</u>
      <u>Quarterly</u>, 1 (Summer-Autumn), 27-42.
            Attempts to discover "What is an American?" from the
      exile. Discusses James' qualifications to write <u>The Ameri-</u>
      <u>can Scene</u>, his detachment, his point of view as that of an
      outsider but also that of a conscious native. "We now live
      in a world that he grasped better than we grasp it our-
      selves." James was the first to view the American scene
      from the <u>present</u>, which resulted in consistently prophetic
      impressions. Reprinted: 1958.B61.

61   MORRIS, WRIGHT. "Objects and Places," in The Territory Ahead.
      New York: Harcourt, Brace and Co., pp. 187-214.
          Reprint of 1958.B60.

62   MORRIS, WRIGHT. "Use of the Past," in The Territory Ahead.
      New York: Harcourt, Brace and Co., pp. 93-112.
          "In Henry James, America had come of age...." His de-
      fect as a novelist is that "The material seems missing,"
      and "...out of craft one cannot conjure up the grand pas-
      sion." James' subject "was consciousness," "the root of
      his style--parenthesis." Describes him as "the bridge
      between the past that made sense, the real past, and the
      present that does not."

63   NOWELL-SMITH, SIMON. "Without Benefit of Bibliography: Some
      Notes on Henry James." Book Collector, 7 (Spring), 64-67.
          Describes his collection of James materials, with ref-
      erence to bibliographies of James' works such as those by
      LeRoy Phillips (1930.A2) and I. R. Brussel (1936.B5).
      Praises the Edel/Laurence volume (see 1957.A3) as "indis-
      pensable" to scholars, and suggests that "The twin Achil-
      les' heels of bibliographers dealing with this period are
      the differentiation of editions, impressions and issues,
      and the description of the colours of cloths."

64   PODHORETZ, NORMAN. "Edmund Wilson, the Last Patrician--II."
      Reporter, 20 (8 January), 32-35.
          "One guesses that Wilson's self-image is of an American
      who has combined the 'internationalist idea of Henry James
      with the 'republican patriotism' of Lincoln...."

65   POWERS, LYALL H. "James's The Tragic Muse: Ave Atque Vale."
      Publications of the Modern Language Association, 73
      (June), 270-74.
          The Tragic Muse heralded the presumed end of novel writ-
      ing and the advent of a dramatic career, and indicates
      James' attitude to this new phase, the central theme of the
      work being the "conflict between art and 'the world.'"
      Examines the relationship between the artist and his in-
      spiration: "The celibate artist, the chaste, and their
      incorporeal, spiritual intercourse" is the prevailing pat-
      tern in the novel. In the Nick/Miriam relationship, James
      projected the problem of approaching the theatre with both
      artistic and mercenary motives, and Nash represents "the
      ultimate author of artistic inspiration--a divinity...."
      See 1959.B19.

1958

66   SLABEY, R. M. "Henry James and 'The Most Impressive Conven-
      tion in All History.'" American Literature, 30 (March),
      89-102.
          Seeks to determine James' attitudes to and opinions re-
      garding Catholicism as revealed in his early work in order
      to explain more fully an important period in his life and
      work, his European stays between 1869 and 1874. Examines
      five short stories set in Italy, Watch and Ward, Roderick
      Hudson, Transatlantic Sketches and contemporary letters.
      Suggests that James was drawn to Catholicism for aesthetic
      reasons and found there many consoling features, and that
      he treated Catholicism with unqualified fairness.

67   SNOW, LOTUS. "The Disconcerting Poetry of Mary Temple: A
      Comparison of the Imagery of The Portrait of a Lady and
      The Wings of the Dove." New England Quarterly, 31 (Sep-
      tember), 312-39.
          Imagery of The Portrait of a Lady and The Wings of the
      Dove compared, with emphasis on the effect Mary Temple had
      as a model for both Isabel Archer and Milly Theale. The
      theme of betrayal in both novels is stressed. Reprinted:
      in Lyall Powers, ed. Studies in "The Portrait of a Lady,"
      pp. 80-93.

68   STAFFORD, WILLIAM T. "James Examines Shakespeare: Notes on
      the Nature of Genius." Publications of the Modern Lan-
      guage Association, 73 (March), 123-28.
          Explores the relationship of James to Shakespeare as
      revealed in James' memoirs, letters, critical prefaces,
      notebooks and literary and dramatic criticism, including
      his introduction to The Tempest, his "most detailed and...
      considered comment." The investigation suggests James'
      view of literary genius and illuminates his story, "The
      Birthplace." Enumerates four attitudes toward literary
      greatness, "all unconventional," and concludes that James
      "was inspired both to project a definition of Shakespeare's
      talent and to make a persuasive plea for the rich rewards
      of proper critical attention to that talent."

69   STAFFORD, WILLIAM T. "The 'Americanism' of Henry James:
      Quentin Anderson and Van Wyck Brooks." Western Review,
      22 (Winter), 155-60.
          Points out "a significant and illuminating relationship"
      between Anderson's The American Henry James (see 1957.A1)
      and Brooks' The Pilgrimage of Henry James (see 1925.A1).
      "Both are centrally concerned with James's American roots.
      Both tie the so-called Jamesian morality to these roots.
      And both attribute the (comparative) artistic failure of

James's last novels to the condition of his relationship
to this American morality." Discusses the thesis of each
work, examines their differences. Paradoxically, "That
which Brooks contends Henry James could not do <u>without</u>
Anderson contends James could not exclusively get along
<u>with</u>," i.e., American sources.

70   STALLMAN, R. W. "Who Was Gilbert Osmond?" <u>Modern Fiction
     Studies</u>, 4 (Summer), 127-35.
         Examines similarities between Gilbert Osmond in <u>The
     Portrait of a Lady</u> and Henry B. Brewster, a friend of
     James', concluding that Brewster's "germinal connection
     with Gilbert Osmond dominates all other potential in-
     spirers including Francis Boott."

71   STALLMAN, R. W. "The Houses that James Built: <u>The Portrait
     of a Lady</u>." <u>Texas Quarterly</u>, 1 (Winter), 176-96.
         Notes that "the scene at the opera house which opens
     Book II of <u>The Portrait of a Lady</u> initiates a decline in
     the heroine's subsequent destiny, a falling away from the
     romantic arch of her soaring aspirations culminating in the
     final scene of Book II at St. Peter's Cathedral." These
     scenes, "pivotal to James's ironic rendering of his hero-
     ines' romantic and self-deluded quest," are related to
     emphasize the reversal of Isabel's intentions. Describes
     the novel as an edifice, demonstrates that the houses in
     the work "serve to interpret their inhabitants metaphoric-
     ally" and "represent the accumulated refinement and cor-
     ruption of civilization, our tragic history echoing through-
     out the House of Experience." The contrast between illu-
     sions and reality provides the substance of the novel.
     Partially reprinted: in Peter Buitenhuis, ed. <u>Twentieth
     Century Interpretations of "The Portrait of a Lady</u>,"
     pp. 37-44.

72   STEWART, RANDALL. "Guilt and Innocence," in <u>American Litera-
     ture and Christian Doctrine</u>. Baton Rouge: Louisiana State
     University Press, pp. 102-106.
         James, like Hawthorne, "was concerned with the loss of
     innocence, and the snares of a refined egotism." Views
     many of James' protagonists as learners in "a variation of
     the theme of the fortunate fall," and notes the author's
     concern with "insidiousness of egotism" in Gilbert Osmond
     and John Marcher, the latter of whom he analyzes in some
     detail. Labels Hawthorne, Melville, and James "'counter-
     romantics' because they recognize Original Sin, because
     they show the conflict between good and evil, because they

1958

show man's struggle toward redemption, because they drama-
tize the necessary role of suffering in the purification
of the self."

73 STOTT, R. TOOLE. "Letter to the Editor." Papers of the Bib-
    liographical Society of America, 52 (October-December),
    29-30.
       Takes exception to Laurence's suggestion (see 1958.B53)
    that Stott's adoption of the "British Colour Council's
    Dictionary of Colours in describing cloths, was arbitrary
    and irrational." A weakness in Laurence's bibliography
    (see 1957.A3) is his use of contradictory terms in describ-
    ing bindings, and Stott defends his own method as "more
    consistent and less liable to error...."

74 SWAN, MICHAEL. "Boasting of Henry James," in A Small Part of
    Time: Essays on Literature, Art, and Travel. London:
    Jonathan Cape, pp. 139-45. Reprinted: Chester Springs,
    Pa.: Dufour Editions, 1961.
       In an essay which originally appeared in Punch, Swan
    reminisces about meeting with an American James enthusiast,
    who recounts his discovery of an item in James' desk, de-
    cribes various boasts concerning James which suggest the
    comments of "rival lovers of the same beautiful women...,"
    and reproduces a conversation with James' valet.

75 SWAN, MICHAEL. "Henry James and H. G. Wells: A Study of
    Their Friendship Based on Their Unpublished Correspond-
    ence," in A Small Part of Time: Essays on Literature, Art,
    and Travel. London: Jonathan Cape, pp. 173-204. Re-
    printed: Chester Springs, Pa.: Dufour Editions, 1961.
       Reprint of 1953.B59.

76 SWAN, MICHAEL. "Henry James and the Heroic Young Master,"
    in A Small Part of Time: Essays on Literature, Art, and
    Travel. London: Jonathan Cape, pp. 43-57. Reprinted:
    Chester Springs, Pa.: Dufour Editions, 1961.
       Reprint of 1955.B66.

77 TAKANO, FUMI. "The Women in the Novels of Henry James."
    Tsuda Review, no. 3 (November), pp. 3-13.
       James' important women characters can be categorized as
    idealists or realists, and "James's novels develop through
    the antagonism and conflict between...these two types."
    Examines The Portrait of a Lady to show how Isabel, the
    idealist, "is created and motivated."

78   TILFORD, JOHN E., JR. "James the Old Intruder." Modern Fic-
     tion Studies, 4 (Summer), 157-64.
        Disputes the view that The Ambassadors is an outstanding
     example of maintainance of a single point of view in
     Strether. Examination of the novel shows that the center
     is by no means always in Strether's consciousness, and that
     James often interposed, that there are authorial intrusions
     throughout the work. Suggests that James was so close to
     the literary conventions of the nineteenth century that he
     couldn't completely eschew them, enjoying the prerogatives
     of intrusive authorship. Reprinted: in Albert E. Stone,
     ed. Twentieth Century Interpretations of "The Ambassadors,"
     pp. 66-74.

79   TILLYARD, E. M. W. "Interlude: Henry James," in The Epic
     Strain in the English Novel. Fair Lawn, N.J.: Essential
     Books, pp. 121-25.
        Although James' best loved work is in the "general idiom
     of comedy," The Bostonians and The Princess Casamassima
     were James' attempts, albeit unsuccessful, at "novelty...of
     the epic kind."

80   TYLER, PARKER. "Texts out of Context." Chicago Review, 12
     (Spring), 67-73.
        In response to 1957.B22, the collection of James' let-
     ters to the New York Tribune, suggests that the newspaper
     achieved in this correspondence "a new literary tone," and
     that James represented "a cult of intelligence isolated
     from its natural habitat of being 'well-informed.'" Ana-
     lyzes James as a journalist, and concludes that his "im-
     portant characters are dedicated to the search for knowl-
     edge of self and others, while epidemic newspaper readers,
     privately as publicly, are dedicated to sampling the day's
     events and guzzling its gossip."

81   TYLER, PARKER. "The Child as 'The Figure in the Carpet.'"
     Chicago Review, 11 (Winter), 31-42.
        Suggests that the child is "the figure" of James' car-
     pet, referring both to that "symbolic offspring of the
     artist, his fictional progeny" as well as to actual chil-
     dren in his stories. Finds authority for his claim in the
     prefaces. Considers James' "acutal and personal views of
     marriage for an artist" in "The Lesson of the Master" and
     examines "The Figure in the Carpet." For James, moral
     character determines sexual virtue. Sex is a "beast in the
     jungle" to James, to be destroyed and "resurrected in a
     higher form. As 'the figure in the carpet," this pattern

1958

of resurrection, this 'child' of the wisdom of life, can
be traced over and over in James's works.

82 VALLETTE, JACQUES. "Une amitie litteraire et sa fin."
    Mercure de France, 333 (August), 706-708. (French)
       In the exchange of letters in Edel and Ray's Henry
    James and H. G. Wells (see 1958.A2), James is "by far the
    stronger because he demolishes systematically, and Wells
    preserves." Describes the relationship between the two
    writers which culminated in Wells' Boon, the result of
    "long exasperation from profound antagonism." The work
    "suggests between the two men a strong difference of moral
    stature."

83 VOLPE, EDMOND L. "The Reception of Daisy Miller." Boston
    Public Library Quarterly, 10 (January), 55-59.
       Notes discrepancy between reports that Daisy Miller was
    objected to on the basis of the portrait of the heroine
    and the generally favorable reviews in contemporary maga-
    zines, and concludes that the work "perturbed many readers,
    particularly women, but not the critics."

84 VOLPE, EDMOND L. "James's Theory of Sex in Fiction."
    Nineteenth-Century Fiction, 13 (June), 36-47.
       Examines James' attitude toward sex in the novel as ex-
    pressed in his essay "The Future of the Novel." James "did
    not deny it [sex] a dominant role in human experience; he
    simply left out of his novels all descriptions of it as a
    physical passion," and his "treatment of sex was delicate,
    subtle, oblique...a logical result of his personal concep-
    tion of the novel and of his artistic aim: to portray
    man's inner world as skillfully and artistically as the
    French writers had depicted man's sensual and physical
    existence."

85 WALBRIDGE, EARLE F. "'The Whole Family' and Henry James."
    Papers of the Bibliographical Society of America, 52
    (April-June), 144-45.
       Points out several errors in Edel/Powers article re-
    printing James' letters to Elizabeth Jordan (see 1958.B28).

86 WEGELIN, CHRISTOF. "Henry James and the Aristocracy." North-
    west Review, 1 (Spring), 5-14.
       James' ties to American tradition are apparent in his
    treatment of the aristocracy. Examines The American as
    illustrative of this point, showing the conflict between a
    "natural" and an "artificial" conception of nobility in

the contrast between Newman and the Bellegardes. Concludes
that for James, "man's nobility lies not in his rank but in
his moral nature," which suggests James' "commitment to the
democratic ideology of his country." Restatement of thesis
in 1958.A7, pp. 38-43.

87 WEGELIN, CHRISTOF. "Henry James's The Wings of the Dove as an
     International Novel." Jahrbuch für Amerikastudien, 3: 151-
     60.
          Slightly altered version of material in 1958.A7. James
     pictured the contrast between "'character' and 'culture'"
     in The Wings of the Dove, a novel of "initiation and con-
     version" which presents "the American experience of Europe,
     the European experience of America."

88 WELLEK, RENÉ. "Henry James's Literary Theory and Criticism."
     American Literature, 30 (November), 293-321.
          A consideration of James' stature as a critic suggests
     that he is "by far the best American critic of the nine-
     teenth century," with a "well-defined theory" and point of
     view allowing him "to characterize sensitively and evaluate
     persuasively a wide range of writers...." Examines James'
     critical aims, the influence of Sainte-Beuve and Arnold,
     among others, his view of art and its function, and con-
     cludes that James "holds fast to the insights of organistic
     aesthetics and thus constitutes a bridge from the early
     nineteenth century to modern criticism."

89 WOODRESS, JAMES. "Henry James." Publication of the Modern
     Language Association, 73 (April), 204-205.
          International listing of books and articles on James
     which appeared during the previous year.

90 WRIGHT, NATHALIA. "Henry James and the Greenough Data."
     American Quarterly, 10 (Fall), 338-43.
          Examines James' relationship with the Greenough family,
     who, like the Jameses, spent much of their time in Europe.
     The acquaintance, which extended over most of James' adult
     life, was "responsible for the development of some of his
     most distinctive characterizations and the creation of some
     of his greatest scenic effects." James gathered data for
     his works from association with the Greenoughs, who repre-
     sented "an international cultural phenomenon" of trans-
     planted Americans with artistic consciousness.

1958

91 ZABEL, MORTON D. "Introduction," in <u>The Art of Travel:
    Scenes and Journeys in America, England, France, and Italy
    from the Travel Writings of Henry James</u>. Doubleday Anchor
    Books. Garden City, N.Y.: Doubleday and Co., pp. 1-48.
    Reprinted: Freeport, N.Y.: Books for Libraries Press,
    1970.
        A consideration of the "special conditions and circum-
    stances of his [James'] life--his origins, his nationality,
    his sense of history, and the moment of modern history he
    was given to record"; his place in the "novel of displace-
    ment," of exploration and travel, which he helped to es-
    tablish; and a description of his travel writings as re-
    vealing "intelligence, sympathy and imagination." Examines
    the relationship of James' travels to his achievement as
    an artist, and suggests that they "obliged him to be crit-
    ic, analyst and moralist."

92 ZABEL, MORTON D. "Introduction," in <u>In the Cage and Other
    Tales</u>. Doubleday Anchor Books. Garden City, N.Y.:
    Doubleday and Co., pp. 1-28.
        In introducing a collection which reprints "eight tales
    of Henry James's high maturity," Zabel discusses his pre-
    sentation of major themes in the concentrated form of the
    <u>nouvelle</u>, and analyzes <u>In the Cage</u>, in which the telegraph-
    ist is a representative of the Jamesian "caged" character.
    The work is an "essential key to reading James," whose
    tales "hinge on the test of spiritual or moral truth and
    the inescapable proof it imposes on characters." Defines
    the central subjects in the stories anthologized, all
    "tales of the crisis, dilemma, isolation, or decision to
    which the necessity of moral choice brings a man...."

1959 A BOOKS

1 BRASCH, JAMES D. "The Relation of Theme and Setting in the
   Major Novels of Henry James." Ph.D. dissertation, University of Wisconsin.
       An investigation of James' theory and use of setting
   reveals the influence of Balzac, Hawthorne and Taine and
   suggests that his "settings, in addition to providing overtones and elucidating character, tempered, embellished and
   illuminated his chosen psychological themes."

2 HOLDER-BARELL, ALEXANDER. <u>The Development of Imagery and Its
   Functional Significance in Henry James's Novels</u>. Cooper
   Monographs on English and American Language and Literature,
   No. 3. Bern: Francke Verlag, 215 pp. Reprinted: New
   York: Haskell House, 1966.

The "development in James's application of imagery" is
traced, demonstrating "how the functional significance of
his metaphors underwent a similar development." James'
imagery functions in many ways, and groups of images are
established and analyzed, including "The Rhetorical Image,"
"The Expanding Image," "The Characterizing Image," and "The
Constructive Image," showing "a rising line in functional
significance up to the transition from mere metaphor into
general symbols." Reviewed: Edwin T. Bowden, <u>American
Literature</u>, 32 (March 1960), 92-93; Harold T. McCarthy,
<u>Modern Language Notes</u>, 75 (November 1960), 615-16.

3   PARQUET, MARY E. "Henry James: The Bliss and the Bale."
    Ph.D. dissertation, University of Nebraska.
        James uses his themes to elucidate his philosophical
    view of life as a mixture of good and evil. His approach
    "accounts not only for his penetrating psychological
    studies of his characters but also for the moral dilemmas
    in which he places his protagonists...." According to
    James, "it is only by accepting the close connexion of the
    bliss and the bale that life may be experienced at all."

1959 B SHORTER WRITINGS

1   ALLOTT, MIRIAM. <u>Novelists on the Novel</u>. London: Routledge
    and Kegan Paul; New York: Columbia University Press,
    passim. Reprinted: 1960, 1962, 1967.
        In a chronological collection of comments on the nature
    and craft of fiction by novelists, prefaced by editorial
    introductions, several excerpts of James' discussions of
    the art of the novel are included, in addition to numerous
    references by Allott to James' descriptions of the genesis
    of the novel and his theory of narrative technique.

2   ALVAREZ, A. "Intelligence on Tour." <u>Kenyon Review</u>, 21 (Win-
    ter), 23-33.
        James' essays on travel (1958.B91) represent what has
    been left out or implied in his novels. The "harmony and
    incandescence" of his work depends upon them. Much of
    James' social analysis and in-depth probings of his sur-
    roundings were prompted by "a distaste for his own fate."

3   BASHORE, J. ROBERT, JR. "The Villains in the Major Works of
    Nathaniel Hawthorne and Henry James." Ph.D. dissertation,
    University of Wisconsin.
        "James's villains develop in fairly regular four-year
    phases marked by aesthetic as well as ethical shifts, each
    major novel subsuming the qualities of villains in a

preceding run of short stories." Contrasts and compares villains in Hawthorne and James.

4   BASKETT, S. S. "The Sense of the Present in 'The Aspern Papers.'" <u>Papers of the Michigan Academy of Science, Arts, and Letters</u>, 44: 381-88.
    The continuing appeal of <u>The Aspern Papers</u> is due not to the atmosphere of early nineteenth-century Venice but to "the moral life of the late nineteenth century narrator," whom Baskett analyzes. His "Prufrockian mannerisms, his aplomb, the gradual revelation of his true moral nature, all obscure his real character" as "a man who inhabits a spiritual wasteland, removed from all meaningful inter-course with human kind, past or present."

5   BAUMGAERTEL, GERHARD. "The Reception of Henry James in Germany." <u>Symposium</u>, 13 (Spring), 19-31.
    A survey of German criticism on James, with remarks on the "strong and rising" contemporary interest which began at the time of recovery from World War II. Notes early attempts to introduce James to the German public, lists works in translation since 1946, notes dramatizations of James' works, and suggests that German critiques generally concentrate on "the collision and beneficial conflict between young, inexperienced, naïve Americans and representatives of mature Europe, the old hierarchy of values...."

6   BAUMGAERTEL, GERHARD. "The Concept of the Pattern in the Carpet: Conclusions from T. S. Eliot." <u>Revue Des Langues Vivantes</u>, 25 (July-August), 300-306.
    An analysis of T. S. Eliot's understanding of the concept of "the pattern in the carpet." "...<u>The pattern</u> is distinguished by the attributes of metaphysical writing," and "produces the immediate experience of life in art--rather than reflections about life. It provides the experience especially of that non-material part of life which signifies a projection beyond a particular occurrence and the cause of which remains concealed. It is, further, a creative inner compulsion...."

7   BELL, MILLICENT. "Edith Wharton and Henry James: The Literary Relation." <u>Publications of the Modern Language Association</u>, 74 (December), 619-37.
    "In the landscape of Edith Wharton's life the figure of Henry James is of almost too-distracting importance." Disputes "the conclusion that she was merely a copy of the master," and examines her works as they do or do not reflect Jamesian concerns, techniques and intentions.

Concludes that "the object most native to her talent from first to last" was "scrutiny of society, the outward rather than the inward gaze."

8   BELL, VEREEN M. "Character and Point of View in Representa-
     tive Victorian Novels." Ph.D. dissertation, Duke Univer-
     sity.
         An examination of "changing concepts of character" and
     "adjustments of fictional method," which suggests that
     James conveyed his personal vision of moral order by re-
     producing the mind's atmosphere; "his standard of behavior
     is relative to the situation in which the moral act is
     conceived."

9   BERKELMAN, ROBERT. "Henry James and 'The Real Thing.'" Uni-
     versity of Kansas City Review, 26 (Winter), 93-95.
         A reexamination of "The Real Thing" reveals that "what
     is real in life does not become real in art until the
     artist not merely duplicates it, but transforms it with
     insight." Concludes that "in art 'the real thing' is in-
     genious make-believe; in life 'the real thing' is quiet
     heroism, a tough grace under pressure."

10   BEWLEY, MARIUS. "The Verb to Contribute." Spectator, (24
     July), pp. 114-15.
         In a review of Mordell's volume (1957.B50), discusses
     James' early reviews, the kind of critic he became, the
     "central proposition" and style of his later criticism,
     and concludes that for James, the "values of art" were
     "its high freedom, its moral seriousness, its organic
     wholeness, its relation with life...."

11   BEWLEY, MARIUS. "Henry James and 'Life,'" in The Eccentric
     Design: Form in the Classic American Novel. New York:
     Columbia University Press, pp. 220-44.
         Reprint of 1958.B9.

12   BEWLEY, MARIUS. "Henry James and the Economic Age," in The
     Eccentric Design: Form in the Classic American Novel.
     New York: Columbia University Press, pp. 243-58.
         Considers James' horror of the economic age as corrupt-
     ing the quality of life, and examines the varying roles
     economic matters play in his work, his "transition from a
     conception of the millionaire as a symbolic embodiment of
     those New World possibilities...to the wistful figure of
     the 'good' American...finding salvation, in the rejection
     of his millions."

1959

13   BLACKMUR, RICHARD P. "Introduction," in The Aspern Papers;
      The Spoils of Poynton. Edited by R. P. Blackmur. New
      York: Dell Publishing Co., pp. 5-18.
           In The Aspern Papers and The Spoils of Poynton, "a con-
      science is created which achieves a deep human action, and
      from one to another there is a rising level of intensity
      and a rising degree of involvement." Describes James as
      "the master of naïvety in the sense that Dante was the
      master of disgust."

14   BLACKMUR, RICHARD P. "Introduction," in Washington Square;
      The Europeans. Edited by R. P. Blackmur. New York: Dell
      Publishing Co., pp. 5-12.
           Urges the reader to read James for pleasure, suggests
      continuity in the characters of Washington Square and The
      Euorpeans and James' later works. Discusses the heroines,
      variations of the "American Princess," in the two novels,
      which incorporate social comedy and instinctive allegory.

15   BRODERICK, J. C. "Nature, Art, and Imagination in The Spoils
      of Poynton." Nineteenth-Century Fiction, 13 (March), 295-
      312.
           The Spoils of Poynton implies "that disembodied artistic
      perceptiveness is more admirable than if it had lost its
      freedom and been committeed [sic] to form...." The novel
      represents "a kind of esthetic parable," a "continuing por-
      trait of the artist" in which Fleda Vetch symbolizes "'im-
      agination' or 'insight,' the indispensable first requisite
      in the art of fiction as understood and practiced by Henry
      James."

16   BUITENHUIS, PETER. "From Daisy Miller to Julia Bride: 'A
      Whole Passage of Intellectual History.'" American Quarter-
      ly, 11 (Summer), 136-46.
           James believed that the manners and talk of American
      women had deteriorated by the early 1900's, and Julia
      Bride, a companion piece to Daisy Miller, chronicled his
      sense of the change in a characteristic type. Julia views
      her society from a new perspective of knowledge and judg-
      ment, thus embodying the transition of consciousness of the
      American girl from innocence to experience.

17   BUITENHUIS, PETER. "Henry James on Hawthorne." New England
      Quarterly, 32 (June), 207-25.
           James' five separate evaluations of Hawthorne's achieve-
      ment at different points in James' life "reveal consider-
      able changes of opinion" and show how he learned "different

things from his predecessor at various stages in his development." In these evaluations a key can be found to the shift in James' attitudes toward America.

18   CANBY, HENRY SEIDEL. "Hero of the Great Know-How," in The Saturday Review Gallery. New York: Simon and Schuster, p. 98.
Reprint of 1951.B6.

19   CARGILL, OSCAR. "Gabriel Nash--Somewhat Less than Angel?" Nineteenth-Century Fiction, 14 (December), 231-39.
Rebuttal of Power's thesis in 1959.B71 that The Tragic Muse is a valedictory to the novelist's art and his view of Nash as "'an angelic messenger'" (see 1958.B65). Enumerates his objections to Power's suggestions, and maintains that Nash has many traits in common with Wilde (see 1957.B11), is "a poseur," "a remarkably resourceful witty human, but not a divine guide."

20   CLAIR, J. A. "The American: A Reinterpretation." Publications of the Modern Language Association, 74 (December), 613-18.
Hypothesizes that Mrs. Bread, the real mother of Claire de Cintre, blackmailed both Newman and the Marquise de Bellegarde; that Newman was taken in by her; and that Claire's refusal to marry Newman was a direct result of her having been informed by the Bellegardes of her true parentage.

21   COONEY, SÉAMUS. "Grammar vs. Style in a Sentence from 'Roderick Hudson.'" Notes and Queries, 204 (January), 32-33.
Points out a "grammatical lapse" in the final sentence of Roderick Hudson which appears in the New York edition, and suggests correction.

22   CROW, CHARLES R. "The Style of Henry James: The Wings of the Dove," in Style in Prose Fiction: English Institute Essays: 1958. New York: Columbia University Press, pp. 172-89.
Reprint of 1958.B24.

23   DAHLBERG, EDWARD and HERBERT READ. "A Literary Correspondence." Sewanee Review, 67 (Spring-Summer), 177-203, 422-45.
In an exchange of letters on literary topics, Dahlberg and Read reveal their views on James. Dahlberg deplores James' lack of energy, describes him as "the canniest peeping male that ever observed feminine habits" and "an

1959

exquisite mediocrity." Read defends James, pointing out
that Dahlberg's is "an argument ad hominem" unsubstantiated
by evidence. "Art...has its saints and martyrs, its proph-
ets and evangelists, and for me Henry James has something
in him of them all."

24   DAVIS, DOUGLAS M. "The Turn of the Screw Controversy: Its
     Implications for the Modern Critic and Teacher." Graduate
     Student of English, 2 (Winter), 7-11.
        Suggests that the controversy over The Turn of the Screw
     "is directly related not only to certain prevalent notions
     about the nature of 'serious' fiction but...to the 'expli-
     cation racket' itself." Surveys the spectrum of interpre-
     tations that refute the idea that James was simply writing
     a ghost story, which interpretations reveal the contemporary
     distaste "for simplicity of motives or form" and the in-
     creasing number of scholarly articles.

25   EDEL, LEON. "Introduction," in The Ambassadors. Edited by
     Leon Edel. Riverside Editions. Boston: Houghton Mifflin
     Co., pp. v-xvi.
        In The Ambassadors, James is concerned "with the process
     of living and with human relations" presented in a "large,
     ironic, comic vision." Describes the work as "the first
     truly 'modern' novel" because of the point of view of mak-
     ing the "reader one with Strether." Examines the style of
     the work and the difficulties of its idiosyncracies. "It
     is seeing that is the subject of the novel, perception at
     the pitch of awareness...."

26   EDEL, LEON. "Introduction," in The Sacred Fount. London:
     Rupert Hart-Davis, pp. 5-15.
        Points out difficulties in The Sacred Fount, which ap-
     peared in 1901 "to be...a wasteful expenditure of great
     novelistic resources...." Presents background information
     on the novel, analyzes the character of the narrator and
     his reliability, and describes the work as "a psychological
     mystery in the tradition...of Sherlock Holmes...." The
     question of reality intrigued James, and The Sacred Fount
     is one of the works in which "the central figure, possessed
     of great curiosity," attempts "to muddle out a human en-
     vironment and human relationships, but not possessed of all
     the necessary data to assuage the curiosity." See
     1953.B18.

*27 EDEL, LEON et al. "Henry James," in Masters of American Lit-
     erature. Shorter Edition. Boston: Houghton Mifflin, The
     Riverside Press, pp. 972-78.

1959

Abridged version of volume edited by Pochmann and Allen, 1949.B42.

28   ELLIOTT, GEORGE P. "Getting Away from the Chickens." <u>Hudson Review</u>, 12 (Autumn), 386-96.
      In a light essay, reminisces about his reactions to <u>The Princess Casamassima</u> and about his summer spent tending chickens. "...The great thing about <u>The Princess</u> seemed to be this: it's Burroughs for sophisticates." Likens James' revolutionaries to the "half-men half-apes" in the Tarzan legend, describes both Burroughs and James as "blatant snobs," and concludes that "...there's a lot more Tarzan to Hyacinth Robinson than they led me to believe."

29   FEUERLICHT, IGNACE. "'Erlkönig' and <u>The Turn of the Screw</u>." <u>Journal of English and Germanic Philology,</u> 58 (January), 68-74.
      Points out similarities between <u>The Turn of the Screw</u> and Goethe's "Erlkönig" "in the mood of old sacred terror,' in the basic themes, in the reality of the 'apparitions,' in the motives of supernatural evil, of extraordinary beauty of children, of sexual perversion, and of sudden and mysterious death," and in the abrupt conclusion.

30   FLINN, H. G. and HOWARD C. KEY. "Henry James and Gestation." <u>College English</u>, 21 (December), 173-75.
      In <u>The Portrait of a Lady</u>, the timetable suggests that Isabel's baby was born just six months after her marriage. Authors point out several possible explanations, including the suggestion that Isabel conceived the child out of wedlock. "...If Henry James seems vague on gestational processes, he has a legitimate excuse. He was, after all, a bachelor."

31   FORSTER, E. M. "Henry James and the Young Men." <u>Listener</u>, 62 (16 July), 103.
      In response to Woolf's recollections (see 1959.B100), describes his own experiences on having tea with James as recorded in his diary.

32   FOX, HUGH, JR. "Henry James and the Antimonian [sic] James Household: A Study of Selfhood and Selflessness." <u>Arizona Quarterly</u>, 15 (Spring), 49-55.
      A moralist writing in the transcendental tradition of selfhood being "man's aim in life," James came from a family tradition which "modified this selfhood to ultimately end in selflessness." Given these terms, Strether "is the ideal man."

33   FRANTZ, JEAN H. "A Probable Source for a James <u>Nouvelle</u>."
      <u>Modern Language Notes</u>, 74 (March), 225-26.
        The telegraphist's dilemma in <u>In the Cage</u> is "inversion"
      of that encountered by the butler in "Brooksmith."

34   FUKUMA, KIN-ICHI. "The Ambiguity of <u>The Princess Casamassima</u>."
      <u>Kyusha American Literature</u> (Fukuoka, Japan), no. 2 (May),
      pp. 6-11.
        In <u>The Princess Casamassima</u>, the major "point is be-
      lieved to be the <u>bewilderment</u> of the people in the novel,
      of the writer himself, and the expected bewilderment on the
      side of the readers--that is nothing but the real experi-
      ences of life." The "<u>doubt</u> [about Christina] becomes one
      great <u>motif</u> of the composition." Examines sources of be-
      wilderment in the novel.

35   GALE, ROBERT L. "Henry James's Dream Children." <u>Arizona</u>
      <u>Quarterly</u>, 15 (Spring), 56-63.
        James' use of children draws upon his remembered child-
      hood, and he often yokes together the world of the child
      and of the adult by observing "curiously mature" children
      and "singularly immature" adults.

36   GALE, ROBERT L. "Henry James and Chess." <u>Chess Life</u>, 14
      (5 December), 12.
        James' "use of chess as the basis for several similes
      and metaphors in his fiction proves that he knew little or
      nothing about it." Gives examples of inappropriateness or
      faulty development of chess images, concluding that James
      "was many things...but he was not a chess-player. His was
      the loss, and so is ours."

37   GARGANO, JAMES W. "Foreshadowing in <u>The American</u>." <u>Modern</u>
      <u>Language Notes</u>, 74 (December), 600-601.
        In The American, the opera scene from <u>Don Giovanni</u>
      forecasts the heroine's final retreat to the convent and
      lays the ground for Newman's suffering. Questions whether
      James fictionally exploited the opera in response to
      Flaubert's use of <u>Lucie de Lammermoor</u> in <u>Madame Bovary</u>.

38   HAFLEY, JAMES. "Malice in Wonderland." <u>Arizona Quarterly</u>,
      15 (Spring), 5-12.
        Poe and James have distinctly American and identical
      views of the "connection between life and art," wherein a
      character must choose either life or art, as demonstrated
      by "The Oval Portrait" and <u>The Portrait of a Lady</u>.

39   HAGOPIAN, JOHN V. "Seeing through 'The Pupil' Again." Modern
      Fiction Studies, 5 (Summer), 169-71.
          Questions Martin's interpretation of "The Pupil" (see
      1958.B58), and suggests that Pemberton "is a villain only
      in terms of modern existentialist tragedy," that his is "a
      tragic decision and a tragic act committed out of stern
      necessity," and that to equate him with the Moreens "is to
      betray a lack of psychological insight and a lack of moral
      compassion for Pemberton's own terrible plight."

40   HARKNESS, BRUCE. "Bibliography and the Novelistic Fallacy."
      Studies in Bibliography: Papers of the Bibliographical
      Society of the University of Virginia, 12: 59-73. The
      "modern critic is apt to be entirely indifferent to the
      textual problems of a novel," as illustrated by F. R.
      Leavis' quoting of James in The Great Tradition.

41   HOLLAND, L. B. "The Wings of the Dove." English Literary
      History, 26 (December), 549-74.
          A consideration of fate or "fortune" in The Wings of
      the Dove, a novel which suggests "that for James an Ameri-
      can heroine's destiny (like the American heritage) could
      be complex, embracing without obliterating the social
      realities that are implicit in the vast fortune she pos-
      sesses." Examines the work in view of "areas of relevance"
      suggested by three phrases, and concludes that "The novel's
      vision yields itself, as the form reveals itself, in its
      spendthrift waste of passion...the tragic waste which is
      the appalling cost of Milly's tragic triumph."

42   HONIG, EDWIN. "Conception," in Dark Conceit: The Making of
      Allegory. Evanston, Ill.: Northwestern University Press,
      pp. 51-52.
          Restates ideas in 1958.B50, in a volume which "explores
      the methods and ideas that go into the making of literary
      allegory."

43   HORNE, HELEN. "Henry James: The Real Thing (1890): An At-
      tempt at Interpretation." Die Neueren Sprachen, 8 (May),
      214-19.
          In "The Real Thing," James proposes "different views
      about art and even the ambiguous nature of art itself."
      The "artist's ideas, not just our own...are gradually
      molded to conform with those of James himself," with the
      suggestion that art is a complicated matter, "a matter of
      experience...born of those rare hours when we pass beyond
      the surfaces of things to the heart beneath."

1959

44   HOVEY, RICHARD B.   "The Voice of One," in <u>John Jay Chapman:</u>
      <u>An American Mind</u>. New York: Columbia University Press,
      pp. 118-19, 152-53, 157.
          Quotes James' reaction to Chapman's essay "Emerson,"
      and remarks on Chapman's view of James as indicated in an
      1883 letter and a "devastating critique of James's drama-
      tised version of <u>Daisy Miller</u>." Compares James and Chap-
      man as critics.

45   JONES, ALEXANDER E.   "Point of View in <u>The Turn of the Screw</u>,"
      <u>Publications of the Modern Language Association</u>, 74
      (March), 112-22.
          Discussion of the critical controversy of the point of
      view in <u>The Turn of the Screw</u>, an analysis of the gover-
      ness' personality, and a consideration of the reality of
      the ghosts concluding that the Freudian view of the tale
      is unjustified, that <u>The Turn of the Screw</u> is a "classical
      ghost story," "fundamentally a study of tone," of "uncer-
      tainty, helplessness, terror," in which the governess saves
      the children, routing the forces of evil in an immortal
      battle. Reprinted: in Gerald Willen, ed. <u>A Casebook on</u>
      "The Turn of the Screw," pp. 298-318.

46   JONES, LLEWELLYN.   "Henry James and Spiritual Democracy."
      <u>Humanist</u>, 19 (June), 156-64.
          Labels James a "symbolist," and asserts that his "spir-
      itual democracy" was "based on a sensibility sharpened by
      the circumstances of his upbringing and given an immense
      gamut by his near-cosmopolitanism."

47   KEYNES, GEOFFREY.   "Henry James in Cambridge."   <u>London Maga-</u>
      <u>zine</u>, 6 (March), 50-61.
          Keynes and two friends met annually in Cambridge on New
      Year's Eve, when each chose someone he admired and sent a
      greeting. James was chosen by one present, and responded.
      Keynes reprints the correspondence which developed as a
      result and describes James' visit to Cambridge in June,
      1909, to meet the trio.

48   KNOX, GEORGE.   "Reverberations and <u>The Reverberator</u>."   <u>Essex</u>
      <u>Institute Historical Collections</u>, 95 (October), 348-54.
          Julian Hawthorne's journalistic career is "the major
      stimulus" in James' drafting of <u>The Reverberator</u>.

49   KOCMANOVÁ, JESSIE.   "The Revolt of the Workers in the Novels
      of Gissing, James, and Conrad."   <u>Brno Studies in English</u>,
      1: 119-39.

Describes the nationwide stirring of workers in the
1880's and '90's in Britain, and examines The Princess
Casamassima, aimed at expressing "the reality he [James]
imagined lay behind the London streets," although James
confused "revolutionary socialism with anarchistic terror-
ism." Like Gissing's Demos, James' novel poses the question of "revolutionary action vs. culture, art, refinement,"
failing, however, to solve or even confront the issue.
"The conspiratorial world which James describes ...is a
revolutionary socialist movement without the workers—a
contradiction in terms."

50   KRETSCH, ROBERT W.   "Political Passion in Balzac and Henry
      James." Nineteenth-Century Fiction, 14 (December), 265-
      70.
          Examines and compares Balzac's Histoire des Treize and
      James' The Princess Casamassima, both fictional treatments
      of politico-revolutionary movements of the nineteenth
      century. Whereas Balzac portrays dynamic unity, James
      offers the reader a contrived unity. Balzac is specific
      and intense, while James is circuitous and external, sug-
      gesting the hopelessness of his characters achieving whole-
      ness. The passionate completeness that intrigued Balzac
      became the fragmentation of the individual in James.

51   KROOK, DOROTHEA.   "Principles and Methods in the Later Works
      of Henry James," in Interpretations of American Literature.
      Edited by Charles Feidelson, Jr. and Paul Brodtkorb, Jr.
      New York: Oxford University Press, pp. 262-79.
          Revised version of 1954.B26, concluding that "in a mind
      like James's the philosophic, analytic passion is all of a
      piece with the poetic and intuitive."

52   LAINOFF, SEYMOUR.   "A Note on Henry James's 'The Pupil.'"
      Nineteenth-Century Fiction, 14 (June), 75-77.
          Although the family is instrumental in causing the boy's
      death in "The Pupil," the tutor/narrator is also culpable
      in that he is incapable of freeing the child from his sur-
      roundings, lacking moral courage. The tale is concerned not
      only with the "triumph of mendacity over sensitivity," but
      also with the eternal loneliness of the human spirit.

53   LANG, HANS-JOACHIM.   "Henry James, 1955-1958: Ein Litera-
      turbericht." Jahrbuch für Amerikastudien, 4: 191-219.
      (German)
          A description of scholarship on James written between
      1955 and 1958, divided into discussions of bibliographies,
      texts and manuscripts, emphasizing the Soho bibliography

1959

(1957.A3); biographical works, stressing the Wells-James
relationship and Edel's biography (1953.A2); and general
studies, including reviews of edited anthologies and collections of James' work, discussions of studies of James'
relationship to America, and surveys of works of Bowden
(1956.A1), Crews (1957.A2), Levy (1957.A6), and Hoffmann
(1957.A4). Also reviews special James numbers of
Nineteenth-Century Fiction and Modern Fiction Studies in
1957.

54 LEWIS, R. W. B. "The Histrionic Vision of Henry James."
Jahrbuch für Amerikastudien, 4: 39-51.
Investigates how religious experience is portrayed in
James' fiction, the means of communicating the experience.
"James and his contemporaries tended to regard the writer
as God..." and his "ardent seekers" have as their goal
that of the pilgrim: "a vision of divine reality" which
they seek "in the world conceived as a stage, and in experience made histrionic." The characters "create afresh,
through the free play of consciousness, the nature and the
names of the sins man is prone to." James possessed a
"histrionic sensibility...of the highest order," the activity of which is the "dialectical process made flesh."
Examines religious experience in The Wings of the Dove,
in which James makes "visible and plausible an experience
of grace."

55 LEYBURN, E. D. "Virginia Woolf's Judgment of Henry James."
Modern Fiction Studies, 5 (Summer), 166-69.
Questions why Woolf failed to acknowledge James, from
whom she learned "one after another of the striking features of her art," in her essay "Mr. Bennett and Mrs.
Brown." Suggests that the omission is due to her viewing
James as a dramatic rather than a lyric genius, and her
instinctive feeling that she could therefore not learn
from him, particularly in regard to method, despite the
similarity of intention and interest. James' "way of revealing human life was not Virginia Woolf's way of ap-
proaching the truth of Mrs. Brown...."

56 LOCHHEAD, MARION. "Stars and Striplings: American Youth in
the Nineteenth Century." Quarterly Review, 297 (April),
180-88.
With reference to James' autobiographical works, remarks on his European visit as a child and its part in
his education. James was reared in an environment "where
literature mattered more than dogma and culture more than
piety; where the puritan heritage was shown not in any

1959

repudiation or prohibition, but in a fastidious selective-
ness from the riches of art and learning.... His genius
could flower only by being transplanted to older soil."

57   LOMBARDO, AGOSTINO. "La critica letteraria di Henry James."
      Belfagor, 14 (31 January), 23-38. (Italian)
         A study of James as a literary critic. Enumerates
      James' critical output, reviews previous judgments of his
      effectiveness as a literary critic. Suggests that James
      was a well-rounded critic of all forms of literary art
      except poetry, and that his critical opinions were chan-
      neled through his emotional sensibilities, thus causing
      him occasionally to get too wrapped up in his own percep-
      tions.

*58   LOMBARDO, AGOSTINO. "Introduction," in L'arte del romanzo.
      Milan: C. M. Lerici editore. Cited in "1959 Annual Bib-
      liography." Publications of the Modern Language Associa-
      tion, 75 (May 1960), 253.

59   LUDWIG, RICHARD M. "Henry James," in Bibliography Supplement:
      Literary History of the United States. Edited by Robert
      Spiller et al. New York: The Macmillan Co., pp. 144-48.
         An updating of the 1948 bibliography (see 1948.B23)
      to 1958.

60   LYDE, MARILYN JONES. "The Artistic Value of the Theory of
      Morality and Convention," in Edith Wharton: Convention
      and Morality in the Work of a Novelist. Norman: Univer-
      sity of Oklahoma Press, pp. 164-65.
         Reference to James in discussion of the manner in which
      Wharton "offset the triviality of American convention...."

61   LYDE, MARILYN JONES. "Effect of Wealth upon Convention and
      Morality," in Edith Wharton: Convention and Morality in
      the Work of a Novelist. Norman: University of Oklahoma
      Press, pp. 118-19.
         Wharton's account of her first meeting with James.

62   MARTIN, W. R. "The Use of the Fairy-Tale: A Note on the
      Structure of The Bostonians, a Novel by Henry James."
      English Studies in Africa, 2 (March), 98-109.
         Examination of the fairy tale elements in The Bostoni-
      ans, including references to "'witches'" and trappings of
      the "romance," Verena as "the fairy-tale heroine," and
      Ransom as the "knight in armour" who must rescue the maiden

1959

in the den. "James uses the submerged archetypal 'tale'" for a moral purpose and to poke sophistaicated fun at his characters and situations."

63   SISTER MARY FRANCIS. "Henry James's Theory of Literary Invention." Greyfriar. Siena Studies in Literature, 2: 3–19.
     Examines James' theory of literary invention, based on his remarks in the prefaces and using examples from The American. Defines and gives background of the term "invention," shows how James' view of the concept differs from Samuel Johnson's. "...Henry James is traditional." Details his view of how the artist gets the idea for a work, its germination, and the process of development. Concludes with an eleven point summary of James' position. Like Pope, he "saw the abiding values in the traditional and made them his own."

64   MILLGATE, MICHAEL. "The Novelist and the Businessman: Henry James, Edith Wharton, Frank Norris." Studi Americani, no. 5, pp. 161–89.
     Discusses the importance of the businessman as subject for the American novelist, notes James' view of the difficulty of writing on a business theme and his romantic conception of business figures. James' comments in his essay "The Question of Opportunities" (1898) assist in an understanding of the "problems of the business novel," and serve as "touchstones in assessing the work of other novelists." Analyzes Christopher Newman of The American and Adam Verver of The Golden Bowl as "the most important of James' business characters," and concludes that James responded "eagerly to the appearance of new novelistic material, however far it might seem to be outside the conceivable boundaries of his own interests as a creative artist."

65   MONTGOMERY, MARION. "The Flaw in the Portrait: Henry James vs. Isabel Archer." University of Kansas City Review, 26 (March), 215–20.
     "A brief survey of Isabel's character will...help demonstrate a serious aesthetic flaw" in The Portrait of a Lady, "which results from James's ultimate failure to let structure as well as subject, characters and setting evolve." Isabel moves from one "romantic extreme" to another, from vague freedom to blind duty, and the novel fails to reach its full potential. James "gives two portraits of Isabel Archer rather than one, the first being considerably out of proportion to the second."

66 MOORE, JOHN ROBERT. "An Imperfection in the Art of Henry
     James." Nineteenth-Century Fiction, 13 (March), 351-56.
          Considers what happens when James dealt with a subject
     with which he lacked familiarity, as in The American,
     which displays inconsistencies, lack of reality, and is
     "essentially as plot-ridden as a conventional melodrama or
     a 'well-made' play by Scribe." Describes Newman as "vague,
     lifeless, and even flatly contradictory." The conclusion
     of the novel is "predestined for the story by a wilfull
     blindness to character or by an imperfect sense of lit-
     erary art."

67 MURAKAMI, FUJIO. "The Creation of The Golden Bowl." Jimbun
     Kenkyu (Osaka City University), 10 (July), 117-31. (Japan-
     ese)
          Comments on James' conception of The Golden Bowl with
     reference to his notebook entries; discusses why the work
     developed from a short story into a novel, changes in the
     original plot, characteristics of James' art such as his
     view of "reality," and the importance of character. Exam-
     ines the symbolic meaning of the golden bowl.

68 NOWELL-SMITH, SIMON. "Editing James." Times Literary Supple-
     ment (3 July), p. 399.
          Disputes Rosenbaum's claim (see 1959.B78) that Jacobean
     scholars generally overlooked James' "variant revisions of
     magazine texts for more or less simultaneous American and
     English book editions," and notes exceptions.

69 OLIVER, CLINTON F. "Introduction," in The Princess Casamas-
     sima. Edited by Clinton F. Oliver. Torchbook Edition.
     New York: Harper and Brothers, pp. 5-22.
          Both The Princess Casamassima and The Bostonians deal
     with social themes, and "James's attitude on social reform
     gathers its fullest expression" in the former work. Ana-
     lyzes the characters in this "elaborate experiment in
     autobiography" in which James imaginatively projects him-
     self into Hyacinth's personality. Notes influence of Zola
     on the novel, with its "biological determinism."

70 PANTER-DOWNES, MOLLIE. "Letter from London." New Yorker,
     35 (12 September), 153-54.
          In Redgrave's adaptation of The Aspern Papers (see
     1959.B75) his "H. J. seems merely an intrusive bounder when
     deprived of the intellectual reasoning that James works out
     in the story--a disturbing thought to James admirers."

1959

71 POWERS, LYALL H. "Mr. James's Aesthetic Mr. Nash--Again."
    Nineteenth-Century Fiction, 13 (March), 341-49.
        Disputes Cargill's thesis that Nash in The Tragic Muse
    is a satiric portrait of Wilde (see 1957.B11), and suggests
    that "James used himself as a model for Nash, particularly
    in view of his life-long admiration of Balzac...." Inter-
    prets novel as "James's metaphoric projection of his prob-
    lem of deciding to give up novel writing to become a
    playwright...." Although Wilde may have influenced the
    depiction of Nash in the early part of the novel, James
    "put too much of himself into Nash to handle him very
    satirically at all." For Cargill's response, see 1959.B19.

72 POWERS, LYALL H. "The Portrait of a Lady: 'The Eternal Mys-
    tery of Things.'" Nineteenth-Century Fiction, 14 (Septem-
    ber), 143-55.
        The form of The Portrait of a Lady is a pattern traced
    by Isabel's career, which is defined in the polarity be-
    tween Ralph Touchett and Gilbert Osmond. Analyzes the
    character of Isabel, who constantly tries to penetrate the
    eternal mystery, to solve the problem of duty to husband
    and the truth of Ralph's sentiments about him. At the
    conclusion of the work, Isabel does not regain her pre-
    lapsarian innocence, but achieves a "higher innocence,
    that superior goodness, which comes to the fallen who are
    saved." Thus, "The career of Isabel Archer has the com-
    pleteness of form of the familiar pattern of redemption, of
    the fortunate fall."

73 RAHV, PHILIP. "Attitudes to Henry James," in Image and Idea:
    Fourteen Essays on Literary Themes. Norfolk, Conn.:
    New Directions Press, pp. 63-70.
        Reprint of 1943.B39.

74 RAHV, PHILIP. "The Cult of Experience in American Writing,"
    in Image and Idea: Fourteen Essays on Literary Themes.
    Norfolk, Conn.: New Directions Press, pp. 42-70.
        Expanded version of 1937.B13.

75 REDGRAVE, MICHAEL, ed. The Aspern Papers; A Comedy of Letters.
    London: Samuel French, 80 pp.
        A theatrical adaptation of The Aspern Papers in three
    acts.

76 ROSENBAUM, S. P. "Two Henry James Letters on The American
    and Watch and Ward." American Literature, 30 (January),
    533-37.

Reprints two letters from James to his publisher discussing arrangement for publication of The American and
Watch and Ward which reveal James' early habit of revision, and his attitude toward his first novel as a "bal-
anced combination of self-confidence and self-criticism."

77 ROSENBAUM, S. P. "Letters to the Pell-Clarkes from their
    'Old Cousin and Friend' Henry James." American Literature,
    31 (March), 46-58.
    A consideration of the relationship between the Temples
    and the Jameses as evidenced in two letters James wrote
    to his first cousin, Henrietta Temple Pell-Clarke and her
    husband, Leslie, which Rosenbaum reprints. "...For James,
    communion with the Pell-Clarkes meant not only the sharing
    of plans, regrets, and other personal details, but also
    the communication of the memories and hopes that prompted
    the tenderness and affection conveyed in these letters to
    old cousins and friends."

78 ROSENBAUM, S. P. "The Spoils of Poynton." Times Literary
    Supplement (26 June), p. 385.
    The Spoils of Poynton was serialized as "The Old Things"
    in The Atlantic Monthly, 1896, and then revised exten-
    sively for variant English and American editions, suggest-
    ing "that the revisions of James's fiction are considerably
    more complex than has generally been realized." Discusses
    nature of textual changes, sequence of revision. See
    1959.B68 for Nowell-Smith's reply.

79 SPANOS, BEBE. "The Real Princess Christina." Philological
    Quarterly, 38 (October), 488-96.
    Identifies the Princess Casamassima with "the 'brilliant,
    delicate, complicated' Princess Belgiojoso, nee Christina
    di Trivulzio." Suggests similarities to James' heroine:
    "the lives of the two match closely in details, both moved
    among many different classes and were artists of 'uncon-
    ventional self-drama,'" scorned convention, moved towards
    political extremism, and had parallel personal relation-
    ships. James described the Princess Belgiojoso in his
    Story biography.

80 STAFFORD, WILLIAM T. "Lowell 'Edits' James: Some Revisions
    in French Poets and Novelists." New England Quarterly,
    32 (March), 92-98.
    Critical comments made by James Russell Lowell in a
    letter to James account for some revisions in the second
    edition of French Poets and Novelists.

1959

81 STAFFORD, WILLIAM T. "William James as Critic of His Brother
    Henry." The Personalist, 40 (Autumn), 341-53.
        A detailed study of William James' criticism of Henry,
    in terms of "intrinsic critical worth as Jamesian criti-
    cism, in terms of the critical Jamesian issues which it
    brings to the front, in terms of its critical method, and
    in terms of William's unusual critical position as member
    of the same family which produced the famous novelist."
    Suggests that William's assessment is "Both sensitive and
    irritatingly obtuse, but always apparently honest," and
    exhibits "some of the best and some of the worst facets
    of American criticism appearing during the lifetime of his
    brother."

82 STEIN, WILLIAM BYSSHE. "The Portrait of a Lady: Vis Iner-
    tiae." Western Humanities Review, 13 (Spring), 177-90.
        Views Isabel as a dramatic embodiment of sexual inertia,
    a version of Henry Adams' caricature of the sexless Ameri-
    can woman who desires to compete with the male on his terms
    and with his same kind of power. Isabel's attitude toward
    normal human emotions betrays her womanhood: She "is a
    product of...indiscriminate meddling with the natural im-
    pulses of the female nature...." Reprinted: in William
    Stafford, ed. Perspectives on James's "The Portrait of a
    Lady," pp. 166-83.

83 STEIN, WILLIAM BYSSHE. "'The Pupil': The Education of a
    Prude." Arizona Quarterly, 15 (Spring), 13-22.
        Views "The Pupil" as a "comedy of Americano-European
    legend." The "prudish" Pemberton is the antithesis of the
    "Bohemian" Moreens, whom James did not intend to be "moral
    criminals." Pemberton is "dupe of a fanciful code of re-
    spectability..." and "ends up holding an untranslatable
    form of experience." Reprinted: in Jane P. Tompkins, ed.
    Twentieth Century Interpretations of "The Turn of the
    Screw" and Other Tales, pp. 22-28.

84 STEIN, WILLIAM BYSSHE. "The Aspern Papers: A Comedy of
    Masks." Nineteenth-Century Fiction, 14 (September), 172-
    78.
        The tone of The Aspern Papers is one of "amusement" and
    irony. Points out facets of comic action in the narrative,
    and suggests that the tone corresponds with the inverted
    Don Juan theme of the novel.

85 THURBER, JAMES. "Onward and Upward with the Arts: The Wings
    of Henry James." New Yorker, 35 (7 November), 188-201.

334

The Wings of the Dove represents "a kind of femme fatale
of literature, exerting a curiously compelling effect upon
authors, critics, playwrights, producers and publishers."
Discusses adaptations of the novel into drama, reminisces
about his experience of reading James in college, remarks
on the "James Revival," and states that "Henry James was
at home in the dark and in the light and in the shadows
that lie between." James chose bachelorhood because his
vocation was inconsonant with marriage. "He loved vicari-
ously, though, and no man more intensely and sensitively."
Reprinted: in Lanterns and Lances, London: Hamish Hamilton, 1961, pp. 88-105.

86 TILLOTSON, KATHLEEN. The Tale and the Teller. London: Rupert Hart-Davis, passim.
    Consideration of narrative in which the teller is appar-
ent, and of the relationship between the teller and the
tale. "Most novel-criticism now takes its criteria from
the later Henry James, applying what might be called late
Jacobean standards to Victorian and eighteenth-century
novelists." James was a decisive force in the repudiation
of authorial intrusion.

87 VANDERBILT, KERMIT. "Norton's Reputation in the Twentieth
Century," in Charles Eliot Norton: Apostle of Culture in
a Democracy. Cambridge, Mass.: Harvard University Press,
The Belknap Press, pp. 225-26 and passim.
    James' sympathetic essay on Norton, written in 1914, is
discussed. Through him, "James had gained a close acquaint-
ance with English society" which he made use of in the international novel.

88 VAN DOREN, MARK. "Introduction," in Washington Square.
Edited by Mark Van Doren. Bantam Classics. New York:
Bantam Books, pp. v-ix.
    Describes Washington Square as "a comedy, obedient to
its author's genius. And James must have aimed in it at
some sort of mastery. Nor did he fail of his aim.... It
is master work." Analyzes Dr. Sloper and Catherine, whose
conflict of wills provides the substance of the novel.

89 VAN GHENT, DOROTHY. "On The Portrait of a Lady," in Interpretations of American Literature. Edited by Charles Feidelson, Jr. and Paul Brodtkorb, Jr. New York: Oxford University Press, pp. 244-61.
    Reprint of 1953.B63.

1959

90   VOLPE, EDMOND L. "The Spoils of Art." <u>Modern Language Notes</u>,
     74 (November), 601-608.
         James' <u>The Spoils of Poynton</u> "does not have one logic,
     one truth, one direction." Demonstrates the "loss of
     artistic authority" in the novel.

91   WALSH, WILLIAM. "Henry James and a Sense of Identity." <u>Lis-
     tener</u>, 62 (6 August), 205-206.
         James' "work is part of the <u>realization</u> of a self [ital-
     ics mine]." Considers "the outer world of American society
     and the inner world of his own family" as the circumstances
     out of which James constructed his sense of identity, and
     between which there existed an "element of discrepancy, of
     stress, a kind of structural paradox..." which was influ-
     ential in his development.

92   WALSH, WILLIAM. "IV [Comment on Henry James]," in <u>Autobiog-
     raphical Literature and Educational Thought</u>. Leeds: Uni-
     versity Press, pp. 20-28.
         "The formation of a personal identity amid the complica-
     tions of society" is the "theme" of James' autobiographical
     works.

93   WALSH, WILLIAM. "Maisie in <u>What Maisie Knew</u>," in <u>The Use of
     Imagination: Educational Thought and the Literary Mind</u>.
     London: Chatto and Windus, pp. 148-63. Reprinted: New
     York: Barnes and Noble, 1960.
         Remarks on the child as a critic of adult society, ex-
     amines James' attempt to solve the "technical problem of
     presenting the relation of child to adult...," and de-
     scribes the plot of <u>What Maisie Knew</u> as having "the charac-
     teristic symmetry of a Jamesian scheme." Analyzes Maisie,
     discusses the stages in her development. The second half
     of the novel focuses on the theme of "existence of Maisie's
     moral sense," as pointed out in three scenes.

94   WARD, JOSEPH A. "Social Criticism in James's London Fiction."
     <u>Arizona Quarterly</u>, 15 (Spring), 36-48.
         In the works of 1897-1901, James uses the egotism, ma-
     terialism and pragmatism of London as the "basis for social
     criticism" in which he moves from the "social flaws of ma-
     terialism" to the very "nature of evil itself."

95   WARD, JOSEPH A. "<u>The Ambassadors</u>: Strether's Vision of
     Evil." <u>Nineteenth-Century Fiction</u>, 14 (June), 45-58.
         Strether deals with two kinds of evil, American and Eu-
     ropean, and ultimately discovers the proper relationship
     between art and morality. His experience yields "a discovery

of the fullness of life, for Europe itself, which embodies
the deeds of man at his finest and of man at his worst."
Madame de Vionnet represents a personal symbol of Europe,
"weak and mortal humanity, redeemed by beauty and grace."

96 WARD, JOSEPH A. "Henry James's America: Versions of Oppres-
    sion." Mississippi Quarterly, 13 (Winter), 30-44.
        Discusses James' "vision of evil in America" as deline-
    ated in his earlier works. Simplicity is the most striking
    feature of James' America, coupled with an America of op-
    pression, where evil results from "an intense provincialism
    that breeds aggressive narrow-mindedness; in moderation, it
    is a complacent ignorance of the value of foreign experi-
    ence." Looks at The Europeans and The Bostonians in which
    James attacked the New England ethos.

97 WASSERSTROM, WILLIAM. "Fortune's Darlings," in Heiress of All
    the Ages: Sex and Sentiment in the Genteel Tradition.
    Minneapolis: University of Minnesota Press, pp. 56-67.
        The Wings of the Dove is viewed as a tragedy in which
    "James mined the vein of materialism inherent in the in-
    ternational plot...." Daisy Miller "announces the central
    motifs of James's imagination, their incorporation in the
    classic international plot."

98 WASSERSTROM, WILLIAM. "Nymph and Nun," in Heiress of all the
    Ages: Sex and Sentiment in the Genteel Tradition. Minne-
    apolis: University of Minnesota Press, pp. 87-98.
        Examines Washington Square (as a counterpart of Howells'
    A Modern Instance) which represents "the nature of love
    itself, its place in human affairs...." Also considers the
    father/daughter relationship in The Golden Bowl, in which
    Maggie "combined the qualities of a nymph and a nun" and
    "fulfilled the American dream of love...." James' career
    expressed "this Socratic vision: before an American woman
    can achieve her destiny--to reorder the world through the
    effect of Love--she must herself learn the meaning of love."

99 WOODRESS, JAMES. "Henry James." Publications of the Modern
    Language Association, 74 (May), 172.
        An international listing of books and articles on James
    which appeared during the previous year.

100 WOOLF, LEONARD. "Henry James and the Young Men." Listener,
    62 (9 July), 53-54.
        Autobiographical account in which Woolf discusses his
    (and his friends') reaction to the "elusive novels" of
    James' last period, describes James' shocked reaction to

1959

daughters of Sir Leslie Stephen and their companions,
Saxon Sydney-Turner and Lytton Strachey. Nevertheless,
James showed "genuine kindliness and real feeling for
Leslie Stephen and for the great beauty of his wife and
daughters." See 1959.B31 for Forster's response.

Appendix A

Critical Anthologies (post 1959)
Referenced in the Text

BUITENHUIS, PETER, ed. Twentieth Century Interpretations of "The Portrait of a Lady": A Collection of Critical Essays. Englewood Cliffs, N.J.: Prentice-Hall, 1968.

EDEL, LEON, ed. Henry James: A Collection of Critical Essays. Twentieth Century Views. Englewood Cliffs, N.J.: Prentice-Hall, 1963.

POWERS, LYALL H., comp. The Merrill Studies in "The Portrait of a Lady." Charles E. Merrill Studies. Edited by Matthew J. Bruccoli and Joseph Katz. Columbus, Ohio: Charles E. Merrill Publishing Co., 1970.

STAFFORD, WILLIAM T., ed. Perspectives on James's "The Portrait of a Lady": A Collection of Critical Essays. New York: New York University Press; London: University of London Press, 1967.

STONE, ALBERT E., JR., ed. Twentieth Century Interpretations of "The Ambassadors": A Collection of Critical Essays. Englewood Cliffs, N.J.: Prentice-Hall, 1969.

TOMPKINS, JANE P., ed. Twentieth Century Interpretations of "The Turn of the Screw" and Other Tales: A Collection of Critical Essays. Englewood Cliffs, N.J.: Prentice-Hall, 1970.

WILLEN, GERALD, ed. A Casebook on Henry James's "The Turn of the Screw." New York: Thomas Y. Crowell Co., 1960.

Appendix B

Dissertations Not Listed in *Dissertation Abstracts*

1   JONES, WALTER P. "An Examination of Henry James's Theory and
     Practice of Fiction." Cornell University, 1925.

2   GARNIER, MARIE-REINE. "Henry James et la France." University
     of Strasbourg, 1927. See 1927.A2.

3   BORCHERS, LOTTE. "Frauengestalten und Frauenprobleme bei Henry
     James (Ein Beitrag zur amerikanischen Literaturgeschichte)."
     Greifswald University, 1929. See 1929.A1.

4   HOFF, LLOYD M. "The Revision of Roderick Hudson: Its Extent,
     Nature, and Result." Ohio State University, 1930.

5   DUB, FRIEDERIKE. "Die Romantechnik bei Henry James." University
     of Vienna, 1933.

6   THOMAS, WILLIAM A. "Henry James: A Study in Realism from the
     Beginnings in the First Quarter of the Nineteenth Century to
     1870." University of Pennsylvania, 1934.

7   BOGOSIAN, EZEKIEL. "The Perfect Gentleman: A Study of an Es-
     thetic Type in the Novels of Richardson, Jane Austen, Trollope,
     and Henry James." University of California at Berkeley, 1937.

8   PENFIELD, LIDA S. "Henry James and the Art of the Critic."
     Boston University, 1938.

9   DIFFENÉ, PATRICIA. "Henry James. Versuch einer Würdigung seiner
     Eigenart." Marburg University, 1939. See 1939.A1.

10 GUTSCHER, MARIANNE. "Henry James und Walter Pater." University
     of Vienna, 1940.

11 DUNBAR, VIOLA. "Studies in Satire and Irony in the Works of
     Henry James." Northwestern University, 1941.

12 NOEL, FRANCE. "Henry James, peintre de la femme." University of
     Paris, 1942. See 1942.A1.

13 FOLEY, RICHARD N. "The Critical Reputation of Henry James in
    American Magazines from 1866 to 1916." Catholic University,
    1943. See 1944.A1.

14 DEMEL, ERIKA VON ELSWEHR. "Die Wertwelt von Henry James." Uni-
    versity of Vienna, 1944.

15 LECLAIR, ROBERT C. "Three American Travellers in England:
    James Russell Lowell, Henry Adams, Henry James." University
    of Pennsylvania, 1944. See 1945.B32.

16 FINCH, GEORGE A. "The Development of the Fiction of Henry James
    from 1879 to 1886." New York University, 1947.

17 WEISSMANN, LEOPOLDINE. "Edith Wharton Romankunst und ihre Beein-
    flussung durch Henry James." University of Vienna, 1947.

18 LIND, SIDNEY E. "The Supernatural Tales of Henry James: Con-
    flict and Fantasy." New York University, 1948.

19 CHEN, LUCY M. "The Ancestry of The Wings of the Dove." Univer-
    sity of Chicago, 1949.

20 FORRESTER, ANDREW D. "Henry James et la France." University of
    Lyon, 1949.

21 LUCAS, JOHN S. "Henry James's Revision of His Short Stories."
    University of Chicago, 1949.

22 McCARTHY, HAROLD T. "The Aesthetic of Henry James." Harvard
    University, 1950. See 1958.A3.

23 STONE, EDWARD. "Henry James and His Sense of the Past." Duke
    University, 1950.

24 KREHAYN, JOACHIM. "Henry James und seine Stellung zu England
    oder der Bürger auf der Suche nach der Bürgerlichkeit."
    University of Berlin, 1951.

25 MURRAY, DONALD M. "The Critical Reception of Henry James in
    English Periodicals, 1875-1916." New York University, 1951.

26 SAUER, EDWIN H. "Henry James: The Symbols of Morality in the
    Novels of the Middle Period, 1881-1900." University of Cin-
    cinnati, 1951.

27 BOWDEN, EDWIN T., JR. "The Novels of Henry James: An Approach
    Through the Visual Arts." Yale University, 1952. See 1956.A1.

28 BÜSCHGES, GISELA. "Die Kultureinwirkung Europas auf den Ameri-
    kaner bei Henry James." Freiburg University, 1952.

29 ELDERDICE, ROBERT A. "Henry James's Revisions of His Early Short
    Stories and Short Novels." University of Maryland, 1952.

30 FIREBAUGH, JOSEPH J. "Henry James and the Law of Freedom."
    University of Washington, 1952.

31 MARKOW, GEORGE. "Henry James et la France (1842-1876)." Uni-
    versity of Paris, 1952.

32   BEEBE, MAURICE L. "The Alienation of the Artist: A Study of
     Portraits of the Artist by Henry James, Marcel Proust and
     James Joyce." Cornell University, 1953.

33   BERLAND, A. "Henry James and the Nature of Civilization."
     Cambridge University, 1953-54.

34   STADER, KARL-HEINZ. "Die Bewusstseinskunst von Henry James."
     University of Bonn, 1953.

35   BAUMGÄRTEL, WERNER. "Henry James im Spiegel moderner englisher
     Literaturkritik." University of Tübingen, 1954.

36   BENNETT, BARBARA L. "The Ethics of Henry James's Novels."
     University of North Carolina, 1954.

37   FICK, OTTO W. "The Clue and the Labyrinth: The Mind and Tem-
     perament of Henry James." University of Chicago, 1954.

38   HALL, WILLIAM F. "Society and the Individual in the English
     Fictions of Henry James, 1885-1901." Johns Hopkins Univer-
     sity, 1954.

39   LEVY, LEO B. "Versions of Melodrama in the Novels, Tales, and
     Plays of Henry James: 1865-1897." University of California
     at Berkeley, 1954. See 1957.A6.

40   SPANOS, B. "The Essential Henry James: The American Years,
     1843-1870." University of London, 1954-55.

41   BUITENHUIS, PETER. "The American Henry James." Yale University,
     1955.

42   LOWE, ALMA L. "The Travel Writing of Henry James." Rice Uni-
     versity, 1955.

43   WOELFEL, KARL. "Dramaturgische Wandlungen eines epischen Themas
     bei Dramatisierung und Verfilmung, dargestellt an Henry
     James's Washington Square." Erlangen University, 1955.

44   PRAUSNITZ, WALTHER G. "The Craftsmanship of Henry James: A
     Study of the Critical Reviews, 1864-1884." University of
     Chicago, 1956.

45   SAVESON, MARILYN B. "The Influence of Emile Zola upon the Theory
     and Practice of Some English Novelists of His Time [Henry
     James, George Moore, George Gissing, and Arnold Bennett]."
     Cambridge University, 1956.

46   SÖLTER, URSULA. "Die Romanauffassung bei Henry James und in der
     englischen Literaturkritik der 1920er Jahre." University of
     Mainz, 1956.

47   STAFFORD, WILLIAM T. "The American Critics of Henry James:
     1864-1943." University of Kentucky, 1956.

48   STEINKAMP, EGON. "Das Fremdheitserlebnis bei Henry James: Die
     Mächte Europa und Amerika im Leben und Work des Schriftstel-
     lers." Münster University, 1956.

49 HOFMANN, GERT. "Interpretationsprobleme bei Henry James ('The Turn of the Screw,' 'The Sacred Fount,' 'The Figure in the Carpet')." Freiburg University, 1957.

50 VON KLEMPERER, ELIZABETH G. "The Fiction of Henry James and Joseph Conrad in France: A Study in Penetration and Reception." Harvard University [Radcliffe], 1958.

51 DANKLEFF, RICHARD. "The Composition, Revisions, Reception, and Reputation of Henry James's The Spoils of Poynton." University of Chicago, 1959.

52 MURPHY, EDWARD F. "Henry James and Katherine Anne Porter: Endless Relations." University of Ottawa, 1959.

53 POIRIER, WILLIAM R. "Fiction of Comedy and the Early Henry James." Harvard University, 1959.

54 RAMADAN, A. M. "The Reception of Henry James's Fiction in the English Periodicals Between 1875 and 1890." University of London, 1959-60.

Index

A

Abel, Darrel, 1957.B1
"The Abyss and The Wings of the
    Dove: The Image as a Rev-
    elation," 1956.B37
Adams, Henry, 1938.B1
Adams, J. R., 1943.B1-2
Adams, Mrs. H., 1936.B1
"Addenda to 'Biographical and
    Critical Studies of Henry
    James, 1941-1948,'" 1950.B30
"Address on Henry James by Clif-
    ton Fadiman," 1947.B11
"Address on Henry James by W. H.
    Auden," 1947.B6
Adeney, Marcus, 1943.B3
"Adventures of an Illustrator.
    II: In London with Henry
    James," 1922.B14
"The Aesthetic Idealism of Henry
    James," 1917.B19
"The Aesthetic Object," 1957.B40
"Aesthetics of the Skyscraper:
    The Views of Sullivan, James
    and Wright," 1957.B9
"Affinities for Henry James?,"
    1957.B4
"An Afternoon with Max,"
    1956.B35
Ähnebrink, Lars, 1950.B1
Aiken, Conrad, 1925.B1; 1935.B1-
    2; 1958.B1-3 (rpt.)
Alice James: Her Brothers--Her
    Journal, 1934.B5
"Alice James, Neglected Sister,"
    1944.B4

Allen, Gay Wilson (with Henry A.
    Pochmann), 1949.B42
Allen, Walter, 1954.B1
Allott, Miriam, 1953.B1-5;
    1955.B1-2; 1956.B1; 1959.B1
"The Altar of Henry James,"
    1943.B52; 1945.A1 (rpt.)
Alvarez, A., 1959.B2
Amacher, Richard E., 1953.B6
The Ambassadors, 1948.B47
    (Swinnerton); 1959.B25 (Edel)
"The Ambassadors," 1928.21 (Wil-
    liams); 1951.B56 (Thurber,
    Van Doren and Bryson)
"The Ambassadors: Project of
    Novel," 1934.B16
"The Ambassadors: Strether's
    Vision of Evil," 1959.B95
"The Ambassadors: The Crucifix-
    ion of Sensibility," 1956.B72
"The Ambiguity of Henry James,"
    1934.B37; 1938.B16 (rpt.);
    1945.A1 (rpt.); 1948.B56
    (rpt.); 1948.B57
"The Ambiguity of The Princess
    Casamassima," 1959.B34
"The American," 1931.B19
"The American," 1949.B65
American and European in the
    Works of Henry James, 1920.A1
"The American: A Reinterpreta-
    tion," 1959.B20
"The American as Artist: Henry
    James," 1952.B65
The American Essays of Henry
    James, 1956.B23

"American First Editions: A
Series of Bibliographic
Check-Lists Edited by Merle
Johnson and Frederick M.
Hopkins. Henry James, 1843–
1916," 1923.B10

The American Henry James, 1957.A1

"The American Henry James: A
Study of the Novelist as a
Moralist," 1953.A1

"An American in Paris," 1954.B42

"The 'Americanism' of Henry
James: Quentin Anderson and
Van Wyck Brooks," 1958.B69

"The American Literary Expatriate," 1955.B9

"American Novelists in Italy:
Nathaniel Hawthorne, Howells,
James, and F. Marion Craw-
ford," 1953.B8

The American Novels and Stories
of Henry James, 1947.B31

"The American Problem," 1952.B2

The American Scene, 1946.B4

Anderson, Charles R., 1955.B3–4

Anderson, Quentin, 1946.B1;
1947.B1–2; 1950.B2; 1953.A1;
1957.A1

Anderson, Sherwood, 1953.B7

Andreas, Osborn, 1948.A1

"Anglo-American Relations before
the War: Henry James,"
1928.B19"

"Anglo-Saxon Spinsters and Anglo-
Saxon Archers," 1949.B58

Anon., 1917,B1–2; 1920.B1–3;
1921.B1–2; 1922.B1; 1923.B1;
1928.B1; 1943.B4–7; 1944.B1;
1945.B1; 1946.B2; 1947.B3–5;
1948.B1–2; 1949.B1; 1950.B3;
1955.B5; 1956.B2–5; 1958.B4–5

"Another Turn on James's 'The
Turn of the Screw,'" 1949.B48

Anstey, F., 1936.B2

Anthony, Katherine, 1938.B2

"An Apology for Henry James's
'Tiger Cat,'" 1953.B24

"Appearance and Reality in Henry
James," 1950.B10; 1952.B3
(rpt.)

"The Appreciation of Henry
James," 1947.B19

"Approaches to Henry James,"
1957.B16

Arader, Harry F., 1953.B8

"Archetypes of American Innocence: Lydia Blood and
Daisy Miller," 1953.B34

"The Architecture of Henry
James's 'New York Edition,'"
1951.B16

"Armor against Time," 1934.B19

Arms, George (with William M.
Gibson), 1953.B9

Arnavon, Cyrille, 1951.B1

Arnold, F., 1953.B10; 1954.B2

"Arnold on Ruskin; and Henry
James," 1943.B33

"Art and the Inner Life: Dickinson, James," 1955.B59

"Artful Virtuosity: Henry
James," 1934.B28

"Arthur Machen Pays Tribute,"
1943.B29

"Art Imagery in Henry James's
Fiction," 1957.B28

"The Artist and the Artistic,"
1957.B61

"Artist of Fiction," 1956.B69

"The Art of Fiction," 1951.B13
(Downing); 1955.B51
(Maugham)

"The Art of Henry James,"
1919.B15 (Waugh); 1924.B5
(Edgar)

"The Art of Henry James: The
Ambassadors," 1956.B9

"The Art of Reflection in James's
The Sacred Fount," 1954.B19

The Art of the Novel: Critical
Prefaces, By Henry James,
1934.B3

The Art of Travel: Scenes and
Journeys in America, Eng-
land, France, and Italy from
the Travel Writings of Henry
James, 1958.B91

Arvin, Newton, 1934.B1; 1950.B4;
1956.B6

"As I Remember Henry James,"
1954.B6-7
"As I Saw It from an Editor's
Desk. X: The Fiction of
the Magazine," 1924.B15
"The Aspern Papers: A Comedy
of Masks," 1959.B84
"The Aspern Papers" and "The
Europeans," 1950.B14
"The Aspern Papers: Great-
Aunt Wyckoff and Juliana
Bordereau," 1952.B17
The Aspern Papers; The Spoils
of Poynton, 1959.B13
Asteldi, Maria L., 1940.B1
Atherton, Gertrude, 1932.B1
"'At Isella': Some Horrible
Printing Corrected,"
1943.B1
Atkinson, Brooks, 1950.B5
"At the Grave of Henry James,"
1941.B1, B2 (rpt.)
"At the Play," 1946.B17;
1952.B29
"At the Theatre," 1950.B5
"Attitudes to Henry James,"
1943.B39; 1945.A1 (rpt.);
1949.B46 (rpt.)
Aubrey, G. Jean, 1926.B1;
1927.B1
Auden, Wystan Hugh, 1941.B1,
B2 (rpt.); 1946.B3, B4
(rpt.); 1947.B6; 1948.B3
"Autobiographies of American
Novelists: Twain, Howells,
James, Adams, and Garland,"
1957.B59
Autobiography, 1956.B20
"Autobiography in Fiction: An
Unpublished Review by Henry
James," 1957.B17
The Awkward Age, 1948.B22
Ayscough, John, 1922.B2

B

B., H. S., 1939.B1
"A Backward Glance," 1934.B34
Bailey, John, 1935.B3
Bain, James S., 1940.B2
Baker, Ernest A., 1938.B3

--(with James Packman), 1932.B2
"Balzac and Henry James,"
1951.B19
"Balzac aux États-Unis,"
1950.B47
Bangs, John Kendrick, 1955.B6
Bantock, G. H., 1953.B11
Barrell, Charles Wisner, 1945.B2
Barrett, Clifton Waller, 1950.B6
Barrett, Laurence, 1949.B2
Barrie, J. M., 1938.B4
Barzun, Jacques, 1943.B8;
1945.A1 (rpt.); 1956.B7,
B8 (rpt.)
Bashore, J. Robert, Jr., 1959.B3
Baskett, S. S., 1959.B4
Baumgaertel, Gerhard, 1959.B5-6
Baxter, Annette K., 1955.B7
Beach, Joseph Warren, 1918.A1;
1921.B3; 1931.B1; 1932.B3-6;
1948.B4-5; 1954.A1
"The Beast in Henry James,"
1956.B59
"'The Beast in the Jungle'
The Limits of Method,"
1947.B42
"The Beautiful Genius: Turgen-
ev's Influence in the Nov-
els and Short Stories of
Henry James," 1956.B54
Beebe, Maurice, 1952.B1;
1954.B3
--(with William T. Stafford),
1957.B2
Beer, Thomas, 1923.B2; 1925.B2
Beerbohm, Max, 1930.B1;1936.B3;
1946.B5
"Before the Dissolution,"
1947.B35
"Before the Play," 1918.B15
Bell, Millicent, 1957.B3;
1959.B7
Bell, Vereen M., 1959.B8
"The Bellegardes' Feud with
Christopher Newman: A
Study of Henry James's Re-
vision of The American,"
1955.B58
Bement, Douglas (with Ross M.
Taylor), 1943.B9
Benedict, Clare, 1930.B2

Bennett, Arnold, 1917.B3;
1920.B4; 1928.B2; 1932.B7
Bennett, Joan, 1954.B4; 1956.B9
Benson, Arthur Christopher,
1924.B1; 1926.B2-3
Benson, Edward Frederic,
1921.B4; 1930.B3-4; 1940.B3
Bergonzi, Beranard, 1958.B6-7
Berkelman, Robert, 1959.B9
Berland, Alwyn, 1950.B7;
1953.B12; 1958.B8
Berryman, John, 1950.B8
Berti, Luigo, 1946.B6
Bertocci, Angelo, 1949.B3
Bethurum, Dorothy, 1923.B3
Bewley, Marius, 1949.B4-5;
1950.B9-11; 1951.B2; 1952.B2-
4 (rpt.), B5, B6-8 (rpt.);
1958.B9; 1959.B10, B11
(rpt.), B12
Beyer, William, 1950.B12
"A Bibliographical Novitiate:
In Search of Henry James,"
1958.B53
"Bibliography and the Novelistic
Fallacy," 1959.B40
A Bibliography of Henry James,
1957.A3
"Bibliography of Henry James,"
1933.B3
A Bibliography of the Writings of
Henry James, 1930.A2
Bielenstein, Gabrielle Maupin,
1957.B4
"Biographical and Critical Stud-
ies of Henry James, 1941-
1948," 1949.B19
Bishop, Ferman, 1955.B8
Black, James O., 1958.A1
"Black Magic and Bundling,"
1950.B39
Blackmur, Richard P., 1934.B2,
B3 (rpt.); 1935.B4 (rpt.);
1942.B1; 1943.B10; 1945.B3;
1948.B6; 1951.B3; 1952.B9;
1955.B9, B10-11 (rpt.);
1959.B13-14
Blanche, Jacques-Émile, 1923.B4;
1928.B3; 1937.B1
Bland, D. S., 1952.B10

Blanke, G. H., 1956.B10
Blathwayt, Raymond, 1935.B5
"'The Blest Group of Us,'"
1956.B7
"'The Blithedale Romance' and
'The Bostonians,'" 1952.B4
Blöcker, Günter, 1955.B12;
1957.B5
Blomfield, Sir Reginald, 1932.B8
Blotner, Joseph L., 1955.B13
Blunden, Mrs. Edmund C. See
Norman, Sylva.
Boas, Ralph Philip, 1931.B2
"Boasting of Henry James,"
1958.B74
Bockes, Douglas, 1954.A2
Bode, Carl, 1954.B5
Bogan, Louise, 1938.B5; 1944.B2;
1948.B7; 1955.B14-16 (rpt.)
Boit, Louise, 1946.B7
Bompard, Paola, 1952.B11;
1956.B11
"Books and Things," 1917.B14;
1920.B19
"Books in General," 1945.B38
(Russell); 1948.B36 (Pritch-
ett), B41 (Sackville-West);
1949.B24 (Hough), B51-52
(Sackville-West); 1950.B40
(Greene)
Booth, Bradford A., 1950.B13;
1953.B13
Borchers, Lotte, 1929.A1
Bosanquet, Theodora, 1917.B4,
B5-6 (rpt.); 1918.B1;
1920.B5; 1924.A1; 1954.B6-7
The Bostonians, 1945.B37 (Rahv);
1952.B63 (Trilling);
1956.B34 (Howe)
"The Bostonians," 1952.B10
"The Bostonians," 1955.B68
Bottkol, Joseph M., 1950.B14
Boughton, Alice, 1934.B4
Bowden, Edwin T., 1953.B14;
1954.B8; 1956.A1
Bowen, Edwin W., 1918.B2
Bowen, Elizabeth, 1946.B8
Bowman, S. E., 1958.B10
Boyd, Ernest Augustus, 1920.B6;
1927.B2 (rpt.)

Boynton, Percy H., 1919.B1
Bradbrook, Frank W., 1955.B17-18
Bradford, Gamaliel, 1921.B5;
Bradley, A. G., 1936.B4
Bragdon, Claude, 1920.B7
Brasch, James D., 1959.A1
Brebner, Adele, 1956.B12
Breit, Harvey, 1955.B19
"Bret Hart and Henry James as
    seen by Marie Belloc Lown-
    des," 1937.B4
Brewster, Dorothy (with John
    Angus Burrell), 1924.B2
Brewster, Henry, 1957.B6-7
"Brief Note," 1918.B20
"The British Ambassador Pays
    Tribute," 1943.B22
Broderick, J. C., 1959.B15
Brodin, Pierre, 1947.B7; 1948.B8
Brogan, D. W., 1958.B11
Brome, Vincent, 1958.B12
"The Bronzino Portrait in Henry
    James's The Wings of the
    Dove," 1953.B1
Brooke, Stopford, 1917.B7
Brookfield, Arthur Montagu,
    1930.B5
Brooks, Van Wyck, 1920.B8;
    1923.B5-7; 1925.A1; 1932.B9;
    1940.B4-5, B6 (rpt.), B7;
    1947.B8; 1957.B8; 1958.B13-
    14
Broun, Heywood, 1930.B6
Brower, Reuben, 1951.B4
Brown, Clarence Arthur, 1954.B9
Brown, E. K., 1945.B4-5;
    1946.B9; 1950.B15
Brown, Ivor, 1928.B4
Brown, John Mason, 1950.B16
Brumm, Ursula, 1958.B15
Brussell, I. R., 1936.B5
Bryson, Lyman (with James Thurber
    and Mark Van Doren), 1951.B56
Buitenhuis, Peter, 1957.B9;
    1959.B16-17
Burke, Kenneth, 1941.B3; 1950.B17
    1950.B17-18
Burlingame, Roger, 1946.B10
Burnham, David, 1948.B9
Burnham, Philip, 1946.B11
Burr, A. R., 1934.B5

Burrell, John Angus, 1917.B8
--(with Dorothy Brewster),
    1924.B2
Burt, Nathaniel, 1958.B16
Butler, John F., 1956.B13
Bynner, Witter, 1943.B11

C

C., R. W., 1951.B5
Cady, Edwin, 1958.B17
Cahen, J. F., 1950.B19
Cairns, William B., 1918.B3
"The Calm within the Cyclone,"
    1932.B15
Canby, Henry Seidel, 1922.B4;
    1943.B12; 1945.B6; 1948.B10;
    1950.B20; 1951.A1, B6-7;
    1959.B18 (rpt.)
Cantwell, Robert, 1933.B1;
    1934.B6-7; 1937.B2; B3 (rpt.)
Cargill, Oscar, 1956.B14-16;
    1957.B10-11; 1958.B18-19;
    1959.B19
--(with Daniel Lerner), 1951.B37
Carr, Mrs. J. Comyns, 1926.B4
Carter, Everett S., 1950.B21
Cary, Joyce, 1958.B20
"The Case of the Haunted Chil-
    dren," 1950.B72
Castiglioni, Giulio, 1944.B3
Catalani, G., 1939.B2
"Catalogue of Henry James Exhibi-
    tion," 1947.B3
"The Caught Image: A Study of
    Figurative Language in the
    Fiction of Henry James,"
    1952.A1
"Caviar to the General,"
    1934.B13
"Celebrities off Parade: Henry
    James," 1934.B22
"The Central Intelligence,"
    1957.B33
Cestre, Charles, 1932.B10
"The Change of Emphasis in the
    Criticism of Henry James,"
    1948.B43
Chapman, R. W., 1940.B8

"Character and Point of View in Representative Victorian Novels," 1959.B8

"Character-Portrayal in the Work of Henry James," 1918.B3

"Charles Dickens and Henry James: Two Approaches to the Art of Fiction," 1950.B60

"Charles DuBos et Henry James," 1951.B41

Charteris, Evan, 1927.B3

Chase, Richard Volney, 1957.B12-13; 1958.B21-22

"A Chat with William Lyon Phelps," 1945.B7

"Cher Maître and Mon Bon," 1948.B2

Chesterton, G. K., 1936.B6; 1950.B22

Chevallez, Abel, 1925.B3

Chew, Samuel C., 1948.B11

"The Child as 'The Figure in the Carpet,'" 1958.B81

"The Childhood of James's American Innocents," 1956.B80

Chislett, William, Jr., 1928.B5

"The Choice So Freely Made," 1955.B24

"Christina Light," 1956.B26

"Christopher Newman's Final Instinct," 1957.B71

Clair, J. A., 1959.B20

Clark, A. F. Bruce, 1919.B2

Clark, Edwin, 1949.B6-7

"The Clearness of Henry James," 1919.B3

Clemens, Cyril, 1937.B4; 1943.B13-14; 1945.B7

Clemens, Katherine, 1944.B4

Clurman, Harold, 1950.B23

"Coburn: Henry James's Photographer," 1955.B33

Coffin, Tristram P., 1958.B23

Cohen, B. Bernard, 1956.B17

Collins, Carvel, 1955.B20

Collins, Norman, 1932.B11

Colum, Mrs. Mary Maguire, 1937.B5

Colvin, Sir Sidney, 1924.B3

Commager, Henry Steele, 1950.B24-25

Commemorative Tribute to Henry James, 1922.A1

"Comment by F. R. Leavis," 1952.B30

"A Comparison of Manners," 1919.B7

"Comparisons and Affinities (Henry James, Conrad Aiken, W. F. Harvey)," 1952.B55

The Complete Plays of Henry James, 1949.B11

The Complex Fate: Hawthorne, Henry James, and Some Other American Writers, 1952.B2-8

"The Concept of the Pattern in the Carpet: Conclusions from T. S. Eliot," 1959.B6

Connell, John, 1951.B8

Connolly, Francis X., 1950.B26

Conrad, Jessie, 1926.B5

Conrad, Joseph, 1921.B6

Cook, Dorothy (wtth Isabel S. Monro), 1953.B15

Cooney, Séamus, 1959.B21

Cooper, Harold, 1943.B15

Cornelius, R. D., 1919.B3

"Correspondence: The Relation between William and Henry James," 1951.B2

"Cosmopolitanism in American Literature before 1880," 1950.B73

Coveney, Peter, 1957.B14

Coward, T. R., 1920.B9

Cowie, Alexander, 1948.B12

Cowley, Malcolm, 1945.B8

Cowser, John, 1957.B15

Cox, C. B., 1955.B21-22

The Craft of Fiction, 1921.B13

Craig, G. Armour, 1952.B12

Crankshaw, Edward, 1947.B9

"The Creation of The Golden Bowl," 1959.B67

Crews, Frederick C., 1957.A2

"A Critical Analysis of the Dislocated Character as Developed in the Novels of Henry James," 1957.A5

"The Critical Faculty of Henry James," 1924.B12

"The Critical Prefaces," 1934.B2;
 1935.B4 (rpt.); 1955.B10
 (rpt.)
Criticism in American Periodicals
 of the Works of Henry James
 from 1866-1916, 1944.A1
"Criticism of Henry James: A
 Selected Checklist with an
 Index to Studies of Separate
 Works," 1957.B2
"Croissance de Henry James,"
 1957.B69
Cromwell, Agnes Whitney, 1951.B9
The Crooked Corridor: A Study
 of Henry James, 1949.A1
Crothers, Samuel McChord,
 1924.B4
Crow, Charles R., 1958.B24;
 1959.B22 (rpt.)
"The Crowner's Quest," 1919.B6
Cube, H. von, 1951.B10
"The Cult of Experience in Ameri-
 can Writing," 1937.B13;
 1940.B9 (rpt.); 1959.B74
Cunliffe, J. W., 1933.B2
Cunliffe, Marcus, 1954.B10
"A Cut Version of What Maisie
 Knew," 1953.B67

D

D., J., 1953.B16
D'Agostino, Nemi, 1956.B18
Dahlberg, Edward (with Herbert
 Read), 1959.B23
Daiches, David, 1943.B16
Daisy Miller; An International
 Episode, 1918.B14 (Howells);'
 1927.B9 (Sampson)
"Daisy Miller, Western Hero,"
 1958.B23
Daly, Joseph Francis, 1917.B9
Daniels, Earl, 1933.B3, B4 (rpt.)
D'Arzo, Silvio, 1950.B27
"Das Drama der differenzierten
 Sicht," 1957.B48
"Das Kind bei Henry James,"
 1956.B64
"Das Pandämonium der Kinder,"
 1954.B43

"Das versäumte Leben," 1957.B60
Dauner, Louise, 1952.B13
Davis, Douglas M., 1959.B24
Davray, Henry D., 1921.B7
"The Days Before," 1943.B38;
 1952.B56
"The Death of Henry James,"
 1943.B4
de Chaignon la Rose, Pierre,
 1921.B8
Decker, Clarence R., 1952.B14
"The Decline of Romantic Ideal-
 ism, 1855-1871," 1953.B56
"Dedicated to Art," 1920.B25
DeFalco, J. M., 1958.B25
de la Roche, Mazo, 1943.B17
Delétang-Tardif, Yanette,
 1950.B28
DeMille, George E., 1931.B3
Demuth, Charles, 1927.B4
"The Demuth Pictures," 1943.B49
"Den Leser zu unterhalten,"
 1957.B37
"The Depth of Henry James,"
 1943.B58
"Der Erzählstandpunkt in der
 neuren englischen
 Prosa," 1956.B42
Derleth, August, 1946.B12
"Der unsichtbare Schatten,"
 1955.B46
The Destructive Element: A
 Study of Modern Writers and
 Beliefs, 1935.B21-26
Deurbergue, Jean, 1956.B19
The Development of Imagery and
 Its Functional Significance
 in Henry James's Novels,
 1959.A2
"The Development toward the Short
 Novel Form in American Liter-
 ature, with Special Reference
 to Hawthorne, Melville and
 James," 1952.B27
DeVoto, Bernard, 1950.B29
Dickinson, Thomas H., 1932.B12
"Die sündigen Engel," 1954.B2
 (Arnold), B21 (Hühnerfeld)
Diffené, Patricia, 1939.A1
"The Difficulties of Henry
 James," 1928.B15

"The Disconcerting Poetry of Mary
   Temple: A Comparison of the
   Imagery of The Portrait of a
   Lady and The Wings of the
   Dove," 1958.B67
"Discriminating Sympathy:
   Charles Eliot Norton's
   Unique Gift," 1958.B57
Dixon, Ella Hepworth, 1930.B7
Dixson, Robert J., 1954.B11
"The Doctrine of Spiritual Man,"
   1951.B57
Dolmatch, Theodore B., 1951.B11
Domke, H., 1952.B15
Dort, B., 1951.B12
Dove, George N., 1958.B26
"The Dove's Flight," 1954.B35
Downing, F., 1951.B13
"Drama," 1950.B56
"The Drama in The Golden Bowl,"
   1934.B11
"Drama of a High Civilization.
   Preliminary Studies in Henry
   James's Fiction," 1958.A6
"Dramatic Lustrum: A Study of
   the Effect of Henry James's
   Theatrical Experience on His
   Later Novels," 1938.B6
"Drama Vs. the Theatre in Henry
   James," 1957.B77
Draper, Muriel, 1928.B6; 1929.B1
   (rpt.)
"Dreiser and the Liberal Mind,"
   1946.B30
"The Dual Aspects of Evil in
   'Rappaccini's Daughter,'"
   1954.B32
"Due Manieristi: Henry James e
   G. M. Hopkins," 1953.B42
Dunbar, Viola, 1948.B13-14;
   1950.B30-31; 1952.B16
Dunlap, George A., 1934.B8-9
"Du nouveau sur Henry James,"
   1953.B62
Dupee, Frederick Wilcox, 1945.A1;
   1950.B32; 1951.A2, B14;
   1956.A2, B20; 1957.B16
Durham, F. H., 1942.B2
Durr, R. A., 1956.B21

E

Eagle, Solomon. See Squire, Sir
   John Collings
"Early and Late Revisions in
   Henry James's 'A Passionate
   Pilgrim,'" 1951.B22
The Early Development of Henry
   James, 1930.A1
"An Early Wells Review of Henry
   James," 1958.B6
"Early Years of Henry James,"
   1949.B26
"Ecrivains américains," 1947.B33
Edel, Leon, 1930.B8; 1931.A1-2;
   1933.B5; 1939.B3; 1941.B4;
   1943.B18; 1947.B10; 1948.B15;
   1949.B8-12; 1951.B15-18;
   1952.B17-18; 1953.A2, B17-
   19; 1954.B12; 1955.B23-27;
   1956.B22-25; 1957.B17-21;
   1958.B27; 1959.B25-26
--(with Harold C. Goddard),
   1957.B31
--(with Dan H. Laurence), 1957.A3
--(with Ilse Dusoir Lind),
   1957.B22
--(with Lyall H. Powers),
   1958.B28, B29 (rpt.)
--(with Gordon N. Ray), 1958.A2
--(with H. L. Rypins), 1953.B50
--et al., 1959.B27
Edgar, Pelham, 1919.B5; 1921.B9;
   1924.B5; 1925.B4; 1927.A1;
   1932.B13; 1933.B6 (rpt.)
"Edith Wharton and Henry James:
   The Literary Relation,"
   1959.B7
"Editing James," 1959.B68
Edmondson, Elsie, 1954.B13
"The Education of Henry James,"
   1930.B14
Edwards, Herbert, 1952.B19
Edwards, Oliver, 1956.B26-27
"Eerie and Arresting--Truly
   Spellbinding," 1950.B38
Egan, Maurice Francis, 1920.B10
Eight Uncollected Tales of Henry
   James, 1950.B50

"Eine Phrase wird angeklagt.
Henry James schreibt gegen
das Jahrhundert des Kindes,"
1956.B2
"Ein Grandseigneur des mensch-
lichen Herzens," 1955.B57
"Ein vollkommener Roman,"
1951.B10
Eliot, T. S., 1918.B4, B5-6
(rpt.); 1923.B8; 1924.B6;
1943.B19 (rpt.)
Elliot, W. G., 1925.B5
Elliott, George P., 1959.B28
Elliott, Maud Howe, 1934.B10
Ellis Stewart Marsh, 1925.B6
Ellison, Ralph, 1957.B23
Emerson, Donald C., 1950.A1
"Emerson and the James Family,"
1953.B55
"The Enchanted Kingdom of Henry
James," 1942.B6
Enck, J. J., 1958.B30
"En kommentar till 'Europa,'"
1948.B16
Enkvist, Nils Enk, 1956.B28
"En Marge des 'Bostoniennes,'"
1955.B52
"The Epigraph to T. S. Eliot's
'Burbank with a Baedeker:
Bleistein with a Cigar,'"
1958.B31
"'Erlkönig' and The Turn of the
Screw," 1959.B29
"An Error in The Ambassadors,"
1950.B74
"Escape from the Commonplace,"
1951.B24
Espey, John J., 1955.B28;
1958.B31
"The Essential Novelist? Henry
James," 1933.B6
Evans, Oliver, 1949.B13
Evans, Patricia, 1955.B29
"Evil and the American Short
Story," 1958.B39
"Evil in the Fiction of Henry
James," 1957.A7
"Excellence of the Point of View
in James' 'The Ambassadors,'"
1928.B7

"The Exile of Henry James,"
1933.B5
"The Expansion of a Situation:
'The Spoils of Poynton,''
1947.B24
"The Expatriates: Henry James,
Edith Wharton, Henry Adams,
Gertrude Stein," 1954.B10
"The Exploration of James,"
1927.B10
"Explorers of the Inner Life,"
1942.B4

F

"The Face in the Mountain,"
1945.B29
Fadiman, Clifton, 1945.B9-27;
1947.B11; 1948.B16, B17
(rpt.); 1950.B33-34; 1955.B30
(rpt.)
Fagin, Nathan Bryllion, 1941.B5
"Fair Comment," 1943.B23
Faison, S. Lane, Jr., 1957.B24
Falk, Robert P., 1950.B35;
1952.B20; 1953.B20; 1955.B31
"False Scent," 1940.B8, B11, B16
Farrell, James T., 1947.B12
Fay, Eliot G., 1949.B14;
1951.B19
Fay, Gerard, 1952.B21
"February Reverie: Henry James--
Thomas Moore," 1925.B6
Feidelson, Charles, Jr., 1953.B21
Ferguson, Alfred R., 1949.B15;
1956.B29
Fergusson, Francis, 1934.B11;
1943.B20; 1949.B16; 1955.B32
Feuerlicht, Ignace, 1959.B29
"Fiction as Fine Art: Henry
James (1843-1916)," 1936.B13
"Fiction is Art--Plus," 1948.B9
"The Fiction of Henry James,"
1945.B4
"Fictitious Americans: 2. Por-
traits From a Family Album,"
1952.B24
Fiedler, Leslie A., 1948.B18;
1958.B32-33
Field, Michael, 1933.B7

"A Final Note on The Ambassadors,"
1952.B71
Finch, George A., 1948.B19
Fiocco, A., 1950.B36
Firebaugh, Joseph J., 1951.B20;
1953.B22; 1954.B14;
1955.B33; 1957.B25;
1958.B34-35
Firkins, Oscar W., 1924.B7
"The First International Novel,"
1958.B19
Fitzpatrick, Kathleen Elizabeth,
1950.B37
FitzRoy, Almeric, 1925.B7
"Five Letters of Henry James,"
1949.B29
"Flaubert's Sundays: Maupassant
and Henry James," 1948.B44
"The Flaw in the Portrait: Henry
James vs. Isabel Archer,"
1959.B65
"Fleda Vetch and Ellen Brown, or,
Henry James and the Soap
Opera," 1956.B77
Fleet, Simon, 1949.B17
Flinn, H. G. (with Howard C.
Key), 1959.B30
Fogle, Richard H., 1955.B34
Foley, Richard Nicholas, 1944.A1
Follett, Helen T. (with Wilson
Follett), 1918.B7
Follett, Wilson, 1917.B10;
1918.B8; 1923.B9; 1936.B7
--(with Helen T. Follett),
1918.B7
"A Footnote to Daisy Miller,"
1934.B12
Forbes, Elizabeth Livermore,
1938.B6
Forbes-Robertson, Sir Johnston,
1925.B8
Ford, Ford Madox. See Hueffer,
Ford Madox
"Foreshadowing in The American,"
1959.B37
"Foreword: The 'Meaning' of The
Innocents," 1950.B33
"A Forgotten Story by Henry
James," 1954.B15
"For H. J.," 1943.B3
Forster, E. M., 1927.B5;

1952.B22 (rpt.); 1956.B30;
1959.B31
Fourteen Stories by Henry James,
1946.B13
Fox, Adam, 1952.B23
Fox, Hugh, Jr., 1959.B32
Frantz, Jean H., 1959.B33
Frauengestalten und Frauenprob-
leme bei Henry James, 1929.A1
Freeman, John, 1917.B11
"Free Will, Determinism and So-
cial Responsibility in the
Writings of Oliver Wendell
Holmes, Sr., Frank Norris,
and Henry James," 1955.B37
"Freudian Imagery in James's
Fiction," 1954.B16
"The Freudian Reading of The
Turn of the Screw," 1947.B18
Fricker, Robert, 1958.B36
Friend, Albert C., 1954.B15
Frierson, William Coleman,
1925.B9; 1942.B3
"From a Publisher's Easy Chair,"
1935.B18
"From Daisy Miller to Julia
Bride: 'A Whole Passage of
Intellectual History,'"
1959.B16
"From Hawthorne to James to
Eliot," 1941.B9
"From Henry James to Gissing,"
1956.B75
"From Henry James to John Bal-
derston: Relativity and the
'20's," 1955.B63
"From Henry James to Paul Rosen-
feld," 1946.B21
"From My Library Walls," 1943.B37
"From Redemption to Initiation,"
1958.B32
Fryckstedt, O. W., 1958.B37
Frye, Northrop, 1957.B26
Fukuma, Kin-ichi, 1959.B34
Fuller, Hester Thackeray,
1955.B35
Fullerton, Bradford M., 1932.B14
"The Function of Slang in the
Dramatic Poetry of 'The
Golden Bowl,'" 1956.B31
Furbank, P. N., 1951.B21

"A Further Note on 'An Error in The Ambassadors,'" 1951.B15
"A Further Note on Daisy Miller and Cherbuliez," 1950.B65
Fussell, Edwin, 1958.B38
"The Future of the Novel: The Political Novel," 1951.B36

G

"Gabriel Nash—Somewhat Less Than Angel?," 1959.B19
Gabrielson, Thor, 1953.B23
Gale, Robert L., 1952.A1; 1954.B16; 1957.B27-30; 1958.B39-40; 1959.B35-36
Gardner, Burdett, 1953.B24
Gargano, James W., 1959.B37
Garland, Hamlin, 1930.B9-10; 1931.B6
Garland, Robert, 1950.B38
Garnett, David, 1946.B13; 1949.B18; 1953.B25
Garnier, M. R., 1927.A2
Gass, William H., 1958.B41
Gegenheimer, Albert Frank, 1951.B22
Geismar, Maxwell, 1947.B13; 1953.B26
Geist, Stanley, 1952.B24
"Genesis of a Henry James Story," 1945.B2
"The Genesis of The Turn of the Screw," 1941.B16
"Genri Dzheims," 1956.B63
"Genri Dzhems (25 let sodnia smerti)," 1941.B12
"George Eliot (IV): 'Daniel Deronda' and 'The Portrait of a Lady,'" 1946.B18
Gerard, Albert, 1953.B27
Gerber, John C., 1930.B11
Gerould, Gordon Hall, 1942.B4
Gerould, Katherine Fullerton, 1927.B6
"Gertrude Atherton and Henry James," 1954.B31
"Getting Away from the Chickens," 1959.B28
Gettman, Royal A., 1945.B28
--(with Bruce Harkness), 1955.B36

Ghiselin, Brewster, 1952.B25
"The Ghost at Brede Place," 1952.B26
The Ghostly Tales of Henry James, 1949.B12
"The Ghost of Henry James," 1943.B4; 1944.B15 (rpt.)
Gibbs, Wolcott, 1950.B39
Gibson, Priscilla, 1954.B17
Gibson, William M., 1951.B23
--(with George Arms), 1953.B9
Gide, André, 1930.B12
Gilman, Lawrence, 1918.B9; 1920.B12
Girling, H. K., 1956.B31; 1958.B42
Gleckner, Robert F., 1958.B43
Goddard, Harold C. (with Leon Edel), 1957.B31
Godley, A. D., 1926.B6
Ghodes, Clarence, 1944.B5; 1951.B24
Goldberg, M. A., 1957.B32
The Golden Bowl, 1952.B9
"The Golden Bowl," 1954.B28
"The Golden Bowl, I," 1955.B56
"The Golden Bowl Revisited," 1955.B32
"The Golden Bowl, II," 1955.B21
Goldsmith, Arnold Louis, 1955.B37; 1958.B44
Gomez, Enrique, 1918.B10
Gomme, Laurence, 1923.B10
Goodspeed, E. J., 1934.B12
Gordon, Caroline, 1953.B28; 1955.B38; 1957.B33-35
Gosse, Edmund, 1920.B13, B14 (rpt.); 1922.B5; 1931.B7
"The Governess Turns the Screws," 1957.B44
Grabo, Carl H., 1928.B7-10
"Grammar vs. Style in a Sentence from 'Roderick Hudson,'" 1959.B21
Grana, Gianni, 1956.B32
Grattan, Clinton Hartley, 1932.B15-16
Gray, James, 1951.B24
"The Great Good Place: A Journey into the Psyche," 1958.B25
The Great Short Novels of Henry James, 1944.B14

The Great Tradition: George
    Eliot, Henry James, Joseph
    Conrad, 1948.B28
Greene, Graham, 1933.B8; 1936.B8;
    1947.B14; 1948.B20; 1950.B40-
    41; 1951.B26, B27-28 (rpt.),
    B29, B30-31 (rpt.)
Gregory, Alyse, 1926.B7
Gregory, Horace (with Marya
    Zaturenska), 1944.B6
The Grolier Club, 1947.B15
Grossman, James, 1945.B29
Guedalla, Philip, 1919.B6;
    1921.B11 (rpt.)
"The Gulf of Henry James,"
    1920.B3
Gurko, Leo, 1947.B16
Guthrie, Thomas Anstey. See
    Anstey, F.
"Guy Domville," 1935.B14

H

H., J., 1943.B21
H., R., 1955.B39
Hackett, Francis, 1918.B11-12;
    1947.B17
Haerdter, R., 1953.B29
Hafley, James, 1959.B38
Hagopian, John V., 1959.B39
Hale, E. E., 1931.B8
Halifax, Viscount, 1943.B22
Hall, James B. (with Joseph
    Langland), 1956.B33
"The 'Hallucination' Theory of
    The Turn of the Screw,"
    1947.B25
Hamalian, L. (with E. L. Volpe),
    1958.B45
Hamblem, Abigail A., 1957.B36
Hamilton, Eunice C., 1949.B19
"Hamlet 1886," 1955.B39
"Hamlin Garland and Henry James,"
    1952.B39
Hansen-Löve, F., 1955.B40
Hardy, Florence Emily, 1928.B11;
    1930.B13
Harkness, Bruce, 1958.B46;
    1959.B40
--(with Royal A. Gettman),
    1955.B36

Harlow, Virginia, 1949.B20;
    1950.B42
Harrier, Richard C., 1953.B30;
    1954.B18
Harris, Joel Chandler, 1931.B9
Harris, Marie P., 1951.B32
Hart, James D., 1941.B6
Hart, James S., 1954.A3
Hartley, L. P., 1951.B33
Hartwick, Harry, 1934.B13;
    1936.B9
Harvitt, Hélène, 1924.B8
Hastings, Katharine, 1924.B9
Hatcher, Harlan Henthorne,
    1935.B8
"The 'Haunted Personality' in
    Henry James," 1958.B26
Havens, Raymond D., 1925.B10;
    1945.B30; 1950.B43;
    1951.B34; 1955.B41
Hawkins, William, 1950.B44
"Hawthorne and James," 1941.B10
"The Hawthorne Aspect," 1918.B5
"Hawthorne, Henry James, and the
    American Novel," 1952.B5
"Hawthorne, James and 'The Com-
    mon Doom,'" 1958.B38
"Hawthorne's 'The Prophetic
    Pictures' and James's 'The
    Liar,'" 1950.B48
Haycraft, Howard, 1938.B7
Hays, H. R., 1934.B14
Heilman, R. B., 1947.B18;
    1948.B21
"The Heiress of All the Ages,"
    1943.B40; 1949.B47 (rpt.)
"The Heiress: Play Based on
    James's Novel Joins Broad-
    way's String of Sober Hits,"
    1947.B4
"He Knew His Women," 1951.B7
Hellman, George S., 1926.B8
"Hemingway and James," 1949.B21
Hemphill, George, 1949.B21
Henderson, Archibald, 1932.B17
Hendrick, Leo T., 1953.A3
Hennecke, H., 1950.B45
"Henry and William (Two Notes),"
    1943.B53; 1955.B70 (rpt.)

Henry James, 1950.A2 (Swan);
  1951.A2 (Dupee); 1952.A2
  (Swan); 1956.A2 (Dupee);
  1958.A4 (Markow-Totevy)
"Henry James," 1917.B3 (Bennett),
  B4 (Bosanquet), B6 (Bosan-
  quet), B11 (Freeman), B18
  (Scott); 1918.B7 (Follett and
  and Follett), B11 (Hackett);
  1919.B2 (Clark), B10 (Lynd);
  1920.B4 (Bennett), B13
  (Gosse), B14 (Gosse, rpt.),
  B15 (Hind), B21 (MacCarthy),
  B27 (Pound, rpt.); 1921.B3
  (Beach), B19 (Van Doren);
  1922.B3 (Bradford), B4 (Can-
  by), B5 (Gosse, rpt.), B13
  (Orage); 1923.B4 (Blanche),
  B13 (Krans), B17 (O'Brien),
  B18 (Paget); 1924.B1 (Ben-
  son), B4 (Crothers); 1925.B9
  (Frierson); 1926.B19 (Williams); 1927.B2 (Boyd);
  1928.B3 (Blanche); 1929.B5
  (Read, rpt.), B7 (Sherman);
  1930.B12 (Gide); 1931.B3
  (DeMille), B10 (Herrick), B17
  (MacCarthy); 1932.B2 (Baker
  and Packman), B11 (Collins),
  B12 (Dickinson), B16 (Grat-
  tan), B18 (Hughes and Lov-
  ett), B19 (Johnson);
  1934.B24 (Pound, rpt.), B29
  (Van Patten); 1935.B10 (Huef-
  fer); 1936.B5 (Brussell), B9
  (Hartwick), B10 (Johnson);
  1937.B1 (Blanche), B9 (Leav-
  is), B15 (Waldock); 1938.B3
  (Baker), B8 (Hoare); 1939.B5
  (Marsh), B8 (Phelps);
  1942.B8 (Woolf); 1943.B19
  (Eliot, rpt.), B30 (MacKen-
  zie), B36 (Mortimer), B50
  (Swinnerton); 1944.B13
  (Qvamme), 1945.B35 (Maurois);
  1947.B44 (Stein); 1948.B6
  (Blackmur), B8 (Brodin),
  B12 (Cowie), B23 (Johnson),
  B28 (Leavis), B29 (Lind);
  1949.B25 (Hough), B33
  (Leavis), B39 (Mencken), B42

(Pochmann and Allen), B49
  (Roberts); 1950.B7 (Berland),
  B22 (Chesterton), B28 (Delé-
  tang-Tardif), B41 (Greene),
  B45 (Hennecke), B75 (Zabel);
  1951.B1 (Arnavon), B33 (Hart-
  ley), B54 (Smith and Parks);
  1952.B34 (Lüdeke), B45
  (Matthiessen), B54 (Pécnik),
  B59 (Scherman and Redlich);
  1953.B15 (Cook and Monro),
  B29 (Haerdter), B47 (Pouil-
  lon); 1955.B74 (Woodress);
  1956.B70 (Spiller), B76
  (Swinnerton), B85 (Woodress),
  B86 (Wright); 1957.B5
  (Blöcker), B54 (Pochmann),
  B57 (Raleigh), B74 (Wood-
  ress); 1958.A1-3 (Aiken,
  rpt.), B36 (Fricker), B89
  (Woodress); 1959.B27 (Edel
  et al.), B59 (Ludwig), B99
  (Woodress)
"Henry James: A Last Glimpse,"
  1919.B17
"Henry James als Schriftsteller
  zwischen Amerika und Europa,"
  1956.B10
"Henry James: A Master of His
  Art," 1939.B7
"Henry James: American Criti-
  cism," 1939.B1 (B.), B2
  (Catalani)
"Henry James--America's Analyti-
  cal Novelist," 1923.B20
"Henry James: An Appreciation,"
  1921.B6
"Henry James--An Aspect," 1933.B8
"Henry James and America,"
  1955.A2
"Henry James and a Sense of
  Identity," 1959.B91
"Henry James and Auden in Amer-
  ica," 1946.B32
"Henry James and Chess," 1959.B36
"Henry James and Dumas, fils,"
  1943.B21
"Henry James and Emile Zola: A
  Parallel," 1956.B50
"Henry James and French Natural-
  ism," 1955.A4

"Henry James and Gestation,"
1959.B30

"Henry James and Herman Melville," 1945.B42

Henry James and H. G. Wells: A
Record of Their Friendship,
Their Debate on the Art of
Fiction, and Their Quarrel,
1958.A2

"Henry James and H. G. Wells: A
Study of their Friendship
Based on Their Unpublished
Correspondence," 1953.B59;
1958.B75 (rpt.)

"Henry James and His Architect,"
1943.B42

"Henry James and His Critics,"
1927.B7 (Livesay); 1957.B34
(Gordon)

"Henry James and His French Contemporaries," 1941.B13

"Henry James and His Letters,"
1920.B29

"Henry James and His Limitations, 1952.B62

"Henry James and His Method,"
1919.B5

"Henry James and His Tiger-Cat,"
1953.B64

"Henry James and Ibsen," 1952.B19

"Henry James and Italy," 1957.B30

"Henry James and Julio Reuter:
Two Notes," 1956.B28

"Henry James and 'Life,'"
1958.B9; 1959.B11 (rpt.)

"Henry James and Max Beerbohm,"
1928.B20

"Henry James and Minny Temple,"
1949.B31

"Henry James and Mr. Van Wyck
Brooks," 1925.B11

"Henry James and Others,"
1958.B13

"Henry James and Owen Wister,"
1954.B5

"Henry James and R. L. Stevenson," 1936.B12

Henry James and Robert Louis
Stevenson: A Record of
Friendship and Criticism,
1948.A3

"Henry James and Rome," 1951.B55

"Henry James and Schulberg's The
Disenchanted," 1952.B58

"Henry James and Spiritual Democracy," 1959.B46

"Henry James and Stanford White,"
1934.B36

"Henry James and Stevenson Discuss 'Vile' Tess," 1953.B37

"Henry James and Stoicism,"
1955.B22

"Henry James and the Actress,"
1949.B6

"Henry James and the 'Age of Innocence,'" 1952.B20

"Henry James and the Almighty
Dollar," 1934.B1

"Henry James and the Antinomian
Household: A Study of Selfhood and Selflessness,"
1959.B32

"Henry James and the Aristocracy," 1958.B86

"Henry James and the Artist in
America," 1948.B3

"Henry James and the Art of Foreshortening," 1946.B26

"Henry James and the Art of Revision," 1956.B78

"Henry James and the Bazar Letters," 1958.B28, B29 (rpt.)

"Henry James and the Conduct of
Life: A Study of the Novelist's Moral Values," 1954.A4

"Henry James and the Conspirators," 1952.B68

"Henry James and the Contemporary
Subject," 1935.B21

"Henry James and the Direct Impression," 1954.B25

"Henry James and the Drama,"
1946.B23

"Henry James and the Economic
Age," 1959.B12

"Henry James and the Economic
Motif," 1953.B13

"Henry James and the English
Association," 1946.B2

"Henry James and the English Reviewers, 1882-1890," 1952.B50

Henry James and the Expanding
  Horizon: A Study of the
  Meaning and Basic Themes of
  James's Fiction, 1948.A1
"Henry James and the Fantastical
  Conceits," 1953.B5
"Henry James and the Fiction of
  International Relations,"
  1936.B11
"Henry James and the Function of
  Criticism," 1948.B25
"Henry James and the Future of
  the Novel," 1946.B14
"Henry James and the Gallo-
  American," 1957.B6
"Henry James and the Garden of
  Death," 1952.B13
"Henry James and the Ghostly,"
  1918.B18; 1953.B45 (rpt.)
"Henry James and the Grand Re-
  nunciation," 1958.B8
"Henry James and the Greenough
  Data," 1958.B90
"Henry James and the Hawthorne
  Centennial," 1956.B17
"Henry James and the Heroic
  Young Master," 1955.B66;
  1958.B76 (rpt.)
"Henry James and the Interna-
  tional Copyright Again,"
  1954.B8
"Henry James and the Jews: A
  Critical Study," 1958.B54
"Henry James and the Leaning
  Tower," 1943.B43
"Henry James and the Life of the
  Imagination," 1950.A1
"Henry James and the Millionaire,"
  1950.B46
"Henry James and 'The Most Im-
  pressive Convention in All
  History,'" 1958.B66
"Henry James and the New Jeru-
  salem: Of Morality and
  Style," 1946.B1
"Henry James and the Nostalgia of
  Culture," 1930.B20
"Henry James and the Observant
  Profession," 1950.B20
"Henry James and The Outcry,"
  1949.B9

"Henry James and 'The Personal
  Equation,'" 1956.B46
"Henry James and the Play,"
  1950.B32
"Henry James and the Poets,"
  1943.B18
"Henry James and the Political
  Vocation," 1954.B20
"Henry James and the Press: A
  Study of Protest," 1957.B36
"Henry James and the Psychologi-
  cal Novel," 1925.B3
"Henry James and 'The Real
  Thing,'" 1959.B9
"Henry James and the Relation of
  Morals to Manners," 1937.B16
"Henry James and the Sophomore,"
  1952.B1
"Henry James and the Struggle
  for International Copyright:
  An Unnoticed Item in the
  James Bibliography," 1953.B14
"Henry James and the Theatre,"
  1920.B22 (Matthews); 1921.B20
  (Walkley); 1923.B15 (Matthews,
  rpt.); 1929.B8 (Walbrook)
"Henry James and the Trapped
  Spectator," 1939.B4
"Henry James and the Undergrad-
  uate," 1952.B48
"Henry James and the Untold
  Story," 1917.B10'
"Henry James and The Whole Fami-
  ly," 1950.B53
"Henry James and the Young Men,"
  1959.B31 (Forster), B100
  (Woolf)
"Henry James and Thomas Hardy,"
  1943.B56
"Henry James and Vernon Lee,"
  1954.B12
"Henry James and Young Writers,"
  1931.B22
"Henry James: An Impression,"
  1917.B21
"Henry James: An International
  Episode," 1923.B7
"Henry James, A Reminiscence,"
  1940.B14
"Henry James: A Rhapsody of
  Youth," 1917.B8

"Henry James as a Characteristic American," 1934.B21; 1937.B11 (rpt.); 1955.B53 (rpt.)

"Henry James as a Critic of French Literature," 1949.B14

"Henry James as a Letter Writer," 1920.B24

"Henry James as a Literary Artist," 1917.B5

"Henry James as a Reviewer," 1932.B9

"Henry James as a Social Critic," 1947.B36

"Henry James as Dramatic Critic," 1943.B54

"Henry James as Freudian Pioneer," 1956.B15

"Henry James as Humanist," 1921.B18

"Henry James as I Knew Him," 1936.B4

"Henry James as Landlord," 1946.B7

"Henry James (As seen from the 'Yellow Book')," 1918.B16

"Henry James as Traveler," 1958.B47

"Henry James at Dinner," 1943.B24

"Henry James at Newport," 1941.B7

"Henry James at Rye," 1930.B10

"Henry James at the Grecian Urn," 1951.B37

"Henry James at the Reform Club," 1925.B14

Henry James at Work, 1924.A1

Henry James Bibliography in Japan, 1958.A5

"Henry James, Book Reviewer," 1921.B15

"Henry James Came Home at Last," 1956.B53

"A Henry James Centenary Exhibition," 1943.B5

"Henry James: Citizen of Two Countries: An Anglo-American Vision," 1943.B2

"The Henry James Collection," 1956.B61

"Henry James: Correction," 1953.B36

"Henry James Criticizes The Tory Lover," 1955.B8

"Henry James deutsch," 1955.B69

"Henry James. Die Gesandten," 1956.B66

"Henry James. Die sündigen Engel," 1954.B24

"Henry James Discoveries," 1939.B3

"Henry James (Di società, di uominie fantasmi)," 1950.B27

"Henry James' Dramatizations of His Novels," 1942.B2

"Henry James, Edith Wharton, William Dean Howells and American Society on Parade," 1928.B18

"Henry James, 1843–1916," 1943.B13

"Henry James e il problema del male," 1952.B11

"Henry James: Ein europäischer Amerikaner," 1950.B49

"Henry James e la grande arte narrativa," 1956.B32

Henry James et la France, 1927.A2

"Henry James et l'athéisme mondain," 1953.B43

"Henry James' Failure as a Dramatist Exposed by a London Critic," 1917.B2

"Henry James: Fourteen Letters," 1957.B7

"Henry James' Ghost Stories," 1921.B22

"Henry James' gjenkomst," 1953.B23

"Henry James, Himself," 1918.B13

"Henry James: His Range and Accomplishments," 1928.B5

"Henry James, His Symbolism and His Critics," 1947.B2

"Henry James in America," 1931.B6

"Henry James in Cambridge," 1959.B47

"Henry James in England," 1940.B5, B6 (rpt.)

"Henry James in Harley Street," 1953.B50

"Henry James in His Letters,"
  1920.B30
"Henry James in Hollywood,"
  1949.B41
"Henry James in Italy," 1933.B10
"Henry James in Paris," 1932.B26
"Henry James in Reverie,"
  1918.B9
"Henry James in the Galleries,"
  1956.B30
"Henry James in the Great Grey
  Babylon," 1951.B14
"Henry James in the World,"
  1934.B17
"Henry James in War Time,"
  1943.B28
"Henry James, Jr.," 1938.B7
"A Henry James Jubilee: I,"
  1946.B24
"A Henry James Jubilee: II,"
  1947.B37
"Henry James, le civilisé,"
  1951.B47
"Henry James, Lecturer,"
  1951.B32
"A Henry James Letter," 1924.B11
"Henry James: Life Refracted by
  Temperament," 1947.B43
Henry James: Man and Author,
  1927.A1
"Henry James: Master Detective,"
  1930.B18
"Henry James: Master of Indirec-
  tion," 1926.B15
"Henry James, Melodramatist,"
  1956.B8
"Henry James: Miss Wenham,"
  1943.B9
"Henry James, 1955-1958: Ein
  Literaturbericht," 1959.B53
"Henry James' Obscurity,"
  1919.B4
"Henry James's Obscurity,"
  1919.B14
"Henry James of Boston," 1940.B4
Henry James, o il proscritto
  voluntario, 1948.A2
"Henry James on Hawthorne,"
  1959.B17
"Henry James on One of His Early
  Stories," 1951.B34
"Henry James on 'The Outcry,'"
  1955.B41

"Henry James on the Poetry of
  Arnold," 1943.B34
"Henry James on Zola," 1943.B26
Henry James, peintre de la femme,
  1942.A1
"Henry James' Place," 1943.B59
Henry James: Representative
  Selections, with Introduc-
  tion, Bibliography, and
  Notes, 1941.B15
"Henry James Reprints," 1949.B1
  (Anon.), B8 (Edel), B18
  (Garnett), B23 (Hoppe), B32
  (Leavis), B34 (Lehmann), B38
  (Maxwell)
"Henry James, Reviewer," 1921.B17
"Henry James Revisited," 1947.B17
"The Henry James Revival: The
  Expatriate Comes Home,"
  1946.B27
"Henry James's America: Versions
  of Oppression," 1959.B96
"Henry James's Ancestry,"
  1957.B15 (Cowser), B18 (Edel)
"Henry James's 'Bostonians,'"
  1922.B16
"Henry James scittore sintatti-
  co," 1956.B36
"Henry James's Comic Discipline:
  The Use of the Comic in the
  Structure of His Early Fic-
  tion," 1955.A1
"Henry James's Confidence and
  the Development of the Idea
  of the Unconscious," 1956.B45
Henry James's Criticism, 1929.A2
"Henry James's Dream Children,"
  1959.B35
Henry James: Selected Short
  Stories, 1950.B2
"Henry James Self-Revealed,"
  1920.B6
"Henry James's Fable of Caro-
  lina," 1955.B3
"Henry James's Failure as a Dra-
  matist," 1920.B1
"Henry James's Final Period,"
  1947.B39
"Henry James's First Novel,"
  1947.B20 (Leavis); 1950.B66
  (Stone)

"Henry James's Heiress: The Importance of Edith Wharton," 1938.B11

"Henry James's High Hat," 1932.B28

"Henry James's Last Novel," 1950.B67

"Henry James's Last Portrait of a Lady: Charlotte Stant in The Golden Bowl," 1957.B41

"Henry James's Later Novels: The Objectifying of Moral Life," 1954.A3

"Henry James's Literary Theory and Criticism," 1958.B88

"Henry James's Metaphysical Romances," 1954.B34

"Henry James's 'Moral Policeman': William Dean Howells," 1958.B18

"Henry James's Neglected Thriller: The Other House," 1952.B43

"Henry James's Portrait of Henry James," 1936.B7

"Henry James's Portrait of the Artist," 1944.B8

"Henry James's Quality," 1919.B8

"Henry James's Reconciliation of Free Will and Fatalism," 1958.B44

"Henry James's Rejection of The Sacred Fount," 1949.B45

"Henry James's Revision of The American," 1945.B28

"Henry James's Revision of Watch and Ward," 1952.B42

"Henry James's Revisions for The Ambassadors," 1954.B23 (Humphreys); 1955.B23 (Edel)

"Henry James's Revisions of The Portrait of a Lady: A Study of Literary Portraiture and Perfectionism," 1956.A3

"Henry James's Romantic 'Vision of the Real' in the 1870's," 1950.B35

"Henry James's 'The American Scene,'" 1946.B3

"Henry James's The American Scene," 1958.B60

"Henry James's 'The Art of Fiction,'" 1958.B56

"Henry James's 'The Jolly Corner,'" 1957.B67

"Henry James's Theory of Literary Invention," 1959.B63

"Henry James's 'The Tragic Muse,'" 1954.B39

"Henry James's The Wings of the Dove as an International Novel," 1958.B87

Henry James: Stories of Writers and Artists, 1944.B10

"Henry James's Version of the Experimental Novel," 1942.B3

"Henry James's What Maisie Knew: A Comparison with the Plans in The Notebooks," 1953.B68

"Henry James's Workshop," 1917.B13 1917.B13

"Henry James's World of Images," 1953.B52

"Henry James's Year in France," 1946.B16

"Henry James: Symbolic Imagery in the Later Novels," 1948.B54

Henry James: Ten Short Stories, 1948.B46

"Henry James: The Act of Life," 1957.B78

"Henry James: The American Scene," 1923.B6

"Henry James' The American Scene: The Vision of Value," 1955.B62

"Henry James the American: Some Views of His Contemporaries," 1955.B61

"Henry James: The Arch-Enemy of 'Low Company,'" 1934.B20

Henry James: The Art of Fiction and Other Essays, 1948.B39

"Henry James: The Art of Revision, a Comparison of the Original and Revised Versions of The American," 1952.A3

"Henry James: The Banquet of Initiation," 1947.B38

"Henry James' 'The Beast in the Jungle,'" 1947.B48

"Henry James: The Bliss and the Bale," 1959.A3

"Henry James: The Breakup of Victorian Tranquillity," 1955.B13

Henry James: The Creative Process, 1958.A3

"Henry James, the Essential Novelist," 1932.B13

"Henry James: The Expatriate as American," 1955.B72

"Henry James: The First Phase," 1923.B5

Henry James: The Future of the Novel: Essays on the Art of Fiction, 1956.B24

"Henry James: The Golden Bowl," 1952.B52

"Henry James' 'The Impressions of a Cousin,'" 1950.B43

"Henry James: The Late and Early Styles," 1953.A3

Henry James: The Major Phase, 1944.A2

"Henry James: The Master," 1937.B7-8

"Henry James: The Novelist as Actor," 1951.B21

"Henry James: The Poetics of Empiricism," 1951.B49

"Henry James: The Political Vocation," 1957.B39

"Henry James: The Portrait of a Lady (1880-81)," 1953.B35

"Henry James: The Private Universe," 1936.B8; 1951.B27 (rpt.)

"Henry James, the Realist: An Appreciation," 1918.B2

"Henry James: The Real Thing (1890): An Attempt at Interpretation," 1959.B43

"Henry James: The Religious Aspect," 1951.B28

"Henry James the Reporter," 1938.B12

"Henry James, the Satirist," 1934.B14

"Henry James: The Stories," 1947.B21

"Henry James: The Sublime Consensus of the Educated," 1957.B56

"Henry James: 'The Turn of the Screw,'" 1924.B16

Henry James: The Untried Years: 1843-1870, 1953.A2

"Henry James: The War Chapter, 1914-1916," 1941.B4

"Henry James to the Ruminant Reader: The Turn of the Screw," 1924.B10

Henry James: Versuch einer Würdigung seiner Eigenart, 1939.A1

"Henry James versus H. G. Wells," 1958.B12

"Henry James, W. D. Howells and the Art of Fiction," 1951.B35

Henze, Helene, 1957.B37

Hermanowski, G., 1955.B42

"Hero of the Great Know-How: Mark Twain's Machine-Age 'Yankee,'" 1951.B6; 1959.B18 (rpt.)

Herrick, Robert, 1922.B6; 1923.B11, B12 (rpt.); 1931.B10

Heyneman, J. H., 1928.B12

Hicks, Granville, 1933.B9; 1958.B47-48

"'The High Bid' and the Forbes-Robertsons," 1947.B23

"The High Brutality of Good Intentions," 1958.B41

Highet, Gilbert, 1953.B31

Hind, Charles Lewis, 1920.B15; 1926.B9

"Hinweis auf Henry James," 1955.B45

"The Histrionic Vision of Henry James," 1959.B54

Hoare, Dorothy Mackenzie, 1929.B2; 1938.B8

Hodge, Alan, 1948.B22

Hoffman, Frederick J., 1951.B35

Hoffmann, Charles G., 1952.B27; 1953.B32; 1954.B19; 1957.A4

Hogarth, Basil, 1934.B15
Holder-Barell, Alexander, 1959.A2
Holland, L. B., 1959.B41
Holliday, Robert Cortes,
    1918.B13
Hølmebakk, Gordon, 1958.B49
Honig, Edwin, 1949.B22; 1958.B50;
    1959.B42 (rpt.)
"Honors for Henry James,"
    1950.B64
Hopkins, Gerard, 1957.B38
Hoppe, A. J., 1949.B23
Horne, Helen, 1959.B43
Hoskins, Katherine, 1946.B14
Hough, Graham, 1949.B24-25
The House of Fiction: Essays on
    the Novel, 1957.B20
Houser, Z. L., 1949.B26
"The Houses that James Built:
    The Portrait of a Lady,"
    1958.B71
Hovey, Richard B., 1959.B44
Howe, Irving, 1950.B46; 1951.B36;
    1954.B20; 1956.B34; 1957.B39
    (rpt.)
Howe, Mark Anthony DeWolfe,
    1922.B7; 1949.B27
Howells, William Dean, 1918.B14;
    1928.B13
"Howells and James," 1940.B7
"'Howells or James?'--An Essay
    by Henry Blake Fuller,"
    1957.B1
"How Henry James Revised Roderick
    Hudson: A Study in Style,"
    1924.B8
"How to Know Maisie," 1956.B12
Hoxie, Elizabeth F., 1946.B15
Hueffer, Ford Madox, 1920.B16;
    1921.B12; 1931.B11-12;
    1935.B9-10; 1937.B7, B8
    (rpt.)
Hughes, Helen Sard (with Robert
    Morss Lovett), 1932.B18
Hughes, Herbert Leland, 1926.A1
"Hugh Walpole and Henry James:
    The Fantasy of the 'Killer
    and the Slain,'" 1951.B18
Hühnerfeld, P., 1954.B21
Humphrey, Robert, 1954.B22
Humphreys, Susan M., 1954.B23

Huneker, James Gibbons, 1917.B12;
    1920.B17; 1922.B8, B9 (rpt.),
    B10
Hunt, Violet, 1926.B10
Hyde, H. Montgomery, 1956.B35
Hyman, Stanley Edgar, 1955.B43

I

"The Idealism of Merton Densher,"
    1958.B34
"An 'Idiosyncrasy' of the Mas-
    ter," 1949.B7
"The Illuminating Letters of
    Henry James," 1920.B2
The Image of Europe in Henry
    James, 1958.A7
"I Meet Henry James," 1928.B6;
    1929.B1 (rpt.)
"An Imperfection in the Art of
    Henry James," 1959.B66
"The Impressionism of Henry
    James," 1931.B8
"Inadequacy in Eden: Knowledge
    and The Turn of the Screw,"
    1957.B25
"The Inadequate Vulgarity of
    Henry James," 1951.B38
"The Inception of 'The Beast in
    the Jungle,'" 1953.B40
"In Defense of Allegory,"
    1958.B50
"Independence vs. Isolation:
    Hawthorne and James on the
    Problem of the Artist,"
    1955.B7
"In Explanation," 1918.B21
"The Influence of Turgenev on
    Henry James," 1941.B8
"In Memory," 1918.B6
"In Memory of Henry James,"
    1918.B4
"Innocence and Evil in James'
    The Turn of the Screw,"
    1953.B32
"Innocent Among the Lions,"
    1951.B9
"The Innocents," 1952.B21
"'The Innocents' Is Splendidly
    Cast," 1950.B44

"The Institution of Henry James,"
1947.B22
"The Intellectual Jameses,"
1947.B5
"Intelligence on Tour," 1959.B2
"Interlude: Henry James,"
1958.B79
"The 'Internationalism' of The
Golden Bowl," 1956.B82
"Interpreting Genius," 1951.B25
In the Cage and Other Tales,
1958.B92
"In the Country of the Blue,"
1943.B10; 1945.A1 (rpt.)
Introducción a Henry James,
1956.A4
"Introduction à Henry James,"
1953.B27
"The Involvular Club; or, the
Return of the Screw,"
1955.B6
"The Ivory Tower and The Sense
of the Past," 1935.B23
Izzo, Carlo, 1956.B36

J

"Jacobean and Shavian," 1930.B1
"James," 1924.B13
James, Henry
--and aesthetics, 1917.B19;
1929.B7; 1932.B18; 1934.B20;
1939.B9; 1948.B40; 1953.B22;
1954.B33; 1957.B9, B40;
1958.A3
--and Edith Wharton, 1920.B30;
1925.B16; 1934.B34, B35
(rpt.);
as subject, 1938.B11;
1941.B11; 1947.B29; 1953.B44;
1957.B3; 1959.B7,* B60-61
--and Nathaniel Hawthorne,
1918.B4; 1941.B5, B10;
1948.B12; 1949.B4, B5;
1950.B9, B48; 1952.B5, B11;
1953.B40; 1955.B7; 1956.B17,
B34; 1958.B38, B43, B72;
1959.B3, B17
--and H. G. Wells, 1934.B32;
1943.B57;

1953.B59; 1958.A2, B4, B6-7,
B12, B49, B82
--and morality, 1923.B3; 1927.B8;
1928.B21; 1929.B2; 1934.B13,
B27, B33; 1935.B22; 1937.B16;
1941.B9; 1943.B8, B47;
1944.B16; 1946.B1, B8;
1947.B2, B12, B39, B43;
1948.B3, B28; 1949.B21;
1950.B2, B45; 1951.B58;
1952.A2, B20, B65; 1953.A1,
B11; 1954.A3-4, B13; 1956.A1;
1957.A2, A6-7, B56; 1958.B69;
1959.B32
--and realism, 1918.B2; 1924.B7;
1931.B13; 1937.B5; 1943.B48;
1947.B36; 1948.B4; 1950.B35;
1953.B20; 1956.B57; 1957.B1;
1958.B17
--and religion, 1920.B10;
1933.B8; 1935.B5; 1953.B28;
1955.B32; B38; 1957.B29;
1958.B54, B66; 1959.B54
--and Robert Louis Stevenson,
1924.B3; 1926.B8; 1928.B17;
1930.B13; 1936.B12; 1948.A3,
B20; 1952.B14; 1953.B37, B51
--and the drama, 1917.B2, B9;
1920.B1, B22; 1923.B21;
1925.B5, B8; 1926.B17;
1928.B14; 1929.B8; 1931.A1;
1932.A1; 1935.B14; 1936.B2;
1938.B6; 1942.B2; 1943.B20,
B54; 1946.B23; 1947.B10, B23;
1949.B6-7, B9-10, B11, B12,
B16, B43; 1950.B3, B5, B32,
B40, B70; 1951.B42, B48;
1952.B19; 1956.B18, B44;
1957.B77
--and the French writers,
1921.B7; 1925.B9; 1927.A2;
1932.B10; 1935.B9; 1941.B13;
1943.B26; 1946.B6, B16;
1948.B39, B44; 1949.B14;
1950.B47, B54; 1951.B19, B41;
1952.B14; 1955.A4; 1956.B16,
B50; 1959.B50
--and Turgenev, 1941.B8;
1949.B55; 1950.B15; 1956.B54-
55; 1958.B10

*The most significant works are underscored.

--and William Dean Howells,
  1918.B14; 1928.B13;
  as subject, 1924.B7; 1930.B9;
  1940.B7; 1952.B69; 1957.B1;
  1958.B17, B18, B19, B37
--as a psychological novelist,
  1925.B3; 1931.B21; 1932.B11;
  1948.A2, B53; 1949.B12;
  1950.A2, B45; 1951.B49
--Bibliography, 1923.B10;
  1930.A1, A2; 1931.A2;
  1932.B2, B14, B19; 1933.B3;
  1934.B18, B29; 1936.B5, B9-
  10; 1939.B3; 1941.B12, B14,
  B15; 1942.B7; 1943.B1, B5;
  1947.B3, B15; 1948.B8, B12,
  B23, B30, B55; 1949.A1, B15,
  B19, B36, B42; 1950.A2, B6,
  B30; 1952.B28, B40, B64;
  1953.B15; 1954.A1, B30;
  1955.B60, B74; 1956.A4, B61,
  B70, B85-86; 1957.A3, B2,
  B74; 1958.A4-5, B5, B53, B63,
  B73; 1959.B40, B59, B99
--Biocritical surveys,
  1920.B13; 1921.B3, B19;
  1926.B19; 1928.B5; 1929.B4;
  1934.B28; 1936.B11; 1937.B15;
  1938.B3; 1941.B6, B15;
  1944.B14; 1945.B10; 1948.B6,
  B8, B11-12; 1949.B42;
  1950.A2; 1951.A2, B24, B58;
  1952.A2, B34; 1953.B23;
  1954.B10; 1955.B59; 1958.A4
--Biography, 1920.B13, B18;
  1922.B12; 1923.B5-6, B22;
  1924.B9; 1925.A1; 1926.B1,
  B12; 1927.A1, B3; 1928.B11,
  B16; 1930.A1, B2, B19;
  1931.B7-8, B11, B19;
  1932.B16, B20, B22; 1933.B10;
  1934.B5, B10, B31; 1935.A1,
  B1, B14, B16, B19-20;
  1936.B8; 1938.B1-2, B7, B11;
  1941.B4, B8; 1943.B13-14,
  B25, B28, B35, B38, B42-43,
  B53; 1944.B4, B14; 1945.B32;
  1946.B1-2; 1947.A1, B1, B5;
  1948.B25, B35, B40, B42;
  1949.B12, B20, B26, B31, B40,
  B55; 1950.B8, B42; 1951.A1-2,

  B14, B32-33, B38, B55;
  1952.B11, B26, B39, B51;
  1953.A1, A2, B14, B24, B50,
  B55, B64; 1954.B5, B12, B18;
  1955.A3, B8, B25, B33, B66;
  1956.A4, B15, B28-29, B74;
  1957.A1, B6, B15, B18, B30,
  B54; 1958.B13-14, B28, B40,
  B57, B90; 1959.B32, B44,
  B77, B81, B87, B91
--Character portrayal, 1918.B3;
  1927.B10; 1929.A1; 1932.B15;
  1934.B14; 1937.B5; 1939.B4;
  1942.A1; 1943.B40; 1944.B8;
  1947.B11; 1950.B27; 1951.B7,
  B21; 1952.B15; 1953.B35;
  1957.A2, B49; 1958.A6, B26,
  B77; 1959.B3
--Correspondence, 1920.B2, B5-10,
  B12, B17, B19, B20, B24, B29-
  32; 1921.B9; 1923.B1, B4;
  1924.B11; 1926.B1; 1930.B3;
  1931.A2; 1932.A1, B27;
  1933.B10; 1935.B20; 1939.B3;
  1946.B2, B7; 1947.B26;
  1949.B10, B27, B29-30;
  1940.B42; 1951.B8, B34, B42;
  1952.B40; 1953.B30, B36, B59;
  1954.B5; 1955.B8, B26, B41,
  B50, B66; 1956.B17, B27, B41,
  B49; 1957.B6-7, B22, B53;
  1958.A4, B28, B40, B80;
  1959.B76-77
--Criticism and literary theory,
  1918.B25; 1921.B8, B15, B17;
  1924.B12; 1926.A1; 1929.A2;
  1931.A2, B3, B8; 1932.B9;
  1934.B2, B32; 1935.B2;
  1939.B9; 1943.B7, B12, B15,
  B26, B54; 1946.B14, B21;
  1948.B9, B39; 1949.B2, B14;
  1950.B62; 1951.B38; 1952.B53;
  1954.B5, B9, B25; 1955.A5,
  B22, B31, B34; 1956.A4, B24,
  B30, B39, B68, B74; 1957.B17,
  B20, B24, B46-47, B50, B57;
  1958.B68, B88; 1959.B1, B10,
  B57, B63
--Expatriation, 1920.B8, B12;
  1922.A1, B1, B12; 1923.B5-7;
  1925.A1, B2, B11, B15;

1926.B7, B12; 1928.B3, B13,
B18; 1930.B14-16, B20-21,
B23; 1932.B9; 1933.B1, B5,
B9; 1934.B17, B19, B21;
1935.B16; 1937.B4; 1938.B15;
1939.B2, B10; 1940.B5;
1942.B4; 1943.B2, B39, B48,
B58; 1944.B11; 1945.B32;
1947.B6-7, B34; 1948.A2,
B19; 1950.B8, B25, B49, B73;
1953.B8, B29, B58; 1955.B9,
B55, B61, B62, B72; 1956.B19,
B23, B32; 1957.B8, B56;
1958.B60, B69
--Imagery and symbolism,
1934.B26; 1943.B32, B52, B55;
1947.B1-2; 1949.A1, B22;
1950.B18; 1951.B23; 1952.A1,
B13; 1953.B3, B52; 1954.B16-
17; 1955.B29; 1956.B37, B78;
1957.A1, B28-29; 1958.B15,
B67; 1959.A2, B36
--Influence, 1925.A3; 1929.B4;
1931.B22; 1934.B27; 1935.B8,
B15, B29; 1936.B11, B13;
1941.B6; 1942.B3-4; 1943.B18,
B37; 1946.B6, B14, B20;
1947.B6, B13; 1948.B6, B18,
B28; 1950.B13; 1951.B35;
1952.B34, B66; 1959.B85
--International theme, 1920.A1;
1921.B3, B19; 1931.B10;
1936.B11; 1937.B16; 1940.B4;
1942.B6; 1943.B39-40, B47;
1944.B14; 1947.B38; 1948.B6,
B37; 1950.B46, B75; 1951.B58;
1952.B5; 1955.A2; 1956.A1,
B10, B19, B36, B80, B82;
1957.B45, B63; 1958.A7, B9,
B87
--Method, technique, 1918.A1;
1919.B5; 1921.B13; 1924.B5;
1925.B16; 1926.A1; 1927.A1,
B6-7; 1928.B7-10, B18;
1929.B5; 1931.B1, B12;
1932.B3-6; 1935.A1, B9, B24;
1938.B3; 1943.B16, B50, B55;
1946.B14, B26; 1947.B46;
1949.B24, B62; 1950.B15, B20;
1951.B3; 1952.B47; 1953.B21,
B38-39; 1954.A2, B22; 1955.A1,

A5-6, B27, B51; 1956.B36,
B42, B71, B83; 1957.A6,
B32-33; 1959.B8, B86
--Psychoanalytic studies,
1924.B10; 1934.B37; 1943.B41;
1947.B48; 1948.B5; 1951.B18,
B53; 1954.B16; 1956.B15, B59;
1957.B31, B62; 1958.B25
--Reminiscences, 1917.B4-6, B21;
1918.B13, B16, B28; 1920.B4,
B13, B15-16, B21, B26;
1921.B4; 1922.B7, B14;
1923.B4, B11, B16; 1924.A1,
B1, B4, B14; 1925.B5, B7-8;
1926.B2-6, B9-10, B14, B17;
1928.B3, B6, B13, B19;
1930.B4, B7, B9, B17;
1931.B6, B11, B18; 1932.B1,
B8, B23, B25-26, B28;
1933.B11; 1934.B4, B22, B34;
1935.B3, B10, B13, B28;
1936.B1-2, B4, B6; 1937.B1,
B4, B10; 1938.B1, B4, B9-10;
1939.B5, B8, B11; 1940.B2-3,
B10, B12-14; 1942.B5;
1943.B11, B24, B27, B30, B37,
B45-46; 1945.B7; 1946.B5, B7,
B19; 1947.A2; 1949.B17;
1951.B9; 1952.B46; 1953.B25,
B41; 1954.B6-7; 1956.B35;
1959.B31, B47, B100
--Reputation, 1918.B7, B11;
1919.B14; 1920.B3, B6, B25;
1926.B13; 1929.B7; 1931.B14;
1932.B14; 1939.B1-2;
1940.B14; 1944.A1, B1-2, B18;
1945.B6, B10, B39-40;
1946.B27, B30; 1947.B7, B9,
B33; 1948.B10, B15, B43;
1950.B7, B60; 1951.B1, B47,
B58; 1952.B35, B50; 1953.B10;
1954.A1, B29; 1955.B43, B69;
1956.B5, B62, B70; 1957.B34,
B50; 1959.B5, B53
--Revisions, 1918.B1; 1923.B11;
1924.B8; 1925.B10; 1944.A2,
B9; 1945.B28; 1949.B1, B8,
B18, B23, B32, B34, B38;
1950.B31; 1951.B16, B22;
1952.A3, B42; 1954.B23, B42;
1955.B23, B58; 1956.A3, B78,
B79; 1958.B52; 1959.B78

--Style, 1917.B1; 1923.B18;
   1926.B15; 1927.A1, B7;
   1935.B11; 1939.A1; 1943.B23,
   B36; 1945.B8; 1946.B28;
   1950.B28; 1953.A3, B42;
   1954.B26; 1955.B6; 1956.B31,
   B38; 1957.B26, B35; 1958.B24;
   1959.B21
--Themes, 1934.B1; 1936.B8;
   1943.B10; 1948.A1; 1949.A1;
   1950.A1, B10, B37, B75;
   1951.B51; 1952.A2, B67;
   1953.B13, B32, B35, B53, B63;
   1954.B1, B3, 1956.A1, B9,
   B21; 1957.A5-6, B25;
   1958.A4, B8, B38-39, B41;
   1959.A3
--Works
   "The Altar of the Dead,"
   1943.B52; 1945.B17; 1949.B22
   The Ambassadors, 1918.A1;
   1919.B5; 1921.B13; 1924.B2;
   1925.B4; 1927.A1, B5;
   1928.B7, B21; 1930.B11, B22;
   1932.B4; 1934.B16; 1935.B26;
   1943.B32; 1944.A2; 1946.B1;
   1947.B1, B27; 1948.B47;
   1950.B7, B15, B63, B74-75;
   1951.A1-2, B3, B12, B15, B23,
   B46, B56; 1952.B18, B71;
   1953.B17, B28; 1954.A4, B23;
   1955.B23, B28-29; 1956.A4,
   B9, B21, B38, B71-72;
   1957.A1-2, B58, B65-66;
   1958.A1, A7, B21, B27, B78;
   1959.B25, B95
   The American, 1918.A1;
   1920.A1; 1927.A1; 1928.B3;
   1929.B4; 1930.A1; 1931.B19;
   1932.B3; 1945.B28; 1949.B60,
   B65; 1950.B46; 1951.A1-2,
   B48; 1952.A2-3; 1954.A4, B42;
   1955.B58; 1956.A1, B78-79;
   1957.A6, B71; 1958.A7, B19,
   B86; 1959.B20, B37, B64, B66
   The American Scene, 1930.B16;
   1934.B19; 1944.A2; 1946.B3-4,
   B11, B32; 1948.B48; 1955.B62;
   1958.B60

"The Art of Fiction," 1931.A2;
1948.B39; 1950.B1; 1958.B56
The Aspern Papers, 1950.B14;
1951.A1-2; 1952.B17, B32;
1955.B73; 1956.B81; 1957.A4,
B51; 1959.B4, B13, B84
"At Isella," 1930.A1; 1943.B1;
1957.A6
Autobiography, 1917.B14;
1918.B9, B19; 1942.B8;
1956.B3-4, B6, B20, B53, B69;
1957.B59, B61, B69, B92
The Awkward Age, 1918.A1;
1921.B13; 1927.A1; 1932.B16;
1945.B30; 1948.B22; 1951.A1-
2, B20; 1952.A2; 1958.B42
"The Beast in the Jungle,"
1939.B4; 1943.B49; 1945.B18;
1947.B42, B48; 1948.B32;
1949.B22; 1950.B51, B68;
1951.B53; 1953.B40; 1954.B41;
1957.A4; 1958.B45
"The Bench of Desolation,"
1952.B38; 1957.A4
"Benvolio," 1930.A1
"The Birthplace," 1945.B2,
B19; 1950.B2; 1958.B68
The Bostonians, 1918.A1;
1922.B16; 1927.A1; 1932.B16;
1934.B8; 1945.B37; 1947.A1,
B31, B36-37; 1948.B7, B28;
1949.B4; 1951.A1-2, B37;
1952.B63; 1955.A4, B4, B52;
1956.B34; 1959.B62, B96
"Brooksmith," 1945.B12
"A Bundle of Letters,"
1930.A1; 1945.B11; 1950.B2
Confidence, 1918.A1; 1930.A1;
1956.B45; 1957.A4, A6
"Crapy Cornelia," 1951.B53
Daisy Miller, 1918.B14;
1920.A1; 1927.B9; 1930.A1;
1934.B12; 1942.B2; 1946.B15;
1948.B13; 1950.B31, B65;
1951.A1-2; 1952.B24;
1953.B34; 1955.B50; 1956.B16,
B47; 1957.A4; 1958.A7, B23,
B83; 1959.B16, B97
"A Day of Days," 1930.A1;
1955.A3

"The Death of the Lion,"
1943.B10
"De Grey, A Romance,"
1930.A1; 1955.A3
Essays in London, 1929.A2
"Eugene Pickering," 1930.A1
"Europe," 1945.B13; 1955.B36
The Europeans, 1918.A1;
1930.A1; 1948.B26, B28;
1950.B14; 1951.A1-2; 1956.A1;
1957.A4, A6; 1959.B14, B96
"The Figure in the Carpet,"
1918.A1; 1927.A1; 1928.B3;
1943.B10; 1952.B36; 1953.B65;
1957.A1; 1958.B81
"Flickerbridge," 1943.B9;
1948.B37
"Four Meetings," 1930.A1;
1945.B14
French Poets and Novelists,
1929.A2; 1949.B14; 1959.B80
"The Friends of the Friends,"
1921.B22
"The Future of the Novel,"
1958.B84
"Gabrielle de Bergerac,"
1930.A1; 1955.A3
The Golden Bowl, 1918.A1
1925.B4; 1927.A1; 1932.B16;
1934.B11; 1935.B26; 1943.B32;
1944.A2; 1945.B5; 1946.B1;
1947.A1, B1; 1948.A1, B49;
1950.A2, B10; 1951.A2, B3;
1952.A2, B9, B52; 1953.B2-3,
B60; 1954.A4, B14, B26, B28;
1955.B21, B32, B38, B56;
1956.B11, B31, B82; 1957.A1-
2, B41, B58, B64, B76;
1958.A7, B15, B30; 1959.B64,
B67, B98
"The Great Good Place,"
1921.B22; 1945.B20; 1948.A1;
1958.B25
"Greville Fane," 1956.B33
Guy Domville, 1920.B4;
1952.B61
The High Bid, 1925.B8;
1947.B23
"The Impressions of a Cousin,"
1950.B43

An International Episode,
1930.A1; 1957.A4; 1958.A7
In the Cage, 1927.A1;
1939.B4; 1954.B15; 1958.B92;
1959.B33
The Ivory Tower, 1917.B10;
1918.B23; 1919.B10; 1927.A1
1935.B23; 1943.B32; 1944.A2;
1949.A1
"The Jolly Corner," 1925.A1;
1944.A2; 1945.B21; 1949.B22;
1951.B53; 1953.A2; 1956.B59;
1957.B67
Julia Bride, 1959.B16
"A Landscape Painter,"
1930.A1; 1955.A3, B1
"The Last of the Valerii,"
1951.B55
"The Lesson of the Master,"
1943.B10; 1958.B81
"The Liar," 1945.B22;
1949.B66; 1950.B48
"A Light Man," 1955.A3
"Louisa Pallant," 1945.B15
Madame de Mauves, 1930.A1;
1934.B26; 1951.A1; 1952.B35;
1957.A4, B45; 1958.A7, B9,
B43
The Madonna of the Future,
1930.A1; 1956.B50
"Master Eustace," 1930.A1
"The Middle Years," 1927.A1;
1945.B23; 1953.B65
"A Most Extraordinary Case,"
1955.A3
"Mrs. Medwin," 1945.B16
"My Friend Bingham,"
1930.A1; 1949.B36; 1955.A3
"The Next Time," 1943.B10;
1951.B38
Notebooks, 1944.A2; 1947.B32,
B49; 1948.B4, B29; 1953.B31,
B68
Notes on Novelists, 1918.B25;
1929.A2
"Osborne's Revenge,"
1949.B36; 1955.A3
The Other House, 1947.B10;
1951.B37; 1952.B43; 1957.A6

The Outcry, 1917.B15;
1918.A1; 1949.B9; 1955.B41;
1957.A4
"Owen Wingrave," 1921.B22;
1937.B2
Partial Portraits, 1929.A1
"A Passionate Pilgrim,"
1930.A1; 1948.B37; 1951.B22;
1958.A7
"Paste," 1957.B42
"The Pension Beaurepas,"
1930.A1
"Poor Richard," 1930.A1;
1953.A2; 1955.A3
The Portrait of a Lady,
1918.A1; 1920.A1; 1927.A1;
1930.A1; 1932.B16; 1943.B16;
1944.A2, B9; 1946.B9, B18;
1947.B14; 1948.B27-28;
1949.B51; 1950.A2, B75;
1951.A1-2, B43; 1952.A2, B12;
1953.B35, B63; 1954.A4, B40;
1955.B24, B47; 1956.A1, A3;
1957.A1-2, A6, B4, B10, B12;
1958.A7, B10, B41, B52, B67,
B70-71, B77; 1959.B30, B65,
B72, B82
Portraits of Places, 1934.B19
Prefaces to the New York
Edition, 1929.A2; 1931.A2;
1934.B2, B16; 1935.B2;
1937.B9
The Princess Casamassima,
1918.A1; 1921.B18; 1927.A1;
1932.B16; 1938.B5; 1946.B24;
1947.B36; 1948.B50;
1949.B28; 1950.B7; 1951.A1-
2, B36; 1952.A2, B68;
1953.B12; 1954.B20; 1955.A4,
B13, B40, B45-46; 1956.B14,
B26; 1957.A2, A6, B73;
1958.B35; 1959.B28, B34, B50,
B69, B79
"The Private Life," 1943.B10;
1951.A1, B40
"A Problem," 1949.B36;
1955.A3
"The Pupil," 1945.B24;
1958.B58; 1959.B39, B52, B83
"The Real Thing," 1945.B25;
1949.B37, B44; 1950.B2, B58;

1956.B40; 1957.B75; 1959.B9,
B43
The Reverberator, 1951.A1;
1955.B3; 1957.A4, B52;
1958.A7; 1959.B48
Roderick Hudson, 1918.A1;
1924.B8; 1925.B10; 1927.A1;
1390.A1; 1932.B16; 1943.B16;
1947.B20; 1948.B14; 1949.B2;
1950.A2; 1951.A1-2; 1952.A2,
B16; 1953.B11, B24; 1954.A4;
1956.A1, B26; 1957.A6;
1959.A2, B21
"The Romance of Certain Old
Clothes," 1930.A1; 1947.A1;
1951.B34; 1955.A3, B2
The Sacred Fount, 1918.A1;
1923.B9; 1927.A1; 1932.B16;
1934.B37; 1936.B7; 1942.B1;
1948.A1, B57; 1949.B45, B52;
1951.A1; 1953.B5; 1954.B19;
1955.B27; 1957.A1, A4;
1959.B26
The Sense of the Past,
1917.B10; 1919.B10; 1935.B23;
1944.A2; 1950.B67; 1955.B2,
B63
The Siege of London, 1953.B58
The Spoils of Poynton,
1918.A1; 1927.A1; 1944.B16;
1947.B24, B28; 1948.A1;
1950.B26; 1951.A2; 1954.A4,
B37; 1956.A1, B77; 1957.A4,
A6; 1959.B13, B15, B78, B90
"The Story of a Masterpiece,"
1930.A1; 1949.B36; 1955.A3
"The Story of a Year,"
1930.A1, 1949.B36; 1953.A2;
1954.B3; 1955.A3
"The Sweetheart of M. Bri-
seux," 1930.A1
"The Tone of the Time,"
1945.B26; 1950.B57
"A Tragedy of Error,"
1953.A2; 1956.B22; 1957.B27
The Tragic Muse, 1918.A1;
1927.A1; 1947.A1; 1951.A1-2;
1952.A2; 1954.B39; 1955.A4;
1956.A1; 1957.A1, B11;
1958.B65; 1959.B19, B71

Transatlantic Sketches,
1958.B66
"Travelling Companions,"
1930.A1; 1955.A3; 1957.A1
"The Tree of Knowledge,"
1945.B27
The Turn of the Screw,
1918.B26; 1921.B22; 1924.B10,
B16; 1928.B10; 1934.B37;
1941.B5, B16; 1943.B49;
1944.B12; 1947.B18, B25,
B47; 1948.B21, B57; 1949.B13,
B48, B50, B63-64; 1950.B10-
11, B37, B52; 1951.A2, B2,
B18; 1953.B32; 1954.B43;
1955.B6, B20, B27; 1956.B15,
B44; 1957.B13, B25, B31,
B44, B62; 1958.B26; 1959.B24,
B29, B45
"The Two Faces," 1953.B6;
1956.B60
Washington Square, 1918.A1;
1930.A1; 1934.B9; 1949.B41;
1950.B34, B47; 1951.A1-2;
1956.B16; 1957.A4, A6,
1959.B14, B88, B98
Watch and Ward, 1930.A1;
1950.B66; 1951.A2; 1952.B42;
1957.A6
What Maisie Knew, 1918.A1;
1921.B22; 1927.A1; 1947.A1;
B45; 1950.B10-11, B52;
1951.A1-2; 1953.B67-68;
1956.B12, B84; 1959.B93
The Wings of the Dove,
1918.A1; 1921.B13; 1925.B4;
1927.A1; 1932.B13, B16;
1935.B26; 1943.B52; 1944.A2;
1945.B5; 1946.B1, B25;
1947.B1, B14; 1948.B38;
1949.B5; 1951.A1-2, B3;
1953.B1, B38, B50; 1954.A1,
A4, B27, B35, B40; 1956.A1,
B1, B37; 1957.A1-2, B43,
B58; 1958.A7, B24, B34, B67,
B87; 1959.B41, B54, B85, B97
"Within the Rim," 1919.B17
James, William, 1920.B18
"James' Ambassadors," 1958.B21

"James: An American in Europe,"
1951.B51
"James and Conrad," 1945.B5
"James and Forster: The Morality
of Class," 1953.B12
"James and Jewett," 1953.B46
"James and Joyce," 1953.B57
"James and Kipling," 1951.B5
"James and the Plastic Arts,"
1943.B32
"James and Whistler at the Gros-
venor Gallery," 1952.B51
"James as a Traveler," 1948.B19
"James as Journalistic Critic,"
1957.B47
"James as Script Writer,"
1950.B70
"The James Brothers," 1948.B35
"The James Collection," 1942.B7
"James Editions," 1933.B4
"The Jameses," 1958.B14
"The Jameses: Financier, Here-
tic, Philosopher," 1932.B20
"James e Trollope," 1957.B79
"James Examines Shakespeare:
Notes on the Nature of Geni-
us," 1958.B68
The James Family: Including
Selections from the Writings
of Henry James, Sr., William,
Henry, and Alice James,
1947.A1
"James for Americans," 1952.B23
"A James 'Gift' to Edith Whar-
ton," 1957.B3
"James, Henry: 'The Portrait
of a Lady,'" 1941.B14
"The Jamesian Revolution,"
1957.B63
"James on a Revolutionary Theme,"
1938.B5; 1955.B14 (rpt.)
"James' Play of Minds," 1935.B17
"The James Revival," 1948.B15
"James Russell Lowell: A Link
between Tennyson and Henry
James," 1955.B2
"James's Air of Evil: The Turn
of the Screw," 1949.B13
"James's Debt to Hawthorne (I):
The Blithedale Romance and
The Bostonians," 1949.B4

"James's Debt to Hawthorne (III): The American Problem," 1950.B9

"James's Debt to Hawthorne (II): The Marble Faun and The Wings of the Dove," 1949.B5

"James's Idea of Dramatic Form," 1943.B20

"James's 'Jungle': The Seasons," 1954.B41

"James's Madame de Mauves and Hawthorne's The Scarlet Letter," 1958.B43

"James's Portrait of the Southerner," 1955.B4

"James's Revisions of the Love Affair in The American," 1956.B79

"James's Revisions of the Style of The Portrait of a Lady," 1958.B52

"James's Rhetoric of 'Quotes,'" 1956.B38

"James's Theory of Sex in Fiction," 1958.B84

"James's 'The Private Life' and Browning," 1951.B40

"James's 'The Pupil': The Art of Seeing Through," 1958.B58

"James's The Tragic Muse: Ave Atque Vale," 1958.B65

"James's 'The Turn of the Screw,'" 1955.B20

"James's 'The Two Faces,'" 1953.B6

"James's The Two Faces," 1956.B60

"James's 'What Maisie Knew': A Disagreement," 1950.B52

"James's 'Woman of Genius,'" 1955.B17-18 (Bradbrook), B35 (Fuller), B48 (Lubbock), B49 (McElderry), B54 (Nobbe)

"James the Dramatist," 1950.B3

"James the Melodramatist," 1943.B8; 1945.A1 (rpt.)

"James the Obscure," 1956.B3

"James the Obscured," 1947.B9

"James the Old Intruder," 1958.B78

"Jane Austen's Novel and the Novel of Henry James," 1938.B14

Jenkins, Iredell, 1957.B40

Jennings, Richard, 1943.B23

"John Cowper Powys on Henry James," 1953.B48

Johnson, Alice E., 1957.A5

Johnson, Arthur, 1919.B7

Johnson, Merle, 1932.B19; 1936.B10

Johnson, Thomas H., 1948.B23

"Jonathan Sturges," 1953.B17

Jones, Alexander E., 1959.B45

Jones, Howard Mumford, 1948.B24

--(with Ernest E. Leisy), 1952.B28

Jones, Llewellyn, 1959.B46

Jones, M., 1950.B47

Jones-Evans, Mervyn, 1946.B16; 1953.B33 (rpt.)

Jordan, Elizabeth, 1938.B9-10; 1943.B24

Josephson, Matthew, 1930.B14-16

K

K., Q., 1917.B13; 1918.B15

Kane, R. J., 1949.B28; 1950.B48

Kar, Annette, 1953.B34

Kästner, E., 1954.B24

Kaufman, Marjorie R., 1955.A1

Kayser, Von Rudolf, 1950.B49

Kazin, Alfred, 1943.B25; 1955.B44 (rpt.)

Kees, Weldon, 1941.B7

Kelley, Cornelia Pulsifer, 1930.A1; 1943.B26

"Kensington to Samoa," 1948.B20

Kenton, Edna, 1924.B10; 1925.B11; 1928.B14; 1934.B16-18; 1950.B50

Keown, Eric, 1946.B17; 1952.B29

Kerner, David, 1950.B51

Kettle, Arnold, 1953.B35

Key, Howard C. (with H. G. Flinn), 1959.B30

Keynes, Geoffrey, 1959.B47

Kimball, Jean, 1956.B37; 1957.B41

Kinnaird, John, 1958.B51
Kirk, Rudolf, 1949.B29; 1953.B36
Knight, Grant Cochran, 1925.B12;
    1931.B13; 1954.B25
Knights, L. C., 1939.B4
Knox, George, 1956.B38; 1959.B48
Kocmanová, Jessie, 1959.B49
Koskimies, Rafael, 1956.B39
Krans, Horatio S., 1923.B13
Kraus, Sydney J., 1956.A3;
    1958.B52
Krauss, W., 1955.B45
Kretsch, Robert W., 1959.B50
Krickel, Edwin F., Jr., 1955.A2
Krook, Dorothea, 1954.B26-28;
    1959.B51
Krutch, Joseph Wood, 1929.B3
Kuhn Bertha M., 1957.B42

L

"The Labyrinthine Spirit: Henry
    James," 1949.B3
"La critica letteraria de Henry
    James," 1959.B57
La Farge, John, 1949.B30
"La France dans l'oeuvre de Henry
    James," 1932.B10
Lainoff, Seymour, 1956.B40;
    1959.B52
"Lamb House, Rye," 1926.B3
A Landscape Painter, 1919.B13
Lang, Hans-Joachim, 1955.B46;
    1959.B53
Langland, Joseph (with James B.
    Hall), 1956.B33
Lanier, Sidney, 1945.B31
Larrabee, Harold A., 1932.B20
"L'art de Henry James," 1918.B17
"L'aspect religieux de Henry
    James," 1951.B26
"The Last Phase of Henry James,"
    1938.B15
Las Vergnas, Raymond, 1954.B29
"The Late Method of Henry James,"
    1954.A2
"L'atene dei James," 1955.B5
Laurence, Dan H., 1953.B37;
    1958.B53
--(with Leon Edel), 1957.A3

Leary, Lewis, 1954.B30; 1956.B41
Leavis, F. Raymond, 1937.B9;
    1946.B18; 1947.B19-20;
    1948.B25-28; 1949.B32-33;
    1950.B52; 1952.B30-31 (rpt.)
Leavis, Queenie D., 1938.B11;
    1947.B21-22; 1955.B47
LeClair, Robert C., 1945.B32;
"Lecture d'Henry James,"
    1954.B36
Lee, Vernon. See Paget, Violet
The Legend of the Master,
    1947.A2
Lehmann, John, 1949.B34;
    1952.B32
Leighton, Lawrence, 1934.B19
Leisi, Ernst, 1956.B42
Leisy, Ernest Erwin, 1929.B4
--(with Howard Mumford Jones),
    1952.B28
Lerner, Daniel, 1941.B8
--(with Oscar Cargill), 1951.B37
"'Les Ambassadeurs,'" 1950.B63
"Les 'Ambassadeurs' et les car-
    nets de James," 1951.B46
Les années dramatiques, 1931.A1
"Les héroines d'Henry James dans
    The Portrait of a Lady et
    d'Yvan Tourguéniev dans A la
    Veille," 1958.B10
Leslie, Shane, 1943.B27
"The Lesson of the Master,"
    1920.B17 (Huneker); 1951.B29
    (Greene); 1957.B12 (Chase)
"Letter: [Henry James],"
    1956.B67
"A Letter from Henry James to
    Francis Marion Crawford,"
    1958.B40
"Letter from London," 1959.B70
"Letter to the Editor," 1958.B73
"A Letter to the Editors,"
    1952.B18
"Letters and Comment," 1923.B1
"Letters in Criticism," 1920.B28
"Letters of Henry James,"
    1953.B30
The Letters of Henry James,
    1920.B20
"The Letters of Henry James,"
    1920.B7 (Bragdon), B9

(Coward), B12 (Gilman), B31
(Whitford), B32 (Woolf);
1921.B9 (Edgar)
"The Letters of Henry James to
Mr. Justice Holmes,"
1949.B27
"Letters to the Pell-Clarkes
from their 'Old Cousin and
Friend' Henry James,"
1959.B77
"Lettre d'Angleterre," 1923.B8
"Lettres anglo-américaines:
Henry James," 1954.B29
"Letters de Tourguéneff à Henry
James," 1949.B55
Levin, Harry, 1956.B43
Levy, B. M., 1947.B23
Levy, Leo B., 1956.B44-45;
1957.A6; 1958.B54
Lewis, J. H., 1928.B15
Lewis, Naomi, 1958.B55
Lewis, R. W. B., 1957.B43;
1959.B54
Lewis, Wyndham, 1934.B20
Lewisohn, Ludwig, 1931.B14;
1932.B21 (rpt.)
Leyburn, E. D., 1959.B55
"L'homme sans présent," 1954.B33
Liddell, Robert, 1947.B24-28;
1953.B38-39
Liljegren, Sten Bodvar, 1920.A1
Lind, Ilse Dusoir, 1951.B38
--(with Leon Edel), 1957.B22
Lind, Sidney E., 1948.B29;
1951.B39-40
Linn, James W. (with H. W. Tay-
lor), 1935.B11
"Literary Consciousness and the
Literary Conscience,"
1950.B26
"The Literary Convictions of
Henry James," 1957.B19
"A Literary Correspondence,"
1959.B23
"Literary Credos: I. Henry
James and 'The Art of Fic-
tion.' 1884," 1950.B1
"The Literary Criticism of the
Genteel Decades, 1870-1900,"
1955.B31

"A Literary Friendship--Henry
James and Paul Bourget,"
1950.B54
"The Literary Life," 1952.B36
"The Literary Orphan," 1953.B26
Literary Reviews and Essays by
Henry James on American,
English, and French Litera-
ture, 1957.B50
"Literature and Morality: A
Crucial Question of our
Times," 1947.B12
Littell, Philip, 1917.B14;
1919.B8, B9 (rpt.); 1920.B19
"A Little Reality," 1934.B6
Livesay, J. F. B., 1927.B7
Lochhead, Marion, 1959.B56
Lombardo, Agostino, 1959.B57-58
"Looking Backward with Henry
James," 1956.B6
"The Loose and Baggy Monsters of
Henry James: Notes on the
Underlying Classic Form in
the Novel," 1951.B3;
1955.B11 (rpt.)
"'The Lord of Burleigh' and Henry
James's 'A Landscape Paint-
er,'" 1955.B1
Lovett, Robert Morss (with Helen
Sard Hughes), 1932.B18
Lowell, James Russell, 1932.B22
"Lowell 'Edits' James: Some Re-
visions in French Poets and
Novelists," 1959.B80
Lowndes, Marie Belloc, 1943.B28;
1946.B19
Lubbock, Percy, 1920.B20;
1921.B13; 1928.B16; 1947.B29;
1952.B33 (rpt.); 1955.B48
Lucas, E. V., 1921.B14; 1928.B17;
1932.B23
Lucke, Jessie Ryon, 1953.B40
"The Lucky Crowd--Contemporary
British Fiction," 1958.B46
Ludeke, Henry, 1952.B34
Ludwig, Richard M., 1959.B59
--(with Marvin B. Perry, Jr.),
1952.B35
Lyde, Marilyn Jones, 1959.B60-61

Lydenberg, John, 1957.B44
Lynd, Robert, 1919.B10; 1952.B36-37
Lynskey, Winifred, 1952.B38

M

MacCarthy, Desmond, 1917.B15; 1920.B21; 1930.B17; 1931.B15-16 (rpt.), B17; 1935.B12; 1949.B35; 1953.B41
McCarthy, Harold T., 1956.B46; 1958.A3
MacColl, D. S., 1945.B33
McCormick, John O., 1957.B45
McCullough, Bruce Walker, 1946.B20
McElderry, Bruce R., Jr. 1949.B36; 1950.B53; 1952.B39-43; 1954.B31; 1955.B49-50; 1958.B56
McFarlane, I. D., 1950.B54
McGill, V. J., 1930.B18
Machen, Arthur, 1943.B29
MacKenzie, Compton, 1943.B30; 1944.B7 (rpt.); 1950.B55 (rpt.)
McLane, James, 1924.B11
McLuhan, H. M., 1947.B30
McMahon, Helen, 1952.B44
"Maggie Verver: Neither Saint nor Witch," 1957.B76
"Maisie in What Maisie Knew," 1959.B93
"Maisie, Miles and Flora, the Jamesian Innocents," 1950.B11
"Maisie, Miles and Flora, the Jamesian Innocents: A Rejoinder," 1952.B6
"The Major James," 1955.B28
Male, Roy R., Jr., 1954.B32
"Malice in Wonderland," 1959.B38
Mallet, Charles, 1935.B13
Manly, John Matthews (with Edith Rickert), 1922.B11
"'The Marble Faun' and 'The Wings of the Dove,'" 1926.B7
Marchand, Leslie, 1948.B30
Markow, Georges, 1951.B41
Markow-Totevy, Georges, 1958.A4

Marquardt, William F., 1949.B37
Marsden, Malcolm M., 1958.B57
Marsh, Edward, 1939.B5
Marshall, Margaret, 1943.B31; 1950.B56
Martin, Terence J., 1958.B58
Martin, W. R., 1959.B62
Mary Francis, Sister, 1959.B63
Mason, A. E. W., 1935.B14
"The Massacre of the Innocents," 1952.B70
Matsuhara, Iwao, 1958.B59
Matthews, Brander, 1920.B22; 1921.B15; 1923.B15 (rpt.)
Matthiessen, F. O., 1935.B15; 1941.B9-10; 1943.B32; 1944.A2, B8-9, B10 (rpt.); 1945.B34; 1947.A1, B31-32; 1948.B31; 1952.B45 (rpt.)
Maugham, Somerset, 1939.B6; 1952.B46; 1955.B51
"Maule's Well; or Henry James and the Relation of Morals to Manners," 1938.B17; 1947.B50 (rpt.)
Mauriac, François, 1955.B52
Maurois, André, 1944.B11; 1945.B35; 1947.B33 (rpt.)
Maxse, Mary, 1939.B7
Maxwell, J. C., 1949.B38
Mayne, Ethel Coburn, 1918.B16
Mayoux, Jean-Jacques, 1954.B33
"The Meaning of the Match Image in James's The Ambassadors," 1955.B29
"Meetings with Some Men of Letters," 1932.B25
"Melancholy of the Masters," 1947.B34
Melchiori, Barbara, 1957.B46
Mellow, James R., 1957.B47
Mellquist, Jerome, 1946.B21
"Memorabilia," 1943.B6-7
Memorabilist, 1943.B33-34
"Memories of a Mandarin," 1956.B4
"Memories of Henry James," 1926.B18 (Waterlow); 1950.B55 (MacKenzie)
Mencken, H. L., 1919.B11; 1920.B23; 1949.B39

Mendilow, A. A., 1952.B47
Mennemeier, F. N., 1957.B48
"The Merciful Fraud in Three
    Stories by James," 1949.B22
"Metaphor in the Plot of The
    Ambassadors," 1951.B23
"The Method of the Later Works
    of Henry James," 1954.B26
Michaels, H. S., 1951.B42
Michaud, Régis, 1918.B17;
    1922.B12; 1926.B11-12;
    1928.B18
"'The Middle Years,'" 1918.B19,
    B22 (rpt.)
"The Middle Years," 1919.B9
Milano, Paolo, 1948.A2
Millar, C. C. Hoyer, 1937.B10
Miller, Betty, 1948.B32;
    1949.B40
Miller, Raymond A., Jr., 1957.B49
Miller, Warren, 1949.B41
Millett, Fred B., 1950.B57;
    1951.B43; 1952.B48
Millgate, Michael, 1959.B64
Mills, J. Saxon, 1921.B16
Miner, Earl R., 1954.B34
"A Misprint in 'The Awkward
    Age,'" 1945.B30
"Miss Savage and Miss Bartram,"
    1948.B32
The Modern Fables of Henry James,
    1935.A1
"The Modern Henry James," 1945.B1
"A Modern Writer in Search of a
    Moral Subject," 1934.B27
Moeller, Charles, 1953.B43
"Moeurs Contemporaines, VII,"
    1926.B16
"Money, Birth, and Henry James,"
    1917.B15
Monroe, Elizabeth N., 1941.B11;
    1956.B49
Montgomery, Marion, 1959.B65
Moore, George, 1923.B16
Moore, John Robert, 1959.B66
Moore, Marianne, 1934.B21;
    1937.B11 (rpt.); 1955.B53
    (rpt.)
"The Moral Aspects of Henry James's
    James's 'International Situa-
    tion,'" 1943.B47

"Morality and Henry James,"
    1923.B3
"Morals and Civilization in
    Henry James," 1953.B11
"Morals and Motives in The Spoils
    of Poynton," 1954.B37
Mordell, Albert, 1919.B12-13;
    1957.B50
Morgan, Charles, 1943.B35
Morgan, Louise, 1926.B13
Morooka, Hirashi, 1952.B49
Morris, Lloyd R., 1947.B34
Morris, Wright, 1958.B60, B61
    (rpt.) B62
Mortimer, Raymond, 1943.B36
Moses, Montrose J., 1920.B24
"The Mote in the Middle Dis-
    tance," 1936.B3
"The Mothers of Henry James,"
    1951.B53
Moult, Thomas, 1920.B25
Mowat, Robert Balmain, 1935.B16
"Mr. Edmund Wilson and The Turn
    of the Screw," 1947.B47
"Mr. H____," 1946.B22
"Mr. James and the London Sea-
    son," 1938.B9
"Mr. James's Aesthetic Mr.
    Nash," 1957.B11
"Mr. James's Aesthetic Mr. Nash
    --Again," 1959.B71
"Mr. Oddy," 1933.B12
"Mrs. Grundy Adopts Daisy Mil-
    ler," 1946.B15
"Mr. Shaw on Printed Plays,"
    1923.B21
"Mr. Verver, Our National Hero,"
    1955.B38
Muecke, D. C., 1954.B35
Muller, Herbert, 1937.B12
Munro, Isabel S. (with Dorothy
    Cook), 1953.B15
Munson, Gorham, 1950.B58
Murakami, Fujio, 1959.B67
Murdock, Kenneth B., 1957.B51
--(with F. O. Matthiessen),
    1947.B32
Murray, Donald M., 1952.B50-51
Mustanoja, Tauno F., 1951.B44
"My Meetings with Henry James,"
    1944.B7
"Myth and Dialectic in the Later
    Novels," 1943.B55

N

Nadal, Elirman Syme, 1920.B26
Naefe, Anneliese, 1951.B45
Narkevich, A. Iu, 1941.B12
Nathan, Monique, 1951.B46
"Nature, Art, and Imagination in
    The Spoils of Poynton,"
    1959.B15
Neff, John C., 1938.B12
Neider, Charles, 1948.B33
"A Nest of Gentlefolk at Cam-
    bridge, Massachusetts: Tur-
    genev's American Reputation
    in the Nineteenth Century--
    His Impact on the Youthful
    Henry James," 1956.B55
Nevins, Allan, 1930.B19
Nevius, Blake, 1953.B44
Newbolt, Henry, 1942.B5
"New Documents on the Jameses,"
    1947.B49
"New Editions," 1951.B50
"New Reflections on The Golden
    Bowl," 1957.B68
"The Nice American Gentleman,"
    1949.B17
Niess, R. J., 1956.B50
"The Night Journey in The Ambas-
    sadors," 1956.B21
Nobbe, Susanne H., 1955.B54
Noel, France, 1942.A1
"No Innocents Abroad," 1958.B11
"No Landmarks," 1933.B1;
    1937.B3 (rpt.)
Norman, Sylva, 1947.B35
The Notebooks of Henry James,
    1947.B32
"The Notebooks of Henry James,"
    1953.B49
"A Note by His Photographer,"
    1934.B4
"A Note on 'A Bundle of Letters,'"
    1945.B11
"A Note on Art and Neurosis,"
    1945.B41
"A Note on 'Brooksmith,'"
    1945.B12
"A Note on 'Europe,'" 1945.B13
"A Note on 'Four Meetings,'"
    1945.B14

"A Note on Henry James," 1917.B12
    (Huneker); 1922.B9 (rpt.);
    1929.B2 (Hoare); 1943.B27
    (Leslie)
"A Note on Henry James's First
    Short Story," 1957.B27
"A Note on Henry James's 'The
    Pupil,'" 1959.B52
"A Note on Henry James's 'The
    Real Thing,'" 1956.B40
"A Note on Literary Indebtedness:
    Dickens, George Eliot, Henry
    James," 1955.B47
"A Note on 'Louisa Pallant,'"
    1945.B15
"A Note on 'Mrs. Medwin,'"
    1945.B16
"A Note on 'The Altar of the
    Dead,'" 1945.B17
"A Note on 'The Beast in the
    Jungle,'" 1945.B18
"A Note on The Beast in the Jun-
    gle," 1950.B51
"A Note on 'The Birthplace,'"
    1945.B19
"A Note on the Freudian Reading
    of 'The Turn of the Screw,'"
    1957.B62
"A Note on the Genesis of Daisy
    Miller," 1948.B13
"A Note on 'The Great Good
    Place,'" 1945.B20; 1948.B17
    (rpt.)
"A Note on 'The Jolly Corner,'"
    1945.B21
"A Note on 'The Liar,'" 1945.B22
"A Note on 'The Middle Years,'"
    1945.B23
"A Note on The Princess Casa-
    massima," 1957.B73
"A Note on 'The Pupil,'" 1945.B24
"A Note on 'The Real Thing,'"
    1945.B25
"A Note on 'The Tone of the
    Time,'" 1945.B26
"A Note on the Translations of
    H. James in France," 1930.B8
"A Note on 'The Tree of Knowl-
    edge,'" 1945.B27
Notes and Reviews by Henry James,
    1921.B8

"Notes by the Way," 1943.B31

"Notes in the Margin," 1920.B23

"Notes on Henry James," 1943.B46

"Notes on Henry James and The Turn of the Screw," 1950.B37

"The Notes on Novelists," 1918.B25

"The Notes To 'The Ivory Tower,'" 1918.B23

"Not Quite the Real Thing," 1945.B34

"A Novel as a 'Work of Art': A Reading of The Ambassadors," 1958.A1

"The Novel as Dramatic Poem (III): The Europeans," 1948.B26

"The Novel from James to Joyce," 1931.B1

"The Novelist and his Subject-Matter: Reflections of Henry James and H. G. Wells," 1958.B7

"The Novelist and the Business-man: Henry James, Edith Wharton, Frank Norris," 1959.B64

"The Novelist as Art Critic," 1957.B24

"The Novelist as Mystic: 'The Song of Henry James,'" 1947.B26

"The Novelist in Search of Perfection," 1946.B20

"Novelists' Thoughts About Their Art. I. Anthony Trollope and Henry James," 1956.B39

"A Novel of Henry Adams," 1925.B17

"Novels of Henry James," 1921.B1

"The Novels of Henry James," 1930.B23

Nowell-Smith, Simon, 1946.B22; 1947.A2; 1957.B52; 1958.B63; 1959.B68

"Now that you've read James' 'The Beast in the Jungle,'" 1958.B45

Nuhn, Ferner, 1942.B6

O

O'Brien, E. J., 1923.B17

Ochshorn, Myron, 1952.B52

O'Connor, Frank. See O'Donovan, Michael

O'Connor, William Van, 1952.B53

O'Donovan, Michael, 1956.B52

O'Faolain, Sean, 1948.B34

"Of Henry James and Howells, 1925," 1925.B15

"Of Some Americans," 1922.B2

Okita, Hajime, 1958.A5

"The Old Masters: Howells and James," 1922.B11

Oliver, Clinton Forrest, 1947.B36; 1959.B69

"On Henry James' Centennial: Lasting Impressions of a Great American Writer," 1943.B11

"On Henry James's Roderick Hudson," 1952.B49

"On James's 'The Great Good Place,'" 1948.B17

"On The Portrait of a Lady," 1953.B63; 1959.B89 (rpt.)

"Onward and Upward with the Arts: The Wings of Henry James," 1959.B85

Orage, Alfred Richard, 1918.B18; 1922.B13; 1935.B17; 1953.B45 (rpt.)

Orcutt, William Dana, 1926.B14; 1934.B22; 1935.B18 (rpt.); 1943.B37; 1945.B36 (rpt.)

"Organic Form in American Criticism, 1840-1870," 1955.B34

"Oscar Wilde and Henry James," 1948.B40

"Other Books," 1956.B49

The Other House, 1947.B10

"Otherness," 1949.B35

"Our Contemporary Henry James," 1948.B53

"Our Illustrious Expatriate," 1920.B8

"Our Passion Is Our Task," 1943.B25

"Over Henry's Shoulder,"
1956.B41
Oxford and Asquith, Earl of,
1928.B19

P

Pacey, W. C. D., 1941.B13
Packman, James (with Ernest A.
Baker), 1932.B2
Paget, Violet, 1923.B18
The Painter's Eye: Notes and
Essays on the Pictorial Arts
by Henry James, 1956.B74
"The Painter's Sponge and Var-
nish Bottle: Henry James'
Revision of The Portrait of
a Lady," 1944.A2; 1944.B9
Palache, John G., 1924.B12
"The Palpitating Divan,"1950.B21
Panter-Downes, Mollie, 1959.B70
"The Paradox of an American
'Identity,'" 1958.B51
Parisian Sketches: Letters to
the New York Tribune, 1875-
1876, 1957.B22
Parkes, Henry Bamford, 1948.B35;
1955.B55
Parks, Edd Winfield (with James
Harry Smith), 1951.B54
Parquet, Mary E., 1959.A3
Parrington, Vernon Louis,
1930.B20
"A 'Passionate Pilgrim,'"
1930.B15
"The Passionate Pilgrim: An
Aspect of Henry James,"
1948.B37
Pattee, Fred L., 1923.B19;
1930.B21
"The Pattern of Innocence
through Experience in the
Characters of Henry James,"
1953.B53
"Patterns of Realism in the At-
lantic," 1952.B44
Patterson, David, 1953.B46
Paulding, Gouverneur, 1956.B53
Peacock, Ronald, 1946.B23
Pécnik, B., 1952.B54

Pennell, Joseph, 1922.B14;
1925.B13 (rpt.)
Penzoldt, Peter, 1952.B55
Perrin, Edwin N., 1955.B56
Perry, Bliss, 1922.A1; 1935.B19
Perry, F. M., 1926.B15
Perry, Marvin, B., Jr. (with
Richard Ludwig), 1952.B35
Perry, Ralph Barton, 1933.B10;
1935.B20; 1942.B7
"The Personality of Henry James,"
1949.B53
"Personal Recollections of Henry
James," 1920.B26
"Petite bibliographe de Henry
James depuis la guerre,"
1952.B64
Phelps, Gilbert, 1956.B54-55
Phelps, William Lyon, 1921.B17;
1923.B20; 1924.B13 (rpt.);
1939.B8
Phillips, J. Nova, 1957.B53
Phillips, LeRoy, 1930.A2
Picon, Gaëtan, 1954.B36
"The Pictorial Element in the
Theory and Practice of Henry
James," 1955.A5
"Pictorial Method in the Novels
of Henry James," 1955.A6
Pierhal, Armand, 1951.B47
"The Pilgrimage," 1957.B8
The Pilgrimage of Henry James,
1925.A1
"The Pilgrimage of Henry James,"
1952.B67
"The 'Plays' of Henry James,"
1928.B14
"The Plays of Henry James,"
1951.B30
Pochmann, Henry A., 1957.B54
--(with Gay Wilson Allen),
1949.B42
Podhoretz, Norman, 1958.B64
"The Poetics of Henry James,"
1935.B29; 1945.A1 (rpt.)
"Point of View in The Turn of
the Screw," 1959.B45
"Point of View: James," 1932.B3
"Point of View: James and
Others," 1932.B4

"Point of View: James, Stendhal," 1932.B5
"Political Passion in Balzac and Henry James," 1959.B50
Popkin, Henry, 1949.B43; 1951.B48
The Portable Henry James, 1951.B58
Porter, Katherine Anne, 1943.B38; 1952.B56
--(with Allen Tate and Mark Van Doren), 1944.B12
The Portrait of a Lady, 1947.B14 (Greene); 1951.B43 (Millett); 1956.B25 (Edel)
"The Portrait of a Lady: A Critical Reappraisal," 1957.B10
"'The Portrait of a Lady' Reprinted," 1948.B27
"The Portrait of a Lady: 'The Eternal Mystery of Things,'" 1959.B72
"The Portrait of a Lady: Vis Inertiae," 1959.B82
"Portrait of Henry James," 1921.B5
"The Portrait of New England," 1948.B7; 1955.B15 (rpt.)
Pouillon, Jean, 1953.B47
Poulet, Georges, 1956.B56
Pound, Ezra, 1918.B19-21, B22 (rpt.), B23-24; 1920.B27 (rpt.); 1926.B16; 1934.B23, B24 (rpt.); 1950.B59
Powers, Lyall H., 1955.A4; 1957.B55; 1958.B65; 1959.B71-72
--(with Leon Edel), 1958.B28, B29 (rpt.)
Powys, John Cowper, 1953.B48
"A Practical Approach to 'The Real Thing,'" 1949.B37
"Pragmatism of Henry James," 1951.B20
Pratt, William C., 1957.B56
"A Prediction in Regard to Three English Authors," 1924.B6
"The Prefaces of George Sand and Henry James," 1955.B71

Prefaces of Henry James, 1931.A2
"Prefatory Note. 'A Tragedy of Error': James's First Story," 1956.B22
"A Pre-Freudian Reading of The Turn of the Screw," 1957.B31
"Preoccupations of Henry James," 1957.B55
"Presence de Henry James," 1947.B7
"Pretender to the Drama," 1949.B43
The Princess Casamassima, 1948.B51 (Trilling); 1959.B69 (Oliver)
"The Princess Casamassima," 1950.B71
"The Princess Casamassima: A Critical Reappraisal," 1956.B14
"The Princess Casamassima: An Introductory Essay," 1948.B50
"The Princess Far Away," 1925.B2
"Principles and Methods in the Later Works of Henry James," 1959.B51
Pritchard, John Paul, 1956.B57
Pritchett, V. S., 1948.B36; 1953.B49
"A Probable Source for a James Nouvelle," 1959.B33
"The Problem in Roderick Hudson," 1952.B16
"The Profanation of the Child," 1958.B33
"A Protest against the James Vogue," 1952.B60
"Psychical Research and 'The Turn of the Screw,'" 1949.B50
"The Psychological Novel," 1931.B21
"The Published Letters of Henry James: A Survey," 1952.B40
"The Published Letters of Henry James: A Survey. Part II," 1952.B41
"'The Pupil': The Education of a Prude," 1959.B83
Putt, S. Gorley, 1946.B24-25; 1947.B37; 1948.B37

Q

"A Question of Covering One's
   Tracks," 1952.B32
The Question of Henry James: A
   Collection of Critical Es-
   says, 1945.A1.
"The Question of James," 1945.B43
"The Quest of Beauty," 1939.B9
Quinn, Arthur Hobson, 1932.B24;
   1936.B11
Quinn, Patrick F., 1954.B37
Qvamme, B., 1944.B13

R

Raeth, Claire J., 1949.B44-45
Rahv, Phillip, 1937.B13; 1940.B9
   (rpt.); 1943.B39-40;
   1944.B14; 1945.B37; 1947.B38;
   1949.B46-47 (rpt.) 1959.B73-
   74 (rpt.)
"A Rainy Afternoon with Truman
   Capote," 1957.B70
Raleigh, John Henry, 1951.B49;
   1957.B57
Randall, D. A. (with J. T. Win-
   terich), 1941.B14
Randell, Wilfrid L., 1921.B18
Rauch, K., 1954.B38
Ray, Gordon, 1952.B57
--(with Leon Edel), 1958.A2
Read, Herbert, 1927.B8; 1929.B5
   (rpt.); 1938.B13 (rpt.);
   1948.B38; 1956.B58 (rpt.);
   1957.B58
--(with Edward Dahlberg),
   1959.B23
"Reading Henry James Aloud,"
   1943.B17
"The Real Approach to The Real
   Thing," 1949.B44
"Realism and Aestheticism: In-
   troduction," 1954.B9
"The Realism War," 1958.B17
"The Realists: Henry James,"
   1956.B57
"The Real Juliana Bordereau,"
   1956.B81
"The Real Princess Christina,"
   1959.B79

"'The Real Thing,'" 1957.B75
"'The Real Thing,': A Parable
   for Writers of Fiction,"
   1950.B58
"The Reception of Daisy Miller,"
   1958.B83
"The Reception of Henry James in
   Germany," 1959.B5
"The Record of Henry James,"
   1920.B5
Redgrave, Michael, 1959.B75
"The Rediscovery of Henry
   James," 1945.B39
Redlich, Rosemarie (with David E.
   Scherman), 1952.B59
Redman, Ben Ray, 1951.B50
"The Redundancy of Henry James,"
   1945.B36
Reed, Glenn A., 1949.B48
Reid, Forrest, 1929.B6; 1940.B10
"The Relation Between William and
   Henry James," 1952.B8
"The Relation of Theme and Setting
   in the Major Novels of Henry
   James," 1959.A1
"The Relativism of Henry James,"
   1953.B22
"Religious Imagery in Henry
   James's Fiction," 1957.B29
"Repeat Performances," 1955.B19
"Representative Tragic Heroines
   in the Work of Brown, Haw-
   thorne, Howells, James, and
   Dreiser," 1957.B49
"The Return of Henry James,"
   1930.B16 (Josephson); 1934.B7
   (Cantwell); 1945.B40 (Stev-
   ens); 1948.B10 (Canby)
   1952.B37 (Lynd)
"The Revelation of an Artist in
   Literature," 1920.B10
"Reverberations and The Rever-
   berator," 1959.B48
The Reverberator, 1957.B52
"A Reviewer's Notebook," 1921.B2;
   1922.B1
"The Revised Version," 1918.B1
"The Revision of Daisy Miller,"
   1950.B31
"The Revision of Roderick Hud-
   son," 1925.B10

"The Revival of Interest in
Henry James," 1945.B9
"The Revolt of the Workers in
the Novels of Gissing, James,
and Conrad," 1959.B49
Richardson, Lyon, 1941.B15
Rickert, Edith (with John Mat-
thews Manly), 1922.B11
"The Rise of Realism, 1871-
1891," 1953.B20
"The Rise of the Novel," 1932.B21
Ritchie, G. S., 1940.B11
"Roadside Meetings of a Literary
Nomad," 1930.B9
"Robert Louis Stevenson and Henry
James, with Some Letters of
Mrs. R. L. Stevenson,"
1924.B3
Roberts, Morley, 1932.B25
Roberts, Morris, 1929.A2;
1946.B26; 1947.B39; 1948.B39;
1949.B49
Robertson, W. Graham, 1931.B18
Robins, Elizabeth, 1932.A1
Robinson, Edwin Arlington,
1947.B40
Robinson, Jean Joseph, 1952.B58
Robson, W. W., 1954.B39
Roditi, Edouard, 1947.B41;
1948.B40
Rodker, John, 1918.B25
Roellinger, F. X., Jr., 1949.B50
Rogers, Robert, 1956.B59
"Romanen som redskap eller erk-
jennelse. Noen notater om
forholdet mellom Henry James
og H. G. Wells," 1958.B49
"'Romola' and 'The Golden Bowl,'"
1953.B2
Roscoe, E. S., 1925.B14
Rosenbaum, S. P., 1959.B76-78
Rosenfeld, Paul, 1946.B27
Rosenzweig, Saul, 1943.B41;
1944.B15 (rpt.)
Rothenstein, William, 1932.B26
"The Rough and Lurid Vision:
Henry James, Graham Greene
and the International Theme,"
1957.B45
Rourke, Constance, 1931.B19
Rouse, Blair, 1950.B60

Routh, Harold Victor, 1937.B14
Rupp, Henry R., 1956.B60
"A Ruskin Echo in The Wings of
the Dove," 1956.B1
Russell, John, 1943.B42-43;
1945.B38
Russell, John R., 1956.B61
"Rye Road," 1931.B12
Rypins, H. L. (with Leon Edel),
1953.B50

S

S., C., 1956.B62
S., W. E., 1953.B58
Sackville-West, Edward, 1948.B41;
1949.B51-53; 1951.B51
"The Sacred and Solitary Ref-
uge," 1948.B4
The Sacred Fount, 1953.B18;
1959.B26
"The Sacred Fount," 1942.B1
"'The Sacred Rage': The Time-
Theme in 'The Ambassadors,'"
1957.B66
Samokhvalov, N. I., 1956.B63
Sampson, George, 1920.B28
Sampson, Martin W., 1927.B9;
1930.B22
"Sanctuary vs. The Turn of the
Screw," 1957.B13
Sandeen, Ernest, 1954.B40
Sarawak, Ranee Margaret of,
1934.B25
Sassoon, Siegfried, 1948.B42
"Saturday Morning: The Illusion
of the Middle Way," 1958.B22
"Saved from the Salvage,"
1943.B44
Savelli, Giovanni, 1949.B54
Scarborough, Dorothy, 1917.B16-17
The Scenic Art, Notes on Acting
and the Drama, 1872-1901,
1948.B52
Schelling, Felix E., 1922.B15
Scherman, David E. (with Rose-
marie Redlich), 1952.B59
Schieber, Alis J., 1957.B59
Schneditz, W., 1955.B57
Schneider, Isidor, 1945.B39

"The School of Experience in the Early Novels," 1934.B26; 1935.B25 (rpt.)

"A Schopenhauerian Novel: James's The Princess Casa-massima," 1958.B35

Schorer, Mark, 1950.B61

Schulz, Max F., 1955.B58

Schürenberg, W., 1957.B60

Scott, Arthur L., 1952.B60

Scott, Dixon, 1917.B18

Scott-James, Rolfe Arnold, 1951.B52

"The Secret of Henry James's Style as Revealed by His Typist," 1917.B1

"Seeing Things," 1950.B16

"Seeing through 'The Pupil' Again," 1959.B39

"Seer of the Gem-like Flame," 1953.B54

"Sehnsucht nach Wirklichkeit," 1956.B65

Selected Fiction, 1953.B19

The Selected Letters of Henry James, 1955.B26

Selected Stories, 1957.B38

"The Sense of the Present in 'The Aspern Papers,'" 1959.B4

"Sensibility and Technique: Preface to a Critique," 1943.B16

"The Sentence Structure of Henry James," 1946.B28

"A Sentimental Contribution," 1934.B33

"A Series of Exercises on The Education of Henry Adams and The Portrait of a Lady," 1952.B12

Seznec, Jean, 1949.B55

"A Shake Down," 1918.B24

"The Shape of a Career," 1958.B48

Shapira, Morris, 1957.B61

Sharp, Robert L., 1953.B51

Shaw, George Bernard, 1923.B21; 1952.B61

Sherman, Stuart Pratt, 1917.B19, B20 (rpt.); 1929.B7; 1934.B27

Short, R. W., 1946.B28; 1950.B62; 1953.B52

The Short Novels of Henry James, 1957.A4

The Short Stories of Henry James, 1945.B10

Shroeder, J. W., 1951.B53

"The 'Shy Incongruous Charm' of Daisy Miller," 1955.B50

Sichel, Walter, 1924.B14

Siedler, W. J., 1956.B64-66

Sigaux, Gilbert, 1950.B63

"The Significance of Henry James," 1927.B8

"'Silas Lapham,' 'Daisy Miller,' and the Jews," 1953.B9

Silver, John, 1957.B62

"The Silver Clue," 1944.B2; 1955.B16 (rpt.)

Simon, Irène, 1949.B56

Simon, Jean, 1949.B57

"The Simplicity of Henry James: Some Notes on a Discovery," 1923.B9

Sinclair, Upton, 1956.B67

Slabey, R. M., 1958.B66

"Slices of Cake," 1943.B45

Smith, Bernard, 1939.B9

Smith, F. E., 1947.B42

Smith, James Harry (with Edd Winfield Parks), 1951.B54

Smith, Janet Adam, 1936.B12; 1948.A3; 1956.B68

Smith, Logan Pearsall, 1931.B20; 1939.B10-11; 1943.B44-46

Smith, Roland M., 1949.B58

Smith, S. Stephenson, 1931.B21

Smyth, Ethel, 1940.B12-13

Snell, Edwin Marion, 1935.A1

Snell, George, 1947.B43

Snow, Lotus, 1953.B53; 1958.B67

"Social Criticism in James's London Fiction," 1959.B94

"The Soho Bibliography of Henry James," 1958.B5

"Some Bibliographical Adventures in Americana," 1950.B6

"Some Bibliographical Notes on Henry James," 1934.B18

"Some Bibliographical Notes on the Short Stories of Henry James," 1949.B15

Index

"Some Comments on B. R. McEl-
derry's 'The Uncollected
Stories of Henry James,'"
1951.B39
"Some Critical Terms of Henry
James," 1950.B62
"Some Forgotten Tales of Henry
James," 1922.B15
"Some Novelists I Have Known,"
1952.B46
"Some Readings and Misreadings,"
1953.B28
"A Source for Roderick Hudson,"
1948.B14
Spanos, Bebe, 1959.B79
"The Special Case of Henry
James," 1932.B27
Specker, Heidi, 1948.B43
Spencer, Benjamin T., 1957.B63
Spencer, James L., 1957.B64
Spender, Stephen, 1934.B26-27;
1935.B21 (rpt.), B22-24,
B25 (rpt.), B26; 1944.B16
"The Sphinx and the Housecat,"
1945.B3
Spiller, Robert, 1953.B54;
1955.B59; 1956.B69-70
"The Spoils of Art," 1959.B90
"The Spoils of Henry James,"
1946.B29
"The Spoils of Poynton,"
1959.B78
Squire, Sir John Collings,
1919.B14
Stafford, William T., 1953.B55;
1955.B60-61; 1958.B68-69;
1959.B80-81
--(with Maurice Beebe), 1957.B2
Stallman, R. W., 1957.B65-66;
1958.B70-71
--(with Ray B. West, Jr.),
1949.B65-66
Stanzel, Franz, 1956.B71
"Stars and Striplings: American
Youth in the Nineteenth Century," 1959.B56
"The State of the Theatre: Actors Take the Honors,"
1950.B12
Steegmuller, Francis, 1948.B44
Stein, Gertrude, 1947.B44

Stein, William Bysshe, 1956.B72;
1959.B82-84
Stevens, A. W., 1955.B62
Stevens, George, 1945.B40
Stevenson, Elizabeth, 1949.A1
"Stevenson and Henry James: The
Rare Friendship Between Two
Famous Stylists," 1926.B8
"Stevenson and James's Child-
hood," 1953.B51
Stewart, Randall, 1943.B47;
1958.B72
Stokes, Donald Hubert, 1950.B64
Stoll, E. E., 1948.B45
Stone, Edward, 1950.B65-67;
1951.B55; 1954.B41; 1955.B63
Stone, Geoffrey, 1949.B59
Stott, R. Toole, 1958.B73
Stovall, Floyd, 1943.B48;
1953.B56; 1957.B67
"Stream of Consciousness,"
1927.B6
Strong, L. A. G., 1953.B57
"Struthers Burt '04: The Lit-
erary Career of a Prince-
tonian," 1958.B16
"Study Questions and Theme As-
signment on Henry James's
'Paste,'" 1957.B42
Sturgis, Howard Overing, 1935.B27
Sturm, Vilma, 1955.B64
"The Style of Henry James: The
Wings of the Dove," 1958.B24
"A Stylist on Tour," 1918.B12
"Subjective Drama: James,"
1932.B6
"Sul teatro di Henry James,"
1956.B18
"A Superb Performance," 1943.B51
"The Supersubtle Fry," 1953.B65
Süsskind, W. E., 1955.B65
Sutro, Alfred, 1933.B11
Swan, Michael, 1947.B45;
1948.B46; 1949.B60; 1950.A2;
1952.A2; 1953.B59; 1955.B66;
1956.B73; 1958.B74, B75-76
(rpt.)
Sweeney, John L., 1943.B49;
1956.B74
Swinnerton, Frank, 1934.B28;
1943.B50-51; 1948.B47;
1956.B75-76

384

"Symbol and Image in the Later
  Work of Henry James,"
  1953.B3
"Symbol and Image in the Later
  Work of Henry James: A Cor-
  rection," 1953.B4 (Allott),
  B61 (Tillotson)
"Symbolism and the Novel,"
  1958.B15
"Symbolism in Coleridge,"
  1948.B45
"Symbolism in James's The Golden
  Bowl," 1957.B64
"The Symington Collection,"
  1948.B30

T

Takano, Fumi, 1958.B77
"Talk at the Martello Tower,"
  1921.B21
"Talk on Parnassus," 1949.B61
Tallman, Warren E., 1958.A6
"The Taste of Henry James,"
  1957.B46
Tate, Allen, 1950.B68, B69 (rpt.)
--(with Katherine Anne Porter and
  Mark Van Doren), 1944.B12
Taylor, Christy M., 1955.A5
Taylor, H. W. (with James W.
  Linn), 1935.B11
Taylor, Walter Fuller, 1936.B13
"Techniques," 1935.B9
Terrie, Henry L., Jr., 1955.A6
"The Text of Henry James's Un-
  published Plays," 1949.B10
"Texts out of Context," 1958.B80
"That One Talent," 1956.B68
Theatre and Friendship: Some
  Henry James Letters, with a
  Commentary, 1932.A1
"Theatre: Change of Mood,"
  1950.B23
"The Theatre: Through the Mill,"
  1928.B4
The Themes of Henry James: A
  System of Observation through
  the Visual Arts, 1956.A1
Theobald, J. R., 1957.B68
Theory and Practice in Henry
  James, 1926.A1
Thersites, 1949.B61

"'Things' and Values in Henry
  James's Universe," 1957.B32
"Thomas Sargeant Perry and Henry
  James," 1949.B20
Thompson, E. R., 1928.B20
Thompson, Francis, 1948.B48-49
Thorp, Margaret Farrand,
  1950.B70
"Three Americans and a Pole,"
  1931.B11
Three American Travellers in
  England: James Russell
  Lowell, Henry Adams, Henry
  James, 1945.B32
"Three Commentaries: Poe,
  James, and Joyce," 1950.B68,
  B69 (rpt.)
"Three Notes on Henry James,"
  1955.B30
"Three Novels of Henry James,"
  1925.B4
Thurber, James, 1959.B85
--(with Mark Van Doren and Lyman
  Bryson, 1951.B56
"Thus to Revisit...," 1920.B16
Ticknor, Caroline, 1922.B16
Tilford, John E., Jr., 1958.B78
Tilley, Winthrop, 1956.B77
Tillotson, Geoffrey, 1952.B62;
  1953.B60-61
Tillotson, Kathleen, 1959.B86
Tillyard, E. M. W., 1958.B79
"Time and The Ambassadors,"
  1958.B27
"Time and the Biographer: Leon
  Edel on Writing about Henry
  James," 1955.B25
"Time and the Unnamed Article in
  The Ambassadors," 1957.B65
"The Timelessness of Henry
  James," 1945.B6
Tindall, William York, 1949.B62;
  1955.B67
Tintner, Adeline R., 1946.B29
"To Henry James," 1932.B22
"Tolstoi and Henry James,"
  1922.B6
Tooker, L. Frank, 1924.B15
The Tragedy of Manners: Moral
  Drama in the Later Novels of
  Henry James, 1957.A2

"Transition: Henry James,"
1956.B52
Traschen, Isadore, 1952.A3;
1954.B42; 1956.B78-79
Travelling Companions, 1919.B12
"A Treatise on Tales of Horror,"
1944.B17
Trevelyan, Janet Penrose,
1923.B22
Trilling, Lionel, 1945.B41;
1946.B30; 1948.B50, B51
(rpt.); 1950.B71 (rpt.);
1952.B63; 1955.B68 (rpt.)
"The Triple Quest of Henry James:
Fame, Art, and Fortune,"
1956.B29
"The Triumph of Realism: Henry
James," 1931.B13
"Trollope and Henry James in
1868," 1943.B15
Troy, William, 1931.B22;
1943.B52
"Truthful James," 1956.B27
"The Turned Back of Henry James,"
1954.B3
The Turn of the Screw, 1949.B63
"'The Turn of the Screw,'"
1918.B26
"The Turn of the Screw,"
1949.B64
The Turn of the Screw and The
Lesson of the Master, 1930.B6
"'The Turn of the Screw' as
Poem," 1948.B21
"The Turn of the Screw as Retali-
ation," 1956.B44
"The Turn of the Screw Contro-
versy: Its Implications for
the Modern Critic and Teach-
er," 1959.B24
The Turn of the Screw--The Aspern
Papers, 1957.B51
Turn West, Turn East: Mark Twain
and Henry James, 1951.A1
"A Twaddle of Graciousness,"
1957.B53
Tweedy, Katherine, 1938.B14
"Two Americans--Henry James and
Stephen Crane," 1921.B12
"Two Fathers and their Sons,"
1949.B40

"Two Formulas for Fiction: Henry
James and H. G. Wells,"
1946.B9
"Two Frontiersmen," 1928.B1
"Two Henry James Letters on The
American and Watch and Ward,"
1959.B76
"The Two Henry Jameses," 1945.B8
(Cowley); 1947.B1 (Anderson)
"The Two Henry Jameses and How-
ells: A Bibliographical
Mix-up," 1955.B60
"Two Mannerists: James and Hop-
kins," 1956.B48
"Two New Plays," 1952.B61
"Two Notes on a Trilogy,"
1957.B58
"Two Short Reminiscences: Henry
James and Rupert Brooke,"
1953.B41
"The Two Theatres of Henry
James," 1951.B48
"The Two Unfinished Novels,"
1918.B10
Tyler, Parker, 1958.B80-81

U

Uhlig, Helmut, 1955.B69
"Una nota su The Golden Bowl,"
1956.B11
"The Uncollected Stories of Henry
James," 1949.B36
"Un déraciné anglo-américain:
Henry James, d'après sa cor-
respondance," 1921.B7
"Une amite litteraire et sa fin,"
1958.B82
"A Unique Henry James Item,"
1948.B55
"Unlautere Unschuld," 1954.B38
"Un personaggio di Henry James,"
1956.B47
"An Unpublished Letter of Henry
James," 1951.B42
"Unpublished Letters," 1951.B8
"Un romancier en porte-à-faux:
Henry James," 1956.B19
"Un roman de la connaissance:
'Les Ambassadeurs' d'Henry
James," 1951.B12

"Un romanzo di James sul palco-scenio," 1950.B36
"Un splendide exile: Henry James," 1926.B12
"The Upholstery of Galsworthy, Contrasted with Henry James," 1947.B28
"The Use of the Fairy-Tale: A Note on the Structure of The Bostonians, a Novel by Henry James," 1959.B62
"The Uses of James's Imagery: Drama through Metaphor," 1954.B17
Uzzell, Thomas H., 1947.B46

V

Vallett, Jacques, 1952.B64; 1953.B62; 1957.B69; 1958.B82
Vanderbilt, Kermit, 1959.B87
Van Doren, Carl, 1921.B19; 1949.B63
Van Doren, Mark, 1959.B88
--(with Allen Tate and Katherine Ann Porter), 1944.B12
--(with James Thurber and Lyman Bryson), 1951.B56
Van Ghent, Dorothy, 1953.B63; 1959.B89 (rpt.)
Van Patten, Nathan, 1934.B29
"The Vein of Comedy in E. A. Robinson's Poetry," 1944.B6
"The Verb to Contribute," 1959.B10
"The Versatile James," 1951.B17
Versions of Melodrama: A Study of the Fiction and Drama of Henry James, 1957.A6
"The Ververs," 1954.B14
"'Very Modern Rome'--An Unpub- lished Essay of Henry James," 1954.B18
Vientós Gastón, Nilita, 1956.A4
"View of America," 1946.B11
"The Villa Barberini. Henry James," 1918.B28
"The Villains in the Major Works of Nathaniel Hawthorne and Henry James," 1959.B3

"Virginia Woolf's Judgment of Henry James," 1959.B55
"Virgin Soil and The Princess Casamassima," 1949.B28
"The Vision of Grace: James's The Wings of the Dove," 1957.B43
"A Visit to Henry James," 1923.B11, B12 (rpt.)
"A Visit to Henry James' Old Home," 1943.B14
Vivas, Eliseo, 1943.B53; 1955.B70 (rpt.)
"The Vogue of Henry James," 1944.B18
Volpe, Edmond L., 1954.A4; 1955.B71; 1956.B80; 1958.B83- 84; 1959.B90
--(with L. Hamalian), 1958.B45

W

Wade, Allen, 1943.B54; 1948.B52 (rpt.)
Wagenknecht, Edward, 1925.B15; 1948.B53; 1952.B65
Walbridge, Earle F., 1958.B85
Walbrook, H. M., 1926.B17; 1929.B8; 1930.B23
Waldock, A. J. A., 1937.B15; 1947.B47
Waley, Arthur, 1918.B26
Walkley, Arthur Bingham, 1920.B29; 1921.B20-21
Wallace, Irving, 1956.B81
Walpole, Hugh, 1932.B28; 1933.B12; 1934.B30; 1940.B14
Walsh, William, 1959.B91-93
Walter, Eugene, 1957.B70
Ward, Alfred C., 1924.B16
Ward, Geneviève (with Richard Whiteing), 1918.B27
Ward, Joseph A., Jr., 1957.A7; 1959.B94-96
Ward, Mrs. Humphry, 1918.B28
"A Warning to Pre-war Novelists," 1937.B2
Warren, Austin, 1934.B31; 1943.B55; 1948.B54 (rpt.)
--(with René Wellek), 1956.B83
Washington Square, 1950.B34 (Fad- iman); 1959.B88 (Van Doren)

Washington Square and Daisy
    Miller, 1956.B16
Washington Square; The Europeans,
    1959.B14
Wasner, E., 1954.B43
Wasserstrom, William, 1959.B97-
    98
Waterlow, Stanley P., 1926.B18
Watkins, Floyd C., 1957.B71
Watts, Richard, Jr., 1950.B72
Waugh, Arthur, 1919.B15
"A Way into The Aspern Papers,"
    1955.B73
"The Weakness of Henry James,"
    1926.B13
Weber, C. J., 1943.B56;
    1948.B55; 1953.B64
Wegelin, Christof, 1955.B72;
    1956.B82; 1958.A7, B86-87
Wellek, René, 1958.B88
--(with Austin Warren), 1956.B83
Wells, H. G., 1934.B32; 1943.B57
"Wells and Henry James,"
    1943.B57
"Wells vs. James," 1958.B4
Wertham, Frederic, 1947.B48
West, Katherine, 1949.B64
West, Ray B., Jr., 1952.B66
--(with R. W. Stallman),
    1949.B65-66
West, Rebecca, 1957.B72
Westbrook, Perry D., 1953.B65
Westcott, Glenway, 1934.B33
Whalley, George, 1953.B66
Wharton, Edith, 1920.B30;
    1925.B16; 1934.B34, B35 (rpt.)
"What Did Maisie Know?,"
    1956.B84
"What Henry James Went Through,"
    1948.B1
What Maisie Knew, 1947.B45
Wheelwright, John, 1934.B36
"Where Henry James Never Entered,"
    1931.B14
Whitall, James, 1935.B28
Whiteing, Richard (with Geneviève
    Ward), 1918.B27
Whitford, Robert Calvin, 1920.B31
The Whole Family, as subject,
    1938.B10; 1950.B53; 1958.B28,
    B85

"'The Whole Family,'" 1938.B10
"'The Whole Family' and Henry
    James," 1958.B85
"Wholeness of Effect in The
    Golden Bowl," 1958.B30
"Who Was Gilbert Osmond?,"
    1958.B70
Wilcox, Thomas W., 1955.B73
Wilde, Oscar, 1946.B31
Wilkins, M. S., 1957.B73
"William and Henry," 1934.B31
"William and Henry James: 'Our
    Passion Is Our Task,'"
    1955.B44
"William et Henry James d'après
    leur correspondance,"
    1922.B12
"William James as Critic of His
    Brother Henry," 1959.B81
"William James of Albany, New
    York, and His Descendants,"
    1924.B9
Williams, Blanche, 1943.B58
Williams, Harold, 1919.B16
Williams, Orlo, 1928.B21
Williams, Owen P. D., 1949.B67
Williams, Stanley Thomas,
    1926.B19; 1950.B73
Wilson, Edmund, 1925.B17;
    1927.B10; 1934.B37; 1938.B15,
    B16 (rpt.); 1944.B17-18;
    1946.B32; 1947.B49; 1948.B56
    (rpt.), B57; 1952.B67
Wilson, Harris W., 1956.B84
Wilson, James Southall, 1945.B42
The Wings of the Dove, 1948.B38
"The Wings of the Dove,"
    1954.B27 (Krook); 1959.B41
    (Holland)
"The Wings of the Dove and The
    Portrait of a Lady: A Study
    of Henry James's Later
    Phase," 1954.B40
"The Wings of the Dove: A Note
    on Henry James," 1946.B25
Winterich, J. T. (with D. A. Ran-
    dall), 1941.B14
Winters, Yvor, 1937.B16;
    1938,B17 (rpt.); 1947.B50
    (rpt.)

"Without Benefit of Bibliography:
Some Notes on Henry James,"
1958.B63
"With Two Countries," 1944.B1
"The Witness of the Notebooks,"
1948.B5
Wolff, R. L., 1941.B16
"The Women in the Novels of
Henry James," 1958.B77
"'Wonder' and 'Beauty' in The
Awkward Age," 1958.B42
Woodcock, George, 1952.B68
Woodress, James L., 1952.B69;
1955.B74; 1956.B85; 1957.B74;
1958.B89; 1959.B99
Woolf, Leonard, 1959.B100
Woolf, Virginia, 1919.B17;
1920.B32; 1921.B22, B23
(rpt.); 1940.B15; 1942.B8
Worden, Ward S., 1953.B67-68
"The World of Henry James,"
1930.B17; 1931.B15-16 (rpt.)
"A World Where the Victor Be-
longed to the Spoils,"
1944.B16
Worsley, T. C., 1952.B70
Wright, Austin, 1956.B86
Wright, Nathalia, 1958.B90
Wright, Walter, 1957.B75-76
"The Writer as Hero in Important
American Fiction Since How-
ells," 1954.B13
"W. Somerset Maugham Portrays
Henry James," 1951.B44
Wyatt, Edith Franklin, 1917.B21
Wyld, L. D., 1957.B77

Y

Young, Frederic Harold, 1951.B57
Young, G. M., 1940.B16
Young, Robert E., 1950.B74;
1952.B71
Young, Vernon, 1945.B43
"Young Henry James, Critic,"
1949.B2
Young Henry James: 1843-1870,
1955.A3

Z

Zabel, Morton D., 1935.B29;
1943.B59; 1950.B75; 1951.B58;
1957.B78; 1958.B91-92
Zaturenska, Marya (with Horace
Gregory), 1944.B6
Zauli-Naldi, Camilla, 1957.B79

DATE			